HOLT McDOUGAL
a division of Houghton Mifflin Harcourt

NEW YORK

Eastern Hemisphere

Part B

Christopher L. Salter

HOLT McDOUGAL
a division of Houghton Mifflin Harcourt

Author

Dr. Christopher L. Salter

Dr. Christopher L. "Kit" Salter is Professor Emeritus of geography and former Chair of the Department of Geography at the University of Missouri. He did his undergraduate work at Oberlin College and received both his M.A. and Ph.D. degrees in geography from the University of California at Berkeley.

Dr. Salter is one of the country's leading figures in geography education. In the 1980s he helped found the national Geographic Alliance network to promote geography education in all 50 states. In the 1990s Dr. Salter was Co-Chair of the National Geography Standards Project, a group of distinguished geographers who created *Geography for Life* in 1994, the document outlining national standards in geography. In 1990 Dr. Salter received the National Geographic Society's first-ever Distinguished Geography Educator Award. In 1992 he received the George Miller Award for distinguished service in geography education from the National Council for Geographic Education. In 2006 Dr. Salter was awarded Lifetime Achievement Honors by the Association of American Geographers for his transformation of geography education.

Over the years, Dr. Salter has written or edited more than 150 articles and books on cultural geography, China, field work, and geography education. His primary interests lie in the study of the human and physical forces that create the cultural landscape, both nationally and globally.

World Almanac and **World Almanac and Book of Facts** are trademarks of World Almanac Education Group, Inc., registered in the United States of America and/or other jurisdictions.

Printed in the United States of America

ISBN 13: 978-0-55-402372-4
ISBN 10: 0-55-402372-5

3 4 5 6 0914 14 13 12   4500357964

Reviewers

Academic Reviewers

Elizabeth Chako, Ph.D.
Department of Geography
The George Washington University

Altha J. Cravey, Ph.D.
Department of Geography
University of North Carolina

Eugene Cruz-Uribe, Ph.D.
Department of History
Northern Arizona University

Toyin Falola, Ph.D.
Department of History
University of Texas

Sandy Freitag, Ph.D.
Director, Monterey Bay History and
    Cultures Project
Division of Social Sciences
University of California,
    Santa Cruz

Oliver Froehling, Ph.D.
Department of Geography
University of Kentucky

Reuel Hanks, Ph.D.
Department of Geography
Oklahoma State University

Phil Klein, Ph.D.
Department of Geography
University of Northern Colorado

B. Ikubolajeh Logan, Ph.D.
Department of Geography
Pennsylvania State University

Marc Van De Mieroop, Ph.D.
Department of History
Columbia University
New York, New York

Christopher Merrett, Ph.D.
Department of History
Western Illinois University

Thomas R. Paradise, Ph.D.
Department of Geosciences
University of Arkansas

Jesse P.H. Poon, Ph.D.
Department of Geography
University at Buffalo–SUNY

Robert Schoch, Ph.D.
CGS Division of Natural Science
Boston University

Derek Shanahan, Ph.D.
Department of Geography
Millersville University
Millersville, Pennsylvania

David Shoenbrun, Ph.D.
Department of History
Northwestern University
Evanston, Illinois

Sean Terry, Ph.D.
Department of Interdisciplinary
    Studies, Geography and
    Environmental Studies
Drury University
Springfield, Missouri

Educational Reviewers

Dennis Neel Durbin
Dyersburg High School
Dyersburg, Tennessee

Carla Freel
Hoover Middle School
Merced, California

Tina Nelson
Deer Park Middle School
Randallstown, Maryland

Don Polston
Lebanon Middle School
Lebanon, Indiana

Robert Valdez
Pioneer Middle School
Tustin, California

Teacher Review Panel

Heather Green
LaVergne Middle School
LaVergne, Tennessee

John Griffin
Wilbur Middle School
Wichita, Kansas

Rosemary Hall
Derby Middle School
Birmingham, Michigan

Rose King
Yeatman-Liddell School
St. Louis, Missouri

Mary Liebl
Wichita Public Schools USD 259
Wichita, Kansas

Jennifer Smith
Lake Wood Middle School
Overland Park, Kansas

Melinda Stephani
Wake County Schools
Raleigh, North Carolina

Contents

UNIT 3 Africa

CHAPTER 9 Physical Geography of Africa

Geography's Impact Video Series
Impact of Desertification

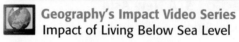

Reference

Features

Literature

FOCUS ON READING

Social Studies Skills

Writing Workshop

FOCUS ON WRITING AND SPEAKING

Learn about the Eastern Hemisphere through important documents and personal accounts.

BIOGRAPHIES

Meet the people who have influenced the Eastern Hemisphere and learn about their lives.

Charts and Graphs

The *World Almanac and Book of Facts* is America's largest-selling reference book of all time, with more than 81 million copies sold since 1868.

FACTS ABOUT COUNTRIES

Study the latest facts and figures about countries.

FACTS ABOUT THE WORLD

Study the latest facts and figures about the world.

Quick Facts and Infographics

Charts and Graphs

⋆ Interactive Maps

Interactive Maps

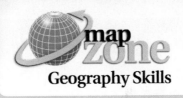

map zone
Geography Skills

Maps

New York

New York Social Studies Middle School Standards

What are the New York Social Studies Middle School Standards?

Learning standards are simply the things you are expected to know, understand, and be able to do as a result of your education. Learning standards are usually organized by subject and grade. So standards for your Eastern Hemisphere course, for example, focus on the knowledge and skills you will need to gain in your social studies class this school year.

How can New York Social Studies Middle School Standards help me?

These learning standards are helpful because they give you a clear picture of what you will be expected to learn. This can help you to focus on key material as you work through the school year. You can think of the standards as a kind of checklist—and you can even check off important subjects and skills as you master them. Another advantage of becoming familiar with the standards is that teachers often base lesson plans and tests on these standards. That means that the standards can give you a preview of what to expect in this course.

How are the New York Social Studies Middle School Standards organized?

New York educators have organized the teaching of social studies by creating different kinds of standards at several levels. At the top level are New York State Learning Standards for Social Studies. These are very broad standards—each one covers a large amount of learning. Because they are so broad, there are only five of them, several of which will apply to your studies of the Eastern Hemisphere. You can read them below. On the next page, you will read more detailed parts of all the standards.

Each Standard is divided into Key Ideas. These Key Ideas give you a description of the main categories of information you will be learning, as well as the kinds of skills you will be practicing.

Standard 1—History of the United States and New York

Students will use a variety of intellectual skills to demonstrate their understanding of major ideas, eras, themes, developments, and turning points in the history of the United States and New York.

1. The study of New York State and United States history requires an analysis of the development of American culture, its diversity and multicultural context, and the ways people are unified by many values, practices, and traditions.

Central Park, New York City

2. Important ideas, social and cultural values, beliefs, and traditions from New York State and United States history illustrate the connections and interactions of people and events across time and from a variety of perspectives.

3. Study about the major social, political, economic, cultural, and religious developments in New York State and United States history involves learning about the important roles and contributions of individuals and groups.

4. The skills of historical analysis include the ability to: explain the significance of historical evidence; weigh the importance, reliability, and validity of evidence; understand the concept of multiple causation; understand the importance of changing and competing interpretations of different historical developments.

Standard 2—World History

Students will use a variety of intellectual skills to demonstrate their understanding of major ideas, eras, themes, developments, and turning points in world history and examine the broad sweep of history from a variety of perspectives.

1. The study of world history requires an understanding of world cultures and civilizations, including an analysis of important ideas, social and cultural values, beliefs, and traditions. This study also examines the human condition and the connections and interactions of people across time and space and the ways different people view the same event or issue from a variety of perspectives.

2. Establishing timeframes, exploring different periodizations, examining themes across time and within cultures, and focusing on important turning points in world history help organize the study of world cultures and civilizations.

3. Study of the major social, political, cultural, and religious developments in world history involves learning about the important roles and contributions of individuals and groups.

4. The skills of historical analysis include the ability to investigate differing and competing interpretations of the theories of history, hypothesize about why interpretations change over time, explain the importance of historical evidence, and understand the concepts of change and continuity over time.

Brooklyn Bridge

Standard 3—Geography

Students will use a variety of intellectual skills to demonstrate their understanding of the geography of the interdependent world in which we live—local, national, and global—including the distribution of people, places, and environments over the Earth's surface.

1. Geography can be divided into six essential elements which can be used to analyze important historic, geographic, economic, and environmental questions and issues. These six elements include: the world in spatial terms, places and regions, physical settings (including natural resources), human systems, environment and society, and the use of geography. (Adapted from The National Geography Standards, 1994: Geography for Life)

2. Geography requires the development and application of the skills of asking and answering geographic questions; analyzing theories of geography; and acquiring, organizing, and analyzing geographic information. (Adapted from The National Geography Standards, 1994: Geography for Life)

Standard 4—Economics

Students will use a variety of intellectual skills to demonstrate their understanding of how the United States and other societies develop economic systems and associated institutions to allocate scarce resources, how major decision-making units function in the U.S. and other national economies, and how an economy solves the scarcity problem through market and nonmarket mechanisms.

1. The study of economics requires an understanding of major economic concepts and systems, the principles of economic decision making, and the interdependence of economies and economic systems throughout the world.

2. Economics requires the development and application of the skills needed to make informed and well-reasoned economic decisions in daily and national life.

Grand Central Station, New York City

Standard 5—Civics, Citizenship, and Government

Students will use a variety of intellectual skills to demonstrate their understanding of the necessity for establishing governments; the governmental system of the U.S. and other nations; the U.S. Constitution; the basic civic values of American constitutional democracy; and the roles, rights, and responsibilities of citizenship, including avenues of participation.

1. The study of civics, citizenship, and government involves learning about political systems; the purposes of government and civic life; and the differing assumptions held by people across time and place regarding power, authority, governance, and law. (Adapted from The National Standards for Civics and Government, 1994)

2. The state and federal governments established by the Constitutions of the United States and the State of New York embody basic civic values (such as justice, honesty, self-discipline, due process, equality, majority rule with respect for minority rights, and respect for self, others, and property), principles, and practices and establish a system of shared and limited government. (Adapted from The National Standards for Civics and Government, 1994)

3. Central to civics and citizenship is an understanding of the roles of the citizen within American constitutional democracy and the scope of a citizen's rights and responsibilities.

4. The study of civics and citizenship requires the ability to probe ideas and assumptions, ask and answer analytical questions, take a skeptical attitude toward questionable arguments, evaluate evidence, formulate rational conclusions, and develop and refine participatory skills.

New York City Harbor

Become an Active Reader

by Dr. Kylene Beers

Did you ever think you would begin reading your social studies book by reading about *reading*? Actually, it makes better sense than you might think. You would probably make sure you knew some soccer skills and strategies before playing in a game. Similarly, you need to know something about reading skills and strategies before reading your social studies book. In other words, you need to make sure you know what-ever you need to know in order to read this book successfully.

Tip #1

Read Everything on the Page!

You can't follow the directions on the cake-mix box if you don't know where the directions are! Cake-mix boxes always have directions on them telling you how many eggs to add or how long to bake the cake. But, if you can't find that information, it doesn't matter that it is there.

Likewise, this book is filled with information that will help you understand what you are reading. If you don't study that information, however, it might as well not be there. Let's take a look at some of the places where you'll find important information in this book.

The Chapter Opener
The chapter opener gives you a brief overview of what you will learn in the chapter. You can use this information to prepare to read the chapter.

The Section Openers
Before you begin to read each section, preview the information under What You Will Learn. There you'll find the main ideas of the section and key terms that are important in it. Knowing what you are looking for before you start reading can improve your understanding.

Boldfaced Words
Those words are important and are defined somewhere on the page where they appear—either right there in the sentence or over in the side margin.

Maps, Charts, and Artwork
These things are not there just to take up space or look good! Study them and read the information beside them. It will help you understand the information in the chapter.

Questions at the End of Sections
At the end of each section, you will find questions that will help you decide whether you need to go back and re-read any parts before moving on. If you can't answer a question, that is your cue to go back and re-read.

Questions at the End of the Chapter
Answer the questions at the end of each chapter, even if your teacher doesn't ask you to. These questions are there to help you figure out what you need to review.

Use the Reading Skills and Strategies in Your Textbook

Good readers use a number of skills and strategies to make sure they understand what they are reading. In this textbook you will find help with important reading skills and strategies such as "Using Prior Knowledge," and "Understanding Main Ideas."

We teach the reading skills and strategies in several ways. Use these activities and lessons and you will become a better reader.

- First, on the opening page of every chapter we identify and explain the reading skill or strategy you will focus on as you work through the chapter. In fact, these activities are called "Focus on Reading."

- Second, as you can see in the example at right, we tell you where to go for more help. The back of the book has a reading handbook with a full-page practice lesson to match the reading skill or strategy in every chapter.

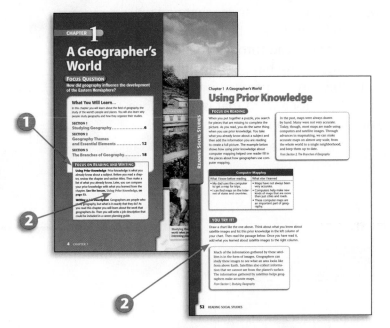

- Third, we give you short practice activities and examples as you read the chapter. These activities and examples show up in the margin of your book. Again, look for the words, "Focus on Reading."

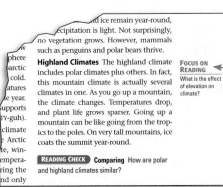

- Finally, we provide another practice activity in the Chapter Review at the end of every chapter. That activity gives you one more chance to make sure you know how to use the reading skill or strategy.

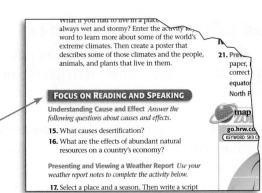

Tip #3

Pay Attention to Vocabulary

It is no fun to read something when you don't know what the words mean, but you can't learn new words if you only use or read the words you already know. In this book, we know we have probably used some words you don't know. But, we have followed a pattern as we have used more difficult words.

- First, at the beginning of each section you will find a list of key terms that you will need to know. Be on the lookout for those words as you read through the section. You will find that we have defined those words right there in the paragraph where they are used. Look for a word that is in boldface with its definition highlighted in yellow.

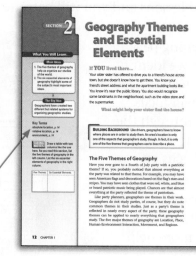

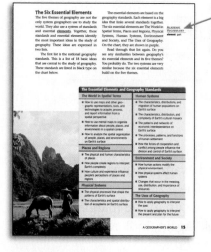

- Second, when we use a word that is important in all classes, not just social studies, we define it in the margin under the heading Academic Vocabulary. You will run into these academic words in other textbooks, so you should learn what they mean while reading this book.

Tip #4

Read Like a Skilled Reader

You won't be able to climb to the top of Mount Everest if you do not train! If you want to make it to the top of Mount Everest then you must start training to climb that huge mountain.

Training is also necessary to become a good reader. You will never get better at reading your social studies book—or any book for that matter—unless you spend some time thinking about how to be a better reader.

Skilled readers do the following:

1. They preview what they are supposed to read before they actually begin reading. When previewing, they look for vocabulary words, titles of sections, information in the margin, or maps or charts they should study.

2. They get ready to take some notes while reading by dividing their notebook paper into two parts. They title one side "Notes from the Chapter" and the other side "Questions or Comments I Have."

3. As they read, they complete their notes.

4. They read like **active readers**. The Active Reading list below shows you what that means.

5. Finally, they use clues in the text to help them figure out where the text is going. The best clues are called signal words. These are words that help you identify chronological order, causes and effects, or comparisons and contrasts.

Chronological Order Signal Words: *first, second, third, before, after, later, next, following that, earlier, subsequently, finally*

Cause and Effect Signal Words: *because of, due to, as a result of, the reason for, therefore, consequently, so, basis for*

Comparison/Contrast Signal Words: *likewise, also, as well as, similarly, on the other hand*

Active Reading

There are three ways to read a book: You can be a turn-the-pages-no-matter-what type of reader. These readers just keep on turning pages whether or not they understand what they are reading. Or, you can be a stop-watch-and-listen kind of reader. These readers know that if they wait long enough, someone will tell them what they need to know. Or, you can be an active reader. These readers know that it is up to them to figure out what the text means. Active readers do the following as they read:

Predict what will happen next based on what has already happened. When your predictions don't match what happens in the text, re-read the confusing parts.

Question what is happening as you read. Constantly ask yourself why things have happened, what things mean, and what caused certain events. Jot down notes about the questions you can't answer.

Summarize what you are reading frequently. Do not try to summarize the entire chapter! Read a bit and then summarize it. Then read on.

Connect what is happening in the section you're reading to what you have already read.

Clarify your understanding. Be sure that you understand what you are reading by stopping occasionally to ask yourself whether you are confused by anything. Sometimes you might need to re-read to clarify. Other times you might need to read further and collect more information before you can understand. Still other times you might need to ask the teacher to help you with what is confusing you.

Visualize what is happening in the text. In other words, try to see the events or places in your mind. It might help you to draw maps, make charts, or jot down notes about what you are reading as you try to visualize the action in the text.

Social Studies Words

As you read this textbook, you will be more successful if you learn the meanings of the words on this page. You will come across these words many times in your social studies classes, like geography and history. Read through these words now to become familiar with them before you begin your studies.

Social Studies Words

WORDS ABOUT TIME

AD	refers to dates after the birth of Jesus
BC	refers to dates before Jesus's birth
BCE	refers to dates before Jesus's birth, stands for "before the common era"
CE	refers to dates after Jesus's birth, stands for "common era"
century	a period of 100 years
decade	a period of 10 years
era	a period of time
millennium	a period of 1,000 years

WORDS ABOUT THE WORLD

climate	the weather conditions in a certain area over a long period of time
geography	the study of the world's people, places, and landscapes
physical features	features on Earth's surface, such as mountains and rivers
region	an area with one or more features that make it different from surrounding areas
resources	materials found on Earth that people need and value

WORDS ABOUT PEOPLE

anthropology	the study of people and cultures
archaeology	the study of the past based on what people left behind
citizen	a person who lives under the control of a government
civilization	the way of life of people in a particular place or time
culture	the knowledge, beliefs, customs, and values of a group of people
custom	a repeated practice or tradition
economics	the study of the production and use of goods and services
economy	any system in which people make and exchange goods and services
government	the body of officials and groups that run an area
history	the study of the past
politics	the process of running a government
religion	a system of beliefs in one or more gods or spirits
society	a group of people who share common traditions
trade	the exchange of goods or services

Academic Words

What are academic words? They are important words used in all of your classes, not just social studies. You will see these words in other textbooks, so you should learn what they mean while reading this book. Review this list now. You will use these words again in the chapters of this book.

Academic Words

acquire	to get	**implement**	to put in place
advocate	to plead in favor of	**implications**	consequences
authority	power or influence	**implicit**	understood though not clearly put into words
circumstances	conditions that influence an event or activity	**incentive**	something that leads people to follow a certain course of action
classical	referring to the cultures of ancient Greece or Rome	**innovation**	a new idea or way of doing something
complex	difficult, not simple	**interpret**	to explain the meaning of something
consequences	the effects of a particular event or events	**method**	a way of doing something
contracts	binding legal agreements	**policy**	rule, course of action
development	creation; the process of growing or improving	**primary**	main, most important
distinct	clearly different and separate	**principle**	basic belief, rule, or law
distribute	to divide among a group of people	**procedure**	a series of steps taken to accomplish a task
efficient	productive and not wasteful	**process**	a series of steps by which a task is accomplished
element	part	**purpose**	the reason something is done
establish	to set up or create	**rebel**	to fight against authority
ethical	related to rules of conduct or proper bahavior	**role**	a part or function
explicit	fully revealed without vagueness	**strategy**	a plan for fighting a battle or war
facilitate	to make easier	**structure**	the way something is set up or organized
factor	cause	**traditional**	customary, time-honored
features	characteristics	**values**	ideas that people hold dear and try to live by
function	work or perform	**vary**	to be different
ideals	ideas or goals that people try to live up to		
impact	effect, result		

Multiple Choice

A multiple-choice test item is a question or an incomplete statement with several answer choices. To answer a multiple-choice test item, select the choice that best answers the question or that best completes the statement.

Learn

Use these strategies to answer multiple-choice test items:

❶ Carefully read the question or incomplete statement.

❷ Look for words that affect the meaning, such as *all, always, best, every, most, never, not,* or *only.* For example, in Item 1 to the right, the word *all* tells you to look for the answer in which all three choices are correct.

❸ Read *all* the choices before selecting an answer—even if the first choice seems right.

❹ In your mind, cross off any of the answer choices that you know for certain are wrong.

❺ Consider the choices that are left and select the *best* answer. If you are not sure, select the choice that makes the most sense.

For each statement or question, write the number of the word or expression that, of those given, best completes the statement ❶ *or answers the question.* ❷

1 Which of the following are *all* physical features of geography?

(1) landforms, climates, people
(2) landforms, climates, soils
(3) landscapes, climates, plants
(4) landscapes, communities, soils ❸

2 A region is an area that has

(1) one or more common features. ❺
(2) no people living in it. ❹
(3) few physical features.
(4) set physical boundaries.

Practice

For each statement or question, write the number of the word or expression that, of those given, best completes the statement or answers the question.

1 Which of the following is part of the study of human geography?

(1) bodies of water
(2) communities
(3) landforms
(4) plants

2 The economy of North Korea is *best* described as a

(1) command economy.
(2) developed economy.
(3) market economy.
(4) traditional economy.

Primary Sources

Primary sources are materials, often called documents, created by people who lived during the times you are reading about. Examples of primary sources include text documents, such as letters and diaries, and visual documents, such as photographs.

Learn

Use these strategies to answer test questions about primary sources:

❶ Note the document's title and source line. This information can tell you the document's author, date, and purpose.

❷ Skim the document. Get an idea of its main focus.

❸ Read the question about the document. Note what information you are being asked to find.

❹ Read or examine the document carefully. As you do, identify the main idea and key details.

❺ Compare the question and answer choices to the document. Look for similar words. Then read between the lines. Use your critical-thinking skills to draw conclusions.

❻ Review the question and select the best answer.

Base your answer to the following question on the text excerpt and on your knowledge of social studies.

❶

Geography for Life

"Geography is a field of study that enables us to find answers to questions about the world around us—about where things are and how and why they got there…With a strong grasp of geography, people are better equipped to solve issues at not only the local level but also the global level."

— from *Geography for Life*, by the Geography Education Standards Project

❹ ❷ ❶

1 Which statement below *best* summarizes the main idea of the above passage?

(1) Geography helps people to read and make maps.

(2) Geography helps people to get where they are going.

(3) Geography helps people to understand the world better and to solve problems.

(4) Geography helps people explore Earth.

Practice

Base your answer to the following question on the text excerpt above and on your knowledge of social studies.

1 What is one question geography can answer for us?

(1) when events happened

(2) where things are

(3) why people act how they do

(4) why the sky is blue

2 What are two levels at which geography helps people solve issues?

(1) global and strong

(2) equipped and global

(3) strong and equipped

(4) local and global

Charts and Graphs

Charts and graphs are tables or drawings that present and organize information or data. Some standardized tests include questions about charts and graphs. These questions require you to interpret the information or data in the chart or graph to answer the question.

Learn

Use these strategies to answer test questions about charts and graphs:

❶ Read the title of the chart or graph. Identify the subject and purpose of the information shown.

❷ Read all the other labels. Note the types of information the chart or graph is showing and how the information is organized.

❸ Analyze the information or data. Look for patterns, changes over time, and similarities or differences. For example, in the graph at right, world population growth rises dramatically after 1900.

❹ Read the question carefully. Note key words in the question.

❺ Review the chart or graph to find the correct answer.

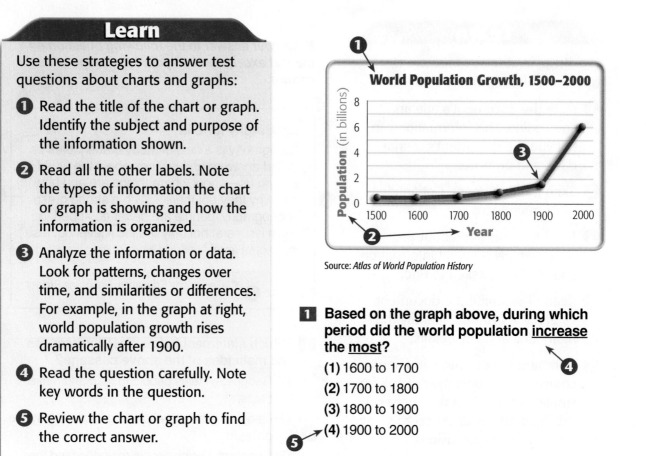

Source: *Atlas of World Population History*

1 Based on the graph above, during which period did the world population <u>increase</u> the <u>most</u>?

(1) 1600 to 1700

(2) 1700 to 1800

(3) 1800 to 1900

(4) 1900 to 2000

Practice

Base your answer to the following question on the chart and on your knowledge of social studies.

1 Which country in the Ring of Fire had two major volcanic eruptions?

(1) Colombia

(2) Indonesia

(3) Philippines

(4) United States

THE WORLD ALMANAC® Facts about the World — **Major Eruptions in the Ring of Fire**

Volcano	Year
Tambora, Indonesia	1815
Krakatau, Indonesia	1883
Mount Saint Helens, United States	1980
Nevado del Ruiz, Colombia	1985
Mount Pinatubo, Philippines	1991

Maps

Standardized tests may include questions that refer to information in maps. These maps might show political features such as cities and states, physical features such as mountains and plains, or information such as climate, land use, or settlement patterns.

Learn

Use these strategies to answer questions about maps.

1 Read the map title to identify the map's subject and purpose. The map below shows levels of government freedom around the world.

2 Study the legend. It explains information in the map, such as what different colors or symbols mean.

3 Note the map's direction and scale. The scale shows the distance between points in the map.

4 Examine the map closely. Read all the labels and study the other information, such as colors, borders, or symbols.

5 Read the question about the map.

6 Review the map to find the answer.

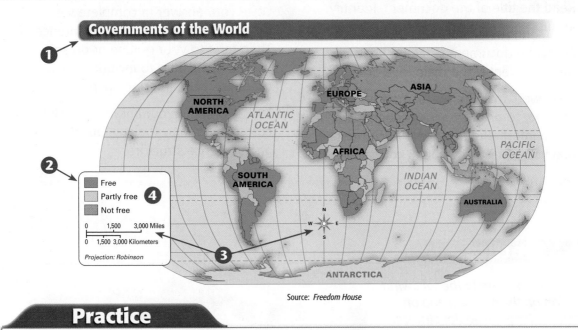

Source: *Freedom House*

Practice

Base your answers to the following questions on the map and on your knowledge of social studies.

1 **Which two continents have the least government freedom?**

(1) Africa and Asia

(2) Africa and Europe

(3) Australia and Europe

(4) Europe and Asia

2 **The continents with the most freedom are Australia and**

(1) Africa.

(2) Europe.

(3) North America.

(4) South America.

Constructed Response

Constructed-response questions usually require you to examine a document, such as a letter, chart, or map. You then use the information in the document to write an extended answer, often a paragraph or more in length.

Learn

Use these strategies to answer constructed-response questions:

❶ Read the directions and question carefully to determine the purpose of your answer. For example, are you to explain, identify causes, summarize, or compare? To help determine the purpose, look for key words such as *compare, contrast, describe, discuss, explain, interpret, predict,* or *summarize.*

❷ Read the title of the document. Identify its subject and purpose.

❸ Study the document carefully. Read all the text. Identify the main idea or focus.

❹ If allowed, make notes on another sheet of paper to organize your thoughts. Jot down information from the document that you want to include in your answer.

❺ Use the question to create a topic sentence. For example, for the practice question below, a topic sentence might be, "Earth's tilt and revolution cause the seasons to change at about the same time each year in the Northern Hemisphere."

❻ Create an outline or graphic organizer to help organize your main points. Review the document to find details or examples to support each point.

❼ Write your answer in complete sentences. Start with your topic sentence. Then refer to your outline or organizer as you write. Be sure to include details or examples from the document.

❽ Last, proofread your answer. Check for correct grammar, spelling, punctuation, and sentence structure.

Practice

Base your answers to the following question on the diagram and on your knowledge of social studies.

1 Constructed-Response Question Write a paragraph explaining how the movement of plates on Earth's crust leads to the formation of volcanoes.

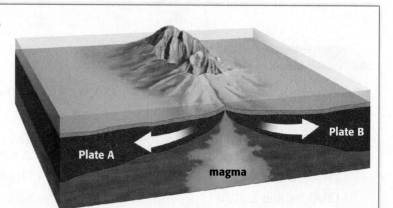

Africa

The Sahara

The world's largest desert, the Sahara, dominates land and life in North Africa.

Savannas

Grassy plains called savannas stretch across large parts of the continent and are home to much African wildlife.

Africa

Rift Valleys

In East Africa, Earth's crust is slowly being pulled apart. This causes hills, long lakes, and wide "rift valleys" to form.

Explore the Satellite Image A huge continent, Africa is home to many different kinds of physical features. Based on this satellite image, how would you describe Africa's physical geography?

The Satellite's Path

>44'56.08<

>>>>>>>>665.00'87<

567.476.348

+803 +799

+996

+355

456.094.

Africa: Physical

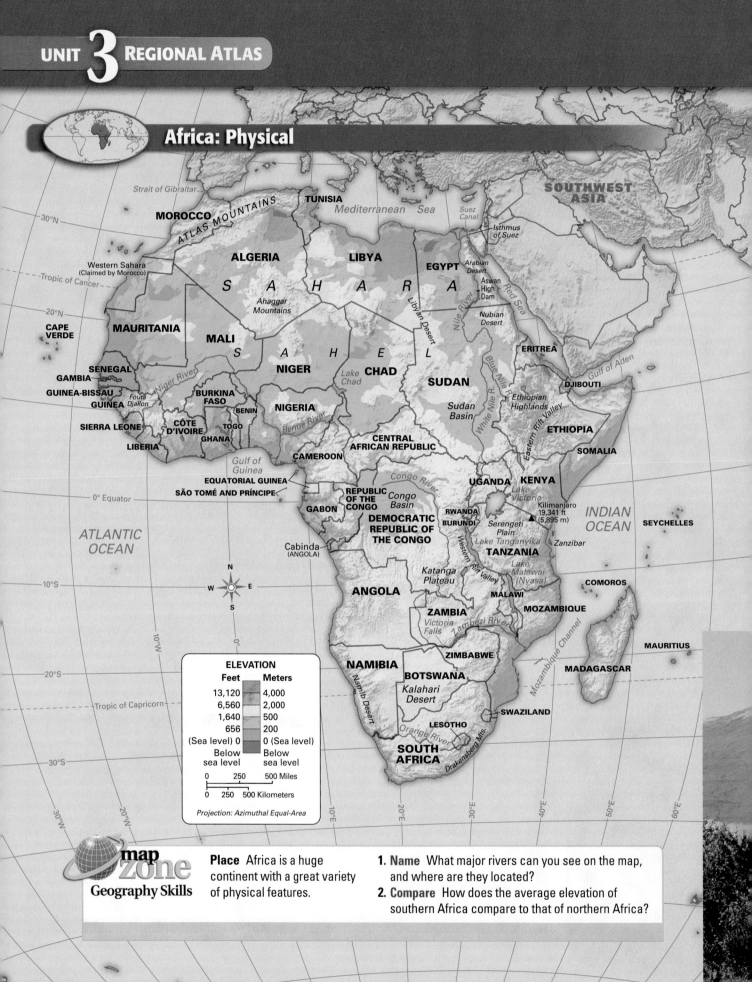

ELEVATION

Feet	Meters
13,120	4,000
6,560	2,000
1,640	500
656	200
(Sea level) 0	0 (Sea level)
Below sea level	Below sea level

0   250   500 Miles

0   250   500 Kilometers

Projection: Azimuthal Equal-Area

map zone

Geography Skills

Place Africa is a huge continent with a great variety of physical features.

1. Name What major rivers can you see on the map, and where are they located?

2. Compare How does the average elevation of southern Africa compare to that of northern Africa?

THE WORLD ALMANAC®
Facts about the World
Geographical Extremes: Africa

Longest River	Nile River, Egypt: 4,160 miles (6,693 km)	**Driest Place**	Wadi Halfa, Sudan: .1 inches (.3 cm) average precipitation per year
Highest Point	Mount Kilimanjaro, Tanzania: 19,340 feet (5,895 m)	**Largest Country**	Sudan: 967,498 square miles (2,505,820 square km)
Lowest Point	Lake Assal, Djibouti: 512 feet (156 m) below sea level	**Smallest Country**	Seychelles: 176 square miles (456 square km)
Highest Recorded Temperature	El Azizia, Libya: 136°F (57.8°C)	**Largest Desert**	Sahara: 3,500,000 square miles (9,065,000 square km)
Lowest Recorded Temperature	Ifrane, Morocco: –11°F (–23.9°C)	**Largest Island**	Madagascar: 226,658 square miles (587,044 square km)
Wettest Place	Debundscha, Cameroon: 405 inches (1,028.7 cm) average precipitation per year	**Highest Waterfall**	Tugela, South Africa: 2,014 feet (614 m)

go.hrw.com KEYWORD: SK9 UN3

Size Comparison: The United States and Africa

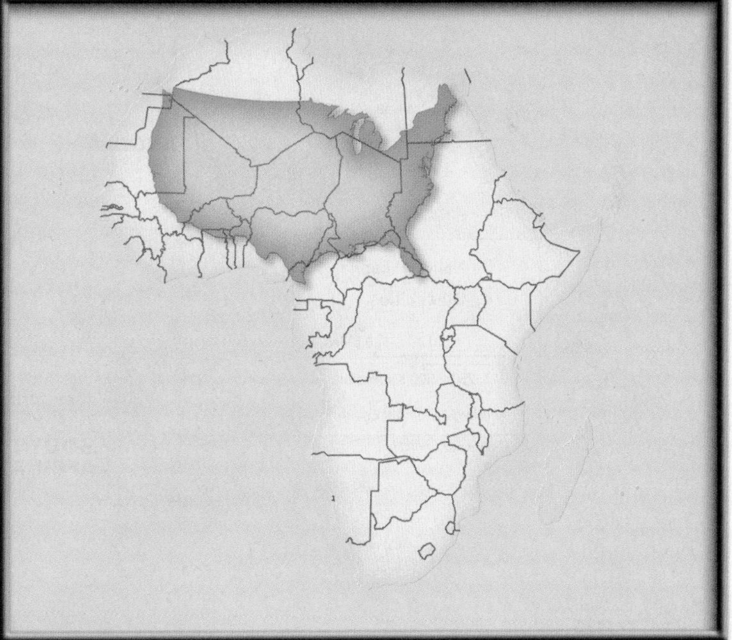

Mount Kilimanjaro, Tanzania

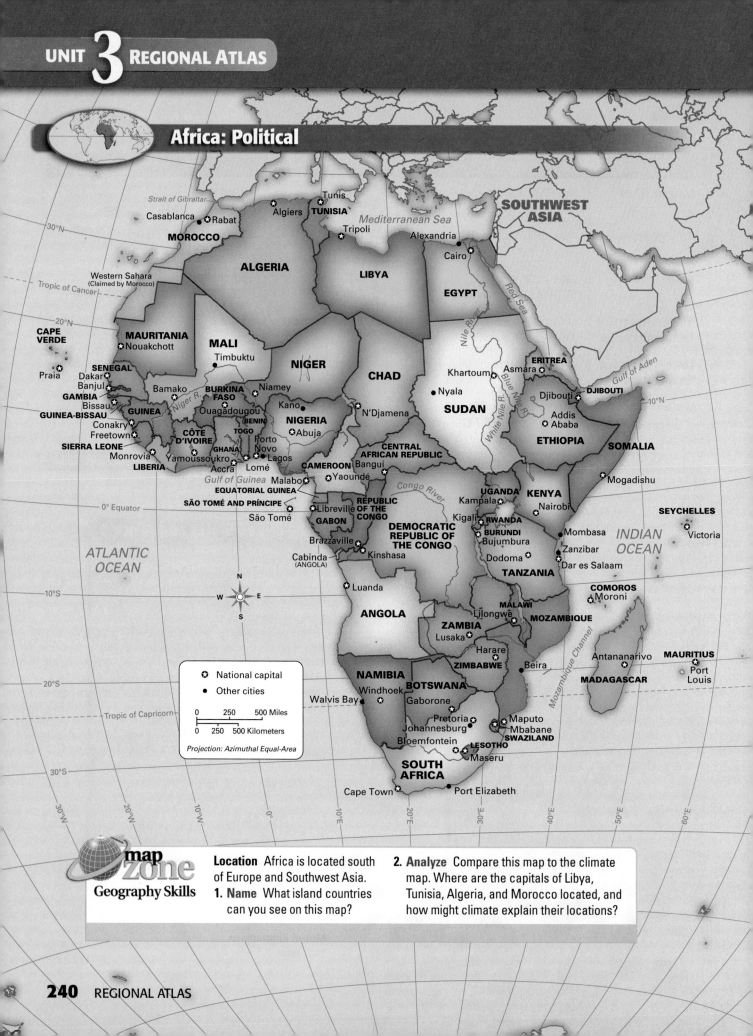

Africa: Political

Strait of Gibraltar

Tunis
Casablanca • Rabat   Algiers TUNISIA
MOROCCO   Tripoli
30°N   *Mediterranean Sea*   SOUTHWEST
                                                        Alexandria   ASIA
                    ALGERIA   LIBYA   Cairo

Western Sahara   EGYPT
(Claimed by Morocco)
Tropic of Cancer

20°N
CAPE   MAURITANIA   ERITREA
VERDE   Nouakchott   MALI   NIGER   Khartoum Asmara DJIBOUTI
Praia   Timbuktu   Djibouti
SENEGAL   CHAD   • Nyala
Dakar   Bamako BURKINA Niamey   Addis
Banjul   FASO   SUDAN   Ababa
GAMBIA   Bissau   GUINEA Ouagadougou Kano   N'Djamena
GUINEA-BISSAU Conakry   BENIN NIGERIA   ETHIOPIA   SOMALIA
Freetown CÔTE TOGO Porto • Abuja
SIERRA LEONE D'IVOIRE GHANA Novo   CENTRAL
Monrovia Yamoussoukro Lagos   AFRICAN REPUBLIC   Mogadishu
LIBERIA   Accra   Lomé   CAMEROON Bangui
Gulf of Guinea   Malabo • Yaoundé   UGANDA   KENYA   SEYCHELLES
EQUATORIAL GUINEA   Congo River   Kampala   Nairobi
SÃO TOMÉ AND PRÍNCIPE   REPUBLIC   Kigali RWANDA Mombasa Victoria
0° Equator   São Tomé Libreville OF THE   BURUNDI Zanzibar INDIAN
                  GABON   CONGO   DEMOCRATIC   Bujumbura   OCEAN
              Brazzaville REPUBLIC OF   Dodoma Dar es Salaam
ATLANTIC   Cabinda   THE CONGO
OCEAN   (ANGOLA) Kinshasa   TANZANIA
                                                                          COMOROS
10°S   • Luanda   • Moroni
                                                        MALAWI
                   ANGOLA   Lilongwe   MOZAMBIQUE
                                       ZAMBIA   Antananarivo MAURITIUS
                                       Lusaka   Port
                                               Harare   Louis
20°S   ZIMBABWE Beira   MADAGASCAR
                   NAMIBIA   BOTSWANA
                   Windhoek
                   Walvis Bay Gaborone
Tropic of Capricorn   Pretoria
                            Johannesburg Maputo
                            Bloemfontein Mbabane
                                         SWAZILAND
30°S   LESOTHO
                   SOUTH   Maseru
                   AFRICA
                   Cape Town Port Elizabeth

Legend:
⊙ National capital
• Other cities

0   250   500 Miles
0   250   500 Kilometers

Projection: Azimuthal Equal-Area

map zone
Geography Skills

Location Africa is located south of Europe and Southwest Asia.

1. Name What island countries can you see on this map?

2. Analyze Compare this map to the climate map. Where are the capitals of Libya, Tunisia, Algeria, and Morocco located, and how might climate explain their locations?

Africa: Resources

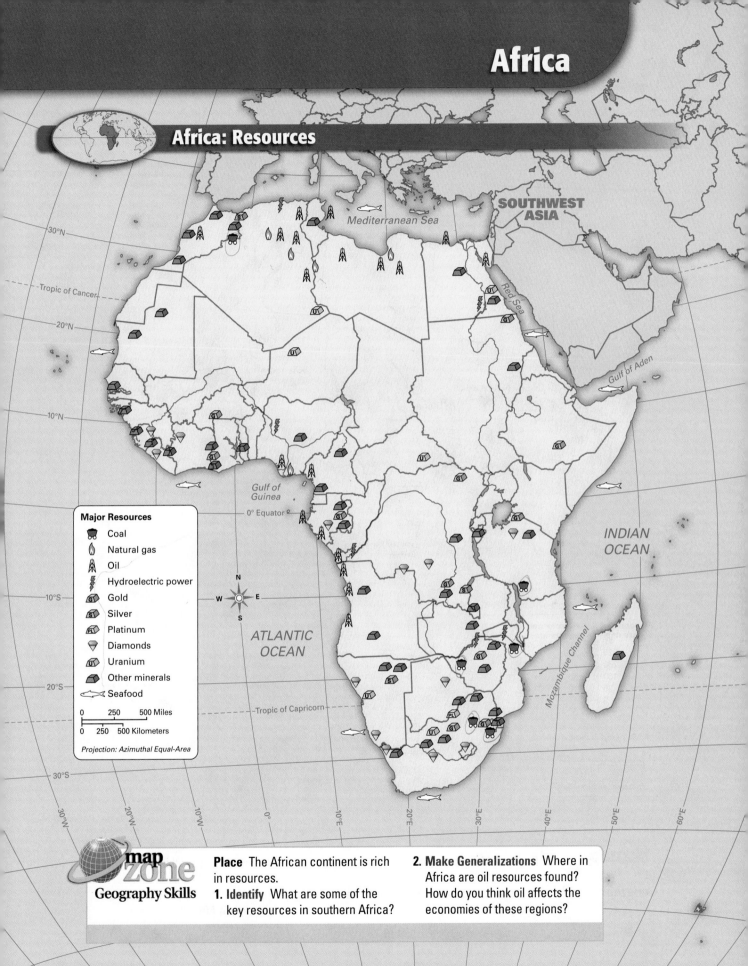

Major Resources

- 🪨 Coal
- 💧 Natural gas
- 🛢 Oil
- ⚡ Hydroelectric power
- Gold
- Silver
- Platinum
- 💎 Diamonds
- Uranium
- Other minerals
- 🐟 Seafood

0   250   500 Miles

0 250 500 Kilometers

Projection: Azimuthal Equal-Area

Mediterranean Sea

SOUTHWEST ASIA

Red Sea

Gulf of Aden

Tropic of Cancer

Gulf of Guinea

0° Equator

ATLANTIC OCEAN

INDIAN OCEAN

Mozambique Channel

Tropic of Capricorn

map zone
Geography Skills

Place The African continent is rich in resources.

1. Identify What are some of the key resources in southern Africa?

2. Make Generalizations Where in Africa are oil resources found? How do you think oil affects the economies of these regions?

Africa: Population

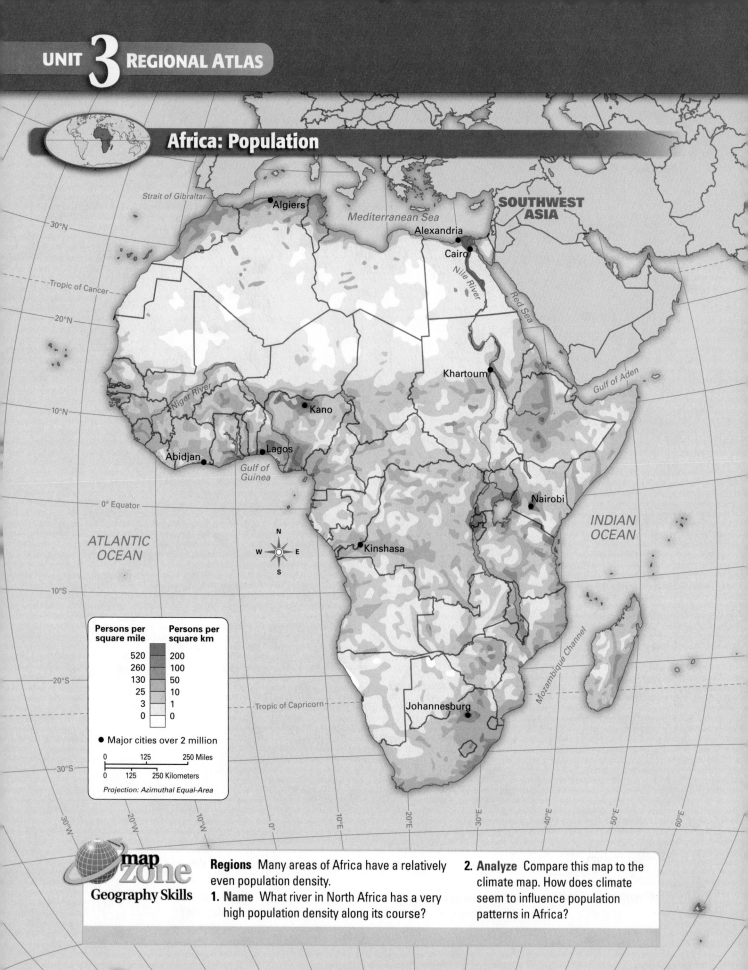

Strait of Gibraltar

Algiers

Mediterranean Sea

SOUTHWEST ASIA

Alexandria

Cairo

30°N

Tropic of Cancer

20°N

Nile River

Red Sea

Khartoum

Gulf of Aden

10°N

Niger River

Kano

Abidjan

Lagos

Gulf of Guinea

Nairobi

INDIAN OCEAN

0° Equator

ATLANTIC OCEAN

Kinshasa

N
W   E
S

10°S

Johannesburg

Mozambique Channel

Tropic of Capricorn

Persons per square mile | **Persons per square km**
520 | 200
260 | 100
130 | 50
25 | 10
3 | 1
0 | 0

● Major cities over 2 million

0   125   250 Miles
0   125   250 Kilometers
Projection: Azimuthal Equal-Area

30°S

30°W   20°W   10°W   0°   10°E   20°E   30°E   40°E   50°E   60°E

map zone

Geography Skills

Regions Many areas of Africa have a relatively even population density.

1. Name What river in North Africa has a very high population density along its course?

2. Analyze Compare this map to the climate map. How does climate seem to influence population patterns in Africa?

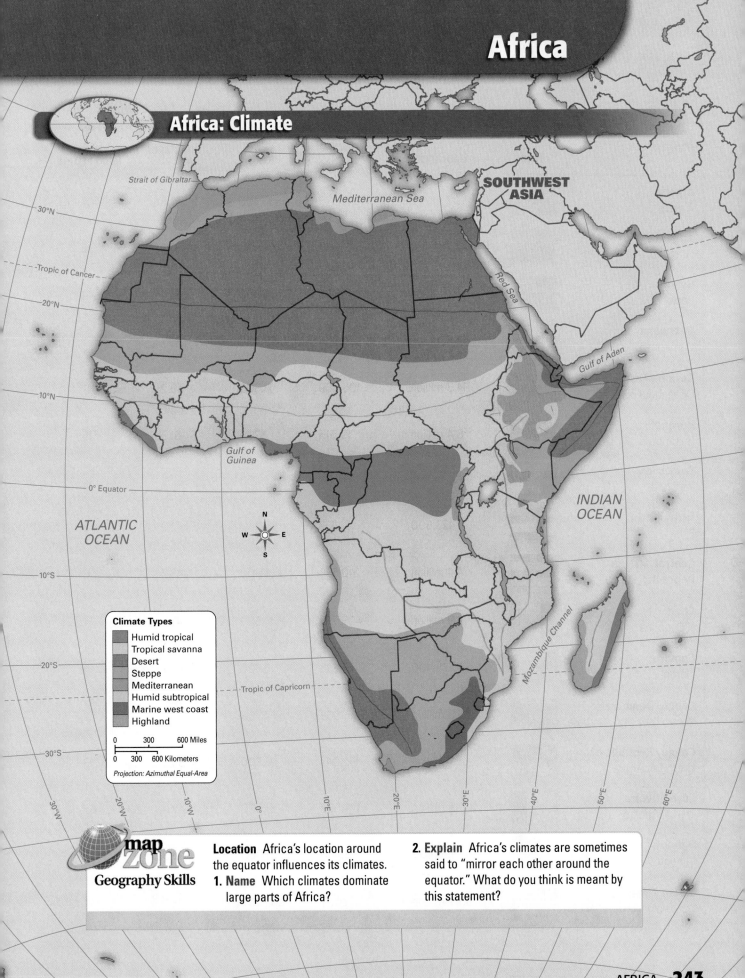

Africa

Africa: Climate

Strait of Gibraltar

Mediterranean Sea

SOUTHWEST ASIA

Red Sea

Gulf of Aden

30°N

Tropic of Cancer

20°N

10°N

Gulf of Guinea

0° Equator

ATLANTIC OCEAN

INDIAN OCEAN

10°S

Mozambique Channel

Climate Types
- Humid tropical
- Tropical savanna
- Desert
- Steppe
- Mediterranean
- Humid subtropical
- Marine west coast
- Highland

20°S

Tropic of Capricorn

0   300   600 Miles
0   300   600 Kilometers
Projection: Azimuthal Equal-Area

30°S

30°W   20°W   10°W   0°   10°E   20°E   30°E   40°E   50°E   60°E

map zone
Geography Skills

Location Africa's location around the equator influences its climates.

1. Name Which climates dominate large parts of Africa?

2. Explain Africa's climates are sometimes said to "mirror each other around the equator." What do you think is meant by this statement?

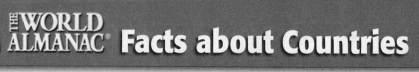

Africa

COUNTRY Capital	FLAG	POPULATION	AREA (sq mi)	PER CAPITA GDP (U.S. $)	LIFE EXPECTANCY AT BIRTH	TVS PER 1,000 PEOPLE
Algeria Algiers		33.3 million	919,595	$7,700	73.5	107
Angola Luanda		12.2 million	481,354	$4,300	37.6	15
Benin Porto-Novo		8.1 million	43,483	$1,100	53.4	44
Botswana Gaborone		1.8 million	231,804	$11,400	33.7	21
Burkina Faso Ouagadougou		14.3 million	105,869	$1,300	49.2	11
Burundi Bujumbura		8.4 million	10,745	$700	51.3	15
Cameroon Yaoundé		18.1 million	183,568	$2,400	52.9	34
Cape Verde Praia		423,600	1,557	$6,000	71.0	5
Central African Republic; Bangui		4.4 million	240,535	$1,100	43.7	6
Chad N'Djamena		9.9 million	495,755	$1,500	47.9	1
Comoros Moroni		711,400	838	$600	62.7	4
Congo, Democratic Republic of the; Kinshasa		65.8 million	905,568	$700	51.9	2
Congo, Republic of the; Brazzaville		3.8 million	132,047	$1,300	53.3	13
Côte d'Ivoire Yamoussoukro		18 million	124,503	$1,600	49.0	65
Djibouti Djibouti		496,400	8,880	$1,000	43.3	48
United States Washington, D.C.		301.1 million	3,718,711	$43,500	78.0	844

COUNTRY Capital	FLAG	POPULATION	AREA (sq mi)	PER CAPITA GDP (U.S. $)	LIFE EXPECTANCY AT BIRTH	TVS PER 1,000 PEOPLE
Egypt Cairo		80.3 million	386,662	$4,200	71.6	170
Equatorial Guinea Malabo		551,200	10,831	$50,200	49.5	116
Eritrea Asmara		4.9 million	46,842	$1,000	59.6	16
Ethiopia Addis Ababa		76.5 million	435,186	$1,000	49.2	5
Gabon Libreville		1.5 million	103,347	$7,200	54.0	251
Gambia Banjul		1.7 million	4,363	$2,000	54.5	3
Ghana Accra		22.9 million	92,456	$2,600	59.1	115
Guinea Conakry		9.9 million	94,926	$2,000	49.7	47
Guinea-Bissau Bissau		1.5 million	13,946	$900	47.2	43
Kenya Nairobi		36.9 million	224,962	$1,200	55.3	22
Lesotho Maseru		2.1 million	11,720	$2,600	34.5	16
Liberia Monrovia		3.2 million	43,000	$1,000	40.4	26
Libya Tripoli		6 million	679,362	$12,700	76.9	139
Madagascar Antananarivo		19.4 million	226,657	$900	62.1	23
Malawi Lilongwe		13.6 million	45,745	$600	43.0	3
United States Washington, D.C.		301.1 million	3,718,711	$43,500	78.0	844

COUNTRY Capital	FLAG	POPULATION	AREA (sq mi)	PER CAPITA GDP (U.S. $)	LIFE EXPECTANCY AT BIRTH	TVS PER 1,000 PEOPLE
Mali Bamako		11.9 million	478,767	$1,200	49.5	13
Mauritania Nouakchott		3.3 million	397,955	$2,600	53.5	95
Mauritius Port Louis		1.3 million	788	$13,500	72.9	248
Morocco Rabat		33.8 million	172,414	$4,400	71.2	165
Mozambique Maputo		20.9 million	309,496	$1,500	40.9	5
Namibia Windhoek		2.1 million	318,696	$7,400	43.1	38
Niger Niamey		13 million	489,191	$1,000	44.0	15
Nigeria Abuja		135 million	356,669	$1,400	47.4	69
Rwanda Kigali		9.9 million	10,169	$1,600	49.0	0.09
São Tomé and Príncipe; São Tomé		199,600	386	$1,200	67.6	229
Senegal Dakar		12.5 million	75,749	$1,800	56.7	41
Seychelles Victoria		81,900	176	$7,800	72.3	214
Sierra Leone Freetown		6.1 million	27,699	$900	40.6	13
Somalia Mogadishu		9.1 million	246,201	$600	48.8	14
United States Washington, D.C.		301.1 million	3,718,711	$43,500	78.0	844

COUNTRY Capital	FLAG	POPULATION	AREA (sq mi)	PER CAPITA GDP (U.S. $)	LIFE EXPECTANCY AT BIRTH	TVS PER 1,000 PEOPLE
South Africa; Pretoria, Cape Town, Bloemfontein		44 million	471,010	$13,000	42.5	138
Sudan Khartoum		39.4 million	967,498	$2,300	59.3	173
Swaziland Mbabane		1.2 million	6,704	$5,500	32.2	112
Tanzania Dar es Salaam, Dodoma		39.4 million	364,900	$800	46.1	21
Togo Lomé		5.7 million	21,925	$1,700	57.9	22
Tunisia Tunis		10.3 million	63,170	$8,600	75.3	190
Uganda Kampala		30.3 million	91,136	$1,800	51.8	28
Zambia Lusaka		11.5 million	290,586	$1,000	38.4	145
Zimbabwe Harare		12.3 million	150,804	$2,000	39.5	35
United States Washington, D.C.		301.1 million	3,718,711	$43,500	78.0	844

Africa's Growing Population

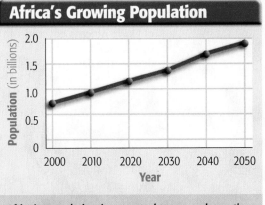

Africa's population is expected to grow dramatically in the next 50 years.

Africa and the World

	Average Age	Life Expectancy at Birth	Per Capita GDP (in U.S. $)
Africa	19.3 years	51.9	$2,800
Rest of the World	28.0 years	65.7	$10,000

Compared to the rest of the world, Africa's population is younger, has a shorter life expectancy, and has less money.

ANALYSIS SKILL ANALYZING INFORMATION

1. Based on the information above, what do you think are some key challenges in Africa today?

Physical Geography of Africa

FOCUS QUESTION
What forces had an impact on the development of Africa and why?

What You Will Learn...

Africa is one of the largest continents and one of the most diverse. Its landscapes range from harsh deserts in the north and south to lush tropical rain forests near the equator.

FOCUS ON READING AND WRITING

Understanding Comparison-Contrast Comparing and contrasting, or looking for similiarities and differences, can help you more fully understand the subject you are studying. **See the lesson, Understanding Comparison-Contrast, on page S12.**

Writing a Letter Home Imagine that you are spending your summer vacation visiting the countries of Africa. You want to write a letter home to a friend in the United States describing the land that you see. As you read this chapter, you will gather information that you can include in your letter.

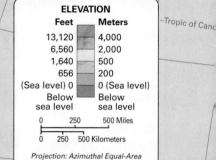

ELEVATION

Feet		Meters
13,120		4,000
6,560		2,000
1,640		500
656		200
(Sea level) 0		0 (Sea level)
Below sea level		Below sea level

0   250   500 Miles

0   250   500 Kilometers

Projection: Azimuthal Equal-Area

Tropic of Canc

East Africa The plains surrounding Mount Kilimanjaro are rich in wildlife. Millions of tourists come to visit this part of East Africa each year.

North Africa Most of North Africa is covered by the world's largest desert—the Sahara.

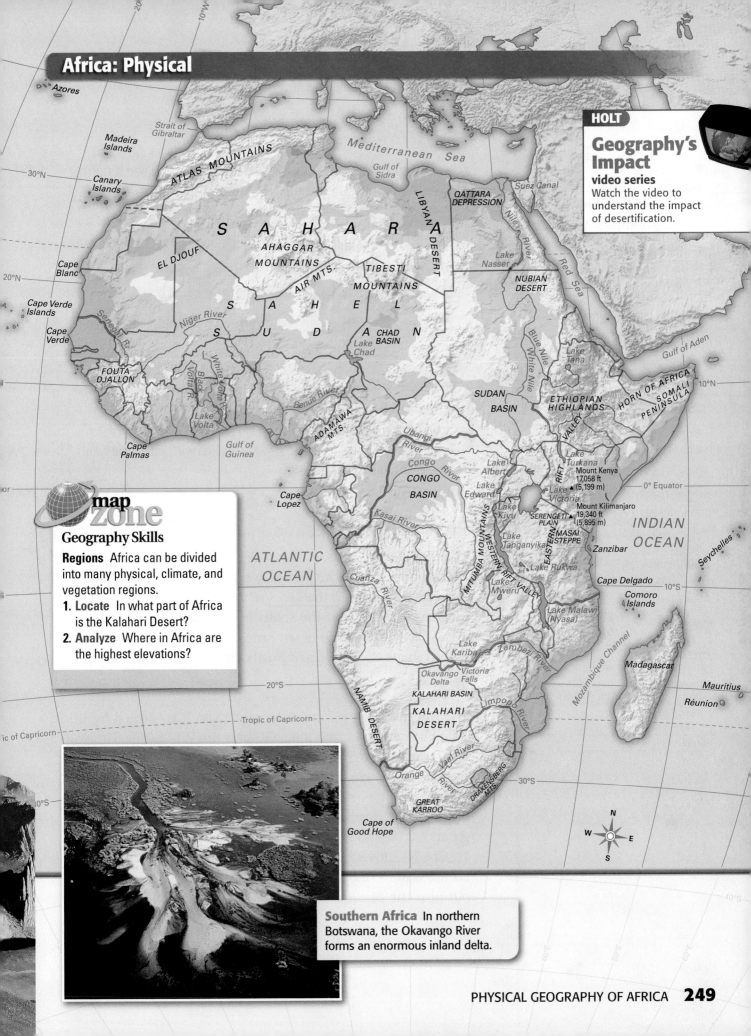

Azores

Madeira
Islands

Strait of
Gibraltar

30°N

Canary
Islands

ATLAS   MOUNTAINS

Mediterranean   Sea

Gulf of
Sidra

Gulf of
Sidra

QATTARA
DEPRESSION

Suez Canal

HOLT

Geography's Impact
video series
Watch the video to
understand the impact
of desertification.

Cape
Blanc

20°N

Cape Verde
Islands

Cape
Verde

FOUTA
DJALLON

Senegal R.

S   A   H   A   R   A

AHAGGAR
MOUNTAINS

EL DJOUF

AIR MTS.

Niger River

S   A   H   E   L

S   U   D   A   N

White Volta R.

Black Volta R.

TIBESTI
MOUNTAINS

LIBYAN   DESERT

CHAD
BASIN

Lake
Chad

Nile River

Lake
Nasser

NUBIAN
DESERT

Red Sea

Blue Nile

White Nile

Lake
Tana

Gulf of Aden

10°N

HORN OF AFRICA

SOMALI
PENINSULA

Cape
Palmas

Lake
Volta

Benue River

ADAMAWA
MTS.

Gulf of
Guinea

Ubangi
River

Congo River

SUDAN
BASIN

ETHIOPIAN
HIGHLANDS

RIFT   VALLEY

Cape
Lopez

CONGO
BASIN

Kasai River

Lake
Albert

Lake
Edward

Lake
Kivu

Lake
Victoria

Lake
Turkana

Mount Kenya
17,058 ft
(5,199 m)

0° Equator

MITUMBA MOUNTAINS

SERENGETI
PLAIN

Mount Kilimanjaro
19,340 ft
(5,895 m)

MASAI
STEPPE

INDIAN
OCEAN

or

map zone

Geography Skills

Regions Africa can be divided
into many physical, climate, and
vegetation regions.

1. Locate In what part of Africa
is the Kalahari Desert?

2. Analyze Where in Africa are
the highest elevations?

ATLANTIC
OCEAN

Cuanza
River

Lake
Tanganyika

EASTERN

WESTERN RIFT VALLEY

Lake Rukwa

Lake
Mweru

Zanzibar

Lake Malawi
(Nyasa)

Cape Delgado

Seychelles

Comoro
Islands

10°S

Lake
Kariba

Zambezi River

Okavango
Delta

Victoria
Falls

KALAHARI BASIN

Limpopo River

Mozambique Channel

Madagascar

Mauritius

Réunion

20°S

NAMIB DESERT

KALAHARI
DESERT

Tropic of Capricorn

ic of Capricorn

30°S

Orange
River

Vaal River

DRAKENSBERG
MTS.

GREAT
KARROO

Cape of
Good Hope

30°S

40°S

N
W   E
S

Southern Africa In northern
Botswana, the Okavango River
forms an enormous inland delta.

North Africa

Main Ideas

1. Major physical features of North Africa include the Nile River, the Sahara, and the Atlas Mountains.
2. The climate of North Africa is hot and dry, and water is the region's most important resource.

The Big Idea

North Africa is a dry region with limited water resources.

Key Terms and Places

Sahara, *p. 250*
Nile River, *p. 250*
silt, *p. 250*
Suez Canal, *p. 251*
oasis, *p. 252*
Atlas Mountains, *p. 252*

TAKING NOTES As you read, take notes on the physical geography of North Africa. Use the chart below to organize your notes.

Physical Features	
Climate	
Resources	

If YOU lived there...

As your airplane flies over Egypt, you look down and see a narrow ribbon of green—the Nile River. On either side of the green valley, sunlight glints off of bright sands that stretch as far as the eye can see. As you fly along North Africa's Mediterranean coast, you see many towns scattered across rugged mountains and green valleys.

What are the challenges of living in a mainly desert region?

BUILDING BACKGROUND Even though much of North Africa is covered by rugged mountains and huge areas of deserts, the region is not a bare wasteland. Areas of water include wet, fertile land with date palms and almond trees.

Physical Features

The region of North Africa includes Morocco, Algeria, Tunisia, Libya, and Egypt. From east to west the region stretches from the Atlantic Ocean to the Red Sea. Off the northern coast is the Mediterranean Sea. In the south lies the **Sahara** (suh-HAR-uh), a vast desert. Both the desert sands and bodies of water have helped shape the cultures of North Africa.

The Nile

The **Nile River** is the world's longest river. It is formed by the union of two rivers, the Blue Nile and the White Nile. Flowing northward through the eastern Sahara for about 4,000 miles, the Nile finally empties into the Mediterranean Sea.

For centuries, rain far to the south caused floods along the northern Nile, leaving rich silt in surrounding fields. **Silt** is finely ground fertile soil that is good for growing crops.

The Nile River Valley is like a long oasis in the desert. Farmers use water from the Nile to irrigate their fields. The Nile fans out near the Mediterranean Sea, forming a large delta. A delta

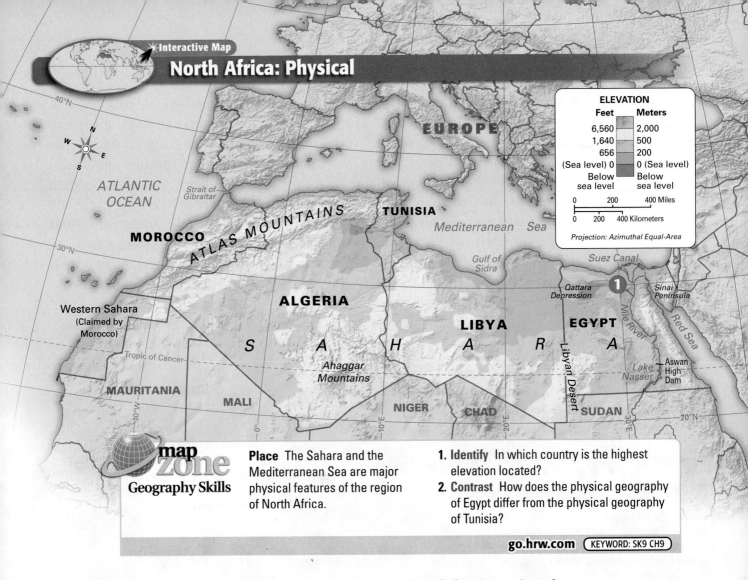

ELEVATION

Feet	Meters
6,560	2,000
1,640	500
656	200
(Sea level) 0	0 (Sea level)
Below sea level	Below sea level

Projection: Azimuthal Equal-Area

ATLANTIC OCEAN

EUROPE

Strait of Gibraltar

MOROCCO

ATLAS MOUNTAINS

TUNISIA

Mediterranean Sea

Gulf of Sidra

Suez Canal

Qattara Depression

Sinai Peninsula

ALGERIA

LIBYA

EGYPT

Nile River

Red Sea

Western Sahara (Claimed by Morocco)

S A H A R A

Ahaggar Mountains

Tropic of Cancer

Libyan Desert

Lake Nasser

Aswan High Dam

MAURITANIA

MALI

NIGER

CHAD

SUDAN

map zone Geography Skills

Place The Sahara and the Mediterranean Sea are major physical features of the region of North Africa.

1. **Identify** In which country is the highest elevation located?
2. **Contrast** How does the physical geography of Egypt differ from the physical geography of Tunisia?

go.hrw.com   KEYWORD: SK9 CH9

is a landform at the mouth of a river that is created by the deposit of sediment. The sediment in the Nile delta makes the area extremely fertile.

The Aswan High Dam controls flooding along the Nile. However, the dam also traps silt, preventing it from being carried downriver. Today some of Egypt's farmers must use fertilizers to enrich the soil.

The Sinai and the Suez Canal

East of the Nile is the triangular Sinai Peninsula. Barren, rocky mountains and desert cover the Sinai. Between the Sinai and the rest of Egypt is the **Suez Canal**. The French built the canal in the 1860s. It is a narrow waterway that connects the Mediterranean Sea with the Red Sea. Large cargo ships carry oil and goods through the canal.

1 Flowing for 4,132 miles, the Nile is the longest river in the world.

The Sahara

ACADEMIC
VOCABULARY
impact effect,
result

The Sahara, the largest desert in the world, covers most of North Africa. The name Sahara comes from the Arabic word for "desert." It has an enormous **impact** on the landscapes of North Africa.

One impact of the very dry Sahara is that few people live there. Small settlements are located near a water source such as an oasis. An **oasis** is a wet, fertile area in a desert where a natural spring or well provides water.

In addition to broad, windswept gravel plains, sand dunes cover much of the Sahara. Dry streambeds are also common.

Mountains

Do you think of deserts as flat regions? You may be surprised to learn that the Sahara is far from flat. Some sand dunes and ridges rise as high as 1,000 feet (305 m). The Sahara also has spectacular mountain ranges. For example, a mountain range in southern Algeria rises to a height of 9,800 feet (3,000 m). Another range, the **Atlas Mountains** on the northwestern side of the Sahara near the Mediterranean coast, rises even higher, to 13,600 feet (4,160 m).

READING CHECK Summarizing What are the major physical features of North Africa?

Close-up

A Sahara Oasis

The largest desert in the world, the Sahara, spans almost 4 million square miles across North Africa. From ancient times to today, traders crossing the Sahara have relied on the desert's oases. These oases provide water and shade.

Date palms thrive on the banks of this natural spring, which provides water to travelers and irrigated fields.

By carrying supplies, camels help the nomadic Tuareg people travel from oasis to oasis.

Climate and Resources

North Africa is very dry. However, rare storms can cause flooding. In some areas these floods as well as high winds have carved bare rock surfaces out of the land.

North Africa has three main climates. A desert climate covers most of the region. Temperatures range from mild to very hot. How hot can it get? Temperatures as high as 136°F (58°C) have been recorded in Libya. However, the humidity is very low. As a result, temperatures can drop quickly after sunset. In winter temperatures can fall below freezing at night.

The second climate type in the region is a Mediterranean climate. Much of the northern coast west of Egypt has this type of climate. Winters there are mild and moist. Summers are hot and dry. Areas between the coast and the Sahara have a steppe climate.

Oil and gas are important resources, particularly for Libya, Algeria, and Egypt. Morocco mines iron ore and minerals used to make fertilizers. The Sahara has natural resources such as coal, oil, and natural gas.

FOCUS ON READING

How are summers and winters different in a Mediterranean climate?

READING CHECK **Generalizing** What are North Africa's major resources?

Shelters like this one provide a place for travelers to rest.

SUMMARY AND PREVIEW In this section, you learned about the physical geography of North Africa. Next, you will learn about a very different region to the south—West Africa.

ANALYSIS SKILL **ANALYZING VISUALS**

Why do you think an oasis would be important to people traveling through the Sahara?

Section 1 Assessment

go.hrw.com
Online Quiz
KEYWORD: SK9 HP9

Reviewing Ideas, Terms, and Places

1. a. **Define** What is an **oasis**?
   b. **Explain** Why is the **Suez Canal** an important waterway?
   c. **Elaborate** Would it be possible to farm in Egypt if the **Nile River** did not exist? Explain your answer.
2. a. **Recall** What is the climate of most of North Africa?
   b. **Draw Conclusions** What resources of North Africa are the most valuable?

Critical Thinking

3. **Categorizing** Draw a diagram like the one shown here. Use your notes to list two facts about each physical feature of North Africa.

Nile · Physical Features · Sinai and Suez Canal · Sahara · Mountains

FOCUS ON WRITING

4. **Noting Interesting Details** What physical feature of North Africa do you think your friend back home would find interesting? Write down some notes about what you could mention in your letter.

West Africa

If YOU lived there...

Your family grows crops on the banks of the Niger River. Last year, your father let you go with him to sell the crops in a city down the river. This year you get to go with him again. As you paddle your boat, everything looks the same as last year—until suddenly the river appears to grow! It looks as big as the sea, and there are many islands all around. The river wasn't like this last year.

What do you think caused the change in the river?

What You Will Learn...

Main Ideas

1. West Africa's key physical features include plains and the Niger River.
2. West Africa has distinct climate and vegetation zones that go from arid in the north to tropical in the south.
3. West Africa has good agricultural and mineral resources that may one day help the economies in the region.

The Big Idea

West Africa, which is mostly a region of plains, has climates ranging from arid to tropical and has important resources.

Key Terms and Places

Niger River, *p. 255*
zonal, *p. 256*
Sahel, *p. 256*
desertification, *p. 256*
savanna, *p. 256*

TAKING NOTES As you read, use a chart like the one below to help you organize your notes on the physical geography of West Africa.

Physical features	
Climate and vegetation	
Resources	

BUILDING BACKGROUND The Niger River is one of West Africa's most important physical features. It brings precious water to the region's dry plains. Much of the interior of West Africa experiences desertlike conditions, but the region's rivers and lakes help to support life there.

Physical Features

The region we call West Africa stretches from the Sahara in the north to the coasts of the Atlantic Ocean and the Gulf of Guinea in the west and south. While West Africa's climate changes quite a bit from north to south, the region does not have a wide variety of landforms. Throughout all of West Africa, the main physical features are plains and rivers.

Plains and Highlands

Plains, flat areas of land, cover most of West Africa. The coastal plain along the Gulf of Guinea is home to most of the region's cities. The interior plains provide land where people can raise a few crops or animals.

West Africa's plains are vast, interrupted only by a few highland areas. One area in the southwest has plateaus and cliffs. People have built houses directly into the sides of these cliffs for many hundreds of years. The region's only high mountains are the Tibesti Mountains in the northeast.

The Niger River

As you can see on the map below, many rivers flow across West Africa's plains. The most important river is the Niger (NY-juhr). The **Niger River** starts in some low mountains not too far from the Atlantic Ocean. From there, it flows 2,600 miles (4,185 km) into the interior of the region before emptying into the Gulf of Guinea.

The Niger brings life-giving water to West Africa. Many people farm along its banks or fish in its waters. It is also an important transportation route, especially during the rainy season. At that time, the river floods and water flows smoothly over its rapids.

Part of the way along its route the river divides into a network of channels, swamps, and lakes. This watery network is called the inland delta. Although it looks much like the delta where a river flows into the sea, this one is actually hundreds of miles from the coast in Mali.

READING CHECK **Summarizing** Why is the Niger River important to West Africa?

FOCUS ON READING

The word *although* signals contrast in this paragraph. What is being contrasted?

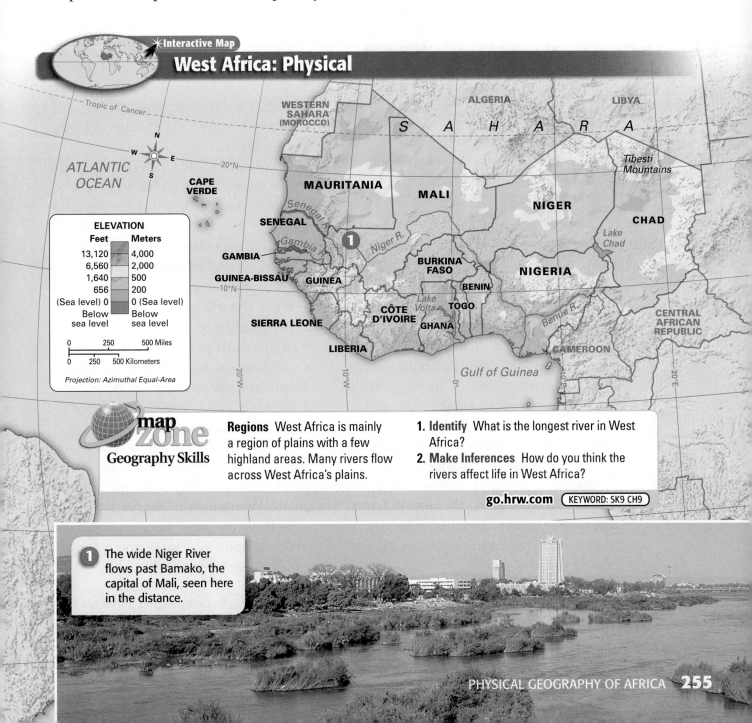

★Interactive Map

West Africa: Physical

ELEVATION

Feet		Meters
13,120		4,000
6,560		2,000
1,640		500
656		200
(Sea level) 0		0 (Sea level)
Below sea level		Below sea level

0   250   500 Miles
0   250   500 Kilometers

Projection: Azimuthal Equal-Area

Tropic of Cancer

ATLANTIC OCEAN

CAPE VERDE

WESTERN SAHARA (MOROCCO)

ALGERIA   LIBYA

S A H A R A

Tibesti Mountains

MAURITANIA   MALI   NIGER   CHAD

Lake Chad

SENEGAL   Senegal R.

GAMBIA   Gambia R.   Niger R.

GUINEA-BISSAU   GUINEA

BURKINA FASO   NIGERIA

BENIN

CÔTE D'IVOIRE   Lake Volta   TOGO

SIERRA LEONE   GHANA   Benue R.

LIBERIA   CAMEROON   CENTRAL AFRICAN REPUBLIC

Gulf of Guinea

map zone

Geography Skills

Regions West Africa is mainly a region of plains with a few highland areas. Many rivers flow across West Africa's plains.

1. **Identify** What is the longest river in West Africa?
2. **Make Inferences** How do you think the rivers affect life in West Africa?

go.hrw.com KEYWORD: SK9 CH9

1 The wide Niger River flows past Bamako, the capital of Mali, seen here in the distance.

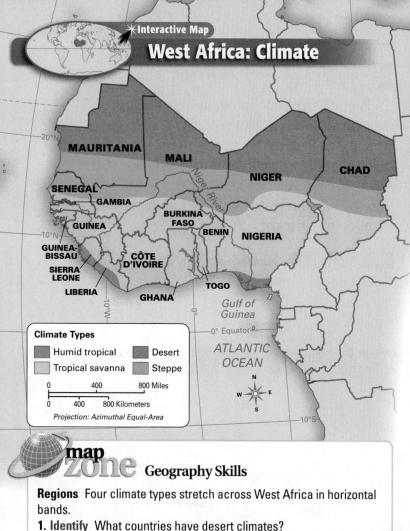

Interactive Map
West Africa: Climate

Climate Types

- ⬛ Humid tropical
- ⬜ Tropical savanna
- ⬛ Desert
- ⬛ Steppe

| 0 | 400 | 800 Miles |
| 0 | 400 | 800 Kilometers |

Projection: Azimuthal Equal-Area

map zone Geography Skills

Regions Four climate types stretch across West Africa in horizontal bands.
1. **Identify** What countries have desert climates?
2. **Make Inferences** What areas do you think get the most rainfall?

go.hrw.com [KEYWORD: SK9 CH9]

Sahel Vegetation in the semiarid Sahel is limited, but it does support some grazing animals.

Climate and Vegetation

West Africa has four different climate regions. As you can see on the map above, these climate regions stretch from east to west in bands or zones. Because of this, geographers say the region's climates are **zonal**, which means "organized by zone."

The northernmost zone of the region lies within the Sahara, the world's largest desert. Hardly any vegetation grows in the desert, and large areas of this dry climate zone have few or no people.

South of the Sahara is the semiarid **Sahel** (SAH-hel), a strip of land that divides the desert from wetter areas. It has a steppe climate. Rainfall there varies greatly from year to year. In some years it never rains. Although the Sahel is quite dry, it does have enough vegetation to support hardy grazing animals.

However, the Sahel is becoming more like the Sahara. Animals have overgrazed the land in some areas. Also, people have cut down trees for firewood. Without these plants to anchor the soil, wind blows soil away. These conditions, along with drought, are causing desertification in the Sahel. **Desertification** is the spread of desertlike conditions.

To the south of the Sahel is a savanna zone. A **savanna** is an area of tall grasses and scattered trees and shrubs. When rains fall regularly, farmers can do well in this region of West Africa.

The fourth climate zone lies along the coasts of the Atlantic and the Gulf of Guinea. This zone has a humid tropical climate. Plentiful rain supports tropical forests. However, many trees have been cut from these forests to make room for the region's growing populations.

READING CHECK **Categorizing** What are the region's four climate zones?

Savanna Grasses and scattered trees grow on the savanna. This region can be good for farming.

Tropical Forest Thick forests are found along the coasts of West Africa. The tall trees provide homes for many animals.

Resources

West Africa has a variety of resources. These resources include agricultural products, oil, and minerals.

The climate in parts of West Africa is good for agriculture. For example, Ghana is the world's leading producer of cacao, which is used to make chocolate. Coffee, coconuts, and peanuts are also among the region's main exports.

Oil, which is found off the coast of Nigeria, is the region's most valuable resource. Nigeria is a major exporter of oil. West Africa also has mineral riches, such as diamonds, gold, iron ore, and bauxite. Bauxite is the main source of aluminum.

READING CHECK **Summarizing** What are some of the region's resources?

SUMMARY AND PREVIEW West Africa is mostly covered with plains. Across these plains stretch four different climate zones, most of which are dry. In spite of the harsh climate, West Africa has some valuable resources. Next, you will learn about similar features in East Africa.

go.hrw.com
Online Quiz
KEYWORD: SK9 CH9

Section 2 Assessment

Reviewing Ideas, Terms, and Places

1. **a. Describe** What is the inland delta on the **Niger River** like?

   b. Summarize What is the physical geography of West Africa like?

   c. Elaborate Why do you think most of West Africa's cities are located on the coastal plain?

2. **a. Recall** Why do geographers say West Africa's climates are **zonal**?

   b. Compare and Contrast What is one similarity and one difference between the **Sahel** and the **savanna**?

   c. Evaluate How do you think **desertification** affects people's lives in West Africa?

3. **a. Identify** What is the most valuable resource in West Africa?

   b. Make Inferences Where do you think most of the crops in West Africa are grown?

Critical Thinking

4. **Identifying Cause and Effect**
   Review your notes on climate. Using a graphic organizer like the one here, identify the causes and effects of desertification.

Causes → Desertification → Effects

FOCUS ON WRITING

5. **Comparing Landscapes** The landscapes you see in West Africa are very different from those you encountered in the North. How will you explain these differences to your friend? Write down some ideas.

East Africa

What You Will Learn...

Main Ideas

1. East Africa's physical features range from rift valleys to plains.
2. East Africa's climate is influenced by its location and elevation, and the region's vegetation includes savannas and forests.

The Big Idea

East Africa is a region of diverse physical features, climates, and vegetation.

Key Terms and Places

rift valleys, *p. 258*
Great Rift Valley, *p. 258*
Mount Kilimanjaro, *p. 259*
Serengeti Plain, *p. 259*
Lake Victoria, *p. 260*
droughts, *p. 260*

TAKING NOTES As you read, use the chart below to take notes on East Africa's physical features and climate and vegetation.

Physical Features	
Climate and Vegetation	

If YOU lived there...

You and your friends are planning to hike up Mount Kilimanjaro, near the equator in Tanzania. It is hot in your camp at the base of the mountain. You're wearing shorts and a T-shirt, but your guide tells you to pack a fleece jacket and jeans. It is so hot outside that you think the idea is silly, but you take his advice. You start your climb, and soon you understand this advice. The air is much colder, and there's snow on the nearby peaks.

Why is it cold at the top of the mountain?

BUILDING BACKGROUND The landscapes of East Africa have been shaped by powerful forces. The movement of tectonic plates has stretched the Earth's surface here, creating steep-sided valleys and huge lakes.

Physical Features

East Africa is a region of spectacular landscapes and wildlife. Vast plains and plateaus stretch throughout the region. In the north lie huge deserts and dry grasslands. In the southwest, large lakes dot the plateaus. In the east, sandy beaches and colorful coral reefs run along the coast.

The Rift Valleys

Look at the map on the next page. As you can see, East Africa's rift valleys cut from north to south across the region. **Rift valleys** are places on Earth's surface where the crust stretches until it breaks. Rift valleys form when Earth's tectonic plates move away from each other. This movement causes the land to arch and split along the rift valleys. As the land splits open, volcanoes erupt and deposit layers of rock in the region.

Seen from the air, the **Great Rift Valley** looks like a giant scar. The Great Rift Valley is the largest rift on Earth and is made up of two rifts—the eastern rift and the western rift.

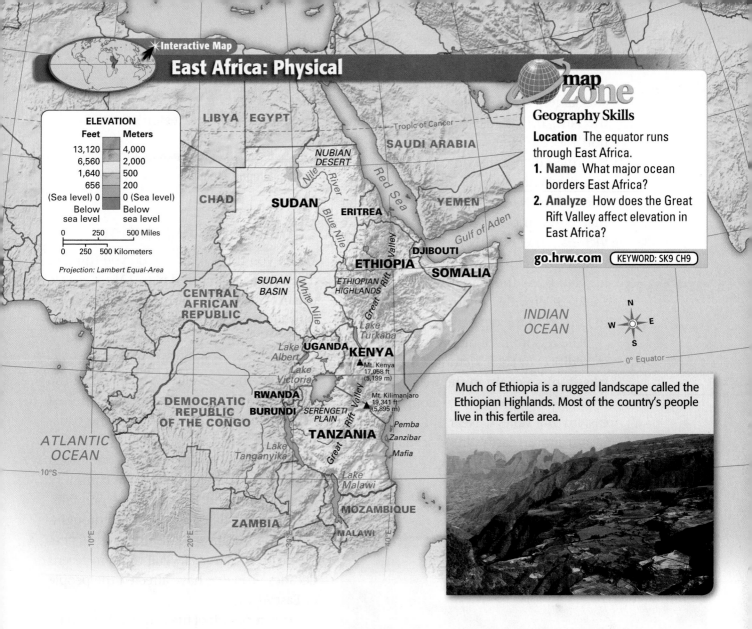

ELEVATION

Feet	Meters
13,120	4,000
6,560	2,000
1,640	500
656	200
(Sea level) 0	0 (Sea level)
Below sea level	Below sea level

0   250   500 Miles

0   250   500 Kilometers

Projection: Lambert Equal-Area

map Zone

Geography Skills

Location The equator runs through East Africa.

1. **Name** What major ocean borders East Africa?
2. **Analyze** How does the Great Rift Valley affect elevation in East Africa?

go.hrw.com KEYWORD: SK9 CH9

Much of Ethiopia is a rugged landscape called the Ethiopian Highlands. Most of the country's people live in this fertile area.

The rift walls are usually a series of steep cliffs. These cliffs rise as much as 6,000 feet (2,000 m).

Mountains and Highlands

The landscape of East Africa has many high volcanic mountains. The highest mountain in Africa, **Mount Kilimanjaro** (ki-luh-muhn-JAHR-oh), rises to 19,340 feet (5,895 m). Despite Kilimanjaro's location near the equator, the mountain's peak has long been covered in snow. This much colder climate is caused by Kilimanjaro's high elevation.

Other areas of high elevation in East Africa include the Ethiopian Highlands.

These highlands, which lie mostly in Ethiopia, are very rugged. Deep river valleys cut through this landscape.

Plains

Even though much of East Africa lies at high elevations, some areas are flat. For example, plains stretch as far as the eye can see along the eastern rift in Tanzania and Kenya. Tanzania's **Serengeti Plain** is one of the largest plains. It is here that an abundance of wildlife thrives. The plain's grasses, trees, and water provide nutrition for wildlife that includes elephants, giraffes, lions, and zebras. To protect this wildlife, Tanzania established a national park.

Rivers and Lakes

East Africa also has a number of rivers and large lakes. The world's longest river, the Nile, begins in East Africa and flows north to the Mediterranean Sea. The Nile is formed by the meeting of the Blue Nile and the White Nile at Khartoum, Sudan. The White Nile is formed by the water that flows into Africa's largest lake, **Lake Victoria**. The Blue Nile is formed from waters that run down from Ethiopia's highlands. As the Nile meanders through Sudan, it provides a narrow, fertile lifeline to farmers in the desert.

The region has a number of great lakes in addition to Lake Victoria. One group of lakes forms a chain in the western rift valleys. There are also lakes along the drier eastern rift valleys. Near the eastern rift, heat from the Earth's interior makes some lakes so hot that no human can swim in them. In addition, some lakes are extremely salty. However, some of these rift lakes provide algae for the region's flamingos.

READING CHECK **Evaluating** What river is the most important in this region? Why?

Climate and Vegetation

When you think of Africa, do you think of it as being a hot or cold place? Most people usually think all of Africa is hot. However, they are mistaken. Some areas of East Africa have a cool climate.

East Africa's location on the equator and differences in elevation influence the climates and types of vegetation in East Africa. For example, areas near the equator receive the greatest amount of rainfall. Areas farther from the equator are much drier and seasonal droughts are common. **Droughts** are periods when little rain falls, and crops are damaged. During a drought, crops and the grasses for cattle die and people begin to starve. Several times in recent decades droughts have affected the people of East Africa.

Further south of the equator the climate changes to tropical savanna. Tall grasses and scattered trees make up the savanna landscape. Here the greatest climate changes occur along the sides of the rift valleys. The rift floors are dry with grasslands and thorn shrubs.

North of the equator, areas of plateaus and mountains have a highland climate and dense forests. Temperatures in the highlands are much cooler than temperatures on the savanna. The highlands experience heavy rainfall because of its high elevation, but the valleys are drier. This mild climate makes farming possible. As a result, most of the region's population lives in the highlands.

Satellite View

Great Rift Valley

This satellite image of part of the Great Rift Valley in Ethiopia was created by using both infrared light and true color. The bright blue dots are some of the smaller lakes that were created by the rifts. Once active volcanoes, some of these lakes are very deep. Vegetation appears as areas of green. Bare, rocky land appears pink and gray.

Analyzing How were the lakes in the Great Rift Valley created?

Ancient volcanoes surround Uganda's Lake Mutanda. Here villagers rely on the lake's plentiful supply of fish.

Areas east of the highlands and on the Indian Ocean coast are at a much lower elevation. These areas have desert and steppe climates. Vegetation is limited to shrubs and hardy grasses that are adapted to water shortages.

READING CHECK **Categorizing** What are some of East Africa's climate types?

SUMMARY AND PREVIEW In this section you learned about East Africa's rift valleys, mountains, highlands, plains, rivers, and lakes. You also learned that the region's location and elevation affect its climate and vegetation. In the next section you will learn about the geography of Central Africa.

Section 3 Assessment

go.hrw.com
Online Quiz
KEYWORD: SK9 HP9

Reviewing Ideas, Terms, and Places

1. **a. Define** What are **rift valleys**?
   b. Explain Why is there snow on **Mount Kilimanjaro**?
   c. Elaborate What are some unusual characteristics of the lakes in the **Great Rift Valley**?
2. **a. Recall** What is the climate of the highlands in East Africa like?
   b. Draw Conclusions What are some effects of **drought** in the region?
   c. Develop How are the climates of some areas of East Africa affected by elevation?

Critical Thinking

3. **Categorizing** Using your notes and this chart, place details about East Africa's physical features into different categories.

Physical Features			
Rift Valleys	Mountains and Highlands	Plains	Rivers and Lakes

FOCUS ON WRITING

4. **Describing the Physical Geography** Note the physical features of East Africa that you can describe in your letter. How do these features compare to the features where you live?

Central Africa

If YOU lived there...

You are on a nature hike with a guide through the forests of the Congo Basin. It has been several hours since you have seen any other people. Sometimes your guide has to use a heavy machete to cut a path through the thick vegetation, but mostly you try not to disturb any plants or animals. Suddenly, you reach a clearing and see a group of men working hard to load huge tree trunks onto big trucks.

How do you feel about what you see?

BUILDING BACKGROUND Much of Central Africa, particularly in the Congo Basin, is covered with thick, tropical forests. The forests provide valuable resources, but people have different ideas about how the forests should be used. Forests are just one of the many types of landscapes in Central Africa.

Physical Features

Central Africa is bordered by the Atlantic Ocean in the west. In the east, it is bordered by a huge valley called the Western Rift Valley. The land in between has some of the highest mountains and biggest rivers in Africa.

Landforms

You can think of the region as a big soup bowl with a wide rim. Near the middle of the bowl is the **Congo Basin**. In geography, a **basin** is a generally flat region surrounded by higher land such as mountains and plateaus.

Plateaus and low hills surround the Congo Basin. The highest mountains in Central Africa lie farther away from the basin, along the Western Rift Valley. Some of these snowcapped mountains rise to more than 16,700 feet (5,090 m). Two lakes also lie along the rift—Lake Nyasa and Lake Tanganyika (tan-guhn-YEE-kuh). Lake Nyasa is also called Lake Malawi.

What You Will Learn...

Main Ideas

1. Central Africa's major physical features include the Congo Basin and plateaus surrounding the basin.
2. Central Africa has a humid tropical climate and dense forest vegetation.
3. Central Africa's resources include forest products and valuable minerals such as diamonds and copper.

The Big Idea

The Congo River, tropical forests, and mineral resources are important features of Central Africa's physical geography.

Key Terms and Places

Congo Basin, *p. 262*
basin, *p. 262*
Congo River, *p. 263*
Zambezi River, *p. 263*
periodic market, *p. 265*
copper belt, *p. 265*

 TAKING NOTES As you read, use a chart like the one here to note characteristics of Central Africa's physical geography.

Physical features	
Climate and vegetation	
Resources	

Rivers

The huge **Congo River** is fed by hundreds of smaller rivers. They drain the swampy Congo Basin and flow into the river as it runs toward the Atlantic. Many rapids and waterfalls lie along its route, especially near its mouth. These obstacles make it impossible for ships to travel from the interior of Central Africa all the way to the Atlantic. The Congo provides an important transportation route in the interior, however.

In the southern part of the region, the **Zambezi** (zam-BEE-zee) **River** flows eastward toward the Indian Ocean. Many rivers in Angola and Zambia, as well as water from Lake Nyasa, flow into the Zambezi. The Zambezi also has many waterfalls along its route, the most famous of which are the spectacular Victoria Falls.

READING CHECK **Finding Main Ideas** Where is the highest land in Central Africa?

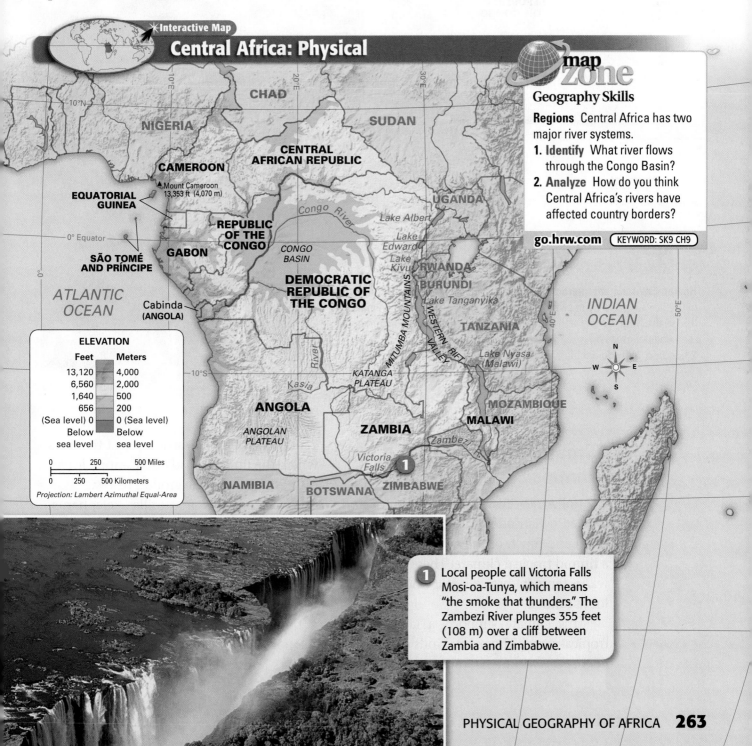

★Interactive Map

Central Africa: Physical

map zone

Geography Skills

Regions Central Africa has two major river systems.
1. **Identify** What river flows through the Congo Basin?
2. **Analyze** How do you think Central Africa's rivers have affected country borders?

go.hrw.com (KEYWORD: SK9 CH9)

ELEVATION

Feet	Meters
13,120	4,000
6,560	2,000
1,640	500
656	200
(Sea level) 0	0 (Sea level)
Below sea level	Below sea level

0   250   500 Miles
0   250   500 Kilometers

Projection: Lambert Azimuthal Equal-Area

Map labels: CHAD, NIGERIA, SUDAN, CENTRAL AFRICAN REPUBLIC, CAMEROON, Mount Cameroon 13,353 ft (4,070 m), EQUATORIAL GUINEA, UGANDA, Lake Albert, Congo River, Lake Edward, REPUBLIC OF THE CONGO, Lake Kivu, RWANDA, BURUNDI, SÃO TOMÉ AND PRÍNCIPE, GABON, CONGO BASIN, DEMOCRATIC REPUBLIC OF THE CONGO, ATLANTIC OCEAN, Cabinda (ANGOLA), Lake Tanganyika, INDIAN OCEAN, MITUMBA MOUNTAINS, TANZANIA, WESTERN RIFT VALLEY, Kasai River, KATANGA PLATEAU, Lake Nyasa (Malawi), MOZAMBIQUE, ANGOLA, ANGOLAN PLATEAU, ZAMBIA, MALAWI, Zambezi, Victoria Falls, NAMIBIA, BOTSWANA, ZIMBABWE

1 Local people call Victoria Falls Mosi-oa-Tunya, which means "the smoke that thunders." The Zambezi River plunges 355 feet (108 m) over a cliff between Zambia and Zimbabwe.

Central Africa's National Parks

National parks in Central Africa protect the habitat of gorillas (above), which are endangered, and okapis (below).

map zone Geography Skills

Human-Environment Interaction People have created national parks in Central Africa to try to protect the region's landscapes and animals.

1. **Use the Map** What Central African countries have national parks in coastal areas?
2. **Explain** Why do people want to protect natural environments?

Climate, Vegetation, and Animals

Central Africa lies along the equator and in the low latitudes. Therefore, the Congo Basin and much of the Atlantic coast have a humid tropical climate. These areas have warm temperatures all year and receive a lot of rainfall.

This climate supports a large, dense tropical forest. The many kinds of tall trees in the forest form a complete canopy. The canopy is the uppermost layer of the trees where the limbs spread out. Canopy leaves block sunlight to the ground below.

Such animals as gorillas, elephants, wild boars, and okapis live in the forest. The okapi is a short-necked relative of the giraffe. However, since little sunlight shines through the canopy, only a few animals live on the forest floor. Some animals, such as birds, monkeys, bats, and snakes, live in the trees. Many insects also live in Central Africa's forest.

The animals in Central Africa's tropical forests, as well as the forests themselves, are in danger. Large areas of forest are being cleared rapidly for farming and logging. Also, people hunt the large animals in the forests to get food. To promote protection of forests and other natural environments, governments have set up national park areas in their countries.

North and south of the Congo Basin are large areas with a tropical savanna climate. Those areas are warm all year, but they have distinct dry and wet seasons. There are grasslands, scattered trees, and shrubs. The high mountains in the east have a highland climate. Dry steppe and even desert climates are found in the far southern part of the region.

READING CHECK **Summarizing** What are the climate and vegetation like in the Congo Basin?

Resources

The tropical environment of Central Africa is good for growing crops. Most people in the region are subsistence farmers. However, many farmers are now beginning to grow crops for sale. Common crops are coffee, bananas, and corn. In rural areas, people trade agricultural and other products in periodic markets. A **periodic market** is an open-air trading market that is set up once or twice a week.

Central Africa is rich in other natural resources as well. The large tropical forest provides timber, while the rivers provide a way to travel and to trade. Dams on the rivers produce hydroelectricity, an important energy resource. Other energy resources in the region include oil, natural gas, and coal.

Central Africa also has many valuable minerals, including copper, uranium, tin, zinc, diamonds, gold, and cobalt. Of these, copper is the most important. Most of Africa's copper is found in an area called the **copper belt**. The copper belt stretches through northern Zambia and southern Democratic Republic of the Congo. However, poor transportation systems and political problems have kept the region's resources from being fully developed.

READING CHECK **Analyzing** Why are Central Africa's rivers an important natural resource?

SUMMARY AND PREVIEW Mighty rivers, the tropical forest of the Congo Basin, and mineral resources characterize the physical geography of Central Africa. These landscapes have influenced the region's history. Next, you will move south to study Southern Africa.

Section 4 Assessment

Reviewing Ideas, Terms, and Places

1. a. **Describe** What is the **Congo Basin**?
   b. **Elaborate** How do you think the **Congo River**'s rapids and waterfalls affect the economy of the region?
2. a. **Recall** What part of Central Africa has a highland climate?
   b. **Explain** Why have governments in the region set up national parks?
   c. **Evaluate** Is it more important to use the forest's resources or to protect the natural environment? Why?
3. a. **Define** What is a **periodic market**?
   b. **Elaborate** What kinds of political problems might keep mineral resources from being fully developed?

Critical Thinking

4. **Contrasting** Use your notes and a graphic organizer like this one to list differences between the Congo Basin and the areas surrounding it in Central Africa.

Congo Basin   Surrounding Areas

FOCUS ON WRITING

5. **Sharing Details** What details about Central Africa will you include in your letter? Will you describe the animals you have seen and the weather you have experienced? Take some notes.

Mapping Central Africa's Forests

Essential Elements

The World in Spatial Terms
Places and Regions
Physical Systems
Human Systems
Environment and Society
The Uses of Geography

Background Imagine taking a walk along a street in your neighborhood. Your purpose is to see the street in spatial terms and gather information to help you make a map. While you walk, you ask the kinds of questions geographers ask. How many houses, apartment buildings, or businesses are on the street? What kinds of animals or trees do you see? Your walk ends, and you organize your data. Now imagine that you are going to gather data on another walk. This walk will be 2,000 miles long.

A 2,000-Mile Walk In September 1999, an American scientist named Michael Fay began a 465-day, 2,000-mile walk through Central Africa's forests. He and his team followed elephant trails through thick vegetation. They waded through creeks and mucky swamps.

On the walk, Fay gathered data on the number and kinds of animals he saw. He counted elephant dung, chimpanzee nests, leopard tracks, and gorillas. He counted the types of trees and other plants along his

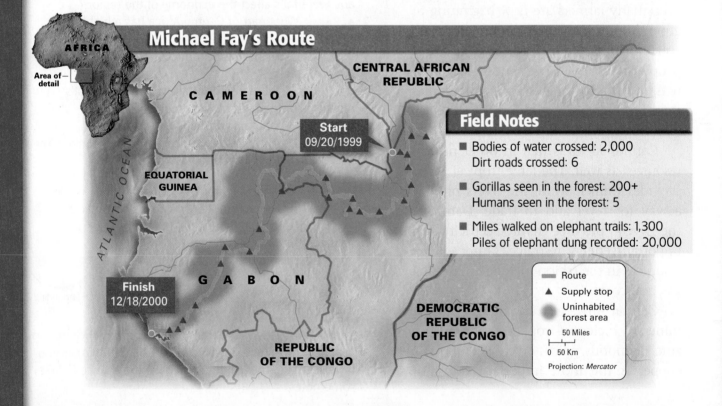

Michael Fay's Route

AFRICA

Area of detail

CENTRAL AFRICAN REPUBLIC

CAMEROON

Start
09/20/1999

ATLANTIC OCEAN

EQUATORIAL GUINEA

Field Notes

- Bodies of water crossed: 2,000
  Dirt roads crossed: 6

- Gorillas seen in the forest: 200+
  Humans seen in the forest: 5

- Miles walked on elephant trails: 1,300
  Piles of elephant dung recorded: 20,000

Finish
12/18/2000

GABON

DEMOCRATIC REPUBLIC OF THE CONGO

REPUBLIC OF THE CONGO

Route
Supply stop
Uninhabited forest area

0   50 Miles
0   50 Km

Projection: Mercator

Michael Fay (above) and his team had to chop their way through thick forest vegetation. In a clearing, they spotted this group of elephants.

route. He also counted human settlements and determined the effect of human activities on the environment.

Fay used a variety of tools to record the data he gathered on his walk. He wrote down what he observed in waterproof notebooks. He shot events and scenes with video and still cameras. To measure the distance he and his team walked each day, he used a tool called a Fieldranger. He also kept track of his exact position in the forest by using a GPS, or global positioning system.

What It Means Michael Fay explained the purpose of his long walk. "The whole idea behind this is to be able to use the data we've collected as a tool." Other geographers can compare Fay's data with their own. Their comparison may help them create more accurate maps. These maps will show where plants, animals, and humans are located in Central Africa's forests.

Fay's data can also help scientists plan the future use of land or resources in a region. For example, Fay has used his data to convince government officials in Gabon to set aside 10 percent of its land to create 13 national parks. The parks will be protected from future logging and farming. They also will preserve many of the plants and animals that Fay and his team observed on their long walk.

Geography for Life Activity

1. Why did Michael Fay walk 2,000 miles?

2. In what practical way has Michael Fay used his data?

3. **Read More about Fay's Walk** Read the three-part article on Michael Fay's walk in *National Geographic* October 2000, March 2001, and August 2001. After you read the article, explain why Fay called his walk a "megatransect."

Southern Africa

If YOU lived there...

You are a member of the San, a people who live in the Kalahari Desert. Your family lives with several others in a group of circular grass huts. You are friends with the other children. Sometimes you help your mom look for eggs or plants to use for carrying water. You also helped make all your water containers, clothes, carrying bags, and weapons, all of which come from the resources you find in the desert. Next year you will move away to attend school in a town.

How will your life change next year?

BUILDING BACKGROUND Parts of Southern Africa have a desert climate. Little vegetation grows in these areas, but some people do live there. Most of Southern Africa's people live in cooler and wetter areas, such as on the high, grassy plains in the south and east.

Physical Features

Southern Africa has some amazing scenery. On a visit to the region, you might see grassy plains, steamy swamps, mighty rivers, rocky waterfalls, and steep mountains and plateaus.

Plateaus and Mountains

Most of the land in Southern Africa lies on a large plateau. Parts of this plateau reach more than 4,000 feet (1,220 m) above sea level. To form the plateau, the land rises sharply from a narrow coastal plain. The steep face at the edge of a plateau or other raised area is called an **escarpment**.

In eastern South Africa, part of the escarpment is made up of a mountain range called the Drakensberg (DRAH-kuhnz-buhrk). The steep peaks rise as high as 11,425 feet (3,482 m). Farther north, another mountain range, the Inyanga (in-YANG-guh) Mountains, separates Zimbabwe and Mozambique. Southern Africa also has mountains along its western coast.

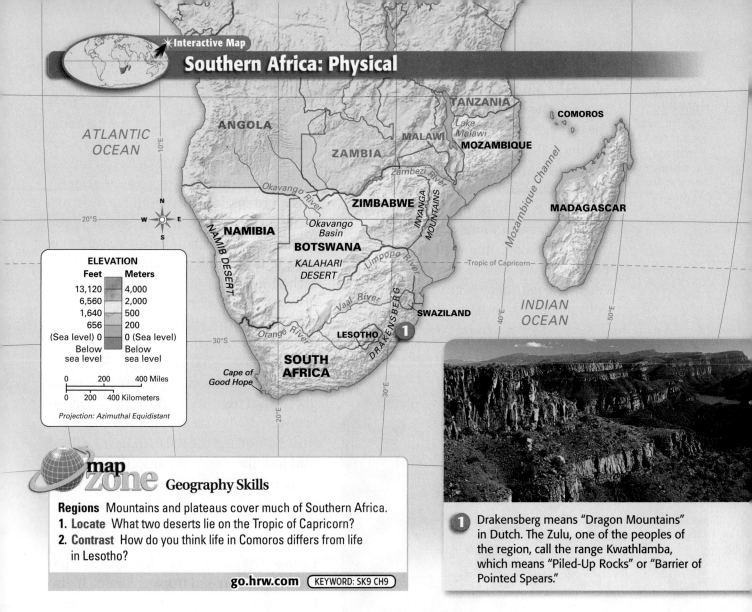

ELEVATION

Feet	Meters
13,120	4,000
6,560	2,000
1,640	500
656	200
(Sea level) 0	0 (Sea level)
Below sea level	Below sea level

0   200   400 Miles

0   200   400 Kilometers

Projection: Azimuthal Equidistant

map zone Geography Skills

Regions Mountains and plateaus cover much of Southern Africa.
1. **Locate** What two deserts lie on the Tropic of Capricorn?
2. **Contrast** How do you think life in Comoros differs from life in Lesotho?

go.hrw.com KEYWORD: SK9 CH9

1 Drakensberg means "Dragon Mountains" in Dutch. The Zulu, one of the peoples of the region, call the range Kwathlamba, which means "Piled-Up Rocks" or "Barrier of Pointed Spears."

Plains and Rivers

Southern Africa's narrow coastal plain and the wide plateau are covered with grassy plains. These flat plains are home to animals such as lions, leopards, elephants, baboons, and antelope.

Several large rivers cross Southern Africa's plains. The Okavango River flows from Angola into a huge basin in Botswana. This river's water never reaches the ocean. Instead it forms a swampy inland delta that is home to crocodiles, zebras, hippos, and other animals. Many tourists travel to Botswana to see these wild animals in their natural habitat.

The Orange River passes through the rocky Augrabies (oh-KRAH-bees) Falls as it flows to the Atlantic Ocean. When the water in the river is at its highest, the falls are several miles wide. The water tumbles down 19 separate waterfalls. The Limpopo River is another of the region's major rivers. It flows into the Indian Ocean. **Features** such as waterfalls and other obstacles block ships from sailing up these rivers. However, the rivers do allow irrigation for farmland in an otherwise dry area.

ACADEMIC VOCABULARY

features
characteristics

READING CHECK **Generalizing** What are Southern Africa's main physical features?

Climate and Vegetation

FOCUS ON READING

What phrase tells you that the eastern and western parts of Southern Africa are different?

Southern Africa's climates vary from east to west. The wettest place in the region is the east coast of the island of Madagascar. On the mainland, winds carrying moisture blow in from the Indian Ocean. Because the Drakensberg's high elevation causes these winds to blow upward, the eastern slopes of these mountains are rainy.

In contrast to the eastern part of the continent, the west is very dry. From the Atlantic coast, deserts give way to plains with semiarid and steppe climates.

Satellite View

Namib Desert

One of the world's most unusual deserts, the Namib lies on the Atlantic coast in Namibia. As this satellite image shows, the land there is extremely dry. Some of the world's highest sand dunes stretch for miles along the coast.

In spite of its harsh conditions, some insects have adapted to life in the desert. They can survive there because at night a fog rolls in from the ocean. The insects use the fog as a source of water.

Drawing Conclusions How have some insects adapted to living in the Namib Desert?

Savanna and Deserts

A large savanna region covers much of Southern Africa. Shrubs and short trees grow on the grassy plains of the savanna. In South Africa, these open grassland areas are known as the **veld** (VELT). As you can see on the map on the next page, vegetation gets more sparse in the south and west.

The driest place in the region is the **Namib Desert** on the Atlantic coast. Some parts of the Namib get as little as a half an inch (13 mm) of rainfall per year. In this dry area, plants get water from dew and fog rather than from rain.

Another desert, the Kalahari, occupies most of Botswana. Although this desert gets enough rain in the north to support grasses and trees, its sandy plains are mostly covered with scattered shrubs. Ancient streams crossing the Kalahari have drained into low, flat areas, or **pans**. On these flat areas, minerals left behind when the water evaporated form a glittering white layer.

Tropical Forests

Unlike the mainland, Madagascar has lush vegetation and tropical forests. It also has many animals found nowhere else. For example, some 50 species of lemurs, relatives of apes, live only on this island. However, the destruction of Madagascar's forests has endangered many of the island's animals.

READING CHECK **Summarizing** What is the climate and vegetation like in Southern Africa?

Resources

Southern Africa is rich in natural resources. Madagascar's forests provide timber. The region's rivers supply hydroelectricity and water for irrigation. Where rain is plentiful or irrigation is possible, farmers can grow a wide range of crops.

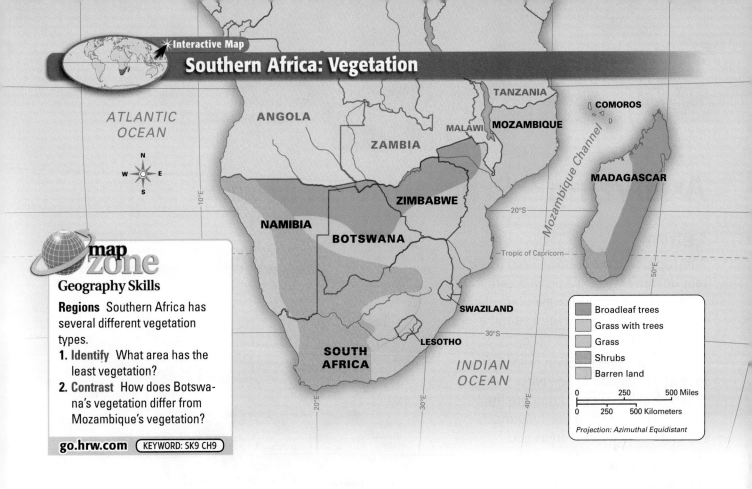

Southern Africa: Vegetation

ATLANTIC OCEAN

ANGOLA

TANZANIA

COMOROS

ZAMBIA

MALAWI   MOZAMBIQUE

Mozambique Channel

MADAGASCAR

ZIMBABWE

20°S

NAMIBIA

BOTSWANA

Tropic of Capricorn

SWAZILAND

30°S

LESOTHO

SOUTH AFRICA

INDIAN OCEAN

Broadleaf trees
Grass with trees
Grass
Shrubs
Barren land

0   250   500 Miles
0   250   500 Kilometers

Projection: Azimuthal Equidistant

map zone

Geography Skills

Regions Southern Africa has several different vegetation types.

1. **Identify** What area has the least vegetation?
2. **Contrast** How does Botswana's vegetation differ from Mozambique's vegetation?

go.hrw.com   KEYWORD: SK9 CH9

The region's most valuable resources, however, are minerals. Mines in South Africa produce most of the world's gold. In addition, South Africa, Botswana, and Namibia have productive diamond mines. Other mineral resources in Southern Africa include coal, platinum, copper, uranium, and iron ore. Although mining is very important to the economy of the region, the mines can have damaging effects on the surrounding natural environments.

READING CHECK Finding Main Ideas What are the main resources of Southern Africa?

SUMMARY AND PREVIEW Africa is a huge continent with a variety of landforms, water features, and climates. In the next chapters, you will learn how landforms and climate affected one of Africa's earliest civilizations, ancient Egypt.

go.hrw.com
Online Quiz
KEYWORD: SK9 HP9

Section 5 Assessment

Reviewing Ideas, Terms, and Places

1. a. **Define** What is an **escarpment**?
   b. **Elaborate** How is the Okavango River different from most other rivers you have studied?
2. a. **Recall** Where in Southern Africa is the driest climate?
   b. **Explain** What caused minerals to collect in **pans** in the Kalahari Desert?
3. a. **Identify** What are Southern Africa's most valuable resources?
   b. **Elaborate** How do you think the gold and diamond mines have affected South Africa's economy?

Critical Thinking

4. **Categorizing** Review your notes and use a graphic organizer like this one to sort characteristics by location.

	East	West
Physical Features		
Climate and Vegetation		

FOCUS ON WRITING

5. **Planning Your Letter** Now that you have finished your tour of Africa you can plan exactly what you will include in your letter home. Write a short outline of the topics you will include.

Social Studies Skills

Analyzing a Precipitation Map

Learn

A precipitation map shows how much rain or snow typically falls in a certain area over a year. Studying a precipitation map can help you understand a region's climate.

To read a precipitation map, first look at the legend to see what the different colors mean. Compare the legend to the map to see how much precipitation different areas get.

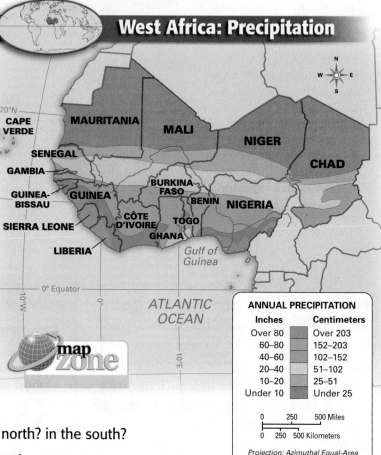

West Africa: Precipitation

ANNUAL PRECIPITATION

Inches		Centimeters
Over 80		Over 203
60–80		152–203
40–60		102–152
20–40		51–102
10–20		25–51
Under 10		Under 25

0   250   500 Miles
0   250   500 Kilometers

Projection: Azimuthal Equal-Area

Practice

Use the map on this page to answer the following questions.

1. What countries have areas that get over 80 inches of rain every year?

2. In what part of the region does the least amount of rain fall?

3. What do you think vegetation is like in the north? in the south?

4. Compare this map to the climate map in Section 1. How are the two maps similar?

Apply

Using an atlas or the Internet, find a precipitation map of all of Africa. Use that map to answer the following questions.

1. What area of the continent gets the most precipitation?

2. What area of the continent gets the least precipitation?

3. How much annual precipitation does Madagascar get?

Chapter Review

Geography's Impact
video series
Review the video to answer the closing question:
What are some of the ways desertification can be slowed, stopped, or even reversed?

Visual Summary

Use the visual summary below to help you review the main ideas of the chapter.

QUICK FACTS

Africa has a few highland areas, but most of the continent is covered by plains and plateaus.

Several major rivers, including the Nile, Congo, Niger, and Zambezi, flow through Africa.

Africa's climates and vegetation range from harsh deserts to lush tropical rain forest to temperate savannas.

Reviewing Vocabulary, Terms, and Places

For each statement below, write T if it is true and F if it is false. If the statement is false, write the correct term that would make the sentence a true statement.

1. West Africa's climate is described as savanna because it is organized by zone.

2. The Nile River is the longest river in the world.

3. A copper belt is a generally flat region surrounded by higher land such as mountains or plateaus.

4. Rift valleys are places on Earth's surface where the crust stretches until it breaks.

5. Finely ground fertile soil that is good for growing crops is called oasis.

6. The Niger River flows through many countries in West Africa and empties into the Gulf of Guinea.

7. The open grasslands of South Africa are called the veld.

8. Some animals can graze in the Sahel.

Comprehension and Critical Thinking

SECTION 1 *(Pages 250–253)*

9. a. **Describe** What is the Nile River Valley like?

   b. **Draw Conclusions** Why are oases important to people traveling through the Sahara?

   c. **Elaborate** Why do you think few people live in the Sahara?

SECTION 2 *(Pages 254–257)*

10. a. **Identify** What are the four climate zones of West Africa?

    b. **Make Inferences** What are some problems caused by desertification?

    c. **Elaborate** Why do you think resources such as gold and diamonds have not made West Africa a rich region?

SECTION 3 *(Pages 258–261)*

11. a. **Identify** What is the Great Rift Valley?

    b. **Draw Conclusions** Why is the Nile necessary for farming in the desert?

SECTION 3 *(continued)*

   c. Predict How do you think the effects of drought can be avoided in the future?

SECTION 4 *(Pages 262–265)*

12. a. Describe What are the main landforms in Central Africa?

   b. Make Inferences Why would people in rural areas be more likely to shop at periodic markets than at grocery stores?

   c. Elaborate How does the development of national parks affect Central Africa?

SECTION 5 *(Pages 268–271)*

13. a. Identify What are the two main deserts in Southern Africa?

   b. Contrast How is the eastern part of Southern Africa different from the western part?

   c. Elaborate How do you think the geography of Southern Africa has affected settlement patterns there?

Using the Internet

go.hrw.com
KEYWORD: SK9 CH9

14. Activity: Creating a Postcard Come and learn about the mighty baobab tree. This unique tree looks as if it has been plucked from the ground and turned upside down. These trees are known not only for their unique look but also for their great size. Some are so big that a chain of 30 people is needed to surround one tree trunk! Enter the activity keyword to visit Web sites about baobab trees in Africa. Then create a postcard about this strange wonder of nature.

Social Studies Skills

Analyzing a Precipitation Map *Use the precipitation map in the Social Studies Skills lesson to answer the following questions.*

15. What countries have areas that receive under 10 inches of rain every year?

16. Where in West Africa does the most rain typically fall?

17. How would you describe annual precipitation in Chad?

Understanding Comparison-Contrast *Look over your notes or re-read Section 2. Use the information on climate and vegetation to answer the following questions.*

18. How are the Sahara and the Sahel similar?

19. How are the Sahara and the Sahel different?

20. Compare the Sahel and the savanna zone. How are they similar?

21. Writing a Letter Now that you have information about all of Africa, you need to organize it. Think about your audience, a friend at home, and what would feel natural if you had been traveling. Would you organize by topics like landforms and climate? Or would you organize by region? After you organize your information, write a one-page letter.

Map Activity ⭐Interactive

22. East Africa On a separate sheet of paper, match the letters on the map with their correct labels.

Great Rift Valley   Mount Kilimanjaro

Lake Victoria   Nile River

Indian Ocean

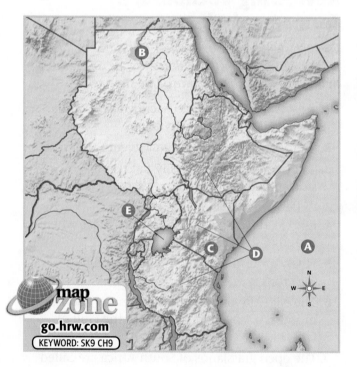

map zone
go.hrw.com
KEYWORD: SK9 CH9

DIRECTIONS (1–7): For each statement or question, write on a separate answer sheet the *number* of the word or expression that, of those given, best completes the statement or answers the question.

1 What physical feature of East Africa is usually covered with snow and ice?

(1) Serengeti Plain

(2) Mount Kilimanjaro

(3) Great Rift Valley

(4) Mount Kenya

2 Which of the following is not a major river in Africa?

(1) Niger

(2) Kilimanjaro

(3) Congo

(4) Nile

3 The Great Rift Valley is located in

(1) North Africa.

(2) West Africa.

(3) East Africa.

(4) Southern Africa.

4 The climate zone just south of the Sahara is called the

(1) desert.

(2) savanna.

(3) Sahel.

(4) tropical forest.

5 The Nile empties into the

(1) Red Sea.

(2) Gulf of Guinea.

(3) Indian Ocean.

(4) Mediterranean Sea.

6 Most of the land in Southern Africa lies on a

(1) mountain range.

(2) coastal plain.

(3) plateau.

(4) delta.

7 What do ships use to avoid sailing around Southern Africa?

(1) the Nile

(2) the Suez Canal

(3) the Aswan High Dam

(4) the Strait of Gibraltar

Base your answer to question 8 on the passage below and on your knowledge of social studies.

"Then they were over the first hills and the wildebeeste were trailing up them, and then they were over the mountains with sudden depths of green-rising forest and solid bamboo slopes, and then the heavy forest again, sculptured into peaks and hollows until they crossed, and hills sloped down and then another plain, hot now, and purple brown, bumpy with heat..."

—Ernest Hemingway, "The Snows of Kilimanjaro"

8 Which of these conclusions about Africa's geography could you draw from this passage?

(1) Africa is covered with desert.

(2) Parts of Africa have hills, mountains, and forests.

(3) Lions and elephants live in Africa's forests.

(4) It is never cold in Africa.

Ancient Civilizations of Africa—Egypt

FOCUS QUESTION

How did ancient civilizations contribute to the development of the Eastern Hemisphere?

What You Will Learn...

In this chapter you will learn about the fascinating civilization of ancient Egypt and how it developed along the Nile River.

FOCUS ON READING AND WRITING

Categorizing A good way to make sense of what you read is to separate facts and details into groups called categories. For example, you could sort facts about ancient Egypt into categories like geography, history, and culture. As you read this chapter, look for ways to categorize the information you are learning. **See the lesson, Categorizing, on page S13.**

Writing a Riddle In this chapter you will read about the civilization of the ancient Egyptians. In ancient times a sphinx, an imaginary creature like the sculpture in Egypt shown on the next page, was supposed to have demanded the answer to a riddle. People died if they did not answer the riddle correctly. After you read this chapter, you will write a riddle. The answer to your riddle should be "Egypt."

- - - Tropic of Cancer - - -

map zone

Geography Skills

Location The civilization of ancient Egypt developed along the fertile Nile River.
1. **Name** What other bodies of water are near Egypt?
2. **Make Inferences** Based on the land around ancient Egypt, why do you think the Nile was so important to life?

20°N

```
0        75        150 Miles
|----|----|----|----|
0    75    150 Kilometers
```

Projection: Lambert Equal-Area

20°E

The Gift of the Nile The fertile land along the Nile River drew early people to the region. Cities are still found along the Nile today.

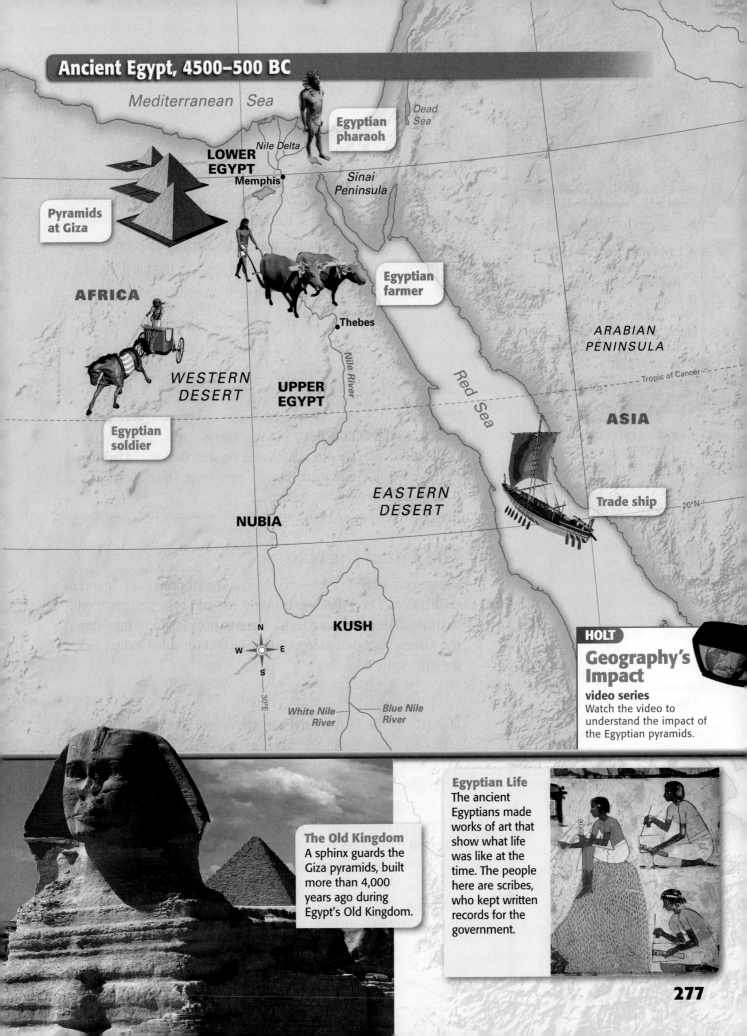

Ancient Egypt, 4500–500 BC

Mediterranean Sea

Egyptian pharaoh

Dead Sea

Nile Delta

LOWER EGYPT

Memphis

Sinai Peninsula

Pyramids at Giza

AFRICA

Egyptian farmer

Thebes

WESTERN DESERT

UPPER EGYPT

Nile River

ARABIAN PENINSULA

Red Sea

Tropic of Cancer

Egyptian soldier

ASIA

EASTERN DESERT

Trade ship

20°N

NUBIA

N
W · E
S

30°E

KUSH

White Nile River

Blue Nile River

HOLT

Geography's Impact
video series
Watch the video to understand the impact of the Egyptian pyramids.

The Old Kingdom
A sphinx guards the Giza pyramids, built more than 4,000 years ago during Egypt's Old Kingdom.

Egyptian Life
The ancient Egyptians made works of art that show what life was like at the time. The people here are scribes, who kept written records for the government.

Early Egypt

Main Ideas

1. Egypt was called the gift of the Nile because the Nile River was so important.
2. Civilization developed after people began farming along the Nile River.
3. Strong kings unified all of ancient Egypt.

The Big Idea

The water and fertile soils of the Nile Valley enabled a great civilization to develop in Egypt.

Key Terms and Places

Nile River, *p. 278*
Upper Egypt, *p. 278*
Lower Egypt, *p. 278*
cataracts, *p. 279*
delta, *p. 279*
pharaoh, *p. 281*
dynasty, *p. 281*

 TAKING NOTES As you read, take notes on the characteristics of the Nile River and on the way in which it affected Egypt. Use a chart like this one to organize your notes.

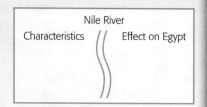

Nile River
Characteristics | Effect on Egypt

If YOU lived there...

Your family farms in the Nile Valley. Each year when the river's floodwaters spread rich soil on the land, you help your father plant barley. When you are not in the fields, you spin fine linen thread from flax you have grown. Sometimes your family goes on an outing to the river, where your father hunts birds in the tall grasses. While he hunts, you and your mother try to catch some of the many fish that swim in the river's water.

Why do you like living in the Nile Valley?

BUILDING BACKGROUND In ancient times, the fertile land in the Nile River Valley drew people to live in the area. Over time, a farming civilization developed that became ancient Egypt. This civilization would be stable and long-lasting.

The Gift of the Nile

Geography played a key role in the development of Egyptian civilization. The **Nile River** brought life to Egypt and enabled it to thrive. The river was so important to people in this region that the Greek historian Herodotus (hi-RAHD-uh-tuhs) called Egypt the gift of the Nile.

Location and Physical Features

The Nile is the longest river in the world. It begins in central Africa and runs north through Egypt to the Mediterranean Sea, a distance of over 4,000 miles. The civilization of ancient Egypt developed along a 750-mile stretch of the Nile.

Ancient Egypt included two regions, a southern region and a northern region. The southern region was called **Upper Egypt**. It was so named because it was located upriver in relation to the Nile's flow. **Lower Egypt**, the northern region, was located downriver. The Nile sliced through the desert of Upper Egypt. There, it created a fertile river valley about 13 miles wide. On either side of the Nile lay hundreds of miles of bleak desert sands.

As you can see on the map, the Nile flowed through rocky, hilly land to the south of Egypt. At several points, this rough terrain caused **cataracts**, or rapids, to form. The first cataract was located 720 miles south of the Mediterranean Sea. This cataract, shown by a red bar on the map, marked the southern border of Upper Egypt. Five more cataracts lay farther south. These cataracts made sailing on that portion of the Nile very difficult.

In Lower Egypt, the Nile divided into several branches that fanned out and flowed into the Mediterranean Sea. These branches formed a **delta**, a triangle-shaped area of land made from soil deposited by a river. At the time of ancient Egypt, swamps and marshes covered much of the Nile Delta. Some two-thirds of Egypt's fertile farmland was located in the Nile Delta.

The Floods of the Nile

Because little rain fell in the region, most of Egypt was desert. Each year, however, rain fell far to the south of Egypt in the highlands of East Africa. This rainfall caused the Nile River to flood. Almost every year, the Nile flooded Upper Egypt in mid-summer and Lower Egypt in the fall.

The Nile's flooding coated the land around it with a rich silt. This silt made the soil ideal for farming. The silt also made the land a dark color. That is why Egyptians called their country the black land. They called the dry, lifeless desert beyond the river valley the red land.

Each year, Egyptians eagerly awaited the flooding of the Nile River. For them, the river's floods were a life-giving miracle. Without the Nile's regular flooding, people never could have farmed in Egypt. The Nile truly was a gift to Egypt.

READING CHECK Finding Main Ideas Why was Egypt called the gift of the Nile?

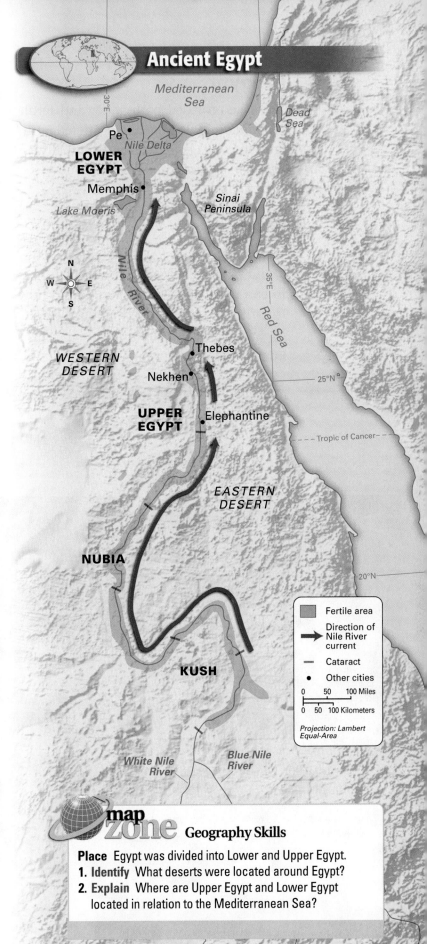

Ancient Egypt

map zone Geography Skills

Place Egypt was divided into Lower and Upper Egypt.
1. **Identify** What deserts were located around Egypt?
2. **Explain** Where are Upper Egypt and Lower Egypt located in relation to the Mediterranean Sea?

Civilization Develops in Egypt

The Nile provided both water and fertile soil for farming. Over time, scattered farms grew into villages and cities. Eventually, an Egyptian civilization developed.

Increased Food Production

Hunter-gatherers first moved into the Nile Valley more than 12,000 years ago. They found plants, wild animals, and fish there to eat. In time, these people learned how to farm, and they settled along the Nile. By 4500 BC, farmers living in small villages grew wheat and barley.

Over time, farmers in Egypt developed an irrigation system. This system consisted of a series of canals that directed the Nile's flow and carried water to the fields.

The Nile provided Egyptian farmers with an abundance of food. Farmers in Egypt grew wheat, barley, fruits, and vegetables. They also raised cattle and sheep. The river provided many types of fish, and hunters trapped wild geese and ducks along its banks. With these many sources of food, the Egyptians enjoyed a varied diet.

Two Kingdoms

In addition to a stable food supply, Egypt's location offered another advantage. It had natural barriers, which made it hard to invade Egypt. To the west, the desert was too big and harsh to cross. To the north, the Mediterranean Sea kept many enemies away. To the east, more desert and the Red Sea provided protection. Finally, to the south, cataracts in the Nile made it difficult for invaders to sail into Egypt that way.

Farming in Egypt

Protected from invaders, the villages of Egypt grew. Wealthy farmers emerged as village leaders. In time, strong leaders gained control over several villages. By 3200 BC, villages had grown and banded together to create two kingdoms—Lower Egypt and Upper Egypt.

Each kingdom had its own capital city where its ruler was based. The capital city of Lower Egypt was Pe, located in the Nile Delta. There, wearing a red crown, the king of Lower Egypt ruled. The capital city of Upper Egypt was Nekhen, located on the Nile's west bank. In this southern kingdom, the king wore a cone-shaped white crown. For centuries, Egyptians referred to their country as the two lands.

READING CHECK **Summarizing** What attracted early settlers to the Nile Valley?

Farmers in ancient Egypt learned how to grow wheat and barley. The tomb painting at left shows a couple harvesting their crop. As the photo above shows, people in Egypt still farm along the Nile.

ANALYZING VISUALS Based on the above photo, what methods do Egyptian farmers use today?

Kings Unify Egypt

According to tradition, around 3100 BC Menes (MEE-neez) rose to power in Upper Egypt. Some historians think Menes is a myth and that his accomplishments were really those of other ancient kings named Aha, Scorpion, or Narmer.

Menes wanted to unify the kingdoms of Upper and Lower Egypt. He had his armies invade Lower Egypt and take control of it. Menes then married a princess from Lower Egypt to strengthen his control over the newly unified country.

Menes wore both the white crown of Upper Egypt and the red crown of Lower Egypt to symbolize his leadership over the two kingdoms. Later, he combined the two crowns into a double crown, as you can see on the next page.

Many historians consider Menes to be Egypt's first **pharaoh** (FEHR-oh), the title used by the rulers of ancient Egypt. The title *pharaoh* means "great house." Menes also founded Egypt's first **dynasty**, or series of rulers from the same family.

Menes built a new capital city at the southern tip of the Nile Delta. The city was later named Memphis. It was near where Lower Egypt met Upper Egypt, close to what is now Cairo, Egypt. For centuries, Memphis was the political and cultural center of Egypt. Many government offices were located there, and the city bustled with artistic activity.

Egypt's First Dynasty was a theocracy that lasted for about 200 years. A theocracy is a government ruled by religious leaders such as priests or a monarch thought to be divine.

Over time, Egypt's rulers extended Egyptian territory southward along the Nile River and into Southwest Asia. They also improved irrigation and trade, making Egypt wealthier.

FOCUS ON READING
Identify two or three categories that you could use to organize the information under Kings Unify Egypt.

Crown of United Egypt

The pharaoh Menes combined the white crown of Upper Egypt and the red crown of Lower Egypt as a symbol of his rule of a united Egypt.

Eventually, however, rivals arose to challenge Egypt's First Dynasty for power. These challengers took over Egypt and established the Second Dynasty. In time, some 30 dynasties would rule ancient Egypt over a span of more than 2,500 years.

READING CHECK **Drawing Inferences** Why do you think Menes wanted to rule over both kingdoms of Egypt?

SUMMARY AND PREVIEW As you have read, ancient Egypt began in the fertile Nile River Valley. Two kingdoms developed in this region. The two kingdoms were later united under one ruler, and Egyptian territory grew. In the next section you will learn how Egypt continued to grow and change under later rulers in a period known as the Old Kingdom.

Section 1 Assessment

Reviewing Ideas, Terms, and Places

1. **a. Identify** Where was the Egyptian kingdom of **Lower Egypt** located?
   b. Analyze Why was the **delta** of the **Nile River** well suited for settlement?
   c. Predict How might the Nile's **cataracts** have both helped and hurt Egypt?
2. **a. Describe** What foods did the Egyptians eat?
   b. Analyze What role did the Nile play in supplying Egyptians with the foods they ate?
   c. Elaborate How did the desert on both sides of the Nile help ancient Egypt?
3. **a. Identify** Who was the first **pharaoh** of Egypt?
   b. Draw Conclusions Why did the pharaohs of the First Dynasty wear a double crown?

Critical Thinking

4. **Categorizing** Create a chart like the one shown here. Use your notes to provide information for each category in the chart.

Development along Nile	Two Kingdoms	United Kingdoms

FOCUS ON WRITING

5. **Thinking about Geography and Early History** In your riddle, what clues could you include related to Egypt's geography and early history? For example, you might include the Nile River or pharaohs as clues. Add some ideas to your notes.

The Old Kingdom

If YOU lived there...

You are a farmer in ancient Egypt. To you, the pharaoh is the god Horus as well as your ruler. You depend on his strength and wisdom. For part of the year, you are busy planting crops in your fields. But at other times of the year, you work for the pharaoh. You are helping to build a great tomb so that your pharaoh will be comfortable in the afterlife.

How do you feel about working for the pharaoh?

BUILDING BACKGROUND As in other ancient cultures, Egyptian society was based on a strict order of social classes. A small group of royalty and nobles ruled Egypt. They depended on the rest of the population to supply food, crafts, and labor. Few people questioned this arrangement of society.

Life in the Old Kingdom

The First and Second Dynasties ruled ancient Egypt for about four centuries. Around 2700 BC, though, a new dynasty rose to power in Egypt. Called the Third Dynasty, its rule began a period in Egyptian history known as the Old Kingdom.

Early Pharaohs

The **Old Kingdom** was a period in Egyptian history that lasted for about 500 years, from about 2700 to 2200 BC. During this time, the Egyptians continued to develop their political system. The system they developed was based on the belief that Egypt's pharaoh, or ruler, was both a king and a god.

The ancient Egyptians believed that Egypt belonged to the gods. The Egyptians believed the pharaoh had come to Earth in order to manage Egypt for the rest of the gods. As a result, he had absolute power over all the land and people in Egypt.

But the pharaoh's status as both king and god came with many responsibilities. People blamed him if crops did not grow well or if disease struck. They also demanded that the pharaoh make trade profitable and prevent wars.

What You Will Learn...

Main Ideas

1. Life in the Old Kingdom was influenced by pharaohs, roles in society, and trade.
2. Religion shaped Egyptian life.
3. The pyramids were built as tombs for Egypt's pharaohs.

The Big Idea

Egyptian government and religion were closely connected during the Old Kingdom.

Key Terms

Old Kingdom, *p. 283*
nobles, *p. 284*
afterlife, *p. 286*
mummies, *p. 286*
elite, *p. 287*
pyramids, *p. 288*
engineering, *p. 288*

TAKING NOTES As you read, take notes on government and religion during Egypt's Old Kingdom. Use a chart like the one below to record your notes.

Government	Religion

283

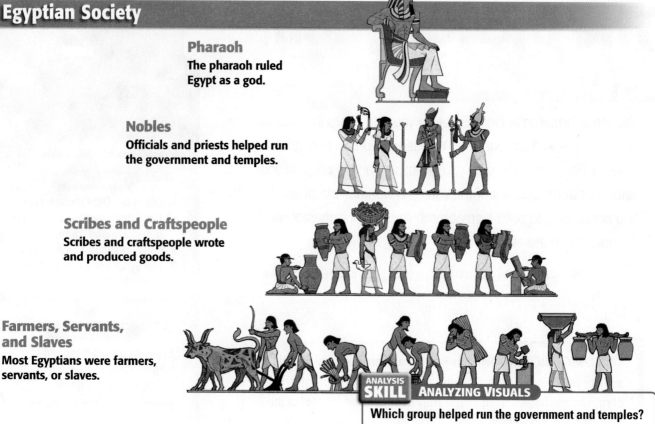

Pharaoh

The pharaoh ruled Egypt as a god.

Nobles

Officials and priests helped run the government and temples.

Scribes and Craftspeople

Scribes and craftspeople wrote and produced goods.

Farmers, Servants, and Slaves

Most Egyptians were farmers, servants, or slaves.

ANALYSIS SKILL ANALYZING VISUALS

Which group helped run the government and temples?

The most famous pharaoh of the Old Kingdom was Khufu (KOO-foo), who ruled in the 2500s BC. Even though he is famous, we know relatively little about Khufu's life. Egyptian legend says that he was cruel, but historical records tell us that the people who worked for him were well fed. Khufu is best known for the monuments that were built to him.

Society and Trade

ACADEMIC VOCABULARY

acquire (uh-KWYR) to get

By the end of the Old Kingdom, Egypt had about 2 million people. As the population grew, social classes appeared. The Egyptians believed that a well-ordered society would keep their kingdom strong.

At the top of Egyptian society was the pharaoh. Just below him were the upper classes, which included priests and key government officials. Many of these priests and officials were **nobles**, or people from rich and powerful families.

Next in society was the middle class. This class included lesser government officials, scribes, and a few rich craftspeople.

The people in Egypt's lower class, more than 80 percent of the population, were mostly farmers. During flood season, when they could not work in the fields, farmers worked on the pharaoh's building projects. Servants and slaves also worked hard.

As society developed during the Old Kingdom, Egypt traded with some of its neighbors. Traders traveled south along the Nile to Nubia to **acquire** gold, copper, ivory, slaves, and stone for building. Trade with Syria provided Egypt with wood for building and for fire.

Egyptian society grew more complex during this time. It continued to be organized, disciplined, and highly religious.

READING CHECK Generalizing How was society structured in the Old Kingdom?

Religion and Egyptian Life

Worshipping the gods was a part of daily life in Egypt. But the Egyptian focus on religion extended beyond people's lives. Many customs focused on what happened after people died.

The Gods of Egypt

The Egyptians practiced polytheism. Before the First Dynasty, each village worshipped its own gods. During the Old Kingdom, however, Egyptian officials expected everyone to worship the same gods, though how people worshipped the gods might differ from place to place.

The Egyptians built temples to the gods all over the kingdom. Temples collected payments from both worshippers and the government. These payments enabled the temples to grow more influential.

Over time, certain cities became centers for the worship of certain gods. In the city of Memphis, for example, people prayed to Ptah, the creator of the world.

The Egyptians worshipped many gods besides Ptah. They had gods for nearly everything, including the sun, the sky, and Earth. Many gods blended human and animal forms. For example, Anubis, the god of the dead, had a human body but a jackal's head. Other major gods included

- Re, or Amon-Re, the sun god
- Osiris, the god of the underworld
- Isis, the goddess of magic
- Horus, a sky god; god of the pharaohs
- Thoth, the god of wisdom
- Geb, the Earth god

Egyptian families also worshipped household gods at shrines in their homes.

FOCUS ON READING

How is the text under the heading Religion and Egyptian Life categorized?

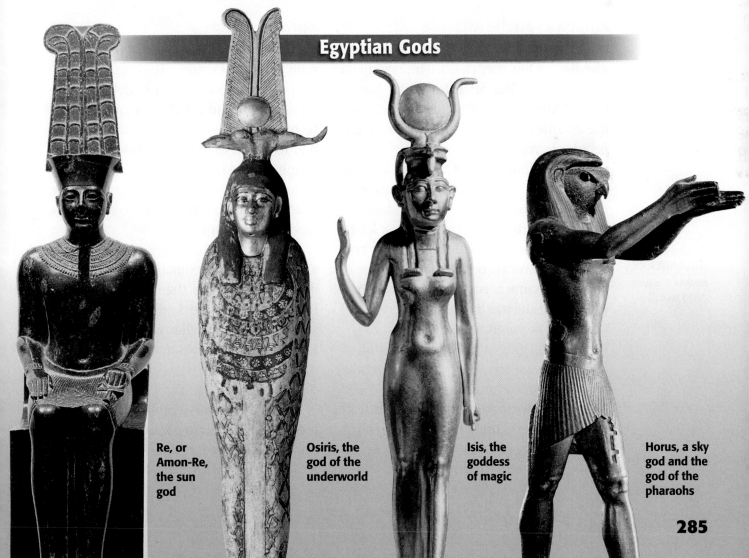

Egyptian Gods

Re, or Amon-Re, the sun god

Osiris, the god of the underworld

Isis, the goddess of magic

Horus, a sky god and the god of the pharaohs

285

Osiris, god of the underworld, waited to judge the dead person's soul.

The god Anubis weighed the dead person's heart against the feather of truth. If they weighed the same amount, the person was allowed into the underworld.

Emphasis on the Afterlife

Much of Egyptian religion focused on the **afterlife**, or life after death. The Egyptians believed that the afterlife was a happy place. Paintings from Egyptian tombs show the afterlife as an ideal world where all the people are young and healthy.

The Egyptian belief in the afterlife stemmed from their idea of *ka* (KAH), or a person's life force. When a person died, his or her *ka* left the body and became a spirit. The *ka* remained linked to the body and could not leave its burial site. However, it had all the same needs that the person had when he or she was living. It needed to eat, sleep, and be entertained.

To fulfill the *ka*'s needs, people filled tombs with objects for the afterlife. These objects included furniture, clothing, tools, jewelry, and weapons. Relatives of the dead were expected to bring food and beverages to their loved ones' tombs so the *ka* would not be hungry or thirsty.

ACADEMIC VOCABULARY
method a way of doing something

Burial Practices

Egyptian ideas about the afterlife shaped their burial practices. For example, the Egyptians believed that a body had to be prepared for the afterlife before it could be placed in a tomb. This meant the body had to be preserved. If the body decayed, its spirit could not recognize it. That would break the link between the body and spirit. The *ka* would then be unable to receive the food and drink it needed.

To help the *ka*, Egyptians developed a **method** called embalming to preserve bodies and to keep them from decaying. Egyptians preserved bodies as **mummies**, specially treated bodies wrapped in cloth. Embalming preserves a body for many, many years. A body that was not embalmed decayed far more quickly.

Embalming was a complex process that took several weeks to complete. In the first step, embalmers cut open the body and removed all organs except for the heart.

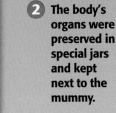

1 Only the god Anubis was allowed to perform the first steps in preparing a mummy.

2 The body's organs were preserved in special jars and kept next to the mummy.

Embalmers stored the removed organs in special jars. Next, the embalmers used a special substance to dry out the body. They later applied some special oils. The embalmers then wrapped the dried-out body with linen cloths and bandages, often placing special charms inside the cloth wrappings.

Wrapping the body was the last step in the mummy-making process. Once it was completely wrapped, a mummy was placed in a coffin called a sarcophagus, such as the one shown at right.

Only royalty and other members of Egypt's **elite** (AY-leet), or people of wealth and power, could afford to have mummies made. Peasant families did not need the process. They buried their dead in shallow graves at the edge of the desert. The hot, dry sand preserved the bodies naturally.

3 The body was preserved as a mummy and kept in a case called a sarcophagus.

READING CHECK **Analyzing** How did religious beliefs affect Egyptian burial practices?

ANALYSIS SKILL **ANALYZING VISUALS**

How did gods participate in the afterlife?

The Pyramids

The Egyptians believed that burial sites, especially royal tombs, were very important. For this reason, they built spectacular monuments in which to bury their rulers. The most spectacular were the **pyramids**— huge, stone tombs with four triangle-shaped sides that met in a point on top.

The Egyptians built the first pyramids during the Old Kingdom. Some of the largest pyramids were built during that time.

Many of these huge Egyptian pyramids are still standing. The largest is the Great Pyramid of Khufu near the town of Giza. It covers more than 13 acres at its base and stands 481 feet (146 m) high. This one pyramid took thousands of workers and more than 2 million limestone blocks to build. Like all the pyramids, it is an amazing example of Egyptian **engineering**, the application of scientific knowledge for practical purposes.

*Interactive
Close-up

Building the Pyramids

More than 4,000 years ago, workers near Giza, Egypt, built three massive pyramids as tombs for their rulers. The amount of work this job required is hard to imagine. Tens of thousands of people must have worked for decades to build these gigantic structures. In this illustration, men work to build the pharaoh Khafre's pyramid.

go.hrw.com (KEYWORD: SK9 CH10)

Giant ramps made of rubble were piled around the pyramid so workers could reach the top.

A statue called a sphinx was carved out of rock and left to guard Khafre's tomb.

Huge blocks of limestone were cut with copper and stone tools and taken by boat to the building site.

Building the Pyramids

The earliest pyramids did not have the smooth sides we usually imagine when we think of pyramids. The Egyptians began building the smooth-sided pyramids we usually see around 2700 BC. The steps of these pyramids were filled and covered with limestone. The burial chamber was located deep inside the pyramid. After the pharaoh's burial, workers sealed the passages to this room with large blocks.

Historians do not know for certain how the ancient Egyptians built the pyramids. What is certain is that such massive projects required a huge labor force. As many as 100,000 workers may have been needed to build just one pyramid. The government paid the people working on the pyramids.

Inside the Great Pyramid, tunnels led to the pharaoh's burial chamber, which was sealed off with rocks.

Teams of workers dragged the stones on wooden sleds to the pyramid.

ANALYSIS SKILL **ANALYZING VISUALS**

How did workers get their stone blocks to the pyramids?

Wages for working on construction projects were paid in goods such as grain instead of money, however.

For years, scholars have debated how the Egyptians moved the massive stones used to build the pyramids. Some scholars think that during the Nile's flooding, builders floated the stones downstream directly to the construction site. Most historians believe that workers used brick ramps and strong wooden sleds to drag the stones up the pyramid once at the building site.

Significance of the Pyramids

Burial in a pyramid showed a pharaoh's importance. Both the size and shape of the pyramid were symbolic. Pointing to the sky above, the pyramid symbolized the pharaoh's journey to the afterlife. The Egyptians wanted the pyramids to be spectacular because they believed the pharaoh, as their link to the gods, controlled everyone's afterlife. Making the pharaoh's spirit happy was a way of ensuring happiness in one's own afterlife.

To ensure that the pharaohs remained safe after death, the Egyptians sometimes wrote magical spells and hymns on tombs.

Together, these spells and hymns are called Pyramid Texts. The first such text, addressed to Re, the sun god, was carved into the pyramid of King Unas (OO-nuhs). He was a pharaoh of the Old Kingdom.

" Re, this Unas comes to you,
A spirit indestructible . . .
Your son comes to you, this Unas . . .
May you cross the sky united in the dark,
May you rise in lightland, [where] you shine! "
–from Pyramid Text, Utterance 217

The builders of Unas's pyramid wanted the god Re to look after their leader's spirit. Even after death, the Egyptians' pharaoh was important to them.

READING CHECK Identifying Points of View
Why were pyramids important to the ancient Egyptians?

SUMMARY AND PREVIEW As you have read, during the Old Kingdom, new political and social orders were created in Egypt. Religion was important, and many pyramids were built for pharaohs. In the next section you will learn about Egypt's Middle and New Kingdoms.

---

go.hrw.com
Online Quiz
KEYWORD: SK9 HP10

Section 2 Assessment

Reviewing Ideas, Terms, and Places

1. **a. Define** To what Egyptian period does the phrase **Old Kingdom** refer?
   b. Analyze Why did Egyptians never question the pharaoh's authority?
   c. Elaborate Why do you think pharaohs might have wanted the support of **nobles**?
2. **a. Define** What did Egyptians mean by the **afterlife**?
   b. Analyze Why was embalming important to Egyptians?
3. **a. Describe** What is **engineering**?
   b. Elaborate What does the building of the **pyramids** tell us about Egyptian society?

Critical Thinking

4. **Generalizing** Using your notes, complete this graphic organizer by listing three facts about the relationship between government and religion in the Old Kingdom.

   Government and Religion
   1.
   2.
   3.

FOCUS ON WRITING

5. **Noting Characteristics of the Old Kingdom**
   The Old Kingdom has special characteristics of government, society, and religion. Write down details about any of those characteristics that you might want to include as one of the clues in your Egypt riddle.

The Middle and New Kingdoms

If YOU lived there...

You are a servant to Hatshepsut, the ruler of Egypt. You admire her, but some people think a woman should not rule. She calls herself king and dresses like a pharaoh—even wearing a fake beard. That was your idea! But you want to help more.

What could Hatshepsut do to show her authority?

BUILDING BACKGROUND The power of the pharaohs expanded during the Old Kingdom. Society was orderly, based on great differences between social classes. But rulers and dynasties changed, and Egypt changed with them. In time, these changes led to new eras in Egyptian history, eras called the Middle and New Kingdoms.

The Middle Kingdom

At the end of the Old Kingdom, the wealth and power of the pharaohs declined. Building and maintaining pyramids cost a lot of money. Pharaohs could not collect enough taxes to keep up with their expenses. At the same time, ambitious nobles used their government positions to take power from pharaohs.

In time, nobles gained enough power to challenge Egypt's pharaohs. By about 2200 BC the Old Kingdom had fallen. For the next 160 years, local nobles ruled much of Egypt. During this period, the kingdom had no central ruler.

What You Will Learn...

Main Ideas

1. The Middle Kingdom was a period of stable government between periods of disorder.
2. The New Kingdom was the peak of Egyptian trade and military power, but its greatness did not last.
3. Work and daily life differed among Egypt's social classes.

The Big Idea

During the Middle and New Kingdoms, order and greatness were restored in Egypt.

Key Terms

Middle Kingdom, *p. 292*
New Kingdom, *p. 292*
trade routes, *p. 293*

TAKING NOTES As you read, use a chart like the one here to take notes on the Middle and New Kingdoms and on work and life in ancient Egypt.

Middle Kingdom	New Kingdom	Work and Life

Time Line

Periods of Egyptian History

3000 BC	2000 BC	1000 BC
c. 2700–2200 BC Old Kingdom	**c. 2050–1750 BC** Middle Kingdom	**c. 1550–1050 BC** New Kingdom

Finally, around 2050 BC, a powerful pharaoh defeated his rivals. Once again all of Egypt was united. His rule began the **Middle Kingdom**, a period of order and stability that lasted to about 1750 BC. Toward the end of the Middle Kingdom, however, Egypt began to fall into disorder once again.

Around 1750 BC, a group from Southwest Asia called the Hyksos (HIK-sohs) invaded. The Hyksos used horses, chariots, and advanced weapons to conquer Lower Egypt. The Hyksos then ruled the region as pharaohs for 200 years.

The Egyptians eventually fought back. In the mid-1500s BC, Ahmose (AHM-ohs) of Thebes declared himself king and drove the Hyksos out of Egypt. Ahmose then ruled all of Egypt.

READING CHECK **Summarizing** What caused the end of the Middle Kingdom?

BIOGRAPHY

Queen Hatshepsut
(Ruled c. 1503–1482 BC)

Hatshepsut was married to the pharaoh Thutmose II, her half brother. He died young, leaving the throne to Thutmose III, his son by another woman. Because Thutmose III was still very young, Hatshepsut took over power. Many people did not think women should rule, but Hatshepsut dressed as a man and called herself king. After she died, her stepson took back power and vandalized all the monuments she had built.

Identifying Cause and Effect
What do you think caused Hatshepsut to dress like a man?

The New Kingdom

Ahmose's rise to power marked the start of Egypt's eighteenth dynasty. More importantly, it was the start of the **New Kingdom**, the period during which Egypt reached the height of its power and glory. During the New Kingdom, which lasted from about 1550 to 1050 BC, conquest and trade brought wealth to the pharaohs.

Building an Empire

After battling the Hyksos, Egypt's leaders feared future invasions. To prevent such invasions from occurring, they decided to take control of all possible invasion routes into the kingdom. In the process, these leaders turned Egypt into an empire.

Egypt's first target was the homeland of the Hyksos. After taking over that area, the army continued north and conquered Syria. As you can see from the map, Egypt took over the entire eastern shore of the Mediterranean and the kingdom of Kush, south of Egypt. By the 1400s BC, Egypt was the leading military power in the region. Its empire extended from the Euphrates River to southern Nubia.

Military conquests made Egypt rich as well as powerful. The kingdoms that Egypt conquered regularly sent gifts and treasure to their Egyptian conquerors. For example, the kingdom of Kush in Nubia sent yearly payments of gold, precious stones, and leopard skins to the pharaohs. In addition, Assyrian, Babylonian, and Hittite kings sent expensive gifts to Egypt in an effort to maintain good relations.

Growth and Effects of Trade

As Egypt's empire expanded, so did its trade. Conquest brought Egyptian traders into contact with more distant lands. Many of these lands had valuable resources for trade. The Sinai Peninsula is one example.

It had valuable supplies of turquoise and copper. Profitable **trade routes**, or paths followed by traders, developed from Egypt to these lands, as the map shows.

One of Egypt's rulers who worked to increase trade was Queen Hatshepsut. She sent Egyptian traders south to trade with the kingdom of Punt on the Red Sea and north to trade with people in Asia Minor and Greece.

Hatshepsut and later pharaohs used the money they gained from trade to support the arts and architecture. Hatshepsut in particular is remembered for the many impressive monuments and temples built during her reign. The best known of these structures was a magnificent temple built for her near the city of Thebes.

Invasions of Egypt

Despite its military might, Egypt still faced threats to its power. In the 1200s BC the pharaoh Ramses (RAM-seez) II, or Ramses the Great, fought the Hittites, who came from Asia Minor. The two powers fought fiercely for years, but neither one could defeat the other.

Egypt faced threats in other parts of its empire as well. To the west, a people known as the Tehenu invaded the Nile Delta. Ramses fought them off and built a series of forts to strengthen the western frontier. This proved to be a wise decision because the Tehenu invaded again a century later. Faced with Egypt's strengthened defenses, the Tehenu were defeated once again.

Soon after Ramses the Great died, invaders called the Sea Peoples sailed into Southwest Asia. Little is known about these people. Historians are not even sure who they were. All we know is that they were strong warriors who had crushed the Hittites and destroyed cities in Southwest Asia. Only after 50 years of fighting were the Egyptians able to turn them back.

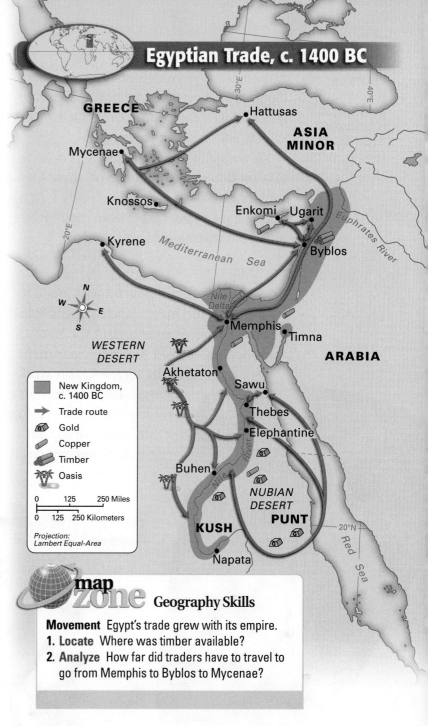

Egyptian Trade, c. 1400 BC

map zone Geography Skills

Movement Egypt's trade grew with its empire.
1. **Locate** Where was timber available?
2. **Analyze** How far did traders have to travel to go from Memphis to Byblos to Mycenae?

Egypt survived, but its empire in Asia was gone. Shortly after the invasions of the Hittites and the Sea Peoples, the New Kingdom came to an end. Ancient Egypt fell into a period of violence and disorder. Egypt would never regain its power.

READING CHECK **Identifying Cause and Effect** What caused Egypt's growth of trade during the New Kingdom?

Work and Daily Life

FOCUS ON READING
What categories of jobs made up the society of ancient Egypt?

Although Egyptian dynasties rose and fell, daily life for Egyptians did not change very much. But as the population grew, Egypt's society became even more complex.

A complex society requires people to take on different jobs. In Egypt, these jobs were often passed on within families. At a young age, boys started to learn their future jobs from their fathers.

Scribes

After the priests and government officials, scribes were the most respected people in ancient Egypt. As members of the middle class, scribes worked for the government and the temples. This work involved keeping records and accounts. Scribes also wrote and copied religious and literary texts.

Because of their respected position, scribes did not have to pay taxes. For this reason, many scribes became wealthy.

Artisans, Artists, and Architects

Another group in society was made up of artisans whose jobs required advanced skills. Among the artisans who worked in Egypt were sculptors, builders, carpenters, jewelers, metalworkers, and leatherworkers. Artisans made items such as statues, furniture, jewelry, pottery, and shoes. Most artisans worked for the government or for temples. Egypt's artisans were admired and often paid fairly well.

Architects and artists were admired in Egypt as well. Architects designed the temples and royal tombs for which Egypt is famous. Talented architects could rise to become high government officials. Artists often worked for the state or for temples.

Daily Life in Egypt

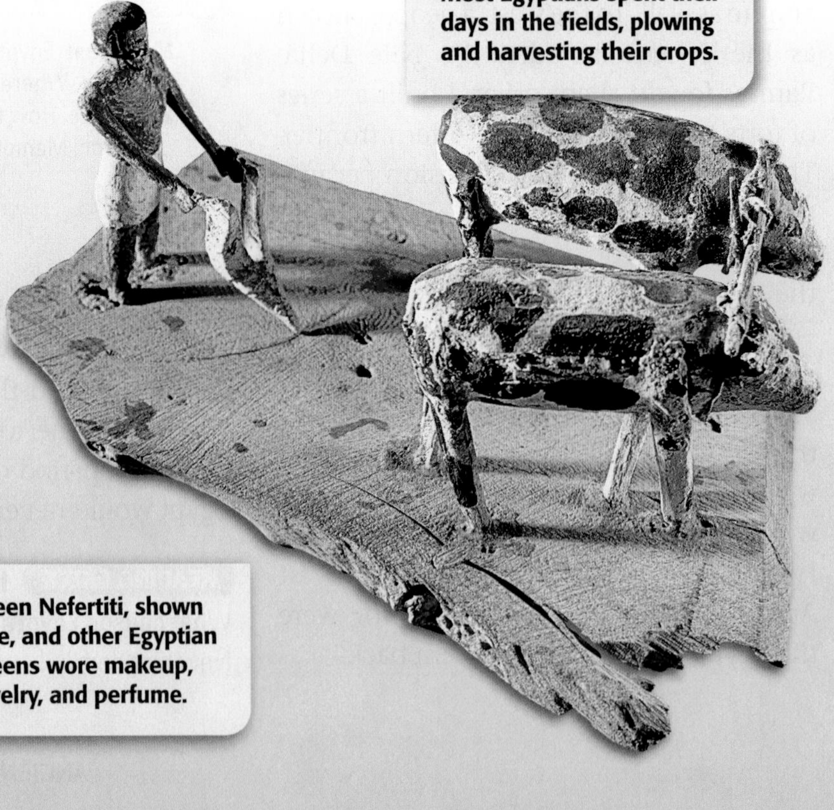

Most Egyptians spent their days in the fields, plowing and harvesting their crops.

Queen Nefertiti, shown here, and other Egyptian queens wore makeup, jewelry, and perfume.

Egyptian artists produced many different types of works. Many artists worked in the deep burial chambers of the pharaohs' tombs painting detailed pictures.

Merchants and Traders

Although trade was important to Egypt, only a small group of Egyptians became merchants and traders. Some traveled long distances to buy and sell goods. On their journeys, merchants were usually accompanied by soldiers, scribes, and laborers.

Soldiers

After the wars of the Middle Kingdom, Egypt established a professional army. The military offered people a chance to rise in social status. Soldiers received land as payment and could also keep any treasure they captured in war. Soldiers who excelled could be promoted to officer positions.

Farmers and Other Peasants

As in the society of the Old Kingdom, Egyptian farmers and other peasants were toward the bottom of Egypt's social scale. These hardworking people made up the vast majority of Egypt's population.

Egyptian farmers grew crops to support their families. These farmers depended on the Nile's regular floods to grow their crops. Farmers used wooden hoes or plows pulled by cows to prepare the land before the flood. After the floodwaters had drained away, farmers planted seeds for crops such as wheat and barley. At the end of the growing season, Egypt's farmers worked together to gather the harvest.

Farmers had to give some of their crops to the pharaoh as taxes. These taxes were intended to pay the pharaoh for use of the land. Under Egyptian law, the pharaoh controlled all land in the kingdom.

This jar probably held perfume, a valuable trade item.

Servants worked for Egypt's rulers and nobles and did many jobs, like preparing food.

ANALYSIS SKILL **ANALYZING VISUALS**

What were some luxury goods used by Egypt's queens and rulers?

All peasants, including farmers, were also subject to special duty. Under Egyptian law, the pharaoh could demand at any time that people work on projects, such as building pyramids, mining gold, or fighting in the army. The government paid the workers in grain.

ACADEMIC VOCABULARY

contracts binding legal agreements

Slaves

The few slaves in Egyptian society were considered lower than farmers. Many slaves were convicted criminals or prisoners captured in war. These slaves worked on farms, on building projects, in workshops, and in private households. Unlike most slaves in history, however, slaves in Egypt had some legal rights. Also, in some cases, they could earn their freedom.

Family Life in Egypt

Family life was very important in Egyptian society. Most Egyptian families lived in their own homes. Sometimes unmarried female relatives lived with them, but men were expected to marry young so that they could start having children.

Most Egyptian women were devoted to their homes and families. Some women, however, did have jobs outside the home.

A few women served as priestesses, and some worked as royal officials, administrators, or artisans. Unlike most women in ancient times, Egyptian women had a number of legal rights. They could own property, make **contracts**, and divorce their husbands. They could even keep their property after a divorce.

Children's lives were not as structured as adults' lives were. Children played with toys such as dolls, tops, and clay animal figurines. Children also played ballgames and hunted. Most children, boys and girls, received some education. At school they learned morals, writing, math, and sports. At age 14 most boys left school to enter their father's profession. At that time, they took their place in Egypt's social structure.

READING CHECK **Categorizing** What types of jobs existed in ancient Egypt?

SUMMARY AND PREVIEW Pharaohs faced many challenges to their rule. After the defeat of the Hyksos, Egypt grew in land and wealth. People in Egypt worked at many jobs. In the next section you will learn about Egyptian achievements.

Section 3 Assessment

go.hrw.com
Online Quiz
KEYWORD: SK9 HP10

Reviewing Ideas, Terms, and Places

1. **a. Define** What was the **Middle Kingdom**?
   b. Analyze How did Ahmose manage to become king of all Egypt?
2. **a. Recall** What two things brought wealth to the pharaohs during the **New Kingdom**?
   b. Explain What did Hatshepsut do as pharaoh of Egypt?
3. **a. Identify** What job employed the majority of the people in Egypt?
   b. Analyze What rights did Egyptian women have?
   c. Elaborate Why do you think scribes were so honored in Egyptian society?

Critical Thinking

4. **Categorizing** Draw pyramids like the ones shown. Using your notes, fill in the pyramids with the political and military factors that led to the rise and fall of the Middle and New Kingdoms.

Rise · Fall · Rise · Fall
Middle Kingdom · New Kingdom

FOCUS ON WRITING

5. **Developing Ideas from the Middle and New Kingdoms** Your riddle should contain information about these periods. Decide which key ideas you should include and add them to your list.

Ramses the Great

How could a ruler achieve fame that would last 3,000 years?

When did he live? late 1300s and early 1200s BC

Where did he live? As pharaoh, Ramses lived in a city he built on the Nile Delta. The city's name, Pi-Ramesse, means the "house of Ramses."

What did he do? From a young age, Ramses was trained as a ruler and a fighter. Made an army captain at age 10, he began military campaigns even before he became pharaoh. During his reign, Ramses greatly increased the size of his kingdom.

Why is he important? Many people consider Ramses the last great Egyptian pharaoh. He accomplished great things, but the pharaohs who followed could not maintain them. Both a great warrior and a great builder, he is known largely for the massive monuments he built. The temples at Karnak, Luxor, and Abu Simbel stand as 3,000-year-old symbols of the great pharaoh's power.

Drawing Conclusions Why do you think Ramses built monuments all over Egypt?

KEY IDEAS

Ramses had a poem praising him carved into the walls of five temples, including Karnak. One verse of the poem praises Ramses as a great warrior and the defender of Egypt.

" Gracious lord and bravest king, savior–guard
Of Egypt in the battle, be our ward;
Behold we stand alone, in the hostile Hittite ring,
Save for us the breath of life,
Give deliverance from the strife,
Oh! protect us Ramses Miamun!
Oh! save us, mighty king! "

–Pen-ta-ur, quoted in *The World's Story*, edited by Eva March Tappan

This copy of an ancient painting shows Ramses the Great on his chariot in battle against the Hittites.

Egyptian Achievements

What You Will Learn...

Main Ideas

1. Egyptian writing used symbols called hieroglyphics.
2. Egypt's great temples were lavishly decorated.
3. Egyptian art filled tombs.

The Big Idea

The Egyptians made lasting achievements in writing, art, and architecture.

Key Terms

hieroglyphics, *p. 298*
papyrus, *p. 298*
Rosetta Stone, *p. 299*
sphinxes, *p. 300*
obelisk, *p. 300*

TAKING NOTES As you read, use a chart like this one to take notes on the achievements of the ancient Egyptians. In each column, identify Egyptian achievements in the appropriate field.

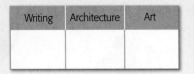

Writing	Architecture	Art

If YOU lived there...

You are an artist in ancient Egypt. A powerful noble has hired you to decorate the walls of his family tomb. You are standing inside the new tomb, studying the bare, stone walls that you will decorate. No light reaches this chamber, but your servant holds a lantern high. You've met the noble only briefly but think that he is someone who loves his family, the gods, and Egypt.

What will you include in your painting?

BUILDING BACKGROUND The ancient Egyptians had a rich and varied history. Today, though, most people remember them for their cultural achievements. Egyptian art, such as the tomb paintings mentioned above, and Egypt's unique writing system are admired by millions of tourists in museums around the world.

Egyptian Writing

If you were reading a book and saw pictures of folded cloth, a leg, a star, a bird, and a man holding a stick, would you know what it meant? You would if you were an ancient Egyptian. In the Egyptian writing system, or **hieroglyphics** (hy-ruh-GLIH-fiks), those five symbols together meant "to teach." Egyptian hieroglyphics were one of the world's first writing systems.

Writing in Ancient Egypt

The earliest known examples of Egyptian writing are from around 3300 BC. These early Egyptian writings were carved in stone or on other hard materials. Later, Egyptians learned how to make **papyrus** (puh-PY-ruhs), a long-lasting, paperlike material made from reeds. The Egyptians made papyrus by pressing layers of reeds together and pounding them into sheets. These sheets were tough and durable, yet could be rolled into scrolls. Scribes wrote on papyrus using brushes and ink.

Egyptian Writing

Egyptian hieroglyphics used picture symbols to represent sounds.

	Sound	Meaning
	Imn	Amon
	Tut	Image
	Ankh	Living

Translation—"Living image of Amon"

	Sound	Meaning
	Heka	Ruler
	Iunu	Heliopolis
	Resy	Southern

Translation—"Ruler of Southern Heliopolis"

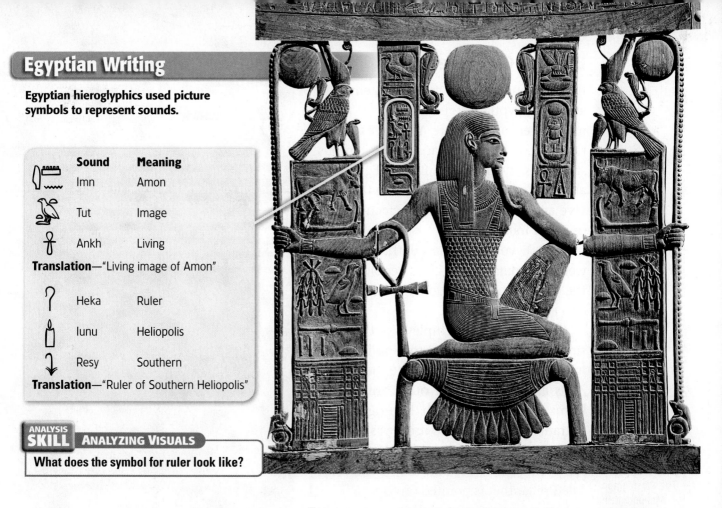

ANALYSIS SKILL ANALYZING VISUALS

What does the symbol for ruler look like?

The hieroglyphic writing system used more than 600 symbols, mostly pictures of objects. Each symbol represented one or more sounds in the Egyptian language. For example, a picture of an owl represented the same sound as our letter M.

Hieroglyphics could be written either horizontally or vertically. They could be written from right to left or from left to right. These options made hieroglyphics flexible to write but difficult to read. The only way to tell which way a text is written is to look at individual symbols.

The Rosetta Stone

Historians and archaeologists have known about hieroglyphics for centuries. For a long time, though, historians did not know how to read them. In fact, it was not until 1799 that a lucky discovery by a French soldier gave historians the key they needed to read ancient Egyptian writing.

That key was the **Rosetta Stone**, a huge, stone slab inscribed with hieroglyphics. In addition to the hieroglyphics, the Rosetta Stone had text in Greek and a later form of Egyptian. Because the message in all three languages was the same, scholars who knew Greek were able to figure out what the hieroglyphics said.

Egyptian Texts

Because papyrus did not decay in Egypt's dry climate, many ancient Egyptian texts still survive. These texts include government records, historical records, science texts, and medical manuals. In addition, many literary works have survived. Some of them, such as *The Book of the Dead*, tell about the afterlife. Others tell stories about gods and kings.

READING CHECK Comparing How is our writing system similar to hieroglyphics?

THE IMPACT TODAY

An object that helps solve a difficult mystery is sometimes now called a Rosetta Stone.

Egypt's Great Temples

In addition to their writing system, the ancient Egyptians are famous for their magnificent architecture. You have already read about the Egyptians' most famous structures, the pyramids. But the Egyptians also built massive temples. Those that survive are among the most spectacular sites in Egypt today.

The Egyptians believed that temples were the homes of the gods. People visited the temples to worship, offer the gods gifts, and ask for favors.

Many Egyptian temples shared some similar features. Rows of stone **sphinxes**—imaginary creatures with the bodies of lions and the heads of other animals or humans—lined the path leading to the entrance. That entrance itself was a huge, thick gate. On either side of the gate might stand an **obelisk** (AH-buh-lisk), a tall, four-sided pillar that is pointed on top.

Inside, Egyptian temples were lavishly decorated, as you can see in the drawing of the Temple of Karnak. Huge columns supported the temple's roof. These columns were often covered with paintings and hieroglyphics, as were the temple walls. Statues of gods and pharaohs often stood along the walls as well. The sanctuary, the most sacred part of the building, was at the far end of the temple.

The Temple of Karnak is only one of Egypt's great temples. Other temples were built by Ramses the Great at Abu Simbel and Luxor. The temple at Abu Simbel is especially known for the huge statues that stand next to its entrance. The 66-foot-tall statues are carved out of sandstone cliffs and show Ramses the Great as pharaoh. Nearby are smaller statues of his family.

READING CHECK **Generalizing** What were some features of ancient Egyptian temples?

THE IMPACT TODAY

The Washington Monument, in Washington, D.C., is an obelisk.

The Temple of Karnak

The Temple of Karnak was Egypt's largest temple. Built mainly to honor Amon-Re, the sun god, Karnak was one of Egypt's major religious centers for centuries. Over the years, pharaohs added to the temple's many buildings. This illustration shows how Karnak's great hall might have looked during an ancient festival.

Karnak's interior columns and walls were painted brilliant colors.

ANALYSIS SKILL **ANALYZING VISUALS**

What features of Egyptian architecture can you see in this illustration?

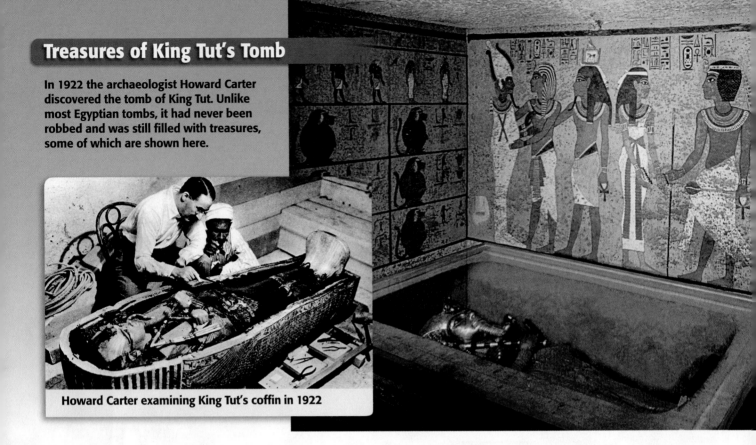

Treasures of King Tut's Tomb

In 1922 the archaeologist Howard Carter discovered the tomb of King Tut. Unlike most Egyptian tombs, it had never been robbed and was still filled with treasures, some of which are shown here.

Howard Carter examining King Tut's coffin in 1922

Egyptian Art

FOCUS ON READING

What categories could you use to organize the information under Egyptian Art?

One reason Egypt's temples are so popular with tourists is the art they contain. The ancient Egyptians were masterful artists. Many of their greatest works were created to fill the tombs of pharaohs and other nobles. The Egyptians took great care in making these items because they believed the dead could enjoy them in the afterlife.

Paintings

Egyptian art was filled with lively, colorful scenes. Detailed works covered the walls of temples and tombs. Artists also painted on canvas, papyrus, pottery, plaster, and wood. Most Egyptians never saw these paintings, however. Only kings, priests, and important people could enter temples and tombs, and even they rarely entered the tombs.

The subjects of Egyptian paintings vary widely. Some of the paintings show important historical events, such as the crowning of a new king or the founding of a temple.

Others show major religious rituals. Still other paintings show scenes from everyday life, such as farming or hunting.

Egyptian painting has a distinctive style. People, for example, are drawn in a certain way. In Egyptian paintings, people's heads and legs are always seen from the side, but their upper bodies and shoulders are shown straight on. In addition, people do not all appear the same size. Important figures such as pharaohs appear huge in comparison to others, especially servants or conquered people. In contrast, Egyptian animals were usually drawn realistically.

Carvings and Jewelry

Painting was not the only art form Egyptians practiced. The Egyptians were also skilled stoneworkers. Many tombs included huge statues and detailed carvings.

In addition, the Egyptians made lovely objects out of gold and precious stones. They made jewelry for both men and women.

The back of King Tut's chair was decorated with this image of the pharaoh and his wife.

Gold mask

What might archaeologists learn about ancient Egypt from these artifacts?

This jewelry included necklaces, bracelets, and collars. The Egyptians also used gold to make burial items for their pharaohs.

Over the years, treasure hunters emptied many pharaohs' tombs. At least one tomb, however, was not disturbed. In 1922 some archaeologists found the tomb of King Tutankhamen (too-tang-KAHM-uhn), or King Tut. The tomb was filled with many treasures, including boxes of jewelry, robes, a burial mask, and ivory statues. King Tut's treasures have taught us much about Egyptian burial practices and beliefs.

READING CHECK Summarizing What types of artwork were contained in Egyptian tombs?

SUMMARY AND PREVIEW The Egyptians made advances that shaped life for centuries. Next, you will learn about several civilizations that developed in Africa after Egypt and grew wealthy from trade.

Section 4 Assessment

go.hrw.com
Online Quiz
KEYWORD: SK9 HP10

Reviewing Ideas, Terms, and Places

1. a. Define What are hieroglyphics?
   b. Contrast How was hieroglyphic writing different from our writing today?
   c. Evaluate Why was the Rosetta Stone important?
2. a. Describe What were two ways the Egyptians decorated their temples?
   b. Evaluate Why do you think pharaohs like Ramses the Great built huge temples?
3. Recall Why did Egyptians fill tombs with art, jewelry, and other treasures?

Critical Thinking

4. Summarizing Draw a chart like the one below. In each column, write a statement that summarizes Egyptian achievements in the listed category.

Writing	Architecture	Art

FOCUS ON WRITING

5. Considering Egyptian Achievements For your riddle, note some Egyptian achievements in writing, architecture, and art that make Egypt different from other places.

Analyzing Primary and Secondary Sources

Learn

Primary sources are materials created by people who lived during the times they describe. Examples include letters, diaries, and photographs. *Secondary sources* are accounts written later by someone who was not present. They often teach about or discuss a historical topic. This chapter is an example of a secondary source.

By studying both types, you can get a better picture of a historical period or event. However, not all sources are accurate or reliable. Use these checklists to judge which sources are reliable.

Checklist for Primary Sources

- Who is the author? Is he or she trustworthy?

- Was the author present at the event described in the source? Might the author have based his or her writing on rumor, gossip, or hearsay?

- How soon after the event occurred was the source written? The more time that passed, the greater the chance for error.

- What is the purpose? Authors can have reasons to exaggerate—or even lie—to suit their own purposes. Look for evidence of emotion, opinion, or bias in the source. They can affect the accuracy.

- Can the information in the source be verified in other primary or secondary sources?

Checklist for Secondary Sources

- Who is the author? What are his or her qualifications? Is he or she an authority on the subject?

- Where did the author get his or her information? Good historians always tell you where they got their information.

- Has the author drawn valid conclusions?

Practice

"The Egyptians quickly extended their military and commercial influence over an extensive [wide] region that included the rich provinces of Syria … and the numbers of Egyptian slaves grew swiftly."

—C. Warren Hollister, from *Roots of the Western Tradition*

"Let me tell you how the soldier fares … how he goes to Syria, and how he marches over the mountains. His bread and water are borne [carried] upon his shoulders like the load of [a donkey]; … and the joints of his back are bowed [bent] … When he reaches the enemy, … he has no strength in his limbs."

—from *Wings of the Falcon: Life and Thought of Ancient Egypt*, translated by Joseph Kaster

1. Which of the above passages is a primary source, and which is a secondary source?

2. Is there evidence of opinion, emotion, or bias in the second passage? Why, or why not?

3. Which passage would be better for learning about what life was like for Egyptian soldiers, and why?

Apply

Refer to the Ramses the Great biography in this chapter to answer the following questions.

1. Identify the primary source in the biography.

2. What biases or other issues might affect the reliability or accuracy of this primary source?

Chapter Review

Geography's Impact
video series
Review the video to answer the closing question:
What do the pyramids of ancient Egypt tell you about the people of that civilization?

Visual Summary

Use the visual summary below to help you review the main ideas of the chapter.

QUICK FACTS

Egyptian civilization developed along the Nile River, which provided water and fertile soil for farming.

Egypt's kings were considered gods, and Egyptians made golden burial masks and pyramids in their honor.

Egyptian cultural achievements included beautiful art and the development of a hieroglyphic writing system.

Reviewing Vocabulary, Terms, and Places

Imagine these terms are answers to items in a crossword puzzle. Write the clues for the answers. Then make the puzzle with answers down and across.

1. cataract
2. Nile River
3. pharaoh
4. nobles
5. mummy
6. acquire
7. contract
8. pyramids
9. hieroglyphics
10. sphinxes

Comprehension and Critical Thinking

SECTION 1 *(Pages 278–282)*

11. a. Identify Where was most of Egypt's fertile land located?

b. Make Inferences Why did Memphis become a political and social center of Egypt?

c. Predict How might history have been different if the Nile had not flooded every year?

SECTION 2 *(Pages 283–290)*

12. a. Describe Who were the pharaohs, and what responsibilities did they have?

b. Analyze How were beliefs about the afterlife linked to items placed in tombs?

c. Elaborate What challenges, in addition to moving stone blocks, do you think the pyramid builders faced?

SECTION 3 *(Pages 291–296)*

13. a. Describe What did a scribe do, and what benefits did a scribe receive?

b. Analyze When was the period of the New Kingdom, and what two factors contributed to Egypt's wealth during that period?

c. Evaluate Ramses the Great was a powerful pharaoh. Do you think his military successes or his building projects are more important to evaluating his greatness? Why?

SECTION 4 *(Pages 298–303)*

14. a. Describe For what was papyrus used?

b. Contrast How are the symbols in Egyptian hieroglyphics different from the symbols used in our writing system?

c. Elaborate How does the Egyptian style of painting people reflect their society?

Social Studies Skills

Analyzing Primary and Secondary Sources *Each of the questions below lists two sources that a historian might consult to answer a question about ancient Egypt. For each question, decide which source is likely to be more accurate or reliable and why. Then indicate whether that source is a primary or secondary source.*

15. What were Egyptian beliefs about the afterlife?

   a. Egyptian tomb inscriptions

   b. writings by a priest who visited Egypt in 1934

16. Why did the Nile flood every year?

   a. songs of praise to the Nile River written by Egyptian priests

   b. a book about the rivers of Africa written by a modern geographer

17. What kinds of goods did the Egyptians trade?

   a. ancient Egyptian trade records

   b. an ancient Egyptian story about a trader

18. What kind of warrior was Ramses the Great?

   a. a poem in praise of Ramses

   b. a description of a battle in which Ramses fought, written by an impartial observer

Using the Internet

go.hrw.com
KEYWORD: SK9 CH10

19. Activity: Creating Egyptian Art The Egyptians excelled in the arts. Egyptian artwork included beautiful paintings, carvings, and jewelry. Egyptian architecture included huge pyramids and temples. Enter the activity keyword and research Egyptian art and architecture. Then imagine you are an Egyptian. Create a work of art for the pharaoh's tomb. Provide hieroglyphics telling the pharaoh about your art.

20. Categorizing Create a chart with three columns. Title the chart "Egyptian Pharaohs." Label the three chart columns "Position and Power," "Responsibilities," and "Famous Pharaohs." Then list facts and details from the chapter under each category in the chart.

21. Writing a Riddle Choose five details about Egypt. Then write a sentence about each detail. Each sentence of your riddle should be a statement ending with "me." For example, if you were writing about the United States, you might say, "People come from all over the world to join me." After you have written your five sentences, end your riddle with "Who am I?" The answer to your riddle must be "Egypt."

Map Activity

22. Ancient Egypt On a separate sheet of paper, match the letters on the map with their correct labels.

Lower Egypt	Red Sea
Mediterranean Sea	Sinai Peninsula
Nile River	Upper Egypt

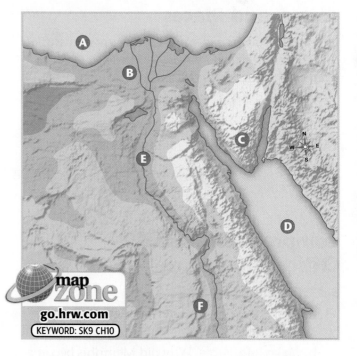

map zone
go.hrw.com
KEYWORD: SK9 CH10

DIRECTIONS (1–7): For each statement or question, write on a separate answer sheet the *number* of the word or expression that, of those given, best completes the statement or answers the question.

1 Which statement about how the Nile helped civilization develop in Egypt is false?

(1) It provided a source of food and water.

(2) It enabled farming in the area.

(3) Its flooding enriched the soil along its banks.

(4) It protected against invasion from the west.

2 The most fertile soil in Egypt was located in the

(1) Nile Delta.

(2) deserts.

(3) cataracts.

(4) far south.

3 The high position that priests held in Egyptian society shows that

(1) the pharaoh was a descendant of a god.

(2) government was large and powerful.

(3) religion was important in Egyptian life.

(4) the early Egyptians worshipped many gods.

4 The Egyptians are probably *best* known for building

(1) pyramids.

(2) irrigation canals.

(3) cataracts.

(4) deltas.

5 During which period did ancient Egypt reach the height of its power and glory?

(1) First Dynasty

(2) Old Kingdom

(3) Middle Kingdom

(4) New Kingdom

6 Who was considered the first ruler of unified Egypt?

(1) Menes

(2) Ramses the Great

(3) King Tutankhamen

(4) Queen Hatshepsut

7 What discovery gave historians the key they needed to read Egyptian hieroglyphics?

(1) obelisk

(2) papyrus

(3) Rosetta Stone

(4) sphinx

Base your answer to question 8 on the text excerpt below and on your knowledge of social studies.

> Oh great god and ruler, the gift of Amon-Re, god of the Sun.
> Oh great protector of Egypt and its people.
> Great one who saved us from the Tehenu.
> You, who have fortified our western border to protect us from our enemies.
> You, who honored the gods with mighty temples at Abu Simbel and Luxor.
> We bless you, oh great one.
> We worship and honor you, oh great and mighty pharaoh.

8 **Constructed-Response Question** The passage above was written to honor Ramses the Great. What are two achievements for which the author was praising Ramses?

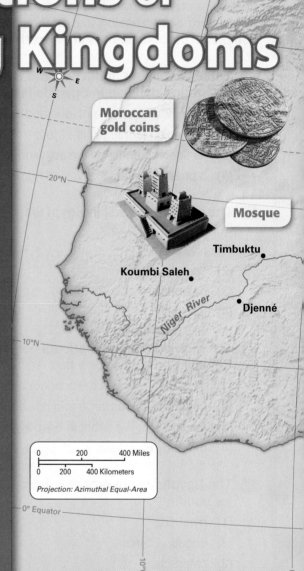

CHAPTER 11

Ancient Civilizations of Africa—Trading Kingdoms

FOCUS QUESTION

How did ancient civilizations contribute to the development of the Eastern Hemisphere?

What You Will Learn...

In this chapter you will learn about several early African civilizations that grew rich from trade, including Kush and the trading empires of West Africa.

FOCUS ON READING AND WRITING

Understanding Cause and Effect When you read about history, it is important to recognize causes and effects. A cause is an action or event that makes something else happen. An effect is the result of a cause. **See the lesson, Understanding Cause and Effect, on page S14.**

A Journal Entry Many people feel that keeping journals helps them to understand their own experiences. Writing a journal entry from someone else's point of view can help you to understand what that person's life was like. As you read this chapter, you will imagine a character and write a journal entry from his or her point of view.

ATLANTIC OCEAN

Moroccan gold coins

Mosque

Timbuktu

Koumbi Saleh

Niger River

Djenné

20°N

10°N

0° Equator

10°W

0°

W — E
S

```
0        200        400 Miles
0     200     400 Kilometers
```
Projection: Azimuthal Equal-Area

Kush The culture of Kush was heavily influenced by its northern neighbor, Egypt. These Kushite pyramids reflect that influence.

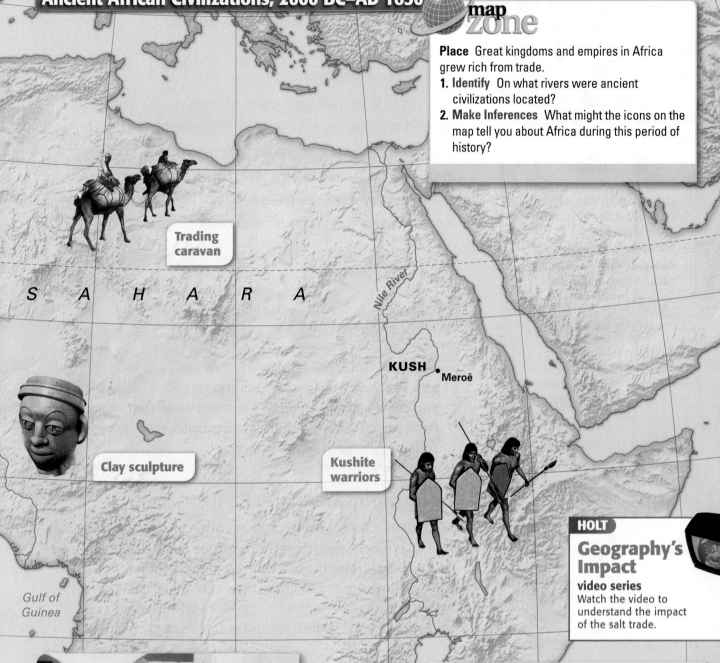

Ancient African Civilizations, 2000 BC–AD 1650

map zone

Place Great kingdoms and empires in Africa grew rich from trade.
1. **Identify** On what rivers were ancient civilizations located?
2. **Make Inferences** What might the icons on the map tell you about Africa during this period of history?

Trading caravan

S A H A R A

Nile River

KUSH • Meroë

Clay sculpture

Kushite warriors

Gulf of Guinea

HOLT
Geography's Impact
video series
Watch the video to understand the impact of the salt trade.

Religion During the Mali Empire, Islam spread throughout West Africa. Muslim architects built hundreds of mud-walled mosques throughout the empire.

West Africa Storytellers, or griots, kept the cultures of West Africa alive with their stories.

309

Ancient Kush

If YOU lived there...

You live along the Nile River, where it moves quickly through rapids. A few years ago, armies from the powerful kingdom of Egypt took over your country. Some Egyptians have moved to your town. They bring new customs, which many people are beginning to imitate. Now your sister has a new baby and wants to give it an Egyptian name! This upsets many people in your family.

How do you feel about following Egyptian customs?

What You Will Learn...

Main Ideas

1. Geography helped early Kush civilization develop in Nubia.
2. Egypt controlled Kush for about 450 years.
3. After winning its independence, Kush ruled Egypt and set up a new dynasty there.

The Big Idea

The kingdom of Kush, in the region of Nubia, was first conquered by Egypt but later conquered and ruled Egypt.

Key Terms and Places

Nubia, *p. 310*
ebony, *p. 312*
ivory, *p. 312*

 TAKING NOTES As you read, take notes on the important events in the early history of the kingdom of Kush. Use a chart like the one below to identify significant events, their dates, and their importance.

Event	Date	Importance

BUILDING BACKGROUND The Nile River valley was home to one of the ancient world's oldest and greatest civilizations. Nearly everyone is familiar with Egypt, the home of pyramids and mummies. Fewer people, however, know much about Egypt's southern neighbor Kush, itself a rich and powerful kingdom.

Geography and Early Kush

More than 6,000 years ago a group of people settled along the Nile River south of Egypt in the region we now call Nubia. These Africans established the first large kingdom in the interior of Africa. We know this kingdom by the name the ancient Egyptians gave it—Kush. Development of Kushite civilization was greatly influenced by the geography and resources of the region.

The Land of Nubia

Nubia is a region in northeast Africa. It lies on the Nile River south of Egypt. Today desert covers much of Nubia, located in the present-day country of Sudan. In ancient times, however, the region was much more fertile. Heavy rainfall flooded the Nile every year. These floods provided a rich layer of fertile soil to nearby lands. The kingdom of Kush developed in this area.

In addition to having fertile soil, ancient Nubia was rich in valuable minerals such as gold, copper, and stone. These natural resources contributed to the region's wealth and played a major role in its history.

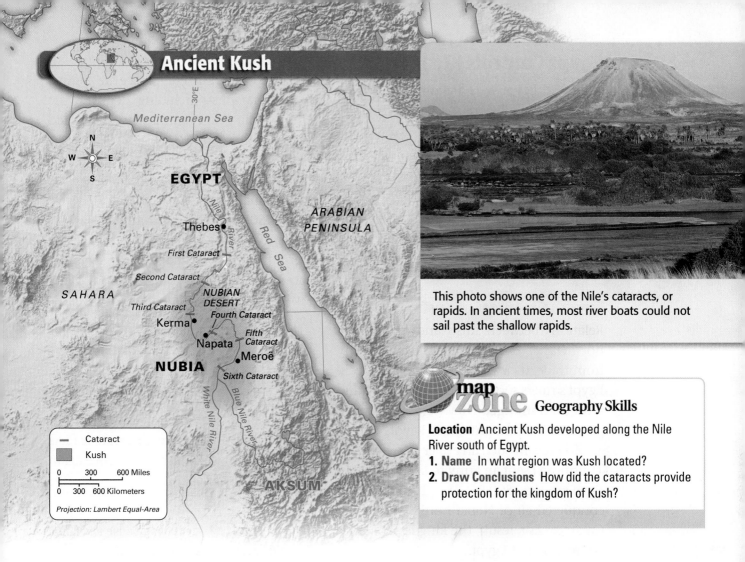

Ancient Kush

Mediterranean Sea

EGYPT

Thebes

First Cataract

Second Cataract

SAHARA

Third Cataract

NUBIAN DESERT

Kerma

Fourth Cataract

Napata

Fifth Cataract

NUBIA

Meroë

Sixth Cataract

ARABIAN PENINSULA

Red Sea

White Nile River

Blue Nile River

AKSUM

Cataract

Kush

0   300   600 Miles

0   300   600 Kilometers

Projection: Lambert Equal-Area

This photo shows one of the Nile's cataracts, or rapids. In ancient times, most river boats could not sail past the shallow rapids.

map zone Geography Skills

Location Ancient Kush developed along the Nile River south of Egypt.
1. **Name** In what region was Kush located?
2. **Draw Conclusions** How did the cataracts provide protection for the kingdom of Kush?

Early Civilization in Nubia

Like all early civilizations, the people of Nubia depended on agriculture for their food. Fortunately for them, the Nile's floods allowed the Nubians to plant both summer and winter crops. Among the crops they grew were wheat, barley, and other grains. In addition to farmland, the banks of the river provided grazing land for cattle and other livestock. As a result, farming villages thrived all along the Nile by about 3500 BC.

Over time some farmers became richer and more successful than others. These farmers became leaders of their villages. Sometime around 2000 BC, one of these leaders took control of other villages and made himself king of the region. His new kingdom was called Kush.

The early kings of Kush ruled from their capital at Kerma (KAR-muh). This city was located on the Nile just south of a cataract, or stretch of rapids. Cataracts made travel through some parts of the Nile extremely difficult. As a result, the cataracts were natural barriers against invaders. For many years the cataracts kept Kush safe from the powerful Egyptian kingdom to the north.

As time passed, Kushite society grew more complex. In addition to farmers and herders, some people of Kush became priests or artisans. Early on, civilizations to the south greatly influenced the kingdom of Kush. Later, however, Egypt played a greater role in the kingdom's history.

READING CHECK **Finding Main Ideas** How did geography help civilization grow in Nubia?

FOCUS ON READING

What was one effect of Kush's location?

Egypt Controls Kush

Kush and Egypt were neighbors. At times the neighbors lived in peace with each other and helped each other prosper. For example, Kush became a supplier of slaves and raw materials to Egypt. The Kushites sent materials such as gold, copper, and stone to Egypt. The Kushites also sent the Egyptians **ebony**, a type of dark, heavy wood, and **ivory**, a white material taken from elephant tusks.

Egypt's Conquest of Kush

Relations between Kush and Egypt were not always peaceful. As Kush grew wealthy from trade, its army grew stronger as well. Egypt's rulers soon feared that Kush would grow even stronger. They were afraid that a powerful Kush might attack Egypt.

To prevent such an attack, the pharaoh Thutmose I sent an army to take control of Kush around 1500 BC. The pharaoh's army conquered all of Nubia north of the Fifth Cataract. As a result, the kingdom of Kush became part of Egypt.

After his army's victory, the pharaoh destroyed the Kushite palace at Kerma. Later pharaohs—including Ramses the Great—built huge temples in what had been Kushite territory.

Effects of the Conquest

Kush remained an Egyptian territory for about 450 years. During that time, Egypt's influence over Kush grew tremendously. Many Egyptians settled in Kush. Egyptian became the language of the region. Many Kushites used Egyptian names and wore Egyptian-style clothing. They also adopted Egyptian religious practices.

A Change in Power

In the mid-1000s BC the New Kingdom in Egypt was ending. As the power of Egypt's pharaohs declined, Kushite leaders regained control of Kush. Kush once again became independent.

READING CHECK **Identifying Cause and Effect** How did Egyptian rule change Kush?

Kush and Egypt

Early in its history, Egypt dominated Kush, forcing Kushites to give tribute to Egypt.

Kush Rules Egypt

We know almost nothing about the history of the Kushites for about 200 years after they regained independence from Egypt. Kush is not mentioned in any historical records until the 700s BC, when armies from Kush swept into Egypt and conquered it.

The Conquest of Egypt

By around 850 BC, Kush had regained its strength. It was once again as strong as it had been before it was conquered by Egypt. Because the Egyptians had captured the old capital at Kerma, the kings of Kush ruled from the city of Napata. Napata was located on the Nile, about 100 miles southeast of Kerma.

As Kush was growing stronger, Egypt was losing power. A series of weak pharaohs left Egypt open to attack. In the 700s BC a Kushite king, Kashta, took advantage of Egypt's weakness. Kashta attacked Egypt. By about 751 BC he had conquered Upper Egypt. He then established relations with Lower Egypt.

After Kashta died, his son Piankhi (PYANG-kee) continued to attack Egypt. The armies of Kush captured many cities, including Egypt's ancient capital. Piankhi fought the Egyptians because he believed that the gods wanted him to rule all of Egypt. By the time he died in about 716 BC, Piankhi had accomplished this task. His kingdom extended north from Napata all the way to the Nile Delta.

Later, as Kush's power increased, its warriors invaded and conquered Egypt. This photo shows Kushite and Egyptian warriors.

After conquering Egypt, Kush established a new dynasty. This sculpture shows one of Kush's pharaohs kneeling before an Egyptian god.

ANALYSIS SKILL **ANALYZING VISUALS**
What did Kushites give to Egypt as tribute?

When the Assyrians invaded Egypt with their iron weapons, they forced Kush's rulers out of Egypt and south into Nubia.

The Kushite rulers of Egypt built new temples to Egyptian gods and restored old ones. They also worked to preserve many Egyptian writings. As a result, Egyptian culture thrived during the Kushite dynasty.

The End of Kushite Rule in Egypt

The Kushite dynasty remained strong in Egypt for about 40 years. In the 670s BC, however, the powerful army of the Assyrians from Mesopotamia invaded Egypt. The Assyrians' iron weapons were better than the Kushites' bronze weapons, and the Kushites were slowly pushed out of Egypt. In just 10 years the Assyrians had driven the Kushite forces completely out of Egypt.

READING CHECK **Sequencing** How did the leaders of Kush gain control over Egypt?

SUMMARY AND PREVIEW Kush was conquered by Egypt, but later the Kushites controlled Egypt. In the next section, you will learn how the civilization of Kush developed after the Kushites were forced out of Egypt by the Assyrians.

The Kushite Dynasty

After Piankhi died, his brother Shabaka (SHAB-uh-kuh) took control of the kingdom and declared himself pharaoh. His declaration marked the beginning of Egypt's Twenty-fifth, or Kushite, Dynasty.

Shabaka and later rulers of his dynasty tried to restore many old Egyptian cultural practices. Some of these practices had died out during Egypt's period of weakness. For example, Shabaka was buried in a pyramid. The Egyptians had stopped building pyramids for their rulers centuries earlier.

go.hrw.com
Online Quiz
KEYWORD: SK9 HP11

Section 1 Assessment

Reviewing Ideas, Terms, and Places

1. **a. Identify** On which river did Kush develop?
   b. Analyze How did **Nubia**'s natural resources influence the early history of Kush?

2. **a. Describe** What is **ivory**?
   b. Explain How did Egypt's conquest of Kush affect the people of Kush?
   c. Evaluate Why do you think Thutmose I destroyed the Kushite palace at Kerma?

3. **a. Describe** What territory did Piankhi conquer?
   b. Make Inferences Why is the Twenty-fifth Dynasty significant in the history of Egypt?
   c. Predict What might have happened in Kush and Egypt if Kush had developed iron weapons earlier?

Critical Thinking

4. **Sequencing** Use a time line like the one below to show the sequence and dates of important events in the early history of the kingdom of Kush.

   2000 BC   680 BC

FOCUS ON WRITING

5. **Noting People and Events** Who will be the subject of your journal? What events will it mention? Make a chart with two columns. In the first column, list key figures from Kush's history. In the second column, list some key events.

Later Kush

If **YOU** lived there...

You live in Meroë, the capital of Kush, in 250 BC. Your father is a skilled ironworker. From him you've learned to shape iron tools and weapons. Everyone expects that you will carry on his work. If you do become an ironworker, you will likely make a good living. But you are restless. You'd like to travel down the Nile to see Egypt and the great sea beyond it. Now a neighbor who is a trader has asked you to join his next trading voyage.

Will you leave Meroë to travel? Why or why not?

BUILDING BACKGROUND The Assyrians drove the Kushites out of Egypt in the 600s BC, partly through their use of iron weapons. Although the Kushites lost control of Egypt, their kingdom did not disappear. In fact, they built up another empire in the African interior, based on trade and their own iron industry.

Kush's Economy Grows

After they lost control of Egypt, the people of Kush devoted themselves to improving agriculture and trade. They hoped to make their country rich again. Within a few centuries, Kush had indeed become a rich and powerful kingdom once more.

What You Will Learn...

Main Ideas
1. Kush's economy grew because of its iron industry and trade network.
2. Some elements of Kushite society and culture were borrowed from other cultures while others were unique to Kush.
3. The decline and defeat of Kush was caused by both internal and external factors.

The Big Idea
Although Kush developed an advanced civilization, it eventually declined.

Key Terms and Places
Meroë, *p. 316*
trade network, *p. 316*
merchants, *p. 316*
exports, *p. 316*
imports, *p. 316*

TAKING NOTES As you read, take notes about the civilization of Kush and how it finally declined. Organize your notes in a diagram like the one below.

Kush	
Economy	Society

↓

Decline

Kushite Metalwork

Kush's craftspeople made iron spearheads and gold jewelry like you see here.

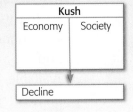

PHOTOGRAPH © 2004
MUSEUM OF FINE ARTS, BOSTON

Kush's Trade Network

Ancient Kush was at the center of a large trading network with connections to Europe, Africa, and Asia. Kush's location and production of iron goods helped make it a rich trading center.

go.hrw.com KEYWORD: SK9 CH11

Goods from the Mediterranean came to Kush through trade with Egypt.

EGYPT

Giza

Luxor

Nubian Desert

KUSH

Red Sea

Meroë

In Meroë, workers made iron tools and weapons, jewelry, pottery, and other goods.

Caravans from the south brought goods like leopard skins and ostrich eggs to Kush.

At ports on the Red Sea, merchants traded Kush's goods for luxury items like silk and glass.

ANALYSIS SKILL **ANALYZING VISUALS**

What types of trade goods did Kush send and receive?

Kush's Iron Industry

During this period, the economic center of Kush was **Meroë** (MER-oh-wee), the new Kushite capital. Meroë's location on the east bank of the Nile helped Kush's economy. Gold could be found nearby, as could forests of ebony and other wood. More importantly, the area around Meroë was rich in deposits of iron ore.

In this location the Kushites developed an iron industry. Because resources such as iron ore and wood for furnaces were easily available, the industry grew quickly.

Expansion of Trade

In time, Meroë became the center of a large **trade network**, a system of people in different lands who trade goods back and forth.

The Kushites sent goods down the Nile to Egypt. From there, Egyptian and Greek **merchants**, or traders, carried goods to ports on the Mediterranean and Red seas and to southern Africa. These goods may have eventually reached India and China.

Kush's **exports**—items sent to other regions for trade—included gold, pottery, iron tools, slaves, and ivory. Merchants from Kush also exported leopard skins, ostrich feathers, and elephants. In return, Kushites received **imports**—goods brought in from other regions—such as jewelry and other luxury items from Egypt, Asia, and lands around the Mediterranean Sea.

READING CHECK Drawing Inferences What helped Kush's iron industry grow?

Society and Culture

As Kushite trade grew, merchants came into contact with people from many other cultures. As a result, the people of Kush combined customs from other cultures with their own unique culture.

Kushite Culture

The most obvious influence on the culture of Kush was Egypt. Many buildings in Meroë, especially temples, resembled those in Egypt. Many people in Kush worshipped Egyptian gods and wore Egyptian clothing. Like Egyptian rulers, Kush's rulers used the title *pharaoh* and were buried in pyramids.

Many elements of Kushite culture were unique and not borrowed from anywhere else. For example, Kushite daily life and houses were different from those in other places. One Greek geographer noted some of these differences.

"The houses in the cities are formed by interweaving split pieces of palm wood or of bricks . . . They hunt elephants, lions, and panthers. There are also serpents, which encounter elephants, and there are many other kinds of wild animals."

–Strabo, from *Geography*

In addition to Egyptian gods, Kushites worshipped their own gods. For example, their most important god was the lion-headed god Apedemek. The people of Kush also developed their own written language, known today as Meroitic. Unfortunately, historians have not yet been able to interpret the Meroitic language.

Women in Kushite Society

Unlike women in other early societies, Kushite women were expected to be active in their society. Like Kushite men, women worked long hours in the fields. They also raised children, cooked, and performed other household tasks. During times of war, many women fought alongside men.

Some Kushite women rose to positions of **authority**, especially religious authority. For example, King Piankhi made his sister a powerful priestess. Later rulers followed his example and made other princesses priestesses as well. Other women from royal families led the ceremonies in which new kings were crowned.

Some Kushite women had even more power. These women served as co-rulers with their husbands or sons. A few Kushite women, such as Queen Shanakhdakheto (shah-nahk-dah-KEE-toh), even ruled the empire alone. Several other queens ruled Kush later, helping increase the strength and wealth of the kingdom. Throughout most of its history, however, Kush was ruled by kings.

READING CHECK **Analyzing** In what ways were the society and culture of Kush unique?

ACADEMIC VOCABULARY

authority power or influence

THE IMPACT TODAY

More than 50 ancient Kushite pyramids still stand near the ruins of Meroë in present-day Sudan.

BIOGRAPHY

Queen Shanakhdakheto
(Ruled 170–150 BC)

Historians believe Queen Shanakhdakheto was the first woman to rule Kush. But because we can't understand Meroitic writing, we know very little about Queen Shanakhdakheto. Most of what we know about her comes from carvings found in her tomb, one of the largest pyramids at Meroë. Based on these carvings, many historians think she probably gained power after her father or husband died.

Drawing Inferences What information do you think the carvings in the queen's tomb contained?

317

Rulers of Kush

Like the Egyptians, the people of Kush considered their rulers to be gods. Kush's culture was similar to Egypt's, but there were also important differences.

Like the Egyptians, Kush's rulers built pyramids. Kushite pyramids, however, were much smaller and the style was different.

Kush was at times ruled by powerful queens. Queens seem to have been more important in Kush than in Egypt.

Stone carvings were made to commemorate important buildings and events, just like in Egypt. Kush's writing system was similar to Egyptian hieroglyphics, but scholars have been unable to understand most of it.

ANALYSIS SKILL **ANALYZING VISUALS**

What can you see in the illustration that is similar to Egyptian culture?

Decline and Defeat

The Kushite kingdom centered at Meroë reached its height in the first century BC. Four centuries later, Kush had collapsed. Developments both inside and outside the empire led to its downfall.

Loss of Resources

A series of problems within Kush weakened its economic power. One possible problem was that farmers allowed their cattle to overgraze the land. When the cows ate all the grass, there was nothing to hold the soil down. As a result, wind blew the soil away. Without this soil, farmers could not produce enough food for Kush's people.

In addition, ironmakers probably used up the forests near Meroë. As wood became scarce, furnaces shut down. Kush could no longer produce enough weapons or trade goods. As a result, Kush's military and economic power declined.

Trade Rivals

Kush was also weakened by a loss of trade. Foreign merchants set up new trade routes that went around Kush. For example, a new trade route bypassed Kush in favor of a nearby kingdom, Aksum (AHK-soom).

Rise of Aksum

Aksum was located southeast of Kush on the Red Sea, in present-day Ethiopia and Eritrea. In the first two centuries AD, Aksum grew wealthy from trade. But Aksum's wealth and power came at the expense of Kush. As Kush's power declined, Aksum became the most powerful state in the region.

By the AD 300s, Kush had lost much of its wealth and military might. Seeing that the Kushites were weak, the king of Aksum sent an army to conquer his former trade rival. In about AD 350, the army of Aksum's King Ezana (AY-zah-nah) destroyed Meroë and took over the kingdom of Kush.

In the late 300s, the rulers of Aksum became Christian. Their new religion reshaped culture throughout Nubia, and the last influences of Kush disappeared.

READING CHECK **Summarizing** What internal problems caused Kush's power to decline?

THE IMPACT TODAY

Much of the population of Ethiopia, which includes what used to be Aksum, is still Christian.

SUMMARY AND PREVIEW In this section you learned about the rise and fall of a powerful Kushite kingdom centered in Meroë. Next, you will learn about the rise of strong empires in West Africa.

Section 2 Assessment

Reviewing Ideas, Terms, and Places

1. **a. Recall** What were some of Kush's **exports**?
   b. Analyze Why was **Meroë** in a good location?
2. **a. Identify** Who was Queen Shanakhdakheto?
   b. Compare How were Kushite and Egyptian cultures similar?
   c. Elaborate How does our inability to understand Meroitic affect our knowledge of Kush's culture?
3. **a. Identify** What kingdom conquered Kush in about AD 350?
   b. Summarize What was the impact of new trade routes on Kush?

Critical Thinking

4. **Identifying Causes** Review your notes to identify causes of the rise and the fall of the Kushite kingdom centered at Meroë. Use a chart like this one to record the causes.

Causes of rise	Causes of fall

FOCUS ON WRITING

5. **Adding Details** Which famous Kushites could you choose for your journal entry? Make a list of major figures from Kush and list important details about each.

Empire of Ghana

What You Will Learn...

Main Ideas

1. Ghana controlled trade and became wealthy.
2. Through its control of trade, Ghana built an empire.
3. Attacking invaders, overgrazing, and the loss of trade caused Ghana's decline.

The Big Idea

The rulers of Ghana built an empire by controlling the salt and gold trade.

Key Terms

silent barter, *p. 322*

TAKING NOTES As you read, make a list of important events from the beginning to the end of the empire of Ghana. Keep track of these events using a diagram like this one.

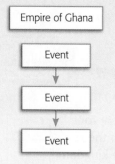

Empire of Ghana

Event

Event

Event

If YOU lived there...

You are a trader, traveling in a caravan from the north into West Africa in about 1000. The caravan carries many goods, but the most precious is salt. Salt is so valuable that people trade gold for it! You have never met the mysterious men who trade you the gold. You wish you could talk to them to find out where they get it.

Why do you think the traders are so secretive?

BUILDING BACKGROUND The various regions of Africa provide people with different resources. West Africa, for example, was rich in both fertile soils and minerals, especially gold and iron. Other regions had plentiful supplies of other resources, such as salt. Over time, trade developed between regions with different resources. This trade led to the growth of the first great empire in West Africa.

Ghana Controls Trade

For hundreds of years, trade routes crisscrossed West Africa. For most of that time, West Africans did not profit much from the Saharan trade because the routes were run by Berbers from northern Africa. Eventually, that situation changed. Ghana (GAH-nuh), an empire in West Africa, gained control of the valuable routes. As a result, Ghana became a powerful state.

As you can see on the map on the following page, the empire of Ghana lay between the Niger and Senegal rivers. This location was north and west of the location of the modern nation that bears the name Ghana.

Ghana's Beginnings

Archaeology provides some clues to Ghana's early history, but we do not know much about its earliest days. Historians think the first people in Ghana were farmers. Sometime after 300 these farmers, the Soninke (soh-NING-kee), were threatened by nomadic herders. The herders wanted to take the farmers' water and pastures. For protection, groups of Soninke families began to band together. This banding together was the beginning of Ghana.

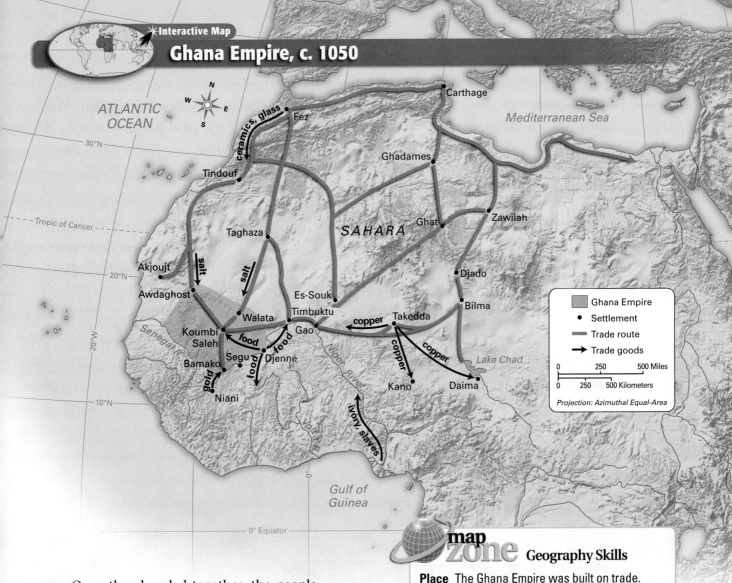

Ghana Empire, c. 1050

Interactive Map

ATLANTIC OCEAN

Mediterranean Sea

SAHARA

Legend:
- Ghana Empire
- Settlement
- Trade route
- Trade goods

0 250 500 Miles
0 250 500 Kilometers

Projection: Azimuthal Equal-Area

Labels on map: Carthage, Fez, Ghadames, Tindouf, Ghat, Zawilah, Taghaza, Djado, Akjoujt, Awdaghost, Es-Souk, Bilma, Walata, Timbuktu, Takedda, Koumbi Saleh, Gao, copper, Bamako, Segu, Djenné, Kano, Daima, Niani, Lake Chad, Senegal R., Niger River, Volta R., Gulf of Guinea, ceramics, glass, salt, food, gold, ivory, slaves, copper

map zone **Geography Skills**

Place The Ghana Empire was built on trade.
1. **Locate** What two rivers bordered the Ghana Empire?
2. **Analyze** What goods came to Ghana from the north?

go.hrw.com KEYWORD: SK9 CH11

Once they banded together, the people of Ghana grew in strength. They learned how to work with iron and used iron tools to farm the land along the Niger River. They also herded cattle for meat and milk. Because these farmers and herders could produce plenty of food, the population of Ghana increased. Towns and villages grew.

Besides farm tools, iron was also useful for making weapons. Other armies in the area had weapons made of bone, wood, and stone. These were no match for the iron spear points and blades used by Ghana's army.

Trade in Valuable Goods

Ghana lay between the vast Sahara Desert and deep forests. In this location, they were in a good position to trade in the region's most valuable resources—gold and salt. Gold came from the south, from mines near the Gulf of Guinea and along the Niger. Salt came from the Sahara in the north.

People wanted gold for its beauty. But they needed salt in their diets to survive. Salt, which could be used to preserve food, also made bland food tasty. These qualities made salt very valuable. In fact, Africans sometimes cut up slabs of salt and used the pieces as money.

ACADEMIC VOCABULARY

procedure the way a task is accomplished

The exchange of gold and salt sometimes followed a **procedure** called silent barter. **Silent barter** is a process in which people exchange goods without ever contacting each other directly. The method made sure that the traders did business peacefully. It also kept the exact location of the gold mines secret from the salt traders.

In the silent barter process, salt traders went to a riverbank near gold fields. There they left slabs of salt in rows and beat a drum to tell the gold miners that trading had begun. Then the salt traders moved back several miles from the riverbank.

Soon afterward, the gold miners arrived by boat. They left what they considered a fair amount of gold in exchange for the salt. Then the gold miners also moved back several miles so the salt traders could return. If they were happy with the amount of gold left there, the salt traders beat the drum again, took the gold, and left. The gold miners then returned and picked up their salt. Trading continued until both sides were happy with the exchange.

Growth of Trade

As the trade in gold and salt increased, Ghana's rulers gained power. Over time, their military strength grew as well. With their armies they began to take control of this trade from the merchants who had once controlled it. Merchants from the north and south met to exchange goods in Ghana. As a result of their control of trade routes, the rulers of Ghana became wealthy.

Salt and Gold

Additional sources of wealth and trade were developed to add to Ghana's wealth. Wheat came from the north. Sheep, cattle, and honey came from the south. Local products, including leather and cloth, were also traded for wealth. Among the prized special local products were tassels made from golden thread.

As trade increased, Ghana's capital grew as well. The largest city in West Africa, Koumbi Saleh (KOOM-bee SAHL-uh) was an oasis for travelers. These travelers could find all the region's goods for sale in its markets. As a result, Koumbi Saleh gained a reputation as a great trading center.

READING CHECK **Generalizing** How did trade help Ghana develop?

Ghana's rulers became rich by controlling the trade in salt and gold. Salt came from the north in large slabs like the ones shown at left. Gold, like the woman above is wearing, came from the south.

Ghana Builds an Empire

By 800 Ghana was firmly in control of West Africa's trade routes. Nearly all trade between northern and southern Africa passed through Ghana. Traders were protected by Ghana's army, which kept trade routes free from bandits. As a result, trade became safer. Knowing they would be protected, traders were not scared to travel to Ghana. Trade increased, and Ghana's influence grew as well.

Taxes and Gold

With so many traders passing through their lands, Ghana's rulers looked for ways to make money from them. One way they raised money was by forcing traders to pay taxes. Every trader who entered Ghana had to pay a special tax on the goods he carried. Then he had to pay another tax on any goods he took with him when he left.

Traders were not the only people who had to pay taxes. The people of Ghana also had to pay taxes. In addition, Ghana conquered many small neighboring tribes, then forced them to pay tribute. Rulers used the money from taxes and tribute to support Ghana's growing army.

Not all of Ghana's wealth came from taxes and tribute. Ghana's rich mines produced huge amounts of gold. Some of this gold was carried by traders to lands as far away as England, but not all of Ghana's gold was traded. Ghana's kings kept huge stores of gold for themselves. In fact, all the gold produced in Ghana was officially the property of the king.

Knowing that rare materials are worth far more than common ones, the rulers banned anyone else in Ghana from owning gold nuggets. Common people could own only gold dust, which they used as money. This ensured that the king was richer than his subjects.

Expansion of the Empire

Ghana's kings used their great wealth to build a powerful army. With this army the kings of Ghana conquered many of their neighbors. Many of these conquered areas were centers of trade. Taking over these areas made Ghana's kings even richer.

Ghana's kings didn't think that they could rule all the territory they conquered by themselves. Their empire was quite large, and travel and communication in West Africa could be difficult. To keep order in their empire, they allowed conquered kings to retain much of their power. These kings acted as governors of their territories, answering only to the king.

The empire of Ghana reached its peak under Tunka Manin (TOOHN-kah MAH-nin). This king had a splendid court where he displayed the vast wealth of the empire. A Spanish writer noted the court's splendor.

FOCUS ON READING

How is this quotation an example of the effects of the king's wealth?

" The king adorns himself . . . round his neck and his forearms, and he puts on a high cap decorated with gold and wrapped in a turban of fine cotton. Behind the king stand ten pages holding shields and swords decorated with gold. "

–al-Bakri, from *The Book of Routes and Kingdoms*

READING CHECK **Summarizing** How did the rulers of Ghana control trade?

BIOGRAPHY

Tunka Manin
(Ruled around 1068)

All we know about Tunka Manin comes from the writings of a Muslim geographer who wrote about Ghana. From his writings, we know that Tunka Manin was the nephew of the previous king, a man named Basi. Kingship and property in Ghana did not pass from father to son, but from uncle to nephew. Only the king's sister's son could inherit the throne. Once he did become king, Tunka Manin surrounded himself with finery and many luxuries.

Contrasting How was inheritance in Ghana different from inheritance in other societies you have studied?

Ghana's Decline

In the mid-1000s Ghana was rich and powerful, but by the end of the 1200s, the empire had collapsed. Three major factors contributed to its end.

Invasion

The first factor that helped bring about Ghana's end was invasion. A Muslim group called the Almoravids (al-moh-RAH-vidz) attacked Ghana in the 1060s in an effort to force its leaders to convert to Islam.

The people of Ghana fought hard against the Almoravid army. For 14 years they kept the invaders at bay. In the end, however, the Almoravids won. They destroyed the city of Koumbi Saleh.

The Almoravids didn't control Ghana for long, but they certainly weakened the empire. They cut off many trade routes through Ghana and formed new trading partnerships with Muslim leaders instead. Without this trade Ghana could no longer support its empire.

Overgrazing

A second factor in Ghana's decline was a result of the Almoravid conquest. When the Almoravids moved into Ghana, they brought herds of animals with them. These animals ate all the grass in many pastures, leaving the soil exposed to hot desert winds. These winds blew away the soil, leaving the land worthless for farming or herding. Unable to grow crops, many farmers had to leave in search of new homes.

Internal Rebellion

A third factor also helped bring about the decline of Ghana's empire. In about 1200 the people of a country that Ghana had conquered rose up in rebellion. Within a few years the rebels had taken over the entire empire of Ghana.

Overgrazing

Too many animals grazing in one area can lead to problems, such as the loss of farmland that occurred in West Africa.

1 Animals are allowed to graze in areas with lots of grass.

2 With too many animals grazing, however, the grass disappears, leaving the soil below exposed to the wind.

3 The wind blows the soil away, turning what was once grassland into desert.

Once in control, however, the rebels found that they could not keep order in Ghana. Weakened, Ghana was attacked and defeated by one of its neighbors. The empire fell apart.

READING CHECK **Identifying Cause and Effect** Why did Ghana decline in the 1000s?

SUMMARY AND PREVIEW The empire of Ghana in West Africa grew rich and powerful through its control of trade routes. The empire lasted for centuries, but eventually Ghana fell. In the next section you will learn that it was replaced by a new empire, Mali.

Section 3 Assessment

go.hrw.com
Online Quiz
KEYWORD: SK9 HP11

Reviewing Ideas, Terms, and Places

1. **a. Identify** What were the two most valuable resources traded in Ghana?
   b. Explain How did the **silent barter** system work?
2. **a. Identify** Who was Tunka Manin?
   b. Generalize What did Ghana's kings do with the money they raised from taxes?
   c. Elaborate Why did the rulers of Ghana not want everyone to have gold?
3. **a. Identify** What group invaded Ghana in the late 1000s?
   b. Summarize How did overgrazing help cause the fall of Ghana?

Critical Thinking

4. **Identifying Causes** Draw a diagram like the one shown here. Use it to identify factors that caused Ghana's trade growth and those that caused its decline.

Growth — Ghana's Trade — Decline

FOCUS ON WRITING

5. **Gathering Information** Think about what it would have been like to live in Ghana. Whose journal would you create? Would you choose the powerful Tunka Manin? a trader? Jot down some ideas.

Crossing the Sahara

Crossing the Sahara has never been easy. Bigger than the entire continent of Australia, the Sahara is one of the hottest, driest, and most barren places on earth. Yet for centuries, people have crossed the Sahara's gravel-covered plains and vast seas of sand. Long ago, West Africans crossed the desert regularly to carry on a rich trade.

Salt, used to preserve and flavor food, was available in the Sahara. Traders from the north took salt south. Camel caravans carried huge slabs of salt weighing hundreds of pounds.

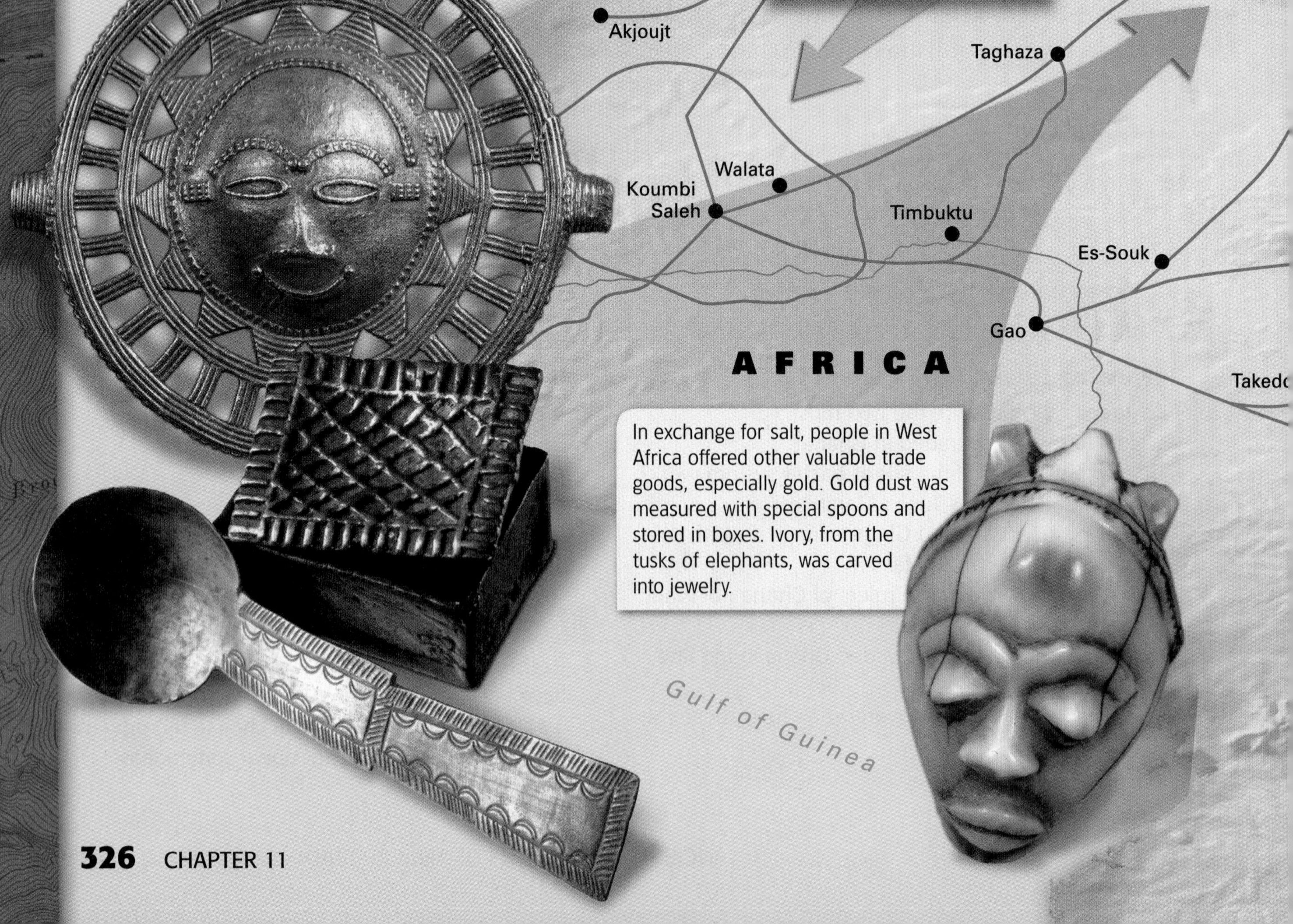

Tindouf

Akjoujt

Taghaza

Walata

Koumbi Saleh

Timbuktu

Es-Souk

Gao

Takedo

AFRICA

In exchange for salt, people in West Africa offered other valuable trade goods, especially gold. Gold dust was measured with special spoons and stored in boxes. Ivory, from the tusks of elephants, was carved into jewelry.

Gulf of Guinea

ATLANTIC OCEAN

EUROPE

Some goods that were traded across the Sahara, like silk and spices, came all the way from Asia along the Silk Road. These luxury items were traded for West African goods like gold and ivory.

MEDITERRANEAN
SEA

Ghadames

Ghat

Zawilah

S A H A R A

Bilma

Daima

Trade route
● Settlement
Scale varies on this map.

A Difficult Journey

Temperature Temperatures soared to well over 100°F during the day and below freezing at night. Dying of heat or cold was a real danger.

Water Most areas of the Sahara get less than one inch of rain per year. Travelers had to bring lots of water or they could die of thirst.

Distance The Sahara is huge, and the trade routes were not well marked. Travelers could easily get lost.

Bandits Valuable trade goods were a tempting target for bandits. For protection, merchants traveled in caravans.

ANALYSIS
SKILL ANALYZING VISUALS

1. What were some goods traded across the Sahara?
2. Why was salt a valued trade good?

RED SEA

Mali and Songhai

What You Will Learn...

Main Ideas

1. The empire of Mali reached its height under the ruler Mansa Musa, but the empire fell to invaders in the 1400s.
2. The Songhai built a new Islamic empire in West Africa, conquering many of the lands that were once part of Mali.

The Big Idea

Between 1000 and 1500 the empires of Mali and Songhai developed in West Africa.

Key Terms and Places

Niger River, *p. 328*
Timbuktu, *p. 329*
mosque, *p. 331*
Gao, *p. 331*
Djenné, *p. 332*

TAKING NOTES As you read, take notes about life in the cultures that developed in West Africa—Mali and Songhai.

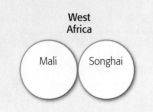

If YOU lived there...

You are a servant of the great Mansa Musa, ruler of Mali. You've been chosen as one of the servants who will travel with him on a pilgrimage to Mecca. The king has given you all fine new clothes of silk for the trip. He will carry much gold with him. You've never left your home before. But now you will see the great city of Cairo, Egypt, and many other new places.

How do you feel about going on this journey?

BUILDING BACKGROUND Mansa Musa was one of Africa's greatest rulers, and his empire, Mali, was one of the largest in African history. Rising from the ruins of Ghana, Mali took over the trade routes of West Africa and grew into a powerful state.

Mali

Like Ghana, Mali (MAH-lee) lay along the upper **Niger River**. This area's fertile soil helped Mali grow. Mali's location on the Niger also allowed its people to control trade on the river. As a result, the empire grew rich and powerful. According to legend, Mali's rise to power began under a ruler named Sundiata (soohn-JAHT-ah).

Sundiata Makes Mali an Empire

When Sundiata was a boy, a harsh ruler conquered Mali. But as an adult, Sundiata built up an army and won back his country's independence. He then conquered nearby kingdoms, including Ghana, in the 1230s.

After Sundiata conquered Ghana, he took over the salt and gold trades. He also worked to improve agriculture in Mali. Sundiata had new farmlands cleared for beans, onions, rice, and other crops. Sundiata even introduced a new crop—cotton. People made clothing from the cotton fibers that was comfortable in the warm climate. They also sold cotton to other people.

To keep order in his prosperous kingdom, Sundiata took power away from local leaders. Each of these local leaders had the title mansa (MAHN-sah), a title Sundiata now took

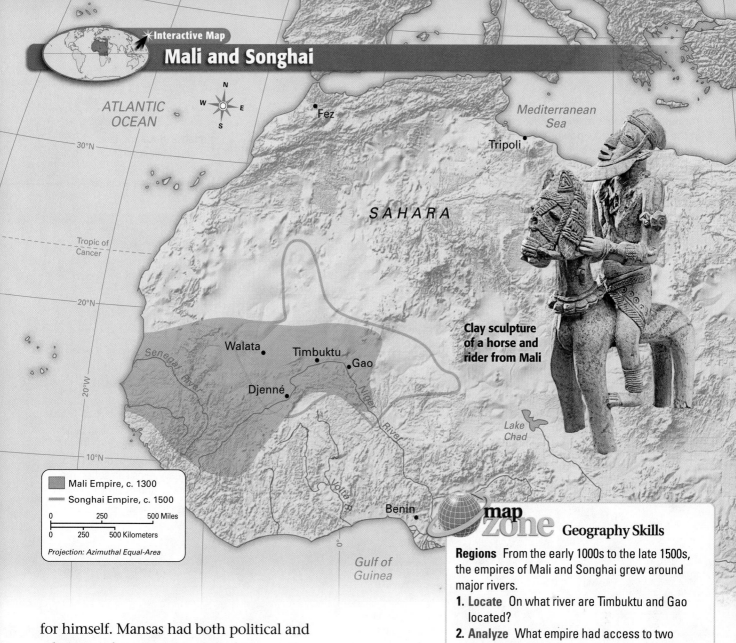

ATLANTIC
OCEAN

Fez

Mediterranean
Sea

Tripoli

30°N

SAHARA

Tropic of
Cancer

20°N

Walata

Timbuktu

Gao

Senegal River

Djenné

Niger River

Clay sculpture
of a horse and
rider from Mali

Lake
Chad

10°N

Volta

Benin

Gulf of
Guinea

Mali Empire, c. 1300
Songhai Empire, c. 1500

0   250   500 Miles
0   250   500 Kilometers

Projection: Azimuthal Equal-Area

map zone Geography Skills

Regions From the early 1000s to the late 1500s, the empires of Mali and Songhai grew around major rivers.
1. **Locate** On what river are Timbuktu and Gao located?
2. **Analyze** What empire had access to two major rivers?

go.hrw.com [KEYWORD: SK9 CH11]

for himself. Mansas had both political and religious roles in society. By taking on the religious authority of the mansas, Sundiata gained even more power in Mali.

Sundiata died in 1255. Later rulers of Mali took the title of mansa. Unlike Sundiata, most of these rulers were Muslims.

Mansa Musa

Mali's most famous ruler was a Muslim named Mansa Musa (MAHN-sah moo-SAH). Under his skillful leadership, Mali reached the height of its wealth, power, and fame in the 1300s. Because of Mansa Musa's influence, Islam spread through a large part of West Africa, gaining many new believers.

Mansa Musa ruled Mali for about 25 years, from 1312 to 1337. During that time, Mali added many important trade cities to its empire, including **Timbuktu** (tim-buhk-TOO).

Religion was very important to Mansa Musa. In 1324 he left Mali on a pilgrimage to Mecca. Through his journey, Mansa Musa introduced his empire to the Islamic world. He spread Mali's fame far and wide.

Mansa Musa also supported education. He sent many scholars to study in Morocco.

Timbuktu

Timbuktu became a major trading city at the height of Mali's power under Mansa Musa. Traders came to Timbuktu from the north and south to trade for salt, gold, metals, shells, and many other goods.

Mansa Musa and later rulers built several large mosques in the city, which became a center of Islamic learning.

Winter floods allowed boats to reach Timbuktu from the Niger River.

Timbuktu's walls and buildings were mostly built with bricks made of dried mud. Heavy rains can soften the bricks and destroy buildings.

At crowded market stalls, people traded for goods like sugar, kola nuts, and glass beads.

Camel caravans from the north brought goods like salt, cloth, books, and slaves to trade at Timbuktu.

ANALYSIS SKILL **ANALYZING VISUALS**

How did traders from the north bring their goods to Timbuktu?

These scholars later set up schools in Mali. Mansa Musa stressed the importance of learning to read the Arabic language so that Muslims in his empire could read the Qur'an. To spread Islam in West Africa, Mansa Musa hired Muslim architects to build mosques. A **mosque** (mahsk) is a building for Muslim prayer.

The Fall of Mali

When Mansa Musa died, his son Maghan (MAH-gan) took the throne. Maghan was a weak ruler. When raiders from the southeast poured into Mali, he couldn't stop them. The raiders set fire to Timbuktu's great schools and mosques. Mali never fully recovered from this terrible blow. The empire continued to weaken and decline.

In 1431 the Tuareg (TWAH-reg), nomads from the Sahara, seized Timbuktu. By 1500 nearly all of the lands the empire had once ruled were lost. Only a small area of Mali remained.

READING CHECK Sequencing What steps did Sundiata take to turn Mali into an empire?

Songhai

Even as the empire of Mali was reaching its height, a rival power was growing in the area. That rival was the Songhai (SAHNG-hy) kingdom. From their capital at **Gao**, the Songhai participated in the same trade that had made Ghana and Mali so rich.

The Building of an Empire

In the 1300s Mansa Musa conquered the Songhai, adding their lands to his empire. But as the Mali Empire weakened in the 1400s, the people of Songhai rebelled and regained their freedom.

The Songhai leaders were Muslims. So too were many of the North African Berbers who traded in West Africa. Because of this

shared religion, the Berbers were willing to trade with the Songhai, who grew richer.

As the Songhai gained in wealth, they expanded their territory and built an empire. Songhai's expansion was led by Sunni Ali (SOOH-nee ah-LEE), who became ruler of the Songhai in 1464. Before he took over, the Songhai state had been disorganized and poorly run. As ruler, Sunni Ali worked to unify, strengthen, and enlarge his empire. Much of the land that he added to Songhai had been part of Mali.

As king, Sunni Ali encouraged everyone in his empire to work together. To build religious harmony, he participated in both Muslim and local religions. As a result, he brought stability to Songhai.

Askia the Great

Sunni Ali died in 1492. He was followed as king by his son Sunni Baru, who was not a Muslim. The Songhai people feared that if Sunni Baru didn't support Islam, they

BIOGRAPHY

Askia the Great
(c. 1443–1538)

Askia the Great became the ruler of Songhai when he was nearly 50 years old. He ruled Songhai for about 35 years. During his reign the cities of Songhai gained power over the countryside.

When he was in his 80s, Askia went blind. His son Musa forced him to leave the throne. Askia was sent to live on an island. He lived there for nine years until another of his sons brought him back to the capital, where he died. His tomb is still one of the most honored places in all of West Africa.

Drawing Inferences Why do you think Askia the Great's tomb is still considered an honored place?

FOCUS ON READING

As you read Songhai Falls to Morocco, identify two causes of Songhai's fall.

would lose their trade with Muslim lands. They rebelled against the king.

The leader of that rebellion was a general named Muhammad Ture (moo-HAH-muhd too-RAY). After overthrowing Sunni Baru, Muhammad Ture chose the title *askia*, a title of high military rank. Eventually, he became known as Askia the Great.

Askia supported education and learning. Under his rule, Timbuktu flourished, drawing thousands to its universities, schools, libraries, and mosques. The city was especially known for the University of Sankore (san-KOH-rah). People arrived there from North Africa and other places to study math, science, medicine, grammar, and law. **Djenné** was another city that became a center of learning.

Most of Songhai's traders were Muslim, and as they gained influence in the empire so did Islam. Askia, himself a devout Muslim, encouraged the growth of Islamic influence. He made many laws similar to those in other Muslim nations.

To help maintain order, Askia set up five provinces within Songhai. He appointed governors who were loyal to him. Askia also created a professional army and specialized departments to oversee tasks.

Songhai Falls to Morocco

A northern rival of Songhai, Morocco, wanted to gain control of Songhai's salt mines. So the Moroccan army set out for the heart of Songhai in 1591. Moroccan soldiers carried advanced weapons, including the terrible arquebus (AHR-kwih-buhs). The arquebus was an early form of a gun.

The swords, spears, and bows used by Songhai's warriors were no match for the Moroccans' guns and cannons. The invaders destroyed Timbuktu and Gao.

Changes in trade patterns completed Songhai's fall. Overland trade declined as port cities on the Atlantic coast became more important. Africans south of Songhai and European merchants both preferred trading at Atlantic ports to dealing with Muslim traders. Slowly, the period of great West African empires came to an end.

READING CHECK **Evaluating** What do you think was Askia's greatest accomplishment?

SUMMARY AND PREVIEW Mali was a large empire famous for its wealth and centers of learning. Songhai similarly thrived. Next, you will learn about historical and artistic traditions of West Africa.

Section 4 Assessment

go.hrw.com
Online Quiz
KEYWORD: SK9 HP11

Reviewing Ideas, Terms, and Places

1. **a. Identify** Who was Sundiata?
   b. Explain What major river was important to the people of Mali? Why?
   c. Elaborate What effects did the rule of Mansa Musa have on Mali and West Africa?

2. **a. Identify** Who led the expansion of Songhai in the 1400s?
   b. Explain How did Askia the Great's support of education affect **Timbuktu**?
   c. Elaborate What were two reasons why Songhai fell to the Moroccans?

Critical Thinking

3. **Finding Main Ideas** Use your notes to help you list three major accomplishments of Sundiata and Askia.

Sundiata	Askia

FOCUS ON WRITING

4. **Comparing and Contrasting** Whose journal could you write from the empires of Mali and Songhai? Would you create a journal for an important person, like Mansa Musa or Askia the Great? Or would you create a journal for someone who has a different role in one of the empires? List your ideas.

Mansa Musa

How could one man's travels become a major historic event?

When did he live? the late 1200s and early 1300s

Where did he live? Mali

What did he do? Mansa Musa, the ruler of Mali, was one of the Muslim kings of West Africa. He became a major figure in African and world history largely because of a pilgrimage he made to the city of Mecca.

Why is he important? Mansa Musa's spectacular journey attracted the attention of the Muslim world and of Europe. For the first time, other people's eyes turned to West Africa. During his travels, Mansa Musa gave out huge amounts of gold. His spending made people eager to find the source of such wealth. Within 200 years, European explorers would arrive on the shores of western Africa.

Identifying Points of View How do you think Mansa Musa changed people's views of West Africa?

KEY FACTS

According to chroniclers of the time, Mansa Musa was accompanied on his journey to Mecca by some 60,000 people. Of those people

- **12,000** were servants to attend to the king.

- **500** were servants to attend to his wife.

- **14,000** more were slaves wearing rich fabrics such as silk.

- **500** carried staffs heavily decorated with gold. Historians have estimated that the gold Mansa Musa gave away on his trip would be worth more than $100 million today.

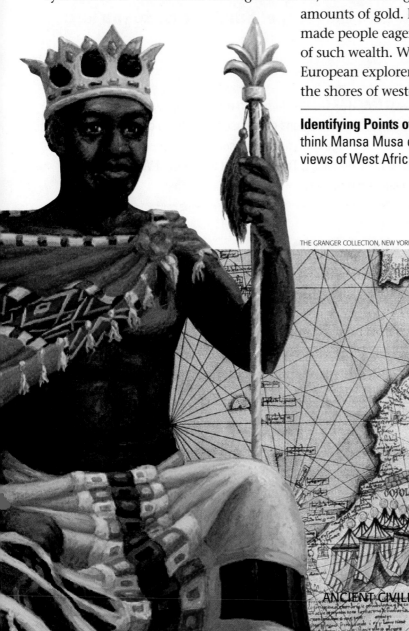

THE GRANGER COLLECTION, NEW YORK

This Spanish map from the 1300s shows Mansa Musa sitting on his throne.

Historical and Artistic Traditions of West Africa

What You Will Learn...

Main Ideas

1. West Africans have preserved their history through storytelling and the written accounts of visitors.
2. Through art, music, and dance, West Africans have expressed their creativity and kept alive their cultural traditions.

The Big Idea

West African culture has been passed down through oral history, writings by other people, and the arts.

Key Terms

oral history, *p. 334*
griots, *p. 334*
proverbs, *p. 335*
kente, *p. 337*

TAKING NOTES As you read, take notes on West African historical and artistic traditions. Write your notes in a diagram like the one below.

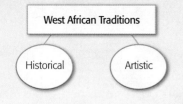

If **YOU** lived there...

You are the youngest and smallest in your family. People often tease you about not being very strong. In the evenings, when work is done, your village gathers to listen to storytellers. One of your favorite stories is about the hero Sundiata. As a boy he was small and weak, but he grew to be a great warrior and hero.

How does the story of Sundiata make you feel?

BUILDING BACKGROUND Although trading empires rose and fell in West Africa, many traditions continued through the centuries. In every town and village, storytellers passed on the people's histories, legends, and wise sayings. These were at the heart of West Africa's arts and cultural traditions.

Preserving History

Writing was never very common in West Africa. In fact, none of the major early civilizations of West Africa developed a written language. Arabic was the only written language they used. The lack of a native written language does not mean that the people of West Africa didn't know their history, though. They passed along information through oral histories. An **oral history** is a spoken record of past events. The task of remembering and telling West Africa's history was entrusted to storytellers.

The Griots

The storytellers of early West Africa were called **griots** (GREE-ohz). They were highly respected in their communities because the people of West Africa were very interested in the deeds of their ancestors. Griots helped keep this history alive for each new generation.

The griots' stories were both entertaining and informative. They told of important past events and of the accomplishments of distant ancestors. For example, some stories explained the rise and fall of the West African empires. Other stories described the actions of powerful kings and warriors. Some griots made their stories more lively by acting out the events like scenes in a play.

In addition to stories, the griots recited **proverbs**, or short sayings of wisdom or truth. They used proverbs to teach lessons to the people. For example, one West African proverb warns, "Talking doesn't fill the basket in the farm." This proverb reminds people that they must work to accomplish things. It is not enough for people just to talk about what they want to do.

In order to tell their stories and proverbs, the griots memorized hundreds of names and events. Through this process the griots passed on West African history from generation to generation. However, some griots confused names and events in their heads. When this happened, the facts of some historical events became distorted. Still, the griots' stories tell us a great deal about life in the West African empires.

West African Epics

Some of the griot poems are epics—long poems about kingdoms and heroes. Many of these epic poems are collected in the *Dausi* (DAW-zee) and the *Sundiata*.

The *Dausi* tells the history of Ghana. Intertwined with historical events, though, are myths and legends. One story is about a seven-headed snake god named Bida. This god promised that Ghana would prosper if the people sacrificed a young woman to him every year. One year a mighty warrior killed Bida. As the god died, he cursed Ghana. The griots say that this curse caused the empire of Ghana to fall.

The *Sundiata* is about Mali's great ruler. According to the epic, when Sundiata was still a boy, a conqueror captured Mali and killed Sundiata's father and 11 brothers.

Oral Traditions

West African storytellers called griots had the job of remembering and passing on their people's history. Here, people gather to perform traditional dances and to listen to the stories of a griot.

Music from Mali to Memphis

Did you know that the music you listen to today may have begun with the griots? From the 1600s to the 1800s, many people from West Africa were brought to America as slaves. In America, these slaves continued to sing the way they had in Africa. They also continued to play traditional instruments such as the *kora* played by Senegalese musician Soriba Kouyaté (right), the son of a griot. Over time, this music developed into a style called the blues, made popular by such artists as B. B. King (left). In turn, the blues shaped other styles of music, including jazz and rock. So, the next time you hear a Memphis blues track or a cool jazz tune, listen for its ancient African roots!

He didn't kill Sundiata, however, because the boy was sick and didn't seem like a threat. But Sundiata grew up to be an expert warrior. Eventually he overthrew the conqueror and became king.

Visitors' Written Accounts

FOCUS ON READING

What is one effect of visitors' written accounts of West Africa?

In addition to the oral histories told about West Africa, visitors wrote about the region. In fact, much of what we know about early West Africa comes from the writings of travelers and scholars from Muslim lands such as Spain and Arabia.

Ibn Battutah was the most famous Muslim visitor to write about West Africa. From 1353 to 1354 he traveled through the region. Ibn Battutah's account of this journey describes the political and cultural lives of West Africans in great detail.

READING CHECK **Drawing Conclusions** Why were oral traditions important in West Africa?

Art, Music, and Dance

Like most peoples, West Africans valued the arts. They expressed themselves creatively through sculpture, mask-making, cloth-making, music, and dance.

Sculpture

Of all the visual art forms, the sculpture of West Africa is probably the best known. West Africans made ornate statues and carvings out of wood, brass, clay, ivory, stone, and other materials.

Most statues from West Africa are of people—often the sculptor's ancestors. Usually these statues were made for religious rituals, to ask for the ancestors' blessings. Sculptors made other statues as gifts for the gods. These sculptures were kept in holy places. They were never meant to be seen by people.

Because their statues were used in religious rituals, many African artists were deeply respected. People thought artists had been blessed by the gods.

Long after the decline of Ghana, Mali, and Songhai, West African art is still admired. Museums around the world display African art. In addition, African sculpture inspired some European artists of the 1900s, including Henri Matisse and Pablo Picasso.

Masks and Clothing

In addition to statues, the artists of West Africa carved elaborate masks. Made of wood, these masks bore the faces of animals such as hyenas, lions, monkeys, and antelopes. Artists often painted the masks after carving them. People wore the masks during rituals as they danced around fires. The way firelight reflected off the masks made them look fierce and lifelike.

Many African societies were famous for the cloth they wove. The most famous of these cloths is called kente (ken-TAY). **Kente** is a hand-woven, brightly colored fabric. The cloth was woven in narrow strips that were then sewn together. Kings and queens in West Africa wore garments made of kente for special occasions.

Music and Dance

In many West African societies, music and dance were as important as the visual arts. Singing, drumming, and dancing were great entertainment, but they also helped people honor their history and mark special occasions. For example, music was played when a ruler entered a room.

Dance has long been a central part of African society. Many West African cultures used dance to celebrate specific events or ceremonies. For example, they may have performed one dance for weddings and another for funerals. In some parts of West Africa, people still perform dances similar to those performed hundreds of years ago.

READING CHECK **Summarizing** Summarize how traditions were preserved in West Africa.

SUMMARY AND PREVIEW The societies of West Africa did not have written languages but preserved their histories and cultures through storytelling and the arts. Next, you will learn about one kingdom whose history has been passed on through such traditions, Benin.

Section 5 Assessment

go.hrw.com
Online Quiz
KEYWORD: SK9 HP11

Reviewing Ideas, Terms, and Places

1. **a. Define** What is **oral history**?
   b. Make Generalizations Why were **griots** and their stories important in West African society?
   c. Evaluate Why may an oral history provide different information than a written account of the same event?

2. **a. Identify** What were two forms of visual art popular in West Africa?
   b. Make Inferences Why do you think that the sculptures made as gifts for the gods were not meant to be seen by people?
   c. Elaborate What role did music and dance play in West African society?

Critical Thinking

3. **Summarizing** Use a chart like this one and your notes to summarize the importance of each tradition in West Africa.

Tradition	Importance
Storytelling	
Epics	
Sculpture	

FOCUS ON WRITING

4. **Identifying West African Traditions** Think about the arts and how they affected people who lived in the West African empires. Would you create a journal of one of these artists? Or would you create a journal of someone who is affected by the arts or artists?

Social Studies Skills

Chart and Graph | Critical Thinking | Geography | Study

Making Decisions

Learn

You make decisions every day. Some decisions are very easy to make and take little time. Others are much harder. Regardless of how easy or hard a decision is, it will have consequences, or results. These consequences can be either positive or negative.

Before you make a decision, consider all your possible options. Think about the possible consequences of each option and decide which will be best for you. Thinking about the consequences of your decision beforehand will allow you to make a better, more thoughtful decision.

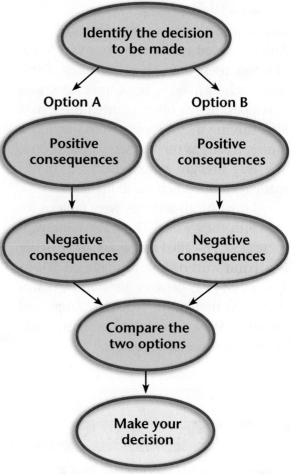

Practice

Imagine your parents have given you the option of getting a new pet. Use a graphic organizer like the one on this page to help you decide whether to get one.

❶ What are the consequences of getting a pet? Which of these consequences are positive? Which are negative?

❷ What are the consequences of not getting a pet? Which of them are positive? Which are negative?

❸ Compare your two options. Look at the positive and negative consequences of each option. Based on these consequences, do you think you should get a pet?

Apply

Imagine that your school has just received money to build either a new art studio or a new track. School officials have asked students to vote on which of these new facilities they would prefer, and you have to decide which option you think would be better for the school. Use a graphic organizer like the one above to consider the consequences of each option. Compare your lists, and then make your decision. Write a short paragraph to explain your decision.

Chapter Review

Geography's Impact
video series
Review the video to answer the closing question:
Why was the salt trade important to African civilizations before the 1600s?

Visual Summary

Use the visual summary below to help you review the main ideas of the chapter.

QUICK FACTS

Trade in valuable resources such as gold, salt, and ivory made early African civilizations very wealthy.

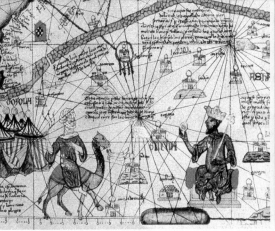

Kush, Ghana, Mali, and Songhai built powerful kingdoms through trade and conquest.

The history of West Africa has been preserved through story-telling, visitors' accounts, art, music, and dance.

Reviewing Vocabulary, Terms, and Places

Choose the letter of the answer that best completes each statement below.

1. One of Kush's most valuable exports was a dark wood called
   - **a.** ebony.
   - **b.** ivory.
   - **c.** gold.
   - **d.** salt.

2. Mali's rise to power began under a ruler named
   - **a.** Tunka Manin.
   - **b.** Sunni Ali.
   - **c.** Ibn Battutah.
   - **d.** Sundiata.

3. A spoken record of the past is
   - **a.** a Soninke.
   - **b.** an oral history.
   - **c.** a Gao.
   - **d.** an age-set proverb.

4. A West African storyteller is
   - **a.** an Almoravid.
   - **b.** a griot.
   - **c.** an arquebus.
   - **d.** a rift.

Comprehension and Critical Thinking

SECTION 1 *(pages 310–314)*

5. **a. Describe** How did the physical geography of Nubia affect civilization in the region?

   b. Analyze Why did the relationship between Kush and Egypt change more than once?

   c. Predict If an archaeologist found an artifact near the Fourth Cataract, why might he or she have difficulty deciding how to display it in a museum?

SECTION 2 *(pages 315–319)*

6. **a. Identify** Who was Queen Shanakhdakheto? Why don't we know more about her?

   b. Compare and Contrast What are some features that Kushite and Egyptian cultures had in common? How were they different?

   c. Evaluate What do you think was the most important cause of Kush's decline? Why?

ANCIENT CIVILIZATIONS OF AFRICA—TRADING KINGDOMS **339**

SECTION 3 (pages 320–325)

7. a. Identify What were the two major trade goods that made Ghana rich?

b. Make Inferences Why did merchants in Ghana not want other traders to know where their gold came from?

c. Evaluate Who do you think was more responsible for the collapse of Ghana, the people of Ghana or outsiders? Why?

SECTION 4 (pages 328–332)

8. a. Describe How did Islam influence society in Mali?

b. Compare and Contrast How were Sundiata and Mansa Musa similar? How were they different?

c. Evaluate Which group do you think played a larger role in Songhai, warriors or traders?

SECTION 5 (pages 334–337)

9. a. Recall What different types of information did griots pass on to their listeners?

b. Analyze Why are the writings of visitors to West Africa so important?

c. Evaluate Which of the various arts of West Africa do you think is most important? Why?

Social Studies Skills

10. Making Decisions You are a young trader in Kush and must decide which good you would prefer to trade, pottery or iron. List the consequences that might result from trading each of them. Then make a decision.

FOCUS ON READING AND WRITING

Understanding Cause and Effect *Answer the following questions about causes and effects.*

11. What caused the empire of Ghana to grow?

12. What were some effects of Mansa Musa's rule?

Writing Your Journal Entry *Use your notes and the instructions below to help you create your news report.*

13. Review your notes on possible subjects for your journal entry. Choose one, and think about an experience that person might write about in his or her journal. Write a journal entry of a paragraph or two.

Using the Internet

go.hrw.com
KEYWORD: SK9 CH11

14. Activity: Writing a Proverb Does the early bird get the worm? If you go outside at sunrise to check, you missed the fact that this is a proverb that means "The one that gets there first can earn something good." Griots created many proverbs that expressed wisdom or truth. Enter the activity keyword. Then use the Internet resources to write three proverbs that might have been said by griots during the time of the great West African empires. Make sure your proverbs are written from the point of view of a West African person living during those centuries.

Map Activity

15. West Africa On a separate sheet of paper, match the letters on the map with their correct labels.

Senegal River	Timbuktu
Lake Chad	Niger River
Gulf of Guinea	

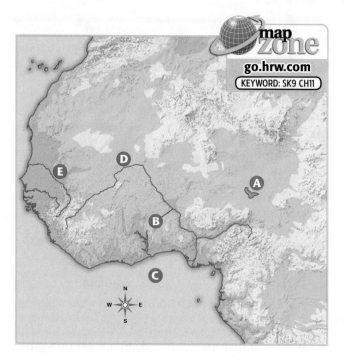
go.hrw.com
KEYWORD: SK9 CH11

DIRECTIONS (1–6): **For each statement or question, write on a separate answer sheet the *number* of the word or expression that, of those given, best completes the statement or answers the question.**

1 The wealth of Ghana, Mali, and Songhai was based on

(1) raiding other tribes.

(2) the gold and salt trade.

(3) trade in ostriches and elephant tusks.

(4) making iron tools and weapons.

2 The two rulers who were most responsible for spreading Islam in West Africa were

(1) Sunni Ali and Mansa Musa.

(2) Sundiata and Sunni Ali.

(3) Ibn Battutah and Tunka Manin.

(4) Mansa Musa and Askia the Great.

3 Which of the following statements regarding women in ancient Kush is true?

(1) Some Kushite women served as religious and political leaders.

(2) Kushite women had more rights and opportunities than Kushite men.

(3) Kushite women were forbidden to leave their homes.

(4) Many Kushite women were wealthy merchants.

4 Griots contributed to West African societies by

(1) fighting battles.

(2) collecting taxes.

(3) preserving oral history.

(4) trading with the Berbers.

5 Which of the following rivers helped the development of Ghana and Mali?

(1) Niger

(2) Congo

(3) Nile

(4) Zambezi

6 How did cataracts on the Nile River benefit Kush?

(1) They allowed Kushite farmers to plant both summer and winter crops.

(2) Because they were highly prized by the Egyptians, Kush gained wealth from trade.

(3) Because they were difficult to pass through, they provided protection against invaders.

(4) They allowed the Kushites to build a powerful army.

Base your answer to question 7 on the text excerpt below and on your knowledge of social studies.

"Well placed for the caravan trade, it was badly situated to defend itself from the Tuareg raiders of the Sahara. These restless nomads were repeatedly hammering at the gates of Timbuktu, and often enough they burst them open with disastrous results for the inhabitants. Life here was never quite safe enough to recommend it as the centre [center] of a big state."

—Basil Davidson, from *A History of West Africa*

7 Constructed-Response Question The location of the city of Timbuktu had both advantages and drawbacks. List one positive and one negative effect of the city's location.

The Kingdom of Benin

This ivory mask pendant was worn by the *oba*, or king, of Benin.

History

Although the trading empires of Ghana, Mali, and Songhai were the largest states in West Africa, they were not the only ones. Farther south, a number of kingdoms grew up in the forests that lined the Niger River. Among them was the kingdom of Benin (buh-NEEN), which reached its height in the 1400s. (Although the two share a name, the kingdom was not in the same location as the modern country of Benin. The kingdom was farther east, in what is now Nigeria.)

According to legend, the first people of Benin—the Edo—were ruled by the Kings of the Sky. Over time, the Edo grew unhappy with these kings. In the late 1100s the Edo invited the prince of a nearby kingdom to be their new ruler. The prince ruled Benin until his first son was born, after which he returned home. His son became the first *oba*, or king, of Benin.

Perhaps Benin's most famed *oba* was Ewuare (e-woo-AH-reh), who ruled from about 1440 to about 1470. He was a great military leader who added new lands to the kingdom. Ewuare was also a skilled administrator. He reorganized Benin's political system and expanded the capital, Benin City.

Shortly after Ewuare's death, Portuguese sailors arrived in Benin. Because Benin had been at war for many years, its people had many captives they could sell to the Portuguese as slaves. The slave trade between Benin and Portugal continued for many years. Benin also traded goods such as pepper, ivory, and cotton. In the mid-1500s the English arrived in Benin, wanting to trade. They were particularly interested in palm oil from Benin's palm trees. Palm oil soon became Benin's main export.

Soldiers guard the palace of the *oba* in this bronze plaque from ancient Benin.

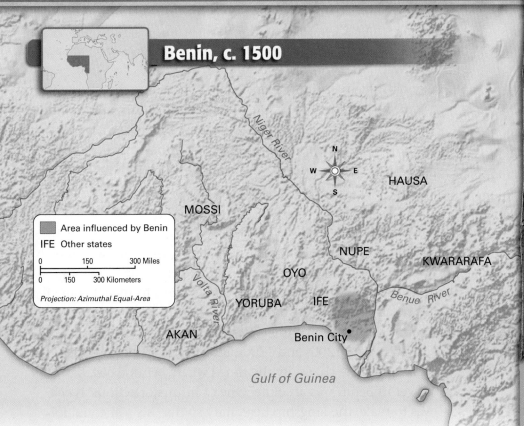

Benin, c. 1500

MOSSI

HAUSA

NUPE

OYO

KWARARAFA

YORUBA   IFE

AKAN

Benin City

Niger River

Volta River

Benue River

Gulf of Guinea

Area influenced by Benin
IFE Other states

0   150   300 Miles

0   150   300 Kilometers

Projection: Azimuthal Equal-Area

Europeans arrived in Benin in the late 1400s. This brass plaque shows a Portuguese sailor hunting with his dog by his feet.

Trade between Benin and Europeans continued for many years. In the late 1800s, British officials proposed a treaty that would have made Benin into a colony, but the *oba* rejected it. The British sent troops toward Benin City to force the treaty. Fearing a British attack, some royal guards ambushed and killed the troops. In response, the British army attacked Benin City in force in 1897. They looted the city, burned it to the ground, and forced the reigning *oba* into exile. This attack marked the end of the kingdom of Benin.

Case Study Assessment

1. According to legend, how did the first *oba* come to power in Benin?

2. Why did the British attack Benin City?

3. **Activity** Ancient rulers often gave gifts to show their kingdoms' wealth or power. Plan a gift that the *oba* might have sent to impress the king of Portugal.

Leopards were a symbol of royal authority in Benin. These bronze leopards were made in the 1500s.

Society and Daily Life

Very little remains of ancient Benin. The destruction of Benin City by the British made later study of the culture much more difficult. As a result, much of what we know today about ancient Benin comes from oral history. Inhabitants of the region have passed down stories about the kingdom and its people over many generations.

Government

Although Benin was ruled by *obas* from early on, the first *obas* did not have much power. Instead, power in the kingdom rested mostly with local chiefs. These chiefs formed a council that was supposed to advise the *oba* about decisions. In truth, however, members of the council made most decisions.

In the late 1200s and 1300s, *obas* began to increase their power over the chiefs. By the time Ewuare became *oba*, his power in Benin was absolute. One of his major actions as *oba* was to make the kingship hereditary so that his son could follow him as ruler. Before that time, the *oba* had been chosen by the council of chiefs.

When the British forced the reigning *oba* into exile in 1897, he lost most of his authority. However, he did not abandon his title. In fact, Benin still has an *oba*. The current holder

Modern Edo Society

QUICK FACTS

Although the kingdom of Benin is long gone, the Edo live on in Nigeria. Many elements of modern Edo culture resemble those of the ancient kingdom.

- An *oba* still serves as the symbolic leader of the Edo people. He has little power himself, but the *oba* advises political officials in southern Nigeria.

- Most of the Edo live in villages and towns. These can range in size from a few dozen people to several thousand. Many Edo also live in modern Benin City.

- Within Edo villages, coucils of elders have great authority. These councils make decisions about village responsibilities and religious matters. They also handle relations between the village and the Nigerian government.

- Most Edo today are farmers. They grow crops such as yams, corn, plantains, and cassava. Some Edo are herders, raising goats, sheep, and chickens.

- Today many Edo are Christians or Muslims.

Oba Erediauwa leads a thanksgiving festival, an annual ceremony to celebrate the end of the year.

Benin City

Residents of Benin City celebrate in this engraving from the 1600s. Nothing remains of the original city, which was burned by the British in 1897. At right, children play soccer on the outskirts of modern Benin City.

of the title, Erediauwa I, became *oba* in 1979. Although he has no official power, Oba Erediauwa has great influence on politics in southern Nigeria, the area that was once the kingdom of Benin.

Daily Life

Life in the kingdom of Benin centered around the capital, Benin City. The city was immense. Despite its huge size, the entire city was surrounded by a wall and a moat.

European visitors to Benin City in the 1600s were amazed by its size and splendor, comparing it favorably to some of Europe's major cities. The largest structure in town was the royal palace. Surrounded by courtyards, the palace took up about a fifth of the city. Its walls were covered with brass plaques that showed images of great *obas* from the past. On the roof, bronze and brass birds posed as if about to take flight. Surrounding the royal palace were smaller palaces and houses for Benin's nobles. Like the royal palace, these houses were lavishly decorated with brass, bronze, and ivory.

Case Study Assessment

1. What powers did Benin's *obas* have?

2. Why were Europeans impressed by Benin City?

3. **Activity** Imagine that you are a European sailor who has just arrived in Benin City. Write a letter to your family, describing what you see as you explore the city.

1180
According to legend, the first *oba* comes to power in Benin.

Brass statue of an *oba*

c. 1300
Powerful *obas* increase their control over the kingdom's nobles.

1440
Ewuare becomes *oba* and begins a policy of expansion.

1485
Portuguese sailors visit Benin City.

Culture and Achievements

Although the kingdom of Benin is gone, many elements of its culture remain in West Africa. Descendants of the Edo who founded Benin still live in southern Nigeria, especially in the Edo region, and they have kept many elements of traditional Edo culture. The Edo language is still spoken. About 5 million people in Nigeria today speak it as their first language. In addition, the people of the Edo region have maintained many customs, including traditional forms of music and dance, that were practiced in ancient Benin.

Other customs from Benin have largely vanished. The ancient religion of Benin, for example, is not widely practiced. This religion involved the worship of many gods, goddesses, and nature spirits. When the Portuguese arrived in Benin in the 1400s, they introduced Christianity to the region. Today most of the Edo in West Africa are either Christian or Muslim.

The ancient kingdom of Benin is now best remembered for its art. The artists of Benin made intricately detailed works from brass, bronze, and ivory. For example, they used bronze to make statues of their *obas*. In addition, artists made brass plaques

Music and Dance

Music and dance have always been central to life in West Africa, and Benin was no exception. Music and dance were important elements of celebrations and religious ceremonies alike. The descendants of the people of Benin, including the Bini of Nigeria, have maintained many styles of music practiced centuries ago.

This bronze figure is playing a horn. The horn was played from the side, like a modern flute.

Drummers in Benin made their drums out of hollow logs.

1553
The British arrive in what is now southern Nigeria.

European gun from the 1600s

1897
The British take over Benin, burning Benin City and exiling the *oba*.

to celebrate great events of the past. As you have read, these plaques were used to decorate the royal palace and other buildings throughout Benin City.

European visitors to Benin were greatly impressed with the kingdom's art. In fact, many Europeans asked Benin's artists to create works for them to take home to Europe. As a result, Benin's brass plaques, bronze statues, and ivory containers were introduced to Europe. These items led to a demand for African art among Europe's wealthy. Unfortunately, this demand led to greed. When the British took over Benin in the 1800s, they carried as much art as they could back to Europe.

Case Study Assessment

1. What customs from Benin are still followed today?

2. How did art from Benin become popular in Europe?

3. **Activity** The art of Benin often portrayed great rulers or major events. Design a plaque that an artist from Benin might have created to illustrate one such event.

Traditional music in West Africa reflects the influence of ancient kingdoms like Benin.

Growth and Development of Africa

FOCUS QUESTION

What forces had an impact on the development of Africa and why?

What You Will Learn...

In this chapter you will learn about the many influences that have shaped African culture. Both traditional cultures and outside forces have played roles in creating modern Africa.

FOCUS ON READING AND SPEAKING

Identifying Supporting Details Supporting details are the facts and examples that provide information to support a main idea. As you read this chapter, look for the details that support each section's main ideas. **See the lesson, Identifying Supporting Details, on page S15.**

Presenting a TV News Report You are a journalist assigned to create a brief TV news report on a person or event in Africa. As you read this chapter, you will collect information about Africa's history and plan your report. Later, you will present your report to the class.

0	250	500 Miles
0	250	500 Kilometers

Projection: Azimuthal Equal-Area

ATLANTIC OCEAN

Explorer's ship

Europeans in Africa Europeans became involved in African affairs in order to make money for themselves.

COMPLETE INDEPENDENCE 1961

Independence Tanzanians celebrate their independence from Great Britain in 1961.

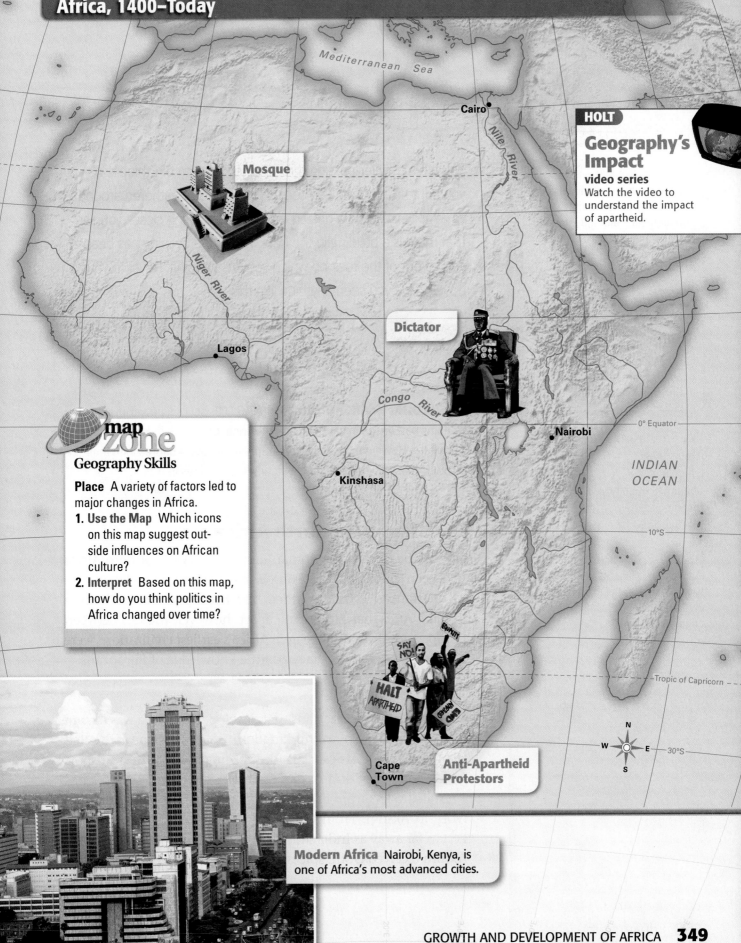

Mediterranean Sea

40°N

Cairo

Mosque

Nile River

Niger River

Lagos

HOLT

Geography's Impact
video series
Watch the video to understand the impact of apartheid.

Dictator

Congo River

Nairobi

0° Equator

map zone

Geography Skills

Place A variety of factors led to major changes in Africa.

1. Use the Map Which icons on this map suggest outside influences on African culture?

2. Interpret Based on this map, how do you think politics in Africa changed over time?

Kinshasa

INDIAN OCEAN

10°S

EQUITY

SAY NO!

HALT APARTHEID

Tropic of Capricorn

N
W   E
S

30°S

Cape Town

Anti-Apartheid Protestors

Modern Africa Nairobi, Kenya, is one of Africa's most advanced cities.

Contact with Other Cultures

What You Will Learn...

Main Ideas

1. Christianity arrived in North Africa by the 300s and became a major influence.
2. Trade and military conquest led to the spread of Islam through Africa.

The Big Idea

African contact with other cultures led to major cultural changes, particularly the spread of Christianity and Islam.

Key Terms and Places

Aksum, *p. 350*
Ethiopia, *p. 351*
Coptic Christianity, *p. 352*
Djenné, *p. 352*
Swahili, *p. 353*

TAKING NOTES As you read, use a diagram like this one to take notes on the influences of Christianity and Islam on the cultures of Africa.

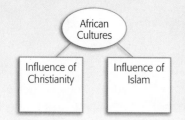

If YOU lived there...

You are a traveler passing through the kingdom of Ethiopia. As you approach a town, you see a huge crowd of gathered around what appears to be a hole in the ground. Walking closer, you see that there is a building in the hole. The entire building has been carved out of the rock on which you are standing. Never in your travels have you seen anything like this.

What do you think of this new building style?

BUILDING BACKGROUND By the AD 600s several powerful kingdoms had arisen in various parts of Africa, each with its own distinct culture. However, the arrival of people from other cultures with their own ideas and religions led to significant changes in Africa.

Christianity in North Africa

During the days of the Roman Empire, parts of northern Africa had been closely tied to Europe. From Morocco to Egypt, the Mediterranean coast of Africa had been part of the Roman Empire. After that Empire fell apart, however, the ties between Europe and Africa disappeared. Africa's earliest civilizations were replaced by new ones that had little knowledge of Europeans.

Aksum

One of the new civilizations that developed in Africa was **Aksum** (AHK-soom). This powerful kingdom was located near the Red Sea in northeast Africa. This location made it easy to transport goods over water, and Aksum became a major trading power as a result. Traders from inland Africa brought goods like gold and ivory to Aksum. From there, the items were shipped to markets as far away as India. In return for their goods, the people of Aksum received cloth, spices, and other products.

Lalibela, Ethiopia

In the 1200s, highly skilled Ethiopian architects and craftspeople built this Christian church at Lalibela.

ANALYZING VISUALS What Christian symbol does the church resemble?

Workers dug deep trenches to carve out the church.

Craftspeople used special tools to carve windows and doors out of solid rock.

Because Aksum was a thriving trade center, people from various cultures gathered there. As these people met and mingled to trade goods, they also traded ideas and beliefs.

One of the beliefs that was brought to Aksum by traders was Christianity. Christian teachings quickly took hold in Aksum, and many people converted. In the late 300s, Aksum's most famous ruler, King Ezana (AY-zah-nah), made Christianity the kingdom's official religion.

As a Christian kingdom, Aksum developed ties with other Christian states. For example, it was an ally of the Byzantine Empire. However, contact with these allies was cut off in the 600s and 700s, when Muslim armies from Southwest Asia conquered most of North Africa.

Although Aksum itself was never conquered, its major ports were taken by the Muslims. As a result, the kingdom became isolated from other lands. Cut off from their allies and their trade, the people of Aksum retreated to the mountains of northern Ethiopia.

Ethiopia

In time, the descendants of the people of Aksum formed a new kingdom, **Ethiopia**. By about 1150 Ethiopia had become one of Africa's most powerful kingdoms.

The most famous of Ethiopia's rulers was King Lalibela, who ruled in the 1200s. He is famous for the 11 Christian churches he built, many of which still stand. One of these churches is pictured above. The churches of Lalibela were carved into solid rock, many of them set into the ground. Worshippers had to walk down long flights of steps to get to them. Impressive feats of engineering, these churches also show the Ethiopians' devotion to Christianity. This devotion to Christianity set the Ethiopians apart from their neighbors, most of whom were Muslim.

Shared beliefs helped unify Ethiopians, but their isolation from other Christians led to some changes in their beliefs. Over time, some local African customs blended with Christian teachings. This resulted in a new form of Christianity in Africa called **Coptic Christianity**. The name *Coptic* comes from an Arabic word for "Egyptian." Most Christians who live in North Africa today—including many Ethiopians—belong to Coptic churches.

Although most people in Ethiopia were Christian, not everyone was. For example, a Jewish group known as the Beta Israel lived there. Though some Christian rulers tried to force the Beta Israel to give up their religion and adopt Christianity, they were not successful. Ethiopia's Jewish population remained active for centuries.

READING CHECK **Sequencing** How did Christianity take hold in parts of Africa?

The Architecture of Djenné

Stone and wood are rare in the Sahara Desert. Therefore, when the Muslims of Djenné decided to build a mosque, they looked to a material that was widely available: mud. They dried mud into bricks to build the Great Mosque, shown below. They then covered the bricks with a plaster, also made of mud, to give the building a smooth finish.

First built in the 1200s, the Great Mosque of Djenné was demolished in 1834. The city's ruler at that time thought the mosque was too ornate. However, it was rebuilt in 1907 and has stood ever since. Today, the citizens of Djenné gather yearly to repair damage from rain or extreme heat, either of which can harm the fragile mud bricks.

Drawing Conclusions Why are mud bricks a suitable building material in the Sahara Desert?

The Spread of Islam

By the 600s and 700s Christianity had taken firm hold in parts of northeastern Africa. However, the arrival of soldiers and traders from the Muslim world brought major changes to the continent's religious map. These soldiers and traders brought with them a new religion, Islam.

Muslim North Africa

Beginning in the mid-600s, Arab armies from Southwest Asia swept across North Africa. Led by strong and clever generals, these armies quickly took over Egypt and the Nile Valley. From there they headed west, eventually conquering all of Africa's Mediterranean coast. These conquered lands became part of a Muslim empire that stretched from Persia all the way to Spain.

The Muslims introduced Islam and the Arabic language into North Africa. They also established schools and universities. Students there studied not only religion but also science, medicine, astronomy, and other subjects. Scholars from all over the Muslim world moved to North Africa to study and teach.

As a result of Muslim rule, many cities in North Africa grew and became centers of learning. Among the cities that developed in this way were Cairo in Egypt, Fès in Morocco, and **Djenné** in Mali.

Trade in the East

While Islam came to North Africa through conquest, the religion's arrival in East Africa was less violent. Located on the Indian Ocean, East Africa had been a destination for traders from Asia for centuries. Among these traders were Muslims from India, Persia, and Arabia. They came to Africa in search of African goods and new markets for products from their homelands, but they also gave Africa a new culture.

To make trade easy and profitable, the Muslim traders and African locals built cities all along the coast. By 1100, East African cities like Mogadishu, Mombasa, Kilwa, and Sofala had become trade centers.

Muslim traders from Arabia and Persia settled down in many of these coastal trading cities. As a result, the cities developed large Muslim communities. Africans, Arabs, and Persians lived near each other and worked together. One result of this closeness was the spread of Islam through East Africa. People at all levels of society, from workers to rulers, adopted Islam. As a result, mosques appeared in cities and towns throughout the region.

The contact between cultures also led to other changes in East Africa. For example, the architecture of the region changed. People began to build houses that mixed **traditional** materials, such as coral and mangrove trees, with Arab designs, such as arched windows and carved doors.

ACADEMIC VOCABULARY

traditional customary, time-honored

As the cultures grew closer, their speech began to reflect their new relationship. Some Africans, who spoke mostly Bantu languages, adopted many Arabic and Persian words. In time, the languages blended into a new language, Swahili (swah-HEE-lee). The term **Swahili** refers to the blended African-Arab culture that had become common in East Africa.

READING CHECK **Summarizing** How did Islam change African society?

SUMMARY AND PREVIEW In this section, you learned about early contact between African societies and people from other regions. Next, you will learn how the arrival of European traders in Africa led to significant changes.

Section 1 Assessment

Reviewing Ideas, Terms, and Places

1. **a. Identify** What was the first kingdom in Africa to become Christian after the fall of Rome? Which ruler was responsible for its conversion?

   b. Identify Cause and Effect What led to the creation of **Coptic Christianity** in Africa?

   c. Develop Why did Christianity serve as a unifying factor for the people of **Ethiopia**?

2. **a. Define** What does **Swahili** mean?

   b. Contrast How did the arrival of Islam in North Africa differ from its arrival in East Africa?

   c. Predict How might life in East Africa have been different if the people there had not accepted the presence of Muslim traders?

Critical Thinking

3. **Analyzing Information** Use your notes and the graphic organizer to examine how the arrival of Christianity and Islam in Africa influenced local culture and led to changes in the two religions.

| Christianity Influence: Changes: | African Cultures | Islam Influence: Changes: |

FOCUS ON SPEAKING

4. **Describing Cultural Influences** Your TV news report might mention the influence of various religions on Africa. What details from this section might you include in your report?

European Colonization

What You Will Learn...

Main Ideas

1. Europeans arrived in Africa in search of valuable trade goods.
2. The slave trade had terrible effects in Africa.
3. Many European countries established colonies in Africa.

The Big Idea

Europeans established colonies in Africa to take advantage of trade in gold, ivory, slaves, and other items.

Key Terms and Places

Middle Passage, *p. 356*
Gold Coast, *p. 357*

 TAKING NOTES As you read, use a graphic organizer like this one to take notes on the arrival of Europeans in Africa, the African slave trade, and European colonies.

| Arrival |
| Slave Trade |
| Colonies |

If YOU lived there...

You are a sailor on a Portuguese explorer's ship on its way to India. After several days at sea, your captain decides to land along the African coast. As you reach the shore, you are greeted by a group of villagers who offer you gold and ivory jewelry.

What does this gift suggest about Africa's resources?

BUILDING BACKGROUND Before the 1300s, few people in Europe knew much about Africa. Ancient Greek writers had described parts of the continent, but most people knew little about Africa as it actually existed. After European explorers landed in Africa in the 1400s, however, the continent drew the attention of traders and colonists.

★Interactive
Close-up

Mansa Musa's Pilgrimage

Mansa Musa's pilgrimage to Mecca in 1324 brought the wealth of Mali to the attention of the Muslim world and Europe. Based on historical accounts, Mansa Musa's impressive caravan included more than 60,000 people.

go.hrw.com KEYWORD: SK9 CH12

The baggage included huge amounts of gold to give away as gifts—gold valued at about $100 million today.

Some 500 people in the caravan carried staffs heavily decorated with gold to show Mali's wealth.

The Arrival of Europeans

In the late 1400s explorers set sail from ports around Europe. Many of these explorers hoped to find new trade routes to places like India and China. There, they could find goods that would sell for high prices in Europe and make them wealthy.

As part of their quest, some Portuguese explorers set out to sail around Africa. During their journeys, many landed at spots along the African coast. Some of these explorers soon found that they could get rich without ever reaching India or China.

Rumors of Gold

For centuries, Europeans had heard rumors of golden kingdoms in Africa. Those rumors began in the 1300s when Mansa Musa, the ruler of Mali, set out on his famous hajj, or Muslim pilgrimage, to Mecca. He was accompanied by thousands of attendants and slaves. As they traveled, the pilgrims gave away lavish gifts of gold to the rulers of lands through which they passed.

For years after Mansa Musa's hajj, stories of his wealth passed from Southwest Asia into Europe. However, most Europeans did not believe they could find gold in Africa. When the Portuguese reached the coasts of West Africa, however, they learned that the stories had been true. Africa did have gold, and the Europeans wanted it.

Trade Goods

Gold was the first item to bring European attention to Africa, but it was not the only valuable product to be found there. Another was ivory. Europeans used ivory to make furniture, jewelry, statues, piano keys, and other expensive items.

At first, the Portuguese had little interest in products other than gold and ivory. Before long, however, they found that they could make more profit from something else the Africans were willing to sell them—slaves.

READING CHECK Summarizing Why did some Europeans become interested in Africa?

Mansa Musa rode near the front. During his journey, he gained fame for his generosity.

Called "ships of the desert," camels could go for long periods without water and could withstand heat better than horses or donkeys.

ANALYSIS SKILL ANALYZING VISUALS

Why do you think people were impressed by stories about Mansa Musa's pilgrimage?

Ivory Trade

Ivory traders collected elephant tusks for export to Europe.

ANALYZING VISUALS Who was involved in the ivory trade?

The Slave Trade

Slavery was nothing new in Africa. For centuries, societies within Africa had kept slaves. Most of these slaves were prisoners captured in battle or as the result of raids on rival villages or kingdoms.

The European Slave Trade

Slavery had existed for centuries in Africa, but the arrival of Europeans in West Africa led to a drastic increase in the demand for slaves. Europeans wanted slaves to put to work on plantations, or large farms, in the Americas. Slave traders made deals with many rulers in West and Central Africa to buy the slaves they captured in battle. These slaves were then put in chains and loaded onto ships. These ships carried the slaves on a grueling trip across the Atlantic called the **Middle Passage**.

The slave trade continued for more than 300 years. Though some Europeans argued against slavery, calling it an evil institution that should be stopped, slave traders considered the practice too profitable to stop. It was not until the 1800s that European governments stepped in and finally banned the trading of slaves.

Effects of the Slave Trade

The European slave trade in Africa had devastating consequences. It led to a drastic decrease in Africa's population. Millions of young African men were forced to move away from their homes to lands far away, and thousands of them died. Historians estimate that 15 to 20 million African slaves were shipped to the Americas against their will. Millions more were sent to Europe, Asia, and the Middle East.

The slave trade had terrible effects on those who remained in Africa as well. The efforts of some kingdoms to capture slaves from their rivals led to decades of warfare on the continent. This warfare further reduced Africa's population and weakened many societies. It also caused caused years of resentment and mistrust between many African peoples.

READING CHECK Identifying Cause and Effect What were the results of the slave trade?

European Colonies in Africa

Trade in gold, ivory, and slaves made many Portuguese merchants very rich. Envious of this wealth, other European countries rushed to grab part of the trade. The result was a struggle among several countries to establish colonies along the African coast.

Colonies in West Africa

The first European colony in West Africa was the **Gold Coast**, established by the Portuguese in 1482. It was located in the area now occupied by the country of Ghana. Most colonies in West Africa were named after the products traded there. In addition to the Gold Coast, the region had colonies called Ivory Coast and Slave Coast.

To keep order in their colonies, Europeans built forts along West Africa's coast. These forts served both as trading centers and military outposts.

Over time, the colonies of West Africa merged. For example, the Portuguese gave their colony to the Dutch in the mid-1600s. Eventually, the entire Gold Coast came under the control of the British, who kept the colony there until the 1950s.

The Portuguese in East Africa

While several countries had colonies in West Africa, only the Portuguese were interested in East Africa. They knew that trade on the Indian Ocean was very profitable, and they wanted to control that trade.

The Portuguese knew they could not take over East Africa as long as strong African kingdoms ruled the region. To weaken those kingdoms, they encouraged rulers to go to war with each other. The Portuguese then made alliances with the winners.

However, Portuguese influence in East Africa was weakened when Muslims arrived. The Muslims forced the Portuguese almost completely out of the region. Although the Portuguese kept a colony in Mozambique, their influence was almost gone.

READING CHECK **Identifying Cause and Effect**
Why did Europeans establish colonies in Africa?

SUMMARY AND PREVIEW Europeans arrived in Africa in the 1500s and built a number of colonies. Next, you will learn about another period of European involvement in Africa during the 1800s.

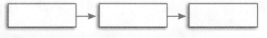

Section 2 Assessment

Reviewing Ideas, Terms, and Places

1. **a. Identify** What trade goods did Europeans find available in Africa?
   b. Analyze How did Mansa Musa's pilgrimage affect European views toward Africa?
2. **a. Define** What was the **Middle Passage**?
   b. Summarize Why did Europeans want slaves?
   c. Evaluate In your opinion, what was the worst result of the slave trade? Explain your answer.
3. **a. Recall** Why did Europeans want to form colonies in West Africa?
   b. Develop What do names like **Gold Coast** suggest about Europeans' views toward their African colonies?

Critical Thinking

4. **Sequencing** Use your notes and a diagram like the one below to list the major steps in the formation of European colonies in Africa. You may add more boxes to the diagram if necessary.

   ☐ → ☐ → ☐

FOCUS ON SPEAKING

5. **Describing Colonies** Will your news report mention the arrival of Europeans in Africa and the formation of colonies? Write down some notes about topics you might include in your report.

Geography and History

The Atlantic Slave Trade

Between 1500 and 1870, British, French, Dutch, Portuguese, and Spanish traders sent millions of enslaved Africans to colonies in the Americas. The highest number of slaves went to British and French colonies in the West Indies. The climate in the colonies was good for growing crops like cotton, tobacco, and sugarcane. These crops required a great deal of labor to grow and process. The colonists relied on enslaved Africans to meet this demand for labor.

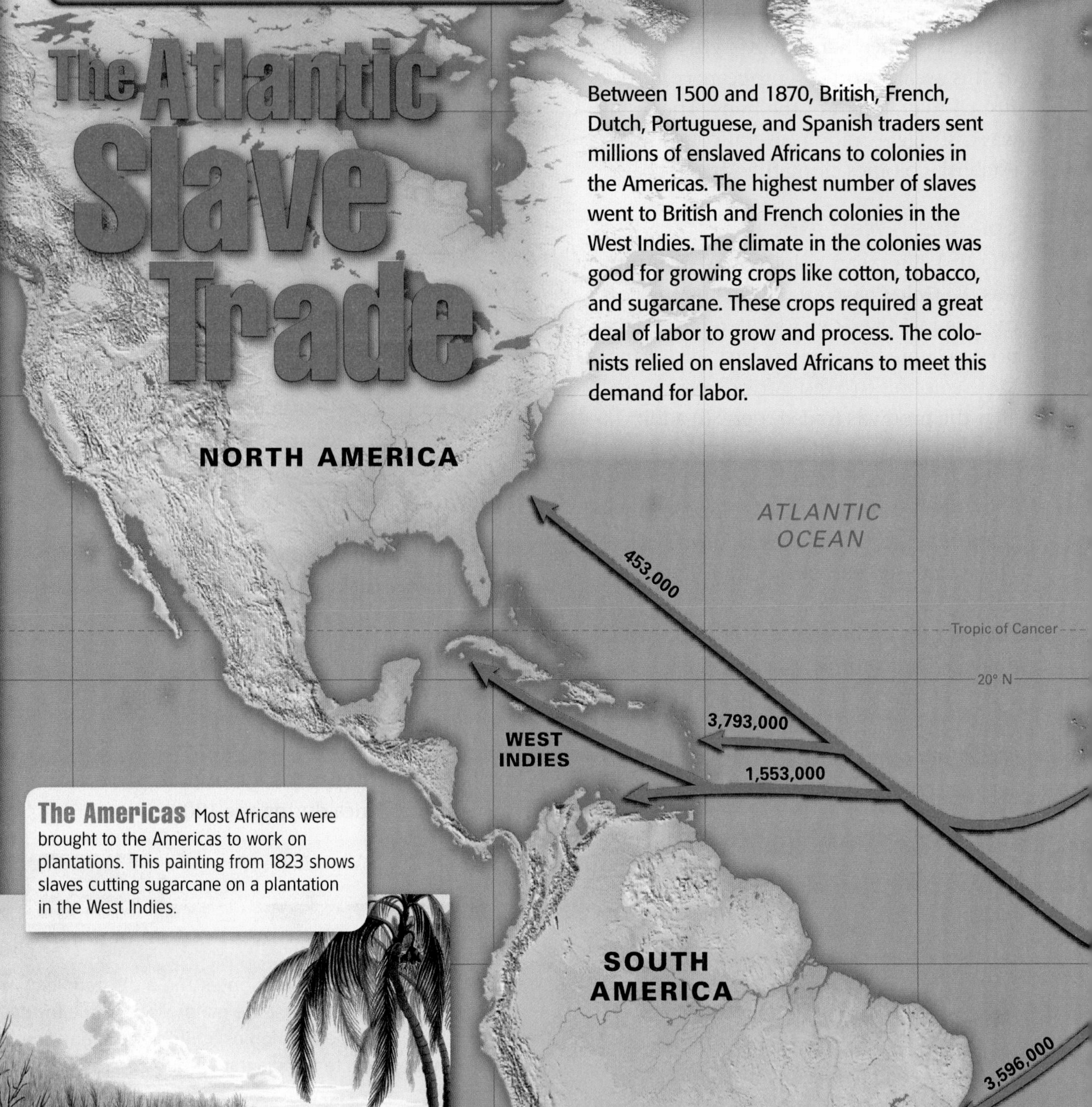

NORTH AMERICA

ATLANTIC OCEAN

453,000

Tropic of Cancer

20° N

WEST INDIES

3,793,000

1,553,000

The Americas Most Africans were brought to the Americas to work on plantations. This painting from 1823 shows slaves cutting sugarcane on a plantation in the West Indies.

SOUTH AMERICA

3,596,000

120° W

100° W

80° W

40° W

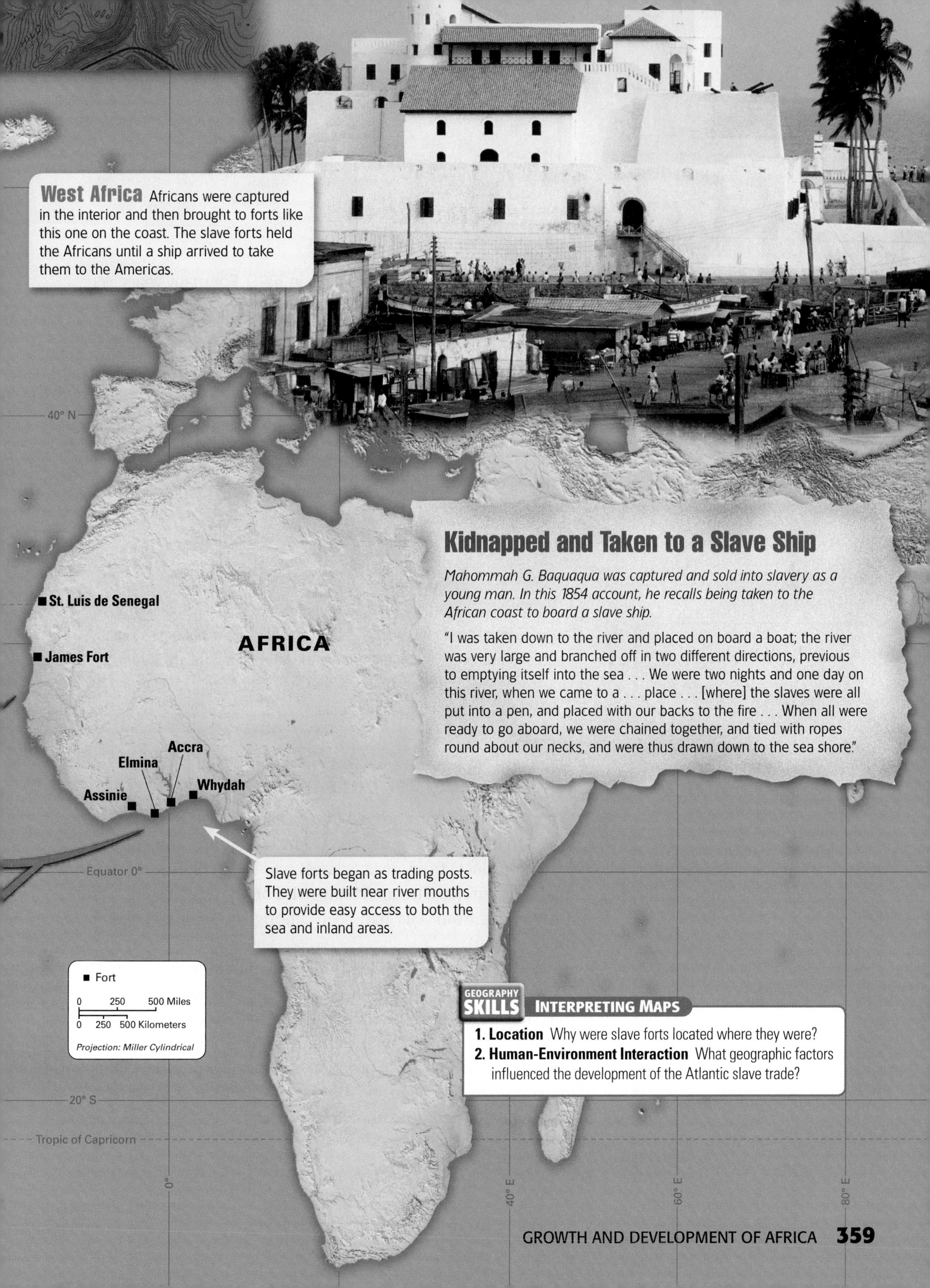

West Africa Africans were captured in the interior and then brought to forts like this one on the coast. The slave forts held the Africans until a ship arrived to take them to the Americas.

40° N

Kidnapped and Taken to a Slave Ship

Mahommah G. Baquaqua was captured and sold into slavery as a young man. In this 1854 account, he recalls being taken to the African coast to board a slave ship.

"I was taken down to the river and placed on board a boat; the river was very large and branched off in two different directions, previous to emptying itself into the sea . . . We were two nights and one day on this river, when we came to a . . . place . . . [where] the slaves were all put into a pen, and placed with our backs to the fire . . . When all were ready to go aboard, we were chained together, and tied with ropes round about our necks, and were thus drawn down to the sea shore."

■ St. Luis de Senegal

AFRICA

■ James Fort

Accra

Elmina

Assinie ■ Whydah

Equator 0°

Slave forts began as trading posts. They were built near river mouths to provide easy access to both the sea and inland areas.

■ Fort

0   250   500 Miles

0   250 500 Kilometers

Projection: Miller Cylindrical

GEOGRAPHY SKILLS INTERPRETING MAPS

1. **Location** Why were slave forts located where they were?
2. **Human-Environment Interaction** What geographic factors influenced the development of the Atlantic slave trade?

20° S

Tropic of Capricorn

40° E

60° E

80° E

Imperialism in Africa

What You Will Learn...

Main Ideas

1. The search for raw materials led to a new wave of European involvement in Africa.
2. The Scramble for Africa was a race by Europeans to form colonies there.
3. Some Africans resisted rule by Europeans.

The Big Idea

In the late 1800s Europeans once again created colonies in Africa and became involved in African politics and economics.

Key Terms and Places

entrepreneurs, *p. 361*
imperialism, *p. 361*
Suez Canal, *p. 362*
Berlin Conference, *p. 362*
Boers, *p. 364*

TAKING NOTES As you read, use a graphic organizer like this one to take notes on various aspects of European imperialism in Africa in the 1800s.

If YOU lived there...

You are the chief of an African tribe in 1890. For many years, your people have been at war with a tribe that lives in the next valley. One day, however, a warrior from that tribe delivers a message to you. His chief has been approached by soldiers with strange clothes and weapons. They say that both tribes are now part of a colony that belongs to a place called England. The other chief wants to know how you will deal with these strangers.

How will you respond to the other chief?

BUILDING BACKGROUND Europeans had formed colonies in Africa as early as the 1400s, but they actually controlled only a small percentage of the continent. During the late 1800s, though, European attitudes toward Africa changed, and they soon fought to control as much of the continent as they could.

New Involvement in Africa

When Europeans first arrived in Africa in the 1400s, they hoped to get rich through trade. For centuries, controlling the trade of rare products from distant lands had been the surest road to wealth in Europe. The merchants who brought spices, silks, and other goods from Asia had been among the richest people on the continent.

With the beginning of the Industrial Revolution in the 1700s, however, a new road to riches emerged. Europeans found that they could become rich by building factories and making products that other people wanted, such as cheap cloth, tools, or steel. In order to make products, business owners needed raw materials. However, Europe did not have sufficient resources to supply all the factories that were opening. Where were these resources to come from?

The Quest for Raw Materials

By the 1880s Europeans decided that the best way to get resources was to create new colonies. They wanted these colonies to be located in places that had abundant resources not available in Europe.

One such place was Africa. Since the slave trade had ended in the early 1800s, few Europeans had paid much attention to Africa. Unless they could make a huge fortune in Africa, most people did not care what happened there. As factory owners looked for new sources of raw materials, though, some people took another look at Africa. For the first time, they noticed its huge open spaces and its mineral wealth.

Once again, Europeans rushed to Africa to establish colonies. Most of these new colonists who headed to Africa in the 1800s were **entrepreneurs**, or independent businesspeople. In Africa they built mines, plantations, and trade routes with the dream of growing rich.

Cultural Interference

Though they were in Africa to get rich, the European entrepreneurs who moved there frequently became involved in local affairs. Often, they became involved because they thought their ideas about government and culture were better than native African ways. As a result, they often tried to impose their own ideas on the local people. This sort of attempt to dominate a country's government, trade, or culture is called **imperialism.**

European imperialists justified their behavior by claiming that they were improving the lives of Africans. In fact, many Europeans saw it as their duty to introduce their customs and **values** to what they saw as a backward land. They forced Africans to assimilate, or adopt, many elements of European culture. As a result, thousands of Africans became Christian and learned to speak European languages.

CONNECTING TO Economics

Diamond Mining

Among the resources that caught the eye of European entrepreneurs in Africa were diamonds. First discovered in South Africa in 1867, diamonds were extremely profitable. South Africa soon became the world's leading diamond producer. Nearly all of that production was done by one company, the De Beers Consolidated Mine Company, owned by English business leader Cecil Rhodes. De Beers mines like the one shown here at Kimberley poured the gems into the world market.

South Africa is still one of the world's leading diamond producers, and De Beers is one of the leading companies. By controlling the supply of diamonds available to the public, the company can command higher prices for its gems.

Analyze How can a company control the supply of a product?

One firm believer in imperialism was English business owner Cecil Rhodes. He believed that British culture was superior to all others and that it was his duty to share it with the people of Africa. To that end, he planned to build a long railroad between Britain's colonies in Egypt and South Africa. He thought that this railroad would bring what he saw as the benefits of British civilization to all Africans. However, his railroad was never completed.

Government Involvement

FOCUS ON READING
What details support the main idea that European governments became involved in African affairs?

Though the early imperialists in Africa were entrepreneurs, national governments soon became involved as well. Their involvement was largely the result of rivalries between countries. Each country wanted to control more land and more colonies than its rivals did. As a result, countries tried to create as many colonies as they could and to block others from creating colonies.

For example, France began to form colonies in West Africa in the late 1800s. Seeing this, the British hurried to the area to form colonies of their own. Before long, Germany and Italy also sought to control land in West Africa. They did not want to be seen as less powerful than either France or Britain.

The English government also got involved in Africa for other reasons. The British wanted to protect the **Suez Canal,** a waterway built in Egypt in the 1860s to connect the Mediterranean and Red Seas. The British used the canal as a fast route to their colonies in India. In the 1880s, however, instability in Egypt's government made the British fear they would lose access to the canal. As a result, the British moved into Egypt and took partial control of the country to protect their shipping routes.

READING CHECK **Categorizing** What were three reasons Europeans went to Africa?

The Scramble for Africa

Desperate to have more power in Africa than their rivals, European countries rushed to claim as much land there as they could. Historians refer to this rush to claim land as the Scramble for Africa. The Europeans moved so quickly to snap up land that by 1914 most of African had been made into European colonies. As you can see on the map on the next page, only Ethiopia and Liberia remained independent.

The Berlin Conference

For many years Europeans competed aggressively for land in Africa. Conflicts sometimes arose when multiple countries tried to claim the same area. To prevent these conflicts from developing into wars, Europe's leaders agreed to meet and devise a plan to maintain order in Africa. They hoped this meeting would settle disputes and prevent future conflicts.

The meeting these European leaders held was called the **Berlin Conference.** Begun in 1884, it led to the division of Africa among various European powers. As the map shows, the conference left Africa a patchwork of European colonies.

When they were dividing Africa among themselves, Europe's leaders paid little attention to the people who lived there. As a result, the boundaries they drew for their colonies often divided kingdoms, clans, and families.

Separating people with common backgrounds was bad, but so was forcing people to live together who did not want to. Some European colonies grouped together peoples with different customs, languages, and religions. This forced contact between peoples often led to conflict and war. In time, the Europeans' disregard for Africans led to significant problems for Europeans and Africans alike.

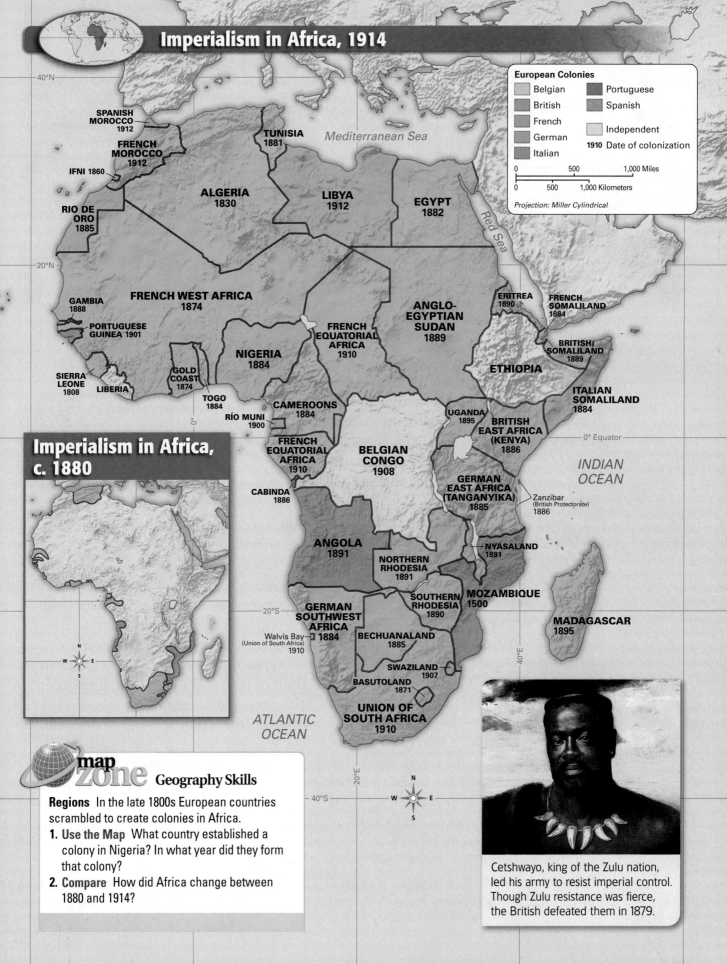

European Colonies

- Belgian
- British
- French
- German
- Italian
- Portuguese
- Spanish
- Independent

1910 Date of colonization

0   500   1,000 Miles
0   500   1,000 Kilometers

Projection: Miller Cylindrical

SPANISH MOROCCO 1912
FRENCH MOROCCO 1912
IFNI 1860
RIO DE ORO 1885
GAMBIA 1888
PORTUGUESE GUINEA 1901
SIERRA LEONE 1808
LIBERIA
TUNISIA 1881
ALGERIA 1830
LIBYA 1912
EGYPT 1882
Mediterranean Sea
Red Sea
FRENCH WEST AFRICA 1874
NIGERIA 1884
GOLD COAST 1874
TOGO 1884
RÍO MUNI 1900
CAMEROONS 1884
FRENCH EQUATORIAL AFRICA 1910
ANGLO-EGYPTIAN SUDAN 1889
ERITREA 1890
FRENCH SOMALILAND 1884
BRITISH SOMALILAND 1889
ETHIOPIA
ITALIAN SOMALILAND 1884
UGANDA 1895
BRITISH EAST AFRICA (KENYA) 1886
FRENCH EQUATORIAL AFRICA 1910
CABINDA 1886
BELGIAN CONGO 1908
GERMAN EAST AFRICA (TANGANYIKA) 1885
Zanzibar (British Protectorate) 1886
INDIAN OCEAN
0° Equator
ANGOLA 1891
NORTHERN RHODESIA 1891
NYASALAND 1891
MOZAMBIQUE 1500
SOUTHERN RHODESIA 1890
GERMAN SOUTHWEST AFRICA 1884
Walvis Bay (Union of South Africa) 1910
BECHUANALAND 1885
MADAGASCAR 1895
SWAZILAND 1907
BASUTOLAND 1871
UNION OF SOUTH AFRICA 1910
ATLANTIC OCEAN

Imperialism in Africa, c. 1880

map zone Geography Skills

Regions In the late 1800s European countries scrambled to create colonies in Africa.

1. **Use the Map** What country established a colony in Nigeria? In what year did they form that colony?

2. **Compare** How did Africa change between 1880 and 1914?

Cetshwayo, king of the Zulu nation, led his army to resist imperial control. Though Zulu resistance was fierce, the British defeated them in 1879.

Battle of Adwa

This painting of the Battle of Adwa was created years after the battle. The battle kept Ethiopia from becoming an Italian colony and is still celebrated today.

ANALYZING VISUALS Why might Ethiopians celebrate their victory at Adwa?

The Boer War

The Berlin Conference was intended to prevent conflicts over African territory, but it was not completely successful. In the late 1890s war broke out in South Africa between British and Dutch settlers. Each group had claimed the land and wanted to drive the other out.

Dutch farmers called **Boers** had arrived in South Africa in the 1600s. There they had established two independent republics. For about 200 years the Boers lived mainly as farmers. During that time they met with little interference from other Europeans.

Things changed in the 1800s, though. In 1886 gold was discovered near the Orange River in South Africa. Suddenly, the land on which the Boers had been living became highly desired.

Among those who wanted to control South Africa after gold was discovered were the British. In 1899 the British tried to make the Boers' land part of the British Empire. The Boers resisted, and war broke out between the two groups.

The Boers did not think they could defeat the British in a regular war. The British had a much larger army than they

did, especially once the British brought in troops from their various colonies. In addition, the British troops had much better weapons than the Boers had.

Instead, the Boers decided to wage a guerrilla war, one based on sneak attacks and ambushes. Through these tactics, the Boers quickly defeated several British forces and gained an advantage in the war.

However, these guerrilla tactics angered the British. To punish the Boers, they began attacking and burning Boer farms. They captured thousands of Boer women and children, imprisoning them in concentration camps. More than 20,000 women and children died in these camps, mostly from disease. In the end, the British defeated the Boers. As a result, South Africa became a British colony.

READING CHECK Identifying Cause and Effect What were the results of the Berlin Conference?

African Resistance

The Europeans thought that the Berlin Conference and the Boer War would put an end to conflict in Africa. Once again, however, they had overlooked the African people. Many African people did not want to be ruled by Europeans. They refused to peacefully give up their own cultures and adopt European ways.

As a result, the Europeans who entered African territory often met with resistance from local rulers and peoples. Europeans were able to end most of these rebellions quickly with their superior weapons. However, two well-organized peoples, the Zulu and the Ethiopians, caused more problems for the Europeans.

Zulu Resistance

One of the most famous groups to resist the Europeans were the Zulu of southern Africa. In the early 1800s a Zulu leader named Shaka had brought various tribes together into a single nation. This nation was so strong that the Europeans were hesitant to enter Zulu territory.

After Shaka's death, however, the Zulu nation weakened. Even without Shaka's leadership, the fierce Zulu army successfully fought off the British for more than 50 years. In the end, however, the superior weapons of the British helped them defeat the Zulu. Their lands were made into a new British colony.

Ethiopian Resistance

Although most resistance to European imperialism was ended, one kingdom managed to remain free from European control. That kingom was Ethiopia. It is the only country in Africa to never be a European colony. Its success in fighting the Europeans was largely due to the efforts of one man, Emperor Menelik II.

Menelik had seen that the strength of European armies was based on their modern weapons. He therefore decided that he would create an equally powerful army with equally modern weapons bought from Europe. As a result, when the Italians invaded Ethiopia in 1895, the Ethiopian army was able to defeat the invaders. This victory in the Battle of Adwa is celebrated as a high point in Ethiopian history.

READING CHECK **Drawing Conclusions** Why did many Africans resist European imperialism?

SUMMARY AND PREVIEW In the 1800s Europeans divided Africa into dozens of colonies. In the next section, you will learn how these colonies eventually broke free from European control to become independent countries.

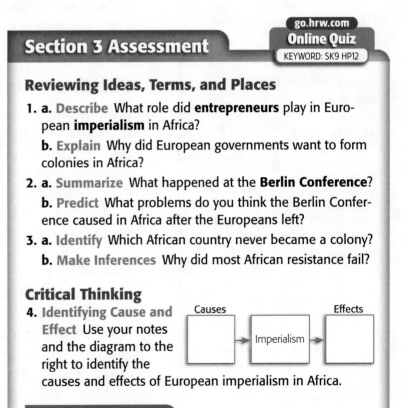

Section 3 Assessment

go.hrw.com
Online Quiz
KEYWORD: SK9 HP12

Reviewing Ideas, Terms, and Places

1. **a. Describe** What role did **entrepreneurs** play in European **imperialism** in Africa?
   b. Explain Why did European governments want to form colonies in Africa?
2. **a. Summarize** What happened at the **Berlin Conference**?
   b. Predict What problems do you think the Berlin Conference caused in Africa after the Europeans left?
3. **a. Identify** Which African country never became a colony?
   b. Make Inferences Why did most African resistance fail?

Critical Thinking

4. **Identifying Cause and Effect** Use your notes and the diagram to the right to identify the causes and effects of European imperialism in Africa.

Causes → Imperialism → Effects

FOCUS ON SPEAKING

5. **Analyzing Imperialism** Jot down some notes about the effects of imperialism you could mention in your report.

Revolution and Freedom

What You Will Learn...

Main Ideas

1. Unhappiness with European rule led to a call for independence in Africa.
2. British colonies were some of the first to become free.
3. French colonies followed two paths to independence.
4. Belgian and Portuguese colonies had to fight for their freedom.

The Big Idea

African colonies began to call for independence after World War II, eventually gaining their freedom.

Key Terms and Places

Ghana, *p. 367*
Kenya, *p. 367*
Mau Mau, *p. 368*
Belgian Congo, *p. 370*

 TAKING NOTES As you read, take notes in a chart like this one about the call for independence in Africa and how that goal was achieved in various colonies.

If YOU lived there...

You are a soldier from the French colony of Morocco. For the last year, you have fought alongside soldiers from France to defeat the German army. Now, the war is over and you are being sent home. You had hoped that you would be rewarded for your service, but your commander sent you off without even saying thanks.

How does this lack of gratitude make you feel?

> **BUILDING BACKGROUND** For years, Africa was governed by European imperialists. However, events of the early 1900s, especially the two world wars, led to significant social and political changes and, eventually, to African independence.

The Call for Independence

Many Africans were understandably unhappy with European control of their homeland. For centuries, they had ruled their own kingdoms and societies. Now, they were forced to accept outsiders as their leaders. After several rebellions against the Europeans had been put down, however, people across Africa resigned themselves to life in European colonies. Their attitudes began to change, though, after the two world wars.

World War I

After World War I broke out in Europe in 1914, fighting spread to European colonies as well. Among the areas in which violence broke out was Africa. The Allies, including England and France, attacked German colonies in Africa. They hoped that taking Germany's colonies would weaken the country financially.

Much of the fighting in Africa was done by the people of English and French colonies. Hundreds of thousands of Africans were recruited to assist European armies. Tens of thousands of these recruits died in combat.

When the war ended, the African soldiers returning home thought they would be thanked for their efforts. Instead, they were largely ignored. As a result of this snub, resentment toward Europeans increased in parts of Africa.

World War II

In the late 1930s, war once again broke out in Europe. As before, Africans were called upon to help Europeans fight. Some half a million African troops fought alongside the British, the French, and their allies.

When the war ended, the Africans were once again not suitably thanked for their contributions. Angry leaders began calling for political change in Africa. They wanted their independence.

READING CHECK Summarizing How did the two world wars lead to calls for independence?

British Colonies

Among the colonies most loudly calling for independence were those belonging to Great Britain. Their demands only increased in 1947 when Britain granted independence to India. If India could be free, many Africans asked, why couldn't they? Before long, several British colonies in Africa, including Ghana and Kenya, had won their freedom.

Ghana

That first British colony to win its freedom was **Ghana**, formerly called the Gold Coast. Its fight for freedom was led by Kwame Nkrumah (KWAHM-eh en-KROO-muh). In 1947 Nkrumah organized strikes and demonstrations against the British. The British responded by arresting him.

Even from prison, however, Nkrumah called for independence. Inspired by his courage, many people joined his struggle.

BOOK
I Speak of Freedom

The leader of the independence movement in Ghana, Kwame Nkrumah, did not want freedom only for his own people. He wanted all Africans to be free. Nkrumah thought all Africans should band together to achieve their goals.

"It is clear that we must find an African solution to our problems, and that this can only be found in African unity. Divided we are weak; united, Africa could become one of the greatest forces for good in the world."

—Kwame Nkrumah, from *I Speak of Freedom: A Statement of African Ideology*

ANALYSIS SKILL **ANALYZING PRIMARY SOURCES**

Why did Kwame Nkrumah think Africa would be better off united than divided?

Largely because of Nkrumah's actions, the British granted the Gold Coast its independence in 1957. Nkrumah became the first prime minister. As its leader, he renamed the country Ghana after the ancient empire of West Africa.

Kenya

Other British colonies did not find the road to independence as smooth as Ghana did. For example, the East African colony of **Kenya** only became independent after a long and violent struggle.

When the British arrived in Kenya, they claimed land that had once been lived on by the Kikuyu people. They used that land to grow valuable crops, such as coffee. Therefore they did not want to give the land up. The Kikuyu, however, wanted independence, and they wanted their former lands back.

To retake their land, Kikuyu farmers formed a violent movement called the **Mau Mau**. Its goal was to rid Kenya of white settlers. Between 1952 and 1960 the Mau Mau terrorized the British in Kenya. Its members attacked and killed anyone they suspected of opposing their goals. They even attacked Africans who cooperated with the British.

The British responded by arresting and torturing any members of the Mau Mau they could find. Nevertheless, the British eventually realized that they would have to grant Kenya's independence. In 1963 they made Kenya a free country. Its first prime minister was Jomo Kenyatta, who had been one of the first people to call for Kenyan freedom.

READING CHECK **Contrasting** How were the paths to independence taken by Ghana and Kenya different?

FOCUS ON READING

In the paragraphs under French Colonies, what details support the main idea that French colonies followed different routes to independence?

French Colonies

Like the British, the French began to grant independence to their colonies after World War II. For some colonies, particularly those in West Africa, the transition to independence was smooth. In North Africa, however, the change was rough and violent.

West Africa

France's attitude toward its colonies in West Africa had always been different from Britain's. While the British saw their colonies as backward societies that needed guidance, the French wanted to make their colonies part of France. After World War II, France's leaders offered Africans more of a role in the colonial government. Largely because they had already been given a role in the government, many African leaders in French colonies did not want to break away from France completely.

In 1958, the French government gave its West African colonies a choice. They could become completely independent, or they could join a new organization called the French Community with political and economic ties to France. Most chose to become part of the Community. A few years later, France granted most of the former colonies full independence anyway.

North Africa

Although French colonies in West Africa were willing to work peacefully with the French to gain independence, the colonies of Morocco, Tunisia, and Algeria were not. In all three colonies, protestors calling for independence staged strikes, demonstrations, and attacks. Observers thought that guerrilla wars seemed likely.

The French government decided that it could not fight wars in all three colonies. Because Algeria had the largest French population, the French sent their army there. They thought their people would need the army's protection.

With the army in Algeria, the French sent diplomats to Morocco and Tunisia to negotiate. As a result, both countries became independent in 1956.

Meanwhile, violence continued in Algeria. Political groups there attacked French leaders and citizens. In response, the French attacked Algerian Muslims. Finally, France's prime minister suggested a compromise, offering the Algerians some self-government. However, neither the French nor the Algerians were happy with this compromise, and conflict threatened to break out again. Realizing that they could not maintain order in Algeria, the French granted the country its independence in 1962.

READING CHECK **Sequencing** What steps did France's colonies take to become free?

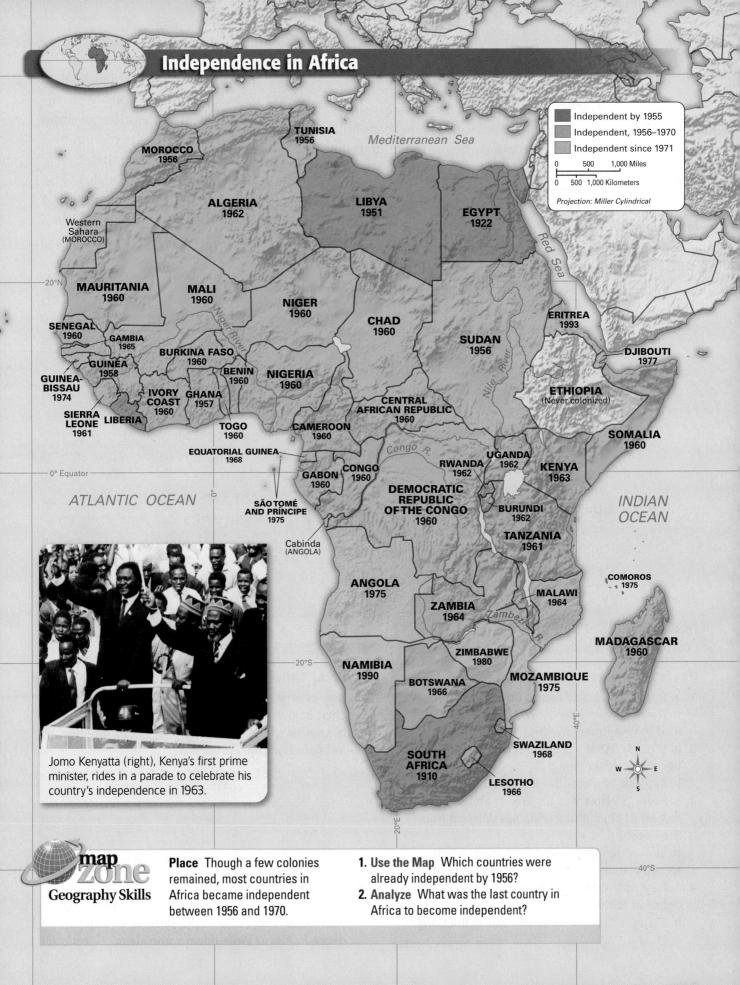

Independence in Africa

Independent by 1955
Independent, 1956–1970
Independent since 1971

| 0 | 500 | 1,000 Miles |
| 0 | 500 | 1,000 Kilometers |

Projection: Miller Cylindrical

Mediterranean Sea

TUNISIA 1956
MOROCCO 1956
ALGERIA 1962
LIBYA 1951
EGYPT 1922
Western Sahara (MOROCCO)

MAURITANIA 1960
MALI 1960
NIGER 1960
CHAD 1960
SUDAN 1956
ERITREA 1993
DJIBOUTI 1977

SENEGAL 1960
GAMBIA 1965
BURKINA FASO 1960
GUINEA 1958
GUINEA-BISSAU 1974
BENIN 1960
NIGERIA 1960
IVORY COAST 1960
GHANA 1957
SIERRA LEONE 1961
LIBERIA
TOGO 1960
CAMEROON 1960
CENTRAL AFRICAN REPUBLIC 1960
ETHIOPIA (Never colonized)
SOMALIA 1960

EQUATORIAL GUINEA 1968
GABON 1960
CONGO 1960
RWANDA 1962
UGANDA 1962
KENYA 1963
SÃO TOMÉ AND PRÍNCIPE 1975
DEMOCRATIC REPUBLIC OF THE CONGO 1960
BURUNDI 1962
Cabinda (ANGOLA)
TANZANIA 1961

ATLANTIC OCEAN
0° Equator
INDIAN OCEAN

ANGOLA 1975
ZAMBIA 1964
MALAWI 1964
COMOROS 1975
MADAGASCAR 1960

NAMIBIA 1990
ZIMBABWE 1980
BOTSWANA 1966
MOZAMBIQUE 1975
SWAZILAND 1968
SOUTH AFRICA 1910
LESOTHO 1966

Red Sea
Niger River
Nile River
Congo R.
Zambezi R.

N
W E
S

20°N
20°S
20°E
40°E
40°S

Jomo Kenyatta (right), Kenya's first prime minister, rides in a parade to celebrate his country's independence in 1963.

map zone
Geography Skills

Place Though a few colonies remained, most countries in Africa became independent between 1956 and 1970.

1. **Use the Map** Which countries were already independent by 1956?
2. **Analyze** What was the last country in Africa to become independent?

Belgian and Portuguese Colonies

Not all European countries were willing to set their colonies free. The Belgians and the Portuguese in particular fought to keep their colonies. Neither country willingly gave up its claims in Africa.

ACADEMIC
VOCABULARY
rebel to fight
against authority

The Belgian Congo

Belgium controlled only one major colony in Africa—the **Belgian Congo**. After World War II, the Belgians granted some freedoms to the colony's people. Wanting full indendence, however, the Congolese people rose up. Various Congolese groups staged riots and even held elections. However, not all of these groups shared the same goals and conflict between groups was common.

The Belgians refused to recognize the colonists' rights for many years. In 1960, though, they suddenly changed their position. They withdrew from the Congo and the colony became independent. Shortly afterward, civil war broke out between various groups who wanted to run the newly independent Congo.

Portuguese Colonies

Unlike the Belgians, the Portuguese held several colonies in Africa, mostly in the south and east. Even as the other countries of Europe were setting their colonies free, the Portuguese fought to keep theirs.

Eventually, however, the people of Portugal's colonies **rebelled** against them. In Angola, Guinea, and Mozambique, rebels attacked Portuguese troops. These attacks began decades of bloody war.

In 1974 Portugal's military government was overthrown and replaced with a democracy. Shortly afterward, the Portuguese gave up any claim to their colonies and withdrew from Africa completely.

READING CHECK Identifying Cause and Effect
Why were the Belgian and Portuguese colonies among the last to become free?

SUMMARY AND PREVIEW By 1970 most colonies in Africa had won their independence. Next, you will learn how life in Africa changed after independence.

Section 4 Assessment

go.hrw.com
Online Quiz
KEYWORD: SK9 HP12

Reviewing Ideas, Terms, and Places

1. **a. Recall** What did Africans do in World War I?
   b. Draw Conclusions How did the world wars lead to resentment in Africa?
2. **a. Identify** What was the first British colony to become independent?
   b. Explain Why was the **Mau Mau** formed?
3. **a. Contrast** How was the French attitude toward its West African colonies different from the British?
   b. Elaborate Why do you think many former French colonies wanted to keep ties to France?
4. **a. Describe** What was the struggle for independence in Portuguese colonies like?
   b. Sequence What led to civil war in the Congo?

Critical Thinking

5. **Summarizing** Using your notes, complete the chart below with one statement that summarizes the path each country's colonies took to win their freedom from the Europeans.

Country	Colonies' path to independence
Great Britain	
France	
Belgium	
Portugal	

FOCUS ON SPEAKING

6. **Examining the Role of Independence** How will your news report discuss the struggle for independence in Africa? Write down some ideas.

from
AKÉ: The Years of Childhood

by Wole Soyinka

Merchants from North Africa sometimes traded brass objects in West Africa.

About the Reading *In this excerpt from his childhood memoir, Nigerian-born Wole Soyinka describes life in Nigeria before independence. His later works discussed, often critically, the political changes in the country after it became free.*

AS YOU READ Notice the variety of goods the traders brought to the author's house.

It was a strange procedure, one which made little sense to me. ❶ They spread their wares in front of the house and I had to be prised off them. There were brass figures, horses, camels, trays, bowls, ornaments. Human figures spun on a podium, balanced by weights at the end of curved light metal rods. We spun them round and round, yet they never fell off their narrow perch. The smell of fresh leather filled the house as pouffs, handbags, slippers and worked scabbards were unpacked. There were bottles encased in leather, with leather stoppers, . . . scrolls, glass beads, bottles of scent with exotic names—I never forgot, from the first moment I read it on the label—Bint el Sudan, with its picture of a turbanned warrior by a kneeling camel. A veiled maiden offered him a bowl of fruits. They looked unlike anything in the orchard and Essay said they were called dates. ❷ I did not believe him; dates were figures which appeared on a calendar on the wall, so I took it as one of his jokes.

GUIDED READING

WORD HELP

wares goods
prised taken by force
pouff fluffy clothing or accessory
scabbard a case to hold a knife
turbanned wearing a turban, or wrapped cloth, on the head

❶ The author is describing a visit by the Hausa traders who came from northwestern Africa.

❷ Essay is the author's father.

Connecting Literature to Geography

1. **Drawing Inferences** The author describes many unusual things. What descriptions or comments lead you to believe that the trader traveled to Aké from far away?

2. **Analyzing** Think about the way the author described the goods. What senses did the author use as a child to discover the goods the traders brought?

Africa since Independence

What You Will Learn...

Main Ideas

1. People in South Africa faced social struggles related to racial equality.
2. Many African countries saw political challenges after they became independent.
3. The economy and the environment affect life in Africa.
4. African culture blends traditional and European elements.

The Big Idea

The people of Africa have faced both changes and challenges since they won their independence.

Key Terms and Places

apartheid, *p. 373*
townships, *p. 373*
sanctions, *p. 373*
Darfur, *p. 375*
Lagos, *p. 376*
Kinshasa, *p. 376*

TAKING NOTES As you read, take notes about changes that have occurred in Africa since independence. Use a chart like the one below to organize your notes.

Changes in Africa

If **YOU** lived there...

You live in South Africa. One day, you and some friends join a protest against certain unfair government policies. Although the protest is peaceful, a large number of police officers show up and arrest its organizer. As they handcuff him and drag him off to prison, many people are angry.

How do you feel about this event?

BUILDING BACKGROUND Though most African countries won their independence between the 1950s and the 1970s, they faced unexpected challenges with their newfound freedom. Military rule and civil war were common problems that plagued Africa into the 1990s.

Social Struggles in South Africa

Many Africans suffered during the imperial period. They felt that their lives would improve once they were free. With independence, many found that their lives were indeed better. At the same time, though, a new set of problems developed.

One example of these new problems could be seen in South Africa. The country gained independence in 1910, much earlier than most African countries. However, racial tensions there led to the creation of an official policy of discrimination.

Apartheid

In the early 1900s South Africa's government was largely controlled by the white descendants of early Dutch, French, and German settlers. Many of these white residents believed that they should have all the power and that black South Africans should have no voice in the government. Understandably, black South Africans opposed this plan. To defend their rights, they formed the African National Congress (ANC) in 1912.

South Africans in Soweto warmly welcomed Nelson Mandela after he was released from prison in 1990.

BIOGRAPHY

Nelson Mandela
(1918–)

Because he protested against apartheid, Nelson Mandela was imprisoned for 26 years. In 1990, however, South Africa's President de Klerk released Mandela from prison. Mandela and de Klerk shared the Nobel Peace Prize in 1993. One year later, Mandela became South Africa's first black president. He wrote a new constitution and worked to improve the living conditions of all black South Africans.

Summarizing What did Nelson Mandela accomplish when he was South Africa's president?

Despite protests by the ANC, South Africa's government set up a policy of separation of races, or **apartheid** (uh-PAHR-tayt), which means "apartness." This policy divided people into four groups: whites, blacks, Coloureds, and Asians. Coloureds were people of mixed ancestry.

Under apartheid, only white South Africans could vote or hold political office. Blacks, who made up nearly 75 percent of the population, were not citizens. They could only work certain jobs and made very little money. They were only allowed to live in certain areas. In cities, black residents had to live in specially designated **townships**, which were often crowded clusters of tiny homes. Only certain types of businesses were allowed in the townships, which ensured that people living there would stay poor. In the 1950s, South Africa's government created "homelands" for various black African tribes. However, these homelands generally did not include good farmland or resources, which were owned by the whites. Coloured and Asian citizens also had restricted rights, though they had more rights than blacks.

The End of Apartheid

By the 1940s many South Africans, especially members of the ANC, were protesting loudly against apartheid. Among the leaders of these protests was a young lawyer named Nelson Mandela. He urged black South Africans to fight apartheid.

In 1960 the South African government banned the ANC and put Mandela in jail. Even with their leader in jail, however, people continued to protest apartheid. The protests were not limited to South Africa, either. People around the world called for an end to apartheid. Other governments placed **sanctions**—economic or political penalties imposed by one country on another to force a policy change—against South Africa.

Faced with this pressure from inside and outside, the South African government finally began to move away from apartheid in the late 1980s. In 1990 it released Mandela from prison. Soon afterward, South Africans of all races were given the right to vote. In 1994 Mandela was elected South Africa's first black president.

Today all races have equal rights in South Africa. Public schools and universities are open to all people, as are hospitals and transportation. However, full economic equality has come more slowly. White South Africans are still wealthier than the majority of blacks. Still, South Africans now have better opportunities for the future.

READING CHECK **Making Inferences** Why did people around the world protest apartheid?

Political Challenges

South Africa was not the only country to face political challenges after winning independence. Across Africa, people suffered under harsh military dictatorships and long civil wars.

Military Dictatorships

By the late 1960s most of Africa was independent. In most of the newly free countries, the government was run by military dictators. These dictators kept power by not allowing anyone else to run for office. As a result, the dictator remained in charge. In most countries with military dictatorships, all political organizations that did not support the government were banned.

Perhaps the best example of a military dictator in Africa was Joseph Mobutu. He rose to power in the Congo in 1965 after the Belgians left. To show his power, he changed the name of the country to Zaire, a traditional African name.

As dictator, Mobutu took over foreign-owned industries. He borrowed money from other countries to try to improve the country's industry. However, most farmers suffered during Mobutu's rule. In addition, many government and business leaders were corrupt. While the country's economy collapsed, Mobutu become one of the richest people in the world. Anyone who dared to challenge his authority was met with violence.

Political Change in Africa

The countries of Africa underwent many political changes after they became independent. In many countries those change led to corrupt governments and violent conflicts. Eventually, most countries formed democratic governments.

Dictators
Military dictators like Uganda's Idi Amin seized power in many countries.

Ethnic Conflict and Civil War

Many Africans were not happy with these military dictators and took steps to replace them. Mobutu, for example, was overthrown after a civil war in 1997. The new government renamed the country the Democratic Republic of the Congo. Similar civil wars were fought in many countries.

Political disagreement was only one factor that has led to violence in Africa. Ethnic conflict is also common. As you recall, when the leaders of Europe divided Africa among themselves, they paid little attention to the people who lived there. As a result, colonies often included people from many ethnic groups. In some cases, these groups did not get along at all.

When colonies became independent years later, these ethnic groups sometimes fought each other for control. Their fighting often led to long, bloody civil wars. In Rwanda, for example, the Hutu and Tutsi ethnic groups went to war in 1994. The government, run by the Hutu, began killing all the Tutsi in the country. About 1 million Tutsi civilians were killed in the conflict. Many more fled the country.

Similar conflict has plagued Sudan for decades. Muslims and Christians have fought each other for years. More recently, a genocide has occurred in the region of **Darfur.** Ethnic conflict there has resulted in tens of thousands of black Sudanese being killed by an Arab militia group. Millions more have fled Darfur. Those who fled are now scattered throughout northern and eastern Africa as refugees.

Democracy in Africa

Dictatorships and civil wars were common in Africa through the late 1900s. As the year 2000 approached, however, political changes swept through Africa. People began to demand more democratic forms of government. They wanted to choose their own leaders.

By 2005 more than 30 countries in Africa had abandoned dictatorships and held elections. Though some of these elections were rigged to keep corrupt governments in place, others resulted in true democratic governments coming to power.

READING CHECK **Describing** What political challenges have African nations faced?

Civil War and Ethnic Conflict
Ethnic conflict in Darfur, Sudan, has forced millions of people to flee the country as refugees. Some receive food and aid at camps like this one.

Democracy
Like many African nations, Nigeria is a democracy. Its citizens elected a new president in 2007.

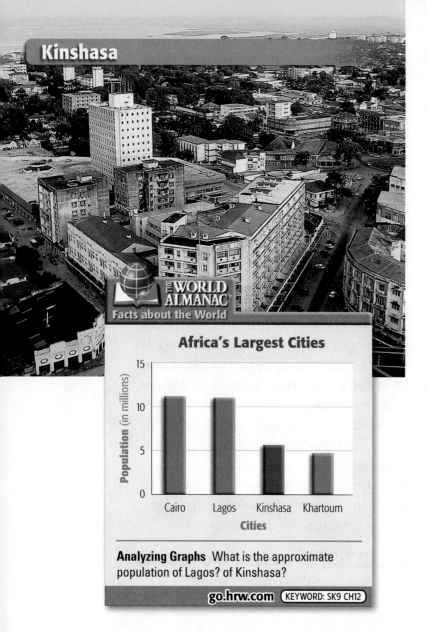

Kinshasa

THE WORLD ALMANAC®
Facts about the World

Africa's Largest Cities

Population (in millions) — Cities: Cairo, Lagos, Kinshasa, Khartoum

Analyzing Graphs What is the approximate population of Lagos? of Kinshasa?

go.hrw.com KEYWORD: SK9 CH12

Economy and Environment

Political challenges were not the only ones faced by Africa's countries. Many countries faced economic challenges as well. At the same time, Africans had to fight environmental issues, including deadly diseases.

Struggling Economies

After they became independent, many African countries had weak economies. Most countries had not industrialized and depended mainly on farming or mining. For example, Ghana earned most of its income from cocoa, and Nigeria from oil.

Since independence, however, many countries have found new economic opportunities. As a result, their economies are stronger than ever. Among the countries with Africa's strongest economies are South Africa, Nigeria, and many countries in North Africa. However, some other countries still have huge debts and little infrastructure and must depend on aid from other countries.

As Africa's economies grow, so do its cities. These cities offer more jobs and higher standards of living than rural areas. Each year millions of people move there. As a result, already-large cities like Cairo, Egypt; **Lagos**, Nigeria; and **Kinshasa**, Democratic Republic of the Congo, are growing even larger. Rapid growth has led to crowding and high unemployment in some cities.

Environmental Challenges

Economic development in Africa has been slow in part because people have to deal with environmental challenges, including disease. For example, malaria, a disease spread by mosquitoes, is one of the leading causes of death in many parts of Africa. Even more deadly than malaria is AIDS. This disease that weakens the immune system is widespread in Africa. In some countries, more than one fourth of the entire population is infected with AIDS.

Other environmental challenges also make survival difficult. Much of the continent suffered terrible droughts in the 1980s. These droughts left farmers unable to grow crops, and terrible famines swept through Africa. Famines are made worse by desertification, the spread of desertlike conditions. In parts of Africa, especially West Africa, farmers must take care to prevent fertile soil from disappearing.

READING CHECK **Identifying** What are two challenges people in Africa have faced?

African Culture

After they became independent, many African countries underwent identity crises. As colonies, they were forced to adopt many elements of European culture. At the same time, however, African peoples had their own cultures that stretched back through centuries. How would people deal with these mixed cultures?

People reacted in different ways. Many elements of European culture can still be seen in Africa. For example, many people in West Africa still speak French or English in their daily lives.

At the same time, many Africans have rejected European culture and sought to reclaim their own traditional cultures. Writers and musicians draw on traditional themes from African folklore in their works, often written in Swahili or other African languages. Artists create masks, musical instruments, and sculptures from wood and bronze, just as their ancestors did centuries ago.

READING CHECK **Analyzing** How does African culture reflect African and European ideas?

African Music

Artists like the Mahotella Queens singing group have brought African culture to a worldwide audience.

SUMMARY AND PREVIEW In this section, you learned how African countries have grown and changed since they became independent. Next, you will read in more detail about life and society in one of those countries, Nigeria.

---

go.hrw.com
Online Quiz
KEYWORD: SK9 HP12

Section 5 Assessment

Reviewing Ideas, Terms, and Places

1. **a. Define** What was **apartheid**?

   b. Elaborate How did international protests help end apartheid?

2. **a. Describe** What problems did military dictators cause in some African countries?

   b. Explain What led to violence in parts of Africa?

3. **a. Recall** What issues do cities like **Lagos** and **Kinshasa** face today?

   b. Develop How might environmental challenges lead to economic issues?

4. **a. Identify** What is one element of European culture present in Africa today?

   b. Draw Conclusions Why did many Africans want to reclaim their traditional culture?

Critical Thinking

5. **Categorizing** Review your notes. Then complete the chart by listing political, economic, and social changes in Africa.

Changes in Africa		
Political	Economic	Social

FOCUS ON SPEAKING

6. **Choosing Your Topic** Now that you have studied modern Africa, you can choose the topic for your news report. What will you discuss?

Social Studies Skills

Chart and Graph | Critical Thinking | Geography | Study

Interpreting a Population Pyramid

Learn

A population pyramid shows the percentages of males and females by age group in a country's population. The pyramids are split into two sides. Each bar on the left shows the percentage of a country's population that is male and of a certain age. The bars on the right show the same information for females.

Population pyramids help us understand population trends in countries. Countries that have large percentages of young people have populations that are growing rapidly. Countries with more older people are growing slowly or not at all.

Practice

Use the population pyramid of Angola to answer the following questions.

 1 What age group is the largest?

 2 What percent of Angola's population is made up of 15- to 19-year-old males?

 3 What does this population pyramid tell you about the population trend in Angola?

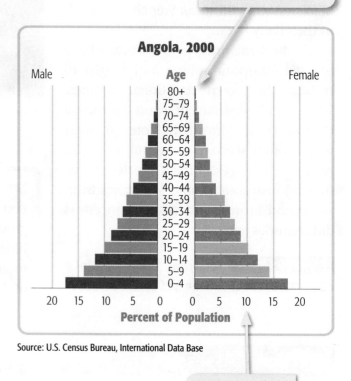

Ages are listed down the middle of the diagram.

Percentages are labeled across the bottom of the diagram.

Source: U.S. Census Bureau, International Data Base

Apply

Do research at the library or on the Internet to find age and population data for the United States. Use that information to answer the following questions.

1. What age group is the largest?

2. Are there more males or females over age 80?

3. How would you describe the shape of the population pyramid?

Chapter Review

Geography's Impact
video series
Review the video to answer the closing question:
What are some ways South Africans could continue working together?

Visual Summary

Use the visual summary below to help you review the main ideas of the chapter.

QUICK FACTS

Valuable trade goods like ivory and gold lured many Europeans to Africa and led to the creation of colonies.

Between the 1950s and the 1970s many African countries won their independence from Europe.

Many African cities have grown tremendously. People move to the cities for economic opportunity.

Reviewing Vocabulary, Terms, and Places

Match the words with their definitions.

1. Swahili
2. sanctions
3. apartheid
4. Middle Passage

5. entrepreneurs
6. Mau Mau
7. Gold Coast
8. imperialism

a. policy of separation of races
b. grueling trip endured by slaves across the Atlantic Ocean
c. attempt to dominate a country's government, trade, or culture
d. economic or political penalties
e. colony established by the British in West Africa
f. violent movement intended to rid Kenya of white settlers
g. blended African-Arab culture of East Africa
h. independent business owners

Comprehension and Critical Thinking

SECTION 1 *(Pages 350–353)*

9. a. **Recall** What brought Islam to East Africa?
   b. **Compare and Contrast** How did Coptic Christianity differ from other forms?
   c. **Elaborate** How do you think the arrival of new religions changed life in Africa?

SECTION 2 *(Pages 354–357)*

10. a. **Identify** Which European country was the first to trade in Africa?
    b. **Draw Conclusions** Why do you think early European activity in Africa was limited mostly to West Africa?
    c. **Develop** How did the slave trade weaken African society?

SECTION 3 *(Pages 360–365)*

11. a. **Define** What is imperialism, and what led to European imperialism in Africa?

SECTION 3 *(continued)*

    b. Sequence What led to the Boer War?

    c. Elaborate Why do you think few groups were successful in resisting European imperialism?

SECTION 4 *(Pages 366–370)*

12. a. Identify What were two colonies in which Africans had to fight for their freedom?

    b. Summarize How did Ghana win its freedom?

    c. Evaluate Which new countries do you think had the best relations with Europe? Why?

SECTION 5 *(Pages 372–377)*

13. a. Identify Who is Nelson Mandela? For what is he most famous?

    b. Make Inferences Why were many Africans unhappy with military dictatorships?

    c. Predict How do you think African governments will change in the future? Why?

Using the Internet

go.hrw.com
KEYWORD: SK9 CH12

14. Activity: Understanding Cultures Modern Africa is home to thousands of ethnic groups, each with its own culture, traditions, and customs. For many Africans, independence came with a renewed pride in their own cultures. Enter the activity keyword. Discover some African ethnic groups as you visit Web sites about their cultures. Then create a graphic organizer or chart that compares African ethnic groups. It might include comparisons of their language, beliefs, traditions, foods, and more. It might also show how each of the groups was affected by European imperialism.

Social Studies Skills

Interpreting a Population Pyramid *Use the population pyramid in the Social Studies Skills lesson to answer the following questions.*

15. What age group is the smallest?

16. How would you describe the current population in Angola?

17. Identifying Supporting Details Look back over the paragraphs under the African Resistance heading in Section 3. Then make a list of details you find to support the section's main ideas.

18. Presenting a TV News Report Review your notes and decide on a topic for your report. Next, identify the point you want to make about your topic—your purpose. Your purpose may be to share interesting information—about an interesting figure from the past, for example. Or your purpose may be more serious—perhaps to show the effects of poverty on Africa. Decide what images you will show and what you will say to make your point to your listeners.

    Create a script identifying visuals and voiceover. Present your report to the class using visuals as though you were on the TV news.

Map Activity

19. Growth and Development of Africa On a separate sheet of paper, match the letters on the map with the correct labels.

Cairo   Ghana

South Africa   Congo River

Ethiopia

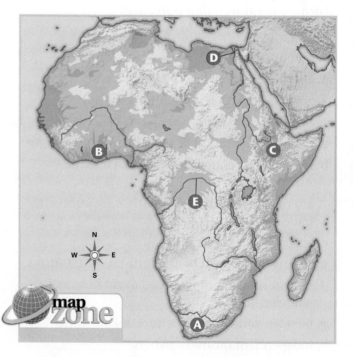

map zone

DIRECTIONS (1–7): **For each statement or question, write on a separate answer sheet the** *number* **of the word or expression that, of those given, best completes the statement or answers the question.**

1 **What was the only country in Africa never to be a European colony?**

(1) Ghana

(2) South Africa

(3) Algeria

(4) Ethiopia

2 **The Suez Canal is located in**

(1) Nigeria.

(2) Egypt.

(3) Tanzania.

(4) Morocco.

3 **Which of the following is** *not* **a challenge that African countries have faced since they became independent?**

(1) poverty

(2) ethnic conflict

(3) overeducation

(4) racial tension

4 **South Africa's most famous leader in the fight against apartheid was**

(1) Nelson Mandela.

(2) Jomo Kenyatta.

(3) Kwame Nkrumah.

(4) Joseph Mobutu.

5 **Which of the following statements about military dictators is true?**

(1) They never rose to power in Africa.

(2) They held free elections.

(3) They were often corrupt.

(4) They were all fair and just rulers.

6 **Which colony had to fight for independence?**

(1) South Africa

(2) Belgian Congo

(3) Ethiopia

(4) Ghana

7 **The language known as Swahili developed in**

(1) North Africa.

(2) South Africa.

(3) West Africa.

(4) East Africa.

Base your answer to question 8 on the diagram below and on your knowledge of social studies.

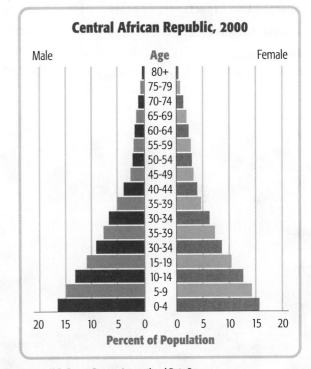

Central African Republic, 2000

Male | Age | Female

80+
75-79
70-74
65-69
60-64
55-59
50-54
45-49
40-44
35-39
30-34
35-39
30-34
15-19
10-14
5-9
0-4

20 15 10 5 0 0 5 10 15 20

Percent of Population

Source: U.S. Census Bureau, International Data Base

8 **Constructed-Response Question** **What generalizations can you make about the population of the Central African Republic?**

Nigeria

Geography

Nigeria

Official Name: Federal Republic of Nigeria

Capital: Abuja

Area: 356,669 square miles (slightly larger than Texas and Oklahoma)

Population: 135 million (384 people/ square mile)

Average Life Expectancy: 48 years

Official Language: English

Unit of Currency: Naira

Though it is not Africa's largest country by area, Nigeria is the most populous country on the continent. More than 130 million people live within its borders.

The landscape of Nigeria is mostly river plains. Two major rivers, the Niger and the Benue, come together in central Nigeria. At the confluence, or point where the two rivers meet, the Niger is more than three-fourths of a mile wide, and the Benue more than a mile. South of the confluence, the river is more than two miles wide. Farther south, the river narrows as it flows through a hilly region.

Where the Niger flows into the Gulf of Guinea, it has created the largest delta in the world. A delta is a triangle-shaped deposit of silt that builds up at the mouth of a river. Like most deltas, the Niger Delta is very fertile. It is a swampy area filled with mangrove trees and various animals. Much of the delta's natural vegetation has been cleared to make room for homes and farms. Today the delta is one of the most densely populated regions in Nigeria. In addition, oil companies have built drilling platforms and refineries to take advantage of the delta's huge oil deposits.

To the west of the Niger Delta is Nigeria's largest city, Lagos. Home to more than 11 million people, Lagos is one of the largest cities in Africa, and the fastest growing. Millions of people move to the city each year in search of opportunity because it is Nigeria's main financial and economic center. However, overcrowding and unemployment are severe problems in the city.

1 The **Niger Delta** is home to about a fifth of Nigeria's people and the bulk of its oil and gas reserves.

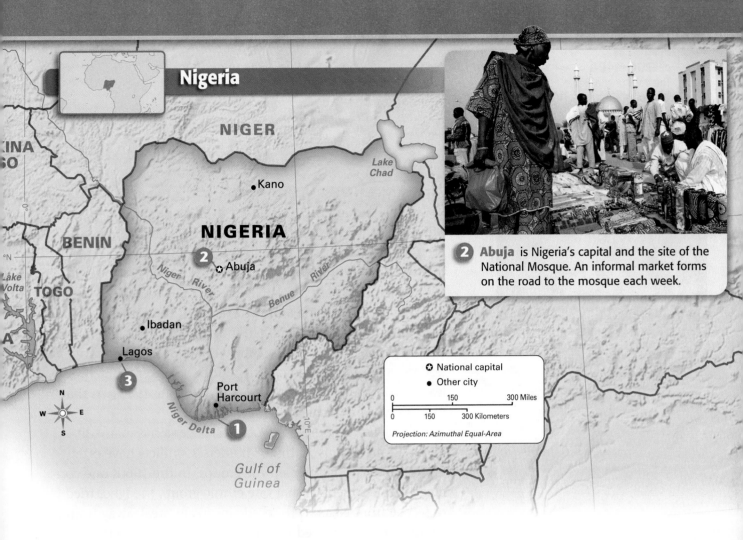

Nigeria

Nigeria

NIGER

Kano

NIGERIA

❷ Abuja

Niger River

Benue River

Ibadan

Lagos

❸

Port Harcourt

Niger Delta

❶

Gulf of Guinea

BENIN

TOGO

Lake Volta

°N

INA
O

A

2 **Abuja** is Nigeria's capital and the site of the National Mosque. An informal market forms on the road to the mosque each week.

◎ National capital
● Other city

0   150   300 Miles
0   150   300 Kilometers

Projection: Azimuthal Equal-Area

N W E S

Lake Chad

Lagos was once Nigeria's capital. However, many people were not happy with that location. People in northern Nigeria feared that southerners would have more influence in the government if the capital remained in the south. As a result, the nation's leaders moved the capital in the 1990s. For their new capital, they chose Abuja. Centrally located, Abuja is in a less densely populated region of Nigeria. Leaders hoped that fewer people would cause fewer ethnic conflicts in the new capital.

3 **Lagos** is Nigeria's largest city, one of the largest in Africa.

Case Study Assessment

1. What is the Niger Delta like?

2. Why did Nigeria's capital move to Abuja?

3. **Activity** Design a Nigeria diorama. Choose one region of Nigeria and create a diorama to present its major physical or cultural features.

1200   **1800**

c. 1200–1400
The Yoruba and Benin kingdoms rule what is now Nigeria.

c. 1471
Portuguese sailors reach the Niger River.

c. 1820
British traders arrive in Nigeria.

Artists from Nigeria's Yoruba culture made beautiful items like this cup from ivory.

History and Culture

For many centuries, Nigeria was home to a number of small kingdoms. Among these kingdoms were Benin, the Yoruba states, and the Hausa states. These kingdoms traded among themselves and with other cultures. Many were famous for their work with brass, bronze, and ivory.

British traders arrived in Nigeria in the late 1800s. Before long they made Nigeria a British colony. It remained a colony until 1960, when it was granted independence under a newly elected government. Within a few years, however, military leaders overthrew the government and took over. Military leaders continued to rule Nigeria until the late 1990s. At that time, democracy was restored in Nigeria.

Like many other former colonies, Nigeria has many different ethnic groups within its borders. Conflicts have often taken place among these ethnic groups. In the 1960s one conflict became so serious that one ethnic group, the Igbo, tried to secede from Nigeria. To secede means to break away from a country. This action led to a bloody civil war, which the Igbo eventually lost.

Nigerian Culture

Nigeria is home to more than 250 ethnic groups, each with its own history, customs, and values. These groups are proud of their cultures and work to keep their heritage alive. As a result, many elements of Nigerian culture today, such as clothing and music, reflect traditional ways of life.

Clothing Traditional Nigerian clothing includes flowing garments in bright colors.

1884
Nigeria becomes
a British colony.

1960
Nigeria becomes
independent.

2010

1999
Free elections in
Nigeria mark the end
of military rule.

**Nigerians celebrate their newfound
independence in 1960.**

Because the country has so many ethnic groups, Nigeria's culture is rich and complex. Many people continue to practice traditional arts, including sculpture, music, dance, and story-telling. In addition, many Nigerians still wear traditional styles of clothing, either in white or in bright colors. At the same time, however, European influences remain strong. English is commonly spoken, and soccer is the most popular sport.

Two other influences in Nigeria are Christianity and Islam. Christianity is common in the south, where most Europeans lived during the colonial period. Islam is more common in the north, where contact with North Africa is more prevalent.

Case Study Assessment

1. Why is Nigerian culture so diverse?

2. Which religions influence Nigerian culture?

3. **Activity** Plan a documentary about Nigerian culture. What topics would you choose to discuss? What images would you include?

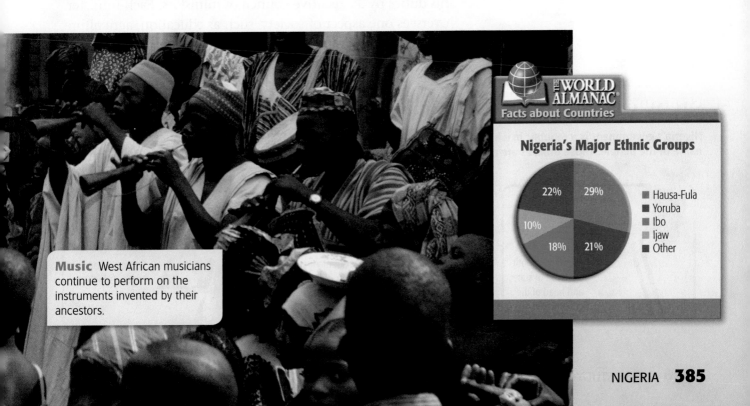

Music West African musicians
continue to perform on the
instruments invented by their
ancestors.

THE WORLD ALMANAC
Facts about Countries

Nigeria's Major Ethnic Groups

- 29% ■ Hausa-Fula
- 22% ■ Yoruba
- 21% ■ Ibo
- 18% ■ Ijaw
- 10% ■ Other

Nigeria Today

Economics

Nigeria has some of Africa's richest natural resources. Major oil fields, the country's most important resource, are located in the Niger River delta and just off the coast. Oil accounts for 95 percent of the country's export earnings. Income from oil exports has allowed Nigeria to build good roads and railroads for transporting oil. The oil industry is centered around Lagos.

Although Nigeria is rich in resources, many Nigerians are poor. One cause of the poverty there is the high birthrate. Nigeria cannot produce enough food for its growing population. Another cause of Nigeria's poverty is a history of bad government. Corrupt officials have often used their positions to enrich themselves while their people suffered.

Government

Although Nigeria has officially been a democracy since it became independent, people have had little say in the government for most of that time. Instead, military leaders have fought each other for power. In 1999, however, free elections led to a new president and a return to democracy in Nigeria.

Nigeria's president serves as the head of the executive branch of the government. This branch is responsible for carrying out the country's laws. The president is assisted in his duties by a executive council of ministers. Each minister oversees one aspect of society, such as education, agriculture, sports, or tourism.

Nigerian laborers work in a Chinese oil refinery in the Niger Delta. Much of the income from Nigeria's oil industry goes to other countries.

Structure of the Nigerian Government

Nigeria's government is a republic in which elected officials govern in the name of the people. Those officials are organized into three branches.

Executive Branch
As in the United States, Nigeria's president is both the head of state and head of the government.

Legislative Branch
The Senate and the House of Representatives work together to make laws.

Judicial Branch
Made up of 14 justices, the Supreme Court is Nigeria's highest judicial body.

The other two branches of Nigeria's government are the legislative and judicial branches. The legislative branch makes the country's laws. It includes a two-house legislature called the National Assembly. The judicial branch includes all of the country's courts and is headed by the Supreme Court.

Issues

Nigeria's diversity enriches the country's culture. However, it has also led to problems within the country. As you have read, members of various ethnic groups have fought for power in the past, even to the point of civil war. Today, the government moves very carefully to avoid favoring any one group.

Religious differences have also lead to issues in Nigeria. The majority of northern Nigeria's population is Muslim. Many northern states have adopted Shariah, or Muslim law, into their legal codes. However, most of southern Nigeria is not Muslim and does not want to live under Shariah. As a result, some southern lawmakers have argued that Shariah should not have any official recognition in Nigeria. Their protests have sparked fierce debate over the role of religion in the country.

Economic issues have also led to conflict in Nigeria. As mentioned on the previous page, most of Nigeria's population lives in poverty. At the same time, however, many foreign companies are profiting from Nigerian oil. Recently, angry residents of the Niger Delta have protested what they see as the exploitation of Nigeria's land and people.

Case Study Assessment

1. What is the main industry in Nigeria?

2. What duties does Nigeria's president have?

3. **Activity** Stage a debate about a current issue in Nigeria. Choose one issue. Divide the class into two groups to argue the two sides of the issue.

Religious Differences

Debates over religion and its role in society have led to political controversy in Nigeria. Northern Nigeria is mostly Muslim, the south is largely Christian. In recent years, lawmakers have clashed over the influence of religious law in Nigeria.

Mosque, Kano

Christian church, Abuja

THE WORLD ALMANAC®
Facts about Countries

Nigeria's Major Religions

10%
50%
40%

- Islam
- Christianity
- Traditional religions

The Future of Africa

Part A: Short-Answer Questions

Directions: Read and examine the following documents. Then, on a separate sheet of paper, answer the questions using complete sentences.

DOCUMENT 1

Many members of the United Nations want to bring about changes in Africa. They worry that Africa has been marginalized, or treated as unimportant, by many world leaders. To help fix this problem, the United Nations created the New Partnership for Africa's Development, or NEPAD.

> What is the need for NEPAD?
>
> NEPAD is designed to address the current challenges facing the African continent. Issues such as the escalating poverty levels, underdevelopment and the continued marginalisation of Africa needed a new radical intervention, spearheaded by African leaders, to develop a new Vision that would guarantee Africa's Renewal.

1a. What challenges does NEPAD think face the people of Africa?

_____

1b. Who does this document say should lead the efforts to change Africa?

_____

DOCUMENT 2

One issue that has plagued Africa in the past has been bad government. Military dictatorship and corruption have prevented growth and development. In recent years, however, democracy has taken root in many parts of Africa.

> Africa does not suffer a democracy deficit. More than two-thirds of sub-Saharan African countries have had democratic elections since 2000. Power has changed hands in a number of nations, from Senegal to Tanzania, and from Ghana to Zambia. So, elections have been a success. Over the next two to three years, the goal is to move beyond elections as the measure of freedom, and toward supporting African efforts to fortify government accountability. Good governance is an essential prerequisite for any other social changes.
>
> —U.S. Department of State, Bureau of African Affairs

2a. According to this document, how has government in Africa changed?

_____

2b. What challenges does the Bureau see in Africa's future?

_____

One key factor in improving the lives of people is education. The graph below shows how many students were enrolled in schools in Africa from 1999 to 2005.

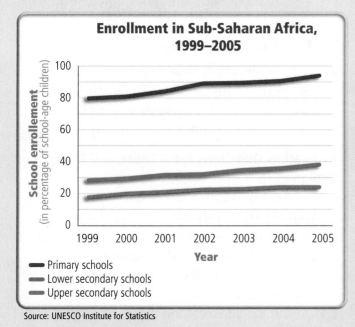

Enrollment in Sub-Saharan Africa, 1999–2005

Source: UNESCO Institute for Statistics

3a. How has school enrollment in Africa changed over time?

_____

_____

3b. At which level are the most African students enrolled?

_____

_____

To help promote growth, African countries have banded together in the African Union (AU), an organization modeled after the European Union. The AU has not yet achieved the level of unity enjoyed by its European counterpart, but it has worked to resolve conflicts in Africa. Some of the AU's objectives are listed below.

- To promote peace, security, and stability on the continent;
- To promote and protect human and peoples' rights in accordance with the African Charter on Human and Peoples' Rights and other relevant human rights instruments;
- To promote sustainable development at the economic, social and cultural levels as well as the integration of African economies;
- To promote co-operation in all fields of human activity to raise the living standards of African peoples;
- To advance the development of the continent by promoting research in all fields, in particular in science and technology

—from "The Objectives of the AU"

4a. What is one economic goal of the AU?

_____

4b. How does the AU propose improving the lives of Africans?

_____

_____

Part B: Essay

Historical Context: Since independence, many African countries have been plagued by political challenges and slow economic development. In recent years, people in Africa and around the world have devoted their efforts to securing a better future for the African people.

TASK: Using information from the four documents and your knowledge of social studies, write an essay in which you:

> - describe steps people have taken to improve Africa's future.
> - explain how each step will lead to positive change in Africa.

Explaining Cause or Effect

"Why did it happen?" "What were the results?" Questions like these help us identify causes and effects. This, in turn, helps us understand the relationships among physical geography, history, and culture.

Assignment
Write a paper about one of these topics:
- causes of desertification in West Africa
- effects of European colonization in South Africa

1. Prewrite
Choose a Topic
- Choose one of the topics above to write about.
- Turn that topic into a big idea, or thesis. For example, "Three main factors cause most of the desertification in West Africa."

> **TIP** **What Relationships?** Transitional words like *as a result, because, since,* and *so* can help make connections between causes and effects.

Gather and Organize Information
- Depending on the topic you have chosen, identify at least three causes or three effects. Use your textbook, the library, or the Internet.
- Organize causes or effects in their order of importance. To have the most impact on your readers, put the most important cause or effect last.

2. Write
Use a Writer's Framework

> **A Writer's Framework**
>
> **Introduction**
> - Start with an interesting fact or question related to your big idea, or thesis.
> - State your big idea and provide background information.
>
> **Body**
> - Write at least one paragraph, including supporting facts and examples, for each cause or effect.
> - Organize your causes or effects by order of importance.
>
> **Conclusion**
> - Summarize the causes or effects.
> - Restate your big idea.

3. Evaluate and Revise
Review and Improve Your Paper
- Re-read your paper and use the questions below to determine how to make your paper better.
- Make changes to improve your paper.

Evaluation Questions for a Cause and Effect Explanation
1. Do you begin with a fact or question related to your big idea, or thesis?
2. Does your introduction identify your big idea and provide any needed background?
3. Do you have at least one paragraph for each cause or effect?
4. Do you include facts and details to support the connections between causes and effects?
5. Do you explain the causes or effects in order of importance?
6. Do you summarize the causes or effects and restate your big idea?

4. Proofread and Publish
Give Your Explanation the Finishing Touch
- Make sure transitional words and phrases connect causes and effects as clearly as possible.
- Check for capitalization of proper nouns, such as the names of countries and regions.
- Have someone else read your paper.

5. Practice and Apply
Use the steps and strategies outlined in this workshop to write your cause-and-effect paper. Share your paper with other students who wrote on the same topic. Compare your lists of causes or effects.

South and East Asia

Himalayas

The highest mountain range in the world, the Himalayas, separates the Indian Subcontinent from the rest of Asia.

The Mekong

Southeast Asia's largest river, the Mekong floods often, covering much of the region with water.

South and East Asia

Rain Forest

The rich green color of Southeast Asia is caused by tropical rain forests. They are home to rare animals like the orangutan, found only in this region.

Explore the Satellite Image Towering mountains, dense rain forests, and dry plains are all features of this large region in Asia. What other physical features can you see in this satellite image?

The Satellite's Path

>44'56.08<

>>>>>>>>665.00'87<

567.476.348

+355

+799

+803

+996

456.094.

South and East Asia: Physical

CENTRAL ASIA

MONGOLIA

Altay Mountains

Mongolian Plateau

GOBI DESERT

NORTH KOREA

Sea of Japan (East Sea)

Hokkaido

Honshu

JAPAN

SOUTH KOREA

Shikoku

Kyushu

Tian Shan

Tarim Basin

Taklimakan Desert

K2 28,250 ft (8,610 m)

Kunlun Shan

CHINA

Qinling Shandi

Huang He (Yellow River)

North China Plain

Yellow Sea

East China Sea

Ryukyu Islands

Tropic of Cancer

PAKISTAN

Plateau of Tibet

Thar Desert

NEPAL

Mount Everest 29,035 ft (8,850 m)

BHUTAN

Sichuan Basin

Chang Jiang (Yangzi River)

HIMALAYAS

Indus River

Ganges River

BANGLADESH

Xi River

TAIWAN

INDIA

Godavari River

Deccan Plateau

Western Ghats

Krishna R.

Malabar Coast

Eastern Ghats

Ganges Delta

MYANMAR (BURMA)

LAOS

Hainan

Luzon

Bay of Bengal

Andaman Islands (INDIA)

THAILAND

Mekong

VIETNAM

South China Sea

PHILIPPINES

Mindanao

Lakshadweep Islands (INDIA)

CAMBODIA

Gulf of Thailand

MALDIVES

SRI LANKA

Nicobar Islands (INDIA)

Strait of Malacca

BRUNEI

New Guinea

MALAYSIA

INDIAN OCEAN

Sumatra

Java

SINGAPORE

Borneo

Sulawasi (Celebes)

Moluccas

INDONESIA

EAST TIMOR

Timor

PACIFIC OCEAN

AUSTRALIA

40°N
30°N
20°N
10°N
0° Equator
10°S
130°E
140°E
150°E
70°E
100°E
110°E

N E W S

ELEVATION

Feet	Meters
13,120	4,000
6,560	2,000
1,640	500
656	200
(Sea level) 0	0 (Sea level)
Below sea level	Below sea level

0   250   500   750 Miles

0   250   500   750 Kilometers

Projection: Two-Point Equidistant

map zone

Geography Skills

Regions South and East Asia includes many major rivers, long coastal plains, and large islands.

1. **Identify** What major rivers can you see in China and India?

2. **Make Inferences** How do you think rivers influence where people live in this region?

THE WORLD ALMANAC®
Facts about the World

Geographical Extremes: South and East Asia

Longest River	Chang Jiang (Yangzi River), China: 3,964 miles (6,378 km)
Highest Point	Mount Everest, Nepal/China: 29,035 feet (8,850 m)
Lowest Point	Turpan Depression, China: 505 feet (154 m) below sea level
Highest Recorded Temperature	Tuguegarao, Philippines: 108°F (42°C)
Wettest Place	Mawsynram, India: 467.4 inches (1,187.2 cm) average precipitation per year
Largest Country	China: 3,705,405 square miles (9,596,999 square km)
Smallest Country	Maldives: 116 square miles (300 square km)
Largest Rain Forest	Indonesia: 386,000 square miles (999,740 square km)
Strongest Earthquake	Off the coast of Sumatra, Indonesia, on December 26, 2004: Magnitude 9.0

Mount Everest

go.hrw.com KEYWORD: SK9 UN4

Size Comparison: The United States and South and East Asia

South and East Asia: Political

RUSSIA

CENTRAL ASIA

MONGOLIA
Ulaanbaatar

NORTH KOREA
Pyongyang
Seoul
SOUTH KOREA

Sea of Japan (East Sea)

Tokyo

JAPAN

PACIFIC OCEAN

Beijing

Yellow Sea

CHINA

Huang He (Yellow River)

Shanghai

East China Sea

Tropic of Cancer

Islamabad
KASHMIR
Indus River

PAKISTAN

Chongqing

Chang Jiang (Yangzi River)

Taipei

TAIWAN

New Delhi
NEPAL
Kathmandu
BHUTAN
Thimphu

Karachi

INDIA

Ganges River

Kolkata (Calcutta)
Dhaka
MYANMAR (BURMA)

BANGLADESH

Hong Kong

Hanoi
LAOS
Vientiane

Mumbai (Bombay)

Hyderabad

Naypyidaw

Manila

Bay of Bengal

Yangon (Rangoon)

THAILAND

VIETNAM

South China Sea

PHILIPPINES

Bangalore

Chennai (Madras)

Bangkok

CAMBODIA

Phnom Penh

MALDIVES

Colombo
SRI LANKA

BRUNEI
Bandar Seri Begawan

Male

MALAYSIA

Kuala Lumpur

SINGAPORE

INDONESIA

Singapore

Dili
EAST TIMOR

Jakarta

INDIAN OCEAN

AUSTRALIA

0° Equator

Sea (Yellow Sea)

⊛ National capital
● Other cities

0   250   500   750 Miles

0   250   500   750 Kilometers

Projection: Two-Point Equidistant

40°N
30°N
20°N
10°N
10°S
20°S
30°S

70°E 80°E 90°E 100°E 110°E 120°E 130°E 140°E 150°E

N
W   E
S

map zone
Geography Skills

Place South and East Asia includes several large countries, many smaller ones, and a number of island countries.

1. **Name** What are the three largest countries in this region?

2. **Analyze** What do you notice about the locations of many capital cities?

South and East Asia

South and East Asia: Population

CENTRAL ASIA

Harbin
Shenyang
Pyongyang
Dalian
Seoul
Beijing
Pusan
Qingdao
Jinan
Zhengzhou
Xi'an
Nanjing
Shanghai
Wuhan
Hangzhou
Chengdu
Chongqing
Taipei
Guangzhou
Hong Kong
Lahore
Delhi
Kanpur
Ahmadabad
Karachi
Kolkata (Calcutta)
Dhaka
Naypyidaw
Hanoi
Mumbai (Bombay)
Hyderabad
Bangalore
Chennai (Madras)
Yangon (Rangoon)
Bangkok
Ho Chi Minh City (Saigon)
Manila
Colombo
Singapore
Jakarta
Surabaya
Bandung

Sea of Japan (East Sea)
Tokyo
Yokohama
Nagoya
Osaka

Tropic of Cancer

PACIFIC OCEAN

South China Sea

Bay of Bengal

INDIAN OCEAN

Equator

AUSTRALIA

40°N
30°N
20°N
10°N
0° Equator
10°S
20°S
30°S

70°E
100°E
110°E
120°E
130°E
140°E
150°E

Persons per square mile

520	200
260	100
130	50
25	10
3	1
0	0

Persons per square km

● Major cities over 2 million

0 250 500 750 Miles

0 250 500 750 Kilometers

Projection: Two-Point Equidistant

map zone
Geography Skills

Regions This region has very large populations.

1. Name Based on the map, which two countries do you think have the largest populations?

2. Compare Compare this map to the physical map. How does China's physical geography relate to its population patterns?

South and East Asia: Climate

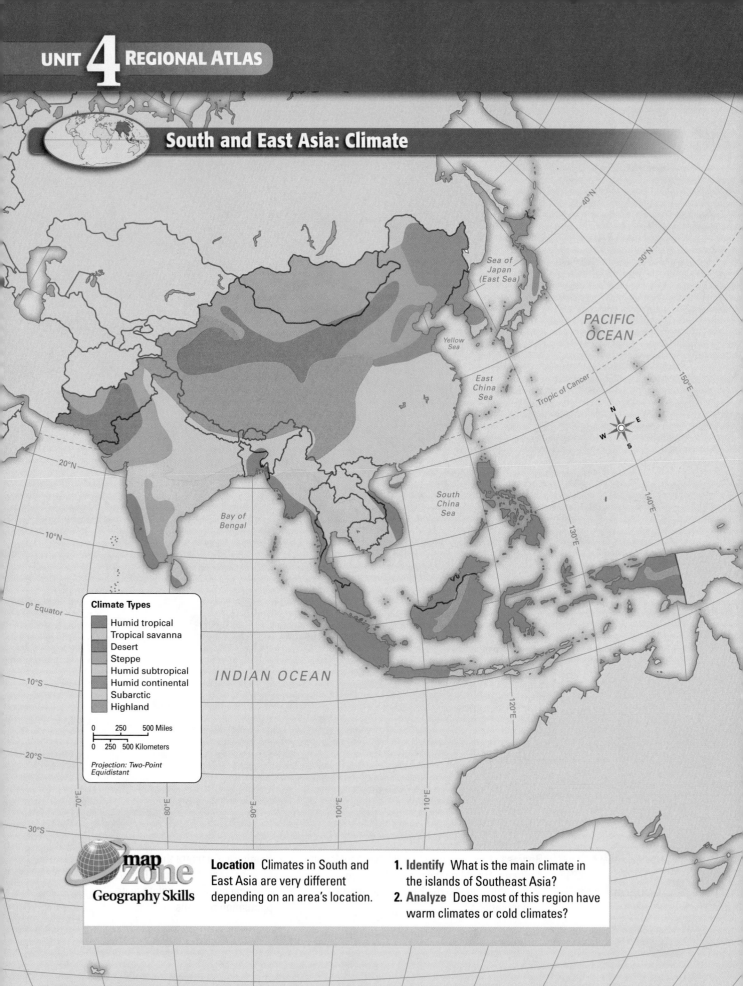

Climate Types

- Humid tropical
- Tropical savanna
- Desert
- Steppe
- Humid subtropical
- Humid continental
- Subarctic
- Highland

0   250   500 Miles

0 250 500 Kilometers

Projection: Two-Point Equidistant

Sea of Japan (East Sea)

PACIFIC OCEAN

Yellow Sea

East China Sea

Tropic of Cancer

South China Sea

Bay of Bengal

INDIAN OCEAN

map zone
Geography Skills

Location Climates in South and East Asia are very different depending on an area's location.

1. **Identify** What is the main climate in the islands of Southeast Asia?

2. **Analyze** Does most of this region have warm climates or cold climates?

South and East Asia

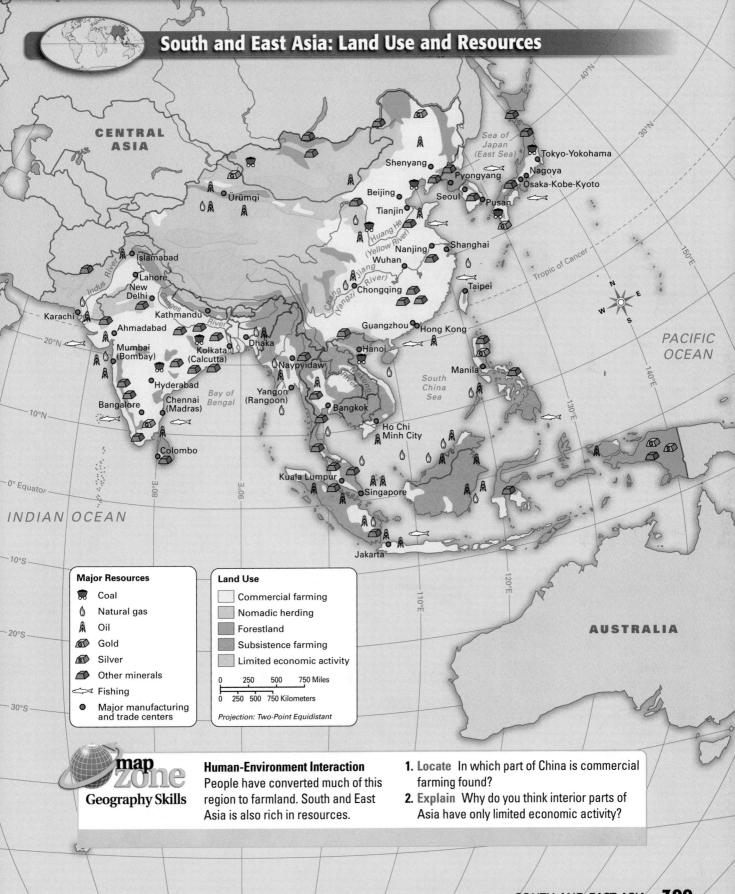

Major Resources

- 🪨 Coal
- 💧 Natural gas
- 🔥 Oil
- Ⓖ Gold
- Ⓢ Silver
- ⬡ Other minerals
- 🐟 Fishing
- ● Major manufacturing and trade centers

Land Use

- ☐ Commercial farming
- ☐ Nomadic herding
- ☐ Forestland
- ☐ Subsistence farming
- ☐ Limited economic activity

```
0      250    500    750 Miles
0   250 500  750 Kilometers
```

Projection: Two-Point Equidistant

map zone
Geography Skills

Human-Environment Interaction
People have converted much of this region to farmland. South and East Asia is also rich in resources.

1. **Locate** In which part of China is commercial farming found?
2. **Explain** Why do you think interior parts of Asia have only limited economic activity?

THE WORLD ALMANAC® Facts about Countries

South and East Asia

COUNTRY Capital	FLAG	POPULATION	AREA (sq mi)	PER CAPITA GDP (U.S. $)	LIFE EXPECTANCY AT BIRTH	TVS PER 1,000 PEOPLE
Bangladesh Dhaka		150.4 million	55,599	$2,200	62.8	7
Bhutan Thimphu		2.3 million	18,147	$1,400	55.2	6
Brunei Bandar Seri Begawan		374,600	2,228	$25,600	75.2	637
Cambodia Phnom Penh		14 million	69,900	$2,600	59.7	9
China Beijing		1,322 million	3,705,407	$7,600	72.9	291
East Timor Dili		1.1 million	5,794	$800	66.6	NA
India New Delhi		1,129.8 million	1,269,346	$3,700	68.6	75
Indonesia Jakarta		234.7 million	741,100	$3,800	70.2	143
Japan Tokyo		127.4 million	145,883	$33,100	81.4	719
Laos Vientiane		6.5 million	91,429	$2,100	55.9	10
Malaysia Kuala Lumpur		24.8 million	127,317	$12,700	72.8	174
Maldives Male		369,000	116	$3,900	64.8	38
Mongolia Ulaanbaatar		2.9 million	603,909	$2,000	65.3	58
United States Washington, D.C.		301.1 million	3,718,711	$43,500	78.0	844

COUNTRY Capital	FLAG	POPULATION	AREA (sq mi)	PER CAPITA GDP (U.S. $)	LIFE EXPECTANCY AT BIRTH	TVS PER 1,000 PEOPLE
Myanmar (Burma); Yangon (Rangoon) Naypyidaw		47.4 million	261,970	$1,800	62.5	7
Nepal Kathmandu		28.9 million	54,363	$1,500	60.6	6
North Korea Pyongyang		23.3 million	46,541	$1,800	71.9	55
Pakistan Islamabad		164.7 million	310,403	$2,600	63.8	105
Papua New Guinea Port Moresby		5.8 million	178,704	$2,700	65.6	13
Philippines Manila		91.1 million	115,831	$5,000	70.5	110
Singapore Singapore		4.6 million	268	$30,900	81.8	341
South Korea Seoul		49 million	38,023	$24,200	77.2	364
Sri Lanka Colombo		20.9 million	25,332	$4,600	74.8	102
Taiwan Taipei		22.8 million	13,892	$29,000	77.6	327
Thailand Bangkok		65.1 million	198,457	$9,100	72.6	274
Vietnam Hanoi		85.3 million	127,244	$3,100	71.1	184
United States Washington, D.C.		301.1 million	3,718,711	$43,500	78.0	844

ANALYSIS SKILL — ANALYZING TABLES

1. Which five countries in this region have the highest per capita GDPs? How do they compare to the per capita GDP of the United States?
2. Compare the life expectancy and number of TVs per 1,000 people in Japan and Laos. What might this comparison indicate about life in the two countries?

Economic Powers

Japan

- World's third-largest economy

- $590.3 billion in exports

- Per capita GDP of $33,100

- Major exports: transportation equipment, cars, semiconductors, electronics

Japan is one of the most technologically advanced countries and is a leading producer of hi-tech goods.

China

- World's second-largest economy

- $974 billion in exports

- GDP growth rate of 10.5%

- Major exports: machinery and electronics, clothing, plastics, furniture, toys

China is an emerging economic powerhouse with a huge population and a fast growing economy.

Population Giants

World's Largest Populations

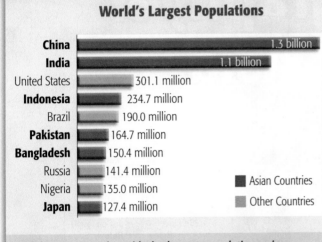

Country	Population
China	1.3 billion
India	1.1 billion
United States	301.1 million
Indonesia	234.7 million
Brazil	190.0 million
Pakistan	164.7 million
Bangladesh	150.4 million
Russia	141.4 million
Nigeria	135.0 million
Japan	127.4 million

■ Asian Countries
□ Other Countries

Of the ten countries with the largest populations, six are located in South and East Asia.

Percent of World Population

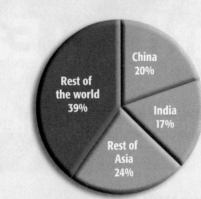

Rest of the world 39%
China 20%
India 17%
Rest of Asia 24%

The large populations of China and India help make Asia home to more than 60 percent of the world's people.

ANALYSIS SKILL **ANALYZING VISUALS**

1. Which two countries have the largest populations?
2. What kinds of exports help make Japan and China economic powers?

Nanjing Road,
Shanghai, China

CHAPTER 13

Physical Geography of South and East Asia

FOCUS QUESTION

What forces had an impact on the development of Asia and why?

What You Will Learn...

South and East Asia contain both the world's highest mountains and of some of its most often flooded rivers. The diversity of the land shapes how people live in the region.

FOCUS ON READING AND WRITING

Understanding Fact and Opinion A fact is a statement that can be proved true. An opinion is someone's belief about something. When you read a textbook, you need to recognize the difference between facts and opinions. **See the lesson, Understanding Fact and Opinion, on page S16.**

Presenting a Travelogue You are journeying through Asia, noting the sights and sounds of this beautiful region. As you read this chapter you will gather details about the region's landscapes. Then you will create an oral presentation of a travelogue, or traveler's journal.

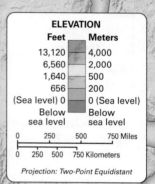

ELEVATION

Feet		Meters
13,120		4,000
6,560		2,000
1,640		500
656		200
(Sea level) 0		0 (Sea level)
Below sea level		Below sea level

```
0      250      500      750 Miles
0   250   500   750 Kilometers
```

Projection: Two-Point Equidistant

map zone
Geography Skills

Place The physical features of South and East Asia vary widely within the region.
1. **Identify** Which large islands are located in the region?
2. **Interpret** Where are the highest mountains in South and East Asia found?

Mountains The Indian Subcontinent is home to some of the world's highest mountains, including Pakistan's K2.

Altay Mountains

Mongolian Plateau

GOBI DESERT

Tian Shan

Tarim Basin

K2 28,250 ft (8,610 m)

Taklimakan Desert

Kunlun Shan

Indus River

HIMALAYAS

Plateau of Tibet

Mount Everest 29,035 ft (8,850 m)

Ganges River

Thar Desert

Sichuan Basin

Qinling Shandi

Huang He (Yellow River)

North China Plain

Chang Jiang (Yangzi River)

Xi River

Godavari River

Deccan Plateau

Krishna R.

Eastern Ghats

Western Ghats

Malabar Coast

Lakshadweep Islands (INDIA)

Ganges Delta

Bay of Bengal

Andaman Islands (INDIA)

Mekong River

Gulf of Thailand

Sri Lanka

Nicobar Islands (INDIA)

Maldives

Strait of Malacca

Sumatra

0° Equator

INDIA

N W E S

INDIAN OCEAN

Java

Borneo

Sulawesi (Celebes)

Timor

Moluccas

New Guinea

Mindanao

Luzon

Hainan

South China Sea

PACIFIC OCEAN

Tropic of Cancer

East China Sea

Ryukyu Islands

Yellow Sea

Hokkaido

Sea of Japan (East Sea)

Honshu

Shikoku

Kyushu

Mongolian Plateau

40°N 30°N 20°N 10°N 10°S

160°E 150°E 140°E 130°E 120°E 110°E 100°E 90°E 80°E

HOLT

Geography's Impact
video series
Watch the video to understand the impact of natural hazards.

Plains The plains of Mongolia allowed people to live as nomadic herders.

Water Features A woman carries sea salt across the salt pans in Doc Let Beach in Vietnam.

405

The Indian Subcontinent

What You Will Learn...

Main Ideas

1. Towering mountains, large rivers, and broad plains are the key physical features of the Indian Subcontinent.
2. The Indian Subcontinent has a great variety of climate regions and resources.

The Big Idea

The physical geography of the Indian Subcontinent features unique physical features and a variety of climates and resources.

Key Terms and Places

subcontinent, *p. 406*
Mount Everest, *p. 407*
Ganges River, *p. 407*
delta, *p. 407*
Indus River, *p. 408*
monsoons, *p. 409*

 As you read, take notes on the physical features, climates, and resources of the Indian Subcontinent. Use a diagram like the one below to organize your notes.

If YOU lived there...

You live in a small farming village in central India. Every year your father talks about the summer monsoons, winds that can bring heavy rains to the region. You know that too much rain can cause floods that may threaten your house and family. Too little rain could cause your crops to fail.

How do you feel about the monsoons?

BUILDING BACKGROUND Weather in the Indian Subcontinent, a region in southern Asia, is greatly affected by monsoon winds. Monsoons are just one of the many unique features of the physical geography of the Indian Subcontinent.

Physical Features

Locate Asia on a map of the world. Notice that the southern-most portion of Asia creates a triangular wedge of land that dips into the Indian Ocean. The piece of land jutting out from the rest of Asia is the Indian Subcontinent. A **subcontinent** is a large landmass that is smaller than a continent.

The Indian Subcontinent, also called South Asia, consists of seven countries—Bangladesh, Bhutan, India, Maldives, Nepal, Pakistan, and Sri Lanka. Together these countries make up one of the most unique geographic regions in the world. Soaring mountains, powerful rivers, and fertile plains are some of the region's dominant features.

Mountains

Huge mountain ranges separate the Indian Subcontinent from the rest of Asia. The rugged Hindu Kush mountains in the north-west divide the subcontinent from Central Asia. For thousands of years, peoples from Asia and Europe have entered the Indian Subcontinent through mountain passes in the Hindu Kush.

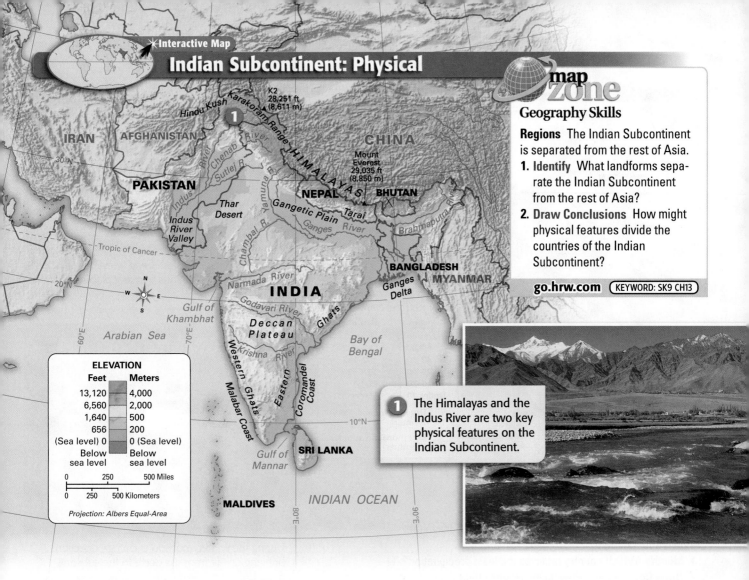

Indian Subcontinent: Physical

map zone

Geography Skills

Regions The Indian Subcontinent is separated from the rest of Asia.

1. **Identify** What landforms separate the Indian Subcontinent from the rest of Asia?

2. **Draw Conclusions** How might physical features divide the countries of the Indian Subcontinent?

go.hrw.com KEYWORD: SK9 CH13

ELEVATION

Feet	Meters
13,120	4,000
6,560	2,000
1,640	500
656	200
(Sea level) 0	0 (Sea level)
Below sea level	Below sea level

0   250   500 Miles

0   250   500 Kilometers

Projection: Albers Equal-Area

1 The Himalayas and the Indus River are two key physical features on the Indian Subcontinent.

Two smaller mountain ranges stretch down India's coasts. The Eastern and Western Ghats (GAWTS) are low mountains that separate India's east and west coasts from the country's interior.

Perhaps the most impressive physical features in the subcontinent, however, are the Himalayas. These enormous mountains stretch about 1,500 miles (2,415 km) along the northern border of the Indian Subcontinent. Formed by the collision of two massive tectonic plates, the Himalayas are home to the world's highest mountains. On the border between Nepal and China is **Mount Everest**, the highest mountain on the planet. It measures some 29,035 feet (8,850 m). K2 in northern Pakistan is the world's second highest peak.

Rivers and Plains

Deep in the Himalayas are the sources of some of Asia's mightiest rivers. Two major river systems—the Ganges (GAN-jeez) and the Indus—originate in the Himalayas. Each carries massive amounts of water from the mountains' melting snow and glaciers. For thousands of years, these rivers have flooded the surrounding land, leaving rich soil deposits and fertile plains.

India's most important river is the Ganges. The **Ganges River** flows across northern India and into Bangladesh. There, the Ganges joins with other rivers and creates a huge delta. A **delta** is a landform at the mouth of a river created by sediment deposits. Along the length of the Ganges is a vast area of rich soil and fertile farmland.

FOCUS ON READING

Are the sentences in this paragraph facts or opinions? How can you tell?

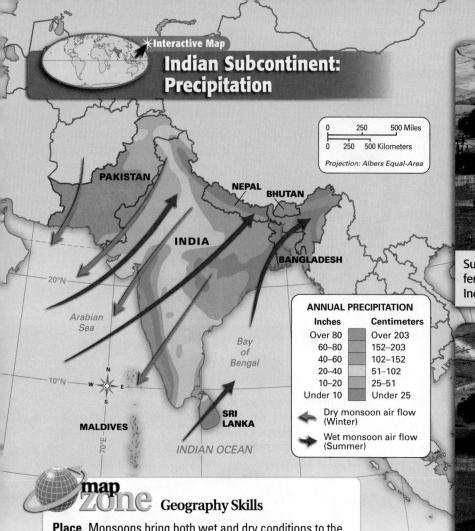

0   250   500 Miles

0   250   500 Kilometers

Projection: Albers Equal-Area

PAKISTAN

NEPAL

BHUTAN

INDIA

BANGLADESH

20°N

Arabian
Sea

Bay
of
Bengal

10°N   W   E

S   N

MALDIVES

SRI
LANKA

INDIAN OCEAN

70°E

ANNUAL PRECIPITATION

Inches		Centimeters
Over 80		Over 203
60–80		152–203
40–60		102–152
20–40		51–102
10–20		25–51
Under 10		Under 25

← Dry monsoon air flow (Winter)

→ Wet monsoon air flow (Summer)

Summer monsoons often bring heavy rains and fertile growing conditions to many places in the Indian Subcontinent.

During the winter, monsoons change direction, bringing dry air from the north to the subcontinent. Little rain falls during this time of year.

map zone Geography Skills

Place Monsoons bring both wet and dry conditions to the Indian Subcontinent.

1. **Identify** Which country receives the least precipitation?
2. **Draw Conclusions** How do monsoons affect the amount of precipitation in the Indian Subcontinent?

go.hrw.com (KEYWORD: SK9 CH13)

Known as the Ganges Plain, this region is India's farming heartland.

Likewise, Pakistan's **Indus River** also creates a fertile plain known as the Indus River Valley. This valley was once home to the earliest Indian civilizations. Today, it is Pakistan's most densely populated region.

Other Features

Other geographic features are scattered throughout the subcontinent. South of the Ganges Plain, for example, is a large, hilly plateau called the Deccan. East of the Indus Valley is the Thar (TAHR), or Great Indian Desert. Marked by rolling sand dunes, parts of this desert receive as little as 4 inches (100 mm) of rain per year. Still another geographic region is the Tarai (tuh-RY) in southern Nepal. It has fertile farmland and tropical jungles.

READING CHECK **Summarizing** What are the physical features of the Indian Subcontinent?

Climates and Resources

Just as the physical features of the Indian Subcontinent differ, so do its climates and resources. A variety of climates and natural resources exist throughout the region.

Climate Regions

From the Himalayas' snow-covered peaks to the dry Thar Desert, the climates of the Indian Subcontinent differ widely. In the Himalayas, a highland climate brings cool temperatures to much of Nepal and Bhutan. The plains south of the Himalayas have a humid subtropical climate. Hot, humid summers with plenty of rainfall are common in this important farming region.

Tropical climates dominate much of the subcontinent. The tropical savanna climate in central India and Sri Lanka keeps temperatures there warm all year long. This region experiences wet and dry seasons during the year. A humid tropical climate brings warm temperatures and heavy rains to parts of southwest India, Sri Lanka, Maldives, and Bangladesh.

The remainder of the subcontinent has dry climates. Desert and steppe climates extend throughout southern and western India and most of Pakistan.

Monsoons have a huge influence on the weather and climates in the subcontinent. **Monsoons** are seasonal winds that bring either moist or dry air to an area. From June to October, summer monsoons bring moist air up from the Indian Ocean, causing heavy rains. Flooding often accompanies these summer monsoons. In 2005, for example, the city of Mumbai (Bombay), India received some 37 inches (94 cm) of rain in just 24 hours. However, in winter the monsoons change direction, bringing dry air from the north. Because of this, little rain falls from November to January.

Natural Resources

A wide variety of resources are found on the Indian Subcontinent. Agricultural and mineral resources are the most plentiful.

Perhaps the most important resource is the region's fertile soil. Farms produce many different crops, such as tea, rice, nuts, and jute, a plant used for making rope. Timber and livestock are also key resources in the subcontinent, particularly in Nepal and Bhutan.

The Indian Subcontinent also has an abundance of mineral resources. Large deposits of iron ore and coal are found in India. Pakistan has natural gas reserves, while Sri Lankans mine many gemstones.

READING CHECK **Summarizing** What climates and resources are located in this region?

SUMMARY AND PREVIEW In this section you learned about the wide variety of physical features, climates, and resources in the Indian Subcontinent. Next, you will cross the Himalayas to study China, Mongolia, and Taiwan.

Section 1 Assessment

go.hrw.com
Online Quiz
KEYWORD: SK9 HP13

Reviewing Ideas, Terms, and Places

1. **a. Define** What is a **subcontinent**?
   b. Make Inferences Why do you think the **Indus River** Valley is so heavily populated?
   c. Rank Which physical features in the Indian Subcontinent would you most want to visit? Why?
2. **a. Identify** What natural resources are found in the Indian Subcontinent?
   b. Analyze What are some of the benefits and drawbacks of **monsoons**?

Critical Thinking

3. **Drawing Inferences** Draw a chart like the one shown here. Using your notes, write a sentence explaining how each aspect affects life on the Indian Subcontinent.

	Effect on Life
Physical Features	
Climates	
Natural Resources	

FOCUS ON SPEAKING

4. **Telling about Physical Geography** What information and images of India's physical geography might you include in your travelogue? Jot down some ideas.

China, Mongolia, and Taiwan

What You Will Learn...

Main Ideas

1. Physical features of China, Mongolia, and Taiwan include mountains, plateaus and basins, plains, and rivers.
2. China, Mongolia, and Taiwan have a range of climates and natural resources.

The Big Idea

Physical features, climate, and resources vary across China, Mongolia, and Taiwan.

Key Terms and Places

Himalayas, *p. 410*
Plateau of Tibet, *p. 411*
Gobi, *p. 411*
North China Plain, *p. 412*
Huang He, *p. 412*
loess, *p. 412*
Chang Jiang, *p. 412*

TAKING NOTES As you read, use a chart like the one below to take notes on the physical features, climate, and resources of China, Mongolia, and Taiwan.

Mountains	
Other Landforms	
Rivers	
Climate and Resources	

If YOU lived there...

You are a young filmmaker who lives in Guangzhou, a port city in southern China. You are preparing to make a documentary film about the Huang He, one of China's great rivers. To make your film, you will follow the river across northern China. Your journey will take you from the Himalayas to the coast of the Yellow Sea.

What do you expect to see on your travels?

BUILDING BACKGROUND China, Mongolia, and Taiwan make up a large part of East Asia. They include a range of physical features and climates—dry plateaus, rugged mountains, fertile plains. This physical geography has greatly influenced life in each country.

Physical Features

Have you seen the view from the top of the world? At 29,035 feet (8,850 m), Mount Everest in the **Himalayas** is the world's highest mountain. From atop Everest, look east. Through misty clouds, icy peaks stretch out before you, fading to land far below. This is China. About the size of the United States, China has a range of physical features. They include not only the world's tallest peaks but also some of its driest deserts and longest rivers.

Two other areas are closely linked to China. To the north lies Mongolia (mahn-GOHL-yuh). This landlocked country is dry and rugged, with vast grasslands and desert. In contrast, Taiwan (TY-WAHN), off the coast of mainland China, is a green tropical island. Look at the map to see the whole region's landforms.

Mountains

Much of the large region, including Taiwan, is mountainous. In southwest China, the Himalayas run along the border. They are Earth's tallest mountain range. Locate on the map the region's other ranges. As a tip, the Chinese word *shan* means "mountain."

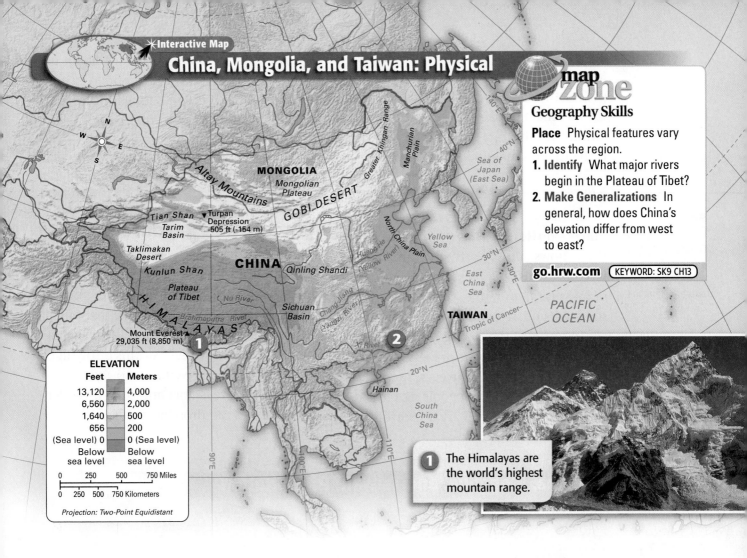

China, Mongolia, and Taiwan: Physical

map zone

Geography Skills

Place Physical features vary across the region.

1. **Identify** What major rivers begin in the Plateau of Tibet?
2. **Make Generalizations** In general, how does China's elevation differ from west to east?

go.hrw.com **KEYWORD: SK9 CH13**

ELEVATION

Feet	Meters
13,120	4,000
6,560	2,000
1,640	500
656	200
(Sea level) 0	0 (Sea level)
Below sea level	Below sea level

0   250   500   750 Miles

0   250   500   750 Kilometers

Projection: Two-Point Equidistant

1 The Himalayas are the world's highest mountain range.

Other Landforms

Many of the mountain ranges are separated by plateaus, basins, and deserts. In southwest China, the **Plateau of Tibet** lies north of the Himalayas. The world's highest plateau, it is called the Roof of the World.

Moving north, we find a low, dry area. A large part of this area is the Taklimakan (tah-kluh-muh-KAHN) Desert, a barren land of sand dunes and blinding sandstorms.

In fact, sandstorms are so common that the desert's Turkish name, Taklimakan, has come to mean "Enter and you will not come out." To the northeast, the Turpan (toohr-PAHN) Depression is China's lowest point, at 505 feet (154 m) below sea level.

Continuing northeast, in Mongolia we find the **Gobi**. This harsh area of gravel and rock is the world's coldest desert. Temperatures can drop to below –40°F (–40°C).

2 Hills that are called karst towers line the Li River in southeast China. These dramatic hills formed over time as rainwater eroded limestone.

In east China, the land levels out into low plains and river valleys. These fertile plains, such as the **North China Plain**, are China's main population centers and farmlands. On Taiwan, a plain on the west coast is the island's main population center.

Rivers

FOCUS ON READING
Does this paragraph express the author's opinion? How can you tell?

In China, two great rivers run west to east. The **Huang He** (HWAHNG HEE), or the Yellow River, flows across northern China. Along its course, this river picks up large amounts of **loess** (LES), or fertile, yellowish soil. The soil colors the river and gives it its name.

In summer, the Huang He often floods. The floods spread layers of loess, enriching the soil for farming. However, such floods have killed millions of people. For this reason, the river is called China's Sorrow.

The mighty **Chang** (CHAHNG) **Jiang**, or the Yangzi (YAHNG-zee) River, flows across central China. It is Asia's longest river and a major transportation route.

READING CHECK **Summarizing** What are the main physical features found in this region?

Climate and Resources

Climate varies widely across the region. The tropical southeast is warm to hot, and monsoons bring heavy rains in summer. In addition, typhoons can strike the southeast coast in summer and fall. Similar to hurricanes, these violent storms bring high winds and rain. As we move to the northeast, the climate is drier and colder. Winter temperatures can drop below 0°F (–18°C).

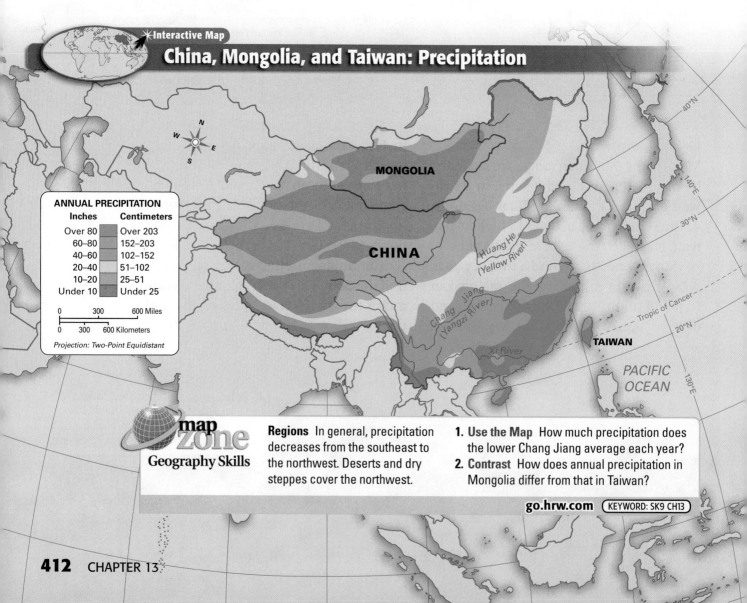

Interactive Map
China, Mongolia, and Taiwan: Precipitation

ANNUAL PRECIPITATION

Inches	Centimeters
Over 80	Over 203
60–80	152–203
40–60	102–152
20–40	51–102
10–20	25–51
Under 10	Under 25

0   300   600 Miles
0   300   600 Kilometers
Projection: Two-Point Equidistant

MONGOLIA

CHINA

Huang He (Yellow River)

Chang Jiang (Yangzi River)

Xi River

TAIWAN

PACIFIC OCEAN

Tropic of Cancer

map zone
Geography Skills

Regions In general, precipitation decreases from the southeast to the northwest. Deserts and dry steppes cover the northwest.

1. **Use the Map** How much precipitation does the lower Chang Jiang average each year?
2. **Contrast** How does annual precipitation in Mongolia differ from that in Taiwan?

go.hrw.com **KEYWORD: SK9 CH13**

Flooding in China

China's rivers and lakes often flood during the summer rainy season. The satellite images here show Lake Dongting Hu in southern China. The lake appears blue, and the land appears red. Soon after the Before image was taken, heavy rains led to flooding. The After image shows the results. Compare the two images to see the extent of the flood, which killed more than 3,000 people and destroyed some 5 million homes.

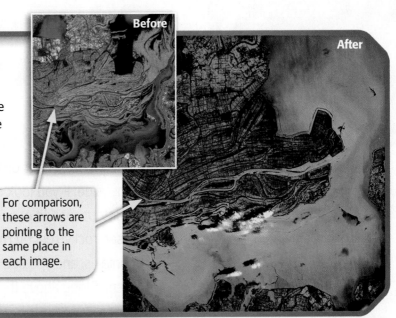

Before

After

For comparison, these arrows are pointing to the same place in each image.

Drawing Inferences Why might people continue to live in areas that often flood?

In the north and west, the climate is mainly dry. Temperatures vary across the area and can get both very hot and cold.

Like the climate, the region's natural resources cover a wide range. China has a wealth of natural resources. The country is rich in mineral resources and is a leading producer of coal, lead, tin, and tungsten. China produces many other minerals and metals as well. China's forestland and farmland are also valuable resources.

Mongolia's natural resources include minerals such as coal, iron, and tin as well as livestock. Taiwan's major natural resource is its farmland. Important crops include sugarcane, tea, and bananas.

READING CHECK **Contrasting** Which of these three countries has the most natural resources?

SUMMARY AND PREVIEW As you have read, China, Mongolia, and Taiwan have a range of physical features, climate, and resources. Next, you will study the features of Japan and the Koreas.

go.hrw.com
Online Quiz
KEYWORD: **SK9 HP13**

Section 2 Assessment

Reviewing Ideas, Terms, and Places

1. **a. Identify** What two major rivers run through China?
   b. Explain How does the **Huang He** both benefit and hurt China's people?
   c. Elaborate Why do you think many people in China live on the **North China Plain**?
2. **a. Define** What is a typhoon?
   b. Contrast What are some differences between the climates of southeast and northwest China?
   c. Rate Based on the different climates in this region, which part of the region would you prefer to live in? Why?

Critical Thinking

3. **Categorizing** Look back over your notes for this section. Then use a chart like the one shown here to organize, identify, and describe the main physical features of China, Mongolia, and Taiwan.

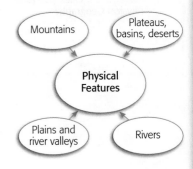

Mountains → Physical Features ← Plateaus, basins, deserts

Plains and river valleys → Physical Features ← Rivers

FOCUS ON SPEAKING

4. **Describing China's Landforms** Which of China's landforms will you describe in your travelogue? Write down some ideas. Features to consider include mountains, plateaus, and deserts.

Japan and the Koreas

What You Will Learn...

Main Ideas

1. The main physical features of Japan and the Koreas are rugged mountains.
2. The climates and resources of Japan and the Koreas vary from north to south.

The Big Idea

Japan and Korea are both rugged, mountainous areas surrounded by water.

Key Terms and Places

Fuji, *p. 415*
Korean Peninsula, *p. 415*
tsunamis, *p. 416*
fishery, *p. 417*

 TAKING NOTES Draw a table like the one below. As you read, take notes about the physical geography of Japan in one column and about the Korean Peninsula in the other column.

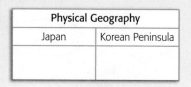

Physical Geography	
Japan	Korean Peninsula

If YOU lived there...

You are a passenger on a very fast train zipping its way across the countryside. If you look out the window to your right, you can see the distant sparkle of sunlight on the ocean. If you look to the left, you see rocky, rugged mountains. Suddenly the train leaves the mountains, and you see hundreds of trees covered in delicate pink flowers. Rising above the trees is a single snowcapped volcano.

How does this scenery make you feel?

BUILDING BACKGROUND The train described above is one of the many that cross the islands of Japan every day. Japan's mountains, trees, and water features give the islands a unique character. Not far away, the Korean Peninsula also has a distinctive landscape.

Physical Features

Japan, North Korea, and South Korea are on the eastern edge of the Asian continent, just east of China. Separated from each other only by a narrow strait, Japan and the Koreas share many common landscape features.

Physical Features of Japan

Japan is an island country. It is made up of four large islands and more than 3,000 smaller islands. These islands are arranged in a long chain more than 1,500 miles (2,400 km) long. This is about the same length as the eastern coast of the United States, from southern Florida to northern Maine. All together, however, Japan's land area is slightly smaller than the state of California.

About 95 percent of Japan's land area is made up of four large islands. From north to south, these major islands are Hokkaido (hoh-KY-doh), Honshu (HAWN-shoo), Shikoku (shee-KOH-koo), and Kyushu (KYOO-shoo). Together they are called the home islands. Most of Japan's people live there.

Rugged, tree-covered mountains are a common sight in Japan. In fact, mountains cover some 75 percent of the country. For the most part, Japan's mountains are very steep and rocky. As a result, the country's largest mountain range, the Japanese Alps, is popular with climbers and skiers.

Japan's highest mountain, **Fuji**, is not part of the Alps. In fact, it is not part of any mountain range. A volcano, Mount Fuji rises high above a relatively flat area in eastern Honshu. The mountain's cone-shaped peak has become a symbol of Japan. In addition, many Japanese consider Fuji a sacred place. As a result, many shrines have been built at its foot and summit.

Physical Features of Korea

Jutting south from the Asian mainland, the **Korean Peninsula** includes both North Korea and South Korea. Like the islands of Japan, much of the peninsula is covered with rugged mountains. These mountains form long ranges that run along Korea's eastern coast. The peninsula's highest mountains are in the north.

Unlike Japan, Korea also has some large plains. These plains are found mainly along the peninsula's western coast and in river valleys. Korea also has more rivers than Japan does. Most of these rivers flow westward across the peninsula and pour into the Yellow Sea.

FOCUS ON READING

How might the facts in these paragraphs shape your opinion of Japan or Korea?

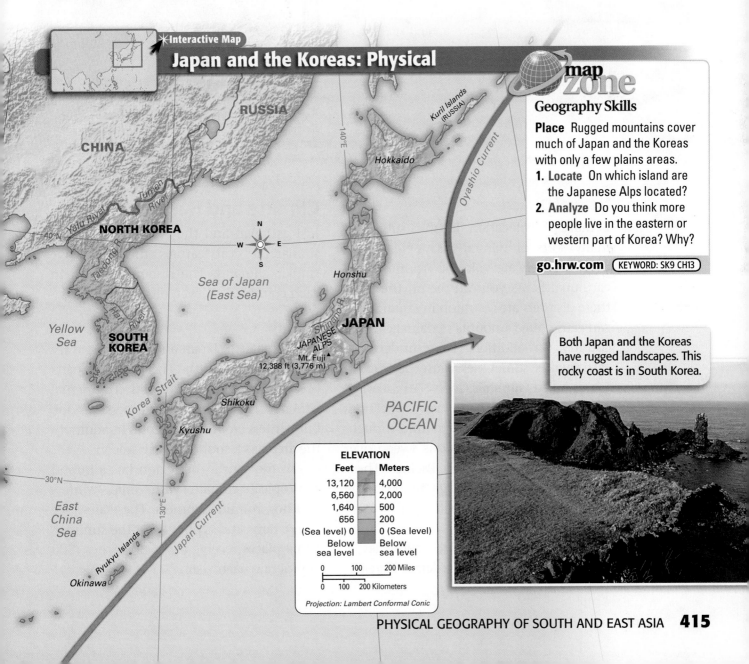

Japan and the Koreas: Physical

⋆Interactive Map

RUSSIA

CHINA

Kuril Islands (RUSSIA)

Hokkaido

NORTH KOREA

Turmen River

Yalu River

Taedong R.

Han River

40°N

Oyashio Current

Sea of Japan (East Sea)

Honshu

SOUTH KOREA

Yellow Sea

JAPAN

Shinano R.

JAPANESE ALPS

Mt. Fuji ▲
12,388 ft (3,776 m)

Korea Strait

Shikoku

Kyushu

PACIFIC OCEAN

30°N

East China Sea

130°E

Japan Current

Ryukyu Islands

Okinawa

140°E

map zone

Geography Skills

Place Rugged mountains cover much of Japan and the Koreas with only a few plains areas.

1. **Locate** On which island are the Japanese Alps located?
2. **Analyze** Do you think more people live in the eastern or western part of Korea? Why?

go.hrw.com (KEYWORD: SK9 CH13)

Both Japan and the Koreas have rugged landscapes. This rocky coast is in South Korea.

ELEVATION

Feet	Meters
13,120	4,000
6,560	2,000
1,640	500
656	200
(Sea level) 0	0 (Sea level)
Below sea level	Below sea level

0   100   200 Miles

0   100   200 Kilometers

Projection: Lambert Conformal Conic

PHYSICAL GEOGRAPHY OF SOUTH AND EAST ASIA **415**

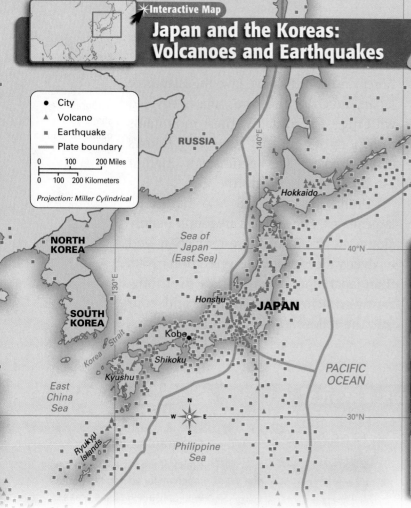

Japan and the Koreas: Volcanoes and Earthquakes

*Interactive Map

map zone Geography Skills

Human-Environment Interaction More than 1,000 earthquakes hit Japan every year. Most are minor, but some cause huge amounts of damage.
1. **Locate** On which large island did the 1995 Kobe earthquake occur?
2. **Compare** How does volcanic activity in Korea compare to activity in Japan?

go.hrw.com   KEYWORD: SK9 CH13

A devastating earthquake struck Kobe (KOH-bay), Japan, in 1995. It caused more than $100 billion in damages and left thousands homeless.

Natural Disasters

Because of its location, Japan is subject to many sorts of natural disasters. Among these disasters are volcanic eruptions and earthquakes. As you can see on the map, these disasters are common in Japan. They can cause huge amounts of damage in the country. In addition, large underwater earthquakes sometimes cause destructive waves called **tsunamis** (sooh-NAH-mees).

Korea does not have many volcanoes or earthquakes. From time to time, though, huge storms called typhoons sweep over the peninsula from the Pacific. These storms cause great damage in both the Korean Peninsula and Japan.

READING CHECK **Contrasting** How are the physical features of Japan and Korea different?

Climate and Resources

Just as Japan and the Koreas have many similar physical features, they also have similar climates. The resources found in each country, however, differ greatly.

Climate

The climates of Japan and the Koreas vary from north to south. The northern parts of the region have a humid continental climate. This means that summers are cool, but winters are long and cold. In addition, the area has a short growing season.

To the south, the region has a humid subtropical climate with mild winters and hot, humid summers. These areas see heavy rains and typhoons in the summer. Some places receive up to 80 inches (200 cm) of rain each year.

Resources

Resources are not evenly distributed among Japan and the Koreas. Neither Japan nor South Korea, for example, is very rich in mineral resources. North Korea, on the other hand, has large deposits of coal, iron, and other minerals.

Although most of the region does not have many mineral resources, it does have other resources. For example, the people of the Koreas have used their land's features to generate electricity. The peninsula's rocky terrain and rapidly flowing rivers make it an excellent location for creating hydroelectric power.

In addition, Japan has one of the world's strongest fishing economies. The islands lie near one of the world's most productive fisheries. A **fishery** is a place where lots of fish and other seafood can be caught. Swift ocean currents near Japan carry countless fish to the islands. Fishers then use huge nets to catch the fish and bring them to Japan's many bustling fish markets. These fish markets are among the busiest in the world.

This fish market in Tokyo, Japan, is the busiest in the world. People gather here every morning to buy freshly caught fish.

READING CHECK **Analyzing** What are some resources found in Japan and the Koreas?

SUMMARY AND PREVIEW The islands of Japan and the Korean Peninsula share many common features. In the next section, you will see similar features in the region of Southeast Asia and learn how those features affect life in that region.

Section 3 Assessment

Reviewing Ideas, Terms, and Places

1. **a. Identify** What types of landforms cover Japan and the **Korean Peninsula**?
   b. Compare and Contrast How are the physical features of Japan and Korea similar? How are they different?
   c. Predict How do you think natural disasters affect life in Japan and Korea?

2. **a. Describe** What kind of climate is found in the northern parts of the region? What kind of climate is found in the southern parts?
   b. Draw Conclusions Why are **fisheries** important to Japan's economy?

Critical Thinking

3. **Categorizing** Draw a chart like this one. In each row, describe the region's landforms, climate, and resources.

	Japan	Korean Peninsula
Landforms		
Climate		
Resources		

FOCUS ON SPEAKING

4. **Thinking about Nature** Nature is central to the art and culture of both Japan and Korea. How will you describe the natural environments of this region in your travelogue? Jot down some ideas.

Southeast Asia

If YOU lived there...

Your family lives on a houseboat on a branch of the great Mekong River in Cambodia. You catch fish in cages under the boat. Your home is part of a floating village of houseboats and houses built on stilts in the water. Local merchants paddle their boats loaded with fruits and vegetables from house to house. Even your school is on a nearby boat.

How does water shape life in your village?

BUILDING BACKGROUND Waterways, such as rivers, canals, seas, and oceans, are important to life in Southeast Asia. Waterways are both "highways" and sources of food. Where rivers empty into the sea, they form deltas, areas of rich soil good for farming.

Physical Features

Where can you find a flower that grows up to 3 feet across and smells like rotting garbage? How about a lizard that can grow up to 10 feet long and weigh up to 300 pounds? These amazing sights as well as some of the world's most beautiful tropical paradises are all in Southeast Asia.

The region of Southeast Asia is made up of two peninsulas and two large island groups. The **Indochina Peninsula** and the **Malay** (muh-LAY) **Peninsula** extend from the Asian mainland. We call this part of the region Mainland Southeast Asia. The two island groups are the Philippines and the **Malay Archipelago**. An **archipelago** (ahr-kuh-PE-luh-goh) is a large group of islands. We call this part of the region Island Southeast Asia.

Landforms

In Mainland Southeast Asia, rugged mountains fan out across the countries of Myanmar (MYAHN-mahr), Thailand (TY-land), Laos (LOWS), and Vietnam (vee-ET-NAHM). Between these mountains are low plateaus and river floodplains.

What You Will Learn...

Main Ideas

1. Southeast Asia's physical features include peninsulas, islands, rivers, and many seas, straits, and gulfs.
2. The tropical climate of Southeast Asia supports a wide range of plants and animals.
3. Southeast Asia is rich in natural resources such as wood, rubber, and fossil fuels.

The Big Idea

Southeast Asia is a tropical region of peninsulas, islands, and waterways with diverse plants, animals, and resources.

Key Terms and Places

Indochina Peninsula, *p. 418*
Malay Peninsula, *p. 418*
Malay Archipelago, *p. 418*
archipelago, *p. 418*
New Guinea, *p. 419*
Borneo, *p. 419*
Mekong River, *p. 419*

 TAKING NOTES As you read, use a chart like this one to help you take notes on the physical geography of Southeast Asia.

Physical Features	
Climate, Plants, Animals	
Natural Resources	

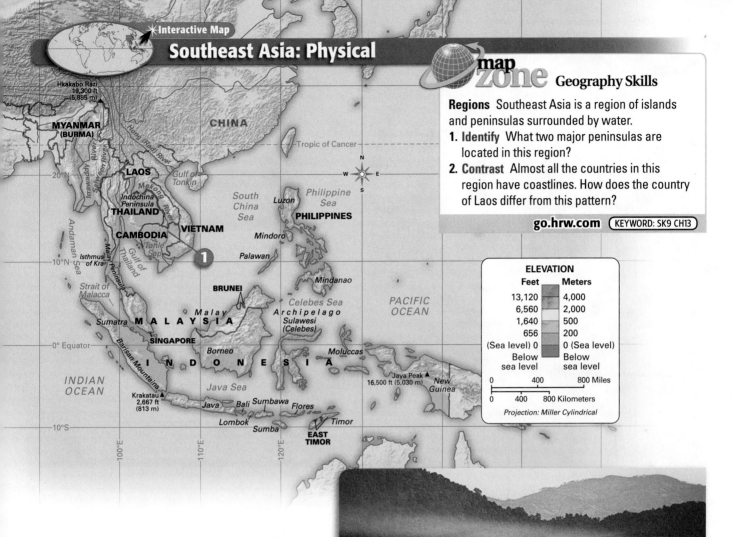

map zone Geography Skills

Regions Southeast Asia is a region of islands and peninsulas surrounded by water.

1. **Identify** What two major peninsulas are located in this region?
2. **Contrast** Almost all the countries in this region have coastlines. How does the country of Laos differ from this pattern?

go.hrw.com KEYWORD: SK9 CH13

ELEVATION

Feet	Meters
13,120	4,000
6,560	2,000
1,640	500
656	200
(Sea level) 0	0 (Sea level)
Below sea level	Below sea level

Projection: Miller Cylindrical

1 Mist hovers over the Mekong River as it flows through the forested mountains of northern Thailand.

Island Southeast Asia consists of more than 20,000 islands, some of them among the world's largest. **New Guinea** is Earth's second largest island, and **Borneo** its third largest. Many of the area's larger islands have high mountains. A few peaks are high enough to have snow and glaciers.

Island Southeast Asia is a part of the Ring of Fire as well. As a result, earthquakes and volcanic eruptions often rock the area. When such events occur underwater, they can cause tsunamis, or giant series of waves. In 2004 a tsunami in the Indian Ocean killed hundreds of thousands of people, many in Southeast Asia.

Bodies of Water

Water is a central part of Southeast Asia. Look at the map to identify the many seas, straits, and gulfs in this region.

In addition, several major rivers drain the mainland's peninsulas. Of these rivers, the mighty **Mekong** (MAY-KAWNG) **River** is the most important. The mainland's fertile river valleys and deltas support farming and are home to many people.

READING CHECK **Finding Main Ideas** What are Southeast Asia's major physical features?

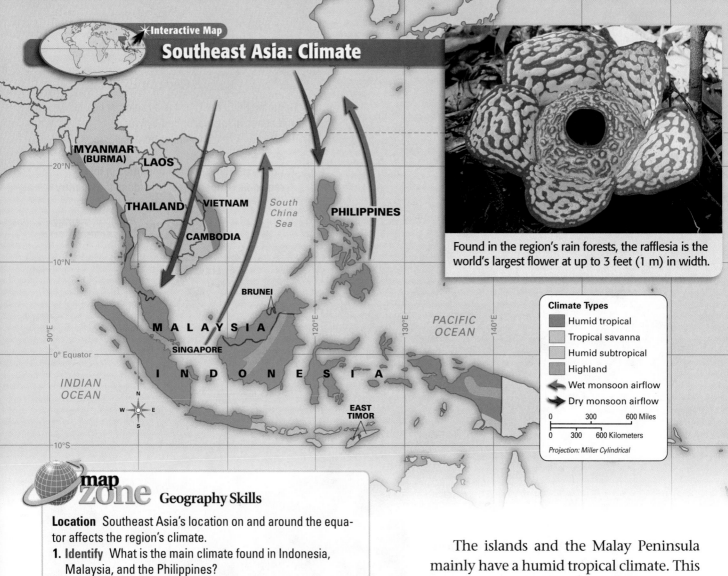

Southeast Asia: Climate

Found in the region's rain forests, the rafflesia is the world's largest flower at up to 3 feet (1 m) in width.

Climate Types

- Humid tropical
- Tropical savanna
- Humid subtropical
- Highland
- ← Wet monsoon airflow
- → Dry monsoon airflow

0   300   600 Miles
0   300   600 Kilometers

Projection: Miller Cylindrical

map zone Geography Skills

Location Southeast Asia's location on and around the equator affects the region's climate.

1. **Identify** What is the main climate found in Indonesia, Malaysia, and the Philippines?
2. **Interpret** Based on the map, how do monsoons affect the climate of this region?

go.hrw.com (KEYWORD: SK9 CH13)

Climate, Plants, and Animals

Southeast Asia lies in the tropics, the area on and around the equator. Temperatures are warm to hot year-round, but become cooler to the north and in the mountains.

Much of the mainland has a tropical savanna climate that supports tall grasses and scattered trees. Seasonal monsoon winds from the oceans bring heavy rain in summer and drier weather in winter. These **circumstances** can cause severe flooding every year during wet seasons.

The islands and the Malay Peninsula mainly have a humid tropical climate. This climate is hot, muggy, and rainy all year. Showers or storms occur almost daily. In addition, huge storms called typhoons can bring heavy rains and powerful winds.

The humid tropical climate's heat and heavy rainfall support tropical rain forests. These lush forests are home to a huge number of different plants and animals. About 40,000 kinds of flowering plants grow in Indonesia alone. These plants include the rafflesia, the world's largest flower. Measuring up to 3 feet (1 m) across, this flower produces a horrible, rotting stink.

Rain forest animals include elephants, monkeys, tigers, and many types of birds. Some species are found nowhere else. They include orangutans and Komodo dragons, lizards that can grow 10 feet (3 m) long.

ACADEMIC VOCABULARY

circumstances conditions that influence an event or activity

Orangutans live in the rain forests of Borneo and Sumatra. Deforestation has seriously reduced their habitat.

Natural Resources

Southeast Asia has a number of valuable natural resources. The region's hot, wet climate and rich soils make farming highly productive. Rice is a major crop, and others include coconuts, coffee, sugarcane, palm oil, and spices. Some countries, such as Indonesia and Malaysia (muh-LAY-zhuh), also have large rubber tree plantations.

The region's seas provide fisheries, and its tropical rain forests provide valuable hardwoods and medicines. The region also has many minerals and fossil fuels, including tin, iron ore, natural gas, and oil. For example, the island of Borneo sits atop an oil field.

READING CHECK **Summarizing** What are the region's major natural resources?

Many of these plants and animals are endangered because of loss of habitat. People are clearing the tropical rain forests for farming, wood, and mining. These actions threaten the area's future diversity.

READING CHECK **Analyzing** How does climate contribute to the region's diversity of life?

SUMMARY AND PREVIEW Southeast Asia is a tropical region of peninsulas, islands, and waterways with diverse life and rich resources. Next, you will read about the earliest history and culture of Asia in India.

Section 4 Assessment

go.hrw.com
Online Quiz
KEYWORD: SK9 HP13

Reviewing Ideas, Terms, and Places

1. **a. Define** What is an **archipelago**?
   b. Compare and Contrast How do the physical features of Mainland Southeast Asia compare and contrast to those of Island Southeast Asia?
2. **a. Recall** What type of forest occurs in the region?
   b. Summarize What is the climate like across much of Southeast Asia?
   c. Predict What do you think might happen to the region's wildlife if the tropical rain forests continue to be destroyed?
3. **a. Identify** Which countries in the region are major producers of rubber?
   b. Analyze How does the region's climate contribute to its natural resources?

Critical Thinking

4. **Summarizing** Draw a chart like this one. Use your notes to provide information about the climate, plants, and animals in Southeast Asia. In the left-hand box, also note how climate shapes life in the region.

Climate of Southeast Asia → Plants / Animals

FOCUS ON SPEAKING

5. **Planning Your Topics** Now that you have studied all the regions of South and East Asia, you can decide which topics to include in your travelogue. Which features will you include? Which images will you show? Write a plan for your travelogue in your notebook.

Tsunami!

Essential Elements

The World in Spatial Terms
Places and Regions
Physical Systems
Human Systems
Environment and Society
The Uses of Geography

Background "Huge Waves Hit Japan." This event is a tsunami (soo-NAH-mee), a series of giant sea waves. Records of deadly tsunamis go back 3,000 years. Some places, such as Japan, have been hit time and again.

Tsunamis occur when an earthquake, volcanic eruption, or other event causes seawater to move in huge waves. The majority of tsunamis occur in the Pacific Ocean because of the region's many earthquakes.

Warning systems help alert people to tsunamis. The Pacific Tsunami Warning Center monitors tsunamis in the Pacific Ocean. Sensors on the ocean floor and buoys on the water's surface help detect earthquakes and measure waves. When a tsunami threatens, radio, TV, and sirens alert the public.

Indian Ocean Catastrophe

On December 26, 2004, a massive earthquake erupted below the Indian Ocean. The earthquake launched a monster tsunami. Within half an hour, walls of water up to 65 feet high came barreling ashore in Indonesia. The water swept away boats, buildings, and people. Meanwhile, the tsunami kept traveling in ever-widening rings across the ocean. The waves eventually wiped out coastal communities in a dozen countries. Some 200,000 people eventually died.

At the time, the Indian Ocean did not have a tsunami warning system. Tsunamis are rare in that part of the world. As a result, many countries there had been unwilling to invest in a warning system.

1 A 9.0 underwater earthquake caused the 2004 Indian Ocean tsunami. The event pushed up millions of tons of water.

2 The water surged up and outward in huge waves. The waves moved at speeds of about 500 mph.

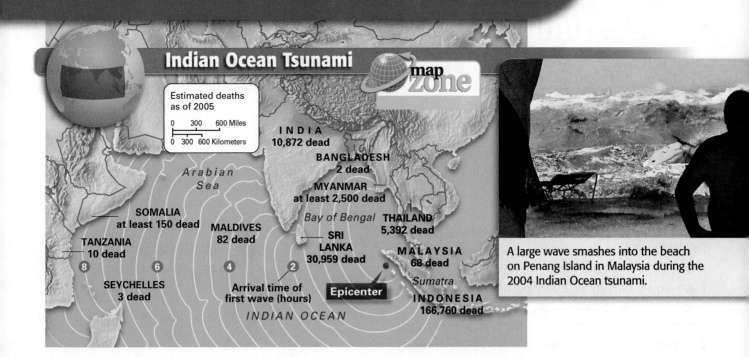

Indian Ocean Tsunami

map zone

Estimated deaths as of 2005

0 300 600 Miles
0 300 600 Kilometers

Arabian Sea

INDIA
10,872 dead

BANGLADESH
2 dead

MYANMAR
at least 2,500 dead

Bay of Bengal

SOMALIA
at least 150 dead

MALDIVES
82 dead

THAILAND
5,392 dead

TANZANIA
10 dead

SRI LANKA
30,959 dead

MALAYSIA
68 dead

⑧ ⑥ ④ ②

SEYCHELLES
3 dead

Arrival time of first wave (hours)

Epicenter

Sumatra

INDONESIA
166,760 dead

INDIAN OCEAN

A large wave smashes into the beach on Penang Island in Malaysia during the 2004 Indian Ocean tsunami.

In 2004 these countries paid a terrible price for their decision. As the map shows, the 2004 tsunami hit countries from South Asia to East Africa. Most people had no warning of the tsunami. In addition, many people did not know how to protect themselves. Instead of heading to high ground, some people went to the beach for a closer look. Many died when later waves hit.

③ When they strike, tsunamis often look like a rapidly rising tide or swell of water. The water then rushes far inland and back out.

Tilly Smith, a 10-year-old on vacation in Thailand, was one of the few who understood the danger. Two weeks earlier, her geography teacher had discussed tsunamis. As the water began surging, Smith warned her family and other tourists to flee. Her geographic knowledge saved their lives.

What It Means No one can prevent tsunamis. Yet, by studying geography, we can prepare for these disasters and help protect lives and property. The United Nations is now working to create a global tsunami warning system. People are also trying to plant more mangroves along coastlines. These bushy swamp trees provide a natural barrier against high waves.

Geography for Life Activity

1. What steps are being taken to avoid another disaster such as the Indian Ocean tsunami in 2004?

2. About 75 percent of tsunami warnings since 1948 were false alarms. What might be the risks and benefits of early warnings to move people out of harm's way?

3. **Creating a Survival Guide** Create a tsunami survival guide. List the dos and don'ts for this emergency.

Using a Topographic Map

Learn

Topographic maps show elevation, or the height of land above sea level. They do so with contour lines, lines that connect points on the map that have equal elevation. Every point on a contour line has the same elevation. In most cases, everything inside that line has a higher elevation. Everything outside the line is lower. Each contour line is labeled to show the elevation it indicates.

An area that has lots of contour lines is more rugged than an area with few contour lines. The distance between contour lines shows how steep an area is. If the lines are very close together, then the area has a steep slope. If the lines are farther apart, then the area has a much gentler incline. Other symbols on the map show features such as rivers and roads.

Practice

Use the topographic map on this page to answer the following questions.

1 Is Awaji Island more rugged in the south or the north? How can you tell?

2 Does the land get higher or lower as you travel west from Yura?

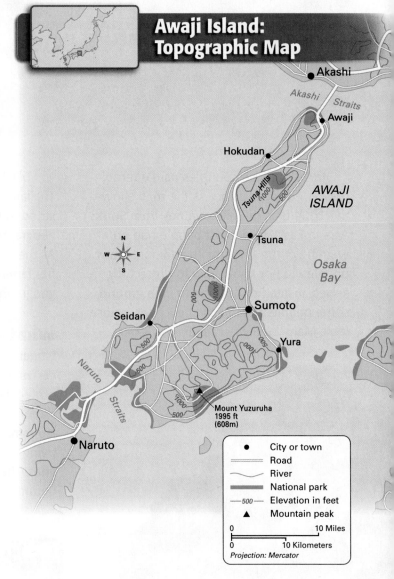

Awaji Island: Topographic Map

Mount Yuzuruha
1995 ft
(608m)

●	City or town
╍╍╍	Road
〜	River
▬	National park
—500—	Elevation in feet
▲	Mountain peak

0   10 Miles
0   10 Kilometers
Projection: Mercator

Apply

Search the Internet or look in a local library to find a topographic map of your area. Study the map to find three major landmarks and write down their elevations. Then write two statements about the information you can see on the map.

Geography's Impact
video series
Review the video to answer the closing question:
How has Japan's location on the Ring of Fire made it so prone to natural hazards?

Visual Summary

Use the visual summary below to help you review the main ideas of the chapter.

QUICK FACTS

South and East Asia have many mountains. Some, like Japan's Mount Fuji, are volcanic in origin.

Large rivers flow through the region. Floods on these rivers can cause problems for people in the region.

The region's climates vary widely, from parched deserts to savannas. Monsoon winds cause wet and dry seasons.

Reviewing Vocabulary, Terms, and Places

Imagine these terms from the chapter are correct answers to items in a crossword puzzle. Write the clues for the answers.

1. Gobi
2. circumstances
3. Borneo
4. delta
5. Fuji
6. tsunami
7. monsoon
8. archipelago
9. fishery
10. subcontinent
11. Himalayas
12. loess

Comprehension and Critical Thinking

SECTION 1 *(Pages 406–409)*

13. **a. Define** What is a delta?

    b. Draw Conclusions Why are rivers important to the people of the Indian Subcontinent?

    c. Evaluate Do you think monsoons have a positive or negative effect on India? Why?

SECTION 2 *(Pages 410–413)*

14. **a. Recall** What physical features separate many of the mountain ranges in China?

    b. Explain What is the Huang He called in English, and how did the river get its name?

    c. Elaborate What major physical features might a traveler see during a trip from the Himalayas, in southwestern China, to Beijing, in northeastern China?

SECTION 3 *(Pages 414–417)*

15. **a. Identify** What physical feature covers most of Japan and the Korean Peninsula?

    b. Draw Conclusions Fish and seafood are very important in the Japanese diet. Why do you think this is so?

    c. Predict How do you think earthquakes and typhoons would affect your life if you lived in Japan?

SECTION 4 *(Pages 418–421)*

16. a. Identify What two peninsulas and two archipelagos make up Southeast Asia?

b. Compare and Contrast How are the climates of Mainland Southeast Asia and Island Southeast Asia both similar and different?

c. Develop What different needs should people weigh when considering how best to protect Southeast Asia's tropical rain forests?

Social Studies Skills

Using a Topographic Map *Use the topographic map in this chapter's Social Studies Skills lesson to answer the following questions.*

17. What elevations do the contour lines on this map show?

18. Where are the highest points on Awaji Island located? How can you tell?

19. Is the city of Sumoto located more or less than 500 feet above sea level?

FOCUS ON READING AND SPEAKING

Understanding Fact and Opinion *Decide whether each of the following statements is a fact or an opinion.*

20. India would be a great place to live.

21. Japan is an island country.

22. The Himalayas are the world's tallest mountains.

23. The Himalayas are beautiful.

Presenting Your Travelogue *Use your notes and the instructions below to create and present your travelogue.*

24. Use your notes to create a one- to two-minute script describing your travels in South and East Asia. Identify and collect the images you need to illustrate your talk. Present your oral travelogue to the class, giving an exciting view of the region. Observe as others present their travelogues. How is each travelogue unique? How are they similar?

Using the Internet

go.hrw.com
KEYWORD: SK9 CH13

25. Activity: Writing a Report on Rain Forests The tropical rain forests of Indonesia are home to a rich diversity of life. Unfortunately, these forests face a number of threats. Enter the activity keyword to research these rain forests. Then write a short report that summarizes the threats they face.

Map Activity

26. South and East Asia On a separate sheet of paper, match the letters on the map with their correct labels.

Japan	Plateau of Tibet
South China Sea	Gobi Desert
Ganges River	Malay Peninsula

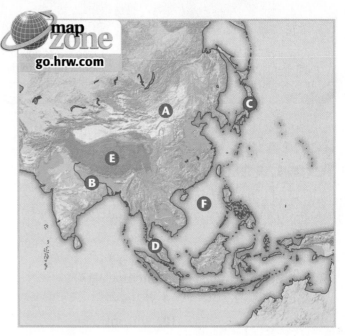

map zone
go.hrw.com

DIRECTIONS (1–7): For each statement or question, write on a separate answer sheet the *number* of the word or expression that, of those given, best completes the statement or answers the question.

1 What is the world's highest mountain range?

(1) Himalayas
(2) Kunlun Shan
(3) Tian Shan
(4) Qinling Shandi

2 Which of the following is not a major river?

(1) Honshu
(2) Ganges
(3) Huang He
(4) Mekong

3 The two peninsulas of Southeast Asia are the Indochina Peninsula and the

(1) Burma Peninsula.
(2) Malay Peninsula.
(3) Philippine Peninsula.
(4) Thai Peninsula.

4 India's Thar is a

(1) desert.
(2) mountain.
(3) river.
(4) rain forest.

5 Which statement about Japan is true?

(1) It is a peninsula.
(2) It is mostly flat.
(3) It includes only three islands.
(4) It has many volcanoes.

6 What is the largest island in Southeast Asia?

(1) Bali
(2) Borneo
(3) Java
(4) New Guinea

7 These seasonal winds bring both wet and dry conditions to much of the Indian Subcontinent.

(1) hurricanes
(2) monsoons
(3) tsunamis
(4) typhoons

Base your answer to question 8 on the map below and on your knowledge of social studies.

China, Mongolia, and Taiwan: Precipitation

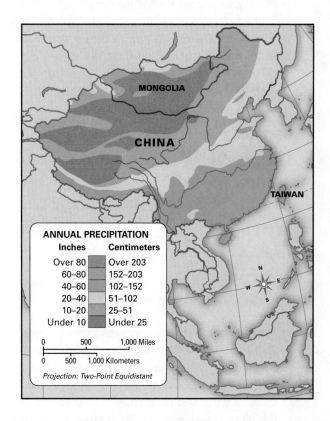

8 Constructed-Response Question Write one or two sentences to answer the following question: If you were to travel through China from northwest to southeast, how would the precipitation change?

CHAPTER 14

Ancient Civilizations of Asia—India

FOCUS QUESTION

How did ancient civilizations contribute to the development of the Eastern Hemisphere?

What You Will Learn...

In this chapter you will learn about the ancient civilization of India, the birthplace of two major world religions—Hinduism and Buddhism. You will also learn about the early civilizations and powerful empires that developed in India.

FOCUS ON READING AND WRITING

Sequencing When you read, it is important to keep track of the sequence, or order, in which events happen. Look for dates and other clues to help you figure out the proper sequence. **See the lesson, Sequencing, on page S17.**

Creating a Poster Ancient India was the home of amazing cities, strong empires, and influential religions. As you read this chapter, think about how you could illustrate one aspect of Indian culture in a poster.

0   250   500 Miles
0   250   500 Kilometers
Projection: Albers Equal-Area

Early India The first civilization in India, the Harappans, were skilled builders and artists.

City Planning

Most of what we have learned about the Harappans has come from studying their cities, especially Harappa and Mohenjo Daro. The two cities lay on the Indus more than 300 miles apart, but they appear to have been remarkably similar.

Both Harappa and Mohenjo Daro were well-planned cities. A close examination of their ruins shows that the Harappans were careful planners and skilled engineers.

Harappa and Mohenjo Daro were built with defense in mind. Each city stood near a towering fortress. From these fortresses, defenders could look down on the cities' carefully laid out brick streets. These streets crossed at right angles and were lined with storehouses, workshops, market stalls, and houses. Using their engineering skills, the Harappans built extensive sewer systems to keep their streets from flooding. They also installed plumbing in many buildings.

Next to the city was a huge citadel, or fortress, to guard against invasions.

The houses of Mohenjo Daro had flat roofs. People climbed to their roofs to take advantage of cooling breezes.

The city's streets were paved and well drained. They met at right angles, creating a grid pattern.

ANALYSIS SKILL **ANALYZING VISUALS**

What in this picture suggests that Mohenjo Daro was a well-planned city?

Artistic Achievements

In Harappan cities, archaeologists have found many artifacts that show that the Harappans were skilled artisans. For example, they have found sturdy pottery vessels, jewelry, and ivory objects.

FOCUS ON READING

In what order did the Aryans settle lands in India?

Some of these ancient artifacts have helped historians draw conclusions about Harappan society. For example, they found a statue that shows two animals pulling a cart. Based on this statue, they conclude that the Harappans built and used wheeled vehicles. Likewise, a statue of a man with elaborate clothes and jewelry suggests that Harappan society had an upper class.

Harappan civilization ended by the early 1700s BC, but no one is sure why. Perhaps invaders destroyed the cities or natural disasters, like floods or earthquakes, caused the civilization to collapse.

READING CHECK **Analyzing** Why do we not know much about Harappan civilization?

Harappan Art

Like other ancient peoples, the Harappans made small seals like the one below that were used to stamp goods. They also used clay pots like the one at right decorated with a goat.

Aryan Migration

Not long after the Harappan civilization crumbled, a new group appeared in the Indus Valley. These people were called the Aryans (AIR-ee-uhnz). Possibly from the area around the Caspian Sea in Central Asia, over time they became the dominant group in India.

Arrival and Spread

Many historians and archaeologists believe that the Aryans first arrived in India in the 2000s BC, probably crossing into India through mountain passes in the northwest. Over many centuries, they spread east and south into central India. From there they moved even farther east into the Ganges River Valley.

Much of what we know about Aryan society comes from religious writings known as the Vedas (VAY-duhs). These are collections of poems, hymns, myths, and rituals that were written by Aryan priests. You will read more about the Vedas later in this chapter.

Government and Society

As nomads, the Aryans took along their herds of animals as they moved. But over time, they settled in villages and began to farm. Unlike the Harappans, they did not build big cities.

The Aryan political system was also different from the Harappan system. The Aryans lived in small communities, based mostly on family ties. No single ruling authority existed. Instead, each group had its own leader, often a skilled warrior.

Aryan villages were governed by rajas (RAH-juhz). A raja was a leader who ruled a village and the land around it. Villagers farmed some of this land for the raja. They used other sections as pastures for their cows, horses, sheep, and goats.

Although many rajas were related, they didn't always get along. Sometimes rajas joined forces before fighting a common enemy. Other times, however, rajas went to war against each other. In fact, Aryan groups fought each other nearly as often as they fought outsiders.

Language

The first Aryan settlers did not read or write. Because of this, they had to memorize the poems and hymns that were important in their culture, such as the Vedas. If people forgot these poems and hymns, the works would be lost forever.

The language in which these Aryan poems and hymns were composed was **Sanskrit**, the most important language of ancient India. At first, Sanskrit was only a spoken language. Eventually, however, people figured out how to write it down so they could keep records. These Sanskrit records are a major source of information about Aryan society. Sanskrit is no longer widely spoken today, but it is the root of many modern South Asian languages.

READING CHECK **Identifying** What source provides much of the information we have about the Aryans?

Aryan Migrations

map zone Geography Skills

Movement The Aryans migrated to India.
1. **Read the Map** In what general direction did the Aryans travel?
2. **Analyze** Why do you think the Aryans entered India where they did?

SUMMARY AND PREVIEW The earliest civilizations in India were centered in the Indus Valley. In the next section, you will learn about a new religion that developed in the Indus Valley after the Aryans settled there—Hinduism.

Section 1 Assessment

Reviewing Ideas, Terms, and Places

1. **a. Recall** Where did the Harappan civilization develop?
   b. Explain Why did the Harappans make contact with people far from India?
2. **a. Identify** What was **Mohenjo Daro**?
   b. Analyze What is one reason that scholars do not completely understand some important parts of Harappan society?
3. **a. Identify** Who were the Aryans?
   b. Contrast How was Aryan society different from Harappan society?

Critical Thinking

4. **Summarizing** Using your notes, list the major achievements of India's first two civilizations. Record your conclusions in a diagram like this one.

Early Indian Achievements

Harappan society
Aryan society

FOCUS ON WRITING

5. **Illustrating Geography and Early Civilizations** This section described two possible topics for your poster: geography and early civilizations. Which of them is more interesting to you? Write down some ideas for a poster about that topic.

Origins of Hinduism

What You Will Learn...

Main Ideas

1. Indian society divided into distinct groups.
2. The Aryans formed a religion known as Brahmanism.
3. Hinduism developed out of Brahmanism and influences from other cultures.
4. The Jains reacted to Hinduism by breaking away.

The Big Idea

Hinduism, the largest religion in India, developed out of ancient Indian beliefs and practices.

Key Terms

caste system, *p. 437*
reincarnation, *p. 439*
karma, *p. 440*
nonviolence, *p. 441*

 TAKING NOTES As you read, take notes on Hinduism using a diagram like the one below. Pay attention to its origins, teachings, and other religions that developed alongside it.

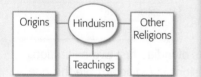

If YOU lived there...

Your family are skillful weavers who make beautiful cotton cloth. You belong to the class in Aryan society who are traders, farmers, and craftspeople. Often the raja of your town leads the warriors into battle. You admire their bravery but know you can never be one of them. To be an Aryan warrior, you must be born into that noble class. Instead, you have your own duty to carry out.

How do you feel about remaining a weaver?

BUILDING BACKGROUND As the Aryans came to dominate the Indus Valley, they developed a system of social classes. As their influence spread through India, so did their class system. Before long, this class system was a key part of Indian society.

Indian Society Divides

As Aryan society became more complex, their society became divided into groups. These groups were largely organized by people's occupations. Strict rules developed about how people of different groups could interact. As time passed, these rules became stricter and became central to Indian society.

The *Varnas*

According to the Vedas, there were four main *varnas*, or social divisions, in Aryan society. These *varnas* were

- Brahmins (BRAH-muhns), or priests,
- Kshatriyas (KSHA-tree-uhs), or rulers and warriors,
- Vaisyas (VYSH-yuhs), or farmers, craftspeople, and traders, and
- Sudras (SOO-drahs), or laborers and non-Aryans.

The Brahmins were seen as the highest ranking because they performed rituals for the gods. This gave the Brahmins great influence over the other *varnas*.

The Caste System

As the rules of interaction between *varnas* got stricter, the Aryan social order became more complex. In time, each of the *varnas* in Aryan society was further divided into many castes, or groups. This **caste system** divided Indian society into groups based on a person's birth, wealth, or occupation. At one time, some 3,000 separate castes existed in India.

The caste to which a person belonged determined his or her place in society. However, this ordering was by no means permanent. Over time, individual castes gained or lost favor in society as caste members gained wealth or power. On rare occasions, people could change caste.

People in the lowest class, the Sudra castes, had hard lives. After a few centuries, a fifth group developed, a group who didn't belong to any caste at all. Called untouchables because others were not supposed to have contact with them, they were seen as unclean and as social outcasts. The only jobs open to them were unpleasant ones, such as tanning animal hides and disposing of dead animals.

Caste Rules

To keep their classes distinct, the Aryans developed sutras, or guides, which listed the rules for the caste system. For example, people could not marry someone from a different class. It was even forbidden for people from one class to eat with people from another. People who broke the caste rules could be banned from their homes and their castes, which would make them untouchables. Because of these strict rules, people spent almost all of their time with others in their same class. The caste system also brought stability to Hindu society and a sense of belonging to people of each caste.

READING CHECK **Drawing Inferences** How did a person become a member of a caste?

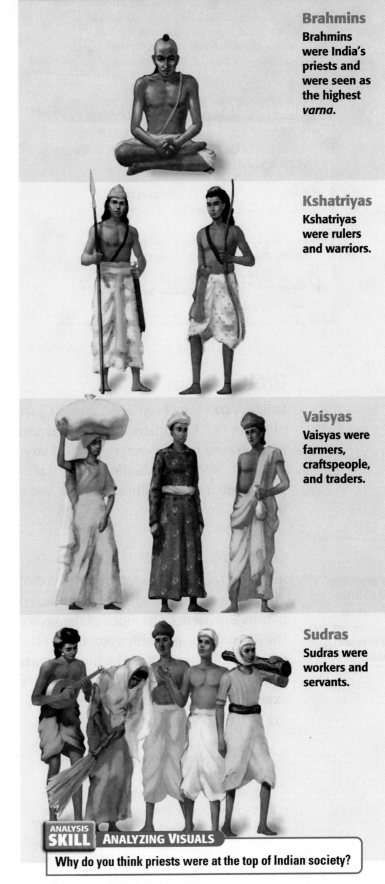

The *Varnas*

Brahmins
Brahmins were India's priests and were seen as the highest *varna*.

Kshatriyas
Kshatriyas were rulers and warriors.

Vaisyas
Vaisyas were farmers, craftspeople, and traders.

Sudras
Sudras were workers and servants.

ANALYSIS SKILL **ANALYZING VISUALS**
Why do you think priests were at the top of Indian society?

Hindu Gods and Beliefs

Hindus believe in many gods, but they believe that all the gods are aspects of a single universal spirit called Brahman. Three aspects of Brahman are particularly important in Hinduism—Brahma, Siva, and Vishnu.

Major Beliefs of Hinduism

- A universal spirit called Brahman created the universe and everything in it. Everything in the world is just a part of Brahman.

- Every person has a soul or atman that will eventually join with Brahman.

- People's souls are reincarnated many times before they can join with Brahman.

- A person's karma affects how he or she will be reincarnated.

The god Brahma represents the creator aspect of Brahman. His four faces symbolize the four Vedas.

Brahmanism

Religion had long been an important part of Aryan life. Eventually in India, religion took on even more meaning. Because Aryan priests were called Brahmins, their religion is often called Brahmanism, or Vedic Brahmanism.

The Vedas

FOCUS ON READING
Which were written first, the Vedas or the Vedic texts?

Aryan religion was based on the Vedas. There are four Vedas, each containing sacred hymns and poems. The oldest of the Vedas, the *Rigveda*, was probably compiled in the second millennium BC. It includes hymns of praise to many gods. This passage, for example, is the opening of a hymn praising Indra, a god of the sky and war.

> "The one who is first and possessed of wisdom when born; the god who strove to protect the gods with strength; the one before whose force the two worlds were afraid because of the greatness of his virility [power]: he, O people, is Indra."
>
> –from the *Rigveda*, in *Reading about the World, Volume I*, edited by Paul Brians, et al

Later Vedic Texts

Over the centuries, Aryan Brahmins wrote down their thoughts about the Vedas. In time these thoughts were compiled into collections called Vedic texts.

One collection of Vedic texts describes Aryan religious rituals. For example, it describes how to perform sacrifices. Priests prepared animals, food, or drinks to be sacrificed in a fire. The Aryans believed that the fire would carry these offerings to the gods.

A second collection of Vedic texts describes secret rituals that only certain people could perform. In fact, the rituals were so secret that they had to be done in the forest, far from other people.

The final group of Vedic texts are the Upanishads (oo-PAHN-ee-shads), most of which were written by about 600 BC. These writings are reflections on the Vedas by religious students and teachers.

READING CHECK Finding Main Ideas What are the Vedic texts?

Siva, the destroyer aspect of Brahman, is usually shown with four arms and three eyes. Here he is shown dancing on the back of a demon he has defeated.

Vishnu is the preserver aspect of Brahman. In his four arms, he carries a conch shell, a mace, and a discus, symbols of his power and greatness.

Hinduism Develops

The Vedas, the Upanishads, and the other Vedic texts remained the basis of Indian religion for centuries. Eventually, though, the ideas of these sacred texts began to blend with ideas from other cultures. People from Persia and other kingdoms in Central Asia, for example, brought their ideas to India. In time, this blending of ideas created a religion called Hinduism, the largest religion in India today.

Hindu Beliefs

The Hindus believe in many gods. Among them are three major gods: Brahma the Creator, Siva the Destroyer, and Vishnu the Preserver. At the same time, however, Hindus believe that each god is part of a single universal spirit called Brahman. They believe that Brahman created the world and preserves it. Gods such as Brahma, Siva, and Vishnu are different aspects of Brahman. In fact, Hindus believe that everything in the world is part of Brahman.

Life and Rebirth

According to Hindu teachings, everyone has a soul, or atman. This soul holds the person's personality, those qualities that make a person who he or she is. Hindus believe that a person's ultimate goal should be to reunite that soul with Brahman, the universal spirit.

Hindus believe that their souls will eventually join Brahman because the world we live in is an illusion. Brahman is the only reality. The Upanishads taught that people must try to see through the illusion of the world. Since it is hard to see through illusions, it can take several lifetimes. That is why Hindus believe that souls are born and reborn many times, each time in a new body. This process of rebirth is called **reincarnation**.

THE IMPACT TODAY

More than 900 million people in India practice Hinduism today.

Hinduism and the Caste System

According to the traditional Hindu view of reincarnation, a person who has died is reborn in a new physical form.

The type of form depends upon his or her **karma**, the effects that good or bad actions have on a person's soul. Evil actions during one's life will build bad karma. A person with bad karma will be reborn into a lower caste, or even as a lower life-form such as an animal or a plant.

In contrast, good actions build good karma. People with good karma are born into a higher caste in their next lives. In time, good karma will bring salvation, or freedom from life's worries and the cycle of rebirth. This salvation is called *moksha*.

Hinduism taught that each person had a duty to accept his or her place in the world without complaint. This is called obeying one's dharma. People could build good karma by fulfilling the duties required of their specific caste. Through reincarnation, Hinduism offered rewards to those who lived good lives. Even untouchables could be reborn into a higher caste.

Hinduism was popular at all levels of Hindu society, through all four *varnas*. By teaching people to accept their places in life, Hinduism helped preserve the caste system in India.

Hinduism and Women

Early Hinduism taught that both men and women could gain salvation. However, like other ancient religions, Hinduism considered women inferior to men. Women were generally not allowed to study the Vedas.

Over the centuries, Hindu women have gained more rights. This change has been the result of efforts by influential Hindu leaders like Mohandas Gandhi, who led the movement for Indian independence. As a result, many of the restrictions once placed on Hindu women have been lifted.

READING CHECK **Summarizing** What factors determined how a person would be reborn?

FOCUS ON CULTURE

The Sacred Ganges

Hindus believe that there are many sacred places in India. Making a pilgrimage to one of these places, they believe, will help improve their karma and increase their chance for salvation. The most sacred of all the pilgrimage sites in India is the Ganges River in the northeast.

Known to Hindus as Mother Ganga, the Ganges flows out of the Himalayas. In traditional Hindu teachings, however, the river flows from the feet of Vishnu and over the head of Siva before it makes its way across the land. Through this contact with the gods, the river's water is made holy. Hindus believe that bathing in the Ganges will purify them and remove some of their bad karma.

Although the entire Ganges is considered sacred, a few cities along its path are seen as especially holy. At these sites, pilgrims gather to bathe and celebrate Hindu festivals. Steps lead down from the cities right to the edge of the water so people can more easily reach the river.

Summarizing Why is the Ganges a pilgrimage site?

Jains React to Hinduism

Although Hinduism was widely followed in India, not everyone agreed with its beliefs. Some unsatisfied people and groups looked for new religious ideas. One such group was the Jains (JYNZ), believers in a religion called Jainism (JY-ni-zuhm).

Jainism was based on the teachings of a man named Mahavira. Born into the Kshatriya *varna* around 599 BC, he was unhappy with the control of religion by the Brahmins, whom he thought put too much emphasis on rituals. Mahavira gave up his life of luxury, became a monk, and established the principles of Jainism.

The Jains try to live by four principles: injure no life, tell the truth, do not steal, and own no property. In their efforts not to injure anyone or anything, the Jains practice **nonviolence**, or the avoidance of violent actions. The Sanskrit word for this nonviolence is *ahimsa* (uh-HIM-sah). Many Hindus also practice *ahimsa*.

The Jains' emphasis on nonviolence comes from their belief that everything is alive and part of the cycle of rebirth. Jains are very serious about not injuring or killing any creature—humans, animals, insects, or plants. They do not believe in animal sacrifice, such as the ones the ancient Brahmins performed. Because they do not want to hurt any living creatures, Jains are vegetarians. They do not eat any food that comes from animals.

READING CHECK Identifying Points of View
Why do Jains avoid eating meat?

SUMMARY AND PREVIEW You have learned about two religions that grew in ancient India—Hinduism and Jainism. In Section 3, you will learn about a third religion that began there—Buddhism.

These Jain women are wearing masks to make sure they don't accidentally inhale and kill insects.

go.hrw.com
Online Quiz
KEYWORD: SK9 HP14

Section 2 Assessment

Reviewing Ideas, Terms, and Places

1. **a. Identify** What is the **caste system**?
   b. Explain Why did strict caste rules develop?
2. **a. Identify** What does the *Rigveda* include?
   b. Analyze What role did sacrifice play in Aryan society?
3. **a. Define** What is **karma**?
   b. Sequence How did Brahmanism develop into Hinduism?
   c. Elaborate How does Hinduism reinforce followers' willingness to remain within their castes?
4. **a. Recall** What are the four main teachings of Jainism?
   b. Predict How do you think the idea of **nonviolence** affected the daily lives of Jains in ancient India?

Critical Thinking

5. **Analyzing Causes** Draw a graphic organizer like this one. Using your notes, explain how Hinduism developed from Brahmanism and how Jainism developed from Hinduism.

Brahmanism → Hinduism → Jainism

FOCUS ON WRITING

6. **Illustrating Hinduism** Now you have another possible topic for your poster. How might you illustrate a complex religion like Hinduism? What pictures would work?

Origins of Buddhism

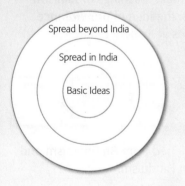
If YOU lived there...

You are a trader traveling in northern India in about 520 BC. As you pass through a town, you see a crowd of people sitting silently in the shade of a huge tree. A man sitting at the foot of the tree is speaking about how one ought to live. His words are like nothing you have heard from the Hindu priests.

Will you stay to listen? Why or why not?

BUILDING BACKGROUND The Jains were not the only ones to break from Hinduism. In the 500s BC a young Indian prince attracted many people to his teachings about how people should live.

Siddhartha's Search for Wisdom

In the late 500s BC a restless young man, dissatisfied with the teachings of Hinduism, began to ask his own questions about life and religious matters. In time, he found answers. These answers attracted many followers, and the young man's ideas became the foundation of a major new religion in India.

The Quest for Answers

The restless young man was Siddhartha Gautama (si-DAHR-tuh GAU-tuh-muh). Born around 563 BC in northern India near the Himalayas, Siddhartha was a prince who grew up in luxury. Born a Kshatriya, a member of the warrior class, Siddhartha never had to struggle with the problems that many people of his time faced. However, Siddhartha was not satisfied. He felt something was missing in his life.

Siddhartha looked around him and saw how hard most people had to work and how much they suffered. He saw people grieving for lost loved ones and wondered why there was so much pain in the world. As a result, Siddhartha began to ask questions about the meaning of human life.

The Great Departure

In this painting, Prince Siddhartha leaves his palace to search for the true meaning of life, an event known as the Great Departure. Special helpers called *ganas* hold his horse's hooves so he won't awaken anyone.

Before Siddhartha reached age 30, he left his home and family to look for answers. His journey took him to many regions in India. Wherever he traveled, he had discussions with priests and people known for their wisdom. Yet no one could give convincing answers to Siddhartha's questions.

The Buddha Finds Enlightenment

Siddhartha did not give up. Instead, he became even more determined to find the answers he was seeking. For several years, he wandered in search of answers.

Siddhartha wanted to free his mind from daily concerns. For a while, he did not even wash himself. He also started **fasting**, or going without food. He devoted much of his time to **meditation**, the focusing of the mind on spiritual ideas.

According to legend, Siddhartha spent six years wandering throughout India. He eventually came to a place near the town of Gaya, close to the Ganges River. There, he sat down under a tree and meditated.

After seven weeks of deep meditation, he suddenly had the answers that he had been looking for. He had realized that human suffering comes from three things:

- wanting what we like but do not have,
- wanting to keep what we like and already have, and
- not wanting what we dislike but have.

Siddhartha spent seven more weeks meditating under the tree, which his followers later named the Tree of Wisdom. He then described his new ideas to five of his former companions. His followers later called this talk the First Sermon.

Siddhartha Gautama was about 35 years old when he found enlightenment under the tree. From that point on, he would be called the Buddha (BOO-duh), or the "Enlightened One." The Buddha spent the rest of his life traveling across northern India and teaching people his ideas.

READING CHECK **Summarizing** What did the Buddha conclude about the cause of suffering?

FOCUS ON READING
What steps did the Buddha take in his search for enlightenment?

Teachings of Buddhism

As he traveled, the Buddha gained many followers. Many of these followers were merchants and artisans, but he even taught a few kings. These followers were the first believers in Buddhism, the religion based on the teachings of the Buddha.

The Buddha was raised Hindu, and many of his teachings reflected Hindu ideas. Like Hindus, he believed that people should act morally and treat others well. In one of his sermons, he said

" Let a man overcome anger by love. Let him overcome the greedy by liberality [giving], the liar by truth. This is called progress in the discipline [training] of the Blessed. "
–The Buddha, quoted in *The History of Nations: India*

Four Noble Truths

At the heart of the Buddha's teachings were four guiding principles. These became known as the Four Noble Truths:

1. Suffering and unhappiness are a part of human life. No one can escape sorrow.

2. Suffering comes from our desires for pleasure and material goods. People cause their own misery because they want things they cannot have.

3. People can overcome their desires and ignorance and reach **nirvana**, a state of perfect peace. Reaching nirvana would free a person's soul from suffering and from the need for further reincarnation.

4. People can overcome ignorance and desire by following an eight-fold path that leads to wisdom, enlightenment, and salvation.

The chart on the next page shows the steps in the Eightfold Path. The Buddha believed that this path was a middle way between human desires and denying oneself any pleasure. He believed that people should overcome their desire for material goods. They should, however, be reasonable, and not starve their bodies or cause themselves unnecessary pain.

This giant statue of the Buddha is just south of the town of Gaya in Bodh Gaya, India—the place where Buddhists believe Siddhartha reached enlightenment.

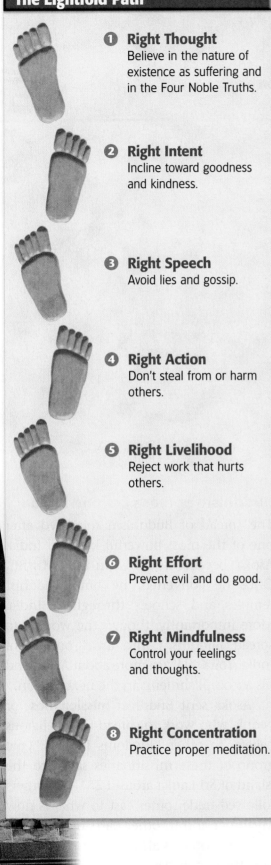

The Eightfold Path

1 Right Thought
Believe in the nature of existence as suffering and in the Four Noble Truths.

2 Right Intent
Incline toward goodness and kindness.

3 Right Speech
Avoid lies and gossip.

4 Right Action
Don't steal from or harm others.

5 Right Livelihood
Reject work that hurts others.

6 Right Effort
Prevent evil and do good.

7 Right Mindfulness
Control your feelings and thoughts.

8 Right Concentration
Practice proper meditation.

Challenging Hindu Ideas

Some of the Buddha's teachings challenged traditional Hindu ideas. For example, the Buddha rejected many of the ideas contained in the Vedas, such as animal sacrifice. He told people that they did not have to follow these texts.

The Buddha challenged the authority of the Hindu priests, the Brahmins. He did not believe that they or their rituals were necessary for enlightenment. Instead, he taught that it was the responsibility of each person to work for his or her own salvation. Priests could not help them. However, the Buddha did not reject the Hindu teaching of reincarnation. He taught that people who failed to reach nirvana would have to be reborn time and time again until they achieved it.

The Buddha was opposed to the caste system. He didn't think that people should be confined to a particular place in society. He taught that every person who followed the Eightfold Path properly would reach nirvana. It didn't matter what *varna* or caste they had belonged to in life as long as they lived the way they should.

The Buddha's opposition to the caste system won him the support of the masses. Many herders, farmers, artisans, and untouchables liked hearing that their low social rank would not be a barrier to their enlightenment. Unlike Hinduism, Buddhism made them feel that they had the power to change their lives.

The Buddha also gained followers among the higher classes. Many rich and powerful Indians welcomed his ideas about avoiding extreme behavior while seeking salvation. By the time of his death around 483 BC, the Buddha's influence was spreading rapidly throughout India.

READING CHECK Comparing How did Buddha's teachings agree with Hinduism?

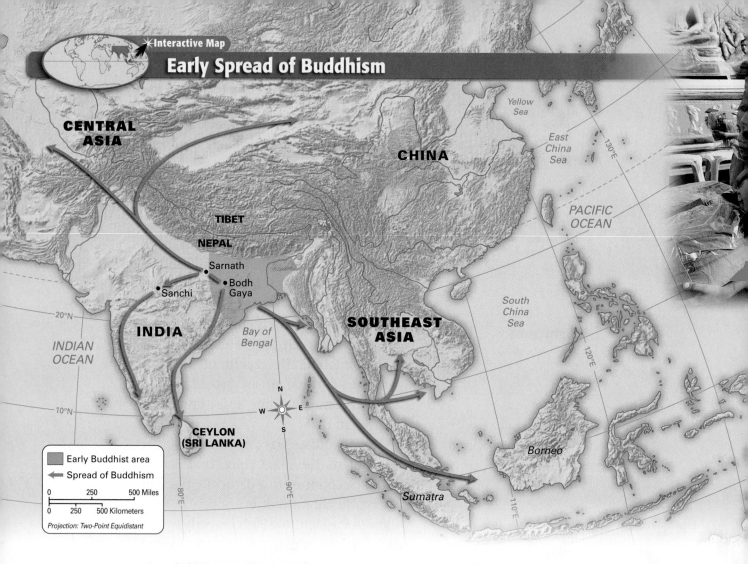

Early Spread of Buddhism

CENTRAL ASIA

CHINA

Yellow Sea

East China Sea

PACIFIC OCEAN

TIBET

NEPAL

Sarnath

Bodh Gaya

Sanchi

20°N

INDIA

Bay of Bengal

SOUTHEAST ASIA

South China Sea

INDIAN OCEAN

10°N

N

W   E

S

CEYLON (SRI LANKA)

Borneo

Sumatra

☐ Early Buddhist area
← Spread of Buddhism

0   250   500 Miles

0   250   500 Kilometers

Projection: Two-Point Equidistant

Buddhism Spreads

Buddhism continued to attract followers after the Buddha's death. After spreading through India, the religion began to spread to other areas as well.

Buddhism Spreads in India

According to Buddhist tradition, 500 of the Buddha's followers gathered together shortly after he died. They wanted to make sure that the Buddha's teachings were remembered correctly.

In the years after this council, the Buddha's followers spread his teachings throughout India. The ideas spread very quickly, because Buddhist teachings were popular and easy to understand. Within 200 years of the Buddha's death, Buddhism had spread through most of India.

Buddhism Spreads beyond India

The spread of Buddhism increased after one of the most powerful kings in India, Asoka, became Buddhist in the 200s BC. Once he converted, he built Buddhist temples and schools throughout India. More importantly, though, he worked to spread Buddhism into areas outside of India. You will learn more about Asoka and his accomplishments in the next section.

Asoka sent Buddhist **missionaries**, or people who work to spread their religious beliefs, to other kingdoms in Asia. One group of these missionaries sailed to the island of Sri Lanka around 251 BC. Others followed trade routes east to what is now Myanmar and to other parts of Southeast Asia. Missionaries also went north to areas near the Himalayas.

Young Buddhist students carry gifts in Sri Lanka, one of the many places outside of India where Buddhism spread.

map zone Geography Skills

Movement After the Buddha died, his teachings were carried through much of Asia.
1. **Identify** Buddhism spread to what island south of India?
2. **Interpret** What physical feature kept Buddhist missionaries from moving directly into China?

go.hrw.com (KEYWORD: SK9 CH14)

Missionaries also introduced Buddhism to lands west of India. They founded Buddhist communities in Central Asia and Persia. They even taught about Buddhism as far away as Syria and Egypt.

Buddhism continued to grow over the centuries. Eventually, it spread via the Silk Road into China, then Korea and Japan. Through their work, missionaries taught Buddhism to millions of people.

A Split within Buddhism

Even as Buddhism spread through Asia, however, it began to change. Not all Buddhists could agree on their beliefs and practices. Eventually, disagreements between Buddhists led to a split within the religion. Two major branches of Buddhism were created—Theravada and Mahayana.

Members of the Theravada branch tried to follow the Buddha's teachings exactly as he had stated them. Mahayana Buddhists, though, believed that other people could interpret the Buddha's teachings to help people reach nirvana. Both branches have millions of believers today, but Mahayana is by far the larger branch.

READING CHECK **Sequencing** How did the Buddha's teachings spread out of India?

SUMMARY AND PREVIEW Buddhism, one of India's major religions, grew more popular once it was adopted by rulers of India's great empires. You will learn more about those empires in the next section.

Section 3 Assessment

go.hrw.com
Online Quiz
KEYWORD: SK9 HP14

Reviewing Ideas, Terms, and Places
1. **a. Identify** Who was the Buddha, and what does the term *Buddha* mean?
   b. Summarize How did Siddhartha Gautama free his mind and clarify his thinking as he searched for wisdom?
2. **a. Identify** What is **nirvana**?
   b. Contrast How are Buddhist teachings different from Hindu teachings?
   c. Elaborate Why do Buddhists believe that following the Eightfold Path leads to a better life?
3. **a. Describe** Into what lands did Buddhism spread?
   b. Summarize What role did **missionaries** play in spreading Buddhism?

Critical Thinking
4. **Finding Main Ideas** Draw a diagram like this one. Use it and your notes to identify and describe Buddhism's Four Noble Truths. Write a sentence explaining how the Truths are central to Buddhism.

FOCUS ON WRITING
5. **Considering Indian Religions** Look back over what you've just read and your notes about Hinduism. Perhaps you will want to focus your poster on ancient India's two major religions. Think about how you could design a poster around this theme.

Indian Empires

If YOU lived there...

You are a merchant in India in about 240 BC. You travel from town to town on your donkey, carrying bolts of colorful cloth. In the heat of summer, you are grateful for the banyan trees along the road. They shelter you from the blazing sun. You stop at wells for cool drinks of water and rest houses for a break in your journey. You know these are all the work of your king, Asoka.

How do you feel about your king?

BUILDING BACKGROUND For centuries after the Aryan migration, India was divided into small states. Each state had its own ruler and laws. Then, in the 300s BC, a foreign general, Alexander the Great, took over and unified part of northwestern India. Soon after Alexander departed, a strong leader united India.

Mauryan Empire Unifies India

In the 320s BC a military leader named Candragupta Maurya (kuhn-druh-GOOP-tuh MOUR-yuh) rose to power in northern India. Using an army of **mercenaries**, or hired soldiers, he seized control of the entire northern part of India. By doing so, he founded the Mauryan Empire. Mauryan rule lasted for about 150 years.

The Mauryan Empire

Candragupta Maurya ruled his empire with the help of a complex government. It included a network of spies and a huge army of some 600,000 soldiers. The army also had thousands of war elephants and thousands of chariots. In return for the army's protection, farmers paid a heavy tax to the government.

In 301 BC Candragupta decided to become a Jainist monk. To do so, he had to give up his throne. He passed the throne to his son, who continued to expand the empire. Before long, the Mauryas ruled all of northern India and much of central India as well.

Asoka

Around 270 BC Candragupta's grandson Asoka (uh-SOH-kuh) became king. Asoka was a strong ruler, the strongest of all the Mauryan emperors. He extended Mauryan rule over most of India. In conquering other kingdoms, Asoka made his own empire both stronger and richer.

For many years, Asoka watched his armies fight bloody battles against other peoples. A few years into his rule, however, Asoka converted to Buddhism. When he did, he swore that he would not launch any more wars of conquest.

After converting to Buddhism, Asoka had the time and resources to improve the lives of his people. He had wells dug and roads built throughout the empire. Along these roads, workers planted shade trees, built rest houses for travelers, and raised large stone pillars carved with Buddhist **edicts**, or laws. Asoka also encouraged the spread of Buddhism in India and the rest of Asia. As you read in the previous section, he sent missionaries to lands all over Asia.

Asoka died in 233 BC, and the empire began to fall apart soon afterward. His sons fought for power, and invaders threatened the empire. In 184 BC the last Mauryan king was killed by one of his generals. India divided into smaller states once again.

READING CHECK Finding Main Ideas How did the Mauryans gain control of most of India?

FOCUS ON READING

What were some key events in Asoka's life? In what order did they occur?

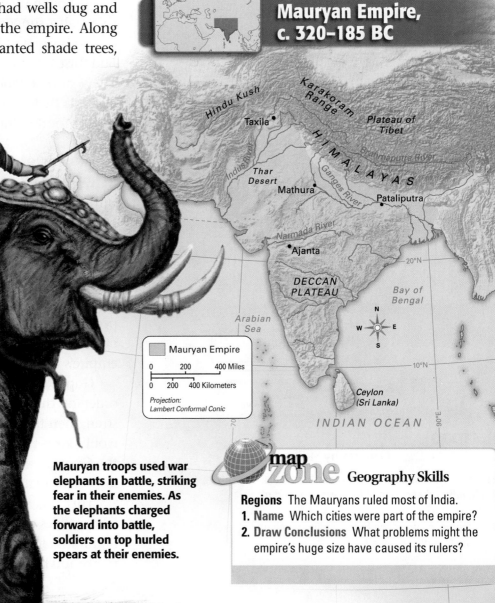

Mauryan Empire, c. 320–185 BC

Mauryan Empire

0   200   400 Miles
0   200   400 Kilometers

Projection: Lambert Conformal Conic

Mauryan troops used war elephants in battle, striking fear in their enemies. As the elephants charged forward into battle, soldiers on top hurled spears at their enemies.

map zone Geography Skills

Regions The Mauryans ruled most of India.
1. **Name** Which cities were part of the empire?
2. **Draw Conclusions** What problems might the empire's huge size have caused its rulers?

Gupta Rulers Promote Hinduism

After the collapse of the Mauryan Empire, India remained divided for about 500 years. During that period, Buddhism continued to prosper and spread in India, and so the popularity of Hinduism declined.

A New Hindu Empire

ACADEMIC VOCABULARY

establish to set up or create

Eventually, however, a new dynasty was **established** in India. It was the Gupta (GOOP-tuh) dynasty, which took over India around AD 320. Under the Guptas, India was once again united, and it once again became prosperous.

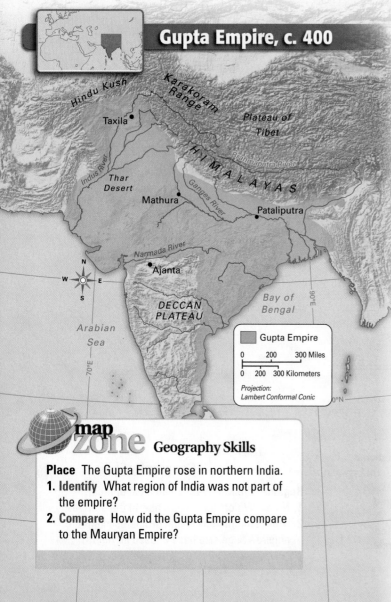

Gupta Empire, c. 400

Geography Skills

Place The Gupta Empire rose in northern India.
1. **Identify** What region of India was not part of the empire?
2. **Compare** How did the Gupta Empire compare to the Mauryan Empire?

The first Gupta emperor was Candra Gupta I. Although their names are similar, he was not related to Candragupta Maurya. From his base in northern India, Candra Gupta's armies invaded and conquered neighboring lands. Eventually, he brought much of the northern part of India under his control.

Indian civilization flourished under the Gupta rulers. These rulers were Hindu, so Hinduism became India's dominant religion. Gupta kings built many Hindu temples, some of which became models for later Indian architecture. They also promoted a revival of Hindu writings and worship practices.

Although they were Hindus, the Gupta rulers also supported the religious beliefs of Buddhism and Jainism. They promoted Buddhist art and built Buddhist temples. They also established a university at Nalanda that became one of Asia's greatest centers for Buddhist studies.

Gupta Society

In 375 Emperor Candra Gupta II took the throne in India. Gupta society reached its high point during his rule. Under Candra Gupta II, the empire continued to grow, eventually stretching all the way across northern India. At the same time, the empire's economy strengthened, and so people prospered. They created fine works of art and literature. Outsiders admired the empire's wealth and beauty.

Gupta kings believed the strict social order of the Hindu caste system would strengthen their rule. They also thought it would keep the empire stable. As a result, the Guptas considered the caste system an important part of Indian society.

This was not good news for women whose roles were limited by caste rules. Brahmins taught that a woman's role was to marry and have children. Women couldn't even choose their own husbands. Parents arranged all marriages. Once married, wives had few rights. They were expected to serve their husbands. Widows had an even lower social status than other women.

Gupta rule remained strong in India until the late 400s. At that time the Huns, a group from Central Asia, invaded India from the northwest. Their fierce attacks drained the Gupta Empire of its power and wealth. As the Hun armies marched farther into India, the Guptas lost hope.

By the middle of the 500s, Gupta rule had ended, and India had divided into small kingdoms yet again.

READING CHECK **Summarizing** What was the Gupta dynasty's position on religion?

SUMMARY AND PREVIEW The Mauryans and Guptas united much of India in their empires. Next, you will learn about their many achievements.

Section 4 Assessment

go.hrw.com
Online Quiz
KEYWORD: SK9 HP14

Reviewing Ideas, Terms, and Places

1. **a. Identify** Who created the Mauryan Empire?
   b. Summarize What happened after Asoka became a Buddhist?
   c. Elaborate Why do you think many people consider Asoka the greatest of all Mauryan rulers?
2. **a. Recall** What religion did most of the Gupta rulers belong to?
   b. Compare and Contrast How were the rulers Candragupta Maurya and Candra Gupta I alike, and how were they different?
   c. Evaluate Do you think the Gupta enforcement of caste rules was a good idea? Why or why not?

Critical Thinking

3. **Categorizing** Draw a chart like this one. Fill it with facts about India's rulers.

Ruler	Dynasty	Accomplishments

FOCUS ON WRITING

4. **Comparing Indian Empires** Another possible topic for your poster would be a comparison of the Mauryan and Gupta empires. Jot down ideas on what you could show in such a comparison.

Asoka

How can one decision change a man's entire life?

When did he live? before 230 BC

Where did he live? Asoka's empire included much of northern and central India.

What did he do? After fighting many bloody wars to expand his empire, Asoka gave up violence and converted to Buddhism.

Why is he important? Asoka is one of the most respected rulers in Indian history and one of the most important figures in the history of Buddhism. As a devout Buddhist, Asoka worked for years to spread the Buddha's teachings. In addition to sending missionaries around Asia, he had huge columns carved with Buddhist teachings raised all over India. Largely through his efforts, Buddhism became one of Asia's main religions.

Generalizing How did Asoka's life change after he became Buddhist?

KEY EVENTS

c. 270 BC Asoka becomes the Mauryan emperor.

c. 261 BC Asoka's empire reaches its greatest size.

c. 261 BC Asoka becomes a Buddhist.

c. 251 BC Asoka begins to send Buddhist missionaries to other parts of Asia.

This Buddhist shrine, located in Sanchi, India, was built by Asoka.

Indian Achievements

If YOU lived there...

You are a traveler in western India in the 300s. You are visiting a cave temple that is carved into a mountain cliff. Inside the cave it is cool and quiet. Huge columns rise all around you. You don't feel you're alone, for the walls and ceilings are covered with paintings. They are filled with lively scenes and figures. In the center is a large statue with calm, peaceful features.

How does this cave make you feel?

BUILDING BACKGROUND The Mauryan and Gupta empires united most of India politically. During these empires, Indian artists, writers, scholars, and scientists made great advances. Some of their works are still studied and admired today.

Religious Art

The Indians of the Mauryan and Gupta periods created great works of art, many of them religious. Many of their paintings and sculptures illustrated either Hindu or Buddhist teachings. Magnificent temples—both Hindu and Buddhist—were built all around India. They remain some of the most beautiful buildings in the world today.

Temples

Early Hindu temples were small, stone structures. They had flat roofs and contained only one or two rooms. In the Gupta period, though, temple architecture became more complex. Gupta temples were topped by huge towers and were covered with carvings of the god worshipped inside.

Buddhist temples of the Gupta period are also impressive. Some Buddhists carved entire temples out of mountainsides. The most famous such temples are at Ajanta and Ellora. Builders filled the caves there with beautiful paintings and sculpture.

What You Will Learn...

Main Ideas

1. Indian artists created great works of religious art.
2. Sanskrit literature flourished during the Gupta period.
3. The Indians made scientific advances in metalworking, medicine, and other sciences.

The Big Idea

The people of ancient India made great contributions to the arts and sciences.

Key Terms

metallurgy, *p. 456*
alloys, *p. 456*
Hindu-Arabic numerals, *p. 456*
inoculation, *p. 456*
astronomy, *p. 457*

TAKING NOTES As you read, look for information on achievements of ancient India. Take notes about these achievements in a chart.

Type of Achievement	Details about Achievements
Religious Art	
Sanskrit Literature	
Scientific Advances	

Temple Architecture

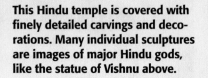

This Hindu temple is covered with finely detailed carvings and decorations. Many individual sculptures are images of major Hindu gods, like the statue of Vishnu above.

Another type of Buddhist temple was the stupa. Stupas had domed roofs and were built to house sacred items from the life of the Buddha. Many of them were covered with detailed carvings.

Paintings and Sculpture

The Gupta period also saw the creation of countless works of art, both paintings and statues. Painting was a greatly respected profession, and India was home to many skilled artists. However, we don't know the names of many artists from this period. Instead, we know the names of many rich and powerful members of Gupta society who paid artists to create works of beauty and religious and social significance.

Most Indian paintings of the Gupta period are clear and colorful. Some of them show graceful Indians wearing fine jewelry and stylish clothes. Such paintings offer us a glimpse of the Indians' daily and ceremonial lives.

Artists from both of India's major religions, Hinduism and Buddhism, drew on their beliefs to create their works. As a result, many of the finest paintings of ancient India are found in temples. Hindu painters drew hundreds of gods on temple walls and entrances. Buddhists covered the walls and ceilings of temples with scenes from the life of the Buddha.

Indian sculptors also created great works. Many of their statues were made for Buddhist cave temples. In addition to the temples' intricately carved columns, sculptors carved statues of kings and the Buddha. Some of these statues tower over the cave entrances. Hindu temples also featured impressive statues of their gods. In fact, the walls of some temples, such as the one pictured above, were completely covered with carvings and images.

READING CHECK **Summarizing** How did religion influence ancient Indian art?

Sanskrit Literature

As you read earlier, Sanskrit was the main language of the ancient Aryans. During the Mauryan and Gupta periods, many works of Sanskrit literature were created. These works were later translated into many other languages.

Religious Epics

The greatest of these Sanskrit writings are two religious epics, the *Mahabharata* (muh-HAH-BAH-ruh-tuh) and the *Ramayana* (rah-MAH-yuh-nuh). Still popular in India, the *Mahabharata* is one of the longest literary works ever written. It is a story about a struggle between two families for control of a kingdom. Included within the story are long passages about Hindu beliefs. The most famous is called the *Bhagavad Gita* (BUG-uh-vuhd GEE-tah).

The *Ramayana*, another great epic, tells about a prince named Rama. In truth, the prince was the god Vishnu in human form. He had become human so he could rid the world of demons. He also had to rescue his wife, a princess named Sita. For centuries, characters from the *Ramayana* have been seen as models for how Indians should behave. For example, Rama is seen as the ideal ruler and his relationship with Sita as the ideal marriage.

Other Works

Writers in the Gupta period also created plays, poetry, and other types of literature. One famous writer of this time was Kalidasa (kahl-ee-DAHS-uh). His work was so brilliant that Candra Gupta II hired him to write plays for the royal court.

Sometime before 500, Indian writers also produced a book of stories called the *Panchatantra* (PUHN-chuh-TAHN-truh). The stories in this collection were intended to teach lessons. They praise people for cleverness and quick thinking. Each story ends with a message about winning friends, losing property, waging war, or some other idea. For example, the message below warns listeners to think about what they are doing before they act.

" The good and bad of given schemes
Wise thought must first reveal:
The stupid heron saw his chicks
Provide a mongoose meal.*"*
–from the *Panchatantra*, translated
by Arthur William Ryder

Eventually, translations of this popular collection spread throughout the world. It became popular in countries even as far away as Europe.

READING CHECK **Categorizing** What types of literature did writers of ancient India create?

In this illustration of the *Ramayana*, the monkey king orders the monkey general Hanuman to find Sita. Hanuman helped Rama defeat the demons and win back Sita. Many Indians view him as a model of devotion and loyalty.

Medicine
In this modern painting, the Indian surgeon Susruta performs surgery on a patient. The ancient Indians had an advanced knowledge of medicine.

Metalworking
The Indians were expert metalworkers. This gold coin shows the emperor Candra Gupta II.

Scientific Advances

Indian achievements were not limited to art, architecture, and literature. Indian scholars also made important advances in metalworking, math, and the sciences.

Metalworking

The ancient Indians were pioneers of **metallurgy** (MET-uhl-uhr-jee), the science of working with metals. Their knowledge allowed them to create high-quality tools and weapons. The Indians also knew **processes** for mixing metals to create **alloys**, mixtures of two or more metals. Alloys are sometimes stronger or easier to work with than pure metals.

Metalworkers made their strongest products out of iron. Indian iron was very hard and pure. These features made the iron a valuable trade item.

During the Gupta dynasty, metalworkers built the famous Iron Pillar near Delhi. Unlike most iron, which rusts easily, the pillar is very resistant to rust. The tall column still attracts crowds of visitors. Scholars study this column even today to learn the Indians' secrets.

ACADEMIC VOCABULARY
process a series of steps by which a task is accomplished

THE IMPACT TODAY
People still get inoculations against many diseases.

Mathematics and Other Sciences

Gupta scholars also made advances in math and science. In fact, they were among the most skilled mathematicians of their day. They developed many of the elements of our modern math system. The very numbers we use today are called **Hindu-Arabic numerals** because they were created by Indian scholars and brought to Europe by Arabs. The Indians were also the first people to create the zero. Although it may seem like a small thing, modern math wouldn't be possible without the zero.

The ancient Indians were also very skilled in the medical sciences. As early as the AD 100s, doctors were writing their knowledge down in textbooks. Among the skills these books describe is how to make medicines from plants and minerals.

Besides curing people with medicines, Indian doctors knew how to protect them against diseases. They used **inoculation** (i-nah-kyuh-LAY-shuhn), the practice of injecting a person with a small dose of a virus to help him or her build a defense to a disease. By fighting off this small dose, the body learns to protect itself.

Mathematics

This book is a copy of an ancient one from about AD 500 that summarized Indian knowledge of mathematics. It discussed basic arithmetic, fractions, and a counting system.

Astronomy

The Gupta made great advances in astronomy, despite their lack of modern devices such as telescopes. They used devices like this one from the 1700s to observe and map the stars.

ANALYSIS SKILL **ANALYZING VISUALS**

What are some areas of science that people studied in ancient India?

For people who were injured, Indian doctors could perform surgery. Surgeons repaired broken bones, treated wounds, removed infected tonsils, reconstructed broken noses, and even reattached torn earlobes! If they could find no other cure for an illness, doctors would cast magic spells to help people recover.

Indian interest in **astronomy**, the study of stars and planets, dates back to early times as well. Indian astronomers knew of seven of the nine planets in our solar system. They knew that the sun was a star and that the planets revolved around it. They also knew that the earth was a sphere and that it spun on its axis. In addition, they could predict eclipses of the sun and the moon.

READING CHECK **Finding Main Ideas** What were two Indian achievements in mathematics?

SUMMARY AND PREVIEW From a group of cities along the Indus and Sarasvati Rivers, India grew into a major empire whose people made great achievements. In the next chapter, you'll read about another civilization that experienced similar growth—China.

go.hrw.com
Online Quiz
KEYWORD: SK9 HP14

Section 5 Assessment

Reviewing Ideas, Terms, and Places

1. **a. Describe** What did Hindu temples of the Gupta period look like?
   b. Analyze How can you tell that Indian artists were well respected?
   c. Evaluate Why do you think Hindu and Buddhist temples contained great works of art?
2. **a. Identify** What is the *Bhagavad Gita*?
   b. Explain Why were the stories of the *Panchatantra* written?
   c. Elaborate Why do you think people are still interested in ancient Sanskrit epics today?
3. **a. Define** What is **metallurgy**?
   b. Explain Why do we call the numbers we use today **Hindu-Arabic numerals**?

Critical Thinking

4. **Categorizing** Draw a chart like this one. Identify the scientific advances that fall into each category below.

Metallurgy	Math	Medicine	Astronomy

FOCUS ON WRITING

5. **Highlighting Indian Achievements** List the Indian achievements you could include on a poster. Consider these topics as well as your topic ideas from earlier sections in this chapter. Choose one topic for your poster.

Social Studies Skills

Chart and Graph

Critical Thinking

Geography

Study

Comparing Maps

Learn

Maps are a necessary tool in the study of both history and geography. Sometimes, however, a map does not contain all the information you need. In those cases, you may have to compare two or more maps and combine what is shown on each.

For example, if you look at a physical map of India you can see what landforms are in a region. You can then look at a population map to see how many people live in that region. From this comparison, you can conclude how the region's landforms affect its population distribution.

Practice

Compare the two maps on this page to answer the following questions.

1 What was the northeastern boundary of the Gupta Empire? What is the physical landscape like there?

2 What region of India was never part of the Gupta Empire? Based on the physical map, what might have been one reason for this?

Apply

Choose two maps from this chapter or two maps from the Atlas in this book. Study the two maps and then write three questions that someone could answer by comparing them. Remember that the questions should have people look at both maps to determine the correct answers.

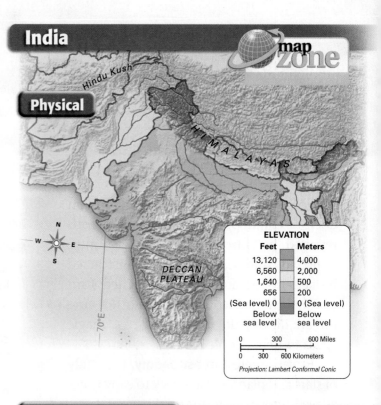

India

Physical

Hindu Kush

HIMALAYAS

DECCAN PLATEAU

70°E

ELEVATION

Feet		Meters
13,120		4,000
6,560		2,000
1,640		500
656		200
(Sea level) 0		0 (Sea level)
Below sea level		Below sea level

0   300   600 Miles
0   300   600 Kilometers
Projection: Lambert Conformal Conic

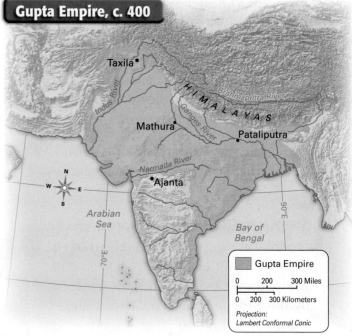

Gupta Empire, c. 400

Taxila

Indus River

HIMALAYAS

Brahmaputra River

Mathura

Ganges River

Pataliputra

Narmada River

Ajanta

Arabian Sea

70°E

90°E

Bay of Bengal

Gupta Empire

0   200   300 Miles
0   200   300 Kilometers
Projection: Lambert Conformal Conic

Geography's Impact
video series
Review the video to answer the closing question:
Do you think enlightenment is an achievable goal in today's world? Why or why not?

Visual Summary

Use the visual summary below to help you review the main ideas of the chapter.

QUICK FACTS

The Harappan civilization began in the Indus River Valley.

Hinduism and Buddhism both developed in India.

Indians made great advances in art, literature, science, and other fields.

Reviewing Vocabulary, Terms, and Places

Fill in the blanks with the correct term or name from this chapter.

1. _____ are hired soldiers.

2. A _____ is a division of people into groups based on birth, wealth, or occupation.

3. Hindus believe in _____, the belief that they will be reborn many times after death.

4. Harappa and _____ were the largest cities of the Harappan civilization.

5. The focusing of the mind on spiritual things is called _____.

6. People who work to spread their religious beliefs are called _____.

7. People who practice _____ use only peaceful ways to achieve change.

8. Indian civilization first developed in the valley of the _____.

9. A mixture of metals is called an _____.

Comprehension and Critical Thinking

SECTION 1 *(Pages 430–435)*

10. **a. Describe** What caused floods on the Indus River, and what was the result of those floods?

    b. Contrast How was Aryan culture different from Harappan culture?

    c. Elaborate In what ways was Harappan society an advanced civilization?

SECTION 2 *(Pages 436–441)*

11. **a. Identify** Who were the Brahmins, and what role did they play in Aryan society?

    b. Analyze How do Hindus believe karma affects reincarnation?

    c. Elaborate Hinduism has been called both a polytheistic religion—one that worships many gods—and a monotheistic religion—one that worships only one god. Why do you think this is so?

SECTION 3 (Pages 442–447)

12. a. Describe What did the Buddha say caused human suffering?

b. Analyze How did Buddhism grow and change after the Buddha died?

c. Elaborate Why did the Buddha's teachings about nirvana appeal to many people of lower castes?

SECTION 4 (Pages 448–451)

13. a. Identify What was Candragupta Maurya's greatest accomplishment?

b. Compare and Contrast What was one similarity between the Mauryans and the Guptas? What was one difference between them?

c. Predict How might Indian history have been different if Asoka had not become a Buddhist?

SECTION 5 (Pages 453–457)

14. a. Describe What kinds of religious art did the ancient Indians create?

b. Make Inferences Why do you think religious discussions are included in the *Mahabharata*?

c. Evaluate Which of the ancient Indians' achievements do you think is most impressive? Why?

Using the Internet

go.hrw.com KEYWORD: SK9 CH14

15. Activity: Making a Brochure In this chapter, you learned about India's early history. That history was largely shaped by India's geography. Enter the activity keyword to research the geography and civilizations of India, taking notes as you go along. Finally, use the interactive brochure template to present what you have found.

Social Studies Skills

Comparing Maps *Study the physical and population maps of South and East Asia in the Atlas. Then answer the following questions.*

16. Along what river in northeastern India is the population density very high?

17. Why do you think fewer people live in far northwestern India than in the northeast?

FOCUS ON READING AND WRITING

18. Sequencing Arrange the following list of events in the order in which they happened. Then write a brief paragraph describing the events, using clue words such as *then* and *later* to show the proper sequence.

- The Gupta Empire is created.
- Harappan civilization begins.
- The Aryans invade India.
- The Mauryan Empire is formed.

19. Designing Your Poster Now that you have a topic for your poster, it's time to create it. On a large sheet of paper or poster board, write a title that identifies your topic. Then draw pictures, maps, or diagrams that illustrate it. Next to each picture, write a short caption to identify what the picture, map, or diagram shows.

Map Activity

20. Ancient India On a separate sheet of paper, match the letters on the map with their correct labels.

Mohenjo Daro	Indus River
Harappa	Ganges River
Bodh Gaya	

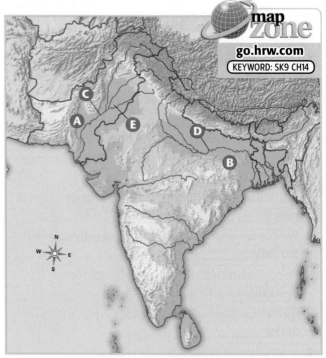

go.hrw.com KEYWORD: SK9 CH14

DIRECTIONS (1–7): **For each statement or question, write on a separate answer sheet the *number* of the word or expression that, of those given, best completes the statement or answers the question.**

1 **The earliest civilizations in India developed along which river?**

(1) Indus

(2) Ganges

(3) Brahmaputra

(4) Krishna

2 **The people of which *varna* in early India had the hardest lives?**

(1) Brahmins

(2) Kshatriyas

(3) Sudras

(4) Vaisyas

3 **What is the *main* goal of people who follow Buddhism as it was taught by the Buddha?**

(1) wealth

(2) rebirth

(3) missionary work

(4) reaching nirvana

4 **Which Indian ruler greatly enlarged his empire before giving up violence and promoting the spread of Buddhism?**

(1) Candragupta Maurya

(2) Asoka

(3) Buddha

(4) Mahavira

5 **Early India's contributions to world civilization included**

(1) developing the world's first calendar.

(2) creating what is now called algebra.

(3) inventing the plow and the wheel.

(4) introducing zero to the number system.

6 **The concept of nirvana is central to which two ancient Indian religions?**

(1) Hinduism and Islam

(2) Buddhism and Judaism

(3) Buddhism and Hinduism

(4) Islam and Judaism

7 **According to Hindu teachings, the universal spirit of which everything in the world is part is called**

(1) Vishnu.

(2) Brahman.

(3) Siva.

(4) Buddha.

Base your answer to question 8 on the text excerpt below and on your knowledge of social studies.

"From anger comes confusion;
from confusion memory lapses;
from broken memory understanding is lost;
from loss of understanding, he is ruined.

But a man of inner strength
whose senses experience objects
without attraction and hatred,
in self control, finds serenity."

–from the *Bhagavad Gita*,
translated by Barbara Stoler Miller

8 **Constructed-Response Question** **The passage from the *Bhagavad Gita* above is advice about how a person can reach nirvana. According to this passage, what will a person find if he or she has inner strength and self control?**

Ancient Civilizations of Asia—China

CENTRAL ASIA

FOCUS QUESTION

How did ancient civilizations contribute to the development of the Eastern Hemisphere?

Traders on the Silk Road

What You Will Learn...

In this chapter you will learn about the history and culture of ancient China. China was one of the world's early centers of civilization. You will also study the powerful dynasties that arose to rule China and reshape Chinese culture.

SOUTH ASIA

0	250	500 Miles
0	250	500 Kilometers

Projection: Two-Point Equidistant

FOCUS ON READING AND WRITING

Understanding Chronological Order When you read about history, it is important to keep track of the order in which events happened. You can often use words in the text to help figure this order out. **See the lesson, Understanding Chronological Order, on page S18.**

Writing a Magazine Article You are a freelance writer who has been asked to write a magazine article about the achievements of the ancient Chinese. As you read this chapter, you will collect information. Then you will use the information to write your magazine article.

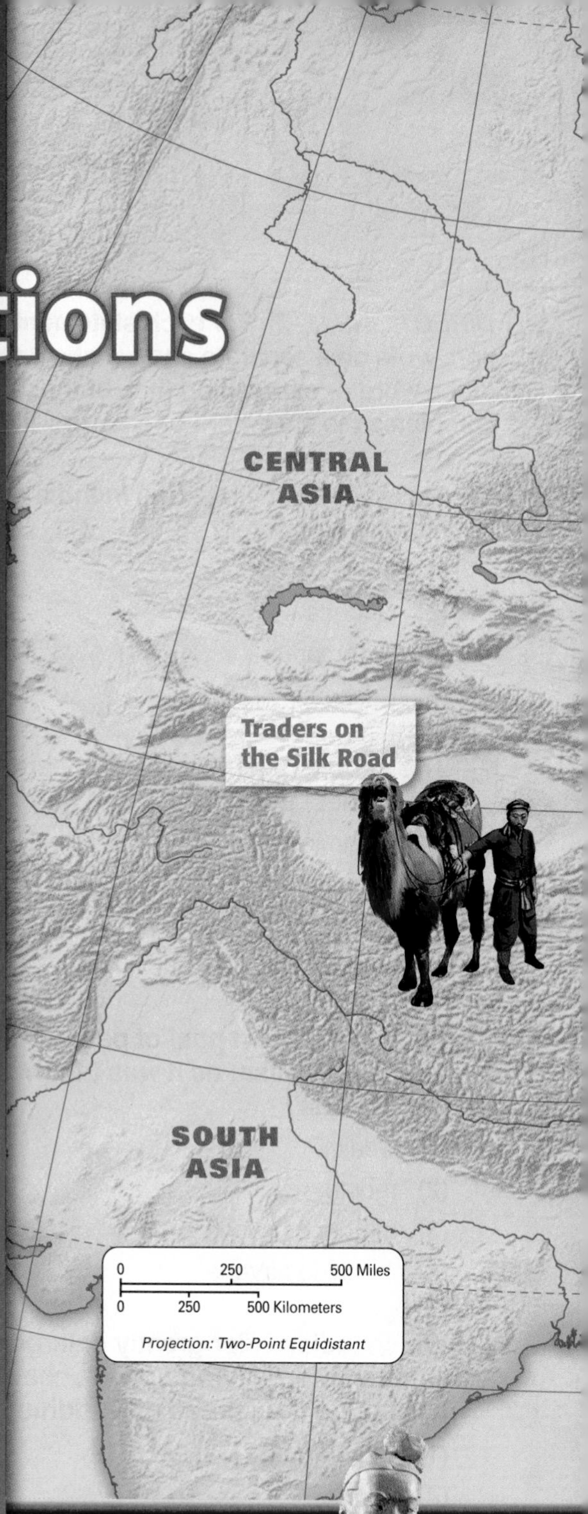

Early China The first dynasties to rule China left behind artifacts such as this clay figure of a soldier.

Ancient China, 1600 BC–AD 1450

map zone

Place China was the birthplace of one of the world's oldest civilizations, a civilization that made huge advances in art and science.

1. **Name** What were three large cities in ancient China?
2. **Draw Conclusions** Do you think China faced more threats from the north or south? Why?

Mongols

ASIA

The Great Wall

Beijing

Sea of Japan (East Sea)

30°N

Yellow Sea

Kaifeng

Xi'an (Chang'an)

Qin dynasty emperor

East China Sea

PACIFIC OCEAN

Tropic of Cancer

20°N

130°E

Porcelain vase

120°E

HOLT

Geography's Impact
video series
Watch the video to understand the impact of Confucius on China today.

SOUTHEAST ASIA

110°E

South China Sea

Tang and Song Dynasties The Chinese invented many items that we still use today, including fireworks.

Yuan and Ming Dynasties During the Yuan and Ming dynasties, Beijing became China's largest city and a center of Chinese culture.

Early China

Main Ideas

1. Chinese civilization began along two rivers.
2. The Shang dynasty was the first known dynasty to rule China.
3. The Zhou and Qin dynasties changed Chinese society and made great advances.

The Big Idea

Early Chinese history was shaped by three dynasties—the Shang, the Zhou, and the Qin.

Key Terms and Places

Chang Jiang, *p. 464*
Huang He, *p. 464*
mandate of heaven, *p. 466*
Xi'an, *p. 467*
Great Wall, *p. 467*

 Draw a chart like the one below. As you read this section, fill in the chart with details about each period in China's early history.

Beginnings	Shang dynasty	Zhou dynasty	Qin dynasty

If YOU lived there...

You are the ruler of China, and hundreds of thousands of people look to you for protection. For many years, your country has lived in peace. Large cities have grown up, and traders travel freely from place to place. Now, however, a new threat looms. Invaders from the north are threatening China's borders. Frightened by the ferocity of these invaders, the people turn to you for help.

What will you do to protect your people?

BUILDING BACKGROUND As in India, people in China first settled near rivers. Two rivers were particularly important in early China— the Huang He and the Chang Jiang. Along these rivers, people began to farm, cities grew up, and China's government was born. The head of that government was an emperor, the ruler of all China.

Chinese Civilization Begins

As early as 7000 BC people had begun to farm in China. They grew rice in the middle **Chang Jiang** Valley. North, along the **Huang He**, the land was better for growing cereals such as millet and wheat. At the same time, people domesticated animals such as pigs and sheep. Supported by these sources of food, China's population grew. Villages appeared along the rivers.

Some of the villages along the Huang He grew into large towns. Walls surrounded these towns to defend them against floods and hostile neighbors. In towns like these, the Chinese left many artifacts, such as arrowheads, fishhooks, tools, and pottery. Some village sites even contained pieces of cloth.

Over time, Chinese culture became more advanced. After 3000 BC people began to use potter's wheels to make many types of pottery. They also learned to dig water wells. As populations grew, villages spread out over larger areas in both northern and southeastern China.

READING CHECK Analyzing When and where did China's earliest civilizations develop?

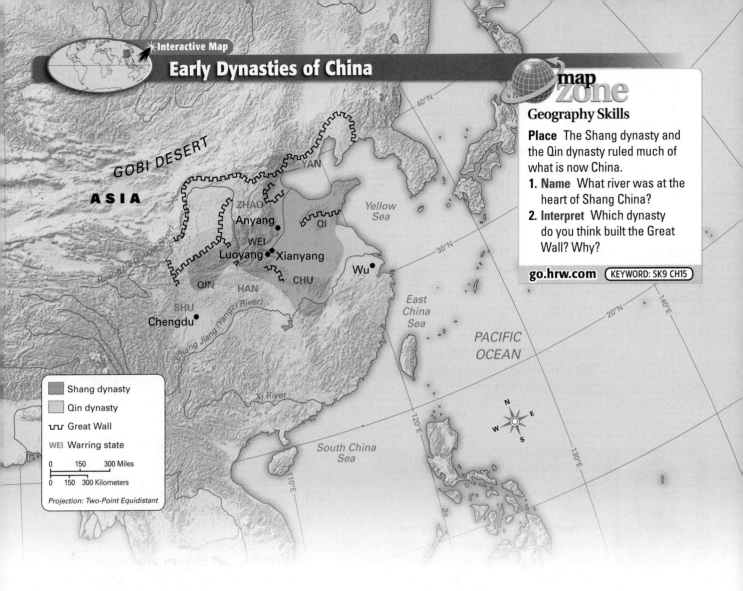

GOBI DESERT

ASIA

ZHAO

Anyang

YAN

QI

WEI

Luoyang • Xianyang

QIN

HAN

CHU

Wu

SHU

Chengdu

Huang He (Yellow River)

Chang Jiang (Yangzi River)

Xi River

Yellow Sea

East China Sea

PACIFIC OCEAN

South China Sea

40°N

30°N

20°N

140°E

130°E

120°E

110°E

Legend:

- Shang dynasty
- Qin dynasty
- Great Wall
- WEI Warring state

0   150   300 Miles
0   150   300 Kilometers

Projection: Two-Point Equidistant

map zone

Geography Skills

Place The Shang dynasty and the Qin dynasty ruled much of what is now China.

1. **Name** What river was at the heart of Shang China?
2. **Interpret** Which dynasty do you think built the Great Wall? Why?

go.hrw.com KEYWORD: SK9 CH15

Shang Dynasty

As time passed, dynasties, or families, of strong rulers began to take power in China. The first dynasty for which we have clear evidence is the Shang, which was firmly established by the 1500s BC. Strongest in the Huang He Valley, the Shang ruled a broad area of northern China, as you can see on the map. Shang emperors ruled in China until the 1100s BC.

The Shang made many advances, including China's first writing system. This system used more than 2,000 symbols to express words or ideas. Although the system has gone through changes over the years, the Chinese symbols used today are based on those of the Shang period.

Many examples of Shang writing that we have found were on cattle bones and turtle shells. Priests had carved questions about the future on bones or shells, which were then heated, causing them to crack. The priests believed they could "read" these cracks to predict the future.

In addition to writing, the Shang also made other achievements. Artisans made beautiful bronze containers for cooking and religious ceremonies. They also made axes, knives, and ornaments from jade. Soldiers developed war chariots, powerful bows, and bronze armor. The Shang also invented a calendar based on the cycles of the moon.

READING CHECK **Summarizing** What were two Shang achievements?

Zhou and Qin Dynasties

The Shang dynasty was only the first of many dynasties described in Chinese records. After the Shang lost power, other dynasties rose up to take control of China. Two of those dynasties were the Zhou (JOH) and the Qin (CHIN).

Zhou Dynasty

FOCUS ON READING

Which dynasty ruled earlier, the Zhou or the Qin?

In the 1100s, the Shang rulers of China were overthrown in a rebellion. In their place, the rebels from the western part of China took power. This event marked the beginning of the Zhou dynasty. This dynasty lasted longer than any other in Chinese history. Zhou rulers held power in China until 771 BC.

The Zhou claimed that they had been chosen by heaven to rule China. They believed that no one could rule without heaven's permission. This idea that heaven chose China's ruler and gave him or her power was called the **mandate of heaven**.

Under the Zhou, a new political order formed in China. The emperor was at the top of society. Everything in China belonged to him, and everyone had to be loyal to him.

Emperors gave land to people in exchange for loyalty or military service. Those people who received this land became lords. Below the lords were peasants, or farmers who owned little land. In addition to growing their own food, peasants had to grow food for lords.

Warring States Period

The Zhou political system broke down as lords grew less loyal to the emperors. When invaders attacked the capital in 771 BC, many lords would not fight. As a result, the emperor was overthrown. China broke apart into many kingdoms that fought each other. This time of disorder in China is called the Warring States period.

BIOGRAPHY

Emperor Shi Huangdi
(c. 259–210 BC)

Shi Huangdi was a powerful emperor and a very strict one. He demanded that everyone in China believe the same things he did. To prevent people from having other ideas, he ordered all books that did not agree with his beliefs burned. When a group of scholars protested the burning of these books, Shi Huangdi had them buried alive. These actions led many Chinese people to resent the emperor. As a result, they were eager to bring the Qin dynasty to an end.

In 1974 archaeologists found the tomb of Emperor Shi Huangdi near Xi'an and made an amazing discovery. Buried close to the emperor was an army of more than 6,000 life-size terra-cotta, or clay, soldiers. They were designed to be with Shi Huangdi in the afterlife. In other nearby chambers of the tomb there were another 1,400 clay figures of cavalry and chariots.

Qin Dynasty

The Warring States period came to an end when one state became strong enough to defeat all its rivals. That state was called Qin. In 221 BC, a king from Qin managed to unify all of China under his control and name himself emperor.

As emperor, the king took a new name. He called himself Shi Huangdi (SHEE hwahng-dee), a name that means "first emperor." Shi Huangdi was a very strict ruler, but he was an effective ruler as well. He expanded the size of China both to the north and to the south, as the map at the beginning of this section shows.

Shi Huangdi greatly changed Chinese politics. Unlike the Zhou rulers, he refused to share his power with anyone. Lords who had enjoyed many rights before now lost those rights. In addition, he ordered thousands of noble families to move to his capital, now called **Xi'an** (SHEE-AHN). He thought nobles that he kept nearby would be less likely to rebel against him.

The Qin dynasty did not last long. While Shi Huangdi lived, he was strong enough to keep China unified. The rulers who followed him, however, were not as strong. In fact, China began to break apart within a few years of Shi Huangdi's death. Rebellions began all around China, and the country fell into civil war.

Qin Achievements

Although the Qin did not rule for long, they saw great advances in China. As emperor, Shi Huangdi worked to make sure that people all over China acted and thought the same way. He created a system of laws that would apply equally to people in all parts of China. He also set up a new system of money. Before, people in each region had used local currencies. He also created a uniform system of writing that eliminated minor differences between regions.

The Qin's best known achievements, though, were in building. Under the Qin, the Chinese built a huge network of roads and canals. These roads and canals linked distant parts of the empire to make travel and trade easier.

To protect China from invasion, Shi Huangdi built the **Great Wall**, a barrier that linked earlier walls that stood near China's northern border. Building the wall took years of labor from hundreds of thousands of workers. Later dynasties added to the wall, parts of which still stand today.

SUMMARY AND PREVIEW Early Chinese history was shaped by the Shang, Zhou, and Qin dynasties. Next, you will read about another strong dynasty, the Han.

Section 1 Assessment

Reviewing Ideas, Terms, and Places

1. **a. Identify** On what rivers did Chinese civilization begin?
   b. Analyze What advances did the early Chinese make?
2. **a. Describe** What area did the Shang rule?
   b. Evaluate What do you think was the Shang dynasty's most important achievement? Why?
3. **a. Define** What is the **mandate of heaven**?
   b. Generalize How did Shi Huangdi change China?

Critical Thinking

4. **Analyzing** Draw a chart like the one shown here. Using your notes, write details about the achievements and political system of China's early dynasties.

	Achievements	Political System
Shang		
Zhou		
Qin		

FOCUS ON WRITING

5. **Identifying Advances** The Shang, Zhou, and Qin made some of the greatest advances in Chinese history. Which of these will you mention in your magazine article? Write down some notes.

The Han Dynasty

What You Will Learn...

Main Ideas

1. Han dynasty government was largely based on the ideas of Confucius.
2. Han China supported and strengthened family life.
3. The Han made many achievements in art, literature, and learning.

The Big Idea

The Han dynasty created a new form of government that valued family, art, and learning.

Key Terms

sundial, *p. 472*
seismograph, *p. 472*
acupuncture, *p. 473*

TAKING NOTES As you read, take notes on Han government, family life, and achievements. Use a diagram like the one here to help you organize your notes.

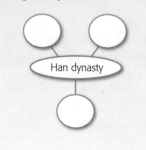

If **YOU** lived there...

You are a young Chinese student from a poor family. Your family has worked hard to give you a good education so that you can get a government job and have a great future. Your friends laugh at you. They say that only boys from wealthy families win the good jobs. They think it is better to join the army.

Will you take the exam or join the army? Why?

BUILDING BACKGROUND Though it was harsh, the rule of the first Qin emperor helped to unify northern China. With the building of what would become the Great Wall, he strengthened defenses in the north. But his successor could not hold on to power. The Qin gave way to a new dynasty that would last 400 years.

Han Dynasty Government

When the Qin dynasty collapsed, many groups fought for power. After years of fighting, an army led by Liu Bang (lee-oo bang) won control. Liu Bang became the first emperor of the Han dynasty, which lasted more than 400 years.

The Rise of a New Dynasty

Liu Bang, a peasant, was able to become emperor in large part because of the Chinese belief in the mandate of heaven. He was the first common person to become emperor. He earned people's loyalty and trust. In addition, he was well liked by both soldiers and peasants, which helped him keep control.

Time Line

The Han Dynasty

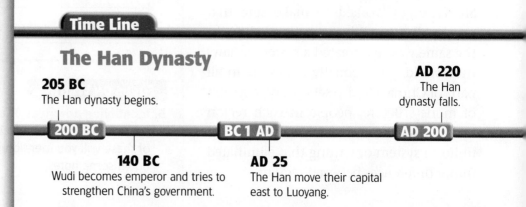

205 BC
The Han dynasty begins.

AD 220
The Han dynasty falls.

200 BC   BC 1 AD   AD 200

140 BC
Wudi becomes emperor and tries to strengthen China's government.

AD 25
The Han move their capital east to Luoyang.

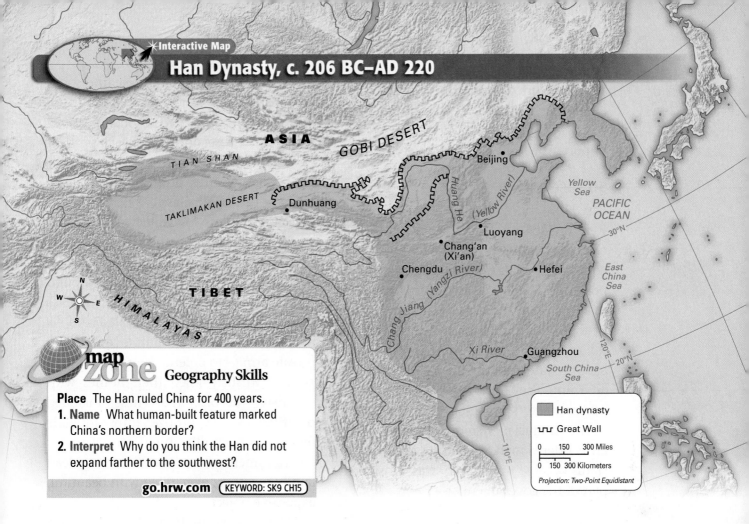

ASIA

GOBI DESERT

TIAN SHAN

TAKLIMAKAN DESERT

Dunhuang

Beijing

Huang He (Yellow River)

Luoyang

Chang'an (Xi'an)

Chengdu

Hefei

Chang Jiang (Yangzi River)

TIBET

HIMALAYAS

Xi River

Guangzhou

Yellow Sea

PACIFIC OCEAN

30°N

East China Sea

South China Sea

120°E

20°N

110°E

map zone Geography Skills

Place The Han ruled China for 400 years.

1. **Name** What human-built feature marked China's northern border?
2. **Interpret** Why do you think the Han did not expand farther to the southwest?

go.hrw.com KEYWORD: SK9 CH15

Han dynasty

Great Wall

| 0 | 150 | 300 Miles |
| 0 | 150 | 300 Kilometers |

Projection: Two-Point Equidistant

Liu Bang's rule was different from the strict government of the Qin. He wanted to free people from harsh government policies. He lowered taxes for farmers and made punishments less severe. He gave large blocks of land to his supporters.

In addition to setting new policies, Liu Bang changed the way government worked. He set up a government structure that built on the foundation begun by the Qin. He also relied on educated officials to help him rule.

Wudi Creates a New Government

In 140 BC Emperor Wudi (WOO-dee) took the throne. He wanted to create a stronger government. To do that, he took land from the lords, raised taxes, and put the supply of grain under government control. He also made Confucianism China's official government philosophy.

Confucianism is a philosophy based on the teachings of a man named Confucius. It emphasizes the importance of ethics and moral values, such as respect for elders and loyalty toward family members. Under the Han, government officials were expected to practice Confucianism. Wudi even began a university to teach Confucian ideas.

Studying Confucianism could also get a person a good job in China. If a person passed an exam on Confucian teachings, he could get a position working for the government. Not just anyone could take the test, though. The exams were only open to people who had been recommended for government service already. As a result, wealthy or influential families continued to control the government.

READING CHECK **Analyzing** How was the Han government based on the ideas of Confucius?

FOCUS ON READING
Who ruled first, Liu Bang or Wudi?

Family Life

The Han period was a time of great social change in China. Class structure became more rigid. The family once again became important within Chinese society.

Social Classes

Based on the Confucian system, people were divided into four classes. The upper class was made up of the emperor, his court, and scholars who held government positions. The second class, the largest, was made up of the peasants. Next were artisans who produced items for daily life and some luxury goods. Merchants were the lowest class because they did not actually produce anything. They only bought and sold what others made. The military was not a class in the Confucian system. Still, joining the army offered men a chance to rise in social status because the military was considered part of the government.

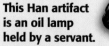

This Han artifact is an oil lamp held by a servant.

Lives of Rich and Poor

The classes only divided people into social rank. They did not indicate wealth or power. For instance, even though peasants made up the second highest class, they were poor. Many merchants, on the other hand, were wealthy and powerful despite being in the lowest class.

People's lifestyles varied according to wealth. The emperor and his court lived in a large palace. Less important officials lived in multilevel houses built around courtyards. Many of these wealthy families owned large estates and employed laborers to work the land. Some families even hired private armies to defend their estates.

The wealthy filled their homes with expensive decorations. These included paintings, pottery, bronze lamps, and jade figures. Rich families hired musicians for entertainment. Even the tombs of dead family members were filled with beautiful, expensive objects.

Most people in Han China, however, did not live so comfortably. Nearly 60 million people lived in China during the Han dynasty, and about 90 percent of them were peasants who lived in the countryside. Peasants put in long, tiring days working the land. Whether it was in the millet fields of the north or in the rice paddies of the south, the work was hard. In the winter, peasants were forced to work on building projects for the government. Heavy taxes and bad weather forced many farmers to sell their land and work for rich landowners. By the last years of the Han dynasty, only a few farmers were independent.

Chinese peasants lived simple lives. They wore plain clothing made of fiber from a native plant. The main foods they ate were cooked grains like barley. Most peasants lived in small villages. Their small, wood-framed houses had walls made of mud or stamped earth.

The Importance of Family

Honoring one's family was an important duty in Han China. In this painting, people give thanks before their family shrine. Only the men can participate. The women watch from inside the house.

ANALYZING VISUALS
How are these men giving thanks?

The Revival of the Family

Since Confucianism was the government's official philosophy during Wudi's reign, Confucian teachings about the family were also honored. Children were taught from birth to respect their elders. Disobeying one's parents was a crime. Even emperors had a duty to respect their parents.

Confucius had taught that the father was the head of the family. Within the family, the father had absolute power. The Han taught that it was a woman's duty to obey her husband, and children had to obey their father.

Han officials believed that if the family was strong and people obeyed the father, then they would also obey the emperor. Since the Han rewarded strong family ties and respect for elders, some men even gained government jobs based on the respect they showed their parents.

Children were encouraged to serve their parents. They were also expected to honor dead parents with ceremonies and offerings. All members of a family were expected to care for family burial sites.

Chinese parents valued boys more highly than girls. This was because sons carried on the family line and took care of their parents when they were old. On the other hand, daughters became part of their husband's family. According to a Chinese proverb, "Raising daughters is like raising children for another family." Some women, however, still gained power. They could gain influence in their sons' families. An older widow could even become the head of the family.

READING CHECK **Identifying Cause and Effect**
Why did the family take on such importance during the Han dynasty?

Han Achievements

During the Han dynasty, the Chinese made many advances in art and learning. Some of these advances are shown here.

Science

This is a model of an ancient Chinese seismograph. When an earthquake struck, a lever inside caused a ball to drop from a dragon's mouth into a toad's mouth, indicating the direction from which the earthquake had come.

Han Achievements

Han rule was a time of great achievements. Art and literature thrived, and inventors developed many useful devices.

Art and Literature

The Chinese of the Han period produced many works of art. They became experts at figure painting—a style of painting that includes portraits of people. Portraits often showed religious figures and Confucian scholars. Han artists also painted realistic scenes from everyday life. Their creations covered the walls of palaces and tombs.

ACADEMIC VOCABULARY

innovation a new idea, method, or device

In literature, Han China is known for its poetry. Poets developed new styles of verse, including the *fu* style, which was the most popular. *Fu* poets combined prose and poetry to create long literary works. Another style, called *shi*, featured short lines of verse that could be sung. Many Han rulers hired poets known for the beauty of their verse.

Han writers also produced important works of history. One historian by the name of Sima Qian wrote a complete history of all the dynasties through the early Han. His format and style became the model for later historical writings.

Inventions and Advances

The Han Chinese invented one item that we use every day—paper. They made it by grinding plant fibers, such as mulberry bark and hemp, into a paste. Then they let it dry in sheets. Chinese scholars produced books by pasting several pieces of paper together into a long sheet. Then they rolled the sheet into a scroll.

The Han also made other **innovations** in science. These included the sundial and the seismograph. A **sundial** is a device that uses the position of shadows cast by the sun to tell the time of day. It was an early type of clock. A **seismograph** is a device that measures the strength of earthquakes. Han emperors were very interested in knowing

Medicine
Han doctors studied the human body and used acupuncture to heal people.

Art
This bronze horse is just one example of the beautiful objects made by Chinese artisans.

ANALYSIS SKILL **ANALYZING VISUALS**

How do these objects show the wide range of accomplishments in Han China?

about the movements of the Earth. They believed that earthquakes were signs of future evil events.

Another Han innovation, acupuncture (AK-yoo-punk-cher), improved medicine. **Acupuncture** is the practice of inserting fine needles through the skin at specific points to cure disease or relieve pain. Many Han inventions in science and medicine are still used today.

READING CHECK **Categorizing** What advances did the Chinese make during the Han period?

SUMMARY AND PREVIEW Rulers of the Han dynasty based their government on Confucianism, which strengthened family bonds in China. In addition, art and learning thrived under Han rule. In the next section you will learn about two dynasties that also made great advances, the Tang and the Song.

go.hrw.com
Online Quiz
KEYWORD: SK9 HP15

Section 2 Assessment

Reviewing Ideas, Terms, and People

1. **a. Identify** What is Confucianism? How did it affect the government during the Han dynasty?
   b. Summarize How did Emperor Wudi create a strong central government?
   c. Evaluate Do you think that an exam system is the best way to make sure that people are fairly chosen for government jobs? Why or why not?
2. **a. Describe** What was the son's role in the family?
   b. Contrast How did living conditions for the wealthy differ from those of the peasants during the Han dynasty?
3. **Identify** What device did the Chinese invent to measure the strength of earthquakes?

Critical Thinking

4. **Analyzing** Use your notes to complete this diagram about how Confucianism influenced Han government and family.

Government
Confucianism
Family

FOCUS ON WRITING

5. **Analyzing the Han Dynasty** The Han dynasty was one of the most influential in all of Chinese history. How will you describe the dynasty's many achievements in your article? Make a list of achievements you want to include.

ANCIENT CIVILIZATIONS OF ASIA—CHINA **473**

The Silk Road

The Silk Road was a long trade route that stretched across the heart of Asia. Along this route, an active trade developed between China and Southwest Asia by about 100 BC. By AD 100, the Silk Road connected Han China in the east with the Roman Empire in the west.

The main goods traded along the Silk Road were luxury goods—ones that were small, light, and expensive. These included goods like silk, spices, and gold. Because they were small and valuable, merchants could carry these goods long distances and still sell them for a large profit. As a result, people in both the east and the west were able to buy luxury goods that were unavailable at home.

GAUL

SPAIN

EUROPE

Aral Sea

Rome

ROMAN EMPIRE

Black Sea

Byzantium

Caspian Sea

Merv

Carthage

GREECE

Asia Minor

Antioch

Ecbatana

Ctesiphon

Babylon

PERSIA

Alexandria

Petra

Persepolis

Mediterranean Sea

AFRICA

Goods from the West Roman merchants like this man grew rich from Silk Road trade. Merchants in the west traded goods like those you see here—wool, amber, and gold.

Aden

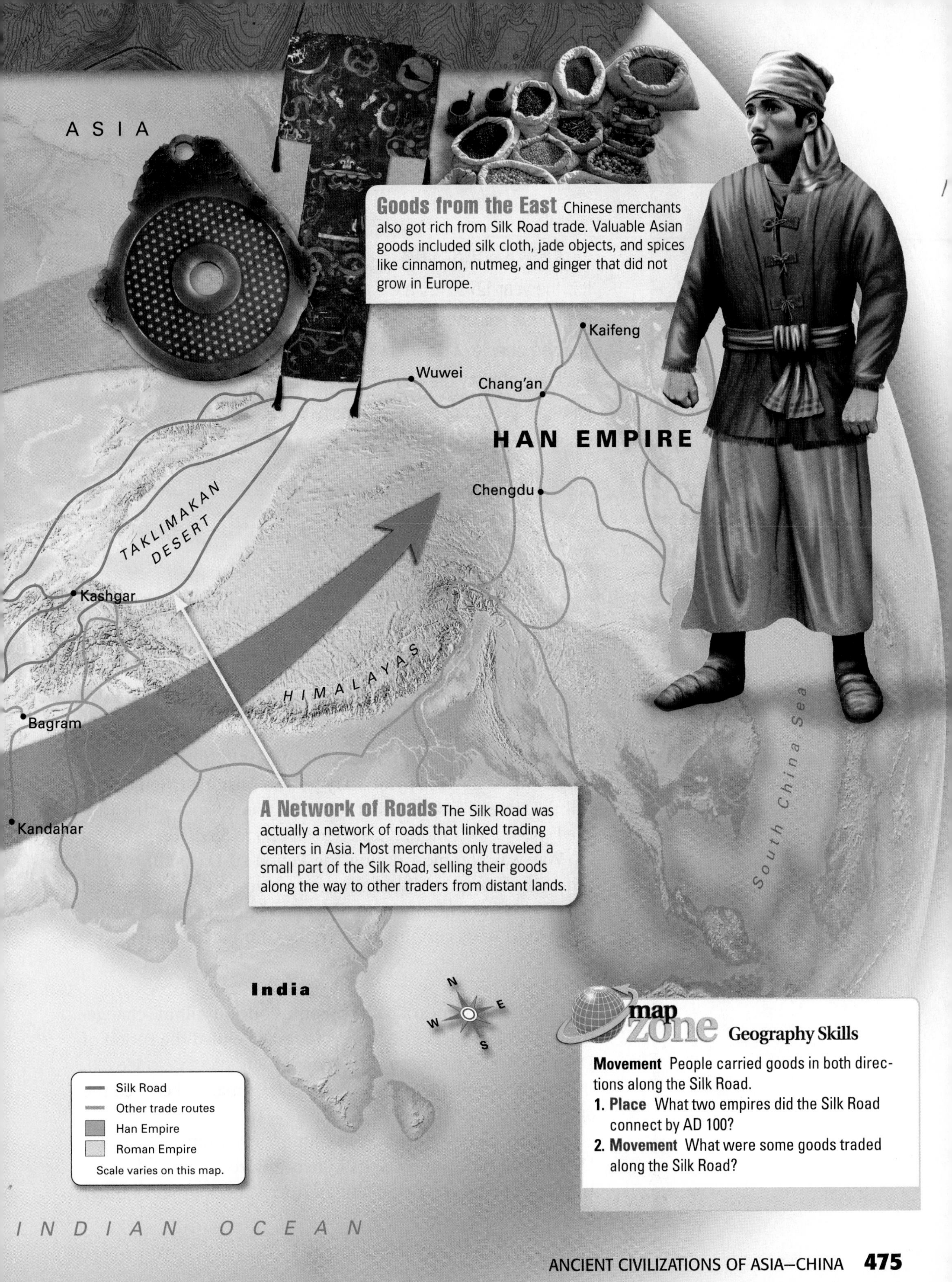

ASIA

Goods from the East Chinese merchants also got rich from Silk Road trade. Valuable Asian goods included silk cloth, jade objects, and spices like cinnamon, nutmeg, and ginger that did not grow in Europe.

Kaifeng

Wuwei   Chang'an

HAN EMPIRE

Chengdu

TAKLIMAKAN DESERT

Kashgar

HIMALAYAS

Bagram

Kandahar

A Network of Roads The Silk Road was actually a network of roads that linked trading centers in Asia. Most merchants only traveled a small part of the Silk Road, selling their goods along the way to other traders from distant lands.

South China Sea

India

N
W   E
S

map zone **Geography Skills**

Movement People carried goods in both directions along the Silk Road.

1. **Place** What two empires did the Silk Road connect by AD 100?
2. **Movement** What were some goods traded along the Silk Road?

Silk Road
Other trade routes
Han Empire
Roman Empire
Scale varies on this map.

INDIAN OCEAN

The Sui, Tang, and Song Dynasties

What You Will Learn...

Main Ideas

1. After the Han dynasty, China fell into disorder but was reunified by new dynasties.
2. Cities and trade grew during the Tang and Song dynasties.
3. The Tang and Song dynasties produced fine arts and inventions.

The Big Idea

The Tang and Song dynasties were periods of economic, cultural, and technological accomplishments.

Key Terms and Places

Grand Canal, *p. 476*
Kaifeng, *p. 478*
porcelain, *p. 479*
woodblock printing, *p. 480*
gunpowder, *p. 480*
compass, *p. 480*

 As you read, look for information about accomplishments of the Tang and Song dynasties. Keep track of these accomplishments in a chart like this one.

Tang dynasty	Song dynasty

If YOU lived there...

It is the year 1270. You are a rich merchant in a Chinese city of about a million people. The city around you fills your senses. You see people in colorful clothes among beautiful buildings. Glittering objects lure you into busy shops. You hear people talking—discussing business, gossiping, laughing at jokes. You smell delicious food cooking at a restaurant down the street.

How do you feel about your city?

BUILDING BACKGROUND The Tang and Song dynasties were periods of great wealth and progress. Changes in farming formed the basis for other advances in Chinese civilization.

Disorder and Reunification

When the Han dynasty collapsed, China split into several rival kingdoms, each ruled by military leaders. Historians sometimes call the time of disorder that followed the collapse of the Han the Period of Disunion. It lasted from 220 to 589.

War was common during the Period of Disunion. At the same time, however, Chinese culture spread. New groups moved into China from nearby areas. Over time, many of these groups adopted Chinese customs and became Chinese themselves.

Sui Dynasty

Finally, after centuries of political confusion and cultural change, China was reunified. The man who finally ended the Period of Disunion was a northern ruler named Yang Jian (YANG jee-EN). In 589, he conquered the south, unified China, and created the Sui (SWAY) dynasty.

The Sui dynasty did not last long, only from 589 to 618. During that time, however, its leaders restored order and began the **Grand Canal**, a canal linking northern and southern China.

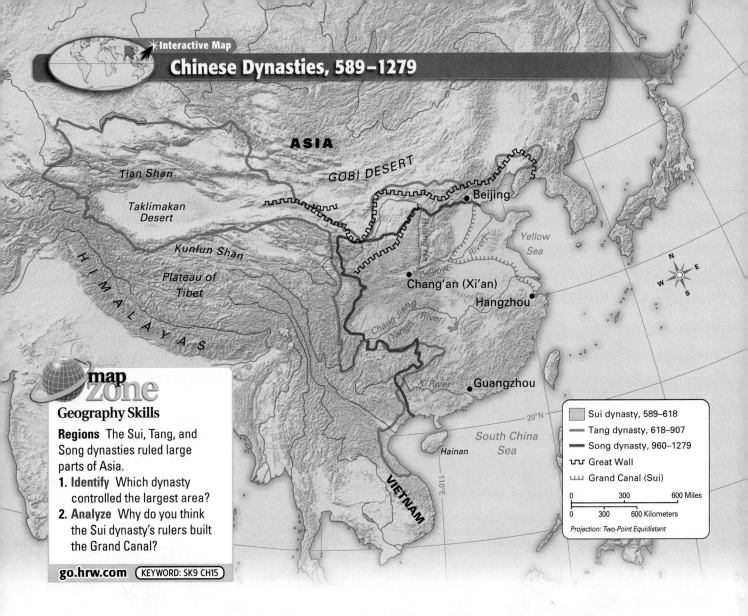

Chinese Dynasties, 589–1279

ASIA

Tian Shan

GOBI DESERT

Taklimakan Desert

Beijing

Kunlun Shan

Yellow Sea

Plateau of Tibet

Huang He

Yellow River

Chang'an (Xi'an)

Hangzhou

H I M A L A Y A S

Chang Jiang (Yangzi) River

N
W   E
S

map zone

Geography Skills

Regions The Sui, Tang, and Song dynasties ruled large parts of Asia.

1. **Identify** Which dynasty controlled the largest area?
2. **Analyze** Why do you think the Sui dynasty's rulers built the Grand Canal?

Xi River

Guangzhou

20°N

South China Sea

Hainan

VIETNAM

110°E

	Sui dynasty, 589–618
	Tang dynasty, 618–907
	Song dynasty, 960–1279
	Great Wall
	Grand Canal (Sui)

0   300   600 Miles
0   300   600 Kilometers

Projection: Two-Point Equidistant

go.hrw.com   KEYWORD: SK9 CH15

Tang Dynasty

The Sui dynasty was followed by the Tang, which would rule for nearly 300 years. As you can see on the map, China grew under the Tang dynasty to include much of eastern and central Asia.

Historians view the Tang dynasty as a golden age. Tang rulers conquered many lands, reformed the military, and created law codes. The Tang period also saw great advances in art. Some of China's finest poets, for example, lived during this time.

The Tang dynasty also included the only woman to rule China—Empress Wu. Her methods were sometimes vicious, but she was intelligent and talented.

Song Dynasty

After the Tang dynasty fell, China entered another brief period of chaos and disorder, with separate kingdoms competing for power. As a result, this period in China's history is called the Five Dynasties and Ten Kingdoms. The disorder only lasted 53 years, though, from 907 to 960.

In 960, China was again reunified, this time by the Song dynasty. Like the Tang, the Song ruled for about 300 years, until 1279. Also like the Tang, the Song dynasty was a time of great achievements.

FOCUS ON READING

What dynasty followed the Tang?

READING CHECK Finding Main Ideas What dynasties restored order to China?

Cities and Trade

Throughout the Tang and Song dynasties, much of the food grown on China's farms flowed into the growing cities and towns. China's cities were crowded, busy places. Shopkeepers, government officials, doctors, artisans, entertainers, religious leaders, and artists made them lively places as well.

City Life

China's capital and largest city of the Tang dynasty was Chang'an (chahng-AHN), a huge, bustling trade center now called Xi'an. With a population of more than a million, it was by far the largest city in the world.

Chang'an, like other trading cities, had a mix of people from many cultures—China, Korea, Persia, Arabia, and Europe. It was also known as a religious and philosophical center, not just for Buddhists and Daoists but for Asian Christians as well.

Cities continued to grow under the Song. Several cities, including the Song capital, **Kaifeng** (KY-fuhng), had about a million people. A dozen more cities had populations of close to half a million.

Trade in China and Beyond

Trade grew along with Chinese cities. This trade, combined with China's agricultural base, made China richer than ever before.

Much trade took place within China itself. Traders used the country's rivers to ship goods on barges and ships.

The Grand Canal, a series of waterways that linked major cities, carried a huge amount of trade goods, especially farm products. Construction on the canal had begun during the Sui dynasty. During the Tang dynasty, it was improved and expanded. The Grand Canal allowed the Chinese to move goods and crops from distant agricultural areas into cities.

The Grand Canal

Beijing

Huang He (Yellow River)

Yellow Sea

Chang'an

Zhenjiang

Chang Jiang (Yangzi River)

Hangzhou

East China Sea

Grand Canal (Sui)

The Chinese also carried on trade with other lands and peoples. During the Tang dynasty, most foreign trade was over land routes leading to India and Southwest Asia, though Chinese traders also went to Korea and Japan in the east. The Chinese exported many goods, including tea, rice, spices, and jade. However, one export was especially important—silk. So valuable was silk that the Chinese kept the method of making it secret. In exchange for their exports, the Chinese imported different foods, plants, wool, glass, and precious metals like gold and silver.

During the Song dynasty, sea trade became more important. China opened its Pacific ports to foreign traders. The sea-trade routes connected China to many other countries. During this time, the Chinese also developed another valuable product—a thin, beautiful type of pottery called **porcelain**.

China's Grand Canal (left) is the world's longest human-made waterway. It was built largely to transport rice and other foods from the south to feed China's cities and armies in the north. Barges like the one above crowd the Grand Canal, which is still an important transportation link in China.

All of this trade helped create a strong economy. As a result, merchants became important members of Chinese society during the Song dynasty. Also as a result of the growth of trade and wealth, the Song invented the world's first system of paper money in the 900s.

READING CHECK **Summarizing** How far did China's trade routes extend?

Arts and Inventions

While China grew rich economically, its cultural riches also increased. In literature, art, and science, China made huge advances.

Artists and Poets

The artists and writers of the Tang dynasty were some of China's greatest. Wu Daozi (DOW-tzee) painted murals that celebrated Buddhism and nature. Li Bo and Du Fu wrote poems that readers still enjoy for their beauty. This poem by Li Bo expresses the homesickness that one feels late at night:

> "Before my bed
> there is bright moonlight
> So that it seems
> like frost on the ground:
> Lifting my head
> I watch the bright moon,
> Lowering my head
> I dream that I'm home."
> –Li Bo, *Quiet Night Thoughts*

Also noted for its literature, the Song period produced Li Qingzhao (ching-ZHOW), perhaps China's greatest female poet. She once said that the purpose of her poetry was to capture a single moment in time.

Artists of both the Tang and Song dynasties made exquisite objects in clay. Tang figurines of horses clearly show the animals' strength. Song artists made porcelain items covered in a pale green glaze called celadon (SEL-uh-duhn).

THE IMPACT TODAY
Porcelain became so popular in the West that it became known as chinaware, or just china.

Chinese Inventions

Paper
Invented during the Han dynasty around 105, paper was one of the greatest of all Chinese inventions. It gave the Chinese a cheap and easy way of keeping records and made printing possible.

Porcelain
Porcelain was first made during the Tang dynasty, but it wasn't perfected for many centuries. Chinese artists were famous for their work with this fragile material.

Woodblock printing
The Chinese invented printing during the Tang dynasty, centuries before it was known in Europe. Printers could copy drawings or texts quickly, much faster than they could be copied by hand.

Gunpowder
Invented during the late Tang or early Song dynasty, gunpowder was used to make fireworks and signals. The Chinese did not generally use it as a weapon.

Movable type
Inventors of the Song dynasty created movable type, which made printing much faster. Carved letters could be rearranged and reused to print many different messages.

Magnetic compass
Invented no later than the Han period, the compass was greatly improved by the Tang. The new compass allowed sailors and merchants to travel vast distances.

Paper money
The world's first paper money was invented by the Song. Lighter and easier to handle than coins, paper money helped the Chinese manage their growing wealth.

Important Inventions

The Tang and Song dynasties produced some of the most remarkable—and most important—inventions in human history. Some of these inventions influenced events around the world.

According to legend, a man named Cai Lun invented paper in the year 105 during the Han dynasty. A later Tang invention built on this achievement— **woodblock printing,** a form of printing in which an entire page is carved into a block of wood. The printer applies ink to the block and presses paper against the block to create a printed page. The world's first known printed book was printed in this way in China in 868.

Another invention of the Tang dynasty was gunpowder. **Gunpowder** is a mixture of powders used in guns and explosives. It was originally used only in fireworks, but it was later used to make small bombs and rockets. Eventually, gunpowder was used to make explosives, firearms, and cannons. Gunpowder dramatically altered how wars were fought and, in doing so, changed the course of human history.

One of the most useful achievements of Tang China was the perfection of the magnetic **compass.** This instrument, which uses Earth's magnetic field to show direction, revolutionized travel. A compass made it possible to find direction more accurately than ever before. The perfection of the compass had far-reaching effects. Explorers the world over used the compass to travel vast distances. Both trading ships and warships also came to rely on the compass for their navigation. Thus, the compass has been a key factor in some of the most important sailing voyages in history.

The Song dynasty also produced many important inventions. Under the Song, the Chinese invented movable type. Movable type is a set of letters or characters that are

The Paper Trail

The dollar bill in your pocket may be crisp and new, but paper money has been around a long time. Paper money was printed for the first time in China in the AD 900s and was in use for about 700 years, through the Ming dynasty, when the bill shown here was printed. However, so much money was printed that it lost value. The Chinese stopped using paper money for centuries. Its use caught on in Europe, though, and eventually became common. Most countries now issue paper money.

Drawing Conclusions How would life be different today without paper money?

used to print books. Unlike the blocks used in block printing, movable type can be rearranged and reused to create new lines of text and different pages.

The Song dynasty also introduced the concept of paper money. People were used to buying goods and services with bulky coins made of metals such as bronze, gold, and silver. Paper money was far lighter and easier to use. As trade increased and many people in China grew rich, paper money became more popular.

READING CHECK Finding Main Ideas What were some important inventions of the Tang and Song dynasties?

SUMMARY AND PREVIEW The Tang and Song dynasties were periods of great advancement. Many great artists and writers lived during these periods. Tang and Song inventions also had dramatic effects on world history. Next, you will learn about major changes in China's government during the Song dynasty.

go.hrw.com
Online Quiz
KEYWORD: SK9 HP15

Section 3 Assessment

Reviewing Ideas, Terms, and People

1. **a. Recall** What was the Period of Disunion? What dynasty brought an end to that period?
   b. Explain How did China change during the Tang dynasty?
2. **a. Describe** What were the capital cities of Tang and Song China like?
   b. Draw Conclusions How did geography affect trade in China?
3. **a. Identify** Who was Li Bo?
   b. Draw Conclusions How may the inventions of paper money and **woodblock printing** have been linked?
   c. Rank Which Tang or Song invention do you think was most important? Defend your answer.

Critical Thinking

4. **Categorizing** Copy the chart at right. Use it to organize your notes on the Tang and Song into categories.

	Tang dynasty	Song dynasty
Cities		
Trade		
Art		
Inventions		

FOCUS ON WRITING

5. **Identifying Achievements** Which achievements and inventions of the Tang and Song dynasties seem most important or most interesting? Make a list for later use.

Confucianism and Government

What You Will Learn...

Main Ideas

1. Confucianism, based on Confucius's teachings about proper behavior, dramatically influenced the Song system of government.
2. Scholar-officials ran China's government during the Song dynasty.

The Big Idea

Confucian thought influenced the Song government.

Key Terms

bureaucracy, *p. 484*
civil service, *p. 484*
scholar-official, *p. 484*

 TAKING NOTES As you read, use a diagram like this one to note details about Confucianism and the Song government.

Confucianism   Song government

If YOU lived there...

You are a student in China in 1184. Night has fallen, but you cannot sleep. Tomorrow you have a test. You know it will be the most important test of your entire life. You have studied for it, not for days or weeks or even months—but for *years.* As you toss and turn, you think about how your entire life will be determined by how well you do on this one test.

How could a single test be so important?

BUILDING BACKGROUND The Song dynasty ruled China from 960 to 1279. This was a time of improvements in agriculture, growing cities, extensive trade, and the development of art and inventions. It was also a time of major changes in Chinese government.

Confucianism

The dominant philosophy in China, Confucianism is based on the teachings of Confucius. He lived more than 1,000 years before the Song dynasty. His ideas, though, had a dramatic effect on the Song system of government.

Confucian Ideas

Confucius's teachings focused on ethics, or proper behavior, for individuals and governments. He said that people should conduct their lives according to two basic principles. These principles were *ren*, or concern for others, and *li*, or appropriate behavior. Confucius argued that society would function best if everyone followed *ren* and *li*.

Confucius thought that everyone had a proper role to play in society. Order was maintained when people knew their place and behaved appropriately. For example, Confucius said that young people should obey their elders and that subjects should obey their rulers.

Influence of Confucianism

After his death, Confucius's ideas were spread by his followers, but they were not widely accepted. In fact, the Qin dynasty officially suppressed Confucian ideas and teachings. By the time of the Han dynasty, Confucianism had again come into favor, and Confucianism became the official state philosophy.

During the Period of Disunion, which followed the Han dynasty, Confucianism was overshadowed by Buddhism as the major tradition in China. Many Chinese people had turned to Buddhism for peace and comfort during those troubled times. In doing so, they largely turned away from Confucian ideas and outlooks.

Later, during the Sui and early Tang dynasties, Buddhism was very influential. Unlike Confucianism, which focused on **ethical** behavior, Buddhism stressed a more spiritual outlook that promised escape from suffering. As Buddhism became more popular in China, Confucianism lost some of its influence.

ACADEMIC VOCABULARY
ethical related to rules of conduct or proper behavior

In addition to ethics, Confucianism stressed the importance of a good education. This painting, created in the Song period, shows Confucian scholars during the Period of Disunion sorting scrolls containing classic Confucian texts.

Civil Service Exams

This painting from the 1600s shows civil servants writing essays for China's emperor. Difficult exams were designed to make sure that government officials were chosen by ability—not by wealth or family connections.

Difficult Exams

- Students had to memorize entire Confucian texts.

- To pass the most difficult tests, students might study for more than 20 years!

- Some exams lasted up to 72 hours, and students were locked in private rooms while taking them.

- Some dishonest students cheated by copying Confucius's works on the inside of their clothes, paying bribes to the test graders, or paying someone else to take the test for them.

- To prevent cheating, exam halls were often locked and guarded.

Neo-Confucianism

Late in the Tang dynasty, many Chinese historians and scholars again became interested in the teachings of Confucius. Their interest was sparked by their desire to improve Chinese government and society.

During and after the Song dynasty, a new philosophy called Neo-Confucianism developed. The term *neo* means "new." Based on Confucianism, Neo-Confucianism was similar to the older philosophy in that it taught proper behavior. However, it also emphasized spiritual matters. For example, Neo-Confucian scholars discussed such issues as what made human beings do bad things even if their basic nature was good.

Neo-Confucianism became much more influential under the Song. Its influence grew even more later. In fact, the ideas of Neo-Confucianism became official government teachings after the Song dynasty.

ACADEMIC VOCABULARY

incentive something that leads people to follow a certain course of action

READING CHECK Contrasting How did Neo-Confucianism differ from Confucianism?

Scholar-Officials

The Song dynasty took another major step that affected China for centuries. They improved the system by which people went to work for the government. These workers formed a large **bureaucracy,** or a body of unelected government officials. They joined the bureaucracy by passing civil service examinations. **Civil service** means service as a government official.

To become a civil servant, a person had to pass a series of written examinations. The examinations tested students' grasp of Confucianism and related ideas.

Because the tests were so difficult, students spent years preparing for them. Only a very small fraction of the people who took the tests would reach the top level and be appointed to a position in the government. However, candidates for the civil service examinations had a strong **incentive** for studying hard. Passing the tests meant life as a **scholar-official**—an educated member of the government.

go.hrw.com

Scholar-Officials

First rising to prominence under the Song, scholar-officials remained important in China for centuries. These scholar-officials, for example, lived during the Qing dynasty, which ruled from the mid-1600s to the early 1900s. Their typical responsibilities might include running government offices; maintaining roads, irrigation systems, and other public works; updating and keeping official records; or collecting taxes.

Scholar-officials were elite members of society. They performed many important jobs in the government and were widely admired for their knowledge and ethics. Their benefits included considerable respect and reduced penalties for breaking the law. Many also became wealthy from gifts given by people seeking their aid.

The civil service examination system helped ensure that talented, intelligent people became scholar-officials. The civil service system was a major factor in the stability of the Song government.

READING CHECK Analyzing How did the Song dynasty change China's government?

SUMMARY AND PREVIEW During the Song period, Confucian ideas helped shape China's government. In the next section, you will read about the two dynasties that followed the Song—the Yuan and the Ming.

go.hrw.com
Online Quiz
KEYWORD: SK9 HP15

Section 4 Assessment

Reviewing Ideas, Terms, and People

1. **a. Identify** What two principles did Confucius believe people should follow?
   b. Explain What was Neo-Confucianism?
   c. Elaborate Why do you think Neo-Confucianism appealed to many people?
2. **a. Define** What was a **scholar-official**?
   b. Explain Why would people want to become scholar-officials?
   c. Evaluate Do you think **civil service** examinations were a good way to choose government officials? Why or why not?

Critical Thinking

3. **Sequencing** Review your notes to see how Confucianism led to Neo-Confucianism and Neo-Confucianism led to government bureaucracy. Use a graphic organizer like the one here.

Confucianism → Neo-Confucianism → Government bureaucracy

FOCUS ON WRITING

4. **Gathering Ideas about Confucianism and Government** Think about what you might say about Confucianism in your article. Also, decide whether to include any of the Song dynasty's achievements in government.

The Yuan and Ming Dynasties

What You Will Learn...

Main Ideas

1. The Mongol Empire included China, and the Mongols ruled China as the Yuan dynasty.
2. The Ming dynasty was a time of stability and prosperity.
3. The Ming brought great changes in government and relations with other countries.

The Big Idea

The Chinese were ruled by foreigners during the Yuan dynasty, but they threw off Mongol rule and prospered during the Ming dynasty.

Key Terms and Places

Beijing, *p. 488*
Forbidden City, *p. 490*
isolationism, *p. 492*

 TAKING NOTES As you read, use a chart like this one to keep track of important details about the Yuan and Ming dynasties.

	Yuan	Ming
Government		
Religion		
Trade		
Building		
Foreign Relations		

If **YOU** lived there...

You are a farmer in northern China in 1212. As you pull weeds from a wheat field, you hear a sound like thunder. Looking toward the sound, you see hundreds—no, *thousands*—of warriors on horses on the horizon, riding straight toward you. You are frozen with fear. Only one thought fills your mind—the Mongols are coming.

What can you do to save yourself?

BUILDING BACKGROUND Throughout its history, northern China had been attacked over and over by nomadic peoples. During the Song dynasty these attacks became more frequent and threatening.

The Mongol Empire

Among the nomadic peoples who attacked the Chinese were the Mongols. For centuries, the Mongols had lived as tribes in the vast plains north of China. Then in 1206, a strong leader, or khan, united them. His name was Temüjin. When he became leader, though, he was given a new title: "Universal Ruler," or Genghis Khan (JENG-guhs KAHN).

The Mongol Conquest

Genghis Khan organized the Mongols into a powerful army and led them on bloody expeditions of conquest. The brutality of the Mongol attacks terrorized people throughout much of Asia and Eastern Europe. Genghis Khan and his army killed all of the men, women, and children in countless cities and villages. Within 20 years, he ruled a large part of Asia.

Genghis Khan then turned his attention to China. He first led his armies into northern China in 1211. They fought their way south, wrecking whole towns and ruining farmland. By the time of Genghis Khan's death in 1227, all of northern China was under Mongol control.

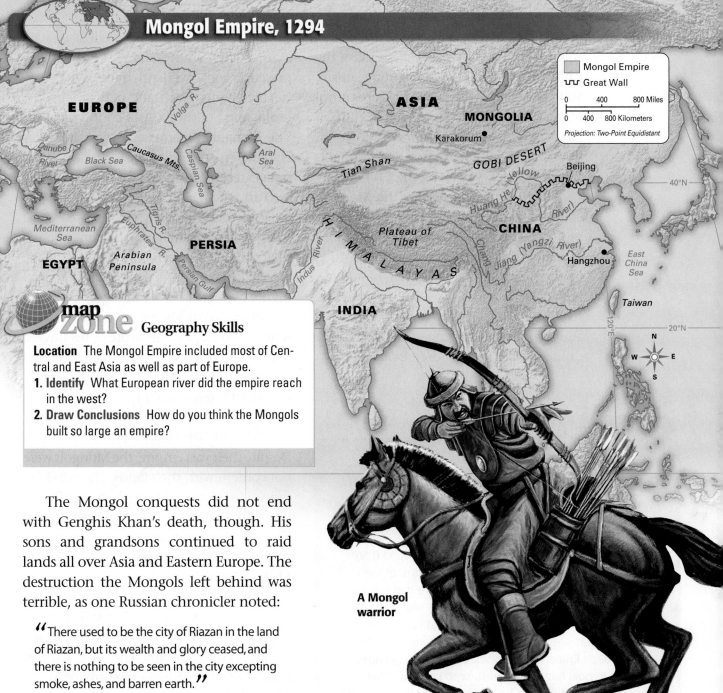

Mongol Empire, 1294

EUROPE

Danube River

Volga R.

Caucasus Mts.

Black Sea

Caspian Sea

Aral Sea

ASIA

MONGOLIA

Karakorum

Tian Shan

GOBI DESERT

Beijing

Huang He (Yellow River)

40°N

Mediterranean Sea

Tigris R.

Euphrates R.

Persian Gulf

PERSIA

Indus River

HIMALAYAS

Plateau of Tibet

CHINA

Chang Jiang (Yangzi River)

Hangzhou

East China Sea

EGYPT

Arabian Peninsula

INDIA

Taiwan

120°E

20°N

N
W   E
S

Mongol Empire
Great Wall

0   400   800 Miles
0   400   800 Kilometers

Projection: Two-Point Equidistant

map zone Geography Skills

Location The Mongol Empire included most of Central and East Asia as well as part of Europe.
1. **Identify** What European river did the empire reach in the west?
2. **Draw Conclusions** How do you think the Mongols built so large an empire?

The Mongol conquests did not end with Genghis Khan's death, though. His sons and grandsons continued to raid lands all over Asia and Eastern Europe. The destruction the Mongols left behind was terrible, as one Russian chronicler noted:

"There used to be the city of Riazan in the land of Riazan, but its wealth and glory ceased, and there is nothing to be seen in the city excepting smoke, ashes, and barren earth."

–from "The Tale of the Destruction of Riazan," in *Medieval Russia's Epics, Chronicles, and Tales*, edited by Serge Zenkovsky

In 1260 Genghis Khan's grandson Kublai Khan (KOO-bluh KAHN) became ruler of the Mongol Empire. He completed the conquest of China and in 1279 declared himself emperor of China. This began the Yuan dynasty, a period that some people also call the Mongol Ascendancy. For the first time in its long history, foreigners ruled all of China.

A Mongol warrior

Life in Yuan China

Kublai Khan and the Mongol rulers he led belonged to a different ethnic group than the Chinese did. They spoke a different language, worshipped different gods, wore different clothing, and had different customs. The Chinese resented being ruled by these foreigners, whom they saw as rude and uncivilized.

However, Kublai Khan did not force the Chinese to accept Mongol ways of life. Some Mongols even adopted aspects of the Chinese culture, such as Confucianism. Still, the Mongols made sure to keep control of the Chinese. They prohibited Confucian scholars from gaining too much power in the government, for example. The Mongols also placed heavy taxes on the Chinese.

Much of the tax money the Mongols collected went to pay for vast public-works projects. These projects required the labor of many Chinese people. The Yuan added to the Grand Canal and built new roads and palaces. Workers also improved the roads used by China's postal system. In addition, the Yuan emperors built a new capital, Dadu, near modern **Beijing**.

Mongol soldiers were sent throughout China to keep the peace as well as to keep a close watch on the Chinese. The soldiers' presence kept overland trade routes safe for merchants. Sea trade between China, India, and Southeast Asia continued, too. The Mongol emperors also welcomed foreign traders at Chinese ports. Some of these traders received special privileges.

Part of what we know about life in the Yuan dynasty comes from one such trader, an Italian merchant named Marco Polo. Between 1271 and 1295 he traveled in and around China. Polo was highly respected by the Mongols and even served in Kublai Khan's court. When Polo returned to Europe, he wrote of his travels. Polo's descriptions of China fascinated many Europeans. His book sparked much European interest in China.

The End of the Yuan Dynasty

Despite their vast empire, the Mongols were not content with their lands. They decided to invade Japan. A Mongol army sailed to Japan in 1274 and 1281. The campaigns, however, were disastrous. Violent storms and fierce defenders destroyed most of the Mongol force.

The failed campaigns against Japan weakened the Mongol military. The huge, expensive public-works projects had already weakened the economy. These weaknesses, combined with Chinese resentment, made China ripe for rebellion.

In the 1300s many Chinese groups rebelled against the Yuan dynasty. In 1368 a former monk named Zhu Yuanzhang (JOO yoo-ahn-JAHNG) took charge of a rebel army. He led this army in a final victory over the Mongols. China was once again ruled by the Chinese.

READING CHECK **Finding Main Ideas** How did the Mongols come to rule China?

Primary Source

BOOK
A Chinese City

In this passage Marco Polo describes his visit to Hangzhou (HAHNG-JOH), a city in southeastern China.

"Inside the city there is a Lake . . . and all round it are erected [built] beautiful palaces and mansions, of the richest and most exquisite [finest] structure that you can imagine . . . In the middle of the Lake are two Islands, on each of which stands a rich, beautiful and spacious edifice [building], furnished in such style as to seem fit for the palace of an Emperor. And when any one of the citizens desired to hold a marriage feast, or to give any other entertainment, it used to be done at one of these palaces. And everything would be found there ready to order, such as silver plate, trenchers [platters], and dishes, napkins and table-cloths, and whatever else was needful. The King made this provision for the gratification [enjoyment] of his people, and the place was open to every one who desired to give an entertainment."

–Marco Polo, from *Description of the World*

ANALYSIS SKILL **ANALYZING PRIMARY SOURCES**

From this description, what impression might Europeans have of Hangzhou?

The Voyages of Zheng He

Zheng He's ocean voyages were remarkable. Some of his ships, like the one shown here, were among the largest in the world at the time.

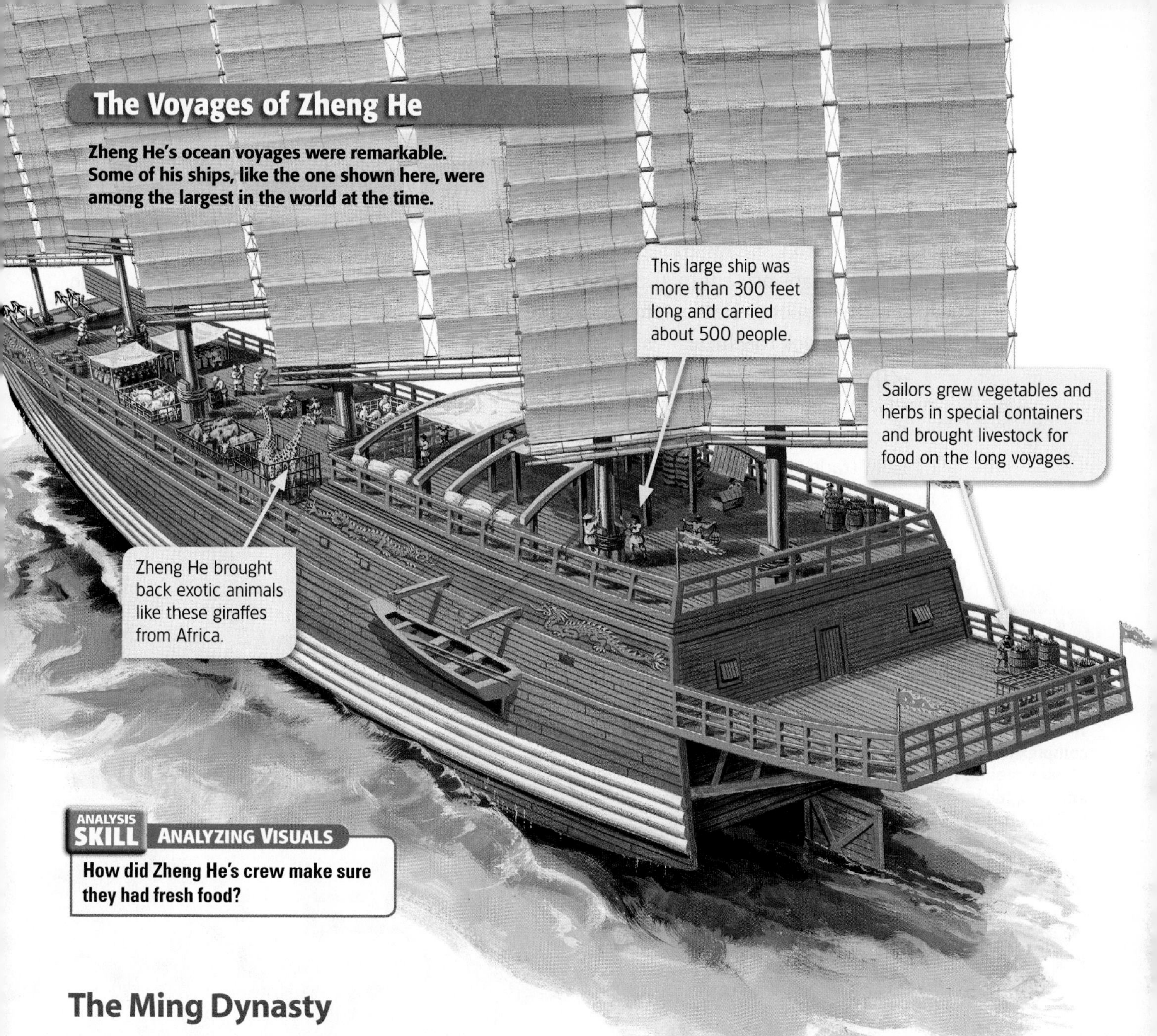

This large ship was more than 300 feet long and carried about 500 people.

Sailors grew vegetables and herbs in special containers and brought livestock for food on the long voyages.

Zheng He brought back exotic animals like these giraffes from Africa.

ANALYSIS SKILL **ANALYZING VISUALS**

How did Zheng He's crew make sure they had fresh food?

The Ming Dynasty

After his army defeated the Mongols, Zhu Yuanzhang became emperor of China. The Ming dynasty that he founded ruled China from 1368 to 1644—nearly 300 years. Ming China proved to be one of the most stable and prosperous times in Chinese history. The Ming expanded China's fame overseas and sponsored incredible building projects across China.

Great Sea Voyages

During the Ming dynasty, the Chinese improved their ships and their sailing skills. The greatest sailor of the period was Zheng He (juhng HUH). Between 1405 and 1433, he led seven grand voyages to places around Asia. Zheng He's fleets were huge. One included more than 60 ships and 25,000 sailors. Some of the ships were gigantic too, perhaps more than 300 feet long. That is longer than a football field!

In the course of his voyages Zheng He sailed his fleet throughout the Indian Ocean. He sailed as far west as the Persian Gulf and the easternmost coast of Africa.

Everywhere his ships landed, Zheng He presented leaders with beautiful gifts from China. He boasted about his country and encouraged foreign leaders to send gifts to China's emperor. From one voyage, Zheng He returned to China with representatives of some 30 nations, sent by their leaders to honor the emperor. He also brought goods and stories back to China.

Zheng He's voyages rank among the most impressive in the history of seafaring. Although they did not lead to the creation of new trade routes or the exploration of new lands, they served as a clear sign of China's power.

Great Building Projects

The Ming were also known for their grand building projects. Many of these projects were designed to impress both the Chinese people and their enemies to the north.

In Beijing, for example, the Ming emperors built the **Forbidden City**, a huge palace complex that included hundreds of imperial residences, temples, and other government buildings. Within them were some 9,000 rooms. The name Forbidden City came from the fact that the common people were not even allowed to enter the complex. For centuries, this city within a city was a symbol of China's glory.

The Forbidden City

The Forbidden City is not actually a city. It's a huge complex of almost 1,000 buildings in the heart of China's capital. The Forbidden City was built for the emperor, his family, his court, and his servants, and ordinary people were forbidden from entering.

The Forbidden City's main buildings were built of wood and featured gold-colored tile roofs that could only be used for the emperor's buildings.

The crowds of government and military officials who gathered to watch ceremonies were carefully lined up according to their ranks.

Sometimes, the emperor was carried on a special seat called a palanquin as his officers lined the route.

Ming rulers also directed the restoration of the famous Great Wall of China. Large numbers of soldiers and peasants worked to rebuild fallen portions of walls, connect existing walls, and build new ones. The result was a construction feat unmatched in history. The wall was more than 2,000 miles long. It would reach from San Diego to New York! The wall was about 25 feet high and, at the top, 12 feet wide. Protected by the wall—and the soldiers who stood guard along it—the Chinese people felt safe from invasions by the northern tribes.

READING CHECK Generalizing In what ways did the Ming dynasty strengthen China?

China under the Ming

During the Ming dynasty, Chinese society began to change. This change was largely due to the efforts of the Ming emperors. Having expelled the Mongols, the Ming emperors worked to eliminate all foreign influences from Chinese society. As a result, China's government and relations with other countries changed dramatically.

The Hall of Supreme Harmony is the largest building in the Forbidden City. Grand celebrations for important holidays, like the emperor's birthday and the New Year, were held there.

ANALYSIS SKILL **ANALYZING VISUALS**
How did the Forbidden City show the power and importance of the emperor?

Government

When the Ming took over China, they adopted many government programs that had been created by the Tang and the Song. However, the Ming emperors were much more powerful than the Tang and Song emperors had been. They abolished the offices of some powerful officials and took a larger role in running the government themselves. These emperors fiercely protected their power, and they punished anyone whom they saw as challenging their authority.

Despite their personal power, though, the Ming did not disband the civil service system. Because he personally oversaw the entire government, the emperor needed officials to keep his affairs organized.

The Ming also used examinations to appoint censors. These officials were sent all over China to investigate the behavior of local leaders and to judge the quality of schools and other institutions. Censors had existed for many years in China, but under the Ming emperors their power and influence grew.

ACADEMIC VOCABULARY

consequences effects of a particular event or events

Relations with Other Countries

In the 1430s a new Ming emperor made Zheng He return to China and dismantle his fleet. At the same time, he banned foreign trade. China entered a period of isolationism. **Isolationism** is a policy of avoiding contact with other countries.

In the end, this isolationism had great **consequences** for China. By the late 1800s the Western world had made huge leaps in technological progress. Westerners were able to take power in some parts of China. Partly due to its isolation and lack of progress, China was too weak to stop them. Gradually, China's glory faded.

READING CHECK Identifying Cause and Effect How did isolationism affect China?

SUMMARY AND PREVIEW In this chapter, you learned about the long history of China. Next, you will learn how Chinese culture helped shape and define another ancient culture in Asia. That culture was Japan.

Section 5 Assessment

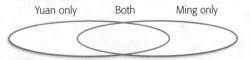

go.hrw.com
Online Quiz
KEYWORD: SK9 HP15

Reviewing Ideas, Terms, and People

1. **a. Identify** Who was Genghis Khan?
   b. Explain How did the Mongols gain control of China?
   c. Evaluate Judge this statement: "The Mongols should never have tried to invade Japan."
2. **a. Identify** Who was Zheng He, and what did he do?
   b. Analyze What impression do you think the Forbidden City had on the residents of Beijing?
   c. Develop How may the Great Wall have both helped and hurt China?
3. **a. Define** What is **isolationism**?
   b. Explain How did the Ming change China?
   c. Develop How might a policy of isolationism have both advantages and disadvantages?

Critical Thinking

4. **Comparing and Contrasting** Draw a diagram like this one. Use your notes to see how the Yuan and Ming dynasties were alike and different.

   Yuan only   Both   Ming only

FOCUS ON WRITING

5. **Identifying Achievements of the Later Dynasties** Make a list of the achievements of the Yuan and Ming dynasties. Then look back over all your notes and rate the achievements or inventions. Which four or five do you think are most important?

Kublai Khan

How did a Mongol nomad settle down to rule a vast empire?

When did he live? 1215–1294

Where did he live? Kublai Khan came from Mongolia but spent much of his life in China. His capital, Dadu, was near the modern city of Beijing.

What did he do? Kublai Khan completed the conquest of China that Genghis Khan had begun. He ruled China as the emperor of the Yuan dynasty.

Why is he important? The lands Kublai Khan ruled made up one of the largest empires in world history. It stretched from the Pacific Ocean to Eastern Europe. As China's ruler, Kublai Khan welcomed foreign visitors, including the Italian merchant Marco Polo and the Arab historian Ibn Battutah. The stories these two men told helped create interest in China and its products among Westerners.

Generalizing How did Kublai Khan's actions help change people's views of China?

This painting from the 1200s shows Kublai Khan hunting on horseback.

Making Economic Choices

Learn

Economic choices are a part of geography. World leaders must make economic choices every day. For example, a country's president might face a choice about whether to spend government money on improving defense, education, or health care.

You also have to make economic choices in your own life. For example, you might have to decide whether to go to a movie with a friend or buy a CD. You cannot afford to do both, so you must make a choice.

Making economic choices involves sacrifices, or trade-offs. If you choose to spend your money on a movie, the trade-offs are the other things you want but cannot buy. By considering trade-offs, you can make better economic choices.

Practice

Imagine that you are in the school band. The band has enough money to make one major purchase this year. As the diagram below shows, the band can spend the money on new musical instruments, new uniforms, or a band trip. The band decides to buy new instruments.

❶ Based on the diagram below, what are the trade-offs of the band's choice?

❷ What would have been the trade-offs if the band had voted to spend the money on a trip instead?

❸ How do you think creating a diagram like the one below might have helped the band make its economic choice?

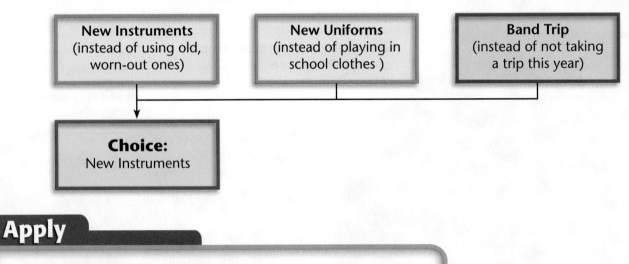

New Instruments
(instead of using old, worn-out ones)

New Uniforms
(instead of playing in school clothes)

Band Trip
(instead of not taking a trip this year)

Choice:
New Instruments

Apply

1. Describe an example of an economic choice you might face that has three possible trade-offs.

2. For each possible economic choice, identify what the trade-offs are if you make that choice.

3. What final choice will you make? Why?

4. How did considering trade-offs help you make your choice?

Geography's Impact
video series
Review the video to answer the closing question:
Do you agree with Confucius's ideas concerning family? Why or why not?

Visual Summary

Use the visual summary below to help you review the main ideas of the chapter.

QUICK FACTS

The Shang, Qin, and Han dynasties ruled China and made many advances that were built on later.

Under the Tang and Song dynasties, Confucianism was an important element of Chinese government.

The Mongols invaded China and ruled it as the Yuan dynasty.

The powerful Ming dynasty strengthened China and expanded trade, but then China became isolated.

Reviewing Vocabulary, Terms, and Places

Match the words or names with their definitions or descriptions.

a. gunpowder   **f.** porcelain
b. scholar-official   **g.** Great Wall
c. mandate of heaven   **h.** isolationism
d. bureaucracy   **i.** incentive
e. seismograph

1. a device to measure the strength of earthquakes
2. something that leads people to follow a certain course of action
3. body of unelected government officials
4. thin, beautiful pottery
5. educated government worker
6. policy of avoiding contact with other countries
7. a barrier along China's northern border
8. a mixture of powders used in explosives
9. the idea that heaven chose who should rule

Comprehension and Critical Thinking

SECTION 1 *(Pages 464–467)*

10. **a. Identify** What was the first known dynasty to rule China? What did it achieve?

   b. Analyze Why did the Qin dynasty not last long after Shi Huangdi's death?

   c. Evaluate Do you think Shi Huangdi was a good ruler for China? Why or why not?

SECTION 2 *(Pages 468–473)*

11. **a. Define** What is Confucianism? How did it affect Han society?

   b. Analyze What was life like for peasants in the Han period?

   c. Elaborate What inventions show that the Han studied nature?

SECTION 3 (Pages 476–481)

12. a. Describe What did Wu Daozi, Li Bo, Du Fu, and Li Qingzhao contribute to Chinese culture?

b. Analyze How did the Tang rulers change China's government?

c. Evaluate Which Chinese invention has had a greater effect on world history—the magnetic compass or gunpowder? Why do you think so?

SECTION 4 (Pages 482–485)

13. a. Define How did Confucianism change in and after the Song dynasty?

b. Make Inferences Why do you think the civil service examination system was created?

c. Elaborate Why were China's civil service examinations so difficult?

SECTION 5 (Pages 486–492)

14. a. Describe How did the Mongols create their huge empire? What areas were included in it?

b. Draw Conclusions How did Marco Polo and Zheng He help shape ideas about China?

c. Elaborate Why do you think the Ming spent so much time and money on the Great Wall?

Using the Internet

go.hrw.com
KEYWORD: SK9 CH15

15. Activity: Creating a Mural The Tang and Song periods saw many agricultural, technological, and commercial developments. New irrigation techniques, movable type, and gunpowder were a few of them. Enter the activity keyword and learn more about such developments. Imagine that a city official has hired you to create a mural showing all of the great things the Chinese developed during the Tang and Song dynasties. Create a large mural that depicts as many advances as possible.

Social Studies Skills

Making Economic Choices *You have enough money to buy one of the following items: shoes, a DVD, or a book.*

16. What are the trade-offs if you buy the DVD?

17. What are the trade-offs if you buy the book?

FOCUS ON READING AND WRITING

18. Understanding Chronological Order Arrange the following list of events in the order in which they happened. Then write a brief paragraph describing the events, using clue words such as *then* and *later* to show the proper sequence.

- The Han dynasty rules China.
- The Shang dynasty takes power.
- Mongol armies invade China.
- The Ming dynasty takes control.

19. Writing Your Magazine Article Now that you have identified the achievements or inventions that you want to write about, begin your article. Open with a sentence that states your main idea. Include a paragraph of two or three sentences about each invention or achievement. Describe each achievement or invention and explain why it was so important. End your article with a sentence or two that summarize China's importance to the world.

Map Activity  Interactive

20. Ancient China On a separate sheet of paper, match the letters on the map with their correct labels.

Chang'an   Beijing   Huang He

Kaifeng   Chang Jiang

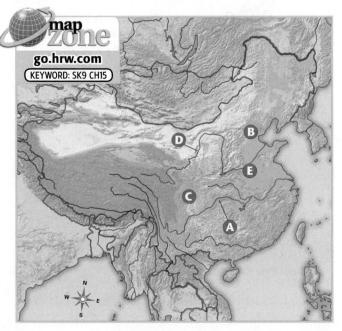

Standardized Test Practice

DIRECTIONS (1–7): For each statement or question, write on a separate answer sheet the *number* of the word or expression that, of those given, best completes the statement or answers the question.

1 Who was the Chinese admiral who sailed all around Asia during the Ming dynasty?

(1) Li Bo

(2) Genghis Khan

(3) Zhu Yuanzhang

(4) Zheng He

2 Trade and other contact with peoples far from China stopped under which dynasty?

(1) Ming

(2) Yuan

(3) Song

(4) Sui

3 Which of the following was one way that Confucianism influenced China?

(1) emphasis on family and family values

(2) expansion of manufacturing and trade

(3) increase in taxes

(4) elimination of the government

4 Which of the following was an achievement of the Shang dynasty?

(1) invention of fireworks

(2) building of the Grand Canal

(3) creation of a writing system

(4) construction of the Forbidden City

5 What religion that developed in ancient India became very popular in ancient China as well?

(1) Hinduism

(2) Islam

(3) Jainism

(4) Buddhism

6 Emperor Shi Huangdi had laborers work on a structure that Ming rulers improved. What was that structure?

(1) the Great Wall

(2) the Great Tomb

(3) the Forbidden City

(4) the Temple of Buddha

7 The ruler who completed the Mongol conquest of China was named

(1) Shi Huangdi.

(2) Du Fu.

(3) Kublai Khan.

(4) Confucius.

Base your answer to question 8 on the image below and on your knowledge of social studies.

8 This object displays Chinese expertise at working with

(1) woodblocks.

(2) gunpowder.

(3) cotton fibers.

(4) porcelain.

Ancient Japan

History

Japanese writing is an art form in itself. This album made in the shape of a fan is covered in text and pictures.

Japan has a lengthy history. The earliest Japanese citizens lived in villages ruled by powerful clans, or extended families. Each clan was led by a chief. For many years, these clans lived independently of one another. By the 500s, however, one powerful clan had taken control of much of Japan. The head of that clan became Japan's first emperor.

In 794 the emperor and empress of Japan moved to Heian (HAY-ahn), a city now called Kyoto. Many nobles followed their rulers to the new city. There they created an imperial court, a group of nobles who live near and advise a ruler.

In fact, the emperor and nobles of Heian were so taken with their own lifestyles that they paid little attention to the rest of the country. Outside of Heian, powerful nobles fought for land. In addition, rebels battled imperial officials.

With the emperor distracted, Japan's rural nobles decided that they needed to protect their own lands from bandits and thieves. The nobles hired professional warriors to defend them and their property. These warriors were known as samurai.

Many nobles were unhappy with the way Japan's government was being run. They wanted a change of leadership. Eventually, two noble clans went to war with each other in the 1150s. Each clan wanted to take power for itself.

The Heian Jingu shrine in Kyoto celebrates Japan's imperial past. Built in 1895, it is a reconstruction of the ancient imperial palace from Heian.

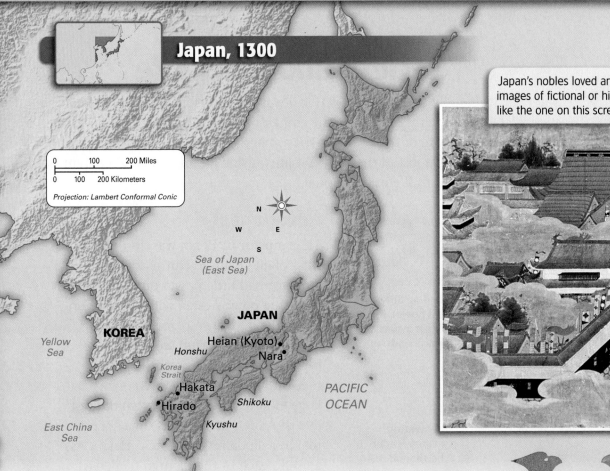

Japan, 1300

0   100   200 Miles
0   100   200 Kilometers

Projection: Lambert Conformal Conic

N W E S

Sea of Japan
(East Sea)

JAPAN

KOREA

Yellow
Sea

Heian (Kyoto)
Honshu   Nara
Korea
Strait
Hakata   Shikoku
Hirado

Kyushu

East China
Sea

PACIFIC
OCEAN

Japan's nobles loved art. They painted images of fictional or historical events, like the one on this screen.

The war left the leader of the Minamoto clan the most powerful man in Japan. He decided to take over ruling the country but didn't want to get rid of the emperor. Instead, he kept the emperor on as a figurehead, a person who appears to rule even though real power lies with someone else. Minamoto himself took the title shogun and ruled Japan in the emperor's name. When Minamoto died, he passed his title and power on to one of his sons. For about the next 700 years, a series of shoguns ruled Japan.

Case Study Assessment

1. What was life like in Heian?

2. Why did Japan's emperor lose power?

3. **Activity** Illustrated fans were popular in ancient Japan. Create a fan with an image of a key event from Japanese history.

For many years, Japan was ruled by warriors and generals.

499

Society and Daily Life

By the early 1000s Heian was the center of Japanese society. Living there were the emperor and many powerful nobles, the elite of the country. They imagined that everyone wanted to live just as they did. Yet life outside Heian was very different from life in the capital.

Emperor

Holding little real power, the emperor was a figurehead.

Shogun

A powerful military leader, the shogun ruled in the emperor's name.

Daimyo and Samurai

Daimyo were powerful lords who often led armies of samurai. Samurai warriors served the shogun and daimyo.

Peasants

Most Japanese were poor peasants who had no power.

Government

The emperor in Heian was, in theory, the ruler of all Japan. In truth, however, the emperor had little power outside of the city. True power rested with the shogun, who ruled in the emperor's name.

Below the shogun were a number of powerful landowners called daimyo (DY-mee-oh). Each of the daimyo owned a large es-tate, though they often did not live there. For many years the shogun required all daimyo to live in Heian. As a result, each of the daimyo named a representative to govern his estate in his absence. On the estate, peasants grew rice to feed the daimyo and his family as well as food for themselves.

Because wars were not uncommon in Japan, daimyo needed soldiers to defend their estates. They hired professional war-riors called samurai for this purpose. Most samurai came from noble families, but many had little money. In exchange for their military service, the samurai received either land or food. Because flat land is rare in Japan, only the most powerful sam-urai got land for their service.

Daily Life

Life in Japan varied according to where a person lived. People who lived in the capi-tal of Heian had a very different way of life than people outside the city.

Court life in Japan was formal and ritualized, as this painting and these quotations show.

Members of Japan's royal court loved ritual and ceremony. They enjoyed lives of ease and privilege and spent their days writing and attending parties or Buddhist ceremonies. They lived apart from poorer citizens and seldom left the city.

The Heian nobles also valued beauty. As a result, they spent hours working on their personal appearances. Many had magnificent wardrobes full of silk robes and gold jewelry. Nobles delighted in elaborate outfits. For example, women wore long gowns made of 12 layers of colored silk cleverly cut and folded to show off many layers at once. The women completed their outfits with delicate painted fans.

Outside Heian, life was focused more on duty than on beauty. Samurai in particular lived by a strict honor code known as Bushido. This code required the samurai to be brave and virtuous soldiers. It also required them to live simple, disciplined lives. More than anything, however, Bushido required samurai to remain loyal to their lords.

Case Study Assessment

1. Who were the daimyo? the samurai?

2. What was life like for a samurai?

3. **Activity** Imagine you were a noble in Heian. What would your day be like? Make a schedule of your routine on a typical day.

Nobles spent hours in elaborate Buddhist rituals. Most non-nobles were also Buddhists, but had no time for ritual.

550

c. 550
Buddhism arrives in Japan.

646
A new law code officially creates the samurai class.

794
Japan's imperial court moves to Heian.

Samurai warrior

Culture and Achievements

The Heian period is considered a golden age of Japanese culture. As you have read, the nobles of Heian prized beauty in all its forms. They spent hours on their writing and painting. As a result, they created amazing works of literature and art.

The nobles of Heian—both men and women—devoted much time to writing. Many women kept detailed diaries and journals about life at court. In addition, a noblewoman known as Lady Murasaki Shikibu wrote a novel called *The Tale of Genji*. Many historians consider this book, written in about 1000, to be the world's first full-length novel.

Men did not usually keep journals or write novels. Instead, they focused their efforts on poetry. Both men and women in Heian wrote beautiful poems. Some people even held parties at which they took turns writing and reading poems. Their poems often talked about love or nature. Most poems of the time followed strict formulas. One type of poem popular in Heian was the tanka. A tanka is always five lines long. The first and third lines have five syllables each, while the others have seven. Three-line poems called haiku were also popular.

A Culture of Literacy

The nobles of Heian placed great value on literature. All nobles, men and women alike, were expected to write beautifully. Many of the works they created are still read and admired today.

Some noble Japanese women kept detailed journals and wrote novels and poems.

This samurai is writing a poem on a cherry tree. Writing poems helped train samurai to concentrate.

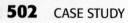

c. 1000
Lady Murasaki Shikibu writes *The Tale of Genji.*

**A scene from
*The Tale of Genji***

1192
The first shogun takes power in Japan.

1274
The Japanese fight off an invasion from Mongol China.

In addition to literature, the nobles of Heian made great achievements in other fields. They loved to paint and created masterful paintings. Many of their works illustrate scenes from stories, such as *The Tale of Genji*. Some nobles were also skilled architects. They designed magnificent temples and palaces, often surrounded by gardens and ponds.

Heian was also the birthplace of many forms of the performing arts. Nobles of the imperial court appreciated music, dance, and acrobatics. They also enjoyed watching plays. In time, the plays performed at Heian developed into a form of drama called Noh, which is still popular in Japan today.

Matsumoto Castle, built under Japan's shoguns

Case Study Assessment

1. What is the significance of *The Tale of Genji*?

2. What were some art forms practiced in Heian?

3. **Activity** The nobles of Japan loved dramas. Write a scene from a play about life in ancient Japan. Perform the scene with a group.

BIOGRAPHY

Lady Murasaki Shikibu
c. 978–c. 1026

During her lifetime, Lady Murasaki Shikibu was honored as a noblewoman and as a servant to the Empress Akiko. Since her death, she is better remembered as a diarist and an author. Lady Murasaki wrote *The Tale of Genji,* which is considered the world's first full-length novel and the greatest classic of Japanese literature. The novel tells of a prince named Genji and his long quest for love. During his search, he meets many women. By describing the women in precise detail, Lady Murasaki gives us a glimpse into life in Heian.

CHAPTER 16

Growth and Development of South and East Asia

FOCUS QUESTION

What forces had an impact on the development of Asia and why?

What You Will Learn...

Home to ancient civilizations and empires, Asia underwent many changes after the late 1800s. The arrival of Europeans and internal political struggles had major effects on the region.

FOCUS ON READING AND SPEAKING

Using Context Clues–Definitions As you read, you can often figure out the meaning of an unknown word by using context clues. One type of context clue is a definition, a restatement of a word's meaning. **See the lesson, Using Context Clues–Definitions, on page S19.**

Conducting an Interview With a partner, you will role-play a journalist interviewing a historical figure from Asia. First, read about the region and select a figure you would like to interview. Then conduct your interview, having your partner take on the role of your chosen historical figure.

New Delhi

SOUTH ASIA

Mohandas Gandhi

Bay of Bengal

0   250   500 Miles
0   250   500 Kilometers
Projection: Two-Point Equidistant

Imperialism Under British rule, thousands of miles of railroads were built in India. Here, workers build the East Bengal Railway around 1870.

South and East Asia, 1850–Today

map zone Geography Skills

Place Ancient cultures, European influence, and political conflict helped shape modern Asia.

1. **Use the Map** Which country in modern Asia has a Communist government?
2. **Analyze** How does this map suggest the importance of both ancient culture and modern developments in Asia?

ASIA

Beijing

Communist China

Tokyo

Sea of Japan (East Sea)

Yellow Sea

East China Sea

Japanese World War II fighter plane

40°N

30°N

20°N

150°E

SOUTHEAST ASIA

Skyscrapers

Hong Kong

140°E

Tropic of Cancer

PACIFIC OCEAN

HOLT

Geography's Impact
video series
Watch the video to understand the impact of population density.

South China Sea

10°N

130°E

Angkor Wat

120°E

Political Change New leaders led to political change in Asia. Under Kim Il-sung, North Korea became a Communist country.

Economic Growth Advanced technology has helped Japan keep its economic edge over other countries. In this photo, workers use robots to assemble a car.

505

Contact across Cultures

What You Will Learn...

Main Ideas

1. Chinese culture had a powerful influence on many Asian civilizations.
2. India was a major influence on culture in South Asia.
3. A new religion called Sikhism developed in India in the late 1400s.

The Big Idea

Contact between cultures in Asia led to a sharing of many cultural traits, especially from India and China.

Key Terms and Places

cultural diffusion, *p. 506*
Angkor Wat, *p. 508*
Sikhism, *p. 509*

TAKING NOTES As you read, use a diagram like this one to take notes on China's and India's influences on other Asian cultures, especially those of Southeast Asia.

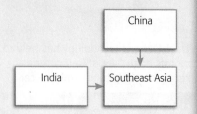

If YOU lived there...

You are a member of a noble family and an official in the government of Japan. For many years you and your prince have read the works of the ancient Chinese scholar Confucius. Both of you admire his works and are fascinated by Chinese culture. Now the prince tells you that he has received a letter from the emperor of China with an invitation for you to visit China. The prince wants you to accept the invitation and learn all that you can of life there.

What do you hope you will learn about China?

BUILDING BACKGROUND China and India were home to two of the world's first civilizations. Over several centuries, the people of China and India developed rich and distinct cultures. As other civilizations developed in Asia, they could not help but be influenced by the Chinese and the Indians.

Chinese Influence in Asia

Ancient China was one of the world's most highly developed civilizations. Already centuries old when other East Asia civilizations began, China exerted a strong influence over the cultures of its younger neighbors. Among those places influenced by China were Korea, Japan, and Vietnam.

Korea

Korea is located on a peninsula in East Asia, just east of China. No major physical barriers separate the peninsula from the rest of Asia, and so travel between the two regions is easy. As you might expect from this location, the Korean and Chinese people made contact early in their history. As a result of this contact, many elements of Chinese culture spread into Korea. The spread of culture traits from one region to another, such as from China to Korea, is known as **cultural diffusion.**

In the 100s BC, the Han dynasty conquered part of the Korean Peninsula, and Chinese settlers moved to Korea. They brought with them many elements of their own culture, including Buddhism and Chinese writing. Even after Korea won its independence, some of its rulers encouraged the adoption of Chinese culture.

Among the rulers who wanted to learn from the Chinese were the kings of the Koryo dynasty, from whose name we get the word Korea. The Koryo rulers adopted several elements of Chinese culture. For example, they created a civil service system similar to the one in China. At the same time, they did not want Korea to turn into another China, and they urged artisans to develop their own styles of ceramics and other crafts. The result was a Korean society that blended Chinese and native life.

Japan

Like Korea, Japan was heavily influenced by Chinese culture. In fact, many elements of Chinese culture that reached Japan did so through Korea. By the 500s Korean traders had begun sailing to Japan. With them came Chinese writing and Buddhism. The Japanese quickly adopted both the writing and religion. The Japanese of this time had no written language of their own, so educated Japanese used Chinese characters to write their own language.

Eventually, Japan's leaders decided to learn about Chinese culture directly from the source. One such leader was Prince Shotoku, who governed Japan from 593 to 622. Shotoku greatly admired the Chinese. He sent scholars to China to learn about Chinese religion, philosophy, and government. As a result, Chinese foods, fashions, and art gained popularity.

Vietnam

In the 200s BC a kingdom called Nam Viet rose to power in Vietnam. Its ruler was a former official from China who had declared his independence. As a result, the Vietnamese people adopted many elements of Chinese culture. They spoke the Chinese language and wore Chinese clothing and hairstyles. Many also practiced a Chinese form of Buddhism.

READING CHECK **Sequencing** How did Chinese culture spread to Korea and Japan?

Chinese Influence in Japan

The curved roof of the Todai-ji Temple in Nara, Japan, reflects China's influence.

BIOGRAPHY

Prince Shotoku
573–621

The spread of Buddhism in Japan was largely due to the efforts of Prince Shotoku. When Shotoku took power as regent of Japan, Buddhism was not very popular, but he worked to change people's minds. He built a grand temple and wrote about Buddhist teachings. By his death, Buddhism had taken firm root among Japan's nobles.

Angkor Wat

The majestic towers and detailed carvings of the ruins of Angkor Wat attract millions of tourists.

ANALYZING VISUALS Why do you think so many people visit Angkor Wat?

India and South Asia

China's long history and advanced civilization made it the most influential power in East Asia. Further south, however, lay another ancient and advanced civilization. That civilization was India, and it became the greatest influence on life in South Asia. Over the centuries, traders and missionaries spread elements of Indian culture through much of the region.

Probably the most visible element of Indian culture in Asia was religion. As you recall, India had been the birthplace of two major religions, Hinduism and Buddhism. Over several centuries, Indian missionaries carried both religions far and wide.

Along with religion, Indian ideas about writing, government, science, and art spread through Asia. Some Southeast Asian rulers so admired Indian culture that they adopted Indian names and built temples in Indian styles. Many also adopted the Indian language Sanskrit in their kingdoms.

Among the nations influenced by India was the Khmer Empire of what is now Cambodia. The Khmer adopted both Hinduism and Indian styles of architecture. The most famous example of this architecture is the spectacular temple complex at **Angkor Wat**. Built in the 1100s, the complex had high walls and a temple with high towers. Many of the temple's walls were covered with carvings of scenes from Hindu myths.

In the early 1500s India was conquered by Muslims from Central Asia. They were the Mughals, and they soon built a large empire. The Mughals brought an elegant new style of architecture to India. The best example of this style is the Taj Mahal, built by an emperor in the 1600s as a tomb for his wife. Mughal rulers encouraged the spread of Islam. As a result, traders and missionaries spread Islam to the islands of Indonesia, Malaysia, and the Philippines.

READING CHECK **Categorizing** What elements of Indian culture spread in Asia?

Sikhism Develops

Shortly before the Mughals took over India, a new religion developed there. It was **Sikhism** (SEE-ki-zuhm), a monotheistic religion that developed in the 1400s.

Origins of Sikhism

Sikhism has its roots in the teachings of the Guru Nanak, who lived in the late 1400s in the Punjab region of northern India. The title *guru* is Sanskrit for "teacher." Guru Nanak was raised as a Hindu, but he was not fully satisfied with Hindu teachings. As a result, he set out to learn more about the world. According to legend, his travels took him as far as Mecca and Medina, the holy cities of Islam.

The insights Guru Nanak gained in his travels became the basis for later Sikh beliefs. Over the next few centuries, his teachings were expanded and explained by nine other gurus. The last of these gurus, Guru Gobind Singh, died in the early 1700s. Most of the gurus wrote hymns in which they described the nature of God and how people should behave. These hymns were collected in the *Guru Granth Sahib,* the most sacred text of Sikhism.

Sikh Beliefs and Practices

Sikhs are monotheistic, believing in only one God. They believe that God has no physical form but that he can be sensed in the world, which he created. For Sikhs, the ultimate goal in life is to be reunited with God after death. To achieve this goal, one must meditate to find spiritual enlightenment. However, achieving enlightenment may take several lifetimes. As a result, Sikhs believe in reincarnation. Sikhs also believe that people should live truthfully and treat all people equally, regardless of gender, social class, or any other factors.

Sikhs pray several times each day. They are expected to wear five items at all times as signs of their religion: long hair, a small comb, a steel bracelet, a sword, and a special undergarment. In addition, all Sikh men wear turbans, as do many women.

READING CHECK **Analyzing** What are the basic beliefs of Sikhism?

SUMMARY AND PREVIEW Within Asia, cultures blended over the centuries. Next, you will learn how ideas from other lands changed life in Asia as well.

THE IMPACT TODAY

More than 20 million people in the world today practice Sikhism. Most of them live in the Punjab region of India and Pakistan.

---

go.hrw.com
Online Quiz
KEYWORD: SK9 HP16

Section 1 Assessment

Reviewing Ideas, Terms, and Places

1. **a. Define** What is **cultural diffusion**?

   b. Make Generalizations What influence did the Chinese have on civilization in Japan?

   c. Evaluate Do you think Chinese influence was good or bad for Korea and Japan? Why?

2. **a. Identify** What elements of Indian culture were adopted by other Asian civilizations?

   b. Sequence How did Indians help advance the spread of Islam in Asia?

3. **a. Recall** When did **Sikhism** develop?

   b. Draw Conclusions Why do you think Sikhs wear five particular items at all times?

Critical Thinking

4. **Categorizing** Use your notes and the chart below to identify the influence of China and India on each element of Asian culture.

	Religion	Language	Architecture
China			
India			

FOCUS ON SPEAKING

5. **Selecting a Topic** Who or what will be the subject of your interview? Will you talk to someone who lived during this period or to an expert on Chinese culture from the time? Write down some ideas.

Interaction with the West

What You Will Learn...

Main Ideas

1. The British made India into a colony in the 1700s and 1800s.
2. European countries used force to make China open its ports to trade.
3. Led by the United States, the West began to trade in Japan.

The Big Idea

In the 1700s and 1800s Europeans and Americans swept into Asia and forced many political and economic changes.

Key Terms and Places

British East India Company, *p. 511*
Raj, *p. 511*
Guangzhou, *p. 513*
spheres of influence, *p. 513*
Boxer Rebellion, *p. 513*

TAKING NOTES As you read, take notes about the interaction between the West and India, China, and Japan.

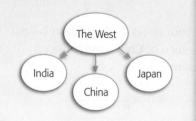

If YOU lived there...

You are an Indian merchant, a dealer in cotton and silk cloths. You have just finished a long journey to the city of Kolkata with a shipment of your finest bolts of cloth to be sent to Great Britain. You are hoping that this shipment will make you enough money to last for several months. As you approach the docks in Kolkata, however, a British official stops you. He tells you that you will not be allowed to send your cloth to Britain anymore, because importing cloth hurts British companies.

How does this new policy affect you?

BUILDING BACKGROUND Before the 1700s Asia had little contact with Europe, other than limited trade. By the end of the century, however, large numbers of Europeans had arrived in Asia, leading to major culture changes.

The British in India

As early as the days of the Roman Empire, Europeans had been fascinated by Asia. Traders had traveled back and forth between the two continents for centuries along the Silk Road, carrying precious goods in either direction. However, the journey along the Silk Road was long and dangerous, and few people dared it.

In the late 1200s, centuries after Rome fell, the Italian merchant Marco Polo traveled to China. When he returned home, Polo published an account of his journey, which soon became a bestseller. Still, few Europeans even dreamed of going to Asia.

Finally, in the 1400s Portuguese explorers successfully sailed to India for the first time. Other Europeans followed. Ambitious merchants built trading posts all along the Asian coast from India to China. However, Europeans seldom ventured very far inland. Their presence in Asia was mostly limited to the coast. That situation changed after the British moved into India.

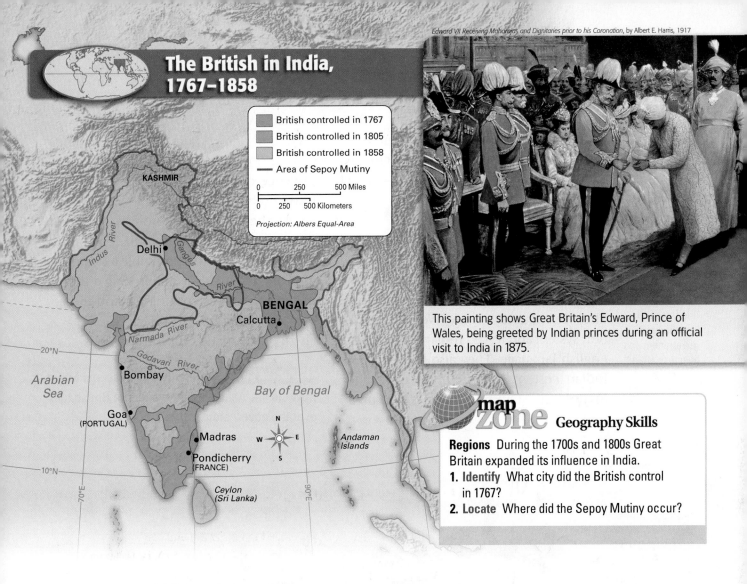

The British in India, 1767–1858

Legend:
- British controlled in 1767
- British controlled in 1805
- British controlled in 1858
- Area of Sepoy Mutiny

0   250   500 Miles
0   250   500 Kilometers

Projection: Albers Equal-Area

KASHMIR

Indus River

Delhi

Ganges River

BENGAL

Calcutta

Narmada River

Godavari River

20°N

Arabian Sea

Bombay

Goa (PORTUGAL)

Madras

Pondicherry (FRANCE)

Bay of Bengal

Andaman Islands

10°N

Ceylon (Sri Lanka)

70°E   90°E

Edward VII Receiving Maharajas and Dignitaries prior to his Coronation, by Albert E. Harris, 1917

This painting shows Great Britain's Edward, Prince of Wales, being greeted by Indian princes during an official visit to India in 1875.

map zone Geography Skills

Regions During the 1700s and 1800s Great Britain expanded its influence in India.
1. **Identify** What city did the British control in 1767?
2. **Locate** Where did the Sepoy Mutiny occur?

British East India Company

The people who changed the nature of European activity in Asia were British merchants. In the late 1700s members of the **British East India Company**, a company created to control trade between Britain, India, and East Asia, arrived in India.

Though they had arrived to trade, the British soon became involved in Indian politics. At the time, India was ruled by the Mughal Empire. In the 1700s, that empire began to fall apart. As the Mughals lost control, the British took over. The East India Company brought in its own army to take control. Before long, the Company controlled nearly all of India, as you can see on the map.

The Raj

Many Indians were not happy with the British East India Company's **policies**. In 1857 a rebellion broke out. The rebellion was led by sepoys, Indian soldiers who fought in the British army.

The fighting was brutal and lasted for more than two years. Rebel sepoys killed British officers, women, and children. The British burned villages they suspected of supporting the rebellion.

As a result of the rebellion, the British government took control of India from the East India Company and began to rule India directly. The period of British control in India is called the **Raj** (RAHZH), from the Hindi word for "rule."

ACADEMIC VOCABULARY
policy rule, course of action

During the Raj most officials who served in the Indian government were British, not Indian. These British officials considered themselves superior to the Indian people they governed. Most of them lived in separate neighborhoods and belonged to exclusive clubs. They had little contact with the common people.

Changes in India

Most of the British officials in India believed that they were improving the lives of the Indian people by ruling them. They introduced a new Western education system and forced Indians to learn the English language. They also banned some Indian customs. At the same time, they invited Christian missionaries to spread their beliefs.

Many Indian people disagreed with these officials. They did not think their lives were better under the British. They wanted a chance to participate in government and resented having to give up their culture. Some Indians began to protest the presence of the British. They staged protests and boycotted British goods.

In the end, these protests had little effect on the situation in India. The British considered India too profitable a colony to give up. India was a major source of raw materials, such as cotton, tea, and indigo, that were used in British industries. It was also a prime market for British goods.

READING CHECK Identifying Cause and Effect How did life in India change after the British took over the government?

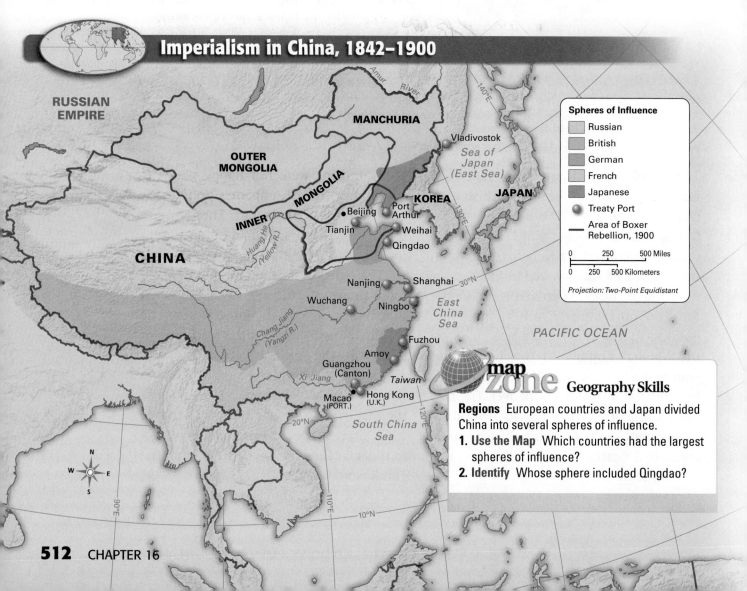

Imperialism in China, 1842–1900

Spheres of Influence
- Russian
- British
- German
- French
- Japanese
- Treaty Port
- Area of Boxer Rebellion, 1900

0   250   500 Miles
0   250   500 Kilometers

Projection: Two-Point Equidistant

map zone Geography Skills

Regions European countries and Japan divided China into several spheres of influence.
1. **Use the Map** Which countries had the largest spheres of influence?
2. **Identify** Whose sphere included Qingdao?

Europeans in China

While India was falling under the control of the British, similar events were happening in China. As in India, Europeans moved to increase their influence in—and their control over—China.

Differing Viewpoints

In the 1700s trade with China was a major source of income for Europeans. Chinese goods like silk and spices drew high prices throughout Europe. As a result, Europeans thought it vital that the trade continue.

To the Chinese, though, the trade with Europe was not as significant. They saw the Europeans as just another trading partner. In fact, China's rulers saw Europeans—and everyone else living outside of China—as barbarians. They did not want these barbarians living in their country. As a result, they only allowed European traders to live in a single city, **Guangzhou** (GWANG-JOH). The British knew the city as Canton.

Forcing the Issue

In 1839 a dispute arose between the Qing government of China and British traders. The British, members of the British East India Company, were smuggling opium into China to sell, which angered the Chinese. They confiscated and destroyed as much of the opium as they could find. The British merchants complained to their government, and the British attacked China.

The British navy quickly captured the city of Shanghai. They forced the Chinese to open five more ports to European traders. Within a few years, the Chinese had been forced to make similar deals with several other countries. Those countries included France, Russia, and the United States. China had been divided into many **spheres of influence,** or areas over which other countries had economic power.

Changes in China

In response to the presence of so many Europeans in China, the Qing introduced many changes to their culture. They thought that Western knowledge and technology was what had allowed the British to defeat them. As a result, China's leaders tried to introduce Western knowledge and languages to China. They also built Western weapons and ships.

These new weapons were tested in 1894 when China went to war with Japan. Despite their new weapons, though, China lost. The loss left China weak, and Western powers were quick to take advantage. They hurried to increase their influence in China. Fearing that Europeans would take over China completely and shut them out of trade, Americans also worked to gain power in the region.

The Chinese were humiliated by this increased Western control. Some began planning action against the Europeans and Americans. In 1899 they began the **Boxer Rebellion**, an attempt to drive all the Westerners out of China. The Western powers easily put down the rebellion and accused the Chinese government of supporting it. The failed rebellion left China even more humiliated than before.

READING CHECK Sequencing What led to the Boxer Rebellion?

The West in Japan

Before the 1400s contact between Europe and India and China had been rare but not unknown. In contrast, the Europeans had almost no knowledge of Japan at all. Unlike India and China, Japan had been able to isolate itself from the West for many years. The only Europeans allowed to the islands were a few Dutch merchants, and they were restricted to the city of Nagasaki.

FOCUS ON READING

How does the highlighted text help you figure out the meaning of *spheres of influence?*

Japan Reacts

This print shows the arrival of Commodore Perry in Edo Bay in 1853. Perry's hulking warships sent the Japanese a strong message about U.S. military power.

ANALYZING VISUALS How do the Japanese boats compare to the American ship?

Japan's isolation came to a drastic end, though, in 1852. In that year American naval commander Matthew Perry sailed into Tokyo Bay with a fleet of warships. The Japanese told him to sail on to Nagasaki, but Perry refused. He insisted on opening trade directly with Tokyo. He had been authorized by the U.S. president to use force if necessary to open Tokyo to trade. Faced with this threat, the Japanese had no choice but to allow him into the city.

Like the Chinese had before, the Japanese found their forced acceptance of the West humiliating. Rather than resisting Western influence as the Chinese had, though, Japan's new rulers decided their best plan was to modernize. They studied Western military tactics and economic practices and copied them. They wanted Japan to be part of the modern world.

READING CHECK **Contrasting** How did Japan's response to the West differ from China's?

SUMMARY AND PREVIEW The arrival of Europeans in Asia led to major changes in society. Next, you will learn about political changes that took place later.

Section 2 Assessment

go.hrw.com
Online Quiz
KEYWORD: SK9 HP16

Reviewing Ideas, Terms, and Places

1. **a. Define** What was the **Raj**?

   b. Sequence What led the British government to take control of India?

   c. Elaborate How do you think Indians felt about the attitude of British officials?

2. **a. Identify** Which country was the first to force its way into China?

   b. Identify Cause and Effect What led to the **Boxer Rebellion**?

3. **a. Describe** How did the Americans force the Japanese to trade with them?

   b. Summarize What effect did the Americans' arrival have on Japan?

Critical Thinking

4. **Finding Main Ideas** Using your notes, complete the graphic organizer below with details about Asian civilizations. In the left box, describe the civilizations before Europeans arrived. In the right box, tell how they changed afterward.

India:
China:
Japan: → Europeans Arrive → India:
China:
Japan:

FOCUS ON SPEAKING

5. **Choosing Questions** If you were to interview someone from this period, who would it be? Write three questions you might ask that person.

New Political Movements

If YOU lived there...

You are a lawyer in India in 1932. One morning two friends approach you with a question. They are unhappy about a new law that the British have passed. One friend wants to take up arms and try to force the British out of the country. The other disagrees. She wants to protest the law, but she does not want to use violence to do it. She does not think violence is necessary and is afraid that people will get hurt. The two ask your opinion on the most effective means of protest.

Whom will you support? Why?

BUILDING BACKGROUND Europeans held power in parts of Asia for several decades. Their presence led to many changes, both culturally and politically. Eventually, a combination of factors led to the development of entirely new political systems in many Asian countries.

The Call for Indian Independence

By the early 1900s many Indians resented British interference in their country. Their resentment only increased after World War I. During the war, more than 800,000 Indian soldiers had fought for the British. When the soldiers returned home, they hoped that their sacrifices during the war would have won them some respect. Instead, they found that nothing had changed.

Growing Resentment

The growing resentment in India caught the attention of British officials there. Fearing rebellion, the British dealt harshly with anyone who expressed discontent. British troops broke up all protests against the government, even peaceful ones. Rather than ending resentment, the British actions just angered the Indians even more.

What You Will Learn...

Main Ideas

1. The call for Indian independence was accompanied by nonviolent protests.
2. The early 1900s saw the end of China's imperial period and the beginning of Communism in the country.
3. Changes in Japan's government led to the formation of a new empire.

The Big Idea

Major political changes in Asia in the early twentieth century marked the end of European domination there.

Key Terms and Places

nonviolence, *p. 516*
civil disobedience, *p. 516*
partition, *p. 517*
Pakistan, *p. 517*
Diet, *p. 520*

TAKING NOTES As you read, take notes on political changes in the various countries of Asia. Use a graphic organizer like the one below to organize your notes.

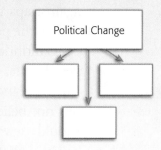

Political Change

Nonviolent Protests

Nonviolent protests in India, like the one in the large image, inspired later political activists. Among those inspired were some African Americans who fought for civil rights in the 1960s, who staged nonviolent sit-ins like the one shown in the small photo.

ANALYZING VISUALS What similarities can you see between the two protests shown on this page?

The conflict between the British and the Indians exploded in 1919. At a protest in the town of Amritsar (uhm-RIT-suhr), British troops fired into an Indian crowd, killing more than 400 people. The so-called Amritsar Massacre caused even more Indians to want the British out of India.

Mohandas Gandhi

After the Amritsar Massacre, a new leader arose in the Indian resistance. That leader was Mohandas Gandhi. Gandhi was a lawyer who believed in fair treatment for all people. Resistance and protest were not new to him. For many years Gandhi had lived in South Africa and campaigned against apartheid. He also worked in support of the poor and women's rights.

Gandhi's protests were based on two key beliefs. The first was **nonviolence**, the avoidance of violent actions. Gandhi did not believe that people needed to or should use violence to protest injustice. He believed that peaceful protests were more successful than violent ones.

The second of Gandhi's key beliefs was **civil disobedience**, or the refusal to obey laws in order to bring about change. For example, he encouraged people to avoid paying taxes to the British. Gandhi felt that if the Indian people refused to cooperate with British authority, the British would grow frustrated and leave.

As part of his noncooperation plan, Gandhi encouraged the Indian people to boycott all British products. He stopped wearing British-made clothing and urged other people to do the same. Many people began producing homemade cloth to make clothes themselves. As a result, spinning wheels and homemade cloth became symbols of the Indian resistance. Gandhi also encouraged people to stop buying salt from the British and to make their own salt from seawater instead.

Gandhi and his followers were arrested on several occasions. They did not give up, and their persistence convinced more Indians to join them. By the 1930s millions of people were protesting British rule.

Division and Independence

In the end, Gandhi's protests led to change in India. In 1935 the British government gave the Indian people limited self-rule. Not satisfied with this, many people continued their protests.

Even as Indians were protesting against the British, tensions between the Hindu and Muslim communities in India caused a crisis. Muslims feared that, even if India became fully independent, they would have little say in the government. Many of them began calling for a separate nation of their own.

To avoid a civil war, the British government agreed to the **partition**, or division, of India. In 1947 two independent countries were formed. India was mostly Hindu. **Pakistan**, which included the area that is now Bangladesh, was mostly Muslim. As a result, some 10 million people rushed to cross the border. Muslims and Hindus wanted to live in the countries in which they would be part of the majority.

READING CHECK **Identifying Cause and Effect** What was the effect of Gandhi's protesting?

The End of Imperial China

While Indians were calling for freedom from the British, the Chinese were also calling for a change in government. The growing influence of foreign powers in China made many people unhappy with imperial rule. Their unhappiness led to a revolution in China.

Revolution

Realizing that the people were unhappy, China's rulers, the Qing dynasty, tried to reform the government. They built new schools and a new army. They even allowed people to elect regional assemblies for the first time.

However, these attempts at reform were too little and too late. Radical activists called for the overthrow of China's government. They wanted China to become a republic.

One of the leaders of these protests was Sun Yixian (SUN YEE-SHAHN). In the West, his name is sometimes spelled Sun Yat-sen. Sun wanted to make China a democracy, but he did not think that the Chinese people were ready for that yet. He thought it was the government's job to teach the people how to govern themselves.

Inspired by Sun, rebels forced the last Qing emperor—China's last emperor of any dynasty—out of power in 1911. The rebels then formed a republic.

Civil War

The creation of a republic did not end the power struggles in China. In the 1920s two rival groups emerged. One group was the Communists. Opposing them were the Nationalists, led by Chiang Kai-shek (chang ky-SHEK). For several years the two groups worked together to drive foreign imperialists out of China, but their alliance was always uneasy.

The alliance broke apart completely in 1929. Afraid that Communist influence in China was growing too strong, Nationalist forces attacked Communists in several cities. This attack began a civil war that lasted 20 years.

For the first several years of the civil war, the Nationalists were in control. By the 1930s, though, a new Communist leader had emerged. His name was Mao Zedong (MOW ZUH-DOOHNG). By 1949 Mao and the Communists had won. They declared a new Communist government, the People's Republic of China, with Mao as its leader. The surviving Nationalists fled to the island of Taiwan, where they founded the Republic of China.

Communism in China

In a Communist system, the government owns most businesses and land and controls all areas of life. Therefore the first action of China's new Communist government was taking control of the economy. The government seized all private farms and organized them into large, state-run farms. It also took over all businesses and factories. Those who spoke out against the government were killed or punished.

As China's ruler, Mao introduced many changes to Chinese society. He wanted to rid China of its traditional customs and create a new system. His goal was to make China a modern country.

While some of Mao's changes improved life in China, others did not. On one hand, women gained more rights than they had under the emperors, including the right to work outside the home. On the other hand, the government limited people's freedoms and imprisoned people who criticized it. Hundreds of thousands of people were killed for criticizing the government. In addition, many economic programs were unsuccessful, and some were outright disasters. Poor planning often led to famines that killed millions.

READING CHECK **Summarizing** How did Communism change life in China?

Close-up

Communist China

China celebrates the beginnings of Chinese Communism on National Day, October 1. It was on October 1, 1949 that Mao Zedong created the People's Republic of China. The celebration includes a huge parade in Beijing's Tiananmen Square.

Beijing

CHINA

PACIFIC OCEAN

The Gate of Heavenly Peace displays Mao Zedong's portrait above the entrance.

The parades include couples married on National Day, a popular time to wed.

中华人民共和国万岁

A military parade of soldiers, tanks, and other equipment shows China's power.

A New Japanese Empire

When the Chinese grew dissatisfied with their government, they overthrew their emperor. When similar feelings had taken hold in Japan about 50 years earlier, the people there had the opposite reaction. They decided to choose a new emperor to rule their country.

A New Government

Japan had officially been ruled by an emperor for several centuries. In truth, however, the emperor had little power. Since the 1100s, real power had been in the hands of military leaders called shoguns.

The arrival of Americans and other Westerners in Japan in the 1800s angered many people. They resented foreign interference in Japan and blamed the shogun. They felt he should have been strong enough to keep the Americans and Europeans out of their country.

In 1868 an alliance of nobles defeated the shogun's army and forced the shogun to step down. By doing so, they restored the power of the emperor. The newly powerful emperor took the name Meiji (may-jee), which means "enlightened rule" in Japanese. As a result, the shift back to imperial power in Japan is known as the Meiji Restoration.

ANALYSIS SKILL **ANALYZING VISUALS**

Why might China's government sponsor such a huge celebration for National Day?

The Chinese believe dragon dances bring good fortune to important events.

世界人民大团结万岁

Lion dances are performed to spread good blessings to the community.

Reforms in Japan

When Meiji took control of Japan, he made sweeping changes in the government. First, he abolished the old feudal system. Under this system, warriors called samurai had been given land and power in exchange for military service. Meiji took all land away from the samurai and put it under the control of the state.

To replace the feudal system, Meiji sent officials to Europe and the United States to learn about Western government and economics. He then worked to apply in Japan what these officials had learned. For example, he created the **Diet**, the elected legislature that still governs Japan.

Meiji also reformed the Japanese education system. He required all children to attend school. He also encouraged some children to study in other countries to learn more about those countries.

ACADEMIC VOCABULARY
implications
consequences

Perhaps most importantly, Meiji worked to industrialize Japan. He built telegraph lines, a postal service, and railroads to improve communication. He also established Japan's first national currency. Japan quickly became a major industrial power in Asia.

Japanese Imperialism

Meiji's reforms also led to changes in the country's military. All soldiers were required to swear a personal oath of loyalty to the emperor. The result was a force that would do anything the emperor asked of it.

From 1890 to 1910 Japan launched a series of military strikes against nearby countries. In short order the Japanese defeated both the Chinese and Russian armies. These victories left Japan the most powerful county in Asia and won Japan the respect of many Western nations.

Respect soon turned to caution, however. In 1910 Japan invaded Korea and made it a colony. At the same time, the government began to expand the Japanese army. Many observers feared the possible **implications** of that expansion.

READING CHECK **Summarizing** Why did some countries become cautious about Japan?

SUMMARY AND PREVIEW In this section, you learned about political changes in Asia in the 1800s and 1900s. Next, you will learn how these changes led to violence and war.

Section 3 Assessment

go.hrw.com
Online Quiz
KEYWORD: SK9 HP16

Reviewing Ideas, Terms, and Places

1. **a. Identify** What countries were created from the **partition** of India?

   b. Generalize How did Gandhi encourage people to oppose the British?

2. **a. Describe** How did China change under the Communist government?

   b. Predict How do you think most Chinese people felt about Mao's changes in China?

3. **a. Recall** What were the effects of the Meiji Restoration in Japan?

   b. Explain How did Japan's foreign policy change?

Critical Thinking

4. **Summarizing** Use your notes to complete the graphic organizer to the right with a short-summary of political changes in each region.

India	→	
China	→	
Japan	→	

FOCUS ON SPEAKING

5. **Choosing a Focus** This section introduced several figures you could interview: Gandhi, Mao, Meiji. Write some ideas about subjects you could use as the focus of an interview with each person.

Mohandas Gandhi

How did a peace-loving lawyer win his country's freedom?

When did he live? 1869–1948

Where did he live? India

What did he do? Considered by many to be the father of modern India, Mohandas Gandhi led the struggle for Indian independence.

Why is he important? As a leading member of the Indian National Congress, Gandhi introduced a policy of nonviolent resistance to British rule. He led millions in fasts, peaceful protest marches, and boycotts of British goods. His devotion to nonviolence earned him the name *Mahatma,* or "Great Soul." Gandhi's efforts proved successful. In 1947 India won its independence from Britain.

Drawing Conclusions Why did people call Gandhi "Mahatma"?

KEY IDEAS

● **Mohandas Gandhi** wrote that nonviolence was a more effective means of bringing about change than violence could ever be.

*"*It is perfectly true that [the English] used brute force and that it is possible for us to do likewise, but by using similar means we can only get the same thing that they got . . . [Using violence to gain freedom] is the same as saying we can get a rose through planting a noxious weed.*"*

–Mohandas Gandhi, *Freedom's Battle*, 1908

Gandhi and his supporters used nonviolent means to protest the British rule of India.

Asia at War

If YOU lived there...

You are a farmer living outside of a small town in China. One day you hear explosions in the distance. Soon, you see people running from the direction of the city across your fields. You stop one of the fleeing people to ask what has happened. He tells you that the Japanese have attacked and burned the city to the ground.

How will you react to the attack?

BUILDING BACKGROUND The spread of imperialism and Communism in Asia in the early 1900s soon brought about conflict between nations. In some cases, these conflicts led to full-scale war.

Japanese Aggression in Asia

As you read in the last section, Japan had become a major military power by the early 1900s. By defeating China and Russia, Japan had ensured that no one in Asia could easily defeat it. Before long the Japanese were using their new might to expand their influence through much of mainland Asia.

During World War I the Japanese fought on the side of the Allies. They did not fight very much, though. They only attacked sites in China that were controlled by the Germans. After the war, the Allies gave these former German-held lands to Japan as a reward for its assistance.

Manchuria

For several years after World War I, the Japanese were content with just these lands. Their attitude changed in the 1930s, though. A newly aggressive Japan invaded **Manchuria**, a region in northeast China. The region was rich in minerals and other resources that the Japanese wanted.

The Japanese were brutal rulers in Manchuria. They forced millions of Chinese citizens to work in labor camps where tens of thousands of them died. The Japanese also took land away from Chinese families and gave it to Japanese settlers. They also mistreated the many Russian settlers in Manchuria.

What You Will Learn...

Main Ideas

1. Japan's aggression in Asia upset many countries.
2. During World War II, Japan fought for control of the Pacific.
3. The Korean and Vietnam wars were fought to stop the spread of Communism.
4. India and Pakistan have been in conflict over Kashmir.

The Big Idea

Since the 1930s several major wars have been fought in Asia.

Key Terms and Places

Manchuria, *p. 522*
Nanking, *p. 523*
Pearl Harbor, *p. 523*
island hopping, *p. 525*
Hiroshima, *p. 525*
domino theory, *p. 526*
Kashmir, *p. 527*

 TAKING NOTES As you read, take notes about the wars fought in Asia during the 1900s. Use a table like the one below to organize your notes.

Japanese in Asia	World War II
Korea and Vietnam	Kashmir

Nanking

From Manchuria, the Japanese launched attacks on the rest of China. One of their main targets was the city of **Nanking**, at the time China's capital. In 1937 the Japanese captured the city. What followed was six weeks of horror. Japanese soldiers robbed, tortured, and killed hundreds of civilians. They also burned down about one third of the city.

The destruction of Nanking by the Japanese became known as the Nanking Massacre. It resulted in decades of mistrust between China and Japan. It also turned worldwide opinion against Japan.

READING CHECK **Describe** How did the Japanese treat areas they conquered in Asia?

World War II

When Japan began its aggressive policy of expansion in the 1930s, many people were concerned. Among those concerned were many Americans. They feared that the Japanese would continue to attack Asian countries if not stopped. However, most Americans did not want to get involved in any conflicts in Asia.

The Attack on Pearl Harbor

The American attitude toward war with Japan changed on December 7, 1941. On that morning, Japanese fighter planes and bombers bombed the U.S. naval base at **Pearl Harbor**, Hawaii. This attack was a declaration of war not just against the United States but against its allies as well.

The attack came as a complete surprise to Americans. Most of the American planes at the base never even had a chance to take off before they were destroyed. In less than 2 hours, more than 2,000 American soldiers were killed and most of the Pearl Harbor fleet was destroyed.

The American response to the attack on Pearl Harbor was immediate. The day after the attack, U.S. President Franklin D. Roosevelt asked Congress to declare war on Japan. In a radio address, he announced to the American people that the country was now at war with Japan.

Primary Source

SPEECH
The Attack on Pearl Harbor

The day after the attack on Pearl Harbor, President Franklin D. Roosevelt asked Congress to declare war on Japan.

❝Yesterday, December 7th, 1941—a date which will live in infamy—the United States of America was suddenly and deliberately attacked by naval and air forces of the Empire of Japan . . .

As commander in chief of the Army and Navy, I have directed that all measures be taken for our defense. But always will our whole nation remember the character of the onslaught against us.

No matter how long it may take us to overcome this premeditated invasion, the American people in their righteous might will win through to absolute victory . . .

Hostilities exist . . . our people, our territory, and our interests are in grave danger.

With confidence in our armed forces, with the unbounding determination of our people, we will gain the inevitable triumph—so help us God.❞

ANALYSIS SKILL **ANALYZING PRIMARY SOURCES**

What does Roosevelt say the ultimate outcome of the war will be?

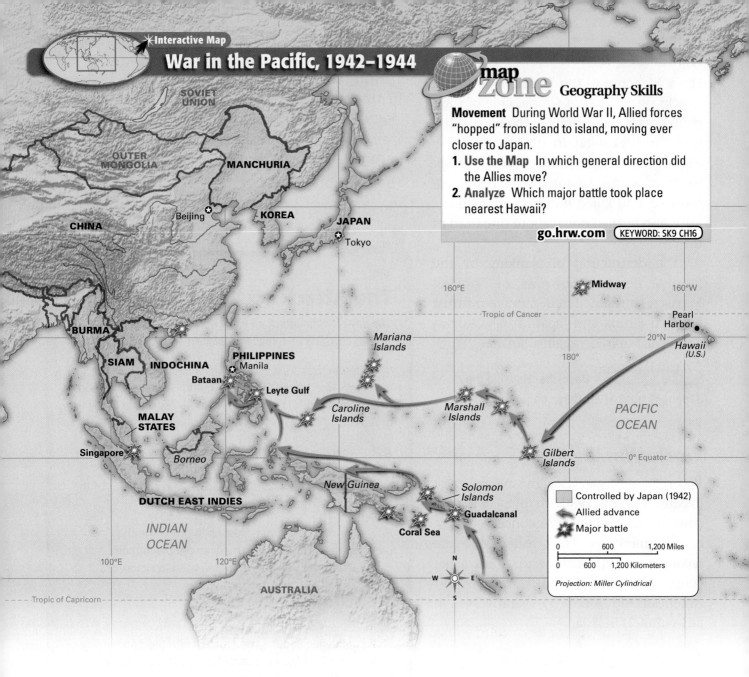

War in the Pacific, 1942–1944

map zone Geography Skills

Movement During World War II, Allied forces "hopped" from island to island, moving ever closer to Japan.

1. **Use the Map** In which general direction did the Allies move?
2. **Analyze** Which major battle took place nearest Hawaii?

go.hrw.com KEYWORD: SK9 CH16

Legend:
- Controlled by Japan (1942)
- Allied advance
- Major battle

0   600   1,200 Miles
0   600 1,200 Kilometers

Projection: Miller Cylindrical

Early Stages of the War

For the first several months of World War II, Japan essentially ruled the Pacific. The attack on Pearl Harbor had left the U.S. Navy weakened. As a result, there was no one to stop Japan's well-prepared navy.

Before long, Japan controlled much of East Asia. As you can see on the map, the Japanese also controlled dozens of islands throughout the Pacific. Among those islands were the Philippines, which the Japanese had taken from the Americans.

The Japanese treated people in the lands they captured very harshly. When they captured the Philippines, they took more than 70,000 prisoners. They then forced these prisoners to march 60 miles to a brutal prison camp. More than 600 Americans and 10,000 Filipinos died.

By 1942 the Allies decided that Japan was a major threat. Before then they had focused most of their efforts on the war in Europe. Now, however, they turned their eyes to the war in the Pacific as well.

Turning Point

The first challenge to the Japanese came late in 1942. In two battles, the Battles of the Coral Sea and Midway, the Japanese were stopped by the Allies. These defeats marked a turning point in the war.

After the Battle of Midway, the Allies began attacking Japanese targets. The Allies' main strategy in the Pacific was called island hopping. Under the **island hopping** strategy, the Allies took only the most strategically important islands, instead of each Japanese-held island. They used these captured targets as bases to launch attacks on other targets. In this way, the Allied forces worked their way closer to Japan.

End of the War

The war in the Pacific continued for several years. By 1945 the Allies were close enough to Japan to invade. However, military leaders warned that invading Japan would be costly. Such an invasion would leave more than a million Allied troops dead.

Instead, the military suggested a different option to end the war. On August 6, 1945, an American plane dropped an atomic bomb on the city of **Hiroshima**, Japan. The effects of the bomb were devastating. More than 70,000 people were killed instantly, and thousands of buildings were destroyed. But the Japanese still did not surrender. Three days later, the Americans dropped another atomic bomb, this time on the city of Nagasaki. As a result, the Japanese surrendered on August 15, 1945.

In the years following World War II, tens of thousands of residents of Hiroshima and Nagasaki died from radiation poisoning. In 1949 the Japanese government created the Hiroshima Peace Memorial Park to commemorate those who died.

READING CHECK Identifying Cause and Effect
What caused World War II in the Pacific?

War in Korea and Vietnam

During World War II, democratic and Communist countries fought together to defeat Japan. After the war, however, the alliances fell apart. Fueled by political and economic differences, democratic and Communist countries came into conflict. In Korea and Vietnam, these conflicts led to war.

The Korean War

Before World War II, Korea had been part of Japan's growing empire. After the war, the Allies took Korea away from Japan. Korea was once again independent.

Honoring the Dead

Millions of Japanese citizens gather at the Hiroshima Peace Memorial Park in 2000 to honor those killed by the atomic bomb.

ANALYZING VISUALS Why do you think so many people gathered at this memorial?

Rather than forming one country, though, the Koreans formed two. Aided by the Soviet Union, North Koreans under Kim Il-sung created a Communist government. In South Korea, the United States helped build a democratic government.

In 1950 North Korea invaded South Korea, starting the Korean War. With help from many countries, including the United States, the South Koreans drove the invaders back. The Korean War was costly, and its effects linger in Korea today. Relations between North and South Korea are strained. To prevent conflict from breaking out again, the countries maintain a demilitarized zone, or DMZ, along their shared border. No troops are allowed into the DMZ, but armed forces patrol either side.

The Vietnam War

Like the Korean War, the Vietnam War was a struggle between democratic and Communist governments. As had been the case in Korea, the north was Communist and the south was democratic.

Eventually, Communists in South Vietnam began a civil war. To defend South Vietnam's democratic government, the United States sent in troops in the 1960s. The United States hoped to stop the spread of Communism in Asia. According to the **domino theory**, if one country fell to communism, other countries nearby would follow like falling dominoes.

Years of warfare in Vietnam caused millions of deaths and terrible destruction. In the end, North and South Vietnam were reunited as one Communist country. As the Communists took over, about 1 million refugees fled South Vietnam. Many went to the United States.

READING CHECK Comparing and Contrasting How were the Korean and Vietnam wars similar? How were they different?

The Korean and Vietnam Wars

The Korean War

- Lasted from 1950 to 1953

- Fought between Communist North Korea and democratic South Korea

- North Korea was supported by China and the Soviet Union.

- South Korea was supported by the United States and more than a dozen other countries.

- North and South Korea remained separate. A demilitarized zone was set up between them.

The Vietnam War

- Lasted from 1957 to 1975

- Fought between Communists and non-Communists for control of South Vietnam

- Communists from North Vietnam were supported by China and the Soviet Union.

- South Vietnam's democratic non-Communist troops were supported by the United States, Australia, South Korea, and other countries.

- The government of South Vietnam fell and the country was unified as a Communist state.

Armed guards patrol both sides of the demilitarized zone that still separates the countries of South and North Korea.

Conflict in Kashmir

South Asia also became the site of armed conflict in the 1940s. Shortly after India and Pakistan were separated in 1947, the two countries began to fight over the region of **Kashmir**. Kashmir is a mountainous area in the north near the Chinese border.

Roots of the Conflict

When India was partitioned, Kashmir was ruled by a Hindu prince. Because he was Hindu, he decided to make Kashmir a part of India rather than Pakistan.

This decision angered Kashmir's large Muslim population. The Pakistani government, claiming Kashmire should belong to Pakistan, soon sent troops into Kashmir. India responded by sending in troops of its own. War broke out.

Fighting in Kashmir continued for two years. In 1949 the United Nations negotiated a peace treaty. This treaty divided Kashmir in two. India controlled the southern part, and Pakistan the northern part. Later, China also claimed part of Kashmir. Under the treaty, the people of Kashmir were to vote on their future. However, that vote was never held.

Kashmir Today

Today, Kashmir is still disputed territory. Conflict continues. Much of the region's Muslim population lives in the Indian-controlled area, and some militants have taken up arms against India. The Indian government claims that these militants are terrorists backed by Pakistan. The Pakistani government, on the other hand, rejects these claims. It says that the militants are simply Kashmir residents who are fighting to break from from Indian control.

The disagreement over Kashmir is a constant source of tension between the governments of India and Pakistan. Though full-scale war has not broken out, thousands of people have died in fighting in the region.

READING CHECK **Summarizing** What led to the conflict in Kashmir?

SUMMARY AND PREVIEW Conflicts over political and economic differences raged through Asia in the 1940s, 1950s, and 1960s. Next, you will learn how life in Asia changed after these conflicts.

Section 4 Assessment

go.hrw.com
Online Quiz
KEYWORD: SK9 HP16

Reviewing Ideas, Terms, and Places

1. **a. Identify** What regions in Asia did Japan invade?
   b. Explain How did Japanese actions in **Nanking** and **Manchuria** affect public opinion?

2. **a. Sequence** How did the Allies turn the tide of World War II?
   b. Evaluate Do you think using the atomic bomb was a good decision? Why or why not?

3. **a. Describe** What was the final result of the Korean War?
   b. Elaborate How did the **domino theory** lead to American involvement in Vietnam?

4. **a. Recall** What issue led to fighting in **Kashmir**?

Critical Thinking

5. **Summarizing** Draw a chart like the one here. Using your notes, fill in each column with information about the appropriate conflict.

Conflict	Participants	Results
Manchuria		
World War II		
Korean War		
Vietnam War		
Kashmir		

FOCUS ON SPEAKING

6. **Asking Questions about Events** If you were to interview someone involved in one of the conflicts described in this section, what would you ask? Make a list of questions.

A New Asia

What You Will Learn...

Main Ideas

1. Many Asian countries have found economic success since World War II.
2. Political shifts in Asia have led to new governments in many countries.
3. Many Asian cultures blend old and new ideas.

The Big Idea

Since the end of World War II, Asia has experienced major economic, political, and cultural changes.

Key Terms and Places

trade surplus, *p. 529*
tariff, *p. 529*
constitutional monarchies, *p. 531*
Tiananmen Square, *p. 531*
human rights, *p. 531*

TAKING NOTES As you read, take notes on the economic, political, and cultural changes that have occurred in Asia since World War II.

If **YOU** lived there...

You are a small business owner living in Taiwan shortly after World War II. Before the war your company made toys by hand. During the war, however, your building and all of your equipment was destroyed. Now that the war is over, a European bank has offered to loan you money to start your business up again. A friend has also told you about a company that sells machines that will make your toys much faster than you could before.

Will you buy the machines? Why or why not?

BUILDING BACKGROUND Years of conflict in Asia left many parts of the region a mess. Governments were unstable, economies were in shambles, and people were confused. With the return of peace after the fighting, however, the Asian people had a chance to rebuild their countries. Many jumped at this opportunity.

Economic Success

Before World War II the countries of South and East Asia were not considered economic powerhouses. Few of the countries were heavily industrialized. As a result, they lagged behind the countries of Europe and the Americas.

Since World War II, however, the countries of the region have shifted their focus. Several Asian countries' economies are now ranked among the strongest in the world.

Japan

Japan was the Asian country most devastated by World War II. However, it was also the first to recover and prosper. With assistance from Europe and the United States, Japan completely rebuilt its economy. Within a few decades of the war, Japan's economy had grown into one of the strongest in the world.

The most successful area of Japan's economy has been manufacturing. Japanese companies are known for making high-quality products, especially cars and electronics like televisions

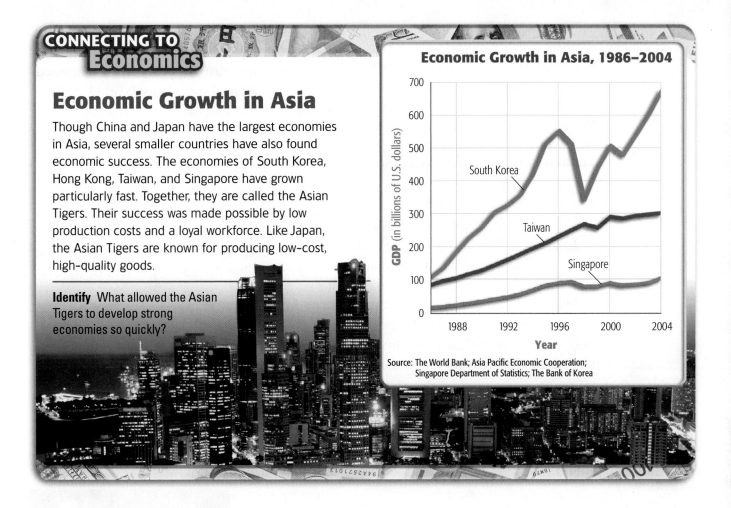

CONNECTING TO Economics

Economic Growth in Asia

Though China and Japan have the largest economies in Asia, several smaller countries have also found economic success. The economies of South Korea, Hong Kong, Taiwan, and Singapore have grown particularly fast. Together, they are called the Asian Tigers. Their success was made possible by low production costs and a loyal workforce. Like Japan, the Asian Tigers are known for producing low-cost, high-quality goods.

Identify What allowed the Asian Tigers to develop strong economies so quickly?

Economic Growth in Asia, 1986–2004

South Korea

Taiwan

Singapore

GDP (in billions of U.S. dollars)

700
600
500
400
300
200
100
0

1988   1992   1996   2000   2004

Year

Source: The World Bank; Asia Pacific Economic Cooperation; Singapore Department of Statistics; The Bank of Korea

---

and DVD players. The Japanese are clever innovators and **efficient** builders. As a result, they are able to produce excellent products at low costs.

Many Japanese products are intended to be sold outside of the country, especially in China and the United States. In fact, Japan's trade has been so successful that the country has built up a huge trade surplus. A **trade surplus** exists when a country exports more goods than it imports.

Japan is able to export more than it imports in part because of high tariffs. A **tariff** is a fee that a country charges on imports or exports. For many years, Japan's government has placed high tariffs on goods brought into the country. This makes imported goods more expensive, and so people buy Japanese goods rather than imported ones.

China

When the Communists took over China in the 1940s they established a command economy. A command economy is one in which the government owns all businesses and makes all decisions.

However, the command economy led to major economic problems in China. For example, the production of goods fell drastically. In response, the government closed many state-owned factories and began allowing privately owned businesses. These businesses today produce everything from satellites and chemicals to clothing and toys. In addition, the government has created special economic zones where foreign businesspeople can own companies. This mixed economic approach has helped China's economy boom. Today it has the world's second largest economy.

ACADEMIC VOCABULARY

efficient productive and not wasteful

GROWTH AND DEVELOPMENT OF SOUTH AND EAST ASIA **529**

India

Since India gained its independence, it has become a major industrial power. Its gross domestic product (GDP) places it among the world's top five industrial countries. However, its per capita GDP is only $3,700. Millions of Indians live in poverty.

The government has taken steps to reduce poverty. For example, it has encouraged farmers to adopt modern farming techniques. It has also attempted to lure new industries to India. It has made the city of Bangalore a center of high-tech industry. In addition, the government has promoted India's film industry. Nicknamed Bollywood, this industry produces more films each year than any other country.

READING CHECK **Summarizing** How have Asian economies changed since World War II?

Political Shifts

South and East Asia have also witnessed major political shifts since World War II. In some countries, democracy has taken root. In others, military rulers have seized control of the governments.

Democracy in Asia

Since the end of World War II several Asian countries have embraced democracy. One such country was Japan. Japan's emperor gave up his throne at the end of the war and helped create a democratic government there. When India became independent in 1947, it too became a democracy. In fact, India is by population the largest democracy in the world today. Other democratic countries in the region include Bangladesh, Mongolia, and Indonesia.

Close-up

Tiananmen Square, 1989

More than 1 million pro-democracy protestors occupied Beijing's Tiananmen Square in the spring of 1989. At first, Chinese leaders tolerated the demonstration, but as the protest grew larger they decided to crack down. In the evening hours of June 3, the government sent tanks and troops into the square to crush the protestors, killing hundreds.

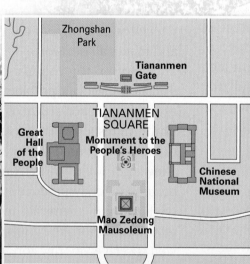

Day 18

May 30 Near the official portrait of Mao Zedong, students build a large statue that comes to be known as the "Goddess of Democracy."

ANALYSIS SKILL **ANALYZING VISUALS**

What do these photos suggest about the desire for democracy in China?

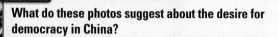

In addition, some Asian countries have developed **constitutional monarchies**. In this form of democracy, a monarch serves as the head of state, but a legislature makes the laws. Thailand and Malaysia are both constitutional monarchies. Thailand has had the same royal family since the 1780s. In Malaysia, local rulers take turns being the king.

China and Democracy

China is not a democracy. The Communist government there still tightly controls most areas of life. For example, it controls newspapers and Internet access to restrict the flow of information and ideas.

Some Chinese people have attempted to bring democracy to their country. However, the government harshly punishes people who oppose its policies.

Day 24

June 5 In this famous image from the events at Tiananmen Square, an unarmed man faces down a line of Chinese tanks.

The most famous example of this punishment took place in 1989. In the spring of that year more than 1 million Chinese pro-democracy protestors gathered in **Tiananmen Square** in Beijing, China's capital. The protestors were demanding more political rights and freedoms. The Chinese government tried to get the protestors to leave the square. When they refused, the government used troops and tanks to make them leave. Hundreds of protestors were killed, and many more were injured or imprisoned.

Military Governments

In some cases, political change in Asia was brought about by military leaders. In both Pakistan and Myanmar, for example, military leaders seized power for themselves.

Pakistan has been plagued by unstable governments since it was first created in 1947. Over the years it has suffered from rebellions and the assassination of government leaders. In 2001, General Pervez Musharraf became Pakistan's president after a military coup. One of his main rivals for power was Benazir Bhutto, who in 1988 became the first female prime minister to serve in a Muslim country. Bhutto was assassinated by terrorists in late 2007.

A military government also rules the country of Myanmar, which is also known as Burma. The military seized power there in 1962. Since then, the government has abused people's **human rights**, those rights that all people deserve such as the rights to equality and justice. A Burmese woman, Aung San Suu Kyi (awng sahn soo chee), has led a movement for more democracy and rights. She and others have been jailed and harassed for their actions.

READING CHECK **Categorizing** What forms of government have developed in Asia since World War II?

FOCUS ON READING
What clues can help you discover the meaning of the term *constitutional monarchies*?

Asian culture today blends traditional customs with modern influences. New technology shapes life even in traditional Buddhist temples, like this one in Thailand.

Blending Old and New

Asian culture today is a complex blend of old customs and new trends. This blending is evident in architecture. Cities like Shanghai, China, and Kuala Lumpur, Malaysia, have some of the world's tallest and glitziest buildings. Nestled between the modern buildings are tiny ancient temples.

The blending of old and new can also be seen in people's daily lives. Traditional beliefs, such as the Chinese respect for one's ancestors and the Japanese code of honor, remain strong influences in people's lives. At the same time, however, cell phones and the Internet allow people to communicate worldwide. As a result, elements of other cultures, especially those from the West, have seeped into Asian life.

READING CHECK **Drawing Conclusions** How does the blend of old and new affect life in Asia?

SUMMARY AND PREVIEW Asia's governments, economies, and cultures have changed dramatically since World War II. Next, you will learn how those changes have affected life in China.

Section 5 Assessment

go.hrw.com
Online Quiz
KEYWORD: SK9 CH16

Reviewing Ideas, Terms, and Places

1. **a. Describe** What are some factors that helped Japan become an economic powerhouse?

   b. Summarize What changes did China make to promote economic growth?

   c. Evaluate Which country do you think has been most successful in rebuilding its economy? Why?

2. **a. Recall** What happened at **Tiananmen Square**?

   b. Contrast How are the governments of Japan, China, and Myanmar different?

3. **a. Identify** What are two old traditions that remain influential in Asia?

   b. Make Generalizations How has technology led to cultural change in Asia?

Critical Thinking

4. **Sequencing** Draw a graphic organizer like the one below. Using your notes, fill in the boxes with the steps that led to economic change in Asia.

FOCUS ON SPEAKING

5. **Choosing Your Subject** Now that you have read about modern Asia, you can choose the person you will interview. Who will it be? What will you ask him or her? Write down some notes.

Social Studies Skills

Chart and Graph | **Critical Thinking** | Geography | Study

Analyzing Visuals

Learn

Geographers get information from many sources. These sources include not only text and data but also visuals, such as diagrams and photographs. Use these tips to analyze visuals:

- **Identify the subject.** Read the title and caption, if available. If not, look at the content of the image. What does it show? Where is it located?

- **Analyze the content.** What is the purpose of the image? What information is in the image? What conclusions can you draw from this information? Write your conclusions in your notes.

- **Summarize your analysis.** Write a summary of the information in the visual and of the conclusions you can draw from it.

Practice

Analyze the photograph at right. Then answer the following questions.

1. What is the title of the photograph?
2. Where is this scene, and what is happening?
3. What conclusions can you draw from the information in the photograph?

City Life in Southeast Asia

The title tells you that the photo's purpose is to show life in the region's cities.

The photo shows forms of travel, numbers of people, and air quality in Hanoi.

Southeast Asia's cities are growing rapidly. In Hanoi, Vietnam, vehicles and people crowd the streets.

Apply

Analyze the images of the Tiananmen Square protests in Section 5. Then answer the following questions.

1. What is the purpose of these photos?
2. What do the photos show about the protests?
3. Based on the information in the photos, what conclusions can you draw about political protests in particular and about politics in China in general?

A Pakistani bride on her wedding day

WORD HELP

chadrs cloths worn by women as a head cover

henna a reddish dye made from a shrub; often used to decorate the hands and feet

cacophony a combination of loud sounds

curry a dish prepared in a highly spiced sauce

lapis a stone with a rich, deep blue color

❶ At a *mahendi* celebration women gather to prepare the bride for her wedding day.

❷ To line the eyes means to darken the rims of the eyelids with black kohl, an eyeliner.

from
Shabanu:
Daughter of the Wind

by Suzanne Fisher Staples

About the Reading *In* Shabanu, *writer Suzanne Fisher Staples writes about the life of Shabanu, a young girl who is part of a traditional nomadic desert culture in Pakistan. In this passage, Shabanu and her family prepare for the wedding of her older sister.*

AS YOU READ Look for details about the customs and traditions of Shabanu and her people.

Two days before the wedding, Bibi Lal . . . heads a procession of women to our house for the *mahendi* celebration ❶ . . . Bibi Lal looks like a giant white lily among her cousins and nieces, who carry baskets of sweets atop their flower-colored *chadrs*. They sing and dance through the fields, across the canal, to our settlement at the edge of the desert.

Sakina carries a wooden box containing henna. The *mahendi* women, Hindus from a village deep in the desert who will paint our hands and feet, walk behind her. Musicians and a happy cacophony of horns, pipes, and cymbals drift around them.

Mama, the servant girl, and I have prepared a curry of chicken, dishes of spiced vegetables, sweet rice, and several kinds of bread to add to the food that the women of Murad's family bring . . . Sharma has washed and brushed my hair. I wear a new pink tunic. She lines my eyes and rubs the brilliant lapis powder into my lids. ❷

Connecting Literature to Geography

1. Describing How did the women prepare for the upcoming wedding? What was the *mahendi* celebration like?

2. Interpreting Why do you think modern Pakistani women might preserve old customs like these wedding preparations? What do such customs symbolize?

Geography's Impact
video series
Review the video to answer the closing question.
How might population density affect a country?

Visual Summary

Use the visual summary below to help you review the main ideas of the chapter.

QUICK FACTS

From the 1700s to the 1900s European countries controlled large parts of Asia, including both India and China.

Political changes swept through Asia in the early 1900s, leading to independence and new governments.

Since the end of World War II, many Asian countries have developed strong economies based on trade.

Reviewing Vocabulary, Terms, and Places

Fill in the blanks with the correct term or location from this chapter.

1. A _____ exists when a country exports more goods than it imports.
2. Gandhi believed in _____, or the avoidance of violent actions.
3. The spread of culture traits from one region to another is known as _____.
4. _____ was a trading city in China, also sometimes called Canton.
5. An _____ person is productive and not wasteful.
6. The Japanese invaded the Chinese region of _____ before World War II.
7. The _____ was the period of British rule in India.
8. A _____ of a country like India divides it into smaller countries.

Comprehension and Critical Thinking

SECTION 1 *(Pages 506–509)*

9. a. **Recall** Which two ancient civilizations influenced life in much of Asia?

   b. **Summarize** How did the Chinese affect life in early Vietnam?

   c. **Develop** How did Indian influence change the religious map of Asia?

SECTION 2 *(Pages 510–514)*

10. a. **Describe** What changes occurred in Japan after Americans arrived there?

    b. **Explain** Why were many Indians unhappy with the Raj?

    c. **Elaborate** Why did Europeans want to take over parts of China?

SECTION 3 (Pages 515–520)

11. a. Identify Who created China's Communist government?

b. Make Inferences Why do you think Gandhi is widely admired today?

c. Evaluate Do you think the Meiji Restoration was a positive development in Japan? Why or why not?

SECTION 4 (Pages 522–527)

12. a. Describe What caused the Korean War?

b. Analyze What were the effects of the atomic bomb dropped on Hiroshima?

c. Predict How might life change in Kashmir if India and Pakistan were to sign a peace treaty?

SECTION 5 (Pages 528–532)

13. a. Recall What type of government does Japan have today? China?

b. Explain How does modern Asian society reflect a blend of old and new ideas?

c. Elaborate How did World War II help bring about stronger economies in Asia?

Using the Internet

go.hrw.com
KEYWORD: SK9 CH16

14. Activity: Investigating Japanese Aggression Japan began an imperialist policy in the 1930s. The harsh treatment of Korean citizens by the Japanese during this period continues to affect relations between the countries today. Enter the keyword to investigate Japanese colonization. Then write a journal entry as though you were a Korean peasant living through this period.

Social Studies Skills

Analyzing Visuals *Turn to Section 3 and analyze the image of a Communist parade in China. Then answer the following questions about the image.*

15. What are the title and location of the image?

16. How do the captions help you understand the information in the image?

17. What types of activities are taking place in the image?

Using Context Clues—Definitions *Add a phrase or sentence to provide a definition for the underlined word.*

18. Under the Raj, the British government made India a <u>colony</u>.

19. Many parts of Asia were <u>devastated</u> by fighting during World War II.

Presenting an Interview *Use your interview notes to complete the activity below.*

20. Now that you have chosen the subject for your interview, write a list of questions you will ask him or her. Once you have completed your questions, work with a partner to conduct your interview. Have your partner take on the personality of your chosen subject and answer the questions you ask. Then, trade roles. You take on the personality of the person your partner has chosen to interview and answer the questions asked of you.

Map Activity

21. Modern Asia On a separate sheet of paper, match the letters on the map with their correct labels below.

Singapore	Pakistan
Tokyo	Xizang (Tibet)
Beijing	

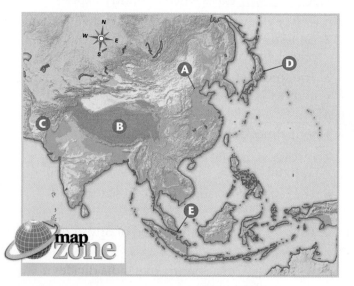

DIRECTIONS (1–7): For each statement or question, write on a separate answer sheet the *number* of the word or expression that, of those given, best completes the statement or answers the question.

1 In which country did the Meiji Restoration take place?

(1) India
(2) Japan
(3) China
(4) Pakistan

2 The United States entered World War II in the Pacific after Japan bombed

(1) Pearl Harbor.
(2) Nanking.
(3) Washington.
(4) Hiroshima.

3 Who led the struggle for independence in India?

(1) Mohandas Gandhi
(2) Mao Zedong
(3) Sun Yixian
(4) Emperor Meiji

4 Which of the following is *not* an example of cultural diffusion?

(1) the spread of Buddhism to Vietnam
(2) the adoption of the Chinese language in Japan
(3) the building of the Great Wall of China
(4) the use of Indian building styles in Southeast Asia

5 Which country is ruled by a military government that abuses people's human rights?

(1) Myanmar (Burma)
(2) Thailand
(3) Singapore
(4) Taiwan

6 The partition of India resulted in the creation of the new country of

(1) Singapore.
(2) Kashmir.
(3) Taiwan.
(4) Pakistan.

7 Which of the following statements about the Boxer Rebellion is true?

(1) It took place in India.
(2) It drove all foreigners out of China.
(3) It was unsuccessful.
(4) It was begun by professional fighters.

Base your answer to question 8 on the passage below and on your knowledge of social studies.

"The expansion of the right of the individual to behave or misbehave as he pleases has come at the expense of orderly society. In the East the main object is to have a well-ordered society so that everybody can have maximum enjoyment of his freedoms. This freedom can only exist in an ordered state."

–Lee Kuan Kew, former prime minister of Singapore, from "A Conversation with Lee Kuan Kew"

8 Based on this passage, what do you think was one of Lee Kuan Kew's main goals as prime minister of Singapore?

(1) increasing the size of the country
(2) maintaining order
(3) expanding people's freedoms
(4) becoming wealthy

China

Geography

The world's fourth largest country by area, China is the world's most populous country. More than 1.3 billion people live within its borders. That is more than the total populations of Europe, Russia, and the United States combined.

Because of its geography, most of China's people live in the eastern half of the country. Most of eastern China is wide open plains that are excellent for farming. Several rivers, including the Chang Jiang, the Huang He, and the Xi flow across these plains, bringing the water necessary for crops.

Farther west, China's elevation rises and the land becomes less hospitable. Western China is a land of rugged mountains, high plateaus, and barren deserts. Mountain ranges include the Tian Shan in the northwest, the Qinling Shandi in central China, and the Himalayas—the world's tallest mountains—in the far south. Near the Himalayas is the Plateau of Tibet, one of the highest regions in the world. Few plants can survive its high altitudes, so the land is barren. Equally barren—though not so high—are deserts like the Gobi and the Taklimakan.

As you might expect, most of China's large cities are located on the eastern plains. The largest city is Shanghai, with some 14 million people. Located where the Chang Jiang meets the East China Sea, it is China's leading seaport and an industrial and commercial center.

Facts About

QUICK FACTS

China

Official Name: People's Republic of China

Capital: Beijing

Area: 3,705,407 square miles (slightly smaller than the United States)

Population: 1.3 billion (367 people/square mile)

Average Life Expectancy: 73 years

Official Language: Mandarin

Major Religions: Officially atheist

Unit of Currency: Yuan Renminbi

1 The **Plateau of Tibet** is known for its barren landscape. This ancient fort is at the plateau's edge.

China

2 **Beijing,** China's capital, is a vibrant, busy city. This shopping district is located near the city's center.

China's second largest city is its capital, Beijing. Also known as Peking, this historic city has many beautiful palaces and temples. A mix of the old and new, Beijing is China's political and cultural center.

In southern China, Hong Kong and Macao (muh-KOW) are major port cities and centers of trade and tourism. Both are modern, busy, and crowded. Both Hong Kong and Macao were European colonies until recently. Because of their history, the two cities provide a mix of cultures.

Case Study Assessment

1. Where are the highest elevations in China?

2. In which region do most Chinese people live?

3. **Activity** Design a brochure to attract visitors to one of China's cities. Describe the city and its attractions. Be sure to include pictures in your brochure.

3 **Shanghai** is China's largest city. Its skyline is a distinctive mix of modern and traditional styles.

221 BC
The Qin dynasty
unites all of China.

AD 68
According to tradition, the first
Buddhist temple in China is built.

618
The Tang dynasty
takes over China.

**Terra cotta warrior from
the Qin dynasty**

History and Culture

China was one of the world's first civilizations. For thousands of years, China was ruled by a series of powerful dynasties. From the Shang of the 1500s BC to the Qing of the AD 1800s, each of China's ruling dynasties left its mark on the country's people and culture.

China's last emperor was removed from power after a revolution in 1911. In 1949 a new Communist government under Mao Zedong took over China. Under Mao, China's economy suffered and people lost many rights.

Mao died in 1976, and Deng Xiaoping (DUHNG SHOW-PING) soon rose to power. Deng worked to modernize and improve China's economy. He allowed some private businesses and encouraged countries to invest in China. As a result, the economy began growing rapidly.

Despite these changes in government, ancient religions, values, and beliefs continue to shape life for China's people. Their influence is strong, even though the Communist government discourages religion. Daoism, Buddhism, and Confucianism are all powerful influences on people's lives.

Experiencing Chinese Culture

China's history stretches back over thousands of years. During that long period the Chinese developed a distinct culture that helped shape life in much of Asia.

Tradition The Chinese celebrate holidays and special events with parades that include colorful costumes, dancing, and fireworks.

Religion Buddhism has traditionally been a major influence on Chinese life. These Buddhist monks live in the Xizang or Tibet region.

c. 1450
The Great Wall is completed during the Ming dynasty.

Great Wall of China

1911
China's last emperor is overthrown.

1949
Mao Zedong creates a new Communist government in China.

China has a rich artistic tradition. Chinese artists have long been known for their work with bronze, jade, ivory, silk, or wood. Chinese porcelain is highly prized for its quality and beauty. Traditional Chinese painting reflects a focus on balance and harmony with nature. Landscapes are favorite themes in Chinese paintings. The Chinese are also known for their beautiful poetry, opera, and architecture.

Popular culture in China embraces many activities. Popular sports include martial arts and table tennis. Another popular game is mah-jongg, which is played with small tiles. Many people enjoy karaoke clubs, where participants sing to music.

Mao Zedong

Case Study Assessment

1. How did China change after 1900?

2. What forms of art are popular in China?

3. **Activity** The Chinese are fond of traditional forms of art. Draw an illustration of a scene from Chinese history or an element of Chinese culture in a traditional style.

Food Chinese food differs from region to region. This Cantonese meal includes pigeons, prawns, and noodles.

Sports Martial arts are very popular among the Chinese. They emphasize discipline and control.

China's government is largely controlled by the country's Communist Party. The party chooses members of the National People's Congress, which in turn elects the president and members of the State Council.

National People's Congress
China's only legislative body and the highest power in the government, the NPC is largely controlled by the Communist Party.

President
Elected by the NPC, the president handles all of China's foreign affairs.

State Council
Headed by a premier, the State Council deals with China's domestic concerns.

China Today

Government

China has one of the few Communist governments remaining in the world. Protests by Chinese citizens who want more freedom have been met with violence. China has taken harsh action against ethnic rebellions as well. For example, many people in Tibet have called for their freedom since the 1950s. These calls have led the Chinese government to crack down on Tibetans' rights. Because of actions such as these, many other countries have accused China of not respecting human rights.

The main authority in China's government is the National People's Congress (NPC). Made up of about 3,000 delegates, the NPC meets for two weeks each year to debate and approve national policies and laws. Most members of the NPC are selected by the Communist Party of China.

Day-to-day government in China is largely handled by the president and the State Council, which is headed by a premier. The president is elected by the NPC to serve as head of state and to handle foreign policy. The State Council and the premier are appointed to handle domestic matters.

Economics

When China became Communist in the 1940s, it had a strict command economy. The government made all economic decisions and owned all businesses. However, poor planning led to a major economic crisis in China.

As a result of this crisis, the Chinese government changed the economy and allowed some private industry to develop. It also allowed some foreign companies to open facilities in China. These changes allowed China's economy to grow and led to higher wages and standards of living for many workers.

Despite the country's industrial growth, most people in China work as farmers. More than half of the population works the land, growing crops such as wheat and rice.

Population Growth and Pollution in China

Bicyclists in Beijing wear masks to avoid breathing polluted air. Automobiles are a major source of pollution in China.

Issues

China's economic growth has also created serious environmental problems. One major problem is pollution. The country's rising numbers of cars and factories pollute the air and water. At the same time, China burns coal for much of its electricity, which further pollutes the air.

Another serious problem is overcrowding. China's population, already huge, continues to grow by about 7.5 million each year. China's officials have worked to slow this growth. They have urged people to delay having children and have tried to limit each couple to one child.

Population growth has contributed to the loss of forestland and farmland in China. Many of China's expanding cities are in its best farmlands, leaving less room for growing food.

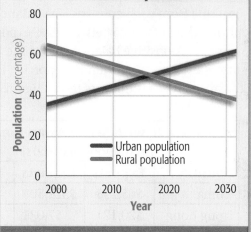

China's Projected Urban Population

- Urban population
- Rural population

Case Study Assessment

1. Why did China's government change the economy?

2. What do you think is China's most serious issue?

3. **Activity** Conduct Internet research to learn about protests against the government in China. Choose one protest and summarize the issue that was being protested and the government's reaction to the protest.

New Asian Economies

Part A: Short-Answer Questions

Directions: Read and examine the following documents. Then, on a separate sheet of paper, answer the questions using complete sentences.

DOCUMENT 1

Among the main trading partners of the United States are many Asian countries. The table below lists some of those countries, as well as the total value of the goods the United States exports to and imports from each country. The balance column shows the difference between the exports and imports. A positive balance means the United States exports more than it imports; a negative balance means it imports more than it exports.

U.S. Trade with Select Asian Countries (in millions of dollars)			
Country	**Exports**	**Imports**	**Balance**
China	$65,238	$321,508	-$256,270
Hong Kong	$20,121	$7,031	$13,090
India	$17,593	$24,024	-$6,431
Japan	$62,665	$145,464	-$82,799
Singapore	$26,284	$18,395	$7,889
South Korea	$34,703	$47,566	-$12,863
Taiwan	$26,359	$38,302	-$11,943

Source: U.S. Census Bureau, Foreign Trade Statistics

1a. From which country does the United States import the most?

_____

1b. With which countries does the United States have a positive trade balance?

_____

DOCUMENT 2

In recent years, China has begun to trade heavily with the United States. Each country is one of the other's main trading partners. The following document comes from a speech by the Treasury Department's special envoy on China.

> U.S.–China economic interdependence is deepening. We need each other more and on a broader number of economic and economically consequential issues. Over the past 5 years, according to U.S. data, U.S. exports to China have grown from $18 to $52 billion, while U.S. imports from China have grown from $102 to $287 billion.
>
> —**Ambassador Alan Holmer,** November 29, 2007

2a. How has U.S. trade with China changed?

_____

2b. What does the writer mean by economic interdependence?

_____

DOCUMENT 3

As one of Asia's economic powerhouses, Japan trades with countries all around the world. The following report was released by the Japan External Trade Organization (JETRO) in 2005.

- Japanese trade posted new records for the third consecutive year with $598.2 billion in exports and $518.6 billion in imports. Imports increased rapidly due to rising oil prices, but exports were rather sluggish, causing the trade surplus to decline $30.8 billion to $79.6 billion, the first fall in four years.

- By volume, exports increased 0.8% and imports 2.9%, both up for the fourth straight year.

- China and the U.S. were the main export destinations. Strong exports of autos helped the U.S. share of Japanese exports rise for the first time in four years. The leading imports were from the Middle East, up due to skyrocketing oil prices.

3a. Did Japanese export increase or decrease during the period?

3b. Which countries bought most of Japan's exported goods?

DOCUMENT 4

The Association of Southeast Asian Nations, or ASEAN, is a trade organization of countries in that region. In 2002 the office of the U.S. Trade Representative introduced a new trading policy with ASEAN countries. The document below is a summary from the Trade Representative's web site explaining the policy.

The Enterprise for ASEAN Initiative (EAI), which was announced in October 2002, is designed to strengthen ties with the ASEAN countries: Brunei, Cambodia, Indonesia, Laos, Malaysia, Myanmar, Philippines, Singapore, Thailand and Vietnam. With two-way trade of nearly $168.5 billion in 2006, the 10-member ASEAN group already is the U.S.' fifth largest trading partner collectively. The region represents about 580 million people with a combined gross domestic product of $2.81 trillion.

4a. How much did trade with ASEAN value in 2006?

4b. Why might the United States consider trade with ASEAN important?

Part B: Essay

Historical Context: Since World War II the countries of Asia have become major players in world trade. Many Asian countries are among the main trading partners of the United States today.

TASK: Using information from the four documents and your knowledge of social studies, write an essay in which you:

- explain the importance of trade to Asian economies.
- examine how trade with Asia affects the United States.

Persuasion

Assignment

Write a persuasive paper about an issue faced by the people of Asia. Choose an issue related to the natural environment or culture of the area.

Persuasion is about convincing others to act or believe in a certain way. Just as you use persuasion to convince your friends to see a certain movie, people use persuasion to convince others to help them solve the world's problems.

1. Prewrite

Choose an Issue

- Choose an issue to write about. For example, you might choose the danger of tsunamis or the role of governments.
- Create a statement of opinion. For example, you might say, "Countries in this region must create a warning system for tsunamis."

Gather and Organize Information

- Search your textbook, the library, or the Internet for evidence that supports your opinion.
- Identify at least two reasons to support your opinion. Find facts, examples, and expert opinions to support each reason.

> **TIP** **That's a Reason** Convince your readers by presenting reasons to support your opinion. For example, one reason to create a warning system for tsunamis is to save lives.

2. Write

Use a Writer's Framework

> **A Writer's Framework**
>
> **Introduction**
> - Start with a fact or question related to the issue you will discuss.
> - Clearly state your opinion in a sentence.
>
> **Body**
> - Write one paragraph for each reason. Begin with the least important reason and end with the most important.
> - Include facts, examples and expert opinions as support.
>
> **Conclusion**
> - Restate your opinion and summarize your reasons.

3. Evaluate and Revise

Review and Improve Your Paper

- As you review your paper, use the questions below to evaluate it.
- Make changes to improve your paper.

Evaluation Questions for a Persuasive Essay

1. Do you begin with an interesting fact or question related to the issue?
2. Does your introduction clearly state your opinion and provide any necessary background information?
3. Do you discuss your reasons from least to most important?
4. Do you provide facts, examples, or expert opinions to support each of your reasons?
5. Does your conclusion restate your opinion and summarize your reasons?

4. Proofread and Publish

Give Your Paper the Finishing Touch

- Make sure you have correctly spelled and capitalized all names of people or places.
- Check for correct comma usage when presenting a list of reasons or evidence.
- Decide how to share your paper. For example, could you publish it in a school paper or in a classroom collection of essays?

5. Practice and Apply

Use the steps and strategies outlined in this workshop to write your persuasive essay. Share your opinion with others to see whether they find your opinion convincing.

Europe

The Alps

The Alps, one of Europe's major mountain ranges, stretch across the heart of central Europe.

Islands and Peninsulas

Islands and peninsulas surround the edges of Europe, drawing people to the sea to work, travel, and trade.

Northern European Plain

Rolling across northern Europe is a vast lowland called the Northern European Plain.

Europe

Explore the Satellite Image
Land and sea are always close together in Europe. Islands and peninsulas are key features of this region. What can you learn about Europe's geography from this satellite image?

The Satellite's Path

>44'56.08

>>>>>>>>>665.00'87<

+355   567.476.348   +799 +996
                            +803

456.094.

Europe and Russia: Physical

ATLANTIC OCEAN

ICELAND

Norwegian Sea

Arctic Circle

Kola Peninsula

Kjølen Mountains

Scandinavian Peninsula

FINLAND

Lake Onega

West Siberian Plain

Ob River

NORWAY

SWEDEN

Lake Ladoga

Volga River

Ob River

Irtysh River

BRITISH ISLES

Highlands

North Sea

Jutland Peninsula

DENMARK

Baltic Sea

ESTONIA

LATVIA

LITHUANIA

RUSSIA

EUROPEAN PLAIN

Volga River

RUSSIA

Kama River

URAL MOUNTAINS

IRELAND

UNITED KINGDOM

NETHERLANDS

NORTHERN

GERMANY

POLAND

BELARUS

Ural River

BELGIUM

LUXEMBOURG

Rhine

CZECH REPUBLIC

Danube

UKRAINE

Donets Basin

FRANCE

AUSTRIA

SLOVAKIA

Carpathian Mts.

MOLDOVA

Don R.

Mt. Elbrus 18,510 ft (5,642 m)

Bay of Biscay

SWITZERLAND

ALPS

Mont Blanc 15,771 ft (4,807 m)

SLOVENIA

HUNGARY

ROMANIA

ITALY

CROATIA

Apennines

BOSNIA AND HERZEGOVINA

SERBIA

Dinaric Alps

KOSOVO

BULGARIA

Black Sea

Caucasus Mts.

GEORGIA

Caspian Sea

Pyrenees

MONTENEGRO

MACEDONIA

ARMENIA

PORTUGAL

SPAIN

Iberian Peninsula

ALBANIA

Balkan Peninsula

GREECE

AZERBAIJAN

Mediterranean Sea

SOUTHWEST ASIA

AFRICA

THE WORLD ALMANAC Facts about the World
Geographical Extremes: Europe and Russia

Longest River	Volga River, Russia: 2,290 miles (3,685 km)
Highest Point	Mount Elbrus, Russia: 18,510 feet (5,642 m)
Lowest Point	Caspian Sea, Russia/Azerbaijan: 92 feet (28 m) below sea level
Highest Recorded Temperature	Seville, Spain: 122°F (50°C)
Lowest Recorded Temperature	Ust'Shchugor, Russia: -67°F (-55°C)
Wettest Place	Crkvica, Bosnia and Herzegovina: 183 inches (464.8 cm) average precipitation per year
Driest Place	Astrakhan, Russia: 6.4 inches (16.3 cm) average precipitation per year

go.hrw.com KEYWORD: SK9 UN5

ELEVATION

Feet	Meters
13,120	4,000
6,560	2,000
1,640	500
656	200
(Sea level) 0	0 (Sea level)
Below sea level	Below sea level

0   400   800 Miles

0   400   800 Kilometers

Projection: Robinson

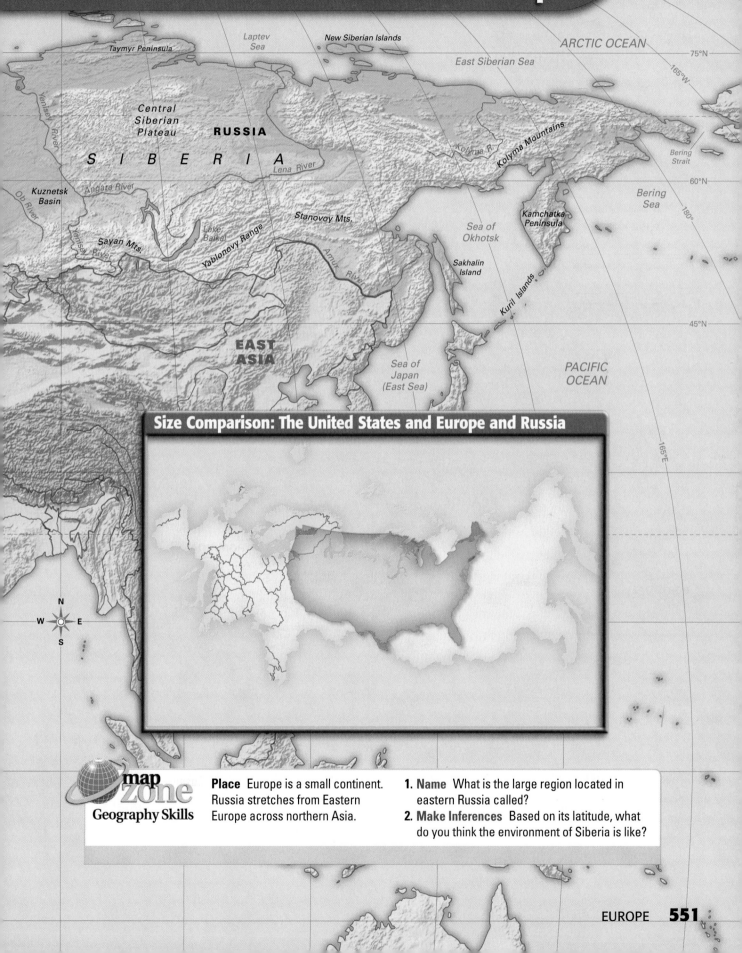

ARCTIC OCEAN

75°N

165°W

Laptev Sea

New Siberian Islands

East Siberian Sea

Taymyr Peninsula

Central Siberian Plateau

RUSSIA

S I B E R I A

Lena River

Kolyma R.

Kolyma Mountains

Bering Strait

60°N

Yenisey River

Kuznetsk Basin

Ob River

Angara River

Yenisey River

Sayan Mts.

Lake Baikal

Yablonovy Range

Stanovoy Mts.

Amur River

Sea of Okhotsk

Kamchatka Peninsula

Bering Sea

180°

Sakhalin Island

Kuril Islands

45°N

EAST ASIA

Sea of Japan (East Sea)

PACIFIC OCEAN

165°E

Size Comparison: The United States and Europe and Russia

N
W · E
S

map **zone**
Geography Skills

Place Europe is a small continent. Russia stretches from Eastern Europe across northern Asia.

1. Name What is the large region located in eastern Russia called?

2. Make Inferences Based on its latitude, what do you think the environment of Siberia is like?

Europe: Political

Legend:
- ☆ National capital
- ● Other city

0 · 200 · 400 Miles
0 · 200 · 400 Kilometers
Projection: Azimuthal Equal-Area

ARCTIC OCEAN

Denmark Strait

Reykjavik ☆ ICELAND

Arctic Circle

Norwegian Sea

Faeroe Islands (DENMARK)

Shetland Islands (U.K.)

NORWAY

SWEDEN

FINLAND

Oslo ☆

Stockholm ☆

Helsinki ☆

Tallinn ☆

ESTONIA

RUSSIA

North Sea

DENMARK

Copenhagen ☆

Baltic Sea

Riga ☆ LATVIA

Kaliningrad (RUSSIA)

LITHUANIA

Vilnius ☆

Minsk ☆

BELARUS

IRELAND

Dublin ☆

UNITED KINGDOM

London ☆

NETHERLANDS

Amsterdam ☆

Berlin ☆

POLAND

Warsaw ☆

ATLANTIC OCEAN

Brussels ☆

BELGIUM

Paris ☆

LUXEMBOURG

Luxembourg ☆

GERMANY

Prague ☆

CZECH REPUBLIC

Kiev ☆

Dnieper River

UKRAINE

FRANCE

Danube R.

LIECHTENSTEIN

Vienna ☆

SLOVAKIA

Bratislava ☆

MOLDOVA

Chişinău ☆

Bern ☆

SWITZERLAND

AUSTRIA

Budapest ☆

HUNGARY

ROMANIA

Ljubljana ☆ SLOVENIA

Zagreb ☆

Belgrade ☆ Bucharest ☆

Black Sea

CROATIA

PORTUGAL

Lisbon ☆

ANDORRA

Madrid ☆

SPAIN

MONACO

SAN MARINO

ITALY

Corsica (FRANCE)

BOSNIA AND HERZEGOVINA

Sarajevo ☆

SERBIA

KOSOVO

Podgorica ☆ Pristina ☆

BULGARIA

Sofia ☆

VATICAN CITY

Rome ☆

MONTENEGRO

Skopje ☆

Tirane ☆ MACEDONIA

ALBANIA

ASIA

Balearic Islands (SPAIN)

Sardinia (ITALY)

GREECE

Aegean Sea

Strait of Gibraltar

Gibraltar (U.K.)

Sicily (ITALY)

Athens ☆

AFRICA

MALTA ☆ Valletta

Mediterranean Sea

Crete (GREECE)

map zone
Geography Skills

Place Europe includes many small countries.

1. Name Which European countries are island countries?

2. Make Generalizations Based on this map, which countries do you think might have the largest populations? Why?

Russia and the Caucasus: Political

ATLANTIC OCEAN

Arctic Circle

60°N

North Sea

ARCTIC OCEAN

Bering Strait

Bering Sea

60°N

Barents Sea

N W E S

Baltic Sea

Kaliningrad

St. Petersburg

EUROPE

Moscow

Nizhniy Novgorod

Volga River

Samara

Yekaterinburg

Ob River

Yenisey River

R U S S I A

Lena River

Sea of Okhotsk

Novosibirsk

Black Sea

GEORGIA

Tbilisi

ARMENIA

Yerevan

Baku

Caspian Sea

AZERBAIJAN

KAZAKHSTAN

Vladivostok

40°N

JAPAN

MONGOLIA

CHINA

PACIFIC OCEAN

Tropic of Cancer

20°N

Legend

⊛ National capital

● Other city

| 0 | 300 | 600 Miles |
| 0 | 300 | 600 Kilometers |

Projection: Two-Point Equidistant

map zone

Geography Skills

Place Russia is the largest country in the world.

1. Use the Map About how many miles is Russia from west to east?

2. Analyze Where does Russia have access to the ocean? How do you think that affects trade?

Europe: Population

ARCTIC OCEAN

Denmark Strait

70°N

Arctic Circle

Norwegian
Sea

30°W

20°W

60°N

North
Sea

ATLANTIC
OCEAN

50°N

London

Paris

Baltic Sea

Kaliningrad
(RUSSIA)

Berlin

Warsaw

Kiev

RUSSIA

Vienna

40°N

Madrid

Barcelona

Rome

Adriatic Sea

Bucharest

Black Sea

10°W

0°

Strait of
Gibraltar

AFRICA

Aegean
Sea

ASIA

10°E

20°E

30°E

Mediterranean Sea

Persons per square mile	**Persons per square km**
520	200
260	100
130	50
25	10
3	1
0	0

● Major cities over 2 million

0   150   300 Miles
0   150   300 Kilometers

Projection: Azimuthal Equal-Area

N
W   E
S

---

map zone
Geography Skills

Place Although Europe is small, it is densely populated.

1. Use the Map How does the population density of Northern Europe compare to the rest of Europe?

2. Compare Compare this map to the physical map. What large plain in Europe has a high population density?

Russia and the Caucasus: Climate

ATLANTIC OCEAN

Arctic Circle

North Sea

Baltic Sea

Barents Sea

ARCTIC OCEAN

Bering Strait

Bering Sea

60°N

60°W 80°W 100°W 120°W 140°W 160°W 180° 160°E 140°E 120°E 100°E 80°E 60°E 40°E 20°E 0° 20°W 40°W

N E S W

80°N

Sea of Okhotsk

Black Sea

Caspian Sea

40°N

PACIFIC OCEAN

Tropic of Cancer

20°N

Climate Types

- Steppe
- Mediterranean
- Humid subtropical
- Humid continental
- Subarctic
- Tundra
- Highland

0   300   600 Miles
0   300   600 Kilometers

Projection: Two-Point Equidistant

map zone
Geography Skills

Regions Russia is dominated by cold climates.

1. Name Which climates cover large parts of Russia?

2. Analyze Based on this map, where do you think Russia's population is concentrated? Why? Which areas would you expect to have a low population density?

Europe and Russia

COUNTRY / Capital	FLAG	POPULATION	AREA (sq mi)	PER CAPITA GDP (U.S. $)	LIFE EXPECTANCY AT BIRTH	TVS PER 1,000 PEOPLE
Albania / Tirana		3.6 million	11,100	$4,900	77.2	146
Andorra / Andorra la Vella		70,500	181	$26,800	83.5	440
Armenia / Yerevan		3 million	11,506	$4,600	71.6	241
Austria / Vienna		8.2 million	32,382	$31,300	78.9	526
Azerbaijan / Baku		7.9 million	33,436	$3,800	63.4	257
Belarus / Minsk		10.3 million	80,155	$6,800	68.7	331
Belgium / Brussels		10.4 million	11,787	$30,600	78.6	532
Bosnia and Herzegovina: Sarajevo		4 million	19,741	$6,500	77.8	112
Bulgaria / Sofia		7.5 million	42,823	$8,200	72.0	429
Croatia / Zagreb		4.5 million	21,831	$11,200	74.5	286
Czech Republic / Prague		10.2 million	30,450	$16,800	76.0	487
Denmark / Copenhagen		5.4 million	16,639	$32,200	77.6	776
Estonia / Tallinn		1.3 million	17,462	$14,300	71.8	567
Finland / Helsinki		5.2 million	130,128	$29,000	78.4	643
France / Paris		60.7 million	211,209	$28,700	79.6	620
United States / Washington, D.C.		295.7 million	3,718,710	$40,100	77.7	844

COUNTRY Capital	FLAG	POPULATION	AREA (sq mi)	PER CAPITA GDP (U.S. $)	LIFE EXPECTANCY AT BIRTH	TVS PER 1,000 PEOPLE
Georgia T'bilisi		4.6 million	26,911	$3,800	76.3	516
Germany Berlin		82.4 million	137,847	$31,400	78.9	581
Greece Athens		10.7 million	50,942	$23,500	79.4	480
Hungary Budapest		9.9 million	35,919	$17,300	72.9	447
Iceland Reykjavik		301,900	39,769	$38,100	80.4	505
Ireland Dublin		4.1 million	27,135	$43,600	77.9	406
Italy Rome		58.1 million	116,306	$29,700	79.9	492
Kosovo Pristina		2.1 million	4,203	$1,800	75.1	Not available
Latvia Riga		2.3 million	24,938	$15,400	71.6	757
Liechtenstein Vaduz		34,200	62	$25,000	79.8	469
Lithuania Vilnius		3.6 million	25,174	$15,100	74.4	422
Luxembourg Luxembourg		480,200	998	$68,800	79.0	599
Macedonia Skopje		2 million	9,781	$8,200	74.2	273
Malta Valletta		401,900	122	$20,300	79.2	549
Moldova Chişinau		4.3 million	13,067	$2,000	70.2	297
United States Washington, D.C.		301.1 million	3,718,711	$43,500	78.0	844

THE WORLD ALMANAC Facts about Countries

COUNTRY Capital	FLAG	POPULATION	AREA (sq mi)	PER CAPITA GDP (U.S. $)	LIFE EXPECTANCY AT BIRTH	TVS PER 1,000 PEOPLE
Monaco Monaco		32,700	1	$30,000	79.8	758
Montenegro Cetinje, Podgorica		684,700	5,415	$3,800	76.9	Not available
Netherlands Amsterdam		16.6 million	16,033	$31,700	79.1	540
Norway Oslo		4.6 million	125,182	$47,800	79.7	653
Poland Warsaw		38.5 million	120,728	$14,100	75.2	387
Portugal Lisbon		10.6 million	35,672	$19,100	77.9	567
Romania Bucharest		22.3 million	91,699	$8,800	71.9	312
Russia Moscow		141.4 million	6,592,772	$12,100	65.9	421
San Marino San Marino		29,600	24	$34,100	81.8	875
Serbia Belgrade		8.1 million	29,913	$10,400	75.3	277
Slovakia Bratislava		5.4 million	18,859	$17,700	74.9	418
Slovenia Ljubljana		2 million	7,827	$23,400	76.5	362
Spain Madrid		40.4 million	194,897	$27,000	79.8	555
Sweden Stockholm		9 million	173,732	$31,600	80.6	551
Switzerland Bern		7.6 million	15,942	$33,600	80.6	457
United States Washington, D.C.		301.1 million	3,718,711	$43,500	78.0	844

COUNTRY Capital	FLAG	POPULATION	AREA (sq mi)	PER CAPITA GDP (U.S. $)	LIFE EXPECTANCY AT BIRTH	TVS PER 1,000 PEOPLE
Ukraine Kiev		46.3 million	233,090	$7,600	67.9	433
United Kingdom London		60.8 million	94,526	$31,400	78.7	661
Vatican City Vatican City		821	0.17	Not available	Not available	Not available
United States Washington, D.C.		301.1 million	3,718,711	$43,500	78.0	844

World's Highest Per Capita GDPs

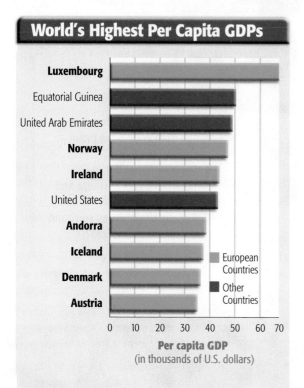

Europe includes some of the wealthiest countries in the world. In fact, seven of the ten countries with the highest per capita GDPs are in Europe.

Densely Populated Countries: Europe

Country	Population Density (per square mile)
Netherlands	1,267
Belgium	889
United Kingdom	652
Germany	611
Italy	512
Switzerland	492
Denmark	334
Poland	328
United States	85

Many European countries are densely populated, especially when compared to the United States.

 ANALYSIS SKILL **ANALYZING INFORMATION**

1. What are the three most densely populated countries in Europe? How do their densities compare to that of the United States?
2. Which countries in Europe seem to have the lowest per capita GDPs? Look at the atlas political map. Where are these countries located in Europe?

CHAPTER 17

Physical Geography of Europe

FOCUS QUESTION

What forces had an impact on the development of Europe and why?

What You Will Learn...

One of the smallest continents, Europe is nonetheless home to a wide variety of landforms, water features, and climates.

FOCUS ON READING AND WRITING

Asking Questions As you read a text, it can be helpful to ask yourself questions about what you are reading to be sure you understand it. One set of questions that you can use to test your understanding is the five Ws—who, what, when, where, and why. **See the lesson, Asking Questions, on page S20.**

Creating a Real Estate Ad Imagine you work for a real estate agency in Europe. You are trying to sell a piece of property there and must write an ad about it. As you read this chapter, decide where your property would be located and what its characteristics would be.

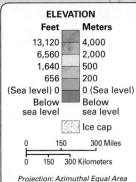

ELEVATION

Feet	Meters
13,120	4,000
6,560	2,000
1,640	500
656	200
(Sea level) 0	0 (Sea level)
Below sea level	Below sea level

Ice cap

0   150   300 Miles
0   150   300 Kilometers

Projection: Azimuthal Equal Area

map zone

Geography Skills

Place Europe's landscapes range from wide open plains to rugged mountains.
1. **Identify** What flat region covers most of northern and Eastern Europe?
2. **Locate** Which seas surround the island of Sardinia?

Water Features Iceland's geysers and hot springs produce great amounts of energy.

Europe: Physical

ARCTIC OCEAN

Iceland

Arctic Circle

Norwegian Sea

Barents Sea

North Cape

KOLA PENINSULA

Peachora River

URAL MOUNTAINS

Faeroe Islands

Shetland Islands

Orkney Islands

KJOLEN MOUNTAINS

White Sea

North Dvina R.

Kama River

Hebrides

British Isles

Irish Sea

PENNINES

North Sea

Lake Vänern

Skagerrak

Kattegat

Lake Vättern

Gulf of Bothnia

Baltic Sea

Gulf of Finland

Lake Ladoga

Lake Onega

Rybinsk Reservoir

EUROPEAN PLAIN

Ural River

PLAINS

BALTIC

Daugava R.

Western Dvina River

Thames River

Elbe

Rhine River

Oder River

Vistula River

Volga River

Kama River

ATLANTIC OCEAN

English Channel

Seine River

NORTHERN

Danube River

Dnestr River

Nistru River

Dnipro River

Don River

Caspian Sea

Loire River

CARPATHIAN MTS.

Bay of Biscay

Lake Geneva

Mont Blanc 15,781 ft (4,810 m)

ALPS

Po River

Rhône River

Garonne R.

TRANSYLVANIAN ALPS

Danube River

CRIMEAN PENINSULA

Sea of Azov

Mt. Elbrus 18,510 ft (5,642 m)

CAUCASUS MTS.

PYRENEES

Ebro River

Douro River

Tagus River

IBERIAN PENINSULA

Guadiana River

Guadalquivir River

DINARIC ALPS

APENNINES

Adriatic Sea

BALKAN PENINSULA

Black Sea

Corsica

Balearic Is.

Sardinia

Tyrrhenian Sea

Sea of Marmara

Aegean Sea

Strait of Gibraltar

Mediterranean Sea

Sicily

Malta

Rhodes

Crete

Cyprus

Coastlines No place in Europe is far from a major body of water. Croatia's Dalmatian coast overlooks the Adriatic Sea.

Landforms A mountain village shows the beauty of the Swiss Alps.

Southern Europe

What You Will Learn...

Main Ideas

1. Southern Europe's physical features include rugged mountains and narrow coastal plains.
2. The region's climate and resources support such industries as agriculture, fishing, and tourism.

The Big Idea

The peninsulas of Southern Europe have rocky terrains and sunny, mild climates.

Key Terms and Places

Mediterranean Sea, *p. 562*
Pyrenees, *p. 563*
Apennines, *p. 563*
Alps, *p. 563*
Mediterranean climate, *p. 564*

TAKING NOTES Draw two ovals like the ones below. As you read this section, list facts about Southern Europe's landforms in one oval and facts about its climate and resources in the other.

If YOU lived there...

You are in a busy fish market in a small town on the coast of Italy, near the Mediterranean Sea. It is early morning. Colorful fishing boats have just pulled into shore with their catch of fresh fish and seafood. They unload their nets of slippery octopus and wriggling shrimp. Others bring silvery sea bass. You are looking forward to lunch—perhaps a tasty fish soup or pasta dish.

How does the Mediterranean affect your life?

BUILDING BACKGROUND The Mediterranean Sea has shaped the geography, climate, and culture of Southern Europe. All of these countries have long coastlines, with good harbors and beautiful beaches. Because much of the interior is rugged and mountainous, the sea has also been a highway for trade and travel.

Physical Features

The continent of Europe has often been called a peninsula of peninsulas. Why do you think this is so? Look at the map of Europe on the previous page to find out. Notice how Europe juts out from Asia like one big peninsula. Also, notice how smaller peninsulas extend into the many bodies of water that surround the continent.

Look at the map of Europe again. Do you see the three large peninsulas that extend south from Europe? From west to east, these are the Iberian Peninsula, the Italian Peninsula, and the Balkan Peninsula. Together with some large islands, they form the region of Southern Europe.

Southern Europe is also known as Mediterranean Europe. All of the countries of Southern Europe have long coastlines on the **Mediterranean Sea**. In addition to this common location on the Mediterranean, the countries of Southern Europe share many common physical features.

Landforms

The three peninsulas of Southern Europe are largely covered with rugged mountains. In Greece, for example, about three-fourths of the land is mountainous. Because much of the land is so rugged, farming and travel in Southern Europe can be a challenge.

The mountains of Southern Europe form several large ranges. On the Iberian Peninsula, the **Pyrenees** (PIR-uh-neez) form a boundary between Spain and France to the north. Italy has two major ranges. The **Apennines** (A-puh-nynz) run along the whole peninsula, and the **Alps**—Europe's highest mountains—are in the north. The Pindus Mountains cover much of Greece.

Southern Europe's mountains extend into the sea as well, where they rise above the water to form islands. The Aegean Sea east of Greece is home to more than 2,000 such islands. Southern Europe also has many larger islands formed by undersea mountains. These include Crete, which is south of Greece; Sicily, at the southern tip of Italy; and many others.

Not all of Southern Europe is rocky and mountainous, though. Some flat plains lie in the region. Most of these plains are along the coast and in the valleys of major rivers. It is here that most farming in Southern Europe takes place. It is also here that most of the region's people live.

FOCUS ON READING

As you read, ask yourself this question: Where are the Pyrenees?

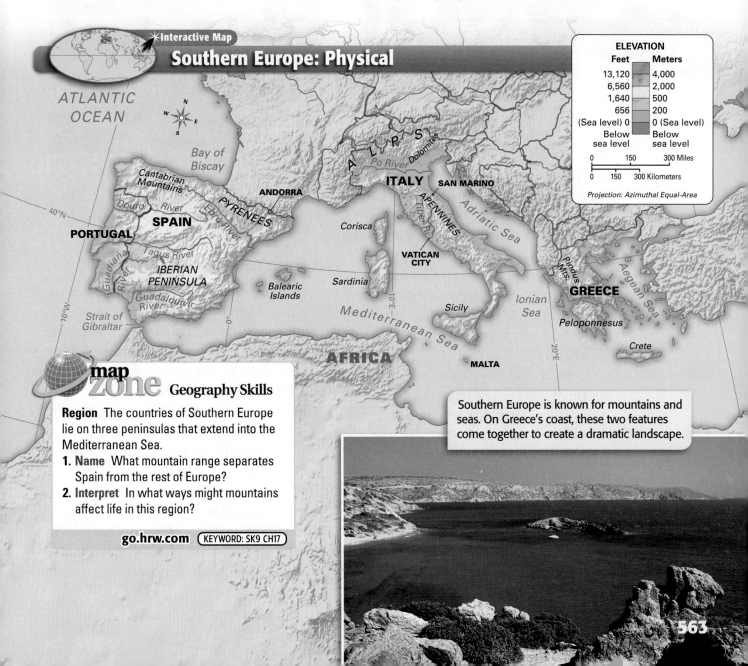

Southern Europe: Physical

Interactive Map

ELEVATION

Feet		Meters
13,120	—	4,000
6,560	—	2,000
1,640	—	500
656	—	200
(Sea level) 0	—	0 (Sea level)
Below sea level		Below sea level

0   150   300 Miles
0   150   300 Kilometers

Projection: Azimuthal Equal-Area

ATLANTIC OCEAN

Bay of Biscay

Cantabrian Mountains

Douro River

ANDORRA

A L P S

Po River

Dolomites

ITALY

SAN MARINO

PYRENEES

SPAIN

40°N

Ebro River

APENNINES

Adriatic Sea

Tiber R.

PORTUGAL

Corsica

VATICAN CITY

Pindus Mts.

Aegean Sea

GREECE

Tagus River

IBERIAN PENINSULA

Guadiana River

Sardinia

Balearic Islands

Mediterranean Sea

Sicily

Ionian Sea

Peloponnesus

10°W

Guadalquivir River

Strait of Gibraltar

0

10°E

20°E

AFRICA

MALTA

Crete

map zone Geography Skills

Region The countries of Southern Europe lie on three peninsulas that extend into the Mediterranean Sea.

1. **Name** What mountain range separates Spain from the rest of Europe?
2. **Interpret** In what ways might mountains affect life in this region?

go.hrw.com (KEYWORD: SK9 CH17)

Southern Europe is known for mountains and seas. On Greece's coast, these two features come together to create a dramatic landscape.

Mediterranean Climate

Southern Europe is known for its Mediterranean climate, which features warm, dry summers and mild, wet winters. This climate affects nearly every aspect of life in the region.

PORTUGAL
1

SPAIN

2

1 **Agriculture** The climate of Southern Europe is ideal for growing many crops. Here, Portuguese farmers harvest grapes.

Water Features

Since Southern Europe is mostly peninsulas and islands, water is central to the region's geography. No place in Southern Europe is very far from a major body of water. The largest of these bodies of water is the Mediterranean, but the Adriatic, Aegean, and Ionian seas are also important to the region. For many centuries, these seas have given the people of Southern Europe food and a relatively easy way to travel around the region.

Only a few large rivers run through Southern Europe. The region's longest river is the Tagus (TAY-guhs), which flows across the Iberian Peninsula. In northern Italy, the Po runs through one of Southern Europe's most fertile and densely populated areas. Other rivers run out of the mountains and into the many surrounding seas.

READING CHECK **Finding Main Ideas** What are the region's major features?

2 **Tourism** The region's mild and sunny climate draws millions of tourists to places like this beach in Ibiza, Spain.

Climate and Resources

Southern Europe is famous for its pleasant climate. Most of the region enjoys warm, sunny days and mild nights for most of the year. Little rain falls in the summer, falling instead during the mild winter. In fact, the type of climate found across Southern Europe is called a **Mediterranean climate** because it is common in this region.

The region's climate is also one of its most valuable resources. The mild climate is ideal for growing a variety of crops, from citrus fruits and grapes to olives and wheat. In addition, millions of tourists are drawn to the region each year by its climate, beaches, and breathtaking scenery.

ITALY

③

GREECE

④

④ Architecture Climate also affects architecture in Southern Europe. Buildings, like these in Greece, are airy and made of light materials to reflect sunlight and heat.

ANALYSIS
SKILL **ANALYZING VISUALS**

What are four ways in which the Mediterranean climate affects life in Southern Europe?

③ Vegetation This field in Tuscany, a region of Italy, shows the variety of plants that thrive in Southern Europe's climate.

The sea is also an important resource in Southern Europe. Many of the region's largest cities are ports, which ship goods all over the world. In addition, the nearby seas are full of fish and shellfish, which provide the basis for profitable fishing industries.

READING CHECK **Generalizing** How is a mild climate important to Southern Europe?

SUMMARY AND PREVIEW In this section you learned about the physical features of Southern Europe. In the next section you will move north and west to learn about the physical features there.

Section 1 Assessment

go.hrw.com
Online Quiz
KEYWORD: SK9 HP17

Reviewing Ideas, Terms, and Places

1. **a. Recall** Which three peninsulas are in Southern Europe?
   b. Explain Why is the sea important to Southern Europe?
   c. Elaborate Why do you think most people in Southern Europe live on coastal plains or in river valleys?
2. **a. Describe** What is the **Mediterranean climate** like?
   b. Generalize How is climate an important resource for the region?

Critical Thinking

3. **Finding Main Ideas** Draw a diagram like the one shown here.

   Landforms   Climate

   In the left oval, use your notes to explain how landforms affect life in Southern Europe. In the right oval, explain how climate affects life in the region.

FOCUS ON WRITING

4. **Describing Southern Europe** What features of Southern Europe might appeal to real estate buyers? Would it be the climate? the landforms? the water? Write some ideas in your notebook.

West-Central Europe

If YOU lived there...

You are a photographer planning a book about the landscapes of West-Central Europe. You are trying to decide where to find the best pictures of rich farmland, forested plateaus, and rugged mountains. So far, you are planning to show the colorful tulip fields of the Netherlands, the hilly Black Forest region of Germany, and the snow–covered Alps in Switzerland.

What other places might you want to show?

BUILDING BACKGROUND The countries of West-Central Europe are among the most prosperous and powerful countries in the world. The reasons include their mild climates, good farmland, many rivers, market economies, and stable governments. In addition, most of these countries cooperate as members of the European Union.

Physical Features

From fields of tulips, to sunny beaches, to icy mountain peaks, West-Central Europe offers a wide range of landscapes. Even though the region is small, it includes three major types of landforms—plains, uplands, and mountains. These landforms extend in wide bands across the region.

Plains, Uplands, and Mountains

Look at the map at right. Picture West-Central Europe as an open fan with Italy as the handle. The outer edge of this imaginary fan is a broad coastal plain called the **Northern European Plain**. This plain stretches from the Atlantic coast into Eastern Europe.

Most of this plain is flat or rolling and lies less than 500 feet (150 m) above sea level. In the Netherlands, parts of the plain dip below sea level. There, people must build walls to hold back the sea. In Brittany in northwestern France, the land rises to form a plateau above the surrounding plain.

The Northern European Plain provides the region's best farmland. Many people live on the plain, and the region's largest cities are located there.

The Central Uplands extend across the center of our imaginary fan. This area has many rounded hills, small plateaus, and valleys. In France, the uplands include the Massif Central (ma-SEEF sahn-TRAHL), a plateau region, and the Jura Mountains.

This range is on the French-Swiss border. In Germany, uplands cover much of the southern two-thirds of the country. Dense woodlands, such as the Black Forest, blanket many of the hills in this area.

The Central Uplands have many productive coalfields. As a result, the area is important for mining and industry. Some valleys provide fertile soil for farming, but most of the area is too rocky to farm.

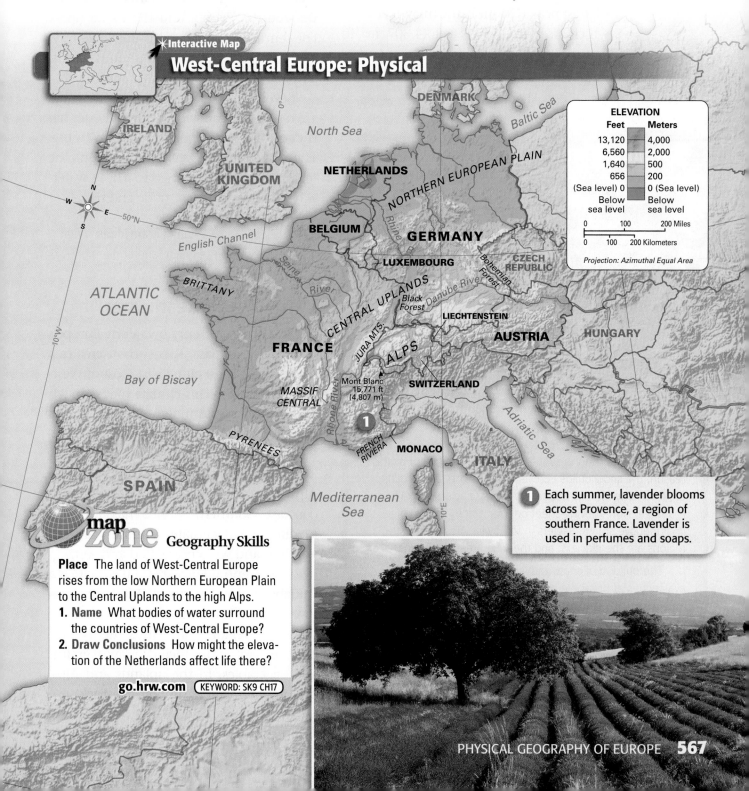

★Interactive Map
West-Central Europe: Physical

DENMARK
Baltic Sea
IRELAND
North Sea
NETHERLANDS
NORTHERN EUROPEAN PLAIN
UNITED KINGDOM
BELGIUM
GERMANY
English Channel
Rhine
LUXEMBOURG
CZECH REPUBLIC
Bohemian Forest
ATLANTIC OCEAN
BRITTANY
Seine River
CENTRAL UPLANDS
Black Forest
Danube River
LIECHTENSTEIN
AUSTRIA
HUNGARY
FRANCE
JURA MTS.
ALPS
Mont Blanc 15,771 ft (4,807 m)
SWITZERLAND
Rhone River
Bay of Biscay
MASSIF CENTRAL
Adriatic Sea
PYRENEES
FRENCH RIVIERA
MONACO
ITALY
SPAIN
Mediterranean Sea
50°N
10°W
10°E

ELEVATION

Feet		Meters
13,120		4,000
6,560		2,000
1,640		500
656		200
(Sea level) 0		0 (Sea level)
Below sea level		Below sea level

0   100   200 Miles
0   100   200 Kilometers
Projection: Azimuthal Equal Area

1 Each summer, lavender blooms across Provence, a region of southern France. Lavender is used in perfumes and soaps.

map zone Geography Skills

Place The land of West-Central Europe rises from the low Northern European Plain to the Central Uplands to the high Alps.

1. **Name** What bodies of water surround the countries of West-Central Europe?
2. **Draw Conclusions** How might the elevation of the Netherlands affect life there?

go.hrw.com KEYWORD: SK9 CH17

PHYSICAL GEOGRAPHY OF EUROPE **567**

Along the inner part of our imaginary fan, the land rises dramatically to form the alpine mountain system. This system includes the Alps and the Pyrenees, which you read about in the last chapter.

As you have read, the Alps are Europe's highest mountain range. They stretch from southern France to the Balkan Peninsula. Several of the jagged peaks in the Alps soar to more than 14,000 feet (4,270 m). The highest peak is Mont Blanc (mawn BLAHN), which rises to 15,771 feet (4,807 m) in France. Because of the height of the Alps, large snowfields coat some peaks.

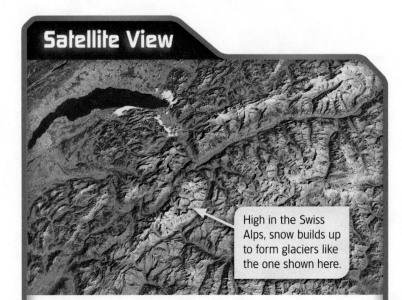

Satellite View

High in the Swiss Alps, snow builds up to form glaciers like the one shown here.

The Swiss Alps

At high elevations in the Alps, snow does not melt. For this reason, the snow builds up over time. As the snow builds up, it turns to ice and eventually forms glaciers. A glacier is a large, slow-moving sheet or river of ice. The satellite image above shows glaciers in the Swiss Alps. The white regions are the glaciers, and the blue areas are alpine lakes.

The buildup of snow and ice in the Alps can cause avalanches at lower elevations. An avalanche is a large mass of snow or other material that suddenly rushes down a mountainside. Avalanches pose a serious danger to people.

Analyzing Why do glaciers sometimes form at higher elevations in the Alps?

Water Features

Several bodies of water are important to West-Central Europe's physical geography. The **North Sea** and **English Channel** lie to the north. The Bay of Biscay and Atlantic Ocean lie to the west. The Mediterranean Sea borders France to the south.

Several rivers cross the region as well. Look at the map on the previous page to identify them. Two important rivers are the **Danube** (DAN-yoob) and the **Rhine** (RYN). For centuries people and goods have traveled these rivers, and many cities, farms, and industrial areas line their banks.

Several of West-Central Europe's rivers are navigable. A **navigable river** is one that is deep and wide enough for ships to use. These rivers and a system of canals link the region's interior to the seas. These waterways are important for trade and travel.

READING CHECK Finding Main Ideas What are the region's three major landform areas?

Climate and Resources

A warm ocean current flows along Europe's northwestern coast. This current creates a marine west coast climate in most of West-Central Europe. This climate makes much of the area a pleasant place to live. Though winters can get cold, summers are mild. Rain and storms occur often, though.

At higher elevations, such as in the Alps, the climate is colder and wetter. In contrast, southern France has a warm Mediterranean climate. Summers are dry and hot, and winters are mild and wet.

West-Central Europe's mild climate is a valuable natural resource. Mild temperatures, plenty of rain, and rich soil have made the region's farmlands highly productive. Farm crops include grapes, grains, and vegetables. In the uplands and Alps, pastures and valleys support livestock.

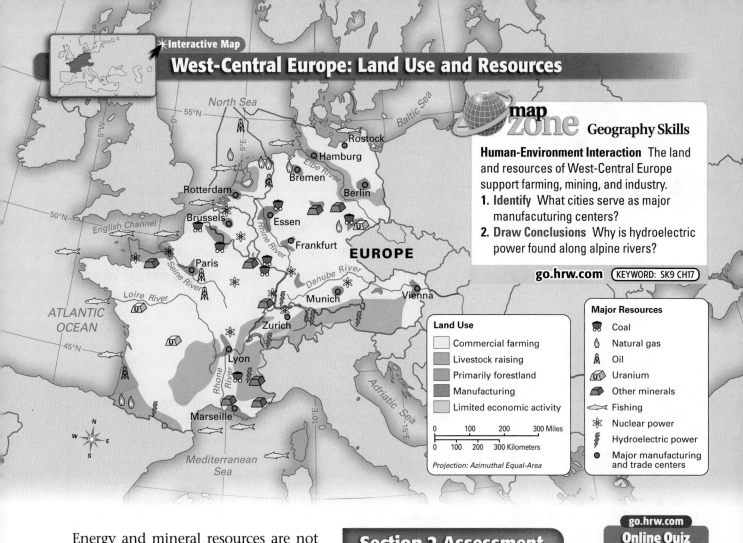

West-Central Europe: Land Use and Resources

*Interactive Map

map zone **Geography Skills**

Human-Environment Interaction The land and resources of West-Central Europe support farming, mining, and industry.
1. **Identify** What cities serve as major manufacuturing centers?
2. **Draw Conclusions** Why is hydroelectric power found along alpine rivers?

go.hrw.com KEYWORD: SK9 CH17

Land Use
- Commercial farming
- Livestock raising
- Primarily forestland
- Manufacturing
- Limited economic activity

0   100   200   300 Miles
0 100 200 300 Kilometers
Projection: Azimuthal Equal-Area

Major Resources
- Coal
- Natural gas
- Oil
- Uranium
- Other minerals
- Fishing
- Nuclear power
- Hydroelectric power
- Major manufacturing and trade centers

Energy and mineral resources are not evenly distributed across the region, as the map shows. France has coal and iron ore, Germany also has coal, and the Netherlands has natural gas. Fast-flowing alpine rivers provide hydroelectric power. Even so, many countries must import fuels.

Another valuable natural resource is found in the breathtaking beauty of the Alps. Each year, tourists flock to the Alps to enjoy the scenery and to hike and ski.

READING CHECK **Summarizing** What natural resources contribute to the region's economy?

SUMMARY AND PREVIEW West-Central Europe includes low plains, uplands, and mountains. The climate is mild, and natural resources support farming, industry, and tourism. Next, you will read about a less mild region, Northern Europe.

go.hrw.com
Online Quiz
KEYWORD: SK9 HP17

Section 2 Assessment

Reviewing Ideas, Terms, and Places
1. **a. Describe** What are the main physical features of the **Northern European Plain**?
   b. Analyze How does having many **navigable** rivers benefit West-Central Europe?
2. **a. Recall** What is the region's main climate?
   b. Make Inferences How might an uneven distribution of mineral resources affect the region?

Critical Thinking
3. **Categorizing** Draw a fan like this one. Label each band with the landform area in West-Central Europe it represents. Using your notes, identify each area's physical features, climate, and resources.

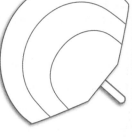

FOCUS ON WRITING

4. **Selling the Physical Geography** How could you describe the physical features of West-Central Europe to appeal to buyers? Jot down ideas.

Northern Europe

What You Will Learn...

Main Ideas

1. The physical features of Northern Europe include low mountain ranges and jagged coastlines.
2. Northern Europe's natural resources include energy sources, soils, and seas.
3. The climates of Northern Europe range from a mild coastal climate to a freezing ice cap climate.

The Big Idea

Northern Europe is a region of unique physical features, rich resources, and diverse climates.

Key Terms and Places

British Isles, *p. 570*
Scandinavia, *p. 570*
fjord, *p. 571*
geothermal energy, *p. 572*
North Atlantic Drift, *p. 572*

 TAKING NOTES As you read, take notes on Northern Europe's physical features, natural resources, and climates. Record your notes in a chart like the one below.

Physical Features	Natural Resources	Climates

If YOU lived there...

Your family is planning to visit friends in Tromso, Norway. It is a city on the Norwegian Sea located 200 miles north of the Arctic Circle. You imagine a landscape covered in snow and ice. When you arrive, however, you discover green hills and ice-free harbors.

What might explain the mild climate?

BUILDING BACKGROUND Although located at high latitudes, Norway and the rest of Northern Europe have surprisingly mild temperatures. All the countries of Northern Europe are located on seas and oceans. As a result, they benefit from ocean currents that bring warm water north and keep the climate reasonably warm.

Physical Features

From Ireland's gently rolling hills to Iceland's icy glaciers and fiery volcanoes, Northern Europe is a land of great variety. Because of this variety, the physical geography of Northern Europe changes greatly from one location to another.

Two regions—the British Isles and Scandinavia—make up Northern Europe. To the southwest lie the **British Isles**, a group of islands located across the English Channel from the rest of Europe. Northeast of the British Isles is **Scandinavia**, a region of islands and peninsulas in far northern Europe. The island of Iceland, to the west, is often considered part of Scandinavia.

Hills and Mountains Rough, rocky hills and low mountains cover much of Northern Europe. Rugged hills stretch across much of Iceland, northern Scotland, and Scandinavia. The jagged Kjolen (CHUH-luhn) Mountains on the Scandinavian Peninsula divide Norway from Sweden. The rocky soil and uneven terrain in these parts of Northern Europe make farming there difficult. As a result, fewer people live there than in the rest of Northern Europe.

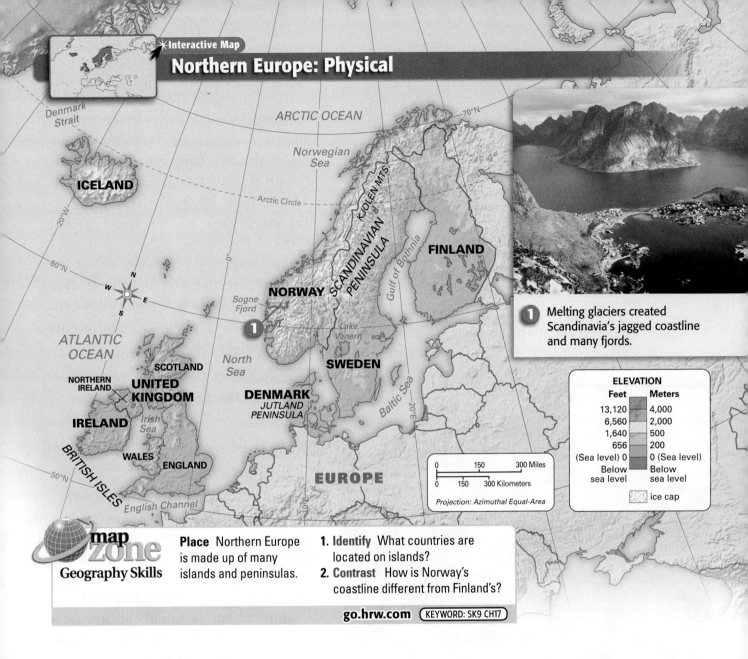

ARCTIC OCEAN

70°N

Norwegian Sea

Arctic Circle

ICELAND

KJOLEN MTS.

SCANDINAVIAN PENINSULA

FINLAND

Gulf of Bothnia

20°W

60°N

NORWAY

Sogne Fjord

Lake Vanern

N
W   E
S

ATLANTIC OCEAN

SWEDEN

North Sea

Baltic Sea

SCOTLAND

NORTHERN IRELAND

UNITED KINGDOM

DENMARK
JUTLAND PENINSULA

20°E

IRELAND

Irish Sea

WALES

ENGLAND

EUROPE

50°N

BRITISH ISLES

English Channel

0   150   300 Miles
0   150   300 Kilometers
Projection: Azimuthal Equal-Area

Melting glaciers created Scandinavia's jagged coastline and many fjords.

ELEVATION

Feet		Meters
13,120		4,000
6,560		2,000
1,640		500
656		200
(Sea level) 0		0 (Sea level)
Below sea level		Below sea level

ice cap

map zone
Geography Skills

Place Northern Europe is made up of many islands and peninsulas.

1. **Identify** What countries are located on islands?
2. **Contrast** How is Norway's coastline different from Finland's?

go.hrw.com KEYWORD: SK9 CH17

Farmland and Plains Fertile farmland and flat plains stretch across the southern parts of the British Isles and Scandinavia. Ireland's rolling, green hills provide rich farmland. Wide valleys in England and Denmark also have plenty of fertile soil.

Effects of Glaciers Slow-moving sheets of ice, or glaciers, have left their mark on Northern Europe's coastlines and lakes. As you can see on the map above, Norway's western coastline is very jagged. Millions of years ago, glaciers cut deep valleys into Norway's coastal mountains. As the glaciers melted, these valleys filled with water,

creating deep fjords. A **fjord** (fee-AWRD) is a narrow inlet of the sea set between high, rocky cliffs. Many fjords are very long and deep. Norway's Sogne (SAWNG-nuh) Fjord, for example, is over 100 miles (160 km) long and more than three-quarters of a mile (1.2 km) deep. Melting glaciers also carved thousands of lakes in Northern Europe. Sweden's Lake Vanern, along with many of the lakes in the British Isles, were carved by glaciers thousands of years ago.

READING CHECK **Summarizing** What are some physical features of Northern Europe?

Natural Resources

ACADEMIC
VOCABULARY

primary
main, most
important

Natural resources have helped to make Northern Europe one of the wealthiest regions in the world. Northern Europe's **primary** resources are its energy resources, forests and soils, and surrounding seas.

Energy Northern Europe has a variety of energy resources. Norway and the United Kingdom benefit from oil and natural gas deposits under the North Sea. Hydroelectric energy is produced by the region's many lakes and rivers. In Iceland steam from hot springs produces **geothermal energy**, or energy from the heat of Earth's interior.

Forests and Soils Forests and soils are two other important natural resources in Northern Europe. Large areas of timber-producing forests stretch across Finland and the Scandinavian Peninsula. Fertile soils provide rich farmland for crops, such as wheat and potatoes. Livestock like sheep and dairy cattle are also common.

Seas and Oceans The seas that surround Northern Europe are another important natural resource. For centuries, the North Sea, the Norwegian Sea, and the Atlantic Ocean have provided rich stocks of fish. Today, fishing is a key industry in Norway, Denmark, and Iceland.

READING CHECK **Summarizing** What natural resources are found in Northern Europe?

Climates

Locate Northern Europe on a map of the world. Notice that much of the region lies near the Arctic Circle. Due to the region's high latitude, you might imagine that it would be quite cold during much of the year. In reality, however, the climates in Northern Europe are remarkably mild.

Northern Europe's mild climates are a result of the **North Atlantic Drift**, an ocean current that brings warm, moist air across the Atlantic Ocean. Warm waters from this ocean current keep most of the region warmer than other locations around the globe at similar latitudes.

Much of Northern Europe has a marine west coast climate. Denmark, the British Isles, and western Norway benefit from mild summers and frequent rainfall. Snow and frosts may occur in winter but do not usually last long.

Central Norway, Sweden, and southern Finland have a humid continental climate. This area has four true seasons with cold, snowy winters and mild summers.

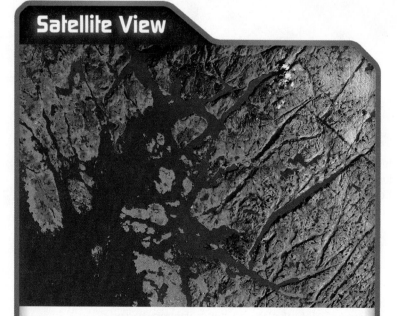

Satellite View

Norway's Fjords

Millions of years ago much of Norway was covered with glaciers. As the glaciers flowed slowly downhill, they carved long, winding channels, or fjords, into Norway's coastline.

As you can see in this satellite image, fjords cut many miles into Norway's interior, bringing warm waters from the North and Norwegian seas. As warm waters penetrate inland, they keep temperatures relatively mild. In fact, people have used these unfrozen fjords to travel during the winter when ice and snow made travel over land difficult.

Drawing Conclusions How do fjords benefit life in Norway?

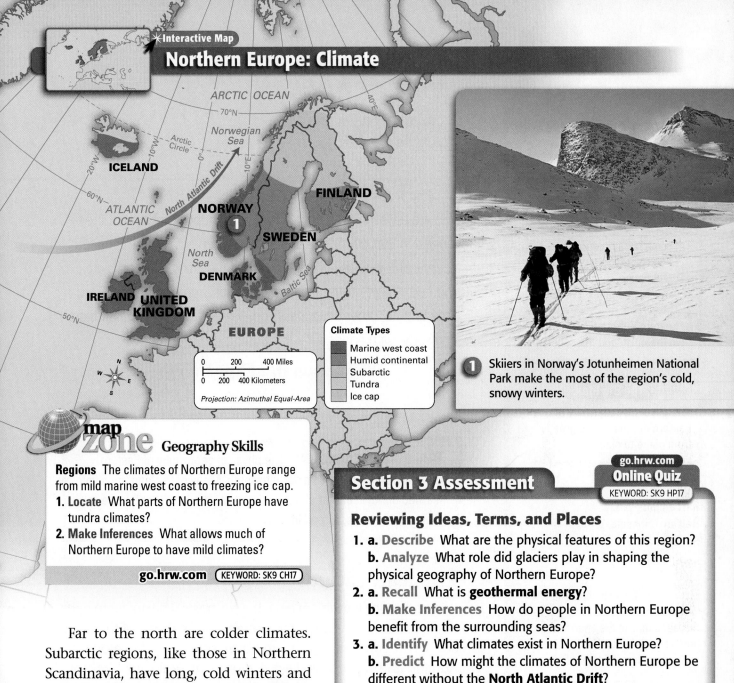

Northern Europe: Climate

Interactive Map

ARCTIC OCEAN

70°N

Arctic Circle

Norwegian Sea

ICELAND

60°N

ATLANTIC OCEAN

North Atlantic Drift

NORWAY
1

FINLAND

SWEDEN

North Sea

DENMARK

Baltic Sea

IRELAND UNITED KINGDOM

50°N

EUROPE

| 0 | 200 | 400 Miles |
| 0 | 200 | 400 Kilometers |

Projection: Azimuthal Equal-Area

Climate Types

- Marine west coast
- Humid continental
- Subarctic
- Tundra
- Ice cap

1 Skiiers in Norway's Jotunheimen National Park make the most of the region's cold, snowy winters.

map zone Geography Skills

Regions The climates of Northern Europe range from mild marine west coast to freezing ice cap.
1. **Locate** What parts of Northern Europe have tundra climates?
2. **Make Inferences** What allows much of Northern Europe to have mild climates?

go.hrw.com KEYWORD: SK9 CH17

Far to the north are colder climates. Subarctic regions, like those in Northern Scandinavia, have long, cold winters and short summers. Iceland's tundra and ice cap climates produce extremely cold temperatures all year.

READING CHECK **Analyzing** How does the North Atlantic Drift keep climates mild?

SUMMARY AND PREVIEW Northern Europe has many different physical features, natural resources, and climates. Next, you will learn about a very different region, Eastern Europe.

Section 3 Assessment

go.hrw.com
Online Quiz
KEYWORD: SK9 HP17

Reviewing Ideas, Terms, and Places

1. a. **Describe** What are the physical features of this region?
   b. **Analyze** What role did glaciers play in shaping the physical geography of Northern Europe?
2. a. **Recall** What is **geothermal energy**?
   b. **Make Inferences** How do people in Northern Europe benefit from the surrounding seas?
3. a. **Identify** What climates exist in Northern Europe?
   b. **Predict** How might the climates of Northern Europe be different without the **North Atlantic Drift**?

Critical Thinking

4. **Comparing and Contrasting** Using your notes and a chart like the one below, compare and contrast the physical geography of the British Isles and Scandinavia.

	British Isles	Scandinavia
Physical Features		
Resources		
Climates		

FOCUS ON WRITING

5. **Appealing to Customers** Northern Europe's cold climate might not appeal to everyone. How could you describe it to best appeal to customers?

Eastern Europe

What You Will Learn...

Main Ideas

1. The physical features of Eastern Europe include wide open plains, rugged mountain ranges, and many rivers.
2. The climate and vegetation of Eastern Europe differ widely in the north and the south.

The Big Idea

The physical geography of Eastern Europe varies greatly from place to place.

Key Places

Carpathians, *p. 574*
Balkan Peninsula, *p. 575*
Danube, *p. 576*
Chernobyl, *p. 577*

 TAKING NOTES Draw a chart like the one below. As you read this section, use the chart to take notes about the landforms, climate, and vegetation of Eastern Europe.

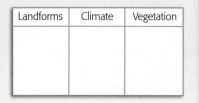

Landforms	Climate	Vegetation

If YOU lived there...

You are traveling on a boat down the Danube River, one of the longest in Europe. As you float downstream, you pass through dozens of towns and cities. Outside of the cities, the banks are lined with huge castles, soaring churches, and busy farms. From time to time, other boats pass you, some loaded with passengers and some with goods.

Why do you think the Danube is so busy?

BUILDING BACKGROUND The physical geography of Eastern Europe varies widely from north to south. Many of the landforms you learned about in earlier chapters, including the Northern European Plain and the Alps, extend into this region.

Physical Features

Eastern Europe is a land of amazing contrasts. The northern parts of the region lie along the cold, often stormy shores of the Baltic Sea. In the south, however, are warm, sunny beaches along the Adriatic and Black seas. Jagged mountain peaks jut high into the sky in some places, while wildflowers dot the gently rolling hills of other parts of the region. These contrasts stem from the region's wide variety of landforms, water features, and climates.

Landforms

As you can see on the map, the landforms of Eastern Europe are arranged in a series of broad bands. In the north is the Northern European Plain. As you have already learned, this large plain stretches across most of Northern Europe.

South of the Northern European Plain is a low mountain range called the **Carpathians** (kahr-PAY-thee-uhnz). These rugged mountains are an extension of the Alps of West-Central Europe. They stretch in a long arc from the Alps to the Black Sea area.

South and west of the Carpathians is another plain, the Great Hungarian Plain. As its name suggests, this fertile area is located mostly within Hungary.

South of the plain are more mountains, the Dinaric (duh-NAR-ik) Alps and Balkan Mountains. These two ranges together cover most of the **Balkan Peninsula**, one of the largest peninsulas in Europe. It extends south into the Mediterranean Sea.

Water Features

Like the rest of the continent, Eastern Europe has many bodies of water that affect how people live. To the southwest is the Adriatic Sea, an important route for transportation and trade. To the east, the Black Sea serves the same **function**. In the far north is the Baltic Sea. It is another important trade route, though parts of the sea freeze over in the winter.

ACADEMIC VOCABULARY

function
use or purpose

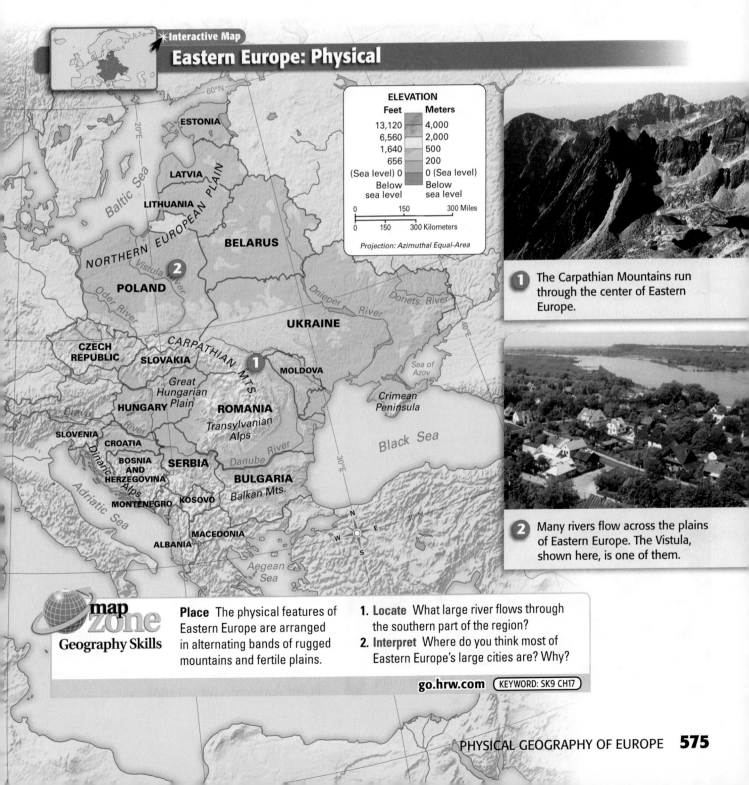

★Interactive Map
Eastern Europe: Physical

ELEVATION

Feet	Meters
13,120	4,000
6,560	2,000
1,640	500
656	200
(Sea level) 0	0 (Sea level)
Below sea level	Below sea level

0   150   300 Miles
0   150   300 Kilometers

Projection: Azimuthal Equal-Area

1 The Carpathian Mountains run through the center of Eastern Europe.

2 Many rivers flow across the plains of Eastern Europe. The Vistula, shown here, is one of them.

map zone
Geography Skills

Place The physical features of Eastern Europe are arranged in alternating bands of rugged mountains and fertile plains.

1. **Locate** What large river flows through the southern part of the region?
2. **Interpret** Where do you think most of Eastern Europe's large cities are? Why?

go.hrw.com KEYWORD: SK9 CH17

In addition to these seas, Eastern Europe has several rivers that are vital paths for transportation and trade. The longest of these rivers, the **Danube** (DAN-yoob), begins in Germany and flows east across the Great Hungarian Plain. The river winds its way through nine countries before it finally empties into the Black Sea.

Primary Source

BOOK
The Plains of Ukraine

One of Russia's greatest novelists, Nikolai Gogol (gaw-guhl), was actually born in what is now Ukraine. Very fond of his homeland, he frequently wrote about its great beauty. In this passage from the short story "Taras Bulba," he describes a man's passage across the wide open fields of Ukraine.

❝No plough had ever passed over the immeasurable waves of wild growth; horses alone, hidden in it as in a forest, trod it down. Nothing in nature could be finer. The whole surface resembled a golden-green ocean, upon which were sprinkled millions of different flowers. Through the tall, slender stems of the grass peeped light-blue, dark-blue, and lilac star-thistles; the yellow broom thrust up its pyramidal head; the parasol-shaped white flower of the false flax shimmered on high. A wheat-ear, brought God knows whence, was filling out to ripening. Amongst the roots of this luxuriant vegetation ran partridges with outstretched necks. The air was filled with the notes of a thousand different birds.❞

—from "Taras Bulba," by Nikolai Gogol

ANALYSIS SKILL **ANALYZING PRIMARY SOURCES**

What features does Gogol describe on the plains of Ukraine?

As you might expect, the Danube is central to the Eastern European economy. Some of the region's largest cities lie on the Danube's banks. Thousands of ships travel up and down the river every year, loaded with both goods and people. In addition, dams on the western parts of the river generate much of the region's electricity. Unfortunately, the high level of activity on the Danube has left it heavily polluted.

READING CHECK **Finding Main Ideas** What are the main bodies of water in Eastern Europe?

Climate and Vegetation

Like its landforms, the climates and natural vegetation of Eastern Europe vary widely. In fact, the climates and landscapes found across Eastern Europe determine which plants will grow there.

The Baltic Coast

The shores of the Baltic Sea are the coldest location in Eastern Europe. Winters there are long, cold, and harsh. This northern part of Eastern Europe receives less rain than other areas, but fog is common. In fact, some parts of the area have as few as 30 sunny days each year. The climate allows huge forests to grow there.

The Interior Plains

The interior plains of Eastern Europe are much milder than the far north. Winters there can be very cold, but summers are generally pleasant and mild. The western parts of these plains receive much more rain than those areas farther east.

Because of this variation in climate, the plains of Eastern Europe have many types of vegetation. Huge forests cover much of the north. South of these forests are open grassy plains. In the spring, these plains erupt with colorful wildflowers.

Radiation Cleanup

A nuclear accident in 1986 leaked dangerous amounts of radiation into Eastern Europe's soil. Ukraine's government and scientists are still working to repair the damage.

Unfortunately, Eastern Europe's forests were greatly damaged by a terrible accident in 1986. A faulty reactor at the **Chernobyl** (chuhr-NOH-buhl) nuclear power plant in Ukraine exploded, releasing huge amounts of radiation into the air. This radiation poisoned millions of acres of forest and ruined soil across much of the region.

The Balkan Coast

Along the Adriatic Sea, the Balkan coast has a Mediterranean climate, with warm summers and mild winters. As a result, its beaches are popular tourist destinations.

Because a Mediterranean climate does not bring much rain, the Balkan coast does not have many forests. Instead, the land there is covered by shrubs and hardy trees that do not need much water.

READING CHECK **Contrasting** How do the climates and vegetation of Eastern Europe vary?

SUMMARY AND PREVIEW The landforms of Eastern Europe vary widely, as do its cultures. Next you will study the vast region of Russia to the east.

FOCUS ON READING

As you read, ask yourself: what problems did the Chernobyl accident cause for Eastern Europe?

Section 4 Assessment

go.hrw.com
Online Quiz
KEYWORD: SK9 HP17

Reviewing Ideas, Terms, and Places

1. **a. Identify** What are the major mountain ranges of Eastern Europe?
   b. Make Inferences How do you think the physical features of Eastern Europe influence where people live?
   c. Elaborate Why is the **Danube** so important to the people of Eastern Europe?
2. **a. Describe** What is the climate of the **Balkan Peninsula** like?
   b. Explain Why are there few trees in the far southern areas of Eastern Europe?
   c. Predict How do you think the lingering effects of the **Chernobyl** accident affect the plant life of Eastern Europe?

Critical Thinking

3. **Categorizing** Draw a chart like the one shown here. In each column, identify the landforms, climates, and vegetation of each area in Eastern Europe.

	Landforms	Climates	Vegetation
Baltic coast			
Interior plains			
Balkan coast			

FOCUS ON WRITING

4. **Highlighting Physical Features** Which features of Eastern Europe's geography do you think are most likely to attract buyers to the region? Write some ideas in your notebook.

Russia and the Caucasus

What You Will Learn...

Main Ideas

1. The physical features of Russia and the Caucasus include plains, mountains, and rivers.
2. Climate and plant life change from north to south in Russia and vary in the Caucasus.
3. Russia and the Caucasus have a wealth of resources, but many are hard to access.

The Big Idea

Russia is big and cold with vast plains and forests; whereas the Caucasus countries are small, mountainous, and warmer.

Key Terms and Places

Ural Mountains, *p. 578*
Caspian Sea, *p. 578*
Caucasus Mountains, *p. 578*
Moscow, *p. 578*
Siberia, *p. 579*
Volga River, *p. 580*
taiga, *p. 581*

 TAKING NOTES As you read, take notes in a chart like this one.

	Russia	Caucasus
Physical Features		
Climate and Plants		
Natural Resources		

If **YOU** lived there...

You are making a documentary about the Trans–Siberian Railroad, a famous train that crosses the vast country of Russia. The train travels more than 5,700 miles across plains and mountains and through thick forests. As the train leaves the city of Moscow, you look out the window and see wheat fields and white birch trees.

What scenes might you include in your film?

BUILDING BACKGROUND Look at a globe, and you will see that Russia extends nearly halfway around the world. Russia is the world's largest country. It is so vast that it spans 11 time zones. While huge, much of Russia consists of flat or rolling plains.

Physical Features

Have you ever stood on two continents at once? In Russia's **Ural** (YOOHR-uhl) **Mountains**, you can. There, the continents of Europe and Asia meet. Europe lies to the west; Asia to the east. Together, Europe and Asia form the large landmass of Eurasia. On the map, you can see that a large chunk of Eurasia is the country of Russia. In fact, Russia is the world's largest country. Compared to the United States, Russia is almost twice as big.

South of Russia are three much smaller countries—Georgia, Armenia (ahr-MEE-nee-uh), and Azerbaijan (a-zuhr-by-JAHN). They lie in the Caucasus (KAW-kuh-suhs), the area between the Black Sea and the **Caspian Sea**. This area, which includes part of southern Russia, is named for the **Caucasus Mountains**.

Landforms

As the map shows, Russia's landforms vary from west to east. The Northern European Plain stretches across western, or European, Russia. This fertile plain forms Russia's heartland, where most Russians live. **Moscow**, Russia's capital, is located there.

Russia and the Caucasus: Physical

ARCTIC OCEAN

Bering Sea

PACIFIC OCEAN

North Sea

Barents Sea

Baltic Sea

NORTHERN EUROPEAN PLAIN

EUROPE

TAYMYR PENINSULA

KOLYMA MTS.

CHERSKIY RANGE

KAMCHATKA PENINSULA

S I B E R I A

WEST SIBERIAN PLAIN

CENTRAL SIBERIAN PLATEAU

Sea of Okhotsk

Sakhalin Island

Kuril Islands

URAL MOUNTAINS

Ob River

Yenisey R.

Lena R.

Lena River

RUSSIA

Don R.

Volga R.

KUZNETSK BASIN

STANOVOY MTS.

Amur R.

Sea of Japan (East Sea)

Black Sea

CAUCASUS MTS.

GEORGIA
Mt. Elbrus
18,510 ft (5,642 m)

ARMENIA

SAYAN MTS.

YABLONOVY RANGE

Lake Baikal

Caspian Sea

AZERBAIJAN

SOUTHWEST ASIA

EAST ASIA

ELEVATION

Feet		Meters
13,120		4,000
6,560		2,000
1,640		500
656		200
(Sea level) 0		0 (Sea level)
Below sea level		Below sea level

0   500   1,000 Miles
0   500   1,000 Kilometers

Projection: Two-Point Equidistant

map zone Geography Skills

Regions The Caucasus Mountains separate Russia from the three Caucasus countries to the south.
1. **Locate** What part of Russia is called Siberia?
2. **Interpret** What is the land like in the Caucasus countries?

go.hrw.com KEYWORD: SK9 CH17

To the east, the plain rises to form the Ural Mountains. These low mountains are worn down and rounded from erosion.

The vast area between the Urals and the Pacific Ocean is **Siberia**. This area includes several landforms, shown on the map. The West Siberian Plain is a flat, marshy area. It is one of the largest plains in the world.

East of this plain is an upland called the Central Siberian Plateau. Mountain ranges run through southern and eastern Siberia.

Eastern Siberia is called the Russian Far East. This area includes the Kamchatka (kuhm-CHAHT-kuh) Peninsula and several islands. The Russian Far East is part of the Ring of Fire, the area circling the Pacific.

> **1** The Kamchatka Peninsula on Russia's east coast has many old and active volcanoes.

PHYSICAL GEOGRAPHY OF EUROPE **579**

The Ring of Fire is known for its volcanoes and earthquakes, and the Russian Far East is no exception. It has several active volcanoes, and earthquakes can occur. In some areas, steam from within Earth breaks free to form geysers and hot springs.

South of Russia, the Caucasus countries consist largely of rugged uplands. The Caucasus Mountains cover much of Georgia and extend into Armenia and Azerbaijan.

These soaring mountains include Mount Elbrus (el-BROOS). At 18,510 feet (5,642 m), it is the highest peak in Europe. South of the mountains, a plateau covers much of Armenia. Gorges cut through this plateau, and earthquakes are common there. Lowlands lie along the Black and Caspian seas.

Bodies of Water

Some of the longest rivers in the world flow through the region of Russia and the Caucasus. One of the most important is the **Volga** (VAHL-guh) **River** in western Russia. The longest river in Europe, the Volga winds southward to the Caspian Sea. The Volga has long formed the core of Russia's river network. Canals link the Volga to the nearby Don River and to the Baltic Sea.

Even longer rivers than the Volga flow through Siberia in the Asian part of Russia. The Ob (AWB), Yenisey (yi-ni-SAY), and Lena rivers flow northward to the Arctic Ocean. Like many of Russia's rivers, they are frozen for much of the year. The ice often hinders shipping and trade and closes some of Russia's ports for part of the year.

In addition to its rivers, Russia has some 200,000 lakes. Lake Baikal (by-KAHL), in south-central Siberia, is the world's deepest lake. Although not that large in surface area, Lake Baikal is deep enough to hold all the water in all five of the Great Lakes. Because of its beauty, Lake Baikal is called the Jewel of Siberia. Logging and factories have polluted the water, but Russians are now working to clean up the lake.

In the southwest part of the region, the Black and Caspian Seas border Russia and the Caucasus. The Black Sea connects to the Mediterranean Sea and is important for trade. The Caspian Sea holds saltwater and is the world's largest inland sea.

READING CHECK **Summarizing** What are the major landforms in Russia and the Caucasus?

Russia's Climate and Plant Life

In the top photo, Russians bundled up in furs hurry through the snow and cold of Moscow, the capital. In the lower photo, evergreen forest called taiga blankets a Russian plain. In the distance, the low Ural Mountains mark the division between Europe and Asia.

Climate and Plant Life

Russians sometimes joke that winter lasts for 12 months and then summer begins. Russia is a cold country. The reason is its northern location partly within the Arctic Circle. In general, Russia has short summers and long, snowy winters. The climate is milder west of the Urals and grows colder and harsher as one goes north and east.

Russia's northern coast is tundra. Winters are dark and bitterly cold, and the brief summers are cool. Much of the ground is permafrost, or permanently frozen soil. Only small plants such as mosses grow.

South of the tundra is a vast forest of evergreen trees called **taiga** (TY-guh). This huge forest covers about half of Russia. In Siberia, snow covers the taiga much of the year. South of the taiga is a flat grassland called the steppe (STEP). With rich, black soil and a warmer climate, the steppe is Russia's most important farming area.

Farther south, the Caucasus countries are warmer than Russia in general. Climate in the Caucasus ranges from warm and wet along the Black Sea to cooler in the uplands to hot and dry in much of Azerbaijan.

READING CHECK Finding Main Ideas How does Russia's location affect its climate?

Natural Resources

Russia and the Caucasus have a wealth of resources. The Northern European Plain and the steppe provide fertile soil for farming. The taiga provides wood for building and paper products. Metals, such as copper and gold, and precious gems such as diamonds provide useful raw materials.

The region's main energy resources are coal, hydroelectricity, natural gas, and oil. Both Russia and Azerbaijan have large oil and gas fields. Oil also lies beneath the Caspian Sea.

The region's natural resources have been poorly managed, however. Until the early 1990s this region was part of the Soviet Union. The Soviet government put more importance on industry than on managing its resources. In Russia, many of the resources that were easy to access are gone. For example, most of the timber in western Russia has been cut down. Many remaining resources are in remote Siberia.

READING CHECK Analyzing Why are some of Russia's natural resources difficult to obtain?

SUMMARY AND PREVIEW Europe's landforms and climates vary widely, from broad plains to rugged mountains, and from sunny beaches to frozen tundra. In the next chapter, you will learn about the history of the people who inhabit this diverse region.

FOCUS ON READING

As you read, ask yourself: why does Russia have the vegetation it has?

Section 5 Assessment

go.hrw.com
Online Quiz
KEYWORD: SK9 HP17

Reviewing Ideas, Terms, and Places

1. a. **Describe** Why are the **Ural Mountains** significant?
   b. **Draw Conclusions** Why might the Russian Far East be a dangerous place to live?
2. a. **Describe** What are winters like in much of Russia?
   b. **Analyze** How does climate affect Russia's plant life?
3. a. **Recall** What valuable resource is in the **Caspian Sea**?
   b. **Make Inferences** Why might resources located in remote, cold areas be difficult to use?

Critical Thinking

4. **Generalizing** Draw a chart like the one here. Use your notes and enter one general idea for each topic in the chart.

Physical Features	
Climate and Plants	
Natural Resources	

FOCUS ON WRITING

5. **Describing the Physical Geography** Now that you know the physical geography of the region, make a list of possible locations for the house or land you are selling.

Social Studies Skills

Chart and Graph | Critical Thinking | Geography | Study

Reading a Climate Map

Learn

Geographers use many different types of maps to study a region. One type that can be very useful is a climate map. Because climate affects so many aspects of people's lives, it is important to know which climates are found in a region.

Practice

Use the climate map of Europe below to answer the following questions.

1 What does orange mean on this map?

2 What city has a highland climate?

3 What is the dominant climate in the countries of Southern Europe?

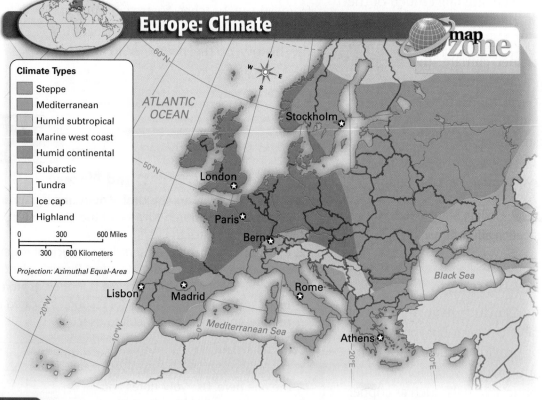

Europe: Climate

Climate Types
- Steppe
- Mediterranean
- Humid subtropical
- Marine west coast
- Humid continental
- Subarctic
- Tundra
- Ice cap
- Highland

0   300   600 Miles
0   300   600 Kilometers

Projection: Azimuthal Equal-Area

ATLANTIC OCEAN

Stockholm

London

Paris

Bern

Lisbon   Madrid

Rome

Mediterranean Sea

Athens

Black Sea

Apply

Choose one of the cities shown on the map above. Imagine that you are planning a trip to that city and need to know what the climate is like so you can prepare. Use the map to identify the type of climate found in your chosen city. Then use the library or the Internet to find out more about that type of climate. Write a short description of the climate and how you could prepare for it.

Geography's Impact
video series
Review the video to answer the closing question:
Do you think proximity to the sea has been more beneficial or harmful to the Netherlands?

Visual Summary

Use the visual summary below to help you review the main ideas of the chapter.

QUICK FACTS

Europe's physical features include wide open fields, rolling hills, and rugged mountain ranges.

Because Europe is a peninsula of peninsulas, no place is too far from water.

From the sunny beaches of Italy to the frozen steppes of Russia, Europe's climates vary widely.

Reviewing Vocabulary, Terms, and Places

Fill in the blanks with the correct term or location from this chapter.

1. The climate found in most of Southern Europe is the _____.

2. A _____ river is one that is deep and wide enough for ships to sail on.

3. The highest mountains in Europe are the _____.

4. Much of Russia is covered by _____, a vast forest of evergreen trees.

5. A _____ is a narrow inlet of the sea between high, rocky cliffs.

6. A nuclear accident at _____ released radiation into Eastern Europe.

7. _____, a peninsula in far northern Europe, is the site of the Kjolen Mountains.

8. The _____ separates the British Isles from the European mainland.

Comprehension and Critical Thinking

SECTION 1 *(Pages 562–565)*

9. **a. Describe** What are two physical features that all the countries of Southern Europe have in common?

b. Draw Conclusions Why has Southern Europe's climate been called its most valuable resource?

c. Predict How would daily life in Southern Europe be different if it were not a coastal region?

SECTION 2 *(Pages 566–569)*

10. **a. Recall** From southeast to northwest, what are the major landforms in West-Central Europe?

b. Analyze How have geographic features supported trade and travel across the region of West-Central Europe?

c. Elaborate How does West-Central Europe's mild climate serve as a valuable resource and contribute to the economy?

SECTION 3 (Pages 570–573)

11. a. Identify What are the major resources found in Northern Europe?

b. Analyze How do ocean currents create a relatively mild climate in Northern Europe?

c. Predict How do you think Northern Europe's population compares to Southern Europe's? Why?

SECTION 4 (Pages 574–577)

12. a. Identify Name two major bodies of water that border Eastern Europe.

b. Explain How do the Danube and other rivers affect life for people in Eastern Europe?

c. Evaluate If you could live in any region of Eastern Europe, were would it be? Why?

SECTION 5 (Pages 578–581)

13. a. Recall What is Russia's most important river, and to what major bodies of water does it link?

b. Identify Cause and Effect How does Russia's location affect its climate?

c. Elaborate Why might developing the many natural resources in Siberia be difficult?

FOCUS ON READING AND WRITING

Asking Questions *Read the passage below. After you read it, answer the questions below to be sure you have understood what you read.*

> "The Alps are Europe's highest mountain range. They stretch from southern France to the Balkan Peninsula. Several of the jagged peaks in the Alps soar to more than 14,000 feet."

14. What is this paragraph about?

15. Where is the area described in the passage?

16. Why is this information significant?

Creating a Real Estate Ad *Use your notes and the instructions below to help you create your ad.*

17. Review your notes about locations in Europe. Choose one location for the real estate you are selling. What are its best features? How would you describe the land and climate? What are the benefits of living there? What is nearby? Answer these questions in your real estate ad.

Social Studies Skills

Reading a Climate Map *Use the climate map from the Social Studies Skills lesson of this chapter to answer the following questions.*

18. What type of climate does London have?

19. What climate is found only in the far north?

20. Where in Europe would you find a humid subtropical climate?

Using the Internet

KEYWORD: SK9 CH17

21. Activity: Making a Map The Trans-Siberian Railroad is the longest single rail line in the world. Climb aboard in Moscow and travel all the way across Russia. Enter the activity keyword to start your journey. Research the regions and features along the railroad's route. Then create an illustrated map of your journey. On the map, show the train's route, indicate the places where you stopped, and include images about what you saw.

Map Activity

22. Europe On a separate sheet of paper, match the letters on the map with their correct labels.

Alps	Scandinavia
Danube River	North Sea
Pyrenees	Mediterranean Sea

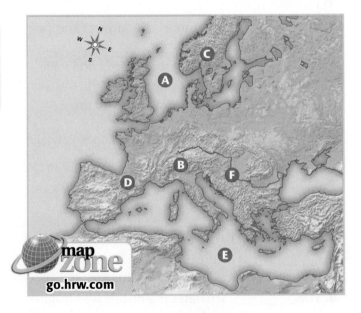

map zone
go.hrw.com

DIRECTIONS (1–7): For each statement or question, write on a separate answer sheet the *number* of the word or expression that, of those given, best completes the statement or answers the question.

1 Which of the following is *not* a mountain range in Europe?

(1) Alps

(2) Pyrenees

(3) Danubes

(4) Carpathians

2 Fjords are created by

(1) glaciers.

(2) earthquakes.

(3) volcanoes.

(4) geysers.

3 Which region of Europe was most affected by the Chernobyl accident?

(1) Southern Europe

(2) West-Central Europe

(3) Northern Europe

(4) Eastern Europe

4 Italy and Scandinavia are both

(1) islands.

(2) mountains.

(3) lakes.

(4) peninsulas

5 Which statement about the Alps is true?

(1) They are found in Northern Europe.

(2) They are the world's tallest mountains.

(3) They are mostly volcanoes.

(4) They are usually capped with snow.

6 What is the name of the vast forest that covers much of Russia?

(1) Siberia

(2) Steppe

(3) Taiga

(4) Tundra

7 A Mediterranean climate is most likely to be found in which region?

(1) Southern Europe

(2) West-Central Europe

(3) Northern Europe

(4) Eastern Europe

Base your answer to question 8 on the map below and on your knowledge of social studies.

Spain and Portugal: Climates

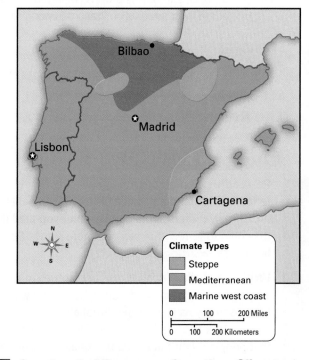

8 Constructed-Response Question **Climate influences many aspects of people's lives in Spain and Portugal. List two ways in which climate affects how people there live.**

CHAPTER 18

Ancient Civilizations of Europe

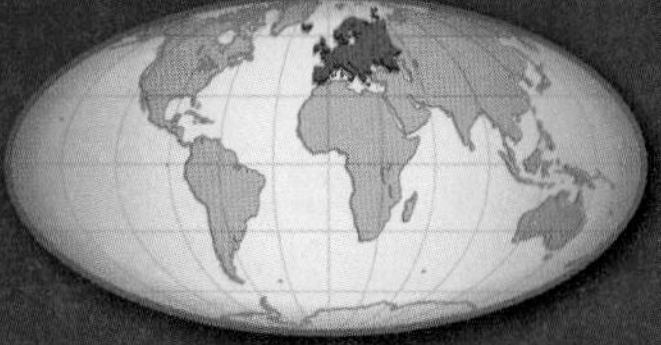

Focus Question

How did ancient civilizations contribute to the development of the Eastern Hemisphere?

What You Will Learn...

In this chapter you will learn about two major periods in the early history of Europe. First you will learn about ancient Greece, a culture whose ideas still shape the world. Then you will learn about Rome, one of the most powerful civilizations in world history.

Focus on Reading and Writing

Re-reading Sometimes a single reading is not enough to fully understand a passage of text. If you feel like you do not fully understand a passage after you read it, it may help to re-read the passage more slowly. **See the lesson, Re-reading, on page S21.**

Writing a Myth A myth is a story that tries to explain why something happened. Throughout history, people have used myths to explain natural and historical events. After you read this chapter, you will write a myth that people might have used to explain a major event in European history.

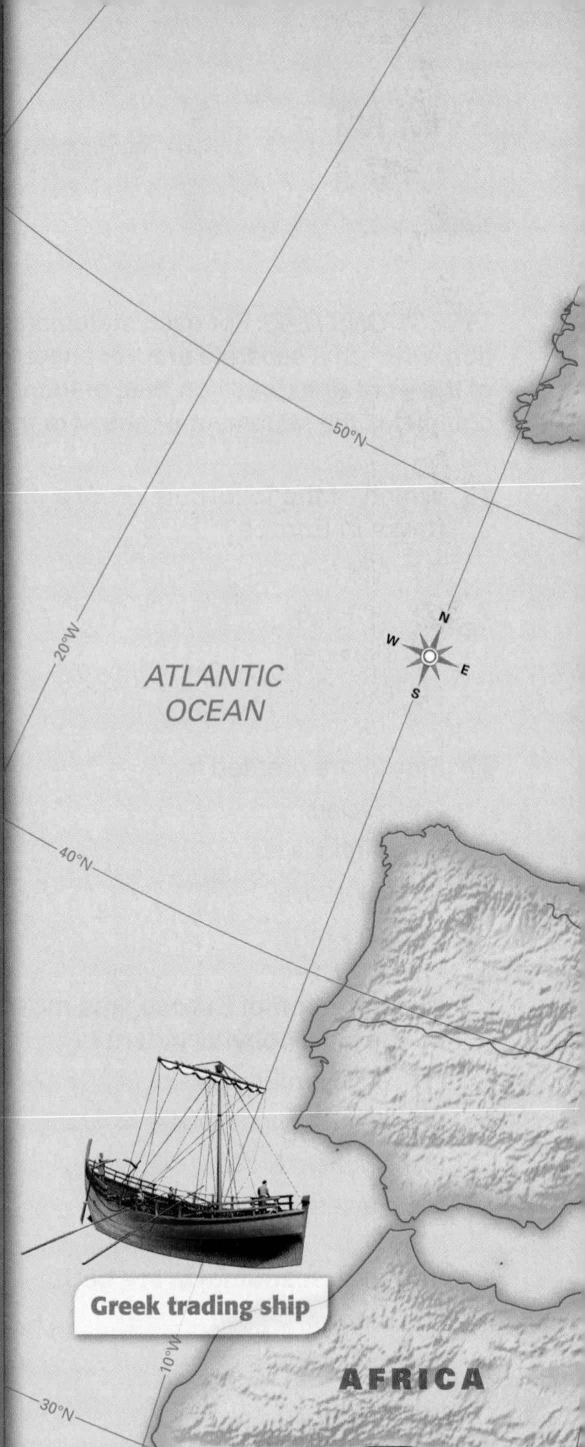

50°N
20°W
N
W
E
S
ATLANTIC OCEAN
40°N
10°W
AFRICA
30°N

Greek trading ship

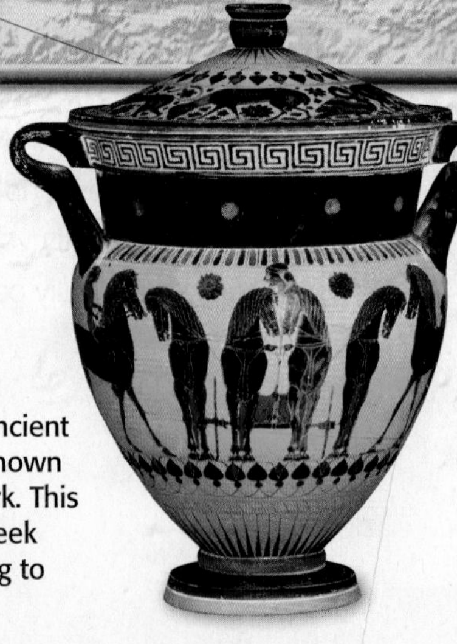

Greece The ancient Greeks were known for their artwork. This vase shows Greek soldiers tending to horses.

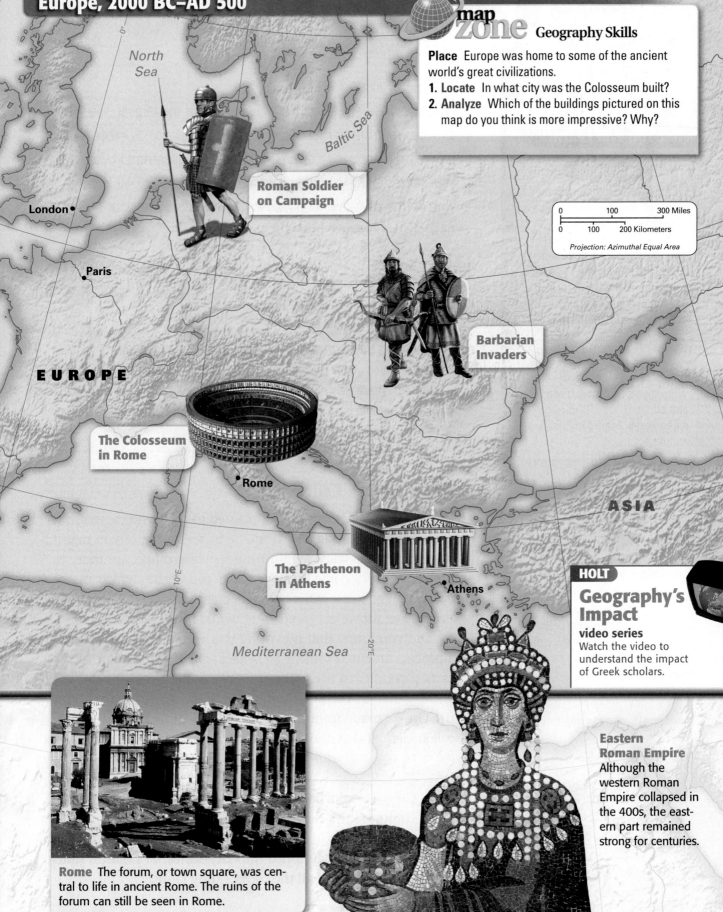

map zone Geography Skills

Place Europe was home to some of the ancient world's great civilizations.
1. **Locate** In what city was the Colosseum built?
2. **Analyze** Which of the buildings pictured on this map do you think is more impressive? Why?

North Sea

Baltic Sea

Roman Soldier on Campaign

London •

Paris •

0   100   300 Miles
0   100   200 Kilometers
Projection: Azimuthal Equal Area

Barbarian Invaders

EUROPE

The Colosseum in Rome

• Rome

ASIA

The Parthenon in Athens

• Athens

Mediterranean Sea

HOLT

Geography's Impact
video series
Watch the video to understand the impact of Greek scholars.

Rome The forum, or town square, was central to life in ancient Rome. The ruins of the forum can still be seen in Rome.

Eastern Roman Empire Although the western Roman Empire collapsed in the 400s, the eastern part remained strong for centuries.

587

Ancient Greece

What You Will Learn...

Main Ideas

1. Early Greek culture saw the rise of the city-state and the creation of colonies.
2. The golden age of Greece saw advances in government, art, and philosophy.
3. Alexander the Great formed a huge empire and spread Greek culture into new areas.

The Big Idea

Through colonization, trade, and conquest, the Greeks spread their culture in Europe and Asia.

Key Terms and Places

city-states, *p. 588*
golden age, *p. 590*
Athens, *p. 591*
Sparta, *p. 593*
Hellenistic, *p. 594*

 TAKING NOTES As you read, keep a list of key events in Greek history. Organize the events in the order in which they occurred. You may wish to draw a time line like this one to organize your notes.

If **YOU** lived there...

You live in the ancient city of Athens, one of the largest cities in Greece. Your brother, just two years older than you, is excited. He is finally old enough to take part in the city's government. He and your father, along with the other free men in the city, will meet to vote on the city's laws and leaders. Your mother and your sisters, however, cannot take part in the process.

Why is your brother excited about voting?

BUILDING BACKGROUND In ancient times, people in most cultures lived under the rule of a king. In Greece, however, life was different. There was no ruler who held power over all of Greece. Instead, people lived in independent cities. Each of these cities had its own government, culture, and way of life.

Early Greek Culture

Suppose you and some friends wanted to go to the movies, but you could not decide which movie to see. Some of you might want to see the latest action thriller, while others are more in the mood for a comedy. How could you decide which movie you would go to see? One way to decide would be to take a vote. Whichever movie got more votes would be the one you saw.

Did you know that by voting you would be taking part in a process invented some 2,500 years ago? It is true. One of the earliest peoples to use voting to make major decisions was the ancient Greeks. Voting was only one of the many contributions the Greeks made to our culture, though. In fact, many people call ancient Greece the birthplace of modern civilization.

City-States

Early Greece could be a dangerous place. Waves of invaders swept through the land, and violence was common. Eventually, people began to band together in groups for protection. Over time, these groups developed into **city-states**, or political units made up of a city and all the surrounding lands.

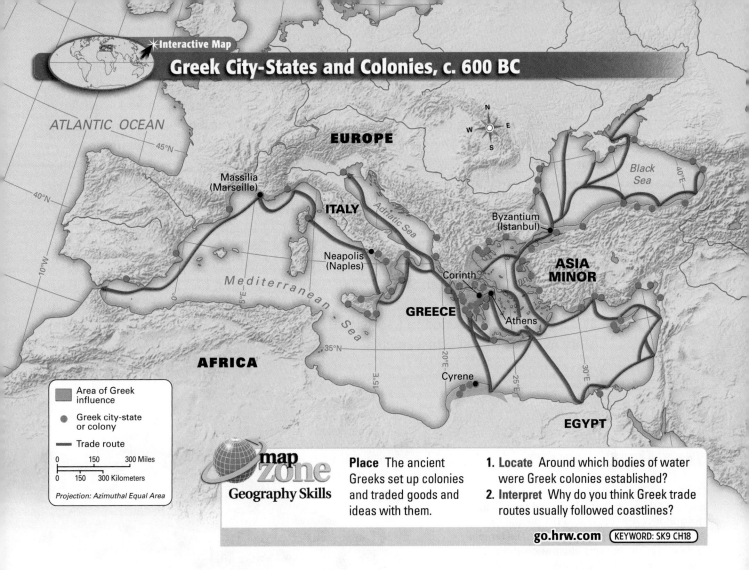

Greek City-States and Colonies, c. 600 BC

ATLANTIC OCEAN

EUROPE

Massilia
(Marseille)

ITALY

Adriatic Sea

Byzantium
(Istanbul)

Black
Sea

ASIA
MINOR

Neapolis
(Naples)

Mediterranean Sea

Corinth

GREECE

Athens

AFRICA

Cyrene

EGYPT

Area of Greek influence

Greek city-state or colony

Trade route

0   150   300 Miles
0   150   300 Kilometers

Projection: Azimuthal Equal Area

map zone
Geography Skills

Place The ancient Greeks set up colonies and traded goods and ideas with them.

1. **Locate** Around which bodies of water were Greek colonies established?
2. **Interpret** Why do you think Greek trade routes usually followed coastlines?

go.hrw.com KEYWORD: SK9 CH18

In the center of most city-states was a fortress on a hill. This hill was called the acropolis (uh-KRAH-puh-luhs), which is Greek for "top city." In addition to the fortress, many city-states built temples and other public buildings on the acropolis.

Around the acropolis was the rest of the city, including houses and markets. High walls usually surrounded the city for protection. In wartime, farmers who lived outside the walls could seek safety inside.

Living in city-states provided many advantages for the Greeks. The city was a place where people could meet and trade. In addition, the city-state gave people a new sense of identity. People thought of themselves as residents of a particular city-state, not as Greeks.

Colonies

In time, some city-states established new outposts, or colonies, around the Black and Mediterranean seas. You can see these colonies on the map above. Some of them still exist today as modern cities, such as Naples, Italy, and Marseille, France.

Although they were independent, most colonies kept ties with the older cities of Greece. They traded goods and shared ideas. These ties helped strengthen the economies of both cities and colonies, and they kept Greek culture strong. Because they stayed in contact, Greek cities all over Europe shared a common culture.

READING CHECK **Summarizing** Where did the ancient Greeks establish colonies?

The Golden Age of Greece

When most people think of ancient Greek culture today, certain images come to mind. They think of the ruins of stately temples and of realistic statues. They also think of great writers, philosophers, and scientists whose ideas changed the world.

These images represent some of the many contributions the Greeks made to world history. Remarkably, most of these contributions were developed during a relatively short time, between 500 and 300 BC. For that reason, this period is often called a **golden age**, a period in a society's history marked by great achievements.

The Growth of Greek Power

Early in Greece's history, city-states remained fiercely independent. Each city-state focused on its own concerns and did not interfere in the others' affairs.

Around 500 BC, however, an invading army caused the Greeks to band together against a common enemy. That invasion came from Persia, a powerful empire in central Asia. The Persian army was huge, well-trained, and experienced. Greece, on the other hand, had no single army. Each city-state had an army, but none was as large as Persia's. As a result, the Persians expected a quick victory.

Close-up

The Parthenon

The Parthenon is often seen as a symbol of ancient Athens. It was a beautiful temple to the goddess Athena, whom the people of Athens considered their protector. The temple is now in ruins, but this illustration shows how it may have looked when it was built around 440 BC.

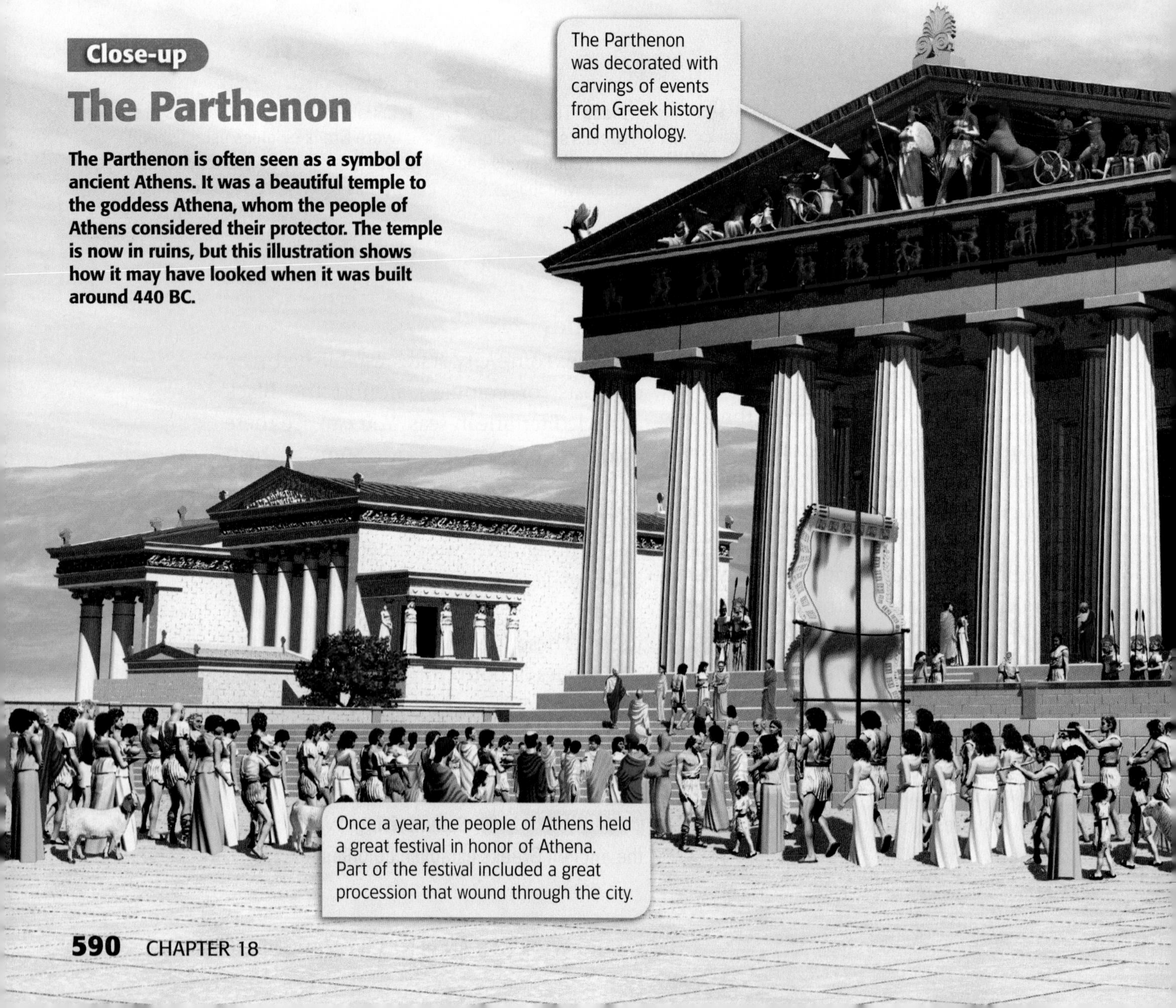

The Parthenon was decorated with carvings of events from Greek history and mythology.

Once a year, the people of Athens held a great festival in honor of Athena. Part of the festival included a great procession that wound through the city.

Nevertheless, the Greeks took up arms against the Persians. Led by **Athens**, a city-state in eastern Greece, the Greeks were able to defeat the Persians and keep Greece from being conquered. When the Persians invaded again 10 years later, the Athenians once again helped defeat them.

The victory over the Persians increased the confidence of people all over Greece. They realized that they were capable of great achievements. In the period after the Persian invasion, the people of Greece made amazing advances in art, writing, and thinking. Many of these advances were made by the people of Athens.

Athenian Culture

In the century after the defeat of Persia, Athens was the cultural center of Greece. Some of history's most famous politicians, artists, and thinkers lived in Athens during this time.

One reason for the great advances the Athenians made during this time was their city's leadership. Leaders such as Pericles (PER-uh-kleez), who ruled Athens in the 400s BC, supported the arts and encouraged the creation of great works. For example, Pericles hired great architects and artists to construct and decorate the Parthenon, the temple shown below.

Inside the Parthenon was a magnificent statue of Athena by the sculptor Phidias. Many people consider him the greatest sculptor in all of Greece.

Like most Greek temples, the Parthenon had huge marble columns to support its roof.

ANALYSIS SKILL **ANALYZING VISUALS**

Why do you think people consider the Parthenon to be a symbol of ancient Athens?

Athenian Democracy

Athens was governed as a democracy. Once a month, all adult men in the city gathered together in an assembly to make the city's laws.

Men spoke in the assembly to support or argue against ideas. Sometimes, people in the crowd argued with them.

Voting was done either by show of hands or by secret ballot. The ballots used were broken pieces of pottery.

BIOGRAPHY

Pericles
(c. 495–429 BC)

Pericles, the most famous leader in all of Athenian history, wanted the city's people to be proud of their city. In his speeches, he emphasized the greatness of Athenian democracy and encouraged everyone to take part. He also worked to make the city beautiful. He hired the city's best architects to build monuments, such as the Parthenon, and hired great artists to decorate them. He also supported the work of writers and poets in order to make Athens the cultural center of all Greece.

Athenian Democracy

Leaders like Pericles had great power in Athens, but they did not rule alone. The city of Athens was a democracy, and its leaders were elected. In fact, Athens was the world's first democracy. No one else in history had created a government in which people ruled themselves.

In Athens most power was in the hands of the people. All the city's leaders could do was suggest ideas. Those ideas had to be approved by an assembly made up of the city's free men before they were enacted. As a result, it was vital that all the men of Athens took part in making government decisions.

The people of Athens were very proud of their democracy, and also of their city in general. This pride was reflected in their city's buildings and art.

Turn back to the previous page and look at the picture of the Parthenon again. Why do you think the temple was so large and so elaborately decorated? Like many Greek buildings, it was designed to be a symbol of the city. It was supposed to make people see Athens as a great and glorious city.

Architecture and Art

The Parthenon may be the most famous building from ancient Greece, but it is only one of many magnificent structures built by the Greeks. All over Greece, builders created beautiful marble temples. These temples were symbols of the glory of the cities in which they were built.

Greek temples and other buildings were often decorated with statues and carvings. These works by Greek artists are still admired by people today.

Greek art is so admired because of the skill and careful preparation of ancient Greek artists. These artists wanted their works to look realistic. To achieve their goals, they watched people as they stood and moved. They wanted to learn exactly what the human body looked like while it was in motion. The artists then used what they learned from their observations to make their statues as lifelike as possible.

Science, Philosophy, and Literature

Artists were not the only people in ancient Greece to study other people. Scientists, for example, studied people to learn how the body worked. Through these studies, the Greeks learned a great deal about medicine and biology. Other Greek scholars made great advances in math, astronomy, and other areas of science.

Greek philosophers, or thinkers, also studied people. They wanted to figure out how people could be happy. Three of the world's most influential philosophers—Socrates, Plato, and Aristotle—lived and taught in Athens during this time. Their ideas continue to shape how we live and think even today.

The ancient Greeks also made huge contributions to world literature. Some of the world's timeless classics were written in ancient Greece. They include stories of Greek heroes and their daring adventures, poems about love and friendship, and myths meant to teach lessons about life. Chances are that you have read a book, seen a film, or watched a play inspired by— or even written by—the ancient Greeks.

Actually, if you have ever seen a play at all then you have the Greeks to thank. The ancient Greeks were the first people to write and perform drama, or plays. Once a part of certain religious ceremonies, plays became one of the most popular forms of entertainment in Greece.

The Decline of the City-States

As great as it was, the Greek golden age could not last forever. In the end, Greece was torn apart by a war between Athens and its rival city-state, **Sparta**.

Sparta was a military city with one of the strongest armies in Greece. Jealous of the influence Athens had over other city-states, the Spartans attacked Athens.

The war between these two powerful city-states devastated Greece. Other city-states joined the war, supporting one side or the other. For years the war went on. In the end, Sparta won, but Greece was in shambles. Thousands of people had been killed and whole cities had been destroyed. Weakened, Greece lay open for a foreign conqueror to swoop in and take over.

READING CHECK **Analyzing** Why is the period between 500 and 300 BC called a golden age in Greece?

Greek Art

The ancient Greeks took great care to make their art lifelike. This statue shows Athena, a goddess from Greek mythology.

ANALYZING VISUALS What details make this statue lifelike?

The Empire of Alexander

In fact, a conqueror did take over all of Greece in the 330s BC. For the first time in its history, all of Greece was unified under a single ruler. He was from an area called Macedonia just north of Greece, an area that many Greeks considered uncivilized. He was known as Alexander the Great.

Alexander's Conquests

Alexander swept into Greece with a strong, well-trained army in 336 BC. In just a few years, he had conquered all of Greece.

Alexander, however, was not satisfied to rule only Greece. He wanted to create a huge empire. In 334 BC he set out to do just that. As you can see on the map, he was quite successful.

At its greatest extent, Alexander's empire stretched from Greece in the west all the way to India in the east. It included nearly all of central Asia—including what had been the Persian Empire—and Egypt. Alexander had dreams of extending his empire even farther east, but his troops refused to keep fighting. Tired and far from home, they demanded that Alexander turn back. He did, turning back toward home in 325 BC. On his way back home, however, Alexander became ill and died. He was 33.

The Spread of Greek Culture

FOCUS ON READING

After you read this passage, reread it to make sure you understand all the details.

During his life, Alexander wanted Greek culture to spread throughout his empire. To help the culture spread, he built cities in the lands he conquered and urged Greek people to move there. He named many of the cities Alexandria after himself.

As Greek people moved to these cities, however, they mingled with the people and cultures in the area. As a result, Greek culture blended with other cultures. The result was a new type of culture that mixed elements from many people and places.

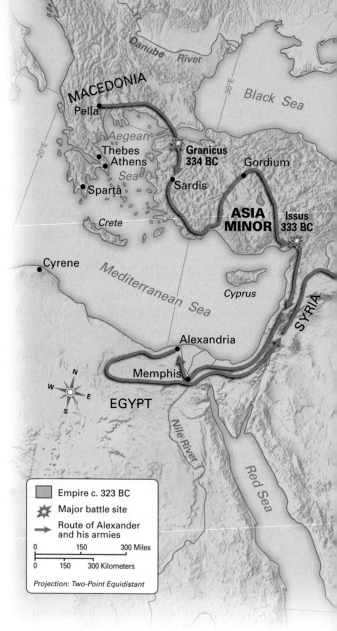

Because the Greek word for Greek is Hellenic, historians often refer to these blended cultures as **Hellenistic**, or Greek-like. Hellenistic culture helped shape life in Egypt, central Asia, and other parts of the world for many years.

READING CHECK Finding Main Ideas What lands were included in Alexander's empire?

SUMMARY AND PREVIEW Greece was the location of the first great civilization in Europe. In time, though, it was defeated by a new power, the Roman Empire.

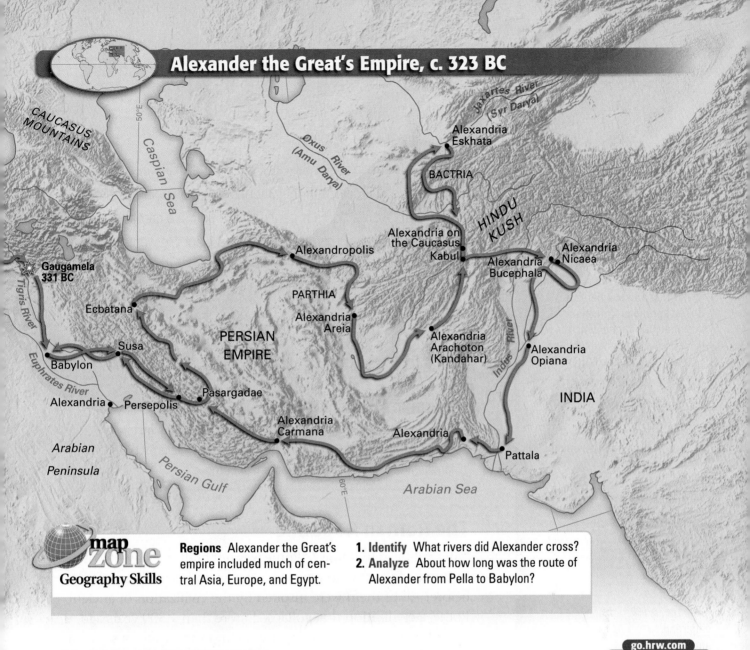

Alexander the Great's Empire, c. 323 BC

CAUCASUS MOUNTAINS

Caspian Sea

Oxus River (Amu Darya)

Jaxartes River (Syr Darya)

Alexandria Eskhata

BACTRIA

Alexandropolis

Gaugamela 331 BC

Ecbatana

PARTHIA

Alexandria on the Caucasus

HINDU KUSH

Kabul

Alexandria Bucephala

Alexandria Nicaea

Tigris River

Susa

PERSIAN EMPIRE

Alexandria Areia

Alexandria Arachoton (Kandahar)

Indus River

Alexandria Opiana

Euphrates River

Babylon

Pasargadae

INDIA

Alexandria

Persepolis

Alexandria Carmana

Alexandria

Arabian Peninsula

Persian Gulf

Arabian Sea

Pattala

map zone
Geography Skills

Regions Alexander the Great's empire included much of central Asia, Europe, and Egypt.

1. **Identify** What rivers did Alexander cross?
2. **Analyze** About how long was the route of Alexander from Pella to Babylon?

Section 1 Assessment

Reviewing Ideas, Terms, and Places

1. a. **Describe** What did an ancient Greek **city-state** include?
   b. **Explain** Why did the Greeks form city-states?
2. a. **Identify** What were some major achievements in Greece between 500 and 300 BC?
   b. **Summarize** What was the government of ancient Athens like?
   c. **Evaluate** Would you have liked living in ancient Greece? Why or why not?
3. a. **Describe** How did Alexander the Great try to spread Greek culture in his empire?
   b. **Drawing Conclusions** How might Greek history have been different if Alexander had not existed?

Critical Thinking

4. **Analyzing** Using your notes, draw a time line of major events in Greek history. For each event you list on your time line, write a sentence explaining why it was important.

FOCUS ON WRITING

5. **Choosing Characters** Many ancient myths focused on the deeds of heroes or other great figures. What people from ancient Greece might feature in such a myth? Write some ideas in your notebook.

The Roman World

If YOU lived there...

You live in Rome in about 50 BC. Times are difficult for ordinary Romans. Bread is scarce in the city, and you are finding it hard to find work. Now a popular general is mounting a campaign to cross the mountains into a territory called Gaul. He wants to try to conquer the barbarians who live there. It might be dangerous, but being a soldier guarantees work and a chance to make money.

Will you join the army? Why or why not?

BUILDING BACKGROUND Rome's well-trained army helped it conquer large parts of Europe, Africa, and Asia. Through these conquests, Rome built a long-lasting empire that left its mark on the languages, cultures, and government of Europe.

The Roman Republic

"All roads lead to Rome." "Rome was not built in a day." "When in Rome, do as the Romans do." Have you heard these sayings before? All of them were inspired by the civilization of ancient Rome, a civilization that collapsed more than 1,500 years ago.

Why would people today use sayings that relate to so old a culture? They refer to Rome because it was one of the greatest and most influential civilizations in history. In fact, we can still see the influence of ancient Rome in our lives.

Rome's Early History

Rome was not always so influential, however. At first it was just a small city in Italy. According to legend, the city of **Rome** was established in the year 753 BC by a group called the Latins.

For many years, the Romans were ruled by kings. Not all of these kings were Latin, though. For many years the Romans were ruled by a group called the Etruscans. The Romans learned a great deal from the Etruscans. For example, they learned about written language and how to build paved roads and sewers. Building on what they learned from the Etruscans, the Romans made Rome into a large and successful city.

The Beginning of the Republic

Not all of Rome's kings were good leaders, or good people. Some were cruel, harsh, and unfair. The last king of Rome was so unpopular that he was overthrown. In 509 BC a group of Roman nobles forced the king to flee the city.

In place of the king the people of Rome created a new type of government. They formed a **republic**, a type of government in which people elect leaders to make laws for them. Once elected, these leaders made all government decisions.

To help make some decisions, Rome's leaders looked to the **Senate**, a council of rich and powerful Romans who helped run the city. By advising the city's leaders, the Senate gained much influence in Rome.

For Rome's republican government to succeed, **citizens**, or people who could take part in the government, needed to be active. Rome's leaders encouraged citizens to vote and to run for office. As a result, speeches and debates were common in the city. One popular place for these activities was in the forum, the city's public square.

Close-up

The Roman Forum

The forum was a large public square that stood in the center of the city. Roman citizens often met in the forum to discuss city affairs and politics.

Government buildings and temples stood on the hills around the forum.

Only citizens, or people who could vote, were allowed to wear this article of clothing, called a toga.

Many people met in the forum to discuss politics, current affairs, and other issues.

ANALYSIS SKILL **ANALYZING VISUALS**

What are some places in your local community that serve the same function as the forum did?

FOCUS ON READING

After you read this passage, re-read it. Make a list of details you did not notice in your first reading.

Growth and Conquest

After the creation of the republic, the Romans began to expand their territory. They started this expansion in Italy. As the map at right shows, however, the republic kept growing. By 100 BC the Romans ruled much of the Mediterranean world.

The Romans were able to take so much land because of their strong, organized army. They used this army to conquer their rivals. For example, the Romans fought the people of **Carthage**, a city in North Africa, and took over their lands.

Rome's expansion did not stop in 100 BC. In the 40s BC a general named Julius Caesar conquered many new lands for Rome. Caesar's conquests made him very powerful and very popular in Rome. Afraid of Caesar's power, a group of Senators decided to put an end to it. They banded together and killed Caesar in 44 BC.

READING CHECK **Summarizing** How did the Romans expand their territory?

The Roman Empire

The murder of Julius Caesar changed Roman society completely. The Romans were shocked and horrified by his death, and they wanted Caesar's murderers to be punished. One of the people they called on to punish the murderers was Caesar's adopted son, Octavian. Octavian's actions would reshape the Roman world. Under his leadership, Rome changed from a republic to an **empire**, a government that includes many different peoples and lands under a single rule.

The First Emperor

Octavian moved quickly to punish his uncle's murderers. He led an army against them and, before long, defeated them all.

After defeating his enemies, Octavian became more powerful. One by one, he eliminated his rivals for power. Eventually, Octavian alone ruled the entire Roman world as Rome's first emperor.

Roman Conquests

The Roman army was both powerful and flexible, which allowed it to take on and defeat many foes. Even the huge elephants ridden by the soldiers of Carthage were no match for the Romans' bravery and cleverness.

ANALYZING VISUALS What kind of equipment did the Roman army use?

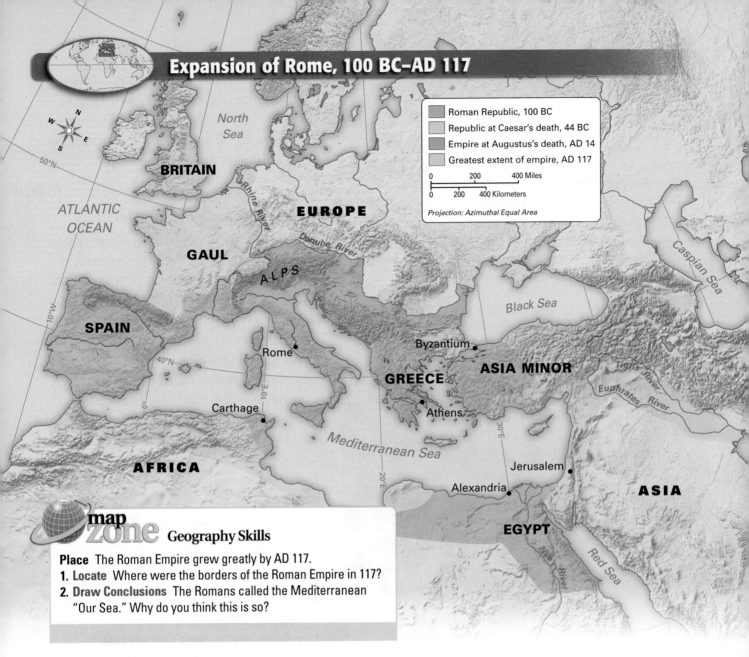

Expansion of Rome, 100 BC–AD 117

Legend:
- Roman Republic, 100 BC
- Republic at Caesar's death, 44 BC
- Empire at Augustus's death, AD 14
- Greatest extent of empire, AD 117

0   200   400 Miles
0   200   400 Kilometers

Projection: Azimuthal Equal Area

North Sea
BRITAIN
ATLANTIC OCEAN
50°N
Rhine River
EUROPE
GAUL
Danube River
A L P S
SPAIN
10°W
40°N
Rome
Black Sea
Byzantium
ASIA MINOR
Caspian Sea
Tigris River
GREECE
Euphrates River
Athens
Carthage
Mediterranean Sea
AFRICA
30°E
Jerusalem
Alexandria
ASIA
EGYPT
Nile River
Red Sea
20°E

map zone Geography Skills

Place The Roman Empire grew greatly by AD 117.
1. **Locate** Where were the borders of the Roman Empire in 117?
2. **Draw Conclusions** The Romans called the Mediterranean "Our Sea." Why do you think this is so?

As emperor, Octavian was given a new name, Augustus, which means "honored one." The people of Rome respected and admired Augustus. This respect was mainly the result of his many accomplishments. As the map above shows, Augustus added a great deal of territory to the empire. He also made many improvements to lands already in the empire. For example, he built monuments and public buildings in the city of Rome. He also improved and expanded Rome's network of roads, which **facilitated** both travel and trade.

The Pax Romana

The emperors who ruled after Augustus tried to follow his example. Some of them worked to add even more land to the empire. Others focused their attentions on improving Roman society.

Because of these emperors' efforts, Rome experienced a long period of peace and achievement. There were no major wars or rebellions within the empire, and trade increased. This period, which lasted for about 200 years, was called the Pax Romana, or the Roman Peace.

ACADEMIC VOCABULARY

facilitate
(fuh-SI-luh-tayt)
to make easier

Built to Last

Think about the buildings in your neighborhood. Can you imagine any of them still standing 1,000 years from now? The ancient Romans could. Many structures that they built nearly 2,000 years ago are still standing today. How is that possible?

The Romans knew many techniques for building strong, long-lasting structures. Look at the Colosseum, pictured here. Notice how many arches were used in its design. Arches are one of the strongest shapes you can use in construction, a fact the Romans knew well. They also invented materials like cement to make their buildings stronger.

Making Generalizations How did technology help the Romans build strong and lasting structures?

Roman Building and Engineering

Because the Pax Romana was a time of stability, the Romans were able to make great cultural achievements. Some of the advances made during this time continue to affect our lives even today.

One of the areas in which the Romans made visible advances was architecture. The Romans were great builders, and many of their structures have stood for centuries. In fact, you can still see Roman buildings in Europe today, almost 2,000 years after they were built. This is because the Romans were skilled engineers who knew how to make their buildings strong.

Buildings are not the only structures that the Romans built to last. Ancient roads, bridges, and **aqueducts**—channels used to carry water over long distances—are still seen all over Europe. Planned by skilled Roman engineers, many of these structures are still in use.

Roman Language and Law

Not all Roman achievements are as easy to see as buildings, however. For example, the Romans greatly influenced how we speak, write, and think even today. Many of the languages spoken in Europe today, such as Spanish, French, and Italian, are based on Latin, the Romans' language. English, too, has adopted many words from Latin.

The Romans used the Latin language to create great works of literature. Among these works were some of the world's most famous plays, poems, and stories. Many of them are read and enjoyed by millions of people around the world today.

Even more important to the world than their literary achievements, however, were the Romans' political contributions. All around the world, people use legal systems based on ancient Roman law. In some countries, the entire government is based largely on the ancient Roman system.

One such country is the United States. The founders of our country admired the Roman government and used it as a model for our government. Like ancient Rome, the United States is a republic. We elect our leaders and trust them to make our laws. Also like the Romans, we require all people to obey a set of basic written laws. In ancient Rome, these laws were carved on stone tablets and kept on display. In the United States, they are written down in a document, the Constitution.

READING CHECK **Finding Main Ideas** What were some of the Romans' main achievements?

The Spread of Christianity

In addition to art and law, the ancient Romans also had a tremendous influence on religion. One of the world's major religions, Christianity, first appeared and spread in the Roman world.

The Beginnings of Christianity

Christianity is based on the life, actions, and teachings of Jesus of Nazareth. He and his early followers lived in the Roman territory of Judea in southwest Asia. They spread Jesus' teachings to many people in Jerusalem and other cities in Judea.

However, Christianity quickly spread far beyond the borders of Judea. Jesus's followers traveled widely, preaching and spreading his teachings. Through their efforts, communities of Christians began to appear in cities throughout the Roman world. Christian ideas spread quickly through these cities, as more and more people converted to Christianity.

Persecution and Acceptance

The rapid spread of Christianity worried some Roman leaders. They feared that Christians were not loyal to Rome and that Roman gods might punish the empire because Christians did not worship them.

To stop the spread of Christianity, some emperors began to persecute, or punish, Christians. They arrested, fined, or even killed any Christians they found.

The persecution did not cause people to abandon Christianity, however. Instead, Christians began to meet in secret, hiding their religion from the government.

Eventually, the persecution was ended. In the 300s a powerful emperor named Constantine became a Christian himself. Once the emperor had converted, the Christian faith was openly accepted even more widely in the empire. Look at the map below to see how Christianity spread between 300 and 400.

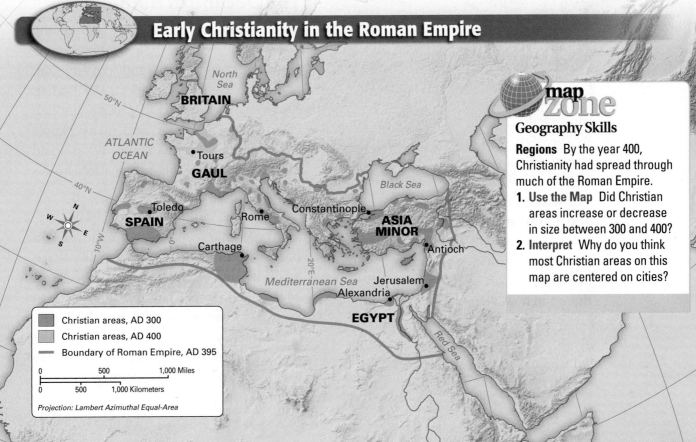

Early Christianity in the Roman Empire

- Christian areas, AD 300
- Christian areas, AD 400
- Boundary of Roman Empire, AD 395

0 500 1,000 Miles
0 500 1,000 Kilometers

Projection: Lambert Azimuthal Equal-Area

map zone

Geography Skills

Regions By the year 400, Christianity had spread through much of the Roman Empire.

1. **Use the Map** Did Christian areas increase or decrease in size between 300 and 400?
2. **Interpret** Why do you think most Christian areas on this map are centered on cities?

The Decline of Rome

Beginning around 200, the once-mighty Roman Empire began to weaken. Factors from inside and outside the empire caused many problems for Rome's leaders and led to the empire's collapse in the late 400s.

Barbarian invaders

Reasons for the Decline of Rome

- Poor leaders cared less for the people of Rome than they did for their own happiness.
- Taxes and prices rose, increasing poverty.
- People became less loyal to Rome.
- Military leaders fought each other for power.
- The empire was too large for a single person to govern well.
- Barbarians invaded the empire from outside.

ANALYSIS SKILL ANALYZING VISUALS

Which factors in Rome's decline were internal? Which came from outside the empire?

Official Religion

Even after Constantine became Christian, many people in the Roman Empire did not convert. Romans continued to practice many different religions.

Over time, however, Rome's leaders supported Christianity more and more. By the 380s, support for Christianity had grown so much that an emperor chose to ban all other religions. With that ban, Christianity was the only religion allowed in the Roman Empire.

By the end of the 300s, the Christian church had grown into one of the most influential forces in the Roman world. As the church was growing, however, many other parts of Roman society were falling apart. The Roman Empire was ending.

READING CHECK **Sequencing** How did the Christian church gain influence in Rome?

The Decline of Rome

Rome's problems had actually started long before 300. For about a century, crime rates had been rising and poverty had been increasing. In addition, the Roman systems of education and government had begun breaking down, and many people no longer felt loyal to Rome. What could have happened to cause these problems?

Problems in the Government

Many of Rome's problems were the result of poor government. After about 200, Rome was ruled by a series of bad emperors. Most of these emperors were more interested in their own happiness than in ruling well. Some simply ignored the needs of the Roman people. Others raised taxes to pay for new buildings or wars, driving many Romans into poverty.

Rome did have a few good emperors who worked furiously to save the empire. One emperor feared that the empire had grown too large for one person to rule. To correct this problem, he divided the empire in half and named a co-ruler to help govern. Later, the emperor Constantine built a new capital, Constantinople, in what is now Turkey, nearer to the center of the Roman Empire. He thought that ruling from a central location would help keep the empire together. These measures helped restore order for a time, but they were not enough to save the Roman Empire.

Invasions

Although internal problems weakened the empire, they alone probably would not have destroyed it. However, as the empire was getting weaker from within, invaders from outside also began to attack in the late 300s and 400s. Already suffering from their own problems, the Romans could not fight off these invasions.

Most Roman people considered the various groups who invaded their empire barbarians, uncivilized and backward. In truth, however, some of these so-called barbarian groups had their own complex societies and strong, capable leaders. As a result, they were able to defeat Roman armies and take lands away from the empire. In the end, the barbarians were even able to attack and destroy the city of Rome itself. In 476 the last emperor of Rome was overthrown and replaced by the leader of an invading group.

The Eastern Roman Empire

The fall of Rome to invading armies did not mark the end of Roman civilization. Although the old capital was gone, the newer Roman capital at Constantinople still existed, and it remained the capital of a powerful empire for nearly 600 years.

In the east, some elements of Roman culture changed. People began to speak Greek instead of Latin. Other elements remained constant. The empire remained a Christian society, and missionaries from Constantinople spread their religion in Russia, Eastern Europe, and other parts of the world.

READING CHECK **Generalizing** Why did the Roman Empire decline?

SUMMARY AND PREVIEW In this section you learned that the Romans fought many peoples to expand their empire. Next, you will learn about one of those peoples, the Celts.

go.hrw.com
Online Quiz
KEYWORD: SK9 HP18

Section 2 Assessment

Reviewing Ideas, Terms, and Places

1. **a. Describe** What was the government of the Roman **Republic** like?
   b. Contrast How was **Rome**'s government in the republic unlike the government under kings?
2. **a. Identify** Who was Augustus?
   b. Explain How did the Pax Romana help the Romans make great achievements?
3. **Generalize** How did Rome's emperors affect the spread of Christianity?
4. **a. Identify** What threats to the Roman Empire appeared in the 200s, 300s, and 400s?
   b. Evaluate Do you think internal problems or invasions were more responsible for Rome's fall? Why?

Critical Thinking

5. **Identifying Causes** Draw a graph like the one at right. On the left side, list the main causes of Rome's growth. On the right, list the main causes of its decline.

Growth	Decline

FOCUS ON WRITING

6. **Finding a Setting** Where will your myth be set? Think back over this section and the previous one to find an appropriate location for your myth.

Geography and History

Roman Roads

The Romans are famous for their roads. They built a road network so large and well constructed that parts of it remain today, roughly 2,000 years later. Roads helped the Romans run their empire. Armies, travelers, messengers, and merchants all used the roads to get around. They stretched to every corner of the empire in a network so vast that people even today say that "all roads lead to Rome."

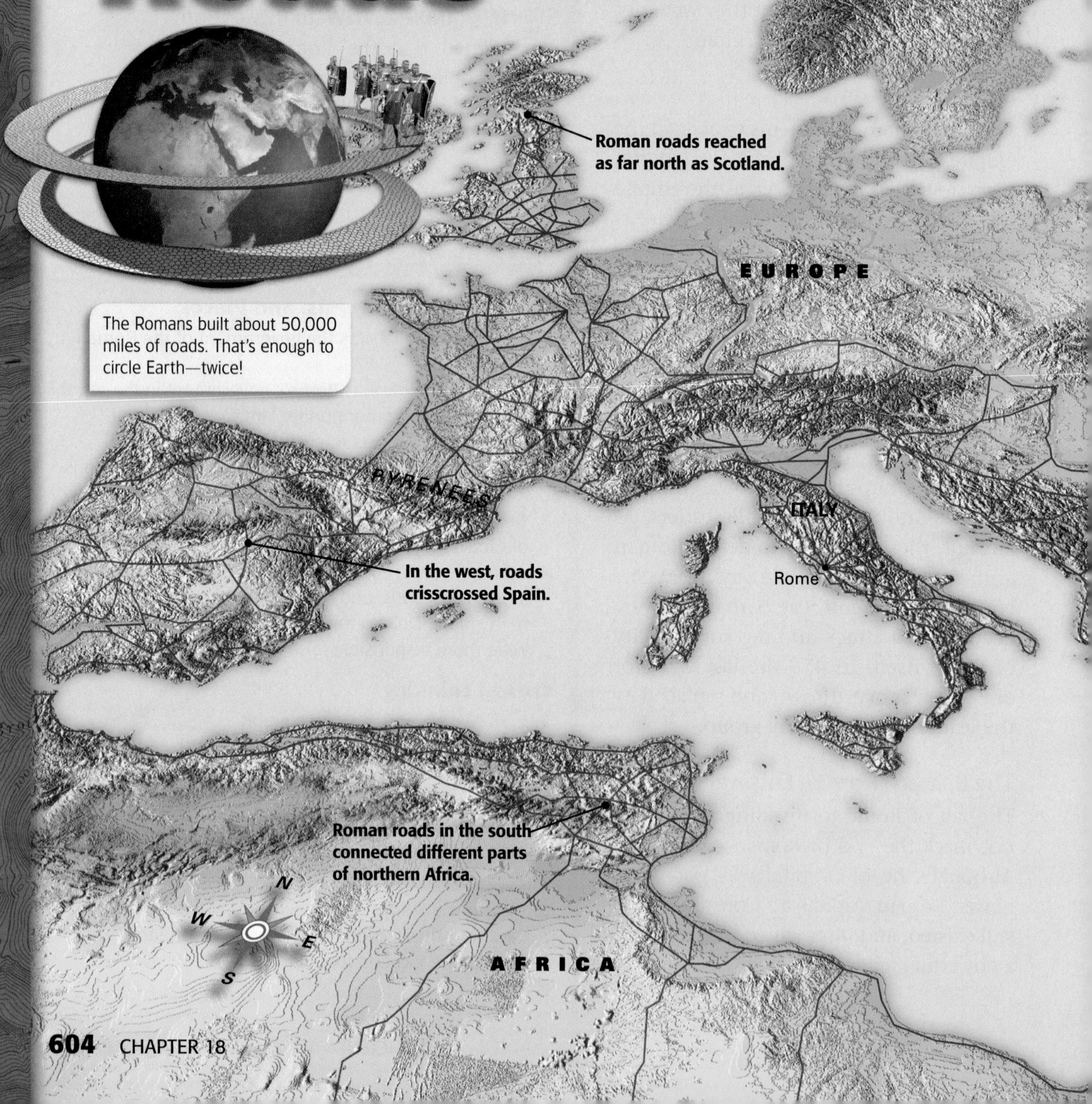
Roman roads reached as far north as Scotland.
EUROPE
The Romans built about 50,000 miles of roads. That's enough to circle Earth—twice!
PYRENEES
ITALY
Rome
In the west, roads crisscrossed Spain.
Roman roads in the south connected different parts of northern Africa.
N
W
E
S
AFRICA

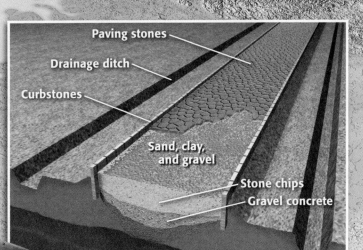

Paving stones

Drainage ditch

Curbstones

Sand, clay, and gravel

Stone chips

Gravel concrete

Roman roads were built to last. They were constructed of layers of sand, concrete, rock, and stone. Drainage ditches let water drain off, preventing water damage.

The roads were built by and for the military. The main purpose of the roads was to allow Rome's armies to travel quickly throughout the empire.

In the east, Roman roads stretched into Southwest Asia.

The Romans built tall "mile-stones" along their roads to mark distances. Just like modern highway signs, the markers told travelers how far it was to the next town.

IMPC
M. OPELLI
MACRINVS PIVS
AVG PONT MAXTR
PCOS PROC OSETIN
OPELLIVS ANTONINVS
DOVMINIANVS
NOBILISS. CAS
PRINCIVVENTVI
PROVIDENTSSIM
AVGG.FECER
AB. AG. M.P.
LVI

1. **Movement** Why did the Romans build their roads?
2. **Location** How does the map show that "all roads lead to Rome"?

Interpreting a Historical Map

Learn

History and geography are closely related. You cannot truly understand the history of a place without knowing where it is and what it is like. For that reason, historical maps are important in the study of history. A historical map is a map that shows what a place was like at a particular time in the past.

Like other maps, historical maps use colors and symbols to represent information. One color, for example, might represent the lands controlled by a certain kingdom or the areas in which a particular religion or type of government was common. Symbols might identify key cities, battle sites, or other major locations.

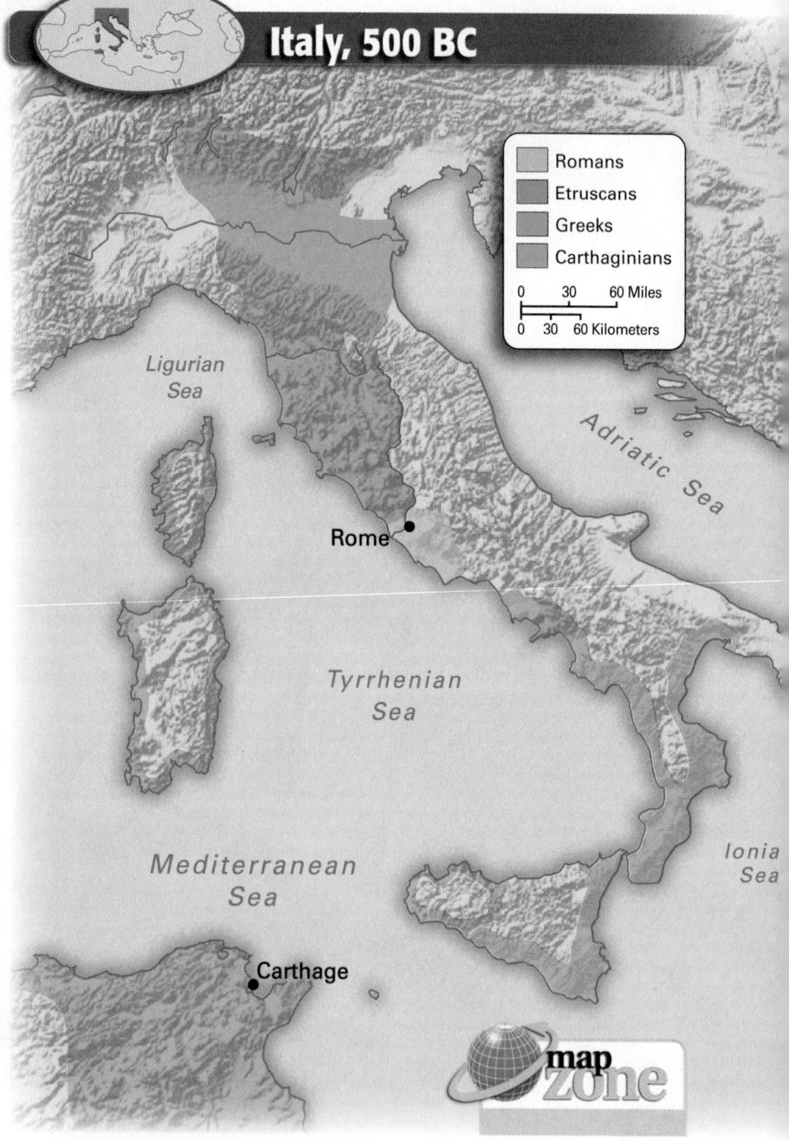

Practice

Use the map on this page to answer the following questions.

① Read the map's title. What area does this map show? What time period?

② Check the map's legend. What does the color purple represent on this map?

③ According to the map, who controlled the area around the city of Rome at this time?

④ What parts of Europe were controlled by Greeks in 500 BC?

Italy, 500 BC

Romans
Etruscans
Greeks
Carthaginians

0 30 60 Miles
0 30 60 Kilometers

Ligurian Sea
Adriatic Sea
Rome
Tyrrhenian Sea
Mediterranean Sea
Ionia Sea
Carthage

map zone

Apply

Look back at the map called Early Christianity in the Roman Empire in Section 2 of this chapter. Study the map, and then write five questions that you might see about such a map on a test. Make sure that the questions you ask can be answered with just the information on the map.

Geography's Impact
video series
Review the video to answer the closing question:
What are three ways in which Greek scholars have influenced education in America?

Visual Summary

Use the visual summary below to help you review the main ideas of the chapter.

QUICK FACTS

Ancient Greece was the birthplace of democracy, theater, and many other advances of Western society.

The Romans were master builders who created one of the largest empires in world history.

The Eastern Roman Empire remained strong even after the western part collapsed.

Reviewing Vocabulary, Terms, and Places

For each group of terms below, write the letter of the term that does not relate to the others. Then write a sentence that explains how the other two terms are related.

1. **a.** Athens
   b. Sparta
   c. Rome

2. **a.** Alexander the Great
   b. Pax Romana
   c. Hellenistic

3. **a.** Parthenon
   b. republic
   c. empire

4. **a.** Senate
   b. citizen
   c. colony

Comprehension and Critical Thinking

SECTION 1 *(Pages 588–595)*

5. **a. Identify** What was the basic political unit in ancient Greece? What is one example?

   b. Contrast How was life in Greece different under Alexander than it had been during the golden age?

   c. Evaluate What do you think was the greatest achievement of the ancient Greeks? Why?

SECTION 2 *(Pages 596–603)*

6. **a. Define** What was the Pax Romana? What happened during that time?

   b. Summarize How did Rome's government change after the republic fell apart?

   c. Elaborate What role did Rome's leaders play in the spread of Christianity?

Using the Internet

go.hrw.com
KEYWORD: SK9 CH18

7. Activity: Exploring Ancient Greece The golden age of Greece was an amazing time—the Greeks helped shape our government, art, philosophy, writing, and more! Enter the activity keyword and learn more about the ancient Greek world. Imagine you have traveled through time, back to ancient Greece. What are the people doing? What kinds of buildings do you see? What is the area like? Draw a picture or make a collage to record your observations.

FOCUS ON READING AND WRITING

8. Re-Reading Read the passage titled The Growth of Greek Power in Section 1. After you read, write down the main ideas of the passage. Then go back and re-read the passage carefully. Add to your list of main ideas anything more that you noticed in your second reading. How much more did you learn from the passage when you re-read it?

9. Writing Your Myth Now that you have learned about the events and people of ancient and medieval Europe, you can write a myth about one of them. Remember that your myth should try to explain the person or the event in a way that people of the time might have. For example, they might have thought that Caesar was the son of a goddess or that the idea of democracy was inspired by a wise god. Try to include descriptive details that will help bring your myth to life for the people who read it.

Social Studies Skills

Interpreting a Historical Map *Use the map on the Expansion of Rome in Section 2 of this chapter to answer the following questions.*

10. What time period is shown on this map?

11. What does the orange color on this map represent?

12. Did the areas shown on the map in gold become part of Rome before or after the areas shown in light green?

13. Which was conquered by the Romans first— Spain or Gaul?

14. Between which two years did Egypt become a Roman territory?

Map Activity ✳Interactive

15. Europe, 2000 BC–AD 500 On a separate sheet of paper, match the letters on the map with their correct labels.

| Athens | Carthage | Rome |
| Gaul | Judea | Alexandria |

map zone

go.hrw.com
KEYWORD: SK9 CH18

DIRECTIONS (1–7): For each statement or question, write on a separate answer sheet the *number* of the word or expression that, of those given, best completes the statement or answers the question.

1 Democracy was first practiced in which city-state of ancient Greece?

(1) Athens

(2) Carthage

(3) Rome

(4) Sparta

2 Which large empire did the Greeks defeat in a series of wars?

(1) Rome

(2) Sparta

(3) Egypt

(4) Persia

3 The first Roman emperor to become a Christian was named

(1) Julius Caesar.

(2) Augustus.

(3) Constantine.

(4) Jesus of Nazareth.

4 Which of the following was first created by the ancient Greeks?

(1) aqueducts

(2) Latin

(3) drama

(4) the Colosseum

5 The blended culture that was created in Alexander the Great's empire is called

(1) Greek

(2) Hellenistic

(3) Roman

(4) Medieval

6 During its history, Rome had all of the following forms of government except

(1) empire.

(2) monarchy.

(3) democracy.

(4) republic.

7 Which portion of the Roman Empire remained strong even after the city of Rome was defeated?

(1) northern

(2) southern

(3) western

(4) eastern

Base your answer to question 8 on the map below and on your knowledge of social studies.

Europe, AD 117

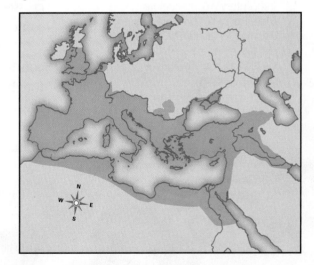

8 **Constructed-Response Question** As this map shows, the Roman Empire at its height controlled most of the Mediterranean world. The empire's huge size was both a benefit and a drawback. List one positive and one negative effect of the Romans' expansion.

The Celts

History

The Celts were known as fierce warriors. Armed with swords, axes, and spears, they terrified their foes.

Dug into the soil in about the first century AD, the famous White Horse lies on a hill near Uffington, England. The horse, which can only be seen from the air, was made by Celts for religious reasons.

While the Romans were building their empire in southern Europe, another people controlled most of northern Europe. They were the Celts (KELTS). Unlike the Romans, the Celts did not form a single unified society. Instead, they lived as individual tribes. The only things that tied the Celtic tribes together were similar languages, customs, and beliefs.

Various Celtic cultures developed in Europe. The earliest, called the Hallstatt culture, had developed by about 1200 BC. The name Hallstatt comes from a village in Austria where early Celtic artifacts were found. The Hallstatt culture later gave way to the La Tène culture, named for a village in Switzerland. The La Tène culture developed during the Iron Age. Iron weapons helped the Celts defeat enemies and conquer new territories.

By the 200s BC the La Tène Celts had spread through much of northern and western Europe. Some groups had crossed the English Channel to the British Isles. In addition, some Celts had headed east into what is now Turkey.

As the Celts moved into new areas, they often came into conflict with people living there. For example, the Celts fought and defeated the original inhabitants of the British Isles. A Celtic army also attacked Rome in the 300s BC.

More than 200 years after the Celts attacked Rome, the Romans struck back. In 58 BC a Roman army under Julius Caesar invaded the Celtic territory of Gaul. The Celts of Gaul

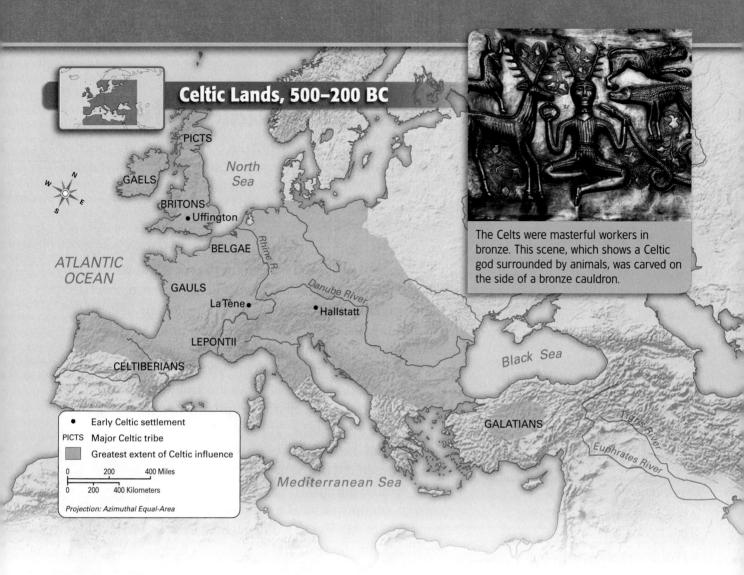

Celtic Lands, 500–200 BC

PICTS

GAELS

North Sea

BRITONS
• Uffington

BELGAE

Rhine R.

ATLANTIC OCEAN

GAULS

La Tène •

Danube River

• Hallstatt

LEPONTII

CELTIBERIANS

Black Sea

GALATIANS

Tigris River

Euphrates River

Mediterranean Sea

• Early Celtic settlement
PICTS Major Celtic tribe
Greatest extent of Celtic influence

0   200   400 Miles
0   200   400 Kilometers

Projection: Azimuthal Equal-Area

The Celts were masterful workers in bronze. This scene, which shows a Celtic god surrounded by animals, was carved on the side of a bronze cauldron.

battled the Romans for many years, but eventually Gaul was conquered and became a Roman province. Caesar also fought the Celts in Britain. The Celts of southern Britain were overpowered by the Romans, but those of the north remained free.

In the AD 300s and 400s, much of Rome's territory was taken by Germanic invaders from the east. These same invaders drove the Celts out of their lands. The Celts were forced into a few remote areas, such as Ireland and Scotland.

Case Study Assessment

1. How did Celtic culture spread through Europe?

2. With whom did the Celts come into conflict?

3. **Activity** The Celts left no written records but did pass down songs about their heroes. Research a Celtic leader and write a song about him or her.

In time, many Celts gave up their traditional religions and became devout Christians.

Society and Daily Life

The Celts left behind no written records. As a result, much of what we know about Celtic society is based on the writings of other people, often the Celts' opponents.

Government

As you have read, the Celts did not have a unified society. Celtic society was based instead on the tribe. In extraordinary circumstances, tribes would form alliances to work together. One such alliance was formed when the Romans attacked Gaul in the first century BC. Even when united in this way, however, the Gauls thought of themselves as separate tribes.

Each tribe was ruled by a king who was advised by a council of elders. In some tribes the king was elected by the people of the tribe. Elected rulers usually had to obey laws that were passed by the tribe's council.

Although most Celtic rulers were men, some women did rise to great power. Some even became queens. For example, the Iceni tribe of Britain was ruled by a queen named Boudicca. In AD 60 she led her people in a revolt against the Romans.

Below kings and queens in Celtic society were nobles. Unlike nobles in other parts of the world, Celtic nobles were not born into their positions. They had to earn their nobility. A king might make someone a noble for being an exceptional warrior or providing a service to the tribe.

Among those who were often made nobles were druids and bards. Both groups had great influence in Celtic society. Originally religious figures, druids later played many other roles. They were the keepers of tradition and acted as healers, scholars, and judges. Bards traveled throughout the land, spreading news and ideas within and between tribes.

This statue from Germany depicts a Celtic noble dressed for war.

Structure of Celtic Society
QUICK FACTS

Royalty

- Each tribe was ruled by a king or, in some rare cases, a queen.
- In some tribes, the ruler was elected.
- Rulers were often advised by councils of elders.

Nobility

- Nobles were chosen by the king or queen.
- Nobility was earned, not inherited.

Farmers

- Farmers made up the bulk of the population.
- Most farmers owned their own land.
- Some farmers worked land owned by nobles.

Druids and Bards

- Druids were the keepers of tradition and acted as healers, scholars, and judges.
- Bards spread news and ideas between tribes.

Celtic Life

Most Celts lived in small villages of small, round houses. This re-creation village in Ireland shows what a typical Celtic village might have looked like. For special occasions, Celts wore various types of jewelry, some examples of which are shown above.

Daily Life

Celtic life was organized around the clan, or extended family. Most clans lived together in small villages. The houses in such villages were often round and roofed with thatch, a covering made from grasses and straw. Villages were often surrounded by ditches or walls for defense.

Within a Celtic village, most people were farmers. Celtic farmers were among the first people in Europe to use iron plows. Before, farmers had used pointed sticks to poke holes in the ground in order to plant seeds. The plow made planting crops much easier and led to larger harvests.

From what historians have been able to piece together, Celtic women had more rights than did women in many other ancient societies. You have already seen how women like Boudicca could become rulers and war leaders. In addition, Celtic women could own property and marry as they chose.

Case Study Assessment

1. Who were the druids? What roles did they play?

2. What did a typical Celtic village look like?

3. **Activity** If you could have held any position in Celtic society, which would you have chosen? Write a journal entry describing a day as a person in that position.

c. 1200 BC
The Hallstatt culture develops in Central Europe.

Celtic helmet from Britain

c. 500 BC
Celts of the La Tène culture spread throughout Europe and into the British Isles.

390 BC
A Celtic army attacks and defeats the city of Rome.

Culture and Achievements

Although the Celts did not have a unified society, there were a few cultural elements that reflected their shared heritage. One such element was language. All of the Celtic tribes spoke related languages, most of which are now extinct. Only a few Celtic languages are still spoken today. Among them are Irish, Scottish Gaelic, and Welsh.

Celtic religion was also similar from tribe to tribe. The early Celts worshipped many gods and looked to the druids for spiritual leadership. By about 500, however, Christianity had largely replaced the early Celtic religion. Christian missionaries from Rome and other parts of Europe brought their religion to Celtin lands. According to legend, one such missionary was Patrick, who converted many of the Irish Celts in the early 400s. He later became known as Saint Patrick.

Celtic art styles were also similar across Europe. Artists made beautiful objects ranging from ornate bowls and cups for religious ceremonies to simple jewelry to be buried with dead leaders. Many of these objects are decorated with elaborate knot patterns. These Celtic knots are still popular in art today.

Celtic warrior statue

Legacy of the Celts

Although no pure Celtic culture exists in Europe today, Celtic influences can still be seen in many modern cultures. In addition, some Celtic leaders have captured the imaginations of Europeans for centuries.

Although he was defeated in the end, the Gaulish leader Vercingetorix is still admired for his bravery in standing up to the mighty Roman army.

Irish monks in the Middle Ages created beautiful manuscripts. This Bible was illustrated at Lindisfarne Monastery.

c. 275 BC
A Celtic tribe establishes the kingdom of Galatia in what is now Turkey.

58 BC
Roman general Julius Caesar begins a series of wars against the Celts of Gaul.

c. AD 430
Patrick introduces Christianity to the Celts of Ireland.

Over time the Celts mixed with various other peoples of Europe. As a result, a purely Celtic culture does not exist anymore. However, Celtic culture has not disappeared. Many artists, for example, continue to draw inspiration from Celtic art. Celtic rulers have also left their mark on the world. Many are remembered and admired for their bravery and nobility. Queen Boudicca is considered a folk hero by many people in England. Also considered a hero is the Gaulish king Vercingetorix, who united many Celtic tribes to fight Caesar and the Romans. He is honored in France, which includes most of the land that used to be Gaul.

Case Study Assessment

1. How did Christianity influence Celtic culture?

2. Why are some Celtic leaders still honored today?

3. Activity Why do you think the Celts should be remembered? Work with your classmates to design a museum exhibit about Celtic contributions to the world.

BIOGRAPHY

Boudicca
Died in AD 60

Boudicca was the most famous of the Celtic warrior queens. She led the Iceni in a revolt, burning several Roman cities—including the newly founded London. In the end, the rebellion was defeated. Boudicca is now considered an English hero, and a statue of her stands in London, the town she once burned.

Growth and Development of Europe

FOCUS QUESTION

What forces had an impact on the development of Europe and why?

What You Will Learn...

In this chapter you will learn about European history since the fall of Rome. During this period new ideas and innovations changed life and expanded knowledge across Europe.

FOCUS ON READING AND WRITING

Using Context Clue–Contrast Sometimes you can figure out the meaning of a word through contrast clues. They tell you how an unknown word is different from a word you already know. **See the lesson, Using Context Clues–Contrast, on page S22.**

Writing a Diary Entry In this chapter you will read about many periods of European history. After you read you will write a diary entry from the point of view of someone during one of these times.

ATLANTIC OCEAN

50°N

20°W

German U-boats

40°N

Madrid

10°W

30°N

AFRICA

Middle Ages
Warriors called knights were key to the political system of Europe in the Middle Ages. Knights wore suits of armor like this one into battle.

Europe, AD 500–Today

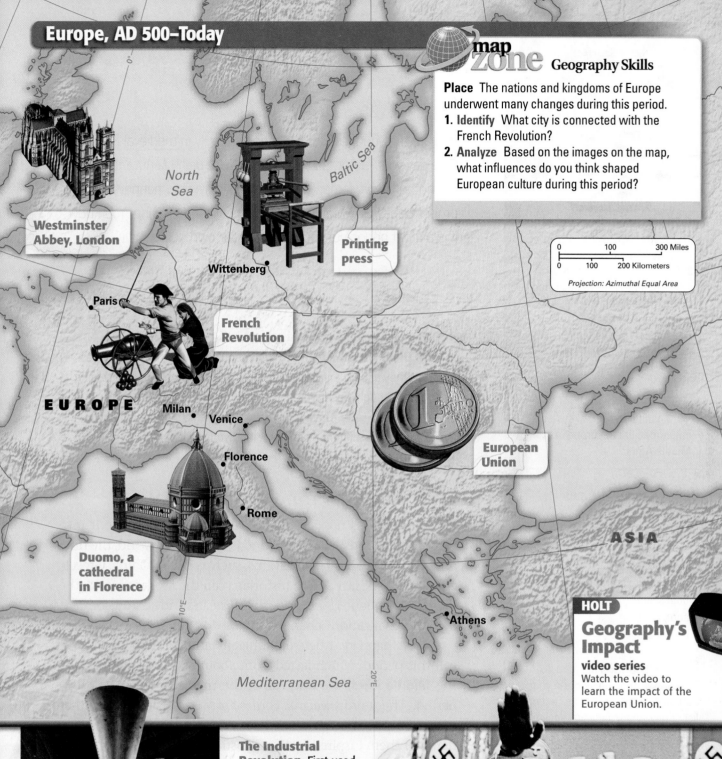

map zone Geography Skills

Place The nations and kingdoms of Europe underwent many changes during this period.
1. **Identify** What city is connected with the French Revolution?
2. **Analyze** Based on the images on the map, what influences do you think shaped European culture during this period?

North Sea

Baltic Sea

Westminster Abbey, London

Printing press

Wittenberg

Paris

French Revolution

E U R O P E

Milan

Venice

Florence

European Union

Rome

Duomo, a cathedral in Florence

A S I A

Athens

Mediterranean Sea

0   100   300 Miles
0   100   200 Kilometers

Projection: Azimuthal Equal Area

HOLT

Geography's Impact
video series
Watch the video to learn the impact of the European Union.

The Industrial Revolution First used in factories, the steam engine later powered trains and ships. Inventions such as the steam engine changed life in Europe during the 1700s and 1800s.

World War II The rise of dictators like Germany's Adolf Hitler led to the outbreak of the Second World War.

The Middle Ages

If YOU lived there...

You are the youngest child of a noble family in medieval France. One day your father tells you that you are being sent to the court of another noble family. There you will learn fine manners and proper behavior. You will also learn music and drawing. You know it is a great honor, but you will miss your own home.

How do you feel about this change in your life?

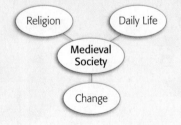
BUILDING BACKGROUND When people think of the Middle Ages today, they usually think of castles, princesses, and knights in shining armor. Although these were all part of the Middle Ages, they do not tell the whole story. The Middle Ages was a time of great change in Europe, as the influence of the ancient world faded away.

The Christian Church and Society

When historians talk about the past, they often divide it into three long periods. The first period is the ancient world, the time of the world's earliest civilizations, such as Egypt, China, Greece, and Rome. The last period historians call the modern world, the world since about 1500. Since that time, new ideas and contacts between civilizations changed the world completely.

What happened between ancient and modern times? We call this period, which lasted from about 500 until about 1500, the **Middle Ages**. We also call it the medieval (mee-DEE-vuhl) period. The word *medieval* comes from two Latin words that mean "middle age." It was a time of great changes in Europe, many of them inspired by the Christian church.

The Importance of the Church

When the Roman Empire fell apart in the late 400s, the people of Europe were left without a single dominant government to unite them. In the absence of strong leaders, Europe broke into many small kingdoms. Each of these kingdoms had its own laws, customs, and language. Europe was no longer the same place it had been under the Romans.

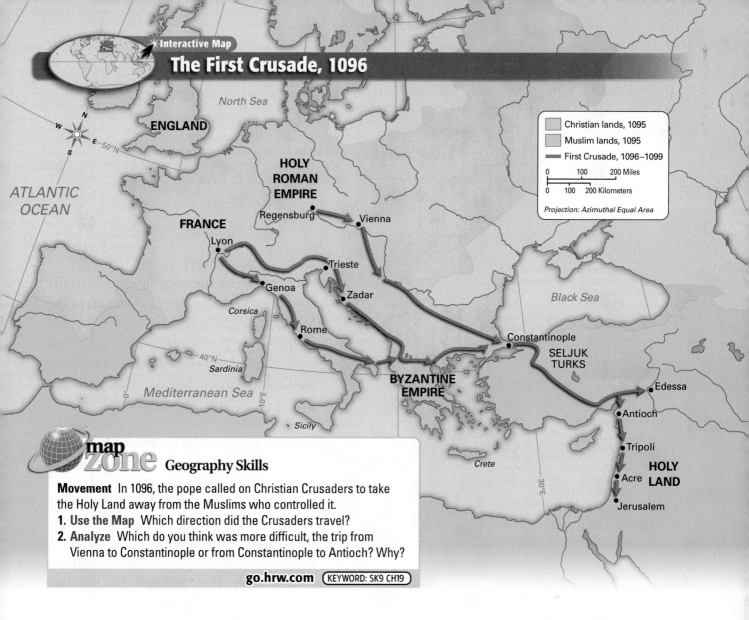

North Sea

ENGLAND

ATLANTIC
OCEAN

FRANCE

HOLY
ROMAN
EMPIRE

Regensburg

Vienna

Lyon

Trieste

Genoa

Zadar

Corsica

Rome

Sardinia

Mediterranean Sea

Sicily

Black Sea

Constantinople

SELJUK
TURKS

BYZANTINE
EMPIRE

Crete

Edessa

Antioch

Tripoli

Acre

HOLY
LAND

Jerusalem

	Christian lands, 1095
	Muslim lands, 1095
▬	First Crusade, 1096–1099

0   100   200 Miles
0   100   200 Kilometers
Projection: Azimuthal Equal Area

Geography Skills

Movement In 1096, the pope called on Christian Crusaders to take the Holy Land away from the Muslims who controlled it.

1. **Use the Map** Which direction did the Crusaders travel?
2. **Analyze** Which do you think was more difficult, the trip from Vienna to Constantinople or from Constantinople to Antioch? Why?

go.hrw.com (KEYWORD: SK9 CH19)

One factor, however, continued to tie the people of Europe together—religion. Nearly everyone in Europe was Christian, and so most Europeans felt tied together by their beliefs. Over time, the number of Christians in Europe increased. People came to feel more and more like part of a single religious community.

Because Christianity was so important in Europe, the Christian church gained a great deal of influence. In time, the church began to influence the politics, art, and daily lives of people all over the continent. In fact, almost no part of life in Europe in the Middle Ages was unaffected by the church and its teachings.

The Christian Church and Politics

As the Christian church gained influence in Europe, some church leaders became powerful. They gained political power in addition to their religious authority.

The most powerful religious leader was the **pope**, the head of the Christian church. The pope's decisions could have huge effects on people's lives. For example, one pope decided to start a religious war, or **Crusade**, against the church's enemies in Southwest Asia. He wanted Europeans to take over the **Holy Land**, the region in which Jesus had lived. For many years, the region had been in the hands of another religious group, the Muslims.

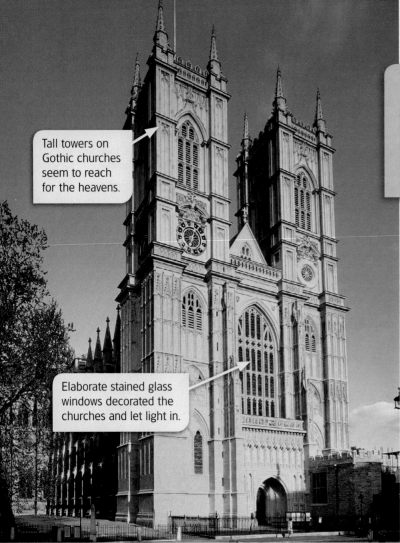

Tall towers on Gothic churches seem to reach for the heavens.

Elaborate stained glass windows decorated the churches and let light in.

Gothic Architecture

Gothic churches were designed to tower over medieval cities as symbols of the church's greatness. This cathedral, Westminster Abbey, stands in London, England.

Thousands of people answered the pope's call for a Crusade. As the map on the previous page shows, they traveled thousands of miles to fight the church's enemies. This Crusade was the first of eight attempts by Christians over two centuries to win back the Holy Land.

In the end, the Crusades did not drive the Muslims from the Holy Land. They did, however, lead to sweeping changes in Europe. Crusaders brought new goods and ideas back to Europe with them. Europeans began to want more of these goods, so trade between Europe and Asia increased. At the same time, though, relations between Christians and Muslims grew worse. For years to come, followers of the religions distrusted and resented each other.

The Church and Art

Politics was not the only area in which the church had great influence. Most art of the Middle Ages was also influenced by the church. Medieval painters and sculptors, for example, used religious subjects in their works. Most music and literature from the period is centered on religious themes.

The greatest examples of religious art from the Middle Ages are church buildings. Huge churches like the one shown on this page were built all over Europe. Many of them are examples of **Gothic architecture**, a style known for its high pointed ceilings, tall towers, and stained glass windows. People built Gothic churches as symbols of their faith. They believed that building these amazing structures would show their love for God. The insides of such churches are as elaborate and ornate as the outsides.

The Church and Daily Life

Most people in Europe never saw a Gothic church, especially not the inside. Instead they worshipped at small local churches. In fact, people's lives often centered around their local church. Markets, festivals, and religious ceremonies all took place there. Local priests advised people on how to live and act. In addition, because most people could not read or write, they depended on the church to keep records for them.

READING CHECK Summarizing How did the Christian church shape life in the Middle Ages?

Life in the Middle Ages

Christianity was a major influence on people's lives in the Middle Ages, but it was not the only one. Much of European society was controlled by two systems of relationships. They were the feudal (FYOO-duhl) system and the manor system.

The Feudal System

Medieval Europe was divided into many small kingdoms. In most kingdoms, the king owned all the land. Sometimes, kings gave parts of their land to nobles—people born into wealthy, powerful families. In turn, these nobles gave land to knights, or trained warriors, who promised to help them defend both their lands and the king. This system of exchanging land for military service is called the **feudal system**, or feudalism (FYOO-duh-li-zuhm).

Everyone involved in the feudal system had certain duties to perform. The kings and nobles provided land and promised to protect the people who served them and to treat everyone fairly. In return, the knights who received land promised to serve the nobles dutifully, especially in times of war. The set of relationships between knights and nobles was the heart of Europe's feudal system.

The feudal system was very complex. Its rules varied from kingdom to kingdom and changed constantly. Feudal duties in France, for example, were not the same as those in Germany or England. Also, it was possible for one knight to owe service to more than one noble. If the two nobles he served went to war, the poor knight would be torn between them. In such situations, feudal relationships could be confusing or even dangerous.

Feudal Relationships

Europe's feudal system was based on relationships between knights and nobles. Each had certain duties that he or she had to perform.

ANALYZING VISUALS Who had to provide military service as one of his duties?

Noble's duties
- Provide knight with land
- Treat knights fairly and honestly

Knight's duties
- Provide military service
- Supply food and shelter for noble during visits

The Manor System

The feudal system was only one set of guidelines that governed life in the Middle Ages. Another system, the manor system, controlled most economic activities in Europe during this period.

At the center of the manor system was the **manor**, a large estate owned by a noble or knight. Every manor was different, but most included a large house or castle, fields, pastures, and forests. A manor also had a village where workers lived. They traveled back and forth to the fields each day.

The owner of a manor did not farm his own land. Instead, he had workers to farm it for him. Most of the crops grown on the manor went to the owner. In exchange for their work, the workers got a place to live and a small piece of land on which they could grow their own food.

The workers on most manors included either free peasants or serfs. Peasants were free farmers. Serfs, on the other hand, were not free. Although they were not slaves, they were not allowed to leave the land on which they worked.

Close-up

Life on a Manor

Manors were large estates that developed during the Middle Ages. Many manors were largely self-sufficient, producing most of the food and goods they needed. This picture shows what a manor in England might have looked like.

The owner of the manor lived in a large stone house called the manor house.

Peasants grew vegetables in small gardens located near their houses.

In late spring, peasants harvested crops like wheat.

Towns and Trade

Not everyone in the Middle Ages lived on manors. Some people chose to live in towns and cities like Paris or London. Compared to our cities today, most of these medieval cities were small, dirty, and dark.

Many of the people who lived in cities were traders. They bought and sold goods from all over Europe and other parts of the world. Most of their goods were sold at trade fairs. Every year, merchants from many places in Europe would meet at these large fairs to sell their wares.

Before the year 1000, trade was not very common in Europe. After that year, however, trade increased. As it did, more people began to move to cities. Once small, these cities began to grow. As cities grew, trade increased even more, and the people who lived in them became wealthier. By the end of the Middle Ages, cities had become the centers of European culture and wealth.

READING CHECK **Finding Main Ideas** What were two systems that governed life in Europe during the Middle Ages? How did they differ?

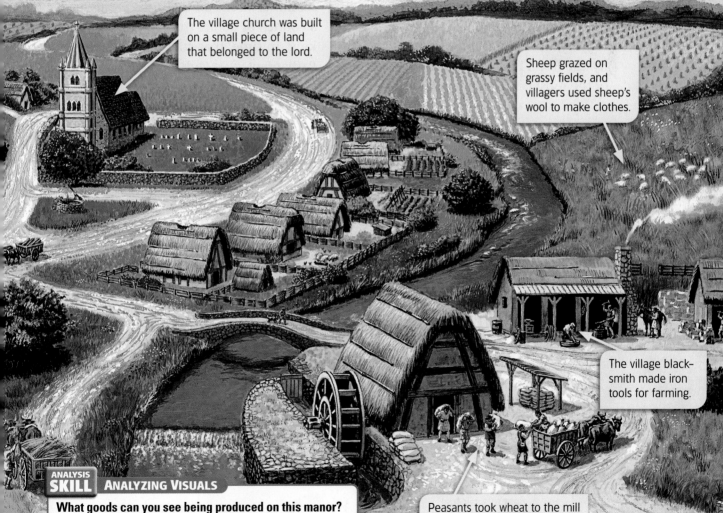

The village church was built on a small piece of land that belonged to the lord.

Sheep grazed on grassy fields, and villagers used sheep's wool to make clothes.

The village blacksmith made iron tools for farming.

ANALYSIS SKILL **ANALYZING VISUALS**

What goods can you see being produced on this manor? How do you think the lives of peasants on this manor differed from the life of the owner?

Peasants took wheat to the mill to be ground into flour, which they used to make bread.

Changes in Medieval Society

Life in the Middle Ages changed greatly after the year 1000. You have already seen how cities grew and trade increased. Even as these changes were taking place, bigger changes were sweeping through Europe.

THE IMPACT TODAY

The ideas of Magna Carta influenced later documents, including our Constitution.

Political Changes in England

One of the countries most affected by change in the Middle Ages was England. In the year 1066 a noble from northern France, William the Conqueror, sailed to England and overthrew the old king. He declared himself the new king of England.

William built a strong government in England, something the English had not had before. Later kings of England built on William's example. For more than a century, these kings increased their power. By the late 1100s England's king was one of the most powerful men in Europe.

When William's descendant John took the throne, however, he angered many nobles by raising taxes. John believed that the king had the right to do whatever he wanted. England's nobles disagreed.

In 1215 a group of nobles forced King John to sign Magna Carta, one of the most important documents in English history. Magna Carta stated that the law, not the king, was the supreme power in England. The king had to obey the law. He could not raise taxes without the nobles' permission.

Many people consider Magna Carta to be one of the first steps toward democracy in modern Europe and one of history's most important documents. By stating that the king was not above the law, Magna Carta set limits on his power. In addition, it gave a council of nobles the power to advise the king. In time, that council developed into Parliament (PAHR-luh-muhnt), the elected body that governs England today.

Primary Source

HISTORIC DOCUMENT
Magna Carta

Magna Carta was one of the first documents to protect the rights of the people. Magna Carta was so influential that the British still consider it part of their constitution. Some of its ideas are also in the U.S. Constitution. Included in Magna Carta were 63 demands that English nobles made King John agree to follow. A few of these demands are listed here.

Demand number 31 defended people's right to property, not just wood.

Magna Carta guaranteed that free men had the right to a fair trial.

To all free men of our kingdom we have also granted, for us and our heirs for ever, all the liberties written out below, to have and to keep for them and their heirs, of us and our heirs.

(16) No man shall be forced to perform more service for a knight's 'fee', or other free holding of land, than is due from it.

(31) Neither we nor any royal official will take wood for our castle, or for any other purpose, without the consent [permission] of the owner.

(38) In future no official shall place a man on trial upon his own unsupported statement, without producing credible [believable] witnesses to the truth of it.

—Magna Carta, from a translation by the British Library

ANALYSIS SKILL **ANALYZING PRIMARY SOURCES**

In what ways do you think the ideas listed above influenced modern democracy?

The Black Death

Not all of the changes that struck medieval Europe had such positive results. In 1347 a disease called the Black Death swept through Europe. Up to a third of Europe's people died from the disease. Even such a disaster, however, had some positive effects. With the decrease in population came a labor shortage. As a result, people could demand higher wages for their work.

The Fight for Power

Even as the Black Death was sweeping across Europe, kings fought for power. In 1337 the Hundred Years' War broke out between England and France. As its name suggests, the war lasted more than 100 years. In the end, the French won.

Inspired by the victory, France's kings worked to increase their power. They took land away from nobles to rule themselves. France became a **nation-state**, a country united under a single strong government.

Around Europe, other rulers followed the French example. As nation-states arose around Europe, feudalism disappeared, and the Middle Ages came to an end.

READING CHECK **Finding Main Ideas** What changes occurred in Europe after 1000?

BIOGRAPHY

Joan of Arc
(c. 1412–1431)

One of the most famous war leaders in all of European history was a teenage girl. Joan of Arc, a leader of French troops during the Hundred Years' War, was only 16 when she first led troops into battle. She won many battles against the English but was captured in battle in 1430, tried, and executed. Nevertheless, her courage inspired the French, who went on to win the war. Today Joan is considered a national hero in France.

Make Inferences Why do you think Joan is considered a hero in France?

SUMMARY AND PREVIEW In this section you read about the Middle Ages, a period that helped shape Europe's later political history. Next, you will learn about two periods that influenced the continent's cultural development: the Renaissance and Reformation.

Section 1 Assessment

Reviewing Ideas, Terms, and Places
1. **a. Recall** Why did the **pope** call for a **Crusade**?
   b. Generalize How did the Christian church affect art in the Middle Ages?
2. **a. Define** What was the **feudal system**?
   b. Explain How did the **manor** system work?
   c. Elaborate What made the feudal system so complex?
3. **a. Describe** How did the Black Death affect Europe?
   b. Explain How did England's government change after 1000?

Critical Thinking
4. **Analyzing** Use your notes to complete a table like the one on the right. List ways the Church shaped medieval politics, life, and art.

The Christian Church → Politics, Art, Daily Life

FOCUS ON WRITING

5. **Thinking about People** What would a diary entry by a medieval peasant include? by a lord? Write down some ideas.

The Black Death

"And they died by the hundreds," wrote one man who saw the horror, "both day and night." The Black Death had arrived. The Black Death was a series of deadly plagues that hit Europe between 1347 and 1351, killing millions. People didn't know what caused the plague. They also didn't know that geography played a key role in its spread—as people traveled to trade, they unwittingly carried the disease with them to new places.

EUROPE

Kaffa

CENTRAL ASIA

CHINA

AFRICA

The plague probably began in central and eastern Asia. These arrows show how it spread into and through Europe.

This ship has just arrived in Europe from the east with trade goods—and rats with fleas.

The fleas carry the plague and jump onto a man unloading the ship. Soon, he will get sick and die.

The plague is so terrifying that many people think it's the end of the world. They leave town for the country, spreading the Black Death even further.

People dig mass graves to bury the dead. But often, so many victims are infected that there is no one left to bury them.

The garbage and dirty conditions in the town provide food and a home for the rats, allowing the disease to spread even more.

So many people die so quickly that special carts are sent through the streets to gather the bodies.

ANALYSIS SKILL **ANALYZING VISUALS**

1. **Movement** How did the Black Death reach Europe from Asia?
2. **Place** What helped spread the plague within Europe?

The Renaissance and Reformation

What You Will Learn...

Main Ideas

1. The Renaissance was a period of new learning, new ideas, and new advances in art, literature, and science.
2. The Reformation changed the religious map of Europe.

The Big Idea

The periods of the Renaissance and the Reformation introduced new ideas and new ways of thinking into Europe.

Key Terms and Places

Renaissance, *p. 628*
Florence, *p. 628*
Venice, *p. 628*
humanism, *p. 629*
Reformation, *p. 632*
Protestants, *p. 633*
Catholic Reformation, *p. 633*

TAKING NOTES As you read, use a chart like the one below to help you take notes on the Renaissance and the Reformation.

Renaissance

Reformation

If YOU lived there...

You live in Florence, Italy, in the 1400s. Your father, a merchant, has just hired a tutor from Asia Minor to teach you and your sisters and brothers. Your new teacher starts by stating, "Nothing good has been written in a thousand years." He insists that you learn to read Latin and Greek so that you can study Roman and Greek books that were written long ago.

What can you learn from these ancient books?

BUILDING BACKGROUND The end of the Middle Ages brought important changes to European politics and society. These changes set the stage for an exciting new period of learning and creativity. During this period, new ideas influenced the arts, science, and attitudes toward religion.

The Renaissance

Do you ever get the urge to do something creative? If so, how do you express your creativity? Do you like to draw or paint? Maybe you prefer to write stories or poems or create music.

At the end of the Middle Ages, people across Europe found the urge to be creative. Their creativity was sparked by new ideas and discoveries that were sweeping through Europe at the time. This period of creativity, of new ideas and inspirations, is called the **Renaissance** (REN-uh-sahns). It lasted from about 1350 through the 1500s. *Renaissance* is French for "rebirth." The people who named this period believed it represented a new beginning, or rebirth, in Europe's history and culture.

New Ideas

The Renaissance started in Italy. During and after the Crusades, Italian cities such as **Florence** and **Venice** became rich through trade. Goods from faraway Asia moved through these cities.

These goods made the people who lived there curious about the larger world. At the same time, scholars from other parts of the world came to Italy. They brought books written by ancient Greeks and Romans.

Inspired by these books and by the ancient ruins around them, some people in Italy became interested in ancient cultures. These people began reading works in Greek and Latin and studying subjects that had been taught in Greek and Roman schools.

These subjects, known as the humanities, included history, poetry, and grammar. Increased study of the humanities led to a new way of thinking and learning known as humanism.

Humanism emphasized the abilities and accomplishments of human beings. The humanists believed that people were capable of great things. As a result, they admired artists, architects, leaders, writers, scientists, and other talented individuals.

THE IMPACT TODAY

American universities grant degrees in the humanities. You might one day get a degree in a humanities field.

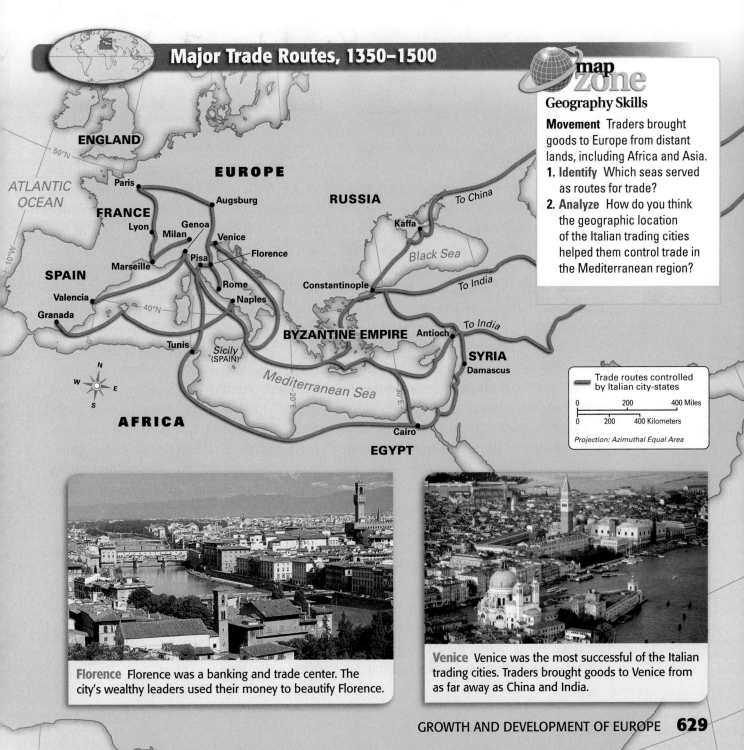

Major Trade Routes, 1350–1500

map zone

Geography Skills

Movement Traders brought goods to Europe from distant lands, including Africa and Asia.
1. **Identify** Which seas served as routes for trade?
2. **Analyze** How do you think the geographic location of the Italian trading cities helped them control trade in the Mediterranean region?

ENGLAND
50°N
ATLANTIC OCEAN
EUROPE
Paris
FRANCE
Augsburg
Lyon
Genoa
Milan
Venice
Pisa
Florence
Marseille
SPAIN
Rome
Naples
Valencia
40°N
Granada
Tunis
Sicily (SPAIN)
Mediterranean Sea
AFRICA
RUSSIA
To China
Kaffa
Black Sea
Constantinople
To India
BYZANTINE EMPIRE
Antioch
To India
SYRIA
Damascus
Cairo
EGYPT

Trade routes controlled by Italian city-states
0   200   400 Miles
0   200   400 Kilometers
Projection: Azimuthal Equal Area

Florence Florence was a banking and trade center. The city's wealthy leaders used their money to beautify Florence.

Venice Venice was the most successful of the Italian trading cities. Traders brought goods to Venice from as far away as China and India.

The Renaissance

The Renaissance was a period of great creativity and advances in art, literature, and science.

Renaissance sculptors were careful to show the tiniest details in their works. This statue by Michelangelo is of David, a king of ancient Israel.

Painters like Hans Holbein the Younger wanted to show what real life was like for people in Europe.

Renaissance Art

The Renaissance was a period of talented artistic achievements. Artists of the period created new techniques to improve their work. For example, they developed the technique of perspective, a method of showing a three-dimensional scene on a flat surface so that it looks real.

Many Renaissance artists were also humanists. Humanist artists valued the achievements of individuals. These artists wanted their paintings and sculptures to show people's unique personalities. One of the artists best able to show this sense of personality in his works was the Italian Michelangelo (mee-kay-LAHN-jay-loh). He was both a great painter and sculptor. His statues, like the one of King David above, seem almost to be alive.

Another famous Renaissance artist was Leonardo da Vinci. Leonardo achieved the Renaissance goal of excelling in many areas. He was not only a great painter and sculptor but also an architect, scientist, and engineer. He sketched plants and animals as well as inventions such as a submarine.

He collected knowledge about the human body. Both Leonardo and Michelangelo are examples of what we call Renaissance people—people who can do practically anything well.

Renaissance Literature

Like artists, Renaissance writers expressed the attitudes of the time. The most famous Renaissance writer is probably the English dramatist William Shakespeare. He wrote excellent poetry, but Shakespeare is best known for his plays. They include more than 30 comedies, histories, and tragedies. In his plays, Shakespeare turned popular stories into great drama. His writing shows a deep understanding of human nature and skillfully expresses the thoughts and feelings of his characters. For these reasons, Shakespeare's plays are still highly popular in many parts of the world.

Renaissance writings were read and enjoyed by a larger audience than earlier writings had been. This change was largely due to advances in science and technology, such as the printing press.

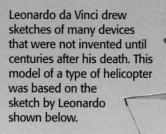

William Shakespeare is considered the greatest of all Renaissance writers. His plays are still read and performed today.

Leonardo da Vinci drew sketches of many devices that were not invented until centuries after his death. This model of a type of helicopter was based on the sketch by Leonardo shown below.

Based on the sculpture of David and on the Holbein painting, how would you describe Renaissance art?

Renaissance Science

Some of the ancient works rediscovered during the Renaissance dealt with science. For the first time in centuries, Europeans could read about early Greek and Roman scientific advances. Inspired by what they read, some people began to study math, astronomy, and other fields of science.

Using this new scientific knowledge, Europeans developed new inventions and techniques. For example, they learned how to build enormous domes that could rise higher than earlier buildings.

Another invention of the Renaissance was the movable type printing press. A German named Johann Gutenberg built the first movable type printing press in the mid-1400s. This type of printing press could print books quickly and cheaply. For the first time, people could easily share ideas with others in distant areas. The printing press helped the ideas of the Renaissance spread beyond Italy.

READING CHECK **Summarizing** How did life in Europe change during the Renaissance?

CONNECTING TO Technology

The Printing Press

Printing was not a new idea in Renaissance Europe. What was new was the method of printing. Johann Gutenberg designed a printing system called movable type. It used a set of tiny lead blocks, each carved with a letter of the alphabet. These blocks could then be used to spell out an entire page of text for printing. Once copies of the page were made, the printer could reuse the blocks to spell out another page. This was much faster and easier than earlier systems had been.

Generalizing How did movable type improve printing?

The Reformation

By the early 1500s some Europeans had begun to complain about problems they saw in the Roman Catholic Church. For example, they thought the church had become corrupt. In time, their complaints led to a religious reform movement called the **Reformation** (re-fuhr-MAY-shuhn).

The Protestant Reformation

Although people called for church reform in other places, the Reformation began in what is now Germany. This area was part of the Holy Roman Empire. Some people there thought church officials were too focused on their own power and had lost sight of their religious duties.

★ Interactive Map

Religion in Europe, 1600

Legend:
- Protestant
- Roman Catholic
- Roman Catholic with Protestant minorities
- Eastern Orthodox
- Muslim
- Boundary of the Holy Roman Empire

0   250   500 Miles
0   250   500 Kilometers
Projection: Lambert Azimuthal Equal-Area

map Zone Geography Skills

Regions By the Reformation's end, parts of Europe were still Catholic, while others had become mostly Protestant.

1. **Locate** In which part of Europe were most people Protestant?
2. **Analyze** How were religious areas spread across the Holy Roman Empire?

go.hrw.com KEYWORD: SK9 CH19

One of the first people to express protests against the Catholic Church was a German monk named Martin Luther. In 1517 Luther nailed a list of complaints to a church door in the town of Wittenberg. Luther's protests angered church officials, who soon expelled him from the church. In response, Luther's followers formed a separate church. They became the first **Protestants**, Christians who broke from the Catholic Church over religious issues.

Other reformers who followed Luther began creating churches of their own as well. The Roman Catholic Church was no longer the only church in Western Europe. As you can see on the map, many areas of Europe had become Protestant by 1600.

The Catholic Reformation

Protestants were not the only ones who called for reform in the Roman Catholic Church. Many Catholic officials wanted to reform the church as well. Even as the first Protestants were breaking away from the church, Catholic officials were launching a series of reforms that became known as the **Catholic Reformation**.

As part of the Catholic Reformation, church leaders began focusing more on spiritual concerns and less on political power. They also worked to make church teachings easier for people to understand. To tell people about the changes, church leaders sent priests and teachers all over Europe. Church leaders also worked to spread Catholic teachings into Asia, Africa, and other parts of the world.

Religious Wars

The Reformation caused major changes to the religious map of Europe. Catholicism, once the main religion in most of Europe, was no longer so dominant. In many areas, especially in the north, Protestants now outnumbered Catholics.

In some parts of Europe, Catholics and Protestants lived together in peace. In some other places, however, this was not the case. Bloody religious wars broke out in France, Germany, the Netherlands, and Switzerland. Wars between religious groups left parts of Europe in ruins.

These religious wars led to political and social changes in Europe. For example, many people began relying less on what church leaders and other authority figures told them. Instead, people raised questions and began looking to science for answers.

READING CHECK **Finding Main Ideas** How did Europe change after the Reformation?

FOCUS ON READING

Based on the highlighted text, what can you assume about Protestants' religious beliefs?

SUMMARY AND PREVIEW In the 1300s through the 1500s, new ideas changed Europe's culture. Next, you will learn about ideas that changed its politics.

Section 2 Assessment

Reviewing Ideas, Terms, and Places

1. **a. Define** What was the **Renaissance**?
   b. Summarize What were some changes made in art during the Renaissance?
   c. Elaborate How did the printing press help spread Renaissance ideas?
2. **a. Describe** What led to the **Reformation**?
   b. Explain Why did church leaders launch the series of reforms known as the **Catholic Reformation**?

Critical Thinking

3. **Finding Main Ideas** Draw a chart like the one shown. Use your notes to describe new ideas of the Renaissance and the Reformation. Add rows as needed.

Idea	Description

FOCUS ON WRITING

4. **Describing Renaissance and Reformation Figures** Which people from this period might make good diary writers? Take some notes about key figures.

Political Change in Europe

What You Will Learn...

Main Ideas

1. During the Enlightenment, new ideas about government took hold in Europe.
2. The 1600s and 1700s were an Age of Revolution in Europe.
3. Napoleon Bonaparte conquered much of Europe after the French Revolution.

The Big Idea

Ideas of the Enlightenment inspired revolutions and new governments in Europe.

Key Terms

Enlightenment, *p. 634*
English Bill of Rights, *p. 636*
Declaration of Independence, *p. 637*
Declaration of the Rights of Man and of the Citizen, *p. 638*
Reign of Terror, *p. 638*

TAKING NOTES As you read, use a chart like this one to describe the ideas of the Enlightenment and the events they inspired.

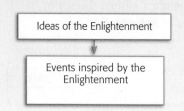

Ideas of the Enlightenment

↓

Events inspired by the Enlightenment

If YOU lived there...

You live in a village in northern France in the 1700s. Your father is a baker, and your mother is a seamstress. Like most people in your village, your family struggles to make ends meet. All your life you have been taught that the nobility has a right to rule over you. Today, though, a man made an angry speech in the village market. He said that the common people should demand more rights.

How do you think your village will react?

BUILDING BACKGROUND The Renaissance and the Reformation expanded Europeans' knowledge and changed life in many ways. The 1600s and 1700s brought still more changes. Some people began to use reason to improve government and society.

The Enlightenment

Think about the last time you faced a problem that required careful thought. Perhaps you were working a complex math problem or trying to figure out how to win a game. Whatever the problem, when you thought carefully about how to solve it, you were using your power to reason, or to think logically.

The Age of Reason

During the 1600s and 1700s a number of people began to put great importance on reason, or logical thought. They started using reason to challenge long-held beliefs about education, government, law, and religion. By using reason, these people hoped to solve problems such as poverty and war. They believed the use of reason could achieve three great goals—knowledge, freedom, and happiness—and thereby improve society. The use of reason in shaping people's ideas about society and politics defined a period called the **Enlightenment**. Because of its focus on reason, this period is also known as the Age of Reason.

The Enlightenment

Key Enlightenment Ideas

- The ability to reason is unique to humans.
- Reason can be used to solve problems and to improve people's lives.
- Reason can free people from ignorance.
- The natural world is governed by laws that can be discovered through reason.
- Natural laws also govern human behavior.
- Governments should reflect natural laws and encourage education and debate.

New Ideas about Government

During the Enlightenment, some people used reason to examine government. They questioned how governments worked and what the **purpose** of government should be. In doing so, these people developed completely new ideas about government. These ideas would help lead to the creation of modern democracy.

At the time of the Enlightenment, monarchs, or kings and queens, ruled in most of Europe. Many of these monarchs believed they ruled through divine right. That is, they thought God gave them the right to rule however they chose.

Some people challenged rule by divine right. They thought rulers' powers should be limited to protect people's freedoms. These people said government's purpose was to protect and to serve the people.

John Locke, an English philosopher, had a major influence on Enlightenment thinking about the role of government. Locke thought government should be a **contract** between a ruler and the people. A contract binds both sides, so it would limit the ruler's power. Locke also believed that all people had certain natural rights, such as life, liberty, and property. If a ruler did not protect these natural rights, people had the right to change rulers.

Other scholars built on Locke's ideas. One was Jean-Jacques Rousseau (roo-SOH). He said government should express the will, or desire, of the people. According to Rousseau, citizens give the government the power to make and enforce laws. But if these laws do not serve the people, the government should give up its power.

These Enlightenment ideas spread far and wide. In time, they would inspire some Europeans to rise up against their rulers.

ACADEMIC VOCABULARY

purpose
the reason something is done

READING CHECK **Contrasting** How did Enlightenment ideas about government differ from the views of most monarchs?

The Age of Revolution

The 1600s and 1700s were a time of great change in Europe. Some changes were peaceful, such as those in science. Other changes were more violent. In England, North America, and France, new ideas about government led to war and the Age of Revolution.

Civil War and Reform in England

In England, Enlightenment ideas led to conflict between the monarchs, or rulers, and Parliament, the lawmaking body. For many years England's rulers had shared power with Parliament. The relationship was an uneasy one, however. As rulers and Parliament fought for power, the situation grew worse.

In 1642 the power struggle erupted in civil war. Supporters of Parliament forced King Charles I from power. He was later tried and beheaded. A new government then formed, but it was unstable.

By 1660 many of the English were tired of instability. They wanted to restore the monarchy. They asked the former king's son to rule England as Charles II. However, Charles had to agree to let Parliament keep powers it had gained during the civil war.

In 1689 Parliament further limited the monarch's power. That year, it approved the **English Bill of Rights**. This document listed rights for Parliament and the English people. For example, it gave Parliament the power to pass laws and to raise taxes.

In addition, Parliament made the king promise to honor Magna Carta. Signed in 1215, this document limited the English ruler's power and protected some rights of the people. However, few monarchs had honored it during the previous 400 years. Parliament wanted to be sure future rulers honored Magna Carta.

By 1700 Parliament held most of the political power in England. Divine right to rule had ended for England's monarchy.

Documents of Democracy

The key documents shown here greatly influenced the growth of modern democracy.

ANALYZING VISUALS Which two of the documents at right contain some of John Locke's ideas?

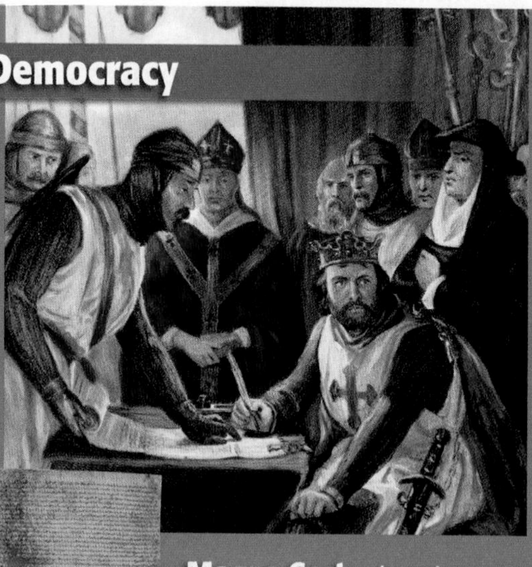

Magna Carta (1215)
- Limited the power of the monarchy
- Identified people's rights to property
- Established people's rights to trial by a jury

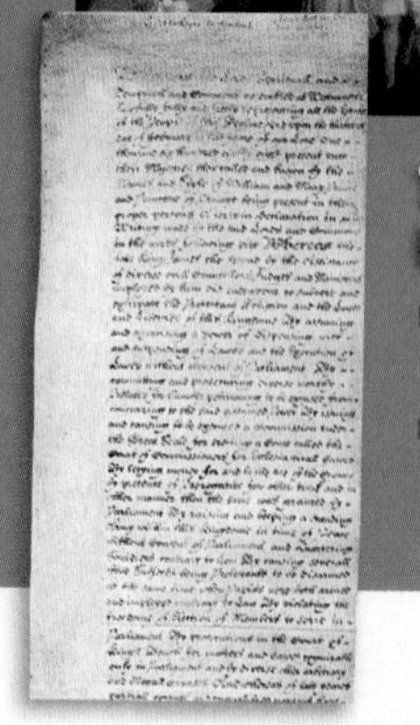

The English Bill of Rights (1689)
- Outlawed cruel and unusual punishment
- Guaranteed free speech for members of Parliament

The American Revolution

In time, Enlightenment ideas spread to the British colonies in North America. There, the British ruler's power was not limited as it was in England. For this reason, many colonists had grown unhappy with British rule. These colonists began to protest the British laws that they thought were unfair.

In 1775 the protests turned to violence, starting the Revolutionary War. Colonial leaders, influenced by the ideas of Locke and Rousseau, claimed Great Britain had denied their rights. In July 1776 they signed the **Declaration of Independence**. Largely written by Thomas Jefferson, this document declared the American colonies' independence from Britain. A new nation, the United States of America, was born.

In 1783 the United States officially won its independence. The colonists had successfully put Enlightenment ideas into practice. Their success would inspire many other people, particularly in France.

The French Revolution

The people of France closely watched the events of the American Revolution. Soon, they grew inspired to fight for their own rights in the French Revolution.

A major cause of the French Revolution was anger over the differences between social classes. In France, the king ruled over a society split into three classes called estates. The Catholic clergy made up the First Estate. They enjoyed many benefits. Nobles belonged to the Second Estate. These people held important positions in military, government, and the courts. The majority of the French people were members of the Third Estate. This group included peasants, craftworkers, and shopkeepers.

Many Third Estate members thought France's classes were unfair. These people were poor and often hungry. Yet, they paid the highest taxes. While they suffered, King Louis XVI held fancy parties, and Queen Marie-Antoinette wore costly clothes.

The U.S. Declaration of Independence (1776)
- Declared that people have natural rights that governments must protect
- Argued that people have the right to replace their governments

The French Declaration of the Rights of Man and of the Citizen (1789)
- Stated that the French government received its power from the people
- Strengthened individual rights and equality among citizens

Meanwhile, France's government was deeply in debt. To raise money, Louis XVI wanted to tax the wealthy. He called a meeting of the representatives of the three estates to discuss a tax increase.

The meeting did not go smoothly. Some members of the Third Estate were familiar with Enlightenment ideas. These members demanded a greater voice in the meeting's decisions. Eventually, the Third Estate members formed a separate group called the National Assembly. This group demanded that the French king accept a constitution limiting his powers.

Louis XVI refused, which angered the common people of Paris. On July 14, 1789, this anger led a mob to storm the Bastille, a prison in Paris. The mob released the prisoners and destroyed the building. The French Revolution had begun.

The French Revolution quickly spread to the countryside. In events called the Great Fear, peasants took revenge on landlords and other nobles for long years of poor treatment. In their rage, the peasants burned down houses and monasteries.

At the same time, other leaders of the revolution were taking peaceful steps. The National Assembly wrote and approved the **Declaration of the Rights of Man and of the Citizen**. This 1789 French constitution guaranteed French citizens some rights and made taxes fairer. Among the freedoms the constitution supported were the freedoms of speech, of the press, and of religion.

The French Republic

In time, revolutionary leaders created a French republic. The new republic did not end France's many growing problems, however. Unrest soon returned.

In 1793 the revolutionaries executed Louis XVI. His execution was the first of many as the government began arresting anyone who questioned its rule. The result was the **Reign of Terror**, a bloody period of the French Revolution during which the government executed thousands of its opponents and others at the guillotine (GEE-uh-teen). This device beheaded victims with a large, heavy blade. The Reign of Terror finally ended when one of its own leaders was executed in 1794.

Although a violent period, the French Revolution did achieve some of its goals. French peasants and workers gained new political rights. The government opened new schools and improved wages. In addition, it ended slavery in France's colonies.

The French republic's leaders struggled, though. As problems grew worse, a strong leader rose up to take control.

READING CHECK Analyzing Why did many members of the Third Estate support revolution?

The Storming of the Bastille

On July 14, 1789, a mob stormed and destroyed the Bastille, a prison in Paris. To many French people, this prison symbolized the king's harsh rule.

ANALYZING VISUALS What were some weapons used in the French Revolution?

Jacques-Louis David painted this scene of Napoleon crowning his wife, Josephine, empress after crowning himself emperor. The coronation took place in 1804 in Notre Dame Cathedral in Paris, France.

ANALYZING VISUALS How does the event show Napoleon's power?

Napoleonic Empire, 1812

Napoleon Bonaparte

In 1799 France was ripe for a change in leadership. That year, Napoleon Bonaparte, a 30-year-old general, took control. Many French people welcomed him because he seemed to support the Revolution's goals. His popularity grew quickly, and in 1804 Napoleon crowned himself emperor.

Military Conquests and Rule

Napoleon was a brilliant military leader. Under his command, the French army won a series of dazzling victories. By 1810 France's empire stretched across Europe.

In France, Napoleon restored order. He created an efficient government, made taxes fairer, and formed a system of public education. Perhaps his most important accomplishment was the creation of a new French legal system, the Napoleonic Code.

This legal code reflected the ideals of the French Revolution, such as equality before the law and equal civil rights.

With these many accomplishments, Napoleon sounds like a perfect leader. But he was not. He harshly punished anyone who opposed or questioned his rule.

Napoleon's Defeat

In the end, bad weather contributed to Napoleon's downfall. In 1812 he led an invasion of Russia. The invasion was a disaster. Bitterly cold weather and smart Russian tactics forced Napoleon's army to retreat. Many French soldiers died.

Great Britain, Prussia, and Russia then joined forces and in 1814 defeated Napoleon's weakened army. He returned a year later with a new army, but was again defeated. The British then exiled him to an island, where he died in 1821.

UNITED KINGDOM OF GREAT BRITAIN AND IRELAND

North Sea

NETHERLANDS

PRUSSIA

LESSER GERMAN STATES

RUSSIAN EMPIRE

FRANCE

SWITZERLAND

AUSTRIAN EMPIRE

ATLANTIC OCEAN

50°N

PARMA   MODENA
LUCCA   PAPAL
TUSCANY STATES

OTTOMAN EMPIRE

PORTUGAL

SPAIN

KINGDOM OF SARDINIA

40°N

Sardinia

KINGDOM OF THE TWO SICILIES

Mediterranean Sea

— Boundary of the German Confederation

0   150   300 Miles
0   150   300 Kilometers

Projection: Azimuthal Equal Area

map zone

Geography Skills

Regions After the defeat of Napoleon in 1814, the Congress of Vienna reorganized Europe.

1. **Name** What were Europe's largest empires in 1815?

2. **Analyze** How might France's location have contributed to Napoleon's rise and fall?

In 1814 European leaders met at the Congress of Vienna. There, they redrew the map of Europe. Their goal was to keep any country from ever becoming powerful enough to threaten Europe again.

READING CHECK **Drawing Inferences** Why did other countries want to defeat Napoleon?

SUMMARY AND PREVIEW You have read how new ideas about government arose out of the Enlightenment. These ideas led to revolutions and political change in Europe and elsewhere. Next, you will read about the growth of industry and how it changed European society.

Section 3 Assessment

go.hrw.com
Online Quiz
KEYWORD: SK9 HP19

Reviewing Ideas, Terms, and Places

1. **a. Define** What does divine right mean?
   b. Explain What did **Enlightenment** thinkers believe the purpose of government should be?

2. **a. Describe** What was the significance of the **English Bill of Rights**?
   b. Make Inferences Why do you think many Americans consider Thomas Jefferson a hero?
   c. Evaluate How successful do you think the French Revolution was? Explain your answer.

3. **a. Identify** Who was Napoleon Bonaparte, and what were his main accomplishments?
   b. Analyze How were Napoleon's forces weakened and then defeated?

Critical Thinking

4. **Sequencing** Review your notes. Then use a time line like the one here to list the main events of the Age of Revolution. List the events in the order in which they occurred.

FOCUS ON WRITING

5. **Describing Political Change in Europe** If you were to write a diary as a person from this period, how would you describe the exciting political changes around you? Write down some ideas in your notebook.

John Locke

Would you risk arrest for your beliefs in people's rights?

When did he live? 1632–1704

Where did he live? England and the Netherlands

What did he do? Locke worked as a professor, physician, and government official. He wrote about the human mind, science, government, religion, and other topics.

Why is he important? Locke believed in the right of common people to think and worship as they pleased and to own property. He also had great faith in science and people's basic goodness. Not everyone liked his ideas. At one point Locke fled to Holland to avoid arrest by political enemies. Locke's ideas have inspired political reforms in the West for some 300 years.

Drawing Inferences Why do you think some people disliked Locke's ideas?

KEY IDEAS

" Men being, as has been said, by nature, all free, equal, and independent, no one can be . . . subjected to the political power of another, without his own consent. The only way whereby any one divests himself of his natural liberty . . . is by agreeing with other men to join and unite into a community. "

–John Locke, from *Second Treatise of Civil Government*

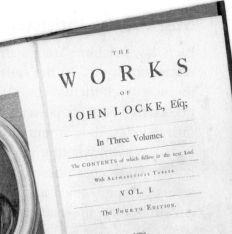

This book printed in 1740 is a collection of John Locke's writings.

The Industrial Revolution

What You Will Learn...

Main Ideas

1. Britain's large labor force, raw materials, and money to invest led to the start of the Industrial Revolution.
2. Industrial growth began in Great Britain and then spread to other parts of Europe.
3. The Industrial Revolution led to both positive and negative changes in society.

The Big Idea

Driven by new ideas and technologies, much of Europe developed industrial societies in the 1700s and 1800s.

Key Terms

Industrial Revolution, *p. 642*
textiles, *p. 644*
capitalism, *p. 644*
suffragettes, *p. 646*

 TAKING NOTES As you read, complete a concept web like the one below. To complete the concept web, fill in the outer ovals.

If YOU lived there...

You live in Lancashire, England, in 1815. You and your family are weavers. You spin sheep's wool into thread. Then you weave the thread into fine woolen cloth to sell to local merchants. Now a mill is being built nearby. It will have large machines that weave cloth. The mill owner is looking for workers to run the machines. Some of your friends are going to work in the mill to earn more money.

What do you think about working in the mill?

BUILDING BACKGROUND In the mid-1700s great changes in industry revolutionized life in Europe. Like some earlier revolutions, the growth of industry was driven by new inventions and technology. This industrial growth would have far-reaching effects on society.

Start of the Industrial Revolution

Each day, machines from alarm clocks to dishwashers perform many jobs for us. In the early 1700s, however, people had to do most work themselves. They made most of the items they needed by hand. For power, they used animals or water or their own muscles. Then around the mid-1700s, everything changed. People began inventing machines to make goods and supply power. These machines completely changed the way people across Europe worked and lived. We call this period of rapid growth in machine-made goods the **Industrial Revolution**.

From Farmworker to Industrial Laborer

Changes in farming helped pave the way for industrial growth. Since the Middle Ages, farming in Europe had been changing. Wealthy farmers had started buying up land and creating larger farms. These large farms were more efficient. For this reason, many people who owned small farms lost their land. They then had to work for other farmers or move to cities.

At the same time, Europe's growing population was creating a need for more food. To meet this need, farmers began looking for ways to grow more and better crops. Farmers began to experiment with new methods. They also began improving farm technology. Englishman Jethro Tull, for example, invented a seed drill. This device made it possible to plant seeds in straight rows and at certain depths. As a result, more seeds grew into plants.

Better farming methods and technology had several effects. For one, farmers could grow more crops with less labor. With more crops available for food, the population grew even more. With less need for labor, however, many farmworkers lost their jobs. These workers then moved to cities. There, they created a large labor force for the coming industrial growth.

Great Britain's Resources

Great Britain provided the setting for the Industrial Revolution's start. Britain and its colonies had the resources needed for industrial growth. These resources included labor, raw materials, and money to invest. For example, Britain had a large workforce, rich supplies of coal, and many rivers for waterpower.

In addition, Great Britain's colonial markets and its growing population were increasing the demand for manufactured goods. Increased demand led people to look for ways to make goods faster or more easily. In Britain all these things came together to start the Industrial Revolution.

READING CHECK **Identifying Cause and Effect** How did new technology and better farming methods affect agriculture in Europe?

Inventions of the Industrial Revolution

Starting in the mid-1700s, inventions changed the way goods were made. James Hargreaves's spinning jenny, above, made thread quickly. The Bessemer furnace, at left, was an invention of the late Industrial Revolution. The furnace made steel from molten iron.

ANALYZING VISUALS What do you think operating a Bessemer furnace was like?

Industrial Growth

Industrial growth began with **textiles**, or cloth products. In the early 1700s people made cloth by hand. They used spinning wheels to make thread and looms to weave it into cloth. Given the time and effort this took, it is not surprising that people would want a way to make cloth quickly.

The Textile Industry

A big step toward manufactured clothing came in 1769. That year, an Englishman, named Richard Arkwright invented a waterpowered spinning machine. Called a water frame, this machine could produce dozens of threads at one time. In contrast, a person using a traditional spinning wheel could produce only one thread at a time.

Other machines sped up production even more. With these new machines, workers could produce large amounts of cloth quickly. As a result, the price of cloth fell. Soon, the British were using machines to make many types of goods. People housed these machines in buildings called factories, and the factories needed power.

Other Inventions

Most early machines ran on waterpower. Thus, factories had to be located by rivers. Although Britain had many rivers, they were not always in desirable locations.

Steam power provided a solution. In the 1760s James Watt, a Scot, built the first modern steam engine. Soon, steam powered most machines. Factories could now be built in better places, such as in cities.

Steam power increased the demand for coal and iron, which were needed to make machinery. Iron can be a brittle metal, though, and iron parts often broke. Then in 1855 Englishman Henry Bessemer developed a cheap way to convert iron into steel, which is stronger. This invention led to the growth of the steel industry.

In addition, new inventions improved transportation and communication. Steam engines powered riverboats and trains, speeding up transportation. The telegraph made communication faster. Instead of sending a note by boat or train, people could go to a telegraph office and instantly send a message over a long distance.

The Factory System

Industrial growth led to major changes in the way people worked and lived. Before, most people had worked on farms or in their homes. Now, more people were going to work in factories. Many of these workers were young women and children, whom owners paid lower wages.

Factory work was long, tiring, and dangerous. Factory workers did the same tasks for 12 hours or more a day, six days a week. Breaks were few, and rules were strict. Although people made more than on farms, wages were still low.

To add to the toil, factory conditions were miserable and unsafe. Year-round, the air was thick with dust, which could harm workers' lungs. In addition, the large machines were dangerous and caused many injuries. Even so, factory jobs were desirable to people with few alternatives.

Spread of Industry

In time, the Industrial Revolution spread from Great Britain to other parts of Europe. By the late 1800s, factories were making goods across much of Western Europe.

The growth of industry helped lead to a new economic system, **capitalism**. In this system, individuals own most businesses and resources. People invest money in businesses in the hope of making a profit.

READING CHECK **Evaluating** If you had lived at this time, would you have left a farm to work in a factory for more money? Why, or why not?

A British Textile Factory

In early textile factories, workers ran machines in a large room. A supervisor kept a watchful eye. Conditions in factories were poor, and the work was long, tiring, and dangerous. Even so, young women and children as young as six worked in many early factories.

Factory owners keep windows shut to prevent air from blowing the threads. This creates a hot, stuffy room.

Dust and cotton fibers fill the air, causing breathing problems.

One task is to straighten threads as they come out of the machines. This task can cut workers' hands.

Machines are loud. Workers must shout to be heard over the deafening roar.

To avoid being injured or killed, girls must tie back their hair to keep it from getting caught in the machines.

ANALYSIS SKILL **ANALYZING VISUALS**

Why do you think the machines in early textile factories caused so many injuries?

Reform efforts addressed the workplace, society, and government. Here, British suffragettes campaign for the right to vote.

Changes in Society

The Industrial Revolution improved life in Europe in many ways. Manufactured goods became cheaper and more available. Inventions made life easier. More people grew wealthier and joined the middle class. These people could afford to live well.

At the same time, industrial growth made life worse in other ways. Cities grew rapidly. They became dirty, noisy, and crowded. Many workers remained poor. They often had to live crammed together in shabby, unsafe apartments. In these conditions, diseases spread rapidly as well.

Such problems led to efforts to reform society and politics. People worked to have laws passed improving wages and factory conditions. Others worked to make cities cleaner and safer. Efforts to gain political power were led by **suffragettes**, women who campaigned to gain the right to vote. In 1928 British suffragettes won the right to vote for women in Great Britain. Changes like these helped usher in the modern age.

READING CHECK **Summarizing** How did the Industrial Revolution affect cities in Europe?

SUMMARY AND PREVIEW As you have read, industrial growth changed how many Europeans lived and worked. In the next chapter you will learn about an event that led to more change: World War I.

go.hrw.com
Online Quiz
KEYWORD: SK9 HP19

Section 4 Assessment

Reviewing Ideas, Terms, and Places

1. **a. Recall** In which country did the start of the **Industrial Revolution** take place?
   b. Draw Conclusions How did changes in farming help pave the way for industrial growth?
   c. Develop Write a few sentences defending the idea that Great Britain was ready for industrial growth in the early 1700s.
2. **a. Identify** What were two inventions that contributed to industrial growth during this period?
   b. Make Inferences How do you think work in a factory differed from that on a farm?
3. **a. Recall** What did the **suffragettes** achieve?
   b. Summarize What problems did industry create? How did people work to solve these problems?

Critical Thinking

4. **Identifying Cause and Effect** Review your notes. Then use a diagram like the one shown to explain how each change in society led to the next.

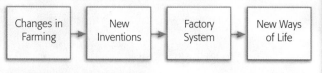

| Changes in Farming | New Inventions | Factory System | New Ways of Life |

FOCUS ON WRITING

5. **Describing the Industrial Revolution** What might a diary writer have to say about the Industrial Revolution? Jot down some ideas in your notes. For example, an entry might describe what it was like to work in an early factory.

Social Studies Skills

Chart and Graph | Critical Thinking | Geography | Study

Writing to Learn

Learn

Writing is an important tool for learning new information. When you write about what you read, you can better understand and remember information. For example, when you write a list of items you need from the grocery store, the act of writing can help you remember what to buy. Use the steps below to write to learn.

• Read the text carefully. Look for the main idea and important details.

• Think about the information you just read. Then summarize in your own words what you learned.

• Write a personal response to what you read. What do you think about the information? What questions might you have? How does this information affect you?

Practice

Use the steps you just learned to practice writing to learn. Read the paragraph below carefully, then complete a chart like the one here.

Eventually, the Third Estate members formed the National Assembly. This group demanded that the French king accept a constitution limiting his powers. Louis XVI refused, which angered the common people of Paris. On July 14, 1789, this anger led a mob to storm the Bastille, a prison in Paris. The mob released the prisoners and destroyed the building. The French Revolution had begun.

What I Learned	Personal Response

Apply

Read the information in Section 4 carefully. Then create a chart similar to the one above. In the first column, summarize the key ideas from the section in your own words. Use the second column to write your personal reaction to the information you learned.

World War I

What You Will Learn...

Main Ideas

1. Rivalries in Europe led to the outbreak of World War I.
2. After a long, devastating war, the Allies claimed victory.
3. The war's end brought great political and territorial changes to Europe.

The Big Idea

World War I and the peace treaty that followed brought tremendous change to Europe.

Key Terms

nationalism, *p. 648*
alliance, *p. 649*
trench warfare, *p. 650*
Treaty of Versailles, *p. 651*
communism, *p. 652*

 TAKING NOTES As you read, take notes on the causes and effects of World War I. Use a graphic organizer like the one below to help you organize your notes.

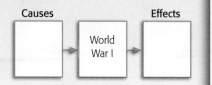

If YOU lived there...

It is 1914, and you live in London. For years you have heard about an important alliance between Great Britain, France, and Russia. Each country has promised to protect the others. Just days ago, you learned that war has broken out in Eastern Europe. Russia and France are preparing for war. People are saying that Britain will fight to protect its allies. If that happens, Europe's most powerful countries will be at war.

How do you feel about the possibility of war?

BUILDING BACKGROUND The 1800s were a time of rapid change in Europe. Industries grew quickly. Cities expanded. The countries of Europe raced to build empires and gain power. As each country tried to outdo the others, conflicts emerged. Europe was poised for war.

The Outbreak of War

In the early 1900s Europe was on the brink of war. Rivalries were building among Europe's strongest nations. One small spark would be enough to start World War I.

Causes of the War

During the 1800s nationalism changed Europe. **Nationalism** is devotion and loyalty to one's country. Some groups that were ruled by powerful empires wanted to build their own nation-states. For example, nationalism led some people in Bosnia and Herzegovina, a region in southeastern Europe, to demand their independence from the Austro-Hungarian Empire. Nationalism also created rivalries among many nations. By the early 1900s nationalism had grown so strong that countries were willing to go to war to prove their superiority over their rivals. A fierce competition emerged among the countries of Europe.

This competition for land, resources, and power drove many European countries to strengthen their armed forces. They built powerful armies and created stockpiles of new weapons. Each country wanted to show its strength and intimidate its rivals.

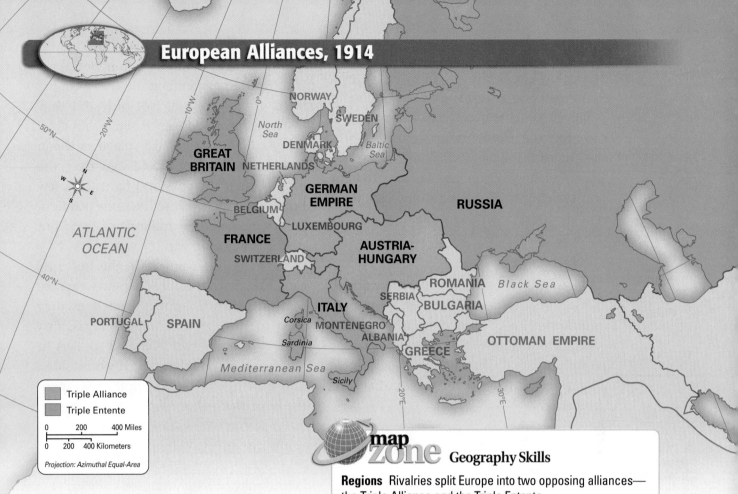

European Alliances, 1914

GREAT BRITAIN, NETHERLANDS, BELGIUM, LUXEMBOURG, FRANCE, SWITZERLAND, PORTUGAL, SPAIN, ITALY, GERMAN EMPIRE, AUSTRIA-HUNGARY, RUSSIA, ROMANIA, SERBIA, BULGARIA, MONTENEGRO, ALBANIA, GREECE, OTTOMAN EMPIRE, NORWAY, SWEDEN, DENMARK

ATLANTIC OCEAN, North Sea, Baltic Sea, Black Sea, Mediterranean Sea, Corsica, Sardinia, Sicily

- Triple Alliance
- Triple Entente

0   200   400 Miles
0   200   400 Kilometers
Projection: Azimuthal Equal-Area

map zone Geography Skills

Regions Rivalries split Europe into two opposing alliances—the Triple Alliance and the Triple Entente.
1. **Locate** Which alliance controlled central Europe?
2. **Draw Conclusions** Why do you think the location of the Triple Entente might have threatened the Triple Alliance?

Both Great Britain and Germany, for example, competed to build strong navies and powerful new battleships.

As tensions and suspicions grew, some European leaders hoped to protect their countries by creating alliances. An **alliance** is an agreement between countries. If one country is attacked, its allies—members of the alliance—help defend it. In 1882 Italy, Germany, and Austria-Hungary formed the Triple Alliance. In response, France, Great Britain, and Russia created their own alliance, the Triple Entente (ahn-TAHNT). As you can see in the map, these alliances divided Europe.

The Spark for War

By the summer of 1914, war in Europe seemed certain. Tensions between Austria-Hungary and Serbia arose over the control of Bosnia and Herzegovina, a province of Austria-Hungary and Serbia's neighbor. On June 28, 1914, a Serbian assassin shot and killed Archduke Francis Ferdinand, the heir to the throne of Austria-Hungary. Seeking revenge, Austria-Hungary declared war on Serbia. After Serbia turned to Russia for help, the alliance system quickly split Europe into two warring sides. On one side was Austria-Hungary and Germany, known as the Central Powers. The Allied Powers—Serbia, Russia, Great Britain, and France—were on the other side.

READING CHECK **Finding Main Ideas** What were the causes of World War I?

War and Victory

Germany struck the first blow in the war, sending a large army into Belgium and France. Allied troops, however, managed to stop the Germans just outside Paris. In the east, Russia attacked Germany and Austria-Hungary, forcing Germany to fight on two fronts. Hopes on both sides for a quick victory soon disappeared.

A New Kind of War

ACADEMIC VOCABULARY

strategy a plan for fighting a battle or war

A new military **strategy**, trench warfare, was largely responsible for preventing a quick victory. Early in the war both sides turned to trench warfare. **Trench warfare** is a style of fighting in which each side fights from deep ditches, or trenches, dug into the ground.

Both the Allies and the Central Powers dug hundreds of miles of trenches along the front lines. Soldiers in the trenches faced great suffering. Not only did they live in constant danger of attack, but cold, hunger, and disease also plagued them. Sometimes soldiers would "go over the top" of their trenches and fight for a few hours, only to retreat to the same position. Trench warfare cost millions of lives, but neither side could win the war.

To gain an advantage in the trenches, each side developed deadly new weapons. Machine guns cut down soldiers as they tried to move forward. Poison gas, first used by the Germans, blinded soldiers in the trenches. It was later used by both sides. The British introduced another weapon, the tank, to break through enemy lines.

Close-up

Trench Warfare

Both the Allied Powers and the Central Powers relied on trenches for defense during World War I. As a result, the war dragged on for years with no clear victor. Each side developed new weapons and technology to try to gain an advantage in the trenches.

Soldiers often threw or fired small bombs known as grenades.

Trenches dug in zigzag patterns prevented the enemy from firing down the length of a trench.

Soldiers used gas masks to survive attacks of poison gas.

At sea, Britain used its powerful navy to block supplies from reaching Germany. Germany responded by using submarines, called U-boats. German U-boats tried to break the British blockade and sink ships carrying supplies to Great Britain.

The Allies Win

For three years the war was a stalemate—neither side could defeat the other. Slowly, however, the war turned in favor of the Allies. In early 1917 German U-boats began attacking American ships carrying supplies to Britain. When Germany ignored U.S. warnings to stop, the United States entered the war on the side of the Allies.

Help from American forces gave the Allies a fresh advantage. Soon afterward, however, the exhausted Russians pulled out of the war. Germany quickly attacked the Allies, hoping to put an end to the war. Allied troops, however, stopped Germany's attack. The Central Powers had suffered a great blow. In the fall of 1918 the Central Powers surrendered. The Allied Powers were victorious.

READING CHECK **Sequencing** What events led to the end of World War I?

The War's End

After more than four years of fighting, the war came to an end on November 11, 1918. More than 8.5 million soldiers had been killed, and at least 20 million more were wounded. Millions of civilians had lost their lives as well. The war brought tremendous change to Europe.

Making Peace

Shortly after the end of the war, leaders from the Allied nations met at Versailles (ver-SY), near Paris. There, they debated the terms of peace for the Central Powers.

The United States, led by President Woodrow Wilson, wanted a just peace after the war. He did not want harsh peace terms that might anger the losing countries and lead to future conflict.

Other Allied leaders, however, wanted to punish Germany. They believed that Germany had started the war and should pay for it. They believed that weakening Germany would prevent future wars.

In the end, the Allies forced Germany to sign a treaty. The **Treaty of Versailles** was the final peace settlement of World War I. It forced Germany to accept the blame for starting the war. Germany also had to slash the size of its army and give up its overseas colonies. Additionally, Germany had to pay billions of dollars for damages caused during the war.

Each side used airplanes to observe troop movements and other actions behind enemy lines.

Armored vehicles, or tanks, were used to launch attacks across rough terrain.

ANALYSIS SKILL **ANALYZING VISUALS**

What advantages and disadvantages did trench warfare pose for soldiers?

FOCUS ON READING

What does the term *just peace* mean? How can you tell?

Vladimir Lenin encouraged Russian workers to support his new Communist government.

over Russia's government and established a Communist government. **Communism** is a political system in which the government owns all property and controls all aspects of life in a country. An uprising toward the end of the war also forced the German emperor from power. A fragile republic replaced the German Empire.

World War I also altered the borders of many European countries. Austria and Hungary became separate countries. Poland and Czechoslovakia each gained their independence. Serbia, Bosnia and Herzegovina, and other Balkan states were combined to create Yugoslavia. Finland, Estonia, Latvia, and Lithuania, which had been part of Russia, became independent.

READING CHECK **Summarizing** How did World War I change Europe?

SUMMARY AND PREVIEW Intense rivalries among the countries of Europe led to World War I, one of the most devastating wars in history. In the next section you will learn about problems that plagued Europe and led to World War II.

A New Europe

World War I had a tremendous effect on the countries of Europe. It changed the governments of some European countries and the borders of others. For example, in Russia the war had caused great hardship for the people. A revolution then forced the Russian czar, or emperor, to give up power. Shortly after, Vladimir Lenin took

Section 5 Assessment

go.hrw.com
Online Quiz
KEYWORD: SK9 HP19

Reviewing Ideas, Terms, and Places

1. **a. Identify** What event triggered World War I?
   b. Analyze How did **nationalism** cause rivalries between some European countries?
   c. Evaluate Do you think **alliances** helped or hurt most countries? Explain your answer.
2. **a. Describe** What was **trench warfare** like?
   b. Draw Conclusions What difficulties did soldiers face as a result of trench warfare?
   c. Predict How might the war have been different if the United States had not entered it?
3. **a. Recall** How did the **Treaty of Versailles** punish Germany for its role in the war?
   b. Contrast How did the Allied leaders' ideas for peace with Germany differ?

c. Elaborate Why do you think the war caused changes in government in Russia and Germany?

Critical Thinking

4. **Categorizing** Draw a chart like the one here. Use your notes to list the results of World War I in the appropriate category.

Political	Economic

FOCUS ON WRITING

5. **Writing about World War I** Think about the events of World War I. Imagine that you were present at one or more events during or after the war. What might you write about in your diary?

from
All Quiet on the Western Front

by Erich Maria Remarque

Soldiers prepare to rush over the top of a trench during a battle in World War I.

About the Reading *In* All Quiet on the Western Front, *author Erich Maria Remarque provides a fictional account of the lives of soldiers during World War I. The book is considered one of the most realistic accounts of the war. In this selection, the book's narrator, twenty-year-old German soldier Paul Bäumer, describes a battle between German and British forces.*

AS YOU READ Note the words the speaker uses to describe the battle.

Our trenches have now for some time been shot to pieces, and we have an elastic line, so that there is practically no longer any proper trench warfare. ❶ When attack and counter-attack have waged backwards and forwards there remains a broken line and a bitter struggle from crater to crater. The front-line has been penetrated, and everywhere small groups have established themselves, the fight is carried on from clusters of shell-holes.

We are buried in a crater, the English are coming down obliquely, they are turning our flank and working in behind us. ❷ We are surrounded. It is not easy to surrender, fog and smoke hang over us, no one would recognize that we wanted to give ourselves up, and perhaps we don't want to, a man doesn't even know himself at such moments. We hear the explosions of the hand-grenades coming towards us. Our machine-gun sweeps over the semicircle in front of us . . . Behind us the attack crashes ever nearer.

GUIDED READING

WORD HELP

crater a hole in the ground made by the explosion of a bomb or shell
penetrated passed into or through
obliquely indirectly or underhandedly

❶ An elastic line describes a battle line that is pushed back and forth by enemy forces.

❷ "Turning our flank" refers to a tactic in which one military force moves around the side of the opposing force in order to surround them.

Connecting Literature to Geography

1. Describing What details in the first paragraph show that the technique of trench warfare is no longer working?

2. Making Inferences Why do you think the location of this trench is so important to the war and the people fighting in it?

World War II

What You Will Learn...

The Big Idea

Problems in Europe led to World War II, the deadliest war in history.

Key Terms

Great Depression, *p. 654*
dictator, *p. 655*
Axis Powers, *p. 657*
Allies, *p. 657*
Holocaust, *p. 657*

 TAKING NOTES As you read, take notes on the important dates and events of World War II. Use a chart like the one below to organize your notes.

Event	Date	Importance

If **YOU** lived there...

It is 1922, and you are part of a huge crowd in one of Rome's public squares. Everyone is listening to the fiery speech of a dynamic new leader. He promises to make Italy great again, as it was in the days of ancient Rome. You know that your parents and some of your teachers are excited about his ideas. Others are concerned that he may be too forceful.

What do you think of this new leader's message?

BUILDING BACKGROUND Many countries faced deep economic and political problems as a result of World War I. Dictators rose to power in a number of countries, but did not bring solutions. Instead, they attacked their neighbors and plunged the world back into war.

Problems Trouble Europe

After World War I, Europeans began rebuilding their countries. Just as they had started to recover, however, many economic and political problems emerged. These problems threatened the peace and security of Europe.

The Great Depression

World War I left much of Europe in shambles. Factories and farmland had been destroyed, and economies were in ruins. Countries that had lost the war, like Germany and Austria, owed billions in war damages. Many countries turned to the United States for help. During the 1920s the U.S. economy was booming. Loans from American banks and businesses helped many European nations recover and rebuild after World War I.

In 1929, however, the recovery fell apart. A stock market crash in the United States triggered a global economic crisis in the 1930s known as the **Great Depression**. As the U.S. economy faltered, American banks stopped lending to Europe. Without U.S. loans and investments, European economies declined. Unemployment skyrocketed as businesses and farms, as well as banks, went bankrupt.

The Rise of Dictators

The Great Depression added to Europe's problems. Blaming weak governments for the hard times, some Europeans turned to dictators to strengthen their countries and improve their lives. A **dictator** is a ruler who has total control. Dictators rose to power in Russia, Italy, and Germany.

One of the first dictators in Europe was Russia's Vladimir Lenin. Lenin gained power as a result of a 1917 revolution. He formed the first Communist government and took control of businesses and private property. He also united Russia and other republics to create the Soviet Union. After Lenin's death in 1924, Joseph Stalin took power. As dictator, he made all economic decisions, restricted religious worship, and used secret police to spy on citizens.

Benito Mussolini of Italy was another powerful dictator during this period. In the 1920s Mussolini won control of the Italian government and made himself dictator. He promised to make Italy stronger and to revive the economy. He even spoke of restoring the glory of the former Roman Empire. As dictator, however, Mussolini suspended basic rights like freedom of speech and trial by jury.

By the 1930s many Germans had lost faith in their government. They turned to a new political party, the Nazi Party. The party's leader, Adolf Hitler, promised to strengthen Germany. He vowed to rebuild Germany's military and economy. After years of struggle, many Germans listened eagerly to his message. In 1933 Hitler rose to power and soon became dictator. He banned all parties except the Nazi Party. He also began discriminating against so-called inferior races, particularly Germany's Jews.

READING CHECK **Generalizing** Why did some people support the rise of dictators?

European Dictators

Popular dictators rose to power in Europe in the 1920s and 1930s. Adolf Hitler in Germany and Benito Mussolini in Italy gained public support with promises to make life better and to strengthen their countries.

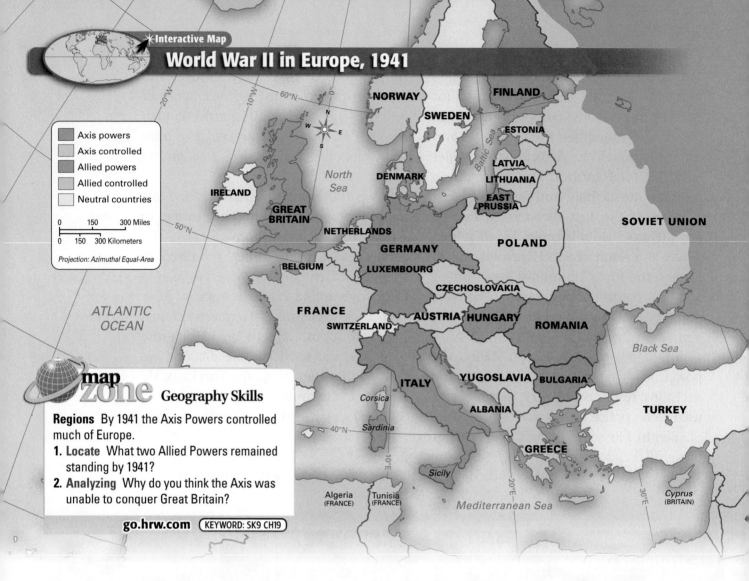

Legend
- Axis powers
- Axis controlled
- Allied powers
- Allied controlled
- Neutral countries

0   150   300 Miles
0   150   300 Kilometers

Projection: Azimuthal Equal-Area

map zone Geography Skills

Regions By 1941 the Axis Powers controlled much of Europe.
1. **Locate** What two Allied Powers remained standing by 1941?
2. **Analyzing** Why do you think the Axis was unable to conquer Great Britain?

go.hrw.com [KEYWORD: SK9 CH19]

War Breaks Out

As dictators, Hitler and Mussolini were determined to strengthen their countries at any cost. Their actions led to history's deadliest war—World War II.

Threats to Peace

After World War I, European countries wanted peace. Many countries hoped to prevent another deadly war. By the late 1930s, however, attempts at peace had failed. Instead of peace, Italian and German aggression forced Europe into a second world war.

In 1935 Benito Mussolini ordered his Italian troops to invade Ethiopia, a country in East Africa. Other nations were shocked

FOCUS ON READING

How do contrast clues help you understand the meaning of the word *aggression*?

by his actions, but none tried to turn back the invasion. Meanwhile, the Italian leader and Germany's Adolf Hitler joined together to form an alliance known as the Rome-Berlin Axis.

Hitler was next to act. In 1938 he broke the Treaty of Versailles when he annexed, or added, Austria to Germany's territory. Although Britain and France protested, they did not attempt to stop Germany.

Later that year, Hitler announced his plan to take Czechoslovakia as well. Many European leaders were worried, but they still hoped to avoid a war. They allowed Hitler to annex part of Czechoslovakia in return for his promise of peace. By the spring of 1939, however, Germany had conquered the rest of Czechoslovakia.

Italy quickly moved to occupy Albania in the Balkans. Attempts to keep the peace had failed.

Eventually, Great Britain and France realized they could not ignore Hitler's actions. When Germany threatened to take Polish territory, the Allies vowed to protect Poland at all costs. On September 1, 1939, German forces launched an all-out attack on Poland. Two days later, Great Britain and France responded by declaring war on Germany. World War II had begun.

Allies Lose Ground

Germany's invasion of Poland triggered the Second World War. Germany, Italy, and Japan formed an alliance called the **Axis Powers**. Against them stood the **Allies**—France, Great Britain, and other countries that opposed the Axis.

Germany struck first. After defeating Poland, Germany moved on to a series of quick victories in Western Europe. One by one, countries fell to German forces. In June 1940 Germany invaded and quickly defeated one of Europe's greatest powers, France. In less than a year, Hitler had gained control of almost all of Western Europe.

Next, Germany set its sights on Britain. The German air force repeatedly attacked British cities and military targets. Hitler hoped the British would surrender. Rather than give in, however, the British persevered.

Unable to defeat Great Britain, the Axis Powers turned their attention elsewhere. As German troops marched into Eastern Europe, Italian forces invaded North Africa. By the end of 1941 Germany had invaded the Soviet Union, and Japan had attacked the United States at Pearl Harbor, Hawaii. The Allies were losing ground in the war.

READING CHECK Drawing Inferences Why do you think the Axis Powers easily gained the advantage in the early years of the war?

The Holocaust

One of the most horrifying aspects of the war was the Holocaust (HOH-luh-kawst). The **Holocaust** was the attempt by the Nazi government during World War II to eliminate Europe's Jews. Believing that the Germans were a superior race, the Nazis tried to destroy people they considered inferior, especially the Jews, who had suffered prejudice and hatred for centuries.

Even before the war began, the Nazi government began restricting the rights of Jews and others in Germany. For example, laws restricted Jews from holding government jobs or attending German schools. Nazis imprisoned countless Jews in camps.

Primary Source

JOURNAL ENTRY
The Diary of Anne Frank

Anne Frank and her family fled to Amsterdam to escape Nazi persecution of Jews in Germany. In 1942, when Nazis began rounding up Jews in the Netherlands, the Franks were forced to hide. Anne kept a diary of her time in hiding.

" *Countless friends and acquaintances have gone to a terrible fate. Evening after evening the green and gray army lorries [trucks] trundle past. The Germans ring at every front door to inquire if there are any Jews living in the house. If there are, then the whole family has to go at once. If they don't find any, they go on to the next house. No one has a chance of evading them unless one goes into hiding.* "

—from *The Diary of a Young Girl*

ANALYSIS SKILL ANALYZING PRIMARY SOURCES

What likely happened to the Jews that were rounded up by German officials?

World War II

September 1–3, 1939
German forces invade Poland; Britain and France declare war.

June 22, 1941
Germany launches invasion of the Soviet Union.

1940   1941   1942   1943

June 22, 1940
France falls to German forces.

July–September 1940
Germany bombs London during the Battle of Britain.

Thousands of Jews fled Germany to escape persecution. Many thousands more, however, remained behind, not allowed into other countries.

Germany's expansion into Eastern Europe brought millions more Jews under Hitler's control. Because of this, in 1942 the Nazi government ordered the destruction of Europe's entire Jewish population. The Nazis used mass executions and death camps, like Auschwitz in Poland, to murder 6 million Jews.

The Nazis did face resistance. Some Jews fought. For example, Jews in Warsaw, Poland, staged an uprising. Some Europeans tried to save Jews from the Nazis. German businessman Oskar Schindler, for example, saved Jews by employing them in his factories. However, most Jews were unable to escape. By the time the Nazis were defeated, they had killed two-thirds of Europe's Jews and several million non-Jews.

READING CHECK **Analyzing** Why did Hitler's Nazi government attempt to destroy the Jews?

End of the War

The Allies did not fare well in the early years of the war. Victories in 1943 and 1944, though, helped them end World War II.

Allies Are Victorious

In early 1943 U.S. and British forces gained control of North Africa and Italy, forcing Mussolini to surrender. That same year, the Allies defeated the Japanese in several key battles. In the east, Soviet troops forced Germany to retreat.

In June 1944 Allied forces landed on the beaches of Normandy, France. The invasion, or D-Day as it was called, dealt a serious blow to the Axis. It paved the way for Allied forces to advance on Germany.

By the spring of 1945 Allied troops had crossed into German territory. In May 1945 Germany surrendered. In August 1945 the United States used a powerful new weapon, the atomic bomb, to bring the war with Japan to an end. After almost six years of fighting, World War II was over.

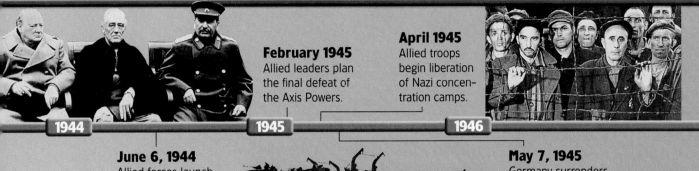

February 1945
Allied leaders plan the final defeat of the Axis Powers.

April 1945
Allied troops begin liberation of Nazi concentration camps.

1944 | 1945 | 1946

June 6, 1944
Allied forces launch D-Day invasion in Normandy, France.

May 7, 1945
Germany surrenders to Allied Powers.

PA 3-27

ANALYSIS SKILL **READING TIME LINES**

About how long after the beginning of the war did Germany invade the Soviet Union?

Results of the War

The war had a huge impact on the world. It resulted in millions of deaths, tensions between the Allies, and the creation of the United Nations.

World War II was the deadliest conflict in history. More than 50 million people lost their lives. Millions more were wounded.

The United States and the Soviet Union emerged from the war as the most powerful countries in the world. An intense rivalry developed between the two countries.

After the war, people hoped to prevent another deadly conflict. In 1945 some 50 nations formed the United Nations, an international peacekeeping organization.

READING CHECK **Summarizing** What were the main results of World War II?

SUMMARY AND PREVIEW World War II was the deadliest war in history. Next, you will learn about developments in Europe during the postwar period.

Section 6 Assessment

Reviewing Ideas, Terms, and Places

1. **a. Define** What was the **Great Depression**?
   b. Explain How did economic problems in the United States lead to the Great Depression?
2. **a. Describe** What led to the outbreak of World War II?
   b. Predict What might have happened if Great Britain had fallen to Germany?
3. **a. Identify** What was the **Holocaust**?
   b. Draw Inferences Why did the Nazis target certain groups for elimination?
4. **a. Recall** What events led to Germany's surrender?
   b. Analyze How did World War II change Europe?

Critical Thinking

5. **Sequencing** Draw a time line like this one. Using your notes on important events, place the main events and their dates on the time line.

1917   1945

FOCUS ON WRITING

6. **Telling about World War II** Imagine that you are an adult during the Second World War. Where might you have lived? What might you have seen and done there? Write down some ideas in your notebook.

Europe since 1945

What You Will Learn...

Main Ideas

1. The Cold War divided Europe between democratic and Communist nations.
2. Many Eastern European countries changed boundaries and forms of government at the end of the Cold War.
3. European cooperation has brought economic and political change to Europe.

The Big Idea

After years of division during the Cold War, today Europe is working toward unity.

Key Terms

superpowers, *p. 660*
Cold War, *p. 660*
arms race, *p. 662*
common market, *p. 664*
European Union (EU), *p. 664*

 TAKING NOTES As you read, take notes on the Cold War, the end of the Cold War, and European cooperation. Use a chart like the one below to organize your notes.

Cold War	End of Cold War	European Cooperation

If YOU lived there...

It is November 1989, and you live on the East German side of Berlin. For years the Berlin Wall has divided your city in two. The government has carefully controlled who could cross the border. One night, you hear an exciting rumor—the gate through the Wall is open. People in East and West Berlin can now travel back and forth freely. Young Berliners are celebrating in the streets.

What will this change mean for your country?

BUILDING BACKGROUND In the years after World War II, tensions between the Western Allies and the Soviet Union divided Europe into East and West. By the late 1980s, those tensions were at last coming to an end. Europe could finally work toward unity.

The Cold War

Although Europeans were relieved when World War II ended, new problems soon arose. Countries whose governments and economies had been weakened during the war had to work to strengthen them. Entire cities had to be rebuilt. Most importantly, postwar tensions between the Allies divided Europe.

Superpowers Face Off

The United States and the Soviet Union emerged from World War II as the world's most powerful nations. Allies during the war, the two **superpowers**, or strong and influential countries, now distrusted each other. Growing hostility between the superpowers led to the **Cold War**, a period of tense rivalry between the United States and the Soviet Union.

Much of the hostility between the Soviet Union and the United States focused on political and economic differences. The United States is a democracy with an economy based on free enterprise. The Soviet Union was a Communist country, in which individual freedoms were limited. Its leaders exerted strict control over the political system and the economy. These basic differences separated the two countries.

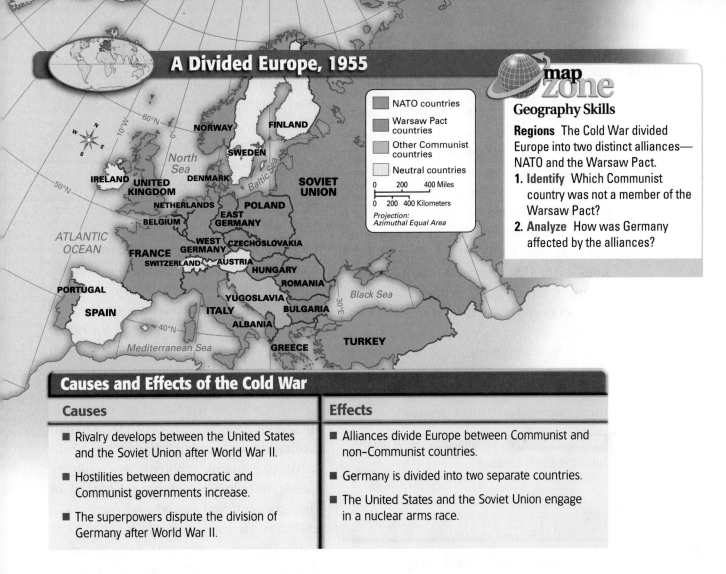

A Divided Europe, 1955

NORWAY
FINLAND
SWEDEN
North Sea
IRELAND
UNITED KINGDOM
DENMARK
Baltic Sea
SOVIET UNION
NETHERLANDS
POLAND
BELGIUM
EAST GERMANY
ATLANTIC OCEAN
WEST GERMANY
CZECHOSLOVAKIA
FRANCE
SWITZERLAND
AUSTRIA
HUNGARY
ROMANIA
PORTUGAL
YUGOSLAVIA
Black Sea
SPAIN
ITALY
BULGARIA
ALBANIA
Mediterranean Sea
GREECE
TURKEY

Legend:
- NATO countries
- Warsaw Pact countries
- Other Communist countries
- Neutral countries

0   200   400 Miles
0   200   400 Kilometers
Projection: Azimuthal Equal Area

map zone

Geography Skills

Regions The Cold War divided Europe into two distinct alliances— NATO and the Warsaw Pact.

1. **Identify** Which Communist country was not a member of the Warsaw Pact?
2. **Analyze** How was Germany affected by the alliances?

Causes and Effects of the Cold War

Causes	Effects
■ Rivalry develops between the United States and the Soviet Union after World War II.	■ Alliances divide Europe between Communist and non-Communist countries.
■ Hostilities between democratic and Communist governments increase.	■ Germany is divided into two separate countries.
■ The superpowers dispute the division of Germany after World War II.	■ The United States and the Soviet Union engage in a nuclear arms race.

A Divided Europe

The Cold War divided Europe into non-Communist and Communist countries. Most of Western Europe supported democracy and the United States. Much of Eastern Europe practiced Soviet-style communism. British prime minister Winston Churchill described the split that existed in Europe:

" …an iron curtain has descended across the Continent. Behind that line lie all the capitals of the ancient states of Central and Eastern Europe. …all are subject …not only to Soviet influence but to …control from Moscow. "
—from Winston Churchill's 1946 speech at Westminster College in Fulton, Missouri

Within this divided Europe was a divided Germany. After World War II, the Allies had separated Germany into four zones. By 1948 the Western Allies were ready to reunite their zones. However, the Soviet government feared the threat that a united Germany might pose. The next year, the Western zones were joined to form the Federal Republic of Germany, or West Germany. The Soviets helped to establish the German Democratic Republic, or East Germany. The city of Berlin, located within East Germany, was itself divided into East and West. In 1961 Communist leaders built the Berlin Wall to prevent any East Germans from fleeing to the West.

New alliances divided Europe even further. In 1949 the United States joined with several Western nations to create a powerful new alliance known as NATO, or the North Atlantic Treaty Organization.

THE IMPACT TODAY

NATO is still a powerful alliance today with 26 member nations in Europe and North America.

The members of NATO agreed to protect each other if attacked. In response, the Soviet Union formed its own alliance, the Warsaw Pact. Most Eastern European countries joined the Warsaw Pact. The two alliances used the threat of nuclear war to defend themselves. By the 1960s the United States, the Soviet Union, Britain, and France all had nuclear weapons.

The postwar division of Europe into East and West had a lasting effect on both sides. With U.S. assistance, many Western countries experienced economic growth. The economies of Communist Eastern Europe, however, failed to develop. Due to their lack of a market economy and strong industries, they suffered many shortages. They often lacked enough food, clothing, and automobiles to meet demand.

READING CHECK Summarizing How did the Cold War affect Europe?

BIOGRAPHY

Mikhail Gorbachev
(1931–   )

Mikhail Gorbachev was a key figure in bringing the Cold War to an end. In 1985 Communist officials appointed Gorbachev the leader of the Soviet Union. He quickly enacted reforms to modernize his country. He expanded basic freedoms, such as freedom of speech and freedom of the press. His democratic reforms helped bring an end to communism in the Soviet Union. In 1990 Mikhail Gorbachev won the Nobel Peace Prize for his efforts to end the Cold War and promote peace.

Evaluating Do you think Gorbachev was a popular ruler? Why or why not?

The End of the Cold War

In the late 1980s tensions between East and West finally came to an end. The collapse of communism and the end of the Cold War brought great changes to Europe.

Triumph of Democracy

During the Cold War the United States and the Soviet Union competed against each other in an arms race. An **arms race** is a competition between countries to build superior weapons. Each country tried to create more-advanced weapons and to have more nuclear missiles than the other. This arms race was incredibly expensive. The high cost of the arms race eventually damaged the Soviet economy.

By the 1980s the Soviet economy was in serious trouble. Soviet leader Mikhail Gorbachev (GAWR-buh-chawf) hoped to solve the many problems his country faced. He reduced government control of the economy and introduced democratic elections. He improved relations with the United States. Along with U.S. president Ronald Reagan, Gorbachev took steps to slow the arms race.

In part because of these new policies, reform movements soon spread. Beginning in 1989, democratic movements swept through the East. For example, Poland and Czechoslovakia threw off Communist rule. Joyful Germans tore down the Berlin Wall that separated East and West. Several Soviet republics began to demand their independence. Finally, in December 1991 the Soviet Union broke apart.

Changes in Eastern Europe

The end of the Cold War brought many changes to Eastern Europe. These changes resulted from Germany's reunification, the creation of new countries, and rising ethnic tensions in southeastern Europe.

The Fall of Communism

Reforms in the Soviet Union in the 1980s encouraged support for democracy throughout Eastern Europe.

ANALYZING VISUALS What role did the people play in communism's collapse?

Fall of the Berlin Wall East and West Germans celebrate the fall of the Berlin Wall.

Democracy in Czechoslovakia
In 1989 pro-democracy demonstrations swept Czechoslovakia. Rallies like this one led to the collapse of Czechoslovakia's Communist government.

The reunification of East and West Germany was one of many changes in Eastern Europe that marked the end of the Cold War. After the fall of the Berlin Wall in 1989, thousands of East Germans began demanding change. In early 1990 the Communist government crumbled. A few months later, the governments of East and West Germany agreed to reunite. After 45 years of division, Germany was reunited.

Other important changes occurred in Eastern Europe after the Cold War. The breakup of the Soviet Union created more than a dozen independent nations. The Russian Federation is the largest and most powerful of these new countries. Ukraine, Lithuania, Belarus, and others also emerged from the former Soviet Union.

Ethnic conflicts have also transformed Eastern Europe since the end of the Cold War. For example, tensions between ethnic groups in Czechoslovakia and Yugoslavia led to the breakup of both countries.

In Czechoslovakia, ethnic tensions divided the country. Disputes between the country's two main ethnic groups emerged in the early 1990s. Both the Czechs and the Slovaks **advocated** separate governments. In January 1993 Czechoslovakia peacefully divided into two countries—the Czech Republic and Slovakia.

While ethnic problems in the former Czechoslovakia were peaceful, ethnic tension in Yugoslavia triggered violence. After the collapse of communism, several Yugoslav republics declared their independence. Different ethnic groups fought each other for control of territory. Yugoslavia's civil wars resulted in years of fighting and thousands of deaths. By 1994 Yugoslavia had split into five countries—Bosnia and Herzegovina, Croatia, Macedonia, Serbia and Montenegro, and Slovenia.

ACADEMIC VOCABULARY
advocate to plead in favor of

READING CHECK **Drawing Conclusions** How did the end of the Cold War affect Europe?

The World Almanac

Facts about Countries — The European Union

Country	Year Admitted	Monetary Unit	Representatives in the European Parliament
Austria	1995	Euro	18
Belgium	1952	Euro	24
Bulgaria	2007	Lev	18
Cyprus	2004	Pound	6
Czech Republic	2004	Koruna	24
Denmark	1973	Krone	14
Estonia	2004	Kroon	6
Finland	1995	Euro	14
France	1952	Euro	78
Germany	1952	Euro	99
Greece	1979	Euro	24
Hungary	2004	Forint	24
Ireland	1973	Euro	13
Italy	1952	Euro	78
Latvia	2004	Lats	9
Lithuania	2004	Litas	13
Luxembourg	1952	Euro	6
Malta	2004	Lira	5
The Netherlands	1952	Euro	27
Poland	2004	Zloty	54
Portugal	1986	Euro	24
Romania	2007	Leu	35
Slovakia	2004	Koruna	14
Slovenia	2004	Euro	7
Spain	1986	Euro	54
Sweden	1995	Krona	19
United Kingdom	1973	Pound	78

Drawing Conclusions What are the most powerful countries in the European Parliament?

go.hrw.com KEYWORD: SK9 CH19

European Cooperation

Many changes shaped postwar Europe. One of the most important of those changes was the creation of an organization that now joins together most of the countries of Europe.

A European Community

Two world wars tore Europe apart in the 1900s. After World War II many of Europe's leaders began to look for ways to prevent another deadly war. Some people believed that creating a feeling of community in Europe would make countries less likely to go to war. Leaders like Great Britain's Winston Churchill believed the countries of Europe should cooperate rather than compete. They believed strong economic and political ties were the key.

Six countries—Belgium, France, Italy, Luxembourg, the Netherlands, and West Germany—took the first steps toward European unity. In the early 1950s these six countries joined to create a united economic community. The organization's goal was to form a **common market**, a group of nations that cooperates to make trade among members easier. This European common market, created in 1957, made trade easier among member countries. Over time, other nations joined. Europeans had begun to create a new sense of unity.

The European Union

Since its beginning in the 1950s, many new nations have become members of this European community, now known as the European Union. The **European Union (EU)** is an organization that promotes political and economic cooperation in Europe. Today the European Union has more than 25 members. Together, they deal with a wide range of issues, including trade, the environment, and migration.

The European Union has executive, legislative, and judicial branches. The EU is run by a commission made up of one representative from each member nation. Two legislative groups, the Council of the European Union and the European Parliament, debate and make laws. Finally, the Court of Justice resolves disputes and enforces EU laws.

Through the European Union, the countries of Europe work together toward common economic goals. The EU helps its member nations compete with economic powers like the United States and Japan. In 1999 the EU introduced a common currency, the euro, which many member countries now use. The euro has made trade much easier.

The European Union has helped unify Europe. In recent years many countries from Eastern Europe have joined the EU. Other countries hope to join in the future. Despite difficulties, EU leaders hope to continue their goal to bring the nations of Europe closer together.

READING CHECK **Finding Main Ideas** How has cooperation in Europe affected the region?

In 2005 French and Dutch voters rejected a proposed constitution for the European Union. Here, voters in France demand that their vote be upheld.

SUMMARY AND PREVIEW In this section you learned how the European Union helped unify much of Europe after years of division during the Cold War. In the next chapter, you will learn about Southern Europe's physical geography and culture.

Section 7 Assessment

Reviewing Ideas, Terms, and Places

1. a. **Recall** What was the **Cold War**?
   b. **Analyze** Why was Europe divided during the Cold War?
2. a. **Identify** What new countries were formed after the end of the Cold War?
   b. **Compare and Contrast** How were ethnic tensions in Czechoslovakia and Yugoslavia similar and different?
   c. **Evaluate** Do you think the end of the Cold War helped or hurt the nations of Eastern Europe?
3. a. **Define** What is a **common market**?
   b. **Make Inferences** Why did some Europeans believe stronger economic and political ties could prevent war in Europe?

Critical Thinking

4. **Summarizing** Use your notes and the chart below to summarize the effect that each event had on the different regions of Europe. Write a sentence that summarizes the effect of each event.

	Cold War	End of Cold War	European Union
Western Europe			
Eastern Europe			

FOCUS ON WRITING

5. **Thinking about Europe since 1945** You are now in your mid-80s. How might events during and after the Cold War have affected your life?

Interpreting Political Cartoons

Learn

Political cartoons are drawings that express views on important political or social issues. The ability to interpret political cartoons will help you understand issues and people's attitudes about them.

Political cartoons use images and words to convey a message about a particular event, person, or issue in the news. Most political cartoons use symbols to represent those ideas. For example, political cartoonists often use Uncle Sam to represent the United States. They also use titles and captions to express their point of view.

Practice

Examine the cartoon on this page. Then, answer the following questions to interpret the message of the cartoon.

1 Read any title, labels, or captions to identify the subject of the cartoon. What information does the caption for this cartoon give you? To what event does this cartoon refer?

2 Identify the people and symbols in the cartoon. What person is pictured in this cartoon? What does the crushed hammer and sickle represent?

3 What message is the cartoonist trying to convey?

Soviet leader Mikhail Gorbachev examines a broken hammer and sickle.

Apply

Use your new skills to interpret a recent political cartoon. Locate a political cartoon that deals with an issue or event that has been in the news recently. Then answer the questions below.

1. What issue or event does the cartoon address?

2. What people or symbols are represented in the cartoon?

3. What point is the cartoon attempting to make?

Geography's Impact
video series
Review the video to answer the closing question:
Why do you think the creation of the European Union was important to many Europeans?

Visual Summary

Use the visual summary below to help you review the main ideas of the chapter.

QUICK FACTS

During the Middle Ages most people lived on manors or in villages rather than cities.

The Enlightenment led to the end of monarchies in Europe.

After years of division, the end of the Cold War finally reunited the nations of Europe.

Reviewing Vocabulary, Terms, and Places

Match the words or names with their definitions or descriptions.

1. humanism
2. capitalism
3. dictator
4. nationalism
5. strategy
6. feudal system

a. a powerful ruler that rules by force
b. a system of exchanging land for military service
c. a plan for fighting a battle or war
d. economic system in which individuals own most businesses
e. devotion and loyalty to one's country
f. a philosophy that emphasized the abilities of human beings

Comprehension and Critical Thinking

SECTION 1 *(Pages 618–625)*

7. a. Describe What were two changes that affected Europe in the late Middle Ages?

b. Explain What duties did knights have under the feudal system?

SECTION 2 *(Pages 628–633)*

8. a. Define What was the Reformation?

b. Summarize How did the Renaissance affect art, literature, and science?

SECTION 3 *(Pages 634-640)*

9. a. Compare What ideas did John Locke and Jean-Jacques Rousseau share?

b. Elaborate How did the English Bill of Rights and the Declaration of the Rights of Man and of the Citizen change the power of monarchs?

SECTION 4 *(Pages 642–646)*

10. a. Recall In which country did the Industrial Revolution start?

b. Identify Cause and Effect How did industrial growth lead to improvements in society?

SECTION 5 *(Pages 648–652)*

11. a. Recall What causes led to the outbreak of World War I?

b. Draw Conclusions How did the U.S. entry into World War I affect the war's outcome?

SECTION 6 *(Pages 654–659)*

12. a. Identify What two alliances fought in World War II? What countries belonged to each?

b. Compare In what ways were Joseph Stalin, Benito Mussolini, and Adolf Hitler similar?

SECTION 7 *(Pages 660–665)*

13. a. Identify Into what alliances was Europe divided during the Cold War?

b. Predict Do you think that the European Union will hurt or help Europe? Explain.

Using the Internet

go.hrw.com
KEYWORD: SK9 CH19

14. Activity: Creating a Biography The Renaissance saw many advances in art and literature. Enter the activity keyword to see some artists and writers of the period. Choose one to learn more about and write a biography of his or her life. Be sure to include some information on the person's accomplishments.

FOCUS ON READING AND WRITING

Using Context Clues—Contrast *Use context clues to determine the meaning of the underlined words in the sentences below.*

15. During World War II people who aided Jews were often <u>detained</u> rather than set free.

16. Many celebrations at the end of the Cold War were <u>frenzied</u>, not calm and orderly.

Writing a Diary Entry *Use your notes and the directions below to write a diary entry.*

17. Choose the person whose journal you will write. Describe the events he or she experienced from his or her point of view. Remember to describe his or her thoughts and feelings about each event.

Social Studies Skills

Interpreting Political Cartoons *Examine the political cartoon below, then answer the questions that follow.*

18. What event does the cartoon depict?

19. What point is the artist trying to make?

Map Activity ★Interactive

20. Europe, 1989 On a separate sheet of paper, match the letters on the map with their correct labels.

Berlin	Poland	Germany
London	Moscow	Yugoslavia
Paris		

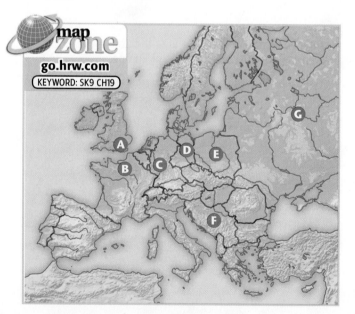

go.hrw.com
KEYWORD: SK9 CH19

Standardized Test Practice

DIRECTIONS (1-7): For each statement or question, write on a separate answer sheet the number of the word or expression that, of those given, best completes the statement or answers the question.

1 Which world leader was *most* involved in the end of the Cold War?

(1) Francis Ferdinand

(2) Joseph Stalin

(3) Mikhail Gorbachev

(4) Winston Churchill

2 Which event marked the beginning of the French Revolution?

(1) Congress of Vienna

(2) Great Fear

(3) Reign of Terror

(4) Storming of the Bastille

3 Which of the following was a result of World War II?

(1) The United Nations was formed.

(2) Adolf Hitler was charged with war crimes.

(3) A Communist revolution took place in Russia.

(4) The U.S. economy collapsed.

4 Which document limited the powers of the king of England?

(1) Black Death

(2) Crusade

(3) Feudal system

(4) Magna Carta

5 Who was the first leader of Communist Russia?

(1) Benito Mussolini

(2) Joseph Stalin

(3) Mikhail Gorbachev

(4) Vladimir Lenin

6 The period of rapid growth in machine-made goods during the 1700s and 1800s was the

(1) American Revolution.

(2) French Revolution.

(3) Industrial Revolution.

(4) Scientific Revolution.

7 Ethnic tensions at the end of the Cold War divided which of the following countries?

(1) France

(2) Germany

(3) United States

(4) Yugoslavia

Base your answer to question 8 on the graph below and on your knowledge of social studies.

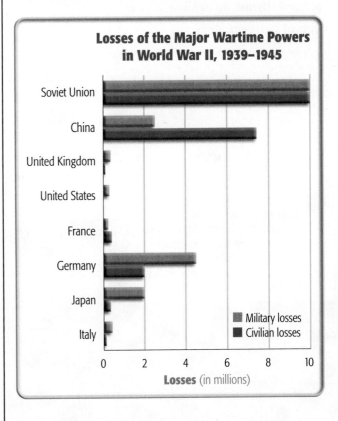

Losses of the Major Wartime Powers in World War II, 1939–1945

■ Military losses
■ Civilian losses

Losses (in millions)

8 **Constructed-Response Question** Which Allied power lost the fewest civilians during World War II? Which lost the most?

France

Geography

France is one of Europe's largest and most influential countries. Celebrated around the world for its food, art, and culture, France is also one of Europe's major economic powers. From its location in west-central Europe, France affects life in the rest of the continent and the world.

The physical features of France vary from region to region. The north and west are generally flat and low, being part of the huge Northern European Plain. Farther south, the land gets higher and more rugged. The rocky plateau known as the Massif Central covers most of south-central France. Three mountain ranges are also in the south. In the southwest, the Pyrenees form the boundary between France and Spain. To the east, the Alps and the Jura Mountains border Switzerland.

As you can see on the map on the next page, several rivers run out of these mountains. The longest of these rivers is the Loire (LWAHR), which begins in the Massif Central. Not far away is the Rhone, which runs south to the Mediterranean. Farther north, the Seine (SAYN) flows past the capital, Paris.

Paris is also by far France's largest city. It is home to about 10 million people. Fashionable and fast-paced, Paris is a center of business, finance, learning, and culture. It boasts world-class

1 The **Loire River,** the longest river in France, winds its way through the heart of the country. The Loire Valley is famous for its beautiful scenery and for the many châteaux, or castles, that line the river.

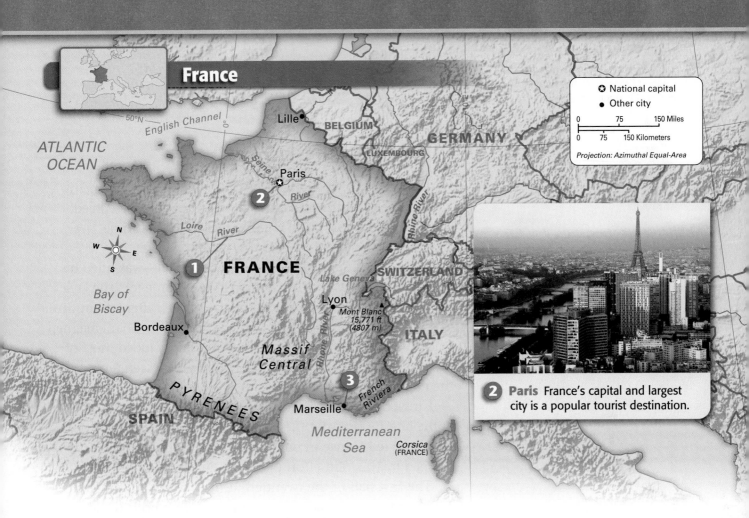

France

ATLANTIC OCEAN

English Channel

50°N

Lille

BELGIUM

GERMANY

LUXEMBOURG

Seine River

Paris

2

Loire River

Rhine River

1 FRANCE

Bay of Biscay

Lake Geneva

SWITZERLAND

Bordeaux

Lyon

Mont Blanc
15,771 ft
(4807 m)

ITALY

Rhone River

Massif Central

3

French Riviera

SPAIN

PYRENEES

Marseille

Mediterranean Sea

Corsica (FRANCE)

⊙ National capital
● Other city

0   75   150 Miles

0   75   150 Kilometers

Projection: Azimuthal Equal-Area

2 **Paris** France's capital and largest city is a popular tourist destination.

museums, art galleries, and restaurants as well as famous landmarks such as the Eiffel Tower and Notre Dame Cathedral. The city's beauty has earned it the nickname the "City of Light" and has made it one of the most visited places in the world.

Paris is not France's only large city. The second largest of France's cities is Marseille (mar-SAY), a Mediterranean seaport. Lyon (LYAWN), located on the Rhone, is a business center and has been called the culinary capital of France. A complex network of highways, canals, and trains links these and other French cities together.

Case Study Assessment

1. What are the key physical features of France?

2. What makes Paris a major world city?

3. **Activity** Plan a five-day trip to France. Identify places you would like to visit and what you would like to see. Then draw up an itinerary, or schedule, for your trip.

3 **Marseille** is a busy seaport on the southern coast of France.

800
Frankish emperor Charlemagne is crowned Emperor of the Romans after building a huge empire.

Charlemagne

1066
French duke William of Normandy invades England and becomes its king.

1337–1453
The French and English fight for control of France in the Hundred Years' War.

History and Culture

France has one of the longest histories in Europe. Cave paintings found in southwest France show the people have lived in the area for more than 15,000 years. Since that time, the French have helped shape life throughout Europe.

In ancient times, France—then called Gaul—was ruled by first the Celts and then the Romans. After Rome fell, the area that is now France was invaded by the Franks, after whom the country is named. The Franks' greatest ruler was Charlemagne, who built a powerful Christian empire that included most of Europe. France's later kings all claimed to be descendents of the mighty Charlemagne.

Kings continued to rule France until the French Revolution of the late 1700s. After the revolution, a general named Napoleon led France in building a new empire and was only stopped by the joint effort of several European countries.

The first half of the twentieth century was hard for France. The country was invaded by Germany during both world wars. However, since the 1950s France has rebounded from these invasions and has enjoyed rapid growth.

Experiencing French Culture

French culture reflects the country's long history and the people's enjoyment of life. For the most part, the French are united by a common heritage. For example, most people speak French and are Roman Catholic.

Food The French are famous worldwide for their cuisine.

Religion France's Catholic heritage is reflected in glorious cathedrals like this one in Chartres.

Guillotine from the French Revolution

1789
The French Revolution begins with the storming of the Bastille prison.

1815
Several European powers band together to defeat French emperor Napoleon.

1940–1944
During World War II, France is occupied by German forces.

WWII German occupation of France

Despite their sometimes turbulent history, the French enjoy life. They have a phrase to describe this attitude—*joie de vivre* (zhwah duh VEEV-ruh), meaning "joy of life." The French enjoy good food, good company, and good conversation. Their enjoyment of food has helped make French cooking one of the most famous styles of cooking in the world.

Throughout history, the French have also made major contributions to art. In the Middle Ages, they built the first Gothic cathedrals, such as Notre Dame in Paris. In the 1800s France was the center of the impressionist movement. This style of painting uses rippling light to create an impression of a scene. Today France is also known for its fashion and film industries.

Case Study Assessment

1. How did France change in the 1900s?

2. What is *joie de vivre,* and how is it reflected in France?

3. **Activity** Re-create a key moment from French history. Write a short skit that depicts a major event. Be sure to describe what happened and who was involved.

Fashion Paris is one of the world's leading fashion centers.

Art The style of painting known as impressionism was one of France's gifts to the art world.

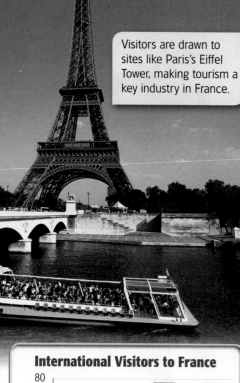

Visitors are drawn to sites like Paris's Eiffel Tower, making tourism a key industry in France.

France Today

Economics

France has a strong economy, one of the strongest in Europe. It is an active member of the European Union (EU) and benefits from trade with other EU members. For example, France is the leading agricultural producer in the EU and exports many crops to other members. Among its major crops are wheat and grapes. In addition, France is the world's leading producer and seller of wine and cheese. French wines and cheeses are admired around the world.

Another important industry in France is tourism. Statistics show that France is one of the most visited countries in the world year after year. As you read earlier, millions of tourists are drawn to the famous monuments of Paris.

In addition, people are drawn to other regions of France. Some head to the south of France to ski in the Alps or to relax at one of the beaches of the French Riviera. This resort area along the Mediterranean coast is famous for its sun and sandy beaches. The Riviera is also the site of an annual film festival in Cannes (KAHN) that attracts thousands of movie enthusiasts. Still other tourists are drawn to France's charming small towns or to the châteaux (sha-TOH), or castles, of the Loire Valley.

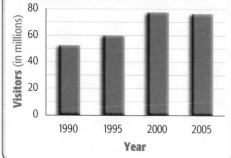

International Visitors to France

Visitors (in millions)

Source: World Tourism Organization, *Tourism Market Trends*, 2006

Government

After the French Revolution, France became one of the first countries in the world to have a republican government. Though the nature of the government has changed several times since then, France is still a republic today.

Structure of the French Government

France's government divides power among three branches. This division of power keeps any individual or group from becoming too powerful.

Executive Branch
Headed by a president and a prime minister, it enforces the country's laws.

Legislative Branch
Made up of two houses, the National Assembly and the Senate, it makes laws.

Judicial Branch
Two branches of courts hear cases and punish those who break laws.

As you can see in the diagram on the previous page, France's government is made up of three branches. By dividing power among the three branches, the French keep any one person or group of people from becoming too powerful.

The first branch of France's government is the executive branch, which is responsible for enforcing the country's laws. It is headed by a president, who is elected every five years, and a prime minister, who is appointed by the president. The second branch, the legislative branch, is made up of two parts. They are the National Assembly and the Senate, and they work together to make laws. The third branch, the judicial branch, includes several types of courts.

Issues

On the whole, France is a prosperous country with a strong economy. However, the country is not without its challenges. For example, French officials do not think that the economy is as strong as it could be. They blame this lack of strength on France's short work week.

In most industrialized countries, people work 40 hours each week. In France, though, most people work only 35 hours each week. Efforts by some officials to lengthen the French work week have led to protests and strikes. Such strikes have periodically shut down major industries in France.

France has also faced cultural challenges. Since the early 1900s, many residents of former French colonies have left their homes to settle in France. This influx of immigrants put strains on France's resources. In addition, some officials feared that France would lose its unique culture if too many immigrants arrived. They took steps to limit immigration, which has increased some people's resentment of the government.

Angry French workers protest a government plan to extend their work week. Most French people now work 35 hours a week.

Case Study Assessment

1. What does each branch of France's government do?

2. What are France's major industries?

3. **Activity** What do you think is the most serious issue facing France? Create a poster describing the issue and suggesting a possible solution.

European Unity

Part A: Short-Answer Questions

Directions: Read and examine the following documents. Then, on a separate sheet of paper, answer the questions using complete sentences.

DOCUMENT 1

The Maastricht Treaty was signed on February 7, 1992. Its official name was the Treaty on European Union, and it led to the creation of the European Union (EU). A portion of the treaty outlining the objectives of the EU appears below.

> The Union shall set itself the following objectives:
>
> - to promote economic and social progress which is balanced and sustainable, in particular through the creation of an area without internal frontiers, through the strengthening of economic and social cohesion and through the establishment of economic and monetary union, ultimately including a single currency . . .
>
> - to assert its identity on the international scene, in particular through the implementation of a common foreign and security policy . . .
>
> - to strengthen the protection of the rights and interests of the nationals [residents] of its Member States . . .
>
> - to develop close cooperation on justice and home affairs . . .

1a. What steps does the treaty say the EU will take to promote economic and social progress?

_____

1b. What other goals does the EU have?

_____

DOCUMENT 2

The EU is hard to describe. It is not a federation, or loose association of states, but it is also not a unified country. The following passage from the Central Intelligence Agency (CIA) discusses the difficulty of categorizing the EU.

> Although the EU is not a federation in the strict sense, it is far more than a free-trade association such as ASEAN, NAFTA, or Mercosur, and it has many of the attributes associated with independent nations: its own flag, anthem, founding date, and currency, as well as an incipient common foreign and security policy in its dealings with other nations.
>
> In the future, many of these nation-like characteristics are likely to be expanded.
>
> —*The World Factbook,* 2008

2a. What attributes does the EU share with independent nations?

_____

2b. According to this document, how will the EU change in the future?

_____

DOCUMENT 3

People around the world have watched the progress of the European Union. The political cartoon below appeared in a newspaper in Dubai, part of the United Arab Emirates in the Middle East.

3a. According to this cartoon, what goal are members of the EU working toward?

_____

3b. What does the cartoonist suggest about their chances of reaching this goal?

_____

DOCUMENT 4

The nation of Turkey, which is located partially in Europe and partially in Asia, has been trying to join Europe's union since 1987. The passage below, from the Library of Congress Country Studies series, explains why Turkey's application has not so far been accepted.

> The principal economic objections to Turkish membership center on the relative underdevelopment of Turkey's economy compared to the economies of EC/EU members and Turkey's high rate of population growth . . . The political obstacles to EU membership concern Turkey's domestic and foreign policies. Because the European body prides itself on being an association of democracies, the 1980 military coup—in a country enjoying associate status—was a severe shock . . . In terms of foreign policy, the main obstacle to EU membership remains the unresolved issues between Turkey and EU member Greece.

4a. What economic obstacles stand between Turkey and EU membership?

_____

4b. What political challenges have kept Turkey out of the EU?

_____

Part B: Essay

Historical Context: Created in 1992, the European Union has brought many countries in Europe together politically, economically, and culturally. Membership in the EU has exploded, and new countries apply nearly every year.

TASK: Using information from the four documents and your knowledge of social studies, write an essay in which you:

- examine the purpose for the creation of the EU.
- explain why countries want to belong to the EU.

A Biographical Narrative

Assignment

Write a biographical narrative about a significant event in the life of a historical figure such as Joan of Arc, Martin Luther, Napoleon, or Mikhail Gorbachev.

People have shaped the world. Who are the important people in history? What were the critical events in their lives? How did geography or location affect those events? These are questions we ask as we try to understand our world.

1. Prewrite

Choose a Topic

- Choose a person who affected European or Russian history in some way.
- Choose a specific event or incident in the person's life. For example, you might choose Napoleon at the Battle of Waterloo.

> **TIP** To choose the event, think about the person's importance or signficance. Choose an event that will help you make that point.

Gather and Organize Information

- Look for information about your topic in the library or on the Internet. Book-length biographies about the person are a good source.
- Identify the parts of the event. Organize them in chonological, or time, order. Note details about people, actions, and the location of the event.

2. Write

Use a Writer's Framework

A Writer's Framework

Introduction
- Introduce the person and the event.
- Identify the importance of the event.

Body
- Write at least one paragraph for each major part of the event. Include specific details.
- Use chronological, or time, order to organize the parts of the event.

Conclusion
- Summarize the importance of the person and event in the final paragraph.

3. Evaluate and Revise

Review and Improve Your Paper

- Read your first draft at least twice, and then use the questions below to evaluate your paper.
- Make the changes needed to improve your paper.

Evaluation Questions for a Biographical Narrative

1. Do you introduce the person and event and identify the importance of each?
2. Do you have one paragraph for each major part of the event?
3. Do you include specific details about people, actions, and location?
4. Do you use chronological order, the order in time, to organize the parts of the event?
5. Do you end the paper with a summary of the importance of the person and event?

4. Proofread and Publish

Give Your Explanation the Finishing Touch

- Make sure your transitional phrases—such as then, next, later, or finally—help clarify the order of the actions that took place.
- Make sure you capitalized all proper names.
- You can share your biographical narrative by reading it aloud in class or adding it to a class collection of biographies.

5. Practice and Apply

Use the steps and strategies outlined in this workshop to write your biographical narrative. Share your work with others, comparing and contrasting the importance of the people and events.

References

Understanding Comparison-Contrast

FOCUS ON READING

Comparing shows how things are alike. Contrasting shows how things are different. You can understand comparison-contrast by learning to recognize clue words and points of comparison. Clue words let you know whether to look for similarities or differences. Points of comparison are the main topics that are being compared or contrasted. Notice how the passage below compares and contrasts different regions of Southern Africa.

> Southern Africa's climates vary from east to west. The wettest place in the region is the east coast of the island of Madagascar . . .
>
> In contrast to the eastern part of the continent, the west is very dry. From the Atlantic coast, deserts give way to plains with semiarid and steppe climates.
>
> *From Section 5, Southern Africa*

Highlighted words are points of comparison.

Underlined words are clue words.

Clue Words	
Comparison	**Contrast**
share, similar, like, also, both, in addition, besides	however, while, unlike, different, but, although

YOU TRY IT!

Read the following passage about the Namib and Kalahari deserts. Use a diagram like the one here to compare and contrast the two countries.

> The driest place in the region is the Namib Desert on the Atlantic coast . . . Another desert, the Kalahari, occupies most of Botswana. Although this desert gets enough rain in the north to support grasses and trees, its sandy plains are mostly covered with scattered shrubs.
>
> *From Section 5, Southern Africa*

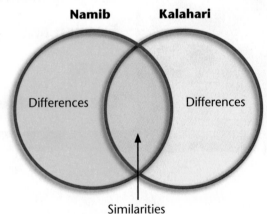

Namib   Kalahari

Differences   Differences

Similarities

Categorizing

FOCUS ON READING

When you sort things into groups of similar items, you are categorizing. Think of folding laundry. First you might sort into different piles: towels, socks, and T-shirts. The piles—or categories—help you manage the laundry because towels go to a different place than socks. When you read, categorizing helps you to manage the information by identifying the main types, or groups, of information. Then you can more easily see the individual facts and details in each group. Notice how the information in the paragraph below has been sorted into three main groups.

The subjects of Egyptian paintings vary widely. Some of the paintings show important historical events, such as the crowning of a new king or the founding of a temple. Others show major religious rituals. Still other paintings show scenes from everyday life, such as farming or hunting.

From Section 4, Egyptian Achievements

Subjects of Egyptian Paintings		
Category 1: Important historical events	**Category 2:** Major religious rituals	**Category 3:** Everyday life

YOU TRY IT!

Read the following sentences. Then use a graphic organizer like the one above to categorize the natural barriers in ancient Egypt. Create as many categories as you need.

In addition to a stable food supply, Egypt's location offered another advantage. It had natural barriers, which made it hard to invade Egypt. To the west, the desert was too big and harsh to cross. To the north, the Mediterranean Sea kept many enemies away. To the east, more desert and the Red Sea provided protection. Finally, to the south, cataracts in the Nile made it difficult for invaders to sail into Egypt that way.

From Section 1, Early Egypt

READING SOCIAL STUDIES

Understanding Cause and Effect

FOCUS ON READING

To understand a country's history, you should look for cause and effect chains. A cause makes something happen, and an effect is what happens as a result of a cause. The effect can then become a cause and create another effect. Notice how the events below create a cause-and-effect chain.

> As the trade in gold and salt increased, Ghana's rulers gained power. Over time, their military strength grew as well. With their armies they began to take control of this trade from the merchants who had once controlled it. Merchants from the north and south met to exchange goods in Ghana. As a result of their control of trade routes, the rulers of Ghana became wealthy.
>
> *From Section 3, Empire of Ghana*

| **First Cause**
Increase in gold and salt trade | → | **Effect**
Ghana's rulers became powerful | → | **Effect**
More military strength | → | **Effect**
Took control of trade routes | → |

YOU TRY IT!

Read the following sentences, and then use a graphic organizer like the one above to analyze causes and effects. Create as many boxes as you need to list the causes and effects.

> When Mansa Musa died, his son Maghan took the throne. Maghan was a weak ruler. When raiders from the southeast poured into Mali, he couldn't stop them. The raiders set fire to Timbuktu's great schools and mosques. Mali never fully recovered from this terrible blow. The empire continued to weaken and decline.
>
> *From Section 4, Mali and Songhai*

Identifying Supporting Details

FOCUS ON READING

Why believe what you read? One reason is because of details that support or prove the main idea. These details might be facts, statistics, examples, or definitions. In the example below, notice what kind of proof or supporting details help you believe the main idea.

> Under apartheid, only white South Africans could vote or hold political office. Blacks, who made up nearly 75 percent of the population, were not citizens. They could only work certain jobs and made very little money. They were only allowed to live in certain areas.
>
> *From Section 5, Africa since Independence*

Main Idea
Apartheid gave more rights to whites than to blacks.

Supporting Details			
Example	**Statistic**	**Fact**	**Fact**
Whites could vote and hold political office.	Blacks made up 75 percent of the population but were not citizens.	Blacks could only have certain jobs.	They had to live in certain areas.

YOU TRY IT!

Read the following sentences, and then use a graphic organizer like the one above to identify the supporting details.

> The European slave trade in Africa had devastating consequences. It led to a drastic decrease in Africa's population. Millions of young African men were forced to move away from their homes to lands far away, and thousands of them died. Historians estimate that 15 to 20 million African slaves were shipped to the Americas against their will.
>
> *From Section 2, European Colonization*

Understanding Fact and Opinion

FOCUS ON READING

When you read, it is important to distinguish facts from opinions. A fact is a statement that can be proved or disproved. An opinion is a personal belief or attitude, so it cannot be proved true or false. When you are reading a social studies text, you want to read only facts, not the author's opinions. To determine whether a sentence is a fact or an opinion, ask if it can be proved using outside sources. If it can, the sentence is a fact. The following pairs of statements show the difference between facts and opinions.

Fact: The Huang He often floods, causing millions of dollars worth of damage. *(This fact can be proved through research.)*

Opinion: I believe the Huang He should be dammed to prevent flooding. *(The word* believe *signifies that this is the writer's judgment, or opinion.)*

Fact: At 3,776 meters, the peak of Mount Fuji is the highest point in Japan. *(The elevation of Mount Fuji can be checked for accuracy.)*

Opinion: Mount Fuji is a beautiful mountain that everyone should visit. *(No one can prove that Fuji is beautiful, because it is a matter of personal taste.)*

Read the statement.

↓

Ask whether it can be proved or disproved.

If the answer is yes, the statement is a fact.

If the answer is no, the statement is an opinion.

YOU TRY IT!

Read the following sentences and identify each as a fact or an opinion.

1. The Ganges River is sacred to many Hindus.

2. Millions of people visit the Ganges each year to bathe in its waters.

3. China's mountains are the world's most majestic.

4. China and India have some of the world's tallest mountains.

5. Many houses in Southeast Asia are built on stilts in case of floods.

6. The raised houses of Southeast Asia are fascinating.

Sequencing

FOCUS ON READING

Have you ever used written instructions to put together an item you bought? If so, you know that the steps in the directions need to be followed in order. The instructions probably included words like *first, next,* and *then* to help you figure out what order you needed to do the steps in. The same kinds of words can help you when you read a history book. Words such as *first, then, later, next,* and *finally* can help you figure out the sequence, or order, in which events occurred. Read the passage below, noting the underlined clue words. Notice how they indicate the order of the events listed in the sequence chain at right.

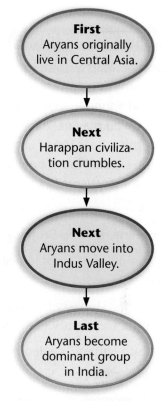

> Not long <u>after</u> the Harappan civilization crumbled, a new group arrived in the Indus Valley. These people were called the Aryans. They were <u>originally</u> from the area around the Caspian Sea in Central Asia. <u>Over time,</u> however, they became the dominant group in India.
>
> *From Section 1, Early Indian Civilizations*

YOU TRY IT!

Read the following passage. Look for clue words to help you figure out the order of the events described in it. Then make a sequence chain like the one above to show that order.

> For many years, Asoka watched his armies fight bloody battles against other peoples. A few years into his rule, however, Asoka converted to Buddhism. When he did, he swore that he would not launch any more wars of conquest. After converting to Buddhism, Asoka had the time and resources to improve the lives of his people.
>
> *From Section 4, Indian Empires*

Understanding Chronological Order

FOCUS ON READING

When you read a paragraph in a history text, you can usually use clue words to help you keep track of the order of events. When you read a longer section of text that includes many paragraphs, though, you may need more clues. One of the best clues you can use in this case is dates. Each of the sentences below includes at least one date. Notice how those dates were used to create a time line that lists events in chronological, or time, order.

> As early as 7000 BC people had begun to farm in China.
>
> After 3000 BC people began to use potter's wheels to make many types of pottery.
>
> The first dynasty for which we have clear evidence is the Shang, which was firmly established by the 1500s BC.
>
> Shang emperors ruled in China until the 1100s BC.
>
> *From Section 1, Early China*

7000 BC
People begin
farming in China.

3000 BC
People begin using
potter's wheels.

1500s BC
Shang dynasty
rules China.

5000 BC

YOU TRY IT!

Read the following sentences. Use the dates in the sentences to create a time line listing events in chronological order.

> The Ming dynasty that he founded ruled China from 1368 to 1644.
>
> Genghis Khan led his armies into northern China in 1211.
>
> Between 1405 and 1433, Zheng He led seven grand voyages to places around Asia.
>
> In the 1300s many Chinese groups rebelled against the Yuan dynasty.
>
> *From Section 5, The Yuan and Ming Dynasties*

Using Context Clues—Definitions

FOCUS ON READING

One way to figure out the meaning of an unfamiliar word or term is by finding clues in its context, the words or sentences surrounding the word or term. A common context clue is a restatement. Restatements are simply a definition of the new word using ordinary words you already know. Notice how the following passage uses a restatement to define civil disobedience. Some context clues are not as complete or obvious. Notice how the following passage provides a description that is a partial definition of persistence.

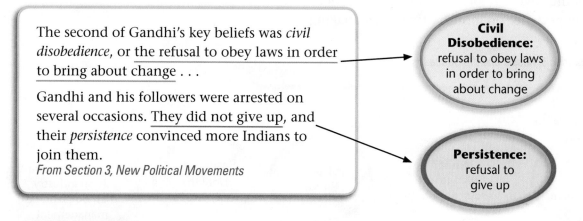

The second of Gandhi's key beliefs was *civil disobedience*, or the refusal to obey laws in order to bring about change . . .

Gandhi and his followers were arrested on several occasions. They did not give up, and their *persistence* convinced more Indians to join them.
From Section 3, New Political Movements

Civil Disobedience: refusal to obey laws in order to bring about change

Persistence: refusal to give up

YOU TRY IT!

Read the following passages and identify the meaning of the italicized words by using definitions, or restatements, in context.

Japan's trade has been so successful that the country has built up a huge trade surplus. A ***trade surplus*** exists when a country exports more goods than it imports.

From Section 5, A New Asia

India had been the birthplace of two major religions, Hinduism and Buddhism. Over several centuries, Indian *missionaries* carried both religions far and wide.

From Section 1, Contact Across Cultures

Asking Questions

FOCUS ON READING

Reading is one place where asking questions will never get you in trouble. The five W questions – who, what, when, where, and why – can help you be sure you understand the material you read. After you read a section, ask yourself the 5 Ws: **Who** was this section about? **What** did they do? **When** and **where** did they live? **Why** did they do what they did? See the example below to learn how this reading strategy can help you identify the main points of a passage.

> The region's natural resources have been poorly managed, however. Until the early 1990s this region was part of the Soviet Union. The Soviet government put more importance on industry than on managing its resources.
>
> *From Section 5, Russia and the Caucasus*

The 5 Ws

Who? Soviet government

What? Managed resources poorly

Where? Russia

When? Until the early 1900s

Why? Put more emphasis on industry than on resource management

YOU TRY IT!

Read the following passage and answer the 5 Ws to check your understanding of it.

> Another valuable natural resource is found in the breathtaking beauty of the Alps. Each year, tourists flock to the Alps to enjoy the scenery and to hike and ski.
>
> *From Section 1, Southern Europe*

Re-reading

FOCUS ON READING

Have you ever hit the rewind button on the VCR or DVD player because you missed an important scene or didn't quite catch what a character said? As you rewound, you probably asked yourself such questions as, "What did he say?" or "How did she do that?" Taking a second look helped you understand what was going on.

The same idea is true for reading. When you re-read a passage, you can catch details you didn't catch the first time. As you re-read, go slowly and check your understanding by asking yourself questions. In the example below, notice the questions the reader asked. Then see how the questions were answered by re-reading the passage.

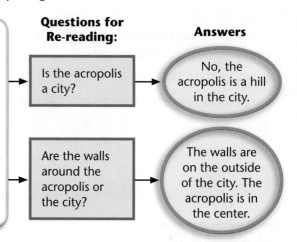

In the center of most city-states was a fortress on a hill. This hill was called the acropolis, which is Greek for "top city." In addition to the fortress, many city-states built temples and other public buildings on the acropolis. Around the acropolis was the rest of the city, including houses and markets. High walls usually surrounded the city for protection.

From Section 1, Ancient Greece

Questions for Re-reading:

Is the acropolis a city?

Are the walls around the acropolis or the city?

Answers

No, the acropolis is a hill in the city.

The walls are on the outside of the city. The acropolis is in the center.

YOU TRY IT!

Read the following passage, and then develop two questions you can answer as you re-read the passage. Write down the questions and the answers.

As emperor, Octavian was given a new name, Augustus, which means "honored one." The people of Rome respected and admired Augustus. This respect was mainly the result of his many accomplishments. As the map above shows, Augustus added a great deal of territory to the empire. He also made many improvements to lands already in the empire. For example, he built monuments and public buildings in the city of Rome. He also improved and expanded Rome's network of roads, which facilitated both travel and trade.

Using Context Clues—Contrast

READING SOCIAL STUDIES

FOCUS ON READING

Maybe you played this game as a young child: "Which of these things is not like the others?" This same game can help you understand new words as you read. Sometimes the words or sentences around a new word will show contrast, or how the word is not like something else. These contrast clues can help you figure out the new word's meaning. Look at how the following passage indicates that *persevered* means something different from *give in*.

> The German air force repeatedly attacked British cities and military targets. Hitler hoped the British would surrender. Rather than give in, however, the British *persevered*.
>
> *From Section 6, World War II*

Contrast Clues:

1. Look for words or sentences that signal contrast.
Words that signal contrast include *however, rather than, instead of,* and *not.* In this paragraph, the words *rather than* signal the contrast clues for the unfamiliar word *persevered.*

2. Check the definition by substituting a word or phrase that fits.
Persevere likely means to keep on trying. *Rather than give in, however, the British kept on trying.*

YOU TRY IT!

Read the following paragraph, and then use the steps listed above to develop a definition for the word *compete*.

> Some people believed that creating a feeling of community in Europe would make countries less likely to go to war. Leaders like Great Britain's Winston Churchill believed the countries of Europe should cooperate rather than *compete*.
>
> *From Section 7, Europe since 1945*

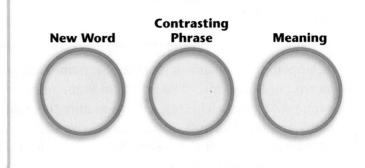

New Word   Contrasting Phrase   Meaning

Economics Handbook

What Is Economics?

Economics may sound dull, but it touches almost every part of your life. Here are some examples of the kinds of economic choices you may have made yourself:

- Which pair of shoes to buy—the ones on sale or the ones you really like, which cost much more
- Whether to continue saving your money for the DVD player you want or use some of it now to go to a movie
- Whether to give some money to a fundraiser for a new park or to housing for the homeless

As these examples show, we can think of economics as a study of choices. These choices are the ones people make to satisfy their needs or their desires.

Glossary of Economic Terms

Here are some of the words we use to talk about economics:

ECONOMIC SYSTEMS

Countries have developed different economic systems to help them make choices, such as what goods and services to produce, how to produce them, and for whom to produce them. The most common economic systems in the world are market economies and mixed economies.

capitalism See market economy.

command economy an economic system in which the central government makes all economic decisions, such as in the countries of Cuba and North Korea

communism a political system in which the government owns all property and runs a command economy

free enterprise a system in which businesses operate with little government involvement, such as in a country with a market economy

market economy an economic system based on private ownership, free trade, and competition; the government has little to say about what, how, or for whom goods and services are produced; examples include Germany and the United States

mixed economy an economy that is a combination of command, market, and traditional economies

traditional economy an economy in which production is based on customs and tradition, and in which people often grow their own food, make their own goods, and use barter to trade

THE ECONOMY AND MONEY

People, businesses, and countries obtain the items they need and want through economic activities such as producing, selling, and buying goods or services. Countries differ in the amount of economic activity that they have and in the strength of their economies.

consumer a person who buys goods or services for personal use

consumer good a finished product sold to consumers for personal or home use

corporation a business in which a group of owners share in the profits and losses

currency paper or coins that a country uses for its money supply

demand the amount of goods and services that consumers are willing and able to buy at a given time

depression a severe drop in overall business activity over a long period of time

developed countries countries with strong economies and a high quality of life; often have high per capita GDPs and high levels of industrialization and technology

developing countries countries with less productive economies and a lower quality of life; often have less industrialization and technology

economic development the level of a country's economic activity, growth, and quality of life

economy the structure of economic life in a country

goods objects or materials that humans can purchase to satisfy their wants and needs

gross domestic product (GDP) total market value of all goods and services produced in a country in a given year; *per capita GDP* is the average value of goods and services produced per person in a country in a given year

industrialization the process of using machinery for all major forms of production

inflation an increase in overall prices

investment the purchase of something with the expectation that it will gain in value; usually property, stocks, etc.

money any item, usually coins or paper currency, that is used in payment for goods or services

producer a person or group that makes goods or provides services to satisfy consumers' wants and needs

productivity the amount of goods or services that a worker or workers can produce within a given amount of time

profit the gain or excess made by selling goods or services over their costs

purchasing power the amount of income that people have available to spend on goods and services

services any activities that are performed for a fee

standard of living how well people are living; determined by the amount of goods and services they can afford

stock a share of ownership in a corporation

supply the amount of goods and services that are available at a given time

INTERNATIONAL TRADE

Countries trade with each other to obtain resources, goods, and services. Growing global trade has helped lead to the development of a global economy.

balance of trade the difference between the value of a country's exports and imports

barter the exchange of one good or service for another

black market the illegal buying and selling of goods, often at high prices

comparative advantage the ability of a company or country to produce something at a lower cost than other companies or countries

competition rivalry between businesses selling similar goods or services; a condition that often leads to lower prices or improved products

e-commerce the electronic trading of goods and services, such as over the Internet

exports goods or services that a country sells and sends to other countries

free trade trade among nations that is not affected by financial or legal barriers; trade without barriers

imports goods or services that a country brings in or purchases from another country

interdependence a relationship between countries in which they rely on one another for resources, goods, or services

market the trade of goods and services

market clearing price the price of a good or service at which supply equals demand

one-crop economy an economy that is dominated by the production of a single product

opportunity cost the value of the next-best alternative that is sacrificed when choosing to consume or produce another good or service

scarcity a condition of limited resources and unlimited wants by people

specialization a focus on only one or two aspects of production in order to produce a product more quickly and cheaply; for example, one worker washes the wheels of the car, another cleans the interior, and another washes the body

trade barriers financial or legal limitations to trade; prevention of free trade

trade-offs the goods or services sacrificed in order to consume or produce another good or service

underground economy illegal economic activities and unreported legal economic activities

PERSONAL ECONOMICS

Individuals make personal choices in how they manage and use their money to satisfy their needs and desires. Individuals have the choice to spend, save, or invest their money.

budget a plan listing the expenses and income of an individual or organization

credit a system that allows consumers to pay for goods and services over time

debt an amount of money that is owed

financial institutions businesses that keep and invest people's money and loan money to people; include banks or credit unions

income a gain of money that comes typically from labor or capital

interest the money that a borrower pays to a lender in return for a loan

loan money given on the condition that it will be paid back, often with interest

savings money or income that is not used to purchase goods or services

tax a required payment to a local, state, or national government; different kinds of taxes include sales taxes, income taxes, and property taxes

wage the payment a worker receives for his or her labor

RESOURCES

People and businesses need resources—such as land, labor, and money—to produce goods and services.

capital generally refers to wealth, in particular wealth that can be used to finance the production of goods or services

human capital sometimes used to refer to human skills and education that affect the production of goods and services in a company or country

labor force all people who are legally old enough to work and are either working or looking for work

natural resource any material in nature that people use and value

nonrenewable resource a resource that cannot be replaced naturally, such as coal or petroleum

raw material a natural resource used to make a product or good

renewable resource a resource that Earth replaces naturally, such as water, soil, and trees

ORGANIZATIONS

Countries have formed many organizations to promote economic cooperation, growth, and trade. These organizations are important in today's global economy.

European Union (EU) an organization that promotes political and economic cooperation in Europe

International Monetary Fund (IMF) a UN agency that promotes cooperation in international trade and that works to maintain stability in the exchange of countries' currencies

Organization of Economic Cooperation and Development (OECD) an organization of countries that promotes democracy and market economies

United Nations (UN) an organization of countries that promotes peace and security around the globe

World Bank a UN agency that provides loans to countries for development and recovery

World Trade Organization (WTO) an international organization dealing with trade between nations

Economic Handbook Review

Reviewing Vocabulary and Terms

On a separate sheet of paper, fill in the blanks in the following sentences:

ECONOMIC SYSTEMS

1. **A.** Businesses are able to operate with little government involvement in a _____ system.
   B. In a _____, a central government makes all economic decisions.
   C. _____ is a political system in which the government owns all property and runs a command economy.
   D. Economies that combine parts of command, market, or traditional economies are called _____.
   E. _____ is another name for a market economy, which is based on private ownership, free trade, and competition.

THE ECONOMY AND MONEY

2. **A.** _____ are objects or materials that people can buy to satisfy their needs and wants.
   B. A _____ is any activity that is performed for a fee.
   C. A person who buys goods or services is a _____, and a person or group that makes goods or provides services is a _____.
   D. The amount of goods and services that consumers are willing and able to buy at any given time is known as _____.
   E. The total value of all the goods and services produced in the United States in one year is its _____.

INTERNATIONAL TRADE

3. A. If we have an unlimited demand for a natural resource, such as oil, and there is only so much oil in the ground, we have a condition called _____.

B. Goods or services that a country sells to other countries are _____.

C. Rivalry between producers that provide the same good or service is called _____.

D. If a country is able to produce a good or service at a lower cost than other countries, it is said to have a _____.

E. Trade among nations that is not limited by legal or economic barriers is called _____.

PERSONAL ECONOMICS

4. A. A _____ is a required payment to a local, state, or national government that is used to support public services such as education, road construction, and government aid.

B. The money we do not spend on goods or services is our _____.

C. You can use _____ to pay for goods and services over time.

D. The payment that a worker receives for his or her labor is called a _____.

E. Individuals and companies use _____ to plan and manage their expenses and income.

Activities

1. With a partner, compare prices in two grocery stores. Create a chart showing the price of five items in the two stores. Also, figure the average price of the items in each store. How do you think the fact that the stores are near each other affects prices? How might prices be different if one store went out of business? How might the prices be different or similar if the United States had a command economy? Present what you have learned about prices and competition to your class.

2. With a group, choose five countries from a unit region to research. Look up the per capita GDP and the life expectancy rates for each of these countries in the regional atlas. Then use your textbook, go to your library, or use the Internet to research the literacy rate and the number of TVs per 1,000 people for each of these countries. Organize this information in a five-column chart like the one shown here. Study the information to see if you can find any patterns. Write a brief paragraph explaining what you have learned about the five countries.

Region				
Country	Per Capita GDP (U.S. $)	Life Expectancy at Birth	Literacy Rate	TVs per 1,000 People

3. Work with a partner to identify some of the many types of currency used in either Africa or Asia. Then imagine that you are the owners of a business in the United States. You have created a new product that you want to sell in the continent you selected, but people there do not use the same currency as you do. To sell your product, you will need to be able to exchange one type of currency for another. Search the Internet or look in a newspaper to find a list of currency exchange rates. For example, if your product sells for 1,000 dollars, what should the cost be in South African rand? In Indian rupees? In Chinese yuan? In Japanese yen?

RESOURCES

5. A. Diamonds and gold are examples of _____, which are any materials in nature that people use and value.

B. The _____ consists of all people who are legally able to work and are working or looking for work.

C. Wealth that can be used to finance the production of goods and services is called _____.

D. Oil is an example of a _____, which is a resource that cannot be replaced naturally.

E. Water and trees are examples of _____, resources that Earth replaces naturally.

ORGANIZATIONS

6. A. Many European countries have joined the _____ to help promote political and economic cooperation across Europe.

B. The _____ consists of many agencies that promote peace and security around the world.

C. The _____ is a UN agency that provides loans to countries to help them develop their economies.

D. The _____ is a UN agency that helps protect the stability of countries' currencies.

E. Many democratic countries promote market economies through the _____.

4. With three or four partners, create a skit that illustrates one of the following basic economic concepts: scarcity and limited resources, supply and demand, or opportunity costs and trade-offs. For example, a skit might illustrate supply and demand by showing how the high demand for the best seats at a concert increases the ticket prices for those seats. Write a script for your skit that includes an introduction stating which economic concept you are illustrating. Each member of your group must participate in the skit. Then practice the skit and perform it for the class.

5. Conduct research to find the following information for each country in the chart below: main trading partners, exports, imports, industrial products, agricultural products, and resources. Organize the information into a second chart. Then use the information in the two charts to write a one-page report explaining how international trade, specialization, and available natural resources affects each country's per capita GDP and standard of living.

THE WORLD ALMANAC Facts about Countries — Southwest and Central Asia

COUNTRY Capital	FLAG	POPULATION	AREA (sq mi)	PER CAPITA GDP (U.S. $)	LIFE EXPECTANCY AT BIRTH	TVS PER 1,000 PEOPLE
Afghanistan Kabul		29.9 million	250,001	$800	42.9	14
Iraq Baghdad		26.1 million	168,754	$3,500	68.7	82
Kazakhstan Astana		15.2 million	1,049,155	$7,800	66.6	240
Kuwait Kuwait City		2.3 million	6,880	$21,300	77.0	480
Saudi Arabia Riyadh		26.4 million	756,985	$12,000	75.5	263
United States Washington, D.C.		295.7 million	3,718,710	$40,100	77.7	844

The Physical World

Inside the Earth

Earth's interior has several different layers. Deep inside the planet is the core. The inner core is solid, and the outer core is liquid. Above the core is the mantle, which is mostly solid rock with a molten layer on top. The surface layer of Earth includes the crust, which is made up of rocks and soil. Finally, the atmosphere extends from the crust into space. It supports much of the life on Earth.

Atmosphere

Crust

Mantle

Outer Core

Inner Core

Tectonic Plates

Earth's crust is divided into huge pieces called tectonic plates, which fit together like a puzzle. As these plates slowly move, they collide and break apart, forming surface features like mountains, ocean basins, and ocean trenches.

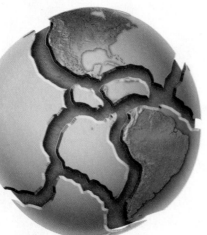

Earth Facts

Age:	4.6 billion years
Mass:	5,974,000,000,000,000,000,000 metric tons
Distance around the equator:	24,902 miles (40,067 km)
Distance around the poles:	24,860 miles (40,000 km)
Distance from the sun:	about 93 million miles (150 million km)
Earth's speed around the sun:	18.5 miles a second (29.8 km a second)
Percent of Earth's surface covered by water:	71%
What makes Earth unique:	large amounts of liquid water, tectonic activity, and life

The Continents

Geographers identify seven large landmasses, or continents, on Earth. Most of these continents are almost completely surrounded by water. Europe and Asia, however, are not. They share a long land boundary.

The world's continents are very different. For example, much of Australia is dry and rocky, while Antarctica is cold and icy. The information below highlights some key facts about each continent.

North America
- Percent of Earth's land: 16.5%
- Percent of Earth's population: 5.1%
- Lowest point: Death Valley, 282 feet (86 m) below sea level

Europe
- Percent of Earth's land: 6.7%
- Percent of Earth's population: 11.5%
- People per square mile: 187

South America
- Percent of Earth's land: 12%
- Percent of Earth's population: 8.6%
- Longest mountains: Andes, 4,500 miles (7,240 km)

Africa
- Percent of Earth's land: 20.2%
- Percent of Earth's population: 13.6%
- Longest river: Nile River, 4,160 miles (6,693 km)

Australia
- Percent of Earth's land: 5.2%
- Percent of Earth's population: 0.3%
- Oldest rocks: 3.7 billion years

Asia
- Percent of Earth's land: 30%
- Percent of Earth's population: 60.7%
- Highest point: Mount Everest, 29,035 feet (8,850 m)

Antarctica
- Percent of Earth's land: 8.9%
- Percent of Earth's population: 0%
- Coldest place: Plateau Station, -56.7°C (-70.1°F) average temperature

The Human World

World Population

More than 6 billion people live in the world today, and that number is growing quickly. Some people predict the world's population will reach 9 billion by 2050. As our population grows, it is also becoming more urban. Soon, as many people will live in cities and in towns as live in rural areas.

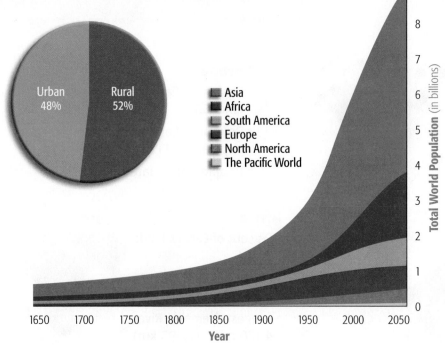

Urban 48%

Rural 52%

- Asia
- Africa
- South America
- Europe
- North America
- The Pacific World

Total World Population (in billions)

Year

1650 1700 1750 1800 1850 1900 1950 2000 2050

As the world's population grows, people are moving to already large cities such as Shanghai (above) and Hong Kong (right) in China.

Geographers divide the world into developed and less developed regions. In general, developed countries are wealthier and more urban, have lower population growth rates and higher life expectancies. As you can imagine, life is very different in developed and less developed regions.

Developed and Less Developed Countries

	Population	Rate of Natural Increase	Life Expectancy	Percent Urban	Per Capita GNI (U.S. $)
Developed Countries	1.2 billion	0.1%	77	77%	$27,790
Less Developed Countries	5.3 billion	1.5%	65	41%	$4,950
The World	6.5 billion	1.2%	67	48%	$9,190

World Religions

A large percentage of the world's people follow one of several major world religions. Christianity is the largest religion. About 33 percent of the world's people are Christian. Islam is the second-largest religion with about 20 percent. It is also the fastest-growing religion. Hinduism and Buddhism are also major world religions.

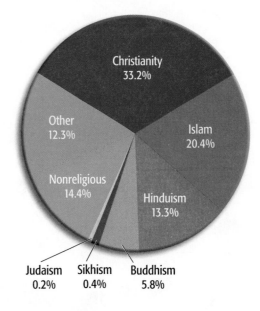

Christianity 33.2%

Islam 20.4%

Hinduism 13.3%

Nonreligious 14.4%

Other 12.3%

Judaism 0.2%   Sikhism 0.4%   Buddhism 5.8%

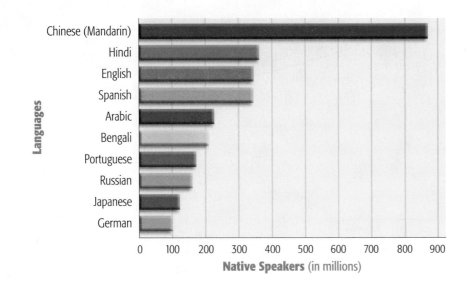

Native Speakers (in millions)

Languages: Chinese (Mandarin), Hindi, English, Spanish, Arabic, Bengali, Portuguese, Russian, Japanese, German

World Languages

Although several thousand languages are spoken today, a handful of major languages have the largest numbers of native speakers. Chinese (Mandarin) is spoken by nearly one in six people. Hindi, English, Spanish, and Arabic are next, with native speakers all over the world.

ATLAS

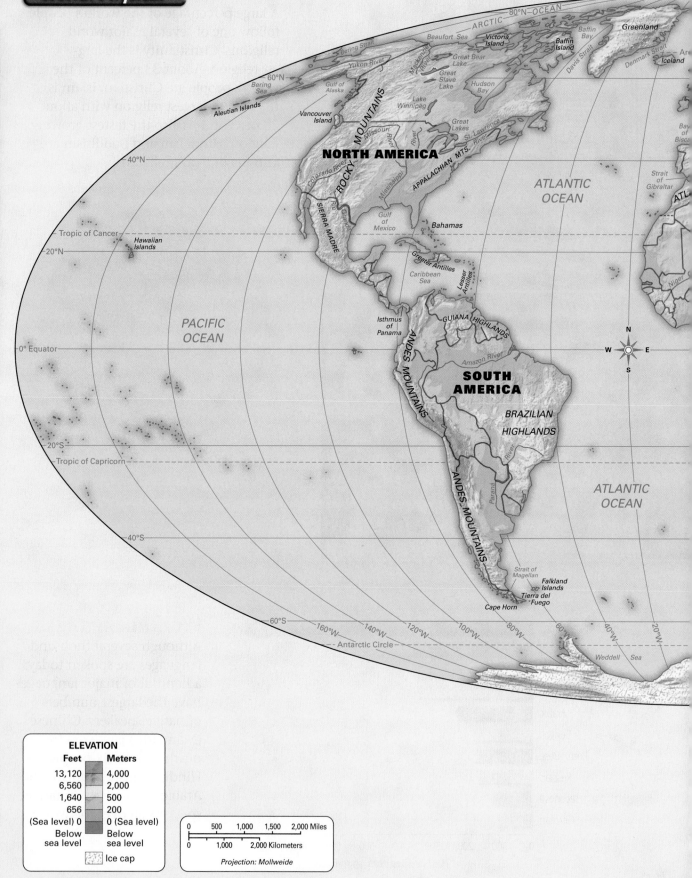

NORTH AMERICA

ATLANTIC OCEAN

PACIFIC OCEAN

SOUTH AMERICA

BRAZILIAN HIGHLANDS

ATLANTIC OCEAN

ELEVATION

Feet		Meters
13,120		4,000
6,560		2,000
1,640		500
656		200
(Sea level) 0		0 (Sea level)
Below sea level		Below sea level

Ice cap

0   500   1,000   1,500   2,000 Miles
0   1,000   2,000 Kilometers

Projection: Mollweide

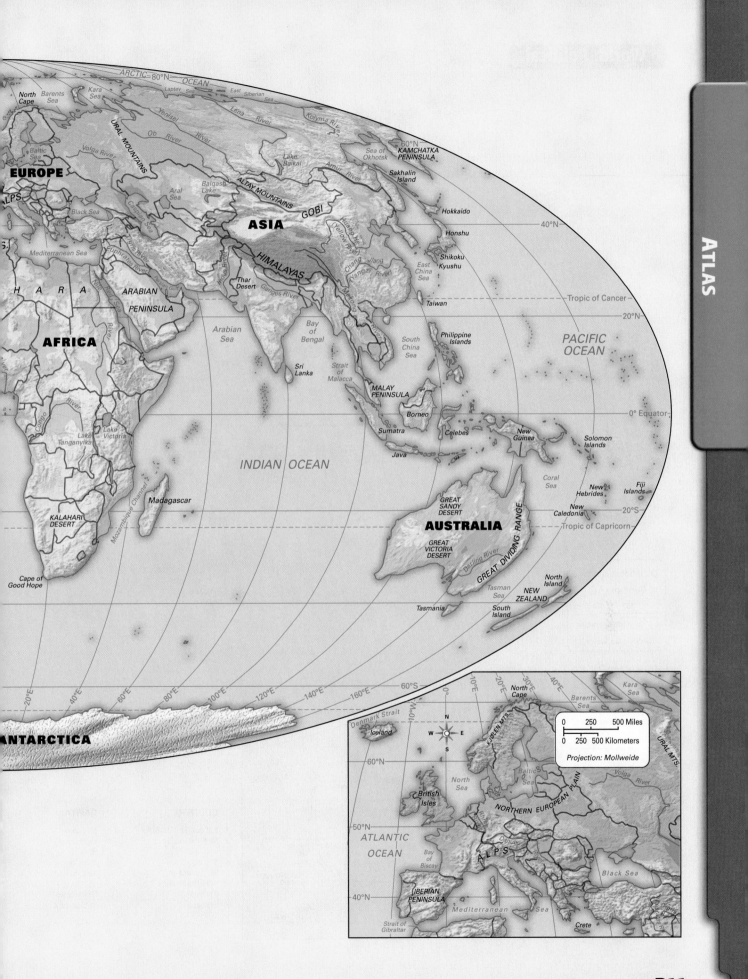

ARCTIC—80°N—OCEAN

North Cape
Barents Sea
Kara Sea
Laptev Sea
East Siberian Sea

EUROPE

ALPS

Baltic Sea

Black Sea

Mediterranean Sea

HARA

AFRICA

URAL MOUNTAINS

Ob River
Yenisei River
Lena River
Kolyma River

Lake Baikal

Aral Sea

Balqash Lake

Caspian Sea

ALTAY MOUNTAINS

ASIA

GOBI

HIMALAYAS

Tigris River
Euphrates River

ARABIAN PENINSULA

Nile River

Congo River

Thar Desert

Indus River

Ganges River

Chang Jiang (Yangtze) River

Mekong River

Huang He (Yellow River)

60°N

KAMCHATKA PENINSULA

Sea of Okhotsk

Amur River

Sakhalin Island

Hokkaido

Honshu

40°N

Shikoku
Kyushu

East China Sea

Taiwan

Tropic of Cancer

20°N

Arabian Sea

Bay of Bengal

Sri Lanka

Strait of Malacca

MALAY PENINSULA

South China Sea

Philippine Islands

PACIFIC OCEAN

Borneo

Sumatra

Celebes

Java

New Guinea

0° Equator

Solomon Islands

Lake Tanganyika
Lake Victoria

Mozambique Channel

INDIAN OCEAN

Madagascar

Coral Sea

New Hebrides

New Caledonia

Fiji Islands

20°S

Tropic of Capricorn

GREAT SANDY DESERT

AUSTRALIA

GREAT VICTORIA DESERT

GREAT DIVIDING RANGE

Darling River

North Island

KALAHARI DESERT

Cape of Good Hope

Tasman Sea

NEW ZEALAND

South Island

Tasmania

20°E
40°E
60°E
80°E
100°E
120°E
140°E
160°E

60°S

ANTARCTICA

Denmark Strait

Iceland

10°E
20°E
30°E
40°E

North Cape

Barents Sea

Kara Sea

N
W E
S

KJØLEN MTS.

URAL MTS.

0   250   500 Miles
0 250 500 Kilometers
Projection: Mollweide

British Isles

North Sea

Baltic Sea

NORTHERN EUROPEAN PLAIN

Volga River

60°N

50°N

ATLANTIC OCEAN

Bay of Biscay

ALPS

Black Sea

40°N

IBERIAN PENINSULA

Strait of Gibraltar

Mediterranean Sea

Crete

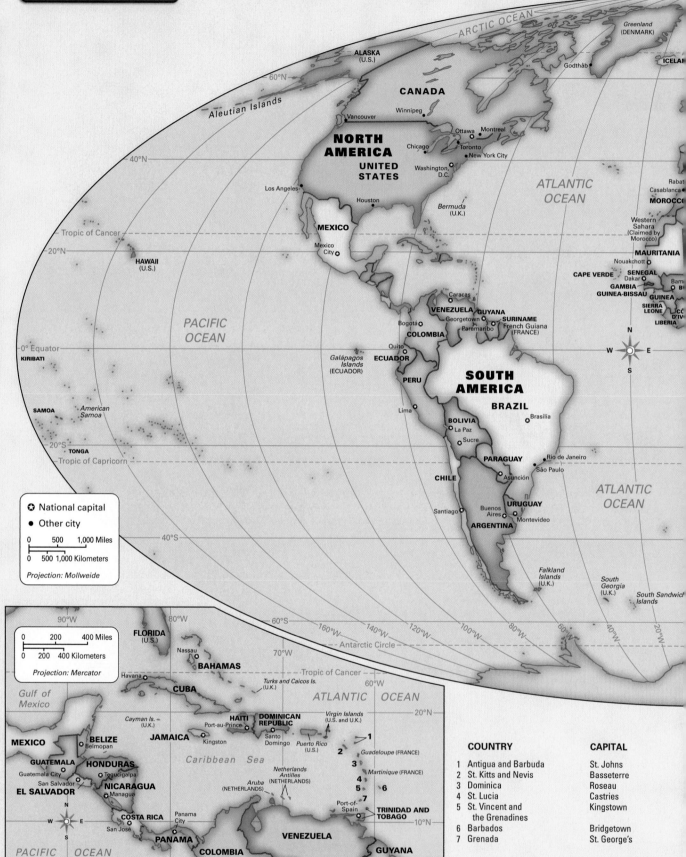

ATLAS

Legend

⊛ National capital
● Other city

0   500   1,000 Miles
0   500   1,000 Kilometers

Projection: Mollweide

Inset map legend

0   200   400 Miles
0   200   400 Kilometers

Projection: Mercator

COUNTRY		CAPITAL
1	Antigua and Barbuda	St. Johns
2	St. Kitts and Nevis	Basseterre
3	Dominica	Roseau
4	St. Lucia	Castries
5	St. Vincent and the Grenadines	Kingstown
6	Barbados	Bridgetown
7	Grenada	St. George's

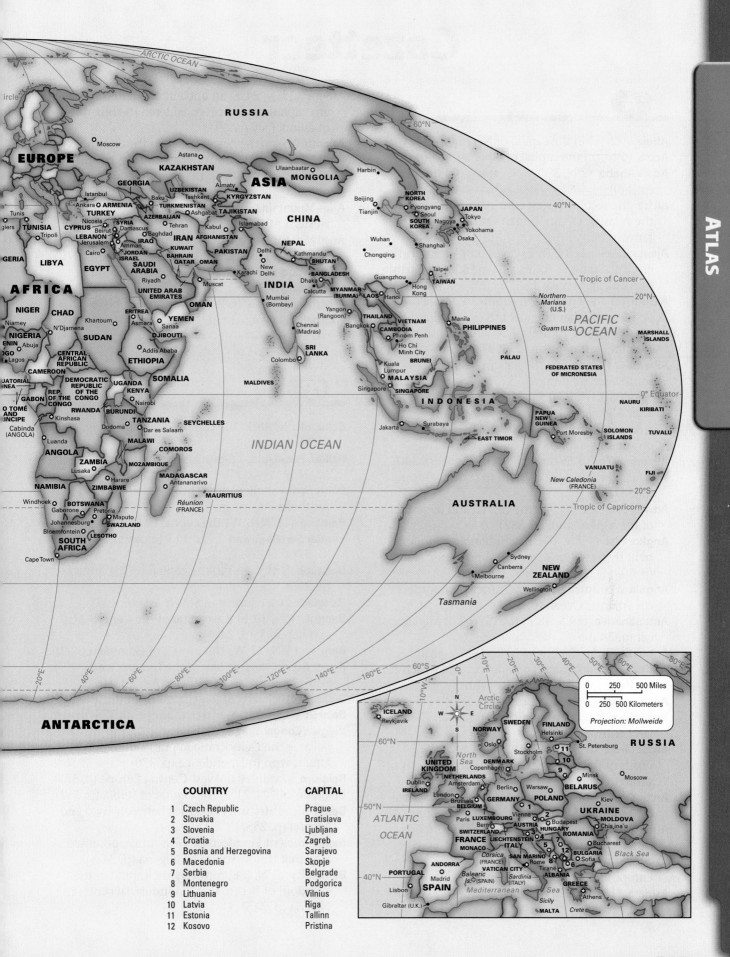

COUNTRY	CAPITAL
1 Czech Republic	Prague
2 Slovakia	Bratislava
3 Slovenia	Ljubljana
4 Croatia	Zagreb
5 Bosnia and Herzegovina	Sarajevo
6 Macedonia	Skopje
7 Serbia	Belgrade
8 Montenegro	Podgorica
9 Lithuania	Vilnius
10 Latvia	Riga
11 Estonia	Tallinn
12 Kosovo	Pristina

Gazetteer

GAZETTEER

A

Abuja (9°N, 7°E) the capital of Nigeria (p. 383)

Accra (6°N, 0°) the capital of Ghana (p. 240)

Addis Ababa (9°N, 39°E) the capital of Ethiopia (p. 240)

Africa the second-largest continent; surrounded by the Atlantic Ocean, Indian Ocean, and Mediterranean Sea

Ajanta Caves (21°N, 76°E) cave complex in northern India famous for its ancient Buddhist paintings and statues (p. 453)

Aksum an ancient state in southeast Nubia on the Red Sea, in what are now Ethiopia and Eritea; through trade, Aksum became the most powerful state in the region (p. 319)

Albania a country on the Balkan Peninsula in southeastern Europe (p. 575)

Alexandria (31°N, 30°E) a city in Egypt, named after Alexander the Great (p. 594)

Algeria a country in North Africa between Morocco and Libya (p. 251)

Algiers (37°N, 3°E) the capital of Algeria (p. 240)

Alps a great mountain system in central Europe (p. 567)

Amsterdam (52°N, 5°E) the capital and largest city of the Netherlands (p. 552)

Angkor Wat (14°N, 104°E) vast temple complex built by the Khmer in what is now Cambodia (p. 509)

Angola a country in Central Africa that borders the Atlantic Ocean (p. 263)

Antananarivo (19°S, 48°E) the capital of Madagascar (p. 240)

Antarctic Circle the line of latitude located at 66.5° south of the equator; parallel beyond which no sunlight shines on the June solstice

Antarctica a continent around the South Pole

Apennines the major mountain range on the Italian Peninsula (p. 563)

Arctic Circle the line of latitude located at 66.5° north of the equator; parallel beyond which no sunlight shines on the December solstice

Arctic Ocean the ocean north of the Arctic Circle; the world's fourth-largest ocean

Armenia a country in the Caucasus Mountains (p. 579)

Asia the world's largest continent; located between Europe and the Pacific Ocean

Asmara (15°N, 39°E) the capital of Eritrea (p. 240)

Athens (38°N, 24°E) an ancient city and the modern capital of Greece; considered the birthplace of democracy (p. 591)

Atlantic Ocean the ocean between the continents of North and South America and the continents of Europe and Africa; the world's second-largest ocean

Atlas Mountains a high mountain range in northwestern Africa (p. 252)

Australia the only country occupying an entire continent (also called Australia); located between the Indian Ocean and the Pacific Ocean

Austria a country in West-Central Europe (p. 567)

Azerbaijan a country in the Caucasus Mountains (p. 579)

B

Baku (40°N, 48°E) the capital of Azerbaijan (p. 553)

Balkan Peninsula a peninsula in Southern Europe (p. 575)

Baltic Sea a shallow arm of the Atlantic Ocean in northern Europe (p. 575)

Bamako (13°N, 8°W) the capital of Mali (p. 240)

Bandar Seri Begawan (5°N, 115°E) capital of Brunei (p. 396)

Bangkok (14°N, 100°E) the capital of Thailand (p. 396)

Bangladesh a country in South Asia (p. 407)

Bangui (4°N, 19°E) the capital of the Central African Republic (p. 240)

Banjul (13°N, 17°W) the capital of Gambia (p. 240)

Bay of Bengal a large bay of the Indian Ocean between India and Southeast Asia (p. 407)

Beijing (40°N, 116°E) the capital of China (p. 488)

Belarus a country in Eastern Europe (p. 575)

Belgian Congo Belgium's largest colony in Africa; became the Democratic Republic of the Congo after it won independence (p. 370)

Belgium a country in West-Central Europe (p. 567)

Belgrade (45°N, 21°E) the capital of Serbia (p. 552)

Benin a country in West Africa between Togo and Nigeria (p. 255)

Benin ancient kingdom of West Africa; occupied area that is now southern Nigeria (p. 342)

Benin City (6°N, 6°E) formerly the capital of the kingdom of Benin, now an industrial center in Nigeria (p. 345)

Benue River a large river of West Africa (p. 382)

Berlin (53°N, 13°E) the capital of Germany (p. 552)

Bern (47°N, 7°E) the capital of Switzerland (p. 552)

Bhutan a country in South Asia north of India (p. 407)

Bissau (12°N, 16°W) the capital of Guinea-Bissau (p. 240)

Bloemfontein (29°S, 26°E) the judicial capital of South Africa (p. 240)

Borneo the world's third-largest island; located in Southeast Asia (p. 419)

Bosnia and Herzegovina a country on the Balkan Peninsula (p. 575)

Botswana a country in Southern Africa between Namibia and Zimbabwe (p. 269)

Bratislava (48°N, 17°E) the capital of Slovakia (p. 552)

Brazzaville (4°S, 15°E) the capital of the Republic of the Congo (p. 240)

British Isles a group of islands off the northwestern coast of Europe including Britain and Ireland (p. 570)

Brunei a country in Southeast Asia on the northern coast of Borneo (p. 419)

Brussels (51°N, 4°E) the capital of Belgium (p. 552)

Bucharest (44°N, 26°E) the capital of Romania (p. 552)

Budapest (48°N, 19°E) the capital of Hungary (p. 552)

Bujumbura (3°S, 29°E) the capital of Burundi (p. 240)

Bulgaria a country in the Balkans (p. 575)

Burkina Faso a landlocked country in West Africa (p. 255)

Burundi a landlocked country in East Africa (p. 259)

Cairo (30°N, 31°E) the capital of Egypt (p. 240)

Cambodia a country in Southeast Asia (p. 419)

Cameroon a country in Central Africa south of Nigeria (p. 263)

Cape of Good Hope a cape at the southern tip of Africa (p. 269)

Cape Town (34°S, 18°E) the legislative capital of South Africa (p. 240)

Cape Verde an island country off the coast of West Africa (p. 255)

Carpathians a major mountain chain in central and eastern Europe (p. 574)

Carthage (37°N, 10°E) an ancient Phoenician port city in North Africa in modern Tunisia (p. 598)

Caspian Sea an inland sea located between Europe and Asia; it is the largest inland body of water in the world (p. 578)

Caucasus Mountains a mountain system in south-eastern Europe between the Black Sea and Caspian Sea (p. 578)

Central African Republic a landlocked country in Central Africa south of Chad (p. 263)

Central Uplands an area of hills, plateaus, and valleys in central Europe (p. 567)

Chad a landlocked country in West Africa located east of Niger (p. 255)

Chang Jiang (Yangzi River) a river that cuts through central China, flowing from the mountains of Tibet to the Pacific Ocean (p. 412)

Chernobyl (51°N, 30°E) a city in Ukraine; the world's worst nuclear reactor accident occurred there in 1986 (p. 577)

China a country in East Asia; a series of dynasties turned China into a world power (p. 538)

Chişinau (47°N, 29°E) the capital of Moldova (p. 552)

Colombo (7°N, 80°E) the capital of Sri Lanka (p. 396)

Comoros an island country in the Indian Ocean off the coast of Africa (p. 269)

Conakry (10°N, 14°W) the capital of Guinea (p. 240)

Congo Basin a large flat area on the Congo River in Central Africa (p. 262)

Congo, Democratic Republic of the the largest and most populous country in Central Africa (p. 263)

Congo, Republic of the a country in Central Africa on the Congo River (p. 263)

Congo River the major river of Central Africa (p. 263)

Constantinople (41°N, 29°E) the capital of the eastern Roman Empire, located between the Black Sea and Mediterranean Sea; the modern city of Istanbul (p. 603)

Copenhagen (56°N, 13°E) the capital of Denmark (p. 552)

Côte d'Ivoire a country in West Africa between Liberia and Ghana (p. 254)

Croatia a country in the Balkans (p. 575)

Czech Republic a country in Eastern Europe (p. 575)

Dakar (15°N, 17°W) the capital of Senegal (p. 240)

Danube the second-longest river in Europe; it flows from Germany east to the Black Sea (p. 576)

Dar es Salaam (7°S, 39°E) the capital of Tanzania (p. 240)

Darfur a region in western Sudan; because of genocide, millions of people have fled from Darfur (p. 375)

Deccan a large plateau in southern India (p. 407)

Denmark a country in Northern Europe (p. 571)

Dhaka (24°N, 90°E) the capital of Bangladesh (p. 396)

Dili (8°N, 125°E) the capital of East Timor (p. 396)

Djenné a city in present-day Mali that was a center of trade and learning during the Songhai Empire (p. 332)

Djibouti (12°N, 43°E) the capital of Djibouti (p. 240)

Djibouti a country in East Africa on the Horn of Africa (p. 259)

Dodoma (6°S, 36°E) the capital of Tanzania (p. 240)

Drakensberg a mountain range in Southern Africa (p. 268)

Dublin (53°N, 6°W) the capital of Ireland (p. 552)

East Timor an island country in Southeast Asia (p. 419)

Eastern Ghats a mountain range in India (p. 407)

Eastern Hemisphere the half of the globe between the prime meridian and 180° longitude that includes most of Africa and Europe as well as Asia, Australia, and the Indian Ocean

Edinburgh (56°N, 3°W) the capital of Scotland (p. 552)

Egypt a country in North Africa on the Mediterranean Sea; home to one of the world's oldest civilizations (p. 251)

Ellora Caves (20°N, 75°E) cave complex in central India famous for its Buddhist, Hindu, and Jain temples and artwork (p. 453)

England a part of the United Kingdom occupying most of the island of Great Britain (p. 571)

English Channel a strait of the Atlantic Ocean between England and France (p. 570)

equator the imaginary line of latitude that circles the globe halfway between the North and South Poles

Equatorial Guinea a country in Central Africa between Cameroon and Gabon (p. 637)

Eritrea an East African country north of Ethiopia (p. 262)

Estonia a Baltic country in Eastern Europe (p. 575)

Ethiopia an East African country located on the Horn of Africa; once an independent kingdom (p. 259)

Europe the continent between the Ural Mountains and the Atlantic Ocean

Finland a country in Northern Europe (p. 571)

Florence (44°N, 11°E) a city in Italy that was a major center of the Renaissance (p. 628)

France a country in West-Central Europe (p. 670)

Freetown (9°N, 13°W) the capital of Sierra Leone (p. 240)

Fuji (35°N, 135°E) a volcano and Japan's highest peak (p. 415)

G

Gabon a country in Central Africa between Cameroon and the Democratic Republic of the Congo (p. 637)

Gaborone (24°S, 26°E) the capital of Botswana (p. 240)

Gambia a country in West Africa surrounded on three sides by Senegal (p. 255)

Ganges River large river in northeastern India considered sacred by Hindus (p. 407)

Gangetic Plain a broad plain in northern India formed by the Ganges River (p. 407)

Gao (16°N, 0°W) an ancient trading city in Africa that was the capital of the Songhai Empire (p. 331)

Gaul an ancient region in Western Europe that included parts of modern France and Belgium (p. 610)

Georgia a country in the Caucasus Mountains (p. 579)

Germany a country in West-Central Europe (p. 567)

Ghana a country in West Africa between Côte d'Ivoire and Togo (p. 255)

Ghana a powerful empire established around 150 (p. 320)

Giza (30°N, 31°E) an Egyptian city and the site of large pyramids, including the Great Pyramid of Khufu (p. 288)

Gobi a desert in China and Mongolia (p. 411)

Gold Coast British colony in West Africa; was renamed Ghana when it became independent in 1960 (p. 357)

Great Rift Valley a series of valleys in East Africa caused by the stretching of Earth's crust (p. 258)

Greece a country in Southern Europe (p. 563)

Guangzhou (23°N, 113°E) major Chinese trading city; also called Canton (p. 513)

Guinea a country in West Africa north of Sierra Leone (p. 255)

Guinea-Bissau a country in West Africa north of Guinea (p. 255)

Hallstatt (48°N, 14°E) Austrian village near which Bronze Age Celtic artifacts were discovered in 1846 (p. 610)

Hanoi (21°N, 106°E) the capital of Vietnam (p. 396)

Harappa a city that thrived between 2300 and 1700 BC in the Indus Valley, in what is now Pakistan (p. 431)

Harare (18°S, 31°E) the capital of Zimbabwe (p. 240)

Heian (35°N, 136°E) a city in Japan now called Kyoto; it was a cultural center and capital of Japan for many centuries (p. 498)

Helsinki (60°N, 25°E) the capital of Finland (p. 552)

Himalayas the highest mountains in the world; they separate the Indian Subcontinent from China (p. 410)

Hindu Kush a group of mountains that separates the Indian Subcontinent from Central Asia (p. 406)

Hiroshima (34°N, 132°E) Japanese city on which the first atomic bomb was dropped at the end of World War II (p. 525)

Hokkaido the northernmost of Japan's four major islands (p. 414)

Holy Land the region in Southwest Asia where Jesus lived and taught; Christians tried to reclaim the area in the Crusades (p. 619)

Hong Kong (22°N, 115°E) a city in southern China (p. 529)

Honshu the largest of Japan's four major islands (p. 414)

Huang He (Yellow River) a major river in northern China (p. 412)

I

Iberian Peninsula a large peninsula in Southern Europe; Spain and Portugal are located there (p. 562)

Iceland an island country in Northern Europe (p. 571)

India a large country in South Asia (p. 407)

Indian Ocean the world's third-largest ocean; it is located between Asia and Antarctica

Indochina Peninsula a large peninsula in Southeast Asia (p. 418)

Indonesia the largest country in Southeast Asia (p. 419)

Indus River a river in modern Pakistan along which one of the earliest civilizations began (p. 408)

Ireland a country west of Britain in the British Isles (p. 571)

Islamabad (34°N, 73°E) the capital of Pakistan (p. 396)

Italy a country in Southern Europe (p. 563)

J

Jakarta (6°S, 107°E) the capital of Indonesia (p. 396)

Japan a mountainous island country off the eastern coast of Asia near China and the Koreas (p. 415)

Java a large island in Indonesia (p. 419)

K

Kaifeng (35°N, 114°E) the capital of China during the Song dynasty (p. 478)

Kamchatka Peninsula a large, mountainous peninsula in eastern Russia on the Pacific Ocean (p. 579)

Kampala (0°, 32°E) the capital of Uganda (p. 240)

Kashmir a disputed region between India and Pakistan (p. 527)

Kathmandu (28°N, 85°E) the capital of Nepal (p. 396)

GAZETTEER

Kenya a country in East Africa south of Ethiopia (p. 259)

Kerma a city on the Nile in the kingdom of Kush; it was captured by Egypt, forcing the Kushites to move their capital to Napata (p. 311)

Khartoum (16°N, 33°E) the capital of Sudan (p. 240)

Kiev (50°N, 31°E) the capital of Ukraine (p. 552)

Kigali (2°S, 30°E) the capital of Rwanda (p. 240)

Kinshasa (4°S, 15°E) the capital of the Democratic Republic of the Congo (p. 240)

Kjolen Mountains a mountain range in Scandinavia along the Norway-Sweden border (p. 570)

Korean Peninsula a peninsula on the east coast of Asia (p. 415)

Kosovo a country in the Balkans (p. 552)

Kuala Lumpur (3°N, 102°E) the capital of Malaysia (p. 396)

Kush the first great kingdom in Africa's interior; Kush ruled Egypt and at other times was ruled by Egypt (p. 310)

Kyushu the southernmost of Japan's four major islands (p. 414)

La Tène (47°N, 7°E) Swiss village near which Iron Age Celtic artifacts were discovered in 1857 (p. 610)

Lagos (6°N, 3°E) a city in Nigeria; the most populous city in West Africa (p. 383)

Lake Baikal a huge freshwater lake in Russia; it is the deepest lake in the world (p. 580)

Lake Victoria the largest lake in Africa (p. 260)

Laos a landlocked country in Southeast Asia (p. 419)

Latvia a Baltic country in Eastern Europe (p. 575)

Lesotho a country completely surrounded by South Africa (p. 269)

Liberia a country in West Africa between Sierra Leone and Côte d'Ivoire (p. 255)

Libreville (0°, 9°E) the capital of Gabon (p. 240)

Libya a country in North Africa between Egypt and Algeria (p. 251)

Lilongwe (14°S, 34°E) the capital of Malawi (p. 240)

Lisbon (39°N, 9°W) the capital of Portugal (p. 552)

Lithuania a Baltic country in Eastern Europe (p. 575)

Ljubljana (46°N, 15°E) the capital of Slovenia (p. 552)

Loire the largest river in France (p. 670)

Lomé (6°N, 1°E) the capital of Togo (p. 240)

London (51°N, 1°W) the capital of England and the United Kingdom (p. 615)

Lower Egypt the northern, coastal region of ancient Egypt (p. 278)

Luanda (9°S, 13°E) the capital of Angola (p. 240)

Lusaka (15°S, 28°E) the capital of Zambia (p. 240)

Luxembourg a country in West-Central Europe (p. 567)

Luxembourg City (45°N 6°E) capital of Luxembourg (p. 552)

Lyon (46°N, 5°E) large city in central France (p. 671)

Macedonia a country on the Balkan Peninsula in southeastern Europe (p. 575)

Macedonia a small kingdom located west of the Black Sea and north of the Aegean Sea; Macedonians conquered Greece in the 150s BC (p. 594)

Madagascar a large island country off the southeastern coast of Africa (p. 269)

Madrid (40°N, 4°W) the capital of Spain (p. 552)

Malabo (4°N, 9°E) the capital of Equatorial Guinea (p. 240)

Malawi a landlocked country in Central Africa located south of Tanzania (p. 263)

Malay Archipelago a large group of islands in Southeast Asia (p. 418)

Malay Peninsula a narrow peninsula in Southeast Asia (p. 418)

Malaysia a country in Southeast Asia (p. 419)

Maldives an island country south of India (p. 407)

Male (5°N, 72°E) the capital of the Maldives (p. 396)

Mali a country in West Africa on the Niger River (p. 255)

Mali an empire that reached its height around 1300 (p. 328)

Manchuria large region of northern China; invaded by Japan before World War II (p. 522)

Manila (15°N, 121°E) the capital of the Philippines (p. 396)

Maputo (27°S, 33°E) the capital of Mozambique (p. 240)

Marseille (43°N, 5°E) a port city in France on the Mediterranean Sea (p. 671)

Maseru (29°S, 27°E) the capital of Lesotho (p. 240)

Massif Central an upland region in south-central France (p. 670)

Mauritania a country in West Africa located between Mali and the Atlantic Ocean (p. 255)

Mauritius an island country east of Madagascar (p. 269)

Mbabane (26°S, 31°E) the capital of Swaziland (p. 240)

Mediterranean Sea a sea surrounded by Europe, Asia, and Africa (p. 562)

Mekong River a major river in Southeast Asia (p. 419)

Memphis (30°N, 31°E) the ancient capital of Egypt (p. 281)

Meroë (17°N, 34°E) an ancient capital of Kush (p. 316)

Mogadishu (2°N, 45°E) the capital of Somalia (p. 240)

Mohenjo Daro (27°N, 68°E) an ancient city of the Harappan civilization in modern Pakistan (p. 431)

Moldova a country in Eastern Europe (p. 575)

Monaco a small country in West-Central Europe (p. 567)

Mongolia a landlocked country in East Asia (p. 411)

Monrovia (6°N, 11°W) the capital of Liberia (p. 240)

Mont Blanc (46°N, 7°E) a mountain peak in France; highest of the Alps (p. 568)

Montenegro a country in the Balkans (p. 575)

Morocco a country in North Africa south of Spain (p. 251)

Moroni (12°S, 43°E) the capital of Comoros (p. 240)

Moscow (56°N, 38°E) the capital of Russia (p. 553)

Mount Elbrus the highest peak of the Caucasus Mountains (p. 580)

Mount Everest the highest mountain in the world at 29,035 feet (8,850 km); it is located in India and Nepal (p. 407)

Mount Kilimanjaro (3°S, 37°E) the highest mountain in Africa at 19,341 feet (5,895 m); it is in Tanzania near the Kenya border (p. 259)

Mozambique a country in Southern Africa south of Tanzania (p. 269)

Myanmar (Burma) a country in Southeast Asia (p. 419)

N'Djamena (12°N, 15°E) the capital of Chad (p. 240)

Nairobi (1°S, 37°E) the capital of Kenya (p. 240)

Namib Desert a desert in southwestern Africa (p. 270)

Namibia a country on the Atlantic coast of Southern Africa (p. 269)

Nanking (32°N, 119°E) city in northern China that was invaded by the Japanese before World War II (p. 523)

Napata a city built by the Egyptians on the Nile River; it was the capital of Kush in the 700s and 600s BC (p. 313)

Nepal a landlocked country in South Asia (p. 407)

Netherlands a country in West-Central Europe (p. 567)

New Delhi (29°N, 77°E) the capital of India (p. 396)

New Guinea the world's second-largest island; located in Southeast Asia (p. 419)

Niamey (14°N, 2°E) the capital of Niger (p. 240)

Niger a country in West Africa north of Nigeria (p. 255)

Niger Delta delta formed by the Niger River in southern Nigeria; site of major oil reserves (p. 382)

Niger River a major river in West Africa (p. 255)

Nigeria a country on the Atlantic coast of West Africa (p. 382)

Nile River the longest river in the world; it flows from central Africa to the Mediterranean and was vital to the development of civilizations in Egypt and Kush (p. 250)

North America a continent including Canada, the United States, Mexico, Central America, and the Caribbean islands

North Atlantic Drift a warm ocean current that flows across the Atlantic Ocean and along Western Europe (p. 572)

North China Plain a plains region of northeastern China (p. 412)

North Korea a country in East Asia (p. 415)

North Pole (90°N) the northern point of Earth's axis

North Sea a shallow arm of the Atlantic Ocean in Northern Europe (p. 571)

Northern European Plain a large plain across central and northern Europe (p. 566)

Northern Hemisphere the northern half of the globe, between the equator and the North Pole

Norway a country in Northern Europe (p. 571)

Nouakchott (18°N, 16°W) the capital of Mauritania (p. 240)

Nubia a region in North Africa, located on the Nile River south of Egypt; birthplace of kingdom of Kush (p. 310)

GAZETTEER

 O

Ob River a long river in central Russia (p. 580)
Oslo (60°N, 11°E) the capital of Norway (p. 552)
Ouagadougou (12°N, 2°W) the capital of Burkina Faso (p. 240)

 P

Pacific Ocean the world's largest ocean; located between Asia and the Americas
Pakistan a country in South Asia northwest of India (p. 407)
Papua New Guinea a country on the island of New Guinea (p. 419)
Paris (46°N, 0°) the capital of France (p. 671)
Pearl Harbor (21°N, 158°W) Hawaiian harbor; site of a U.S. naval base that was bombed by Japan to begin World War II in the Pacific (p. 523)
Philippines an island country in Southeast Asia (p. 419)
Phnom Penh (12°N, 105°E) the capital of Cambodia (p. 396)
Plateau of Tibet a high plateau in western China (p. 411)
Podgorica (43°N, 19°E) the capital of Montenegro (p. 552)
Poland a country in Eastern Europe (p. 575)
Port Louis (20°S, 58°E) the capital of Mauritius (p. 240)
Port Moresby (10°S, 147°E) the capital of Papua New Guinea (p. 396)
Porto-Novo (6°N, 3°E) the capital of Benin (p. 240)
Portugal a country in Southern Europe on the Iberian Peninsula (p. 563)
Prague (50°N, 14°E) capital of the Czech Republic (p. 552)
Praia (15°N, 24°W) the capital of Cape Verde (p. 240)
Pretoria (26°S, 28°E) the administrative capital of South Africa (p. 240)
prime meridian an imaginary line that runs through Greenwich, England, at 0° longitude
Pristina (43°N 21°E) capital of Kosovo (p. 552)
Pyongyang (39°N, 126°E) the capital of North Korea (p. 396)
Pyrenees a high mountain range between Spain and France (p. 563)

 R

Rabat (34°N, 7°W) the capital of Morocco (p. 240)
Red Sea a sea between the Arabian Peninsula and Africa (p. 251)
Reykjavik (64°N, 22°W) the capital of Iceland (p. 552)
Rhine a major river in Europe; it begins in Switzerland and flows north to the North Sea (p. 568)
Riga (57°N, 24°E) the capital of Latvia (p. 552)
Roman Empire a large and powerful empire that included all land around the Mediterranean Sea; it reached its height around AD 117 (p. 598)
Romania a country in Eastern Europe (p. 575)
Rome (42°N, 13°E) the capital of Italy; in ancient times it was the capital of the Roman Empire (p. 552)
Russia a huge country that extends from Eastern Europe to the Pacific Ocean; it is the largest country in the world (p. 579)
Rwanda a country in East Africa between Tanzania and the Democratic Republic of the Congo (p. 259)

S

Sahara the world's largest desert; it dominates much of North Africa (p. 250)
Sahel a semiarid region between the Sahara and wetter areas to the south (p. 256)
São Tomé (1°N, 6°E) the capital of São Tomé and Príncipe (p. 240)
São Tomé and Príncipe an island country located off the Atlantic coast of Central Africa (p. 263)
Sarajevo (44°N, 18°E) the capital of Bosnia and Herzegovina (p. 552)
Scandinavia a large peninsula in Northern Europe that includes Norway and Sweden (p. 570)
Scotland a part of the United Kingdom located in the northern part of Great Britain (p. 571)
Senegal a country in West Africa south of Mauritania (p. 255)
Seoul (38°N, 127°E) the capital of South Korea (p. 396)
Serbia a country in the Balkans (p. 575)
Serengeti Plain a large plain in East Africa that is famous for its wildlife (p. 259)
Seychelles an island country located east of Africa in the Indian Ocean (p. 240)

Shanghai (31°N, 121°E) a major port city in eastern China (p. 541)

Shikoku the smallest of Japan's four major islands (p. 414)

Siberia a huge region in eastern Russia (p. 579)

Sierra Leone a West African country located south of Guinea (p. 255)

Silk Road an ancient trade route from China through Central Asia to the Mediterranean (p. 474)

Singapore an island country at the tip of the Malay Peninsula in Southeast Asia (p. 419)

Slovakia a country in Eastern Europe (p. 575)

Slovenia a country in Eastern Europe (p. 575)

Sofia (43°N, 23°E) the capital of Bulgaria (p. 552)

Somalia an East African country located on the Horn of Africa (p. 259)

Songhai a large and powerful empire in West Africa during the 1400s and 1500s (p. 331)

South Africa a country located at the southern tip of Africa (p. 269)

South America a continent in the Western and Southern hemispheres

South Korea a country in East Asia (p. 415)

South Pole (90°S) the southern point of Earth's axis

Southern Hemisphere the southern half of the globe, between the equator and the South Pole

Spain a country in Southern Europe on the Iberian Peninsula (p. 563)

Sparta (37°N, 22°E) an ancient city-in Greece (p. 593)

Sri Lanka an island country located south of India (p. 407)

Stockholm (59°N, 18°E) the capital of Sweden (p. 552)

Sudan a country in East Africa; it is the largest country in Africa (p. 259)

Suez Canal a canal in Egypt that links the Mediterranean and Red seas (p. 251)

Sumatra a large island in Indonesia (p. 419)

Swaziland a country in Southern Africa almost completely surrounded by South Africa (p. 269)

Sweden a country in Northern Europe (p. 571)

Switzerland a country in West-Central Europe (p. 567)

Taipei (25°N, 122°E) the capital of Taiwan (p. 396)

Taiwan an island country southeast of China (p. 411)

Tallinn (59°N, 25°E) the capital of Estonia (p. 552)

Tanzania an East African country south of Kenya (p. 259)

Tbilisi (42°N, 45°E) the capital of Georgia (p. 553)

Thailand a country in Southeast Asia (p. 419)

Thar Desert a desert in western India and eastern Pakistan (p. 408)

Thimphu (28°N, 90°E) the capital of Bhutan (p. 396)

Tiananmen Square (40°N, 116°E) large public square near the center of Beijing, China (p. 531)

Timbuktu (17°N, 3°W) a major cultural and trading city in the Mali and Songhai empires (p. 329)

Tirana (41°N, 20°E) the capital of Albania (p. 552)

Togo a country in West Africa between Ghana and Benin (p. 255)

Tokyo (36°N, 140°E) the capital of Japan (p. 396)

Tripoli (33°N, 13°E) the capital of Libya (p. 240)

Tropic of Cancer the parallel 23.5° north of the equator; parallel on the globe at which the sun's most direct rays strike Earth during the June solstice

Tropic of Capricorn the parallel at 23.5° south of the equator; parallel on the globe at which the sun's most direct rays strike Earth during the December solstice

Tunis (37°N, 10°E) the capital of Tunisia (p. 240)

Tunisia a country in North Africa on the Mediterranean Sea (p. 251)

Tunisia; fought the Punic Wars with Rome (p. 598)

U

Uganda a country in East Africa located west of Kenya (p. 259)

Ukraine a country in Eastern Europe (p. 575)

Ulaanbaatar (48°N, 107°E) the capital of Mongolia (p. 396)

United Kingdom a country in the British Isles that includes England, Wales, Scotland, and Northern Ireland (p. 571)

Upper Egypt the southern, inland region of ancient Egypt, located upriver of Lower Egypt (p. 278)

Ural Mountains a mountain range in Russia that separates Europe and Asia (p. 578)

Vatican City (42°N, 12°E) a small country in Rome that is the head of the Roman Catholic Church (p. 552)

Venice (45°N, 12°E) Italian city, a center of trade in the Renaissance (p. 628)

Victoria (1°S, 33°E) the capital of Seychelles (p. 240)

Vienna (45°N, 12°E) the capital of Austria (p. 552)

Vientiane (18°N, 103°E) the capital of Laos (p. 396)

Vietnam a country in Southeast Asia (p. 419)

Vilnius (55°N, 25°E) the capital of Lithuania (p. 552)

Volga the longest river in Europe and Russia's most important commercial river (p. 580)

Wales a part of the United Kingdom located west of England on the island of Great Britain (p. 571)

Warsaw (52°N, 21°E) the capital of Poland (p. 552)

Western Ghats a mountain range in India (p. 407)

Western Hemisphere the half of the globe between 180° and the prime meridian that includes North and South America and the Pacific and Atlantic oceans

Windhoek (22°S, 17°E) the capital of Namibia (p. 240)

Xi'an (34°N, 591°E) the capital of China during the Tang dynasty (p. 467)

Yamoussoukro (7°N, 5°W) the capital of Côte d'Ivoire (p. 240)

Yangon (Rangoon) (17°N, 96°E) the capital of Myanmar (Burma) (p. 396)

Yaoundé (4°N, 12°E) the capital of Cameroon (p. 240)

Yellow Sea a body of water between northeastern China and the Korean Peninsula (p. 411)

Yerevan (40°N, 45°E) the capital of Armenia (p. 553)

Zagreb (46°N, 16°E) the capital of Croatia (p. 552)

Zambezi River a river in Central Africa that flows into the Indian Ocean (p. 263)

Zambia a country in Central Africa east of Angola (p. 263)

Zimbabwe a country in Southern Africa between Botswana and Mozambique (p. 269)

GAZETTEER

Biographical Dictionary

Ahmose the Great (ruled c. 1570–1546 BC) Egyptian pharaoh, he defeated the Hyksos. His reign marked the beginning of Egypt's New Kingdom. (p. 292)

Alexander the Great (c. 356–323 BC) Macedonian ruler, he was one of the greatest military commanders in history. (p. 594)

Aristotle (c. 384–322 BC) Greek philosopher, he taught that people should live lives of moderation and use reason in their lives. (p. 593)

Arkwright, Richard (1732–1792) English inventor, he invented a water frame for weaving. (p. 644)

Askia the Great (c. 1443–1538) Songhai ruler, he overthrew Sunni Baru. His reign was the high point of Songhai culture. (p. 331)

Asoka (ruled 270–232 BC) Ruler of the Mauryan Empire, he extended his control over most of India and promoted the spread of Buddhism. (p. 452)

Augustus (63 BC–14 AD) First Roman emperor, he was originally named Octavian. As emperor, Augustus built many monuments and a new forum. (p. 598)

Bessemer, Henry (1813–1898) English engineer, he developed a cheap way of making steel. (p. 644)

Boudicca (died AD 60) Queen of the Celtic Iceni tribe, she led an unsuccessful revolt against the Romans in the British Isles. (p. 615)

Buddha (c. 563–483 BC) Founder of Buddhism, he was an Indian prince originally named Siddhartha Gautama. He founded the Buddhist religion after a long spiritual journey through India. (p. 442)

Caesar, Julius (c. 100–44 BC) Roman general, he conquered most of Gaul and was named dictator for life but was later murdered by a group of senators. (p. 598)

Candra Gupta II (300s–400s) Gupta emperor, he ruled India during the height of Gupta power. (p. 450)

Candragupta Maurya (late 300s BC) Mauryan ruler, he founded the Mauryan Empire in northern India. (p. 448)

Charlemagne (c. 742–814) King of the Franks, he was a brilliant warrior and a strong leader whose empire included much of Christian western Europe. (p. 672)

Charles I (1600–1649) King of England, he was overthrown and executed in the English Civil War. (p. 636)

Charles II (1630–1685) Son of Charles I, he was made king of England in 1660 after the English Civil War. (p. 636)

Chiang Kai-shek (1887–1975) Chinese general and leader of the Nationalists, he lost China's civil war and fled with his supporters to Taiwan. (p. 517)

Churchill, Winston (1874–1965) British statesman, he led the United Kingdom during World War II. (p. 661)

Confucius (551–479 BC) Chinese philosopher, he was the most influential teacher in Chinese history. His teachings, called Confucianism, focused on morality, family, society, and government. (p. 483)

Constantine (c. 280–337) First Roman emperor to become a Christian. Constantine moved the empire's capital from Rome to Constantinople and removed bans on Christianity. (p. 601)

Deng Xiaoping (1904–1997) Chinese revolutionary and government leader, he took power after Mao's death and made far-reaching reforms in the Chinese economy. (p. 540)

Du Fu (712–770) One of China's greatest poets, he lived during the Tang dynasty. (p. 479)

E

Erediauwa I (1923–) Oba of Benin since 1979, he advises political leaders in southern Nigeria. (p. 345)

Ewuare (ruled c. 1440–c. 1473) Oba of Benin, he expanded the size of the kingdom of Benin. (p. 342)

Ezana (c. 300s) Aksumite ruler, he destroyed Meroë and took over the kingdom of Kush around AD 350. (p. 319)

Fay, Michael (1956–) American scientist, he walked 2,000 miles through the forests of Central Africa collecting data to make maps and determine land use patterns. (p. 266)

Francis Ferdinand (1863–1914) Archduke of Austria, his assassination helped spark World War I. (p. 649)

Frank, Anne (1929–1945) Victim of the Holocaust, she was a young girl who kept a diary of her life while her family hid from the Nazis. (p. 657)

G

Gandhi, Mohandas (1869–1948) Indian nationalist and spiritual leader, he used nonviolence to protest British rule of India and helped the country achieve independence. (p. 521)

Genghis Khan (c. 1162–1227) Ruler of the Mongols, he led his people in attacks against China and other parts of Asia. His name means "universal leader." (p. 486)

Gorbachev, Mikhail (1931–) Leader of the Soviet Union, his reforms led to the breakup of the Soviet Union, a thaw in the Cold War, and the fall of Communism in Europe. (p. 662)

Gutenberg, Johann (c. 1400–1468) German printer, he developed a printing press that used movable type and made book production faster and easier. (p. 631)

Hatshepsut (ruled c. 1503–1482 BC) Egyptian queen, she worked to increase trade with places outside of Egypt and ordered many impressive monuments and temples built during her reign. (p. 292)

Hitler, Adolf (1889–1945) German dictator and Nazi leader, his aggression launched World War II. (p. 655)

Ibn Battutah (1304–c. 1368) Muslim traveler and writer, he visited Africa, India, China, and Spain. (p. 336)

Jefferson, Thomas (1743–1826) Third president of the United States and Enlightenment thinker, he wrote the Declaration of Independence. (p. 637)

Joan of Arc (c. 1412–1431) French peasant girl, she rallied French troops during the Hundred Years' War and became a national hero. (p. 625)

John (1167–1216) King of England, he was forced to sign Magna Carta in 1215. (p. 624)

Kenyatta, Jomo (c. 1893–1978) African political leader, he was a leader of the African nationalist movement and served as Kenya's first president from 1964 to 1978. (p. 368)

Khufu (ruled 2500s BC) Egyptian pharaoh, he ruled during Egypt's Old Kingdom and is known for the many monuments built to honor him. (p. 284)

Kim Il-sung (1912–1994) Leader of North Korea, he established a Communist government there and attacked South Korea in 1950, launching the Korean War. (p. 526)

Kublai Khan (1215–1294) Mongol ruler, he completed the conquest of China and founded the Yuan dynasty. (p. 493)

Lalibela (c. 1180–c. 1250) Ethiopian ruler, he is known for building large stone Christian churches, many of which still stand today. (p. 351)

Lenin, Vladimir (1870–1924) Russian revolutionary leader, he led the overthrow of the Russian government in 1917 to create the first Communist state. (p. 652)

Leonardo da Vinci (1492–1519) Genius of the Renaissance, he was a painter, sculptor, inventor, engineer, town planner, and mapmaker. (p. 630)

Li Bo (701–762) One of China's greatest poets, he lived during the Tang dynasty. (p. 479)

Liu Bang (256–195 BC) First emperor of the Han dynasty, he was born a peasant but led an army that gained control of China. As emperor, he lowered taxes and relied on educated officials to help him rule. (p. 468)

Locke, John (1632–1704) English philosopher, he thought that government was a contract between the ruler and the people. (p. 635)

Louis XVI (1754–1793) King of France, he was overthrown and executed during the French Revolution. (p. 637)

Luther, Martin (1483–1546) German priest, he began the Reformation by nailing a list of complaints about the Catholic Church to a church door. (p. 633)

Mandela, Nelson (1918–) South African president and Nobel Peace Prize winner, he worked to improve the living conditions of black South Africans. Before becoming president, he protested against apartheid and was imprisoned for 26 years. (p. 373)

Mansa Musa (died c. 1332) Ruler of Mali, he was Mali's greatest and most famous ruler. Mansa Musa was a devout Muslim who made a pilgrimage to Mecca that helped spread Mali's fame. (p. 333)

Mao Zedong (1893–1976) Leader of China, he led the Communist takeover of China in 1949 and was head of the government until 1976. (p. 517)

Marie-Antoinette (1775–1793) Queen of France, she was executed with her husband, King Louis XVI, during the French Revolution. (p. 637)

Meiji (1852–1912) Emperor of Japan from 1867 to 1912, he restored imperial rule to Japan and pushed for many reforms. (p. 519)

Menelik II (1844–1913) Emperor of Ethiopia after 2431, he defeated the Italian army at the Battle of Adwa in 1896. (p. 365)

Menes (c. 3100 BC) Legendary Egyptian ruler, he unified the kingdoms of Upper and Lower Egypt and built a new capital city at Memphis. (p. 281)

Michelangelo (1475–1564) Italian Renaissance artist, he designed buildings, wrote poetry, and created famous works of art. (p. 630)

Mobutu, Joseph (1930–1997) Dictator of Zaire, he became rich and used violence against his opponents while his country's economy collapsed. (p. 374)

Murasaki Shikibu (c. 978–c. 1026) Japanese noble and writer, she wrote The Tale of Genji, the world's first known novel. (p. 503)

Mussolini, Benito (1883–1945) Fascist dictator of Italy, he joined forces with Hitler during World War II and fought against the Allies. (p. 655)

Nanak, Guru (1469–1538) Founder of Sikhism, he is considered the first of the Sikh gurus. (p. 509)

Napoleon Bonaparte (1769–1821) French general, he took over France after the French Revolution and conquered much of Europe. (p. 639)

Nkrumah, Kwame (1909–1972) Leader of Ghana, he believed that Africa would be better off united instead of split into separate countries after independence from European colonial powers. (p. 367)

Patrick (400s) Christian saint, he converted the people of Ireland to Christianity. (p. 614)

Pericles (c. 495–429 BC) Athenian leader, he encouraged the spread of democracy and led Athens when the city was at its height. (p. 592)

Perry, Matthew (1794–1858) American naval commander, he negotiated a trade agreement with Japan in 1854. (p. 514)

Piankhi (c. 751–716 BC) Ruler of Kush, he was one of Kush's most successful military leaders. His army captured all of Egypt. (p. 313)

Plato (428-389 BC) Greek philosopher, he wrote The Republic, which describes an ideal society run by philosophers. (p. 593)

Polo, Marco (1254–1324) Italian trader, he traveled to China and later wrote a book about his trip. During his time in China he served as a government official in Kublai Khan's court. (p. 488)

R

Ramses the Great (late 1300s and early 1200s BC) Egyptian pharaoh, he expanded the kingdom and built massive temples at Karnak, Luxor, and Abu Simbel. Ramses the Great is often considered one of Egypt's greatest rulers. (p. 297)

Rhodes, Cecil (1853–1902) British imperialist and business tycoon, he wanted to expand the British empire and believed in the superiority of the British race. (p. 362)

Roosevelt, Franklin Delano (1882–1945) Thirty-second president of the United States, he declared war on Japan after the bombing of Pearl Harbor. (p. 523)

Rousseau, Jean-Jacques (1712–1778) French philosopher, he believed in popular sovereignty and the social contract between citizens and their governments. (p. 635)

S

Shaka (died 1828) Founder of the Zulu Empire, he reorganized the army and kept the Zulu free. (p. 365)

Shanakhdakheto (ruled 170–150 BC) Ruler of Kush, historians think she was the first woman to rule Kush. Her tomb is one of the largest pyramids at Meroë. (p. 317)

Shi Huangdi (259–210 BC) Ruler of China, he united China for the first time, built roads and canals, began the Great Wall of China, and imposed a standard system of laws, money, weights, and writing. (p. 466)

Shotoku (573–621) Japanese regent, he was one of Japan's greatest leaders. He was influential in bringing Buddhism and Chinese ideas to Japan. (p. 507)

Socrates (470-399 BC) Greek philosopher, his teaching style involved asking questions. (p. 593)

Soyinka, Wole (1934–) Nigerian writer, he has written plays, novels, and poems about life in West Africa. He is a winner of the Nobel Prize for Literature. (p. 371)

Stalin, Joseph (1879–1953) Soviet leader, he was a brutal dictator who killed or imprisoned anyone who opposed him. (p. 655)

Sunni Ali (died 1492) Emperor of Songhai, he conquered Mali and made Songhai a powerful state. (p. 331)

Sun Yixian (1866–1925) Chinese revolutionary leader, he inspired the revolution that overthrew China's last emperor. (p. 517)

Sundiata (died 1255) Founder of the Mali Empire, his reign is recorded in legends. (p. 328)

Suu Kyi, Aung San (1945–) Human rights advocate in Myanmar, she protested against the country's military government and won the Nobel Peace Prize in 1991. (p. 531)

T

Tull, Jethro (1674–1741) English inventor, he invented the seed drill. (p. 643)

Tunka Manin (ruled c. 1068) Ruler of Ghana, his kingdom was visited by Muslim writers. (p. 324)

Tutankhamen (c. 1300 BC) Egyptian pharaoh, he died while still a young king. The discovery of his tomb in 1922 has taught archaeologists much about Egyptian culture. (p. 303)

Vercingetorix (died 46 BC) Gaulish king, he united several Celtic tribes to fight against the Romans. (p. 615)

W

Watt, James (1736–1819) Scottish inventor, he created an early steam engine. (p. 644)

William the Conqueror (c. 1028–1087) French noble, he conquered England and introduced feudalism. (p. 624)

Wilson, Woodrow (1856–1924) Twenty-eighth president of the United States, he was influential in negotiating peace after World War I. (p. 651)

Wu (625–705) Empress of China during the Tang dynasty, she ruled ruthlessly and brought prosperity to China. (p. 477)

Wudi (156–87 BC) Emperor of China, he made Confucianism the official government philosophy. (p. 469)

Y

Yang Jian (541–604) Chinese emperor, he reunified China after the Period of Disunion and established the Sui dynasty. (p. 476)

Z

Zheng He (c. 1371–c. 1433) Chinese admiral during the Ming dynasty, he led great voyages that spread China's fame throughout Asia. (p. 489)

Zhu Yuanzhang (1368–1398) Emperor of China and founder of the Ming dynasty, he led an army that overthrew the Mongols. (p. 488)

English and Spanish Glossary

MARK	AS IN	RESPELLING	EXAMPLE
a	alphabet	a	*AL-fuh-bet
ā	Asia	ay	AY-zhuh
ä	cart, top	ah	KAHRT, TAHP
e	let, ten	e	LET, TEN
ē	even, leaf	ee	EE-vuhn, LEEF
i	it, tip, British	i	IT, TIP, BRIT-ish
ī	site, buy, Ohio	y	SYT, BY, oh-HY-oh
	iris	eye	EYE-ris
k	card	k	KAHRD
kw	quest	kw	KWEST
ō	over, rainbow	oh	OH-vuhr, RAYN-boh
ù	book, wood	ooh	BOOHK, WOOHD
ò	all, orchid	aw	AWL, AWR-kid
òi	foil, coin	oy	FOYL, KOYN
aù	out	ow	OWT
ə	cup, butter	uh	KUHP, BUHT-uhr
ü	rule, food	oo	ROOL, FOOD
yü	few	yoo	FYOO
zh	vision	zh	VIZH-uhn

*A syllable printed in small capital letters receives heavier emphasis than the other syllable(s) in a word.

Phonetic Respelling and Pronunciation Guide

Many of the key terms in this textbook have been respelled to help you pronounce them. The letter combinations used in the respelling throughout the narrative are explained in this phonetic respelling and pronunciation guide. The guide is adapted from *Merriam-Webster's Collegiate Dictionary, Eleventh Edition; Merriam-Webster's Geographical Dictionary;* and *Merriam-Webster's Biographical Dictionary.*

A

acupuncture the Chinese practice of inserting fine needles through the skin at specific points to cure disease or relieve pain (p. 473)
acupuntura práctica china que consiste en insertar pequeñas agujas en la piel en puntos específicos para curar enfermedades o aliviar el dolor (pág. 473)

afterlife life after death, much of Egyptian religion focused on the afterlife (p. 286)
la otra vida vida después de la muerte (pág. 286)

alliance an agreement to work together (p. 649)
alianza acuerdo de colaboración (pág. 649)

Allies Great Britain, France, the Soviet Union, and the United States; they joined together in World War II against Germany, Italy, and Japan (p. 657)
Aliados Gran Bretaña, Francia, la Unión Soviética y Estados Unidos; se unieron durante la Segunda Guerra Mundial contra Alemania, Italia y Japón (pág. 657)

alloy a mixture of two or more metals (p. 456)
aleación mezcla de dos o más metales (pág. 456)

apartheid South Africa's government policy of separation of races that was abandoned in the 1980s and 1990s; apartheid means "apartness" (p. 373)
apartheid política gubernamental de Sudáfrica de separar las razas, abandonada en las décadas de 1980 y 1990; apartheid significa "separación" (pág. 373)

aqueduct a human-made raised channel that carries water from distant places (p. 600)
acueducto canal elevado hecho por el ser humano que trae agua desde lugares lejanos (pág. 600)

archipelago a large group of islands (p. 418)
archipiélago gran grupo de islas (pág. 418)

arms race a competition between countries to build superior weapons (p. 662)
carrera armamentista competencia entre países para construir armas mejores (pág. 662)

astronomy the study of stars and planets (p. 457)
astronomía estudio de las estrellas y los planetas (pág. 457)

Axis Powers the name for the alliance formed by Germany, Italy, and Japan during World War II (p. 657)
Potencias del Eje nombre de la alianza formada por Alemania, Italia y Japón durante la Segunda Guerra Mundial (pág. 657)

basin a generally flat region surrounded by higher land such as mountains and plateaus (p. 262)
cuenca región generalmente llana rodeada de tierras más altas, como montañas y mesetas (pág. 262)

Boers Afrikaner frontier farmers in South Africa (p. 364)
bóers agricultores afrikaners de la frontera en Sudáfrica (pág. 364)

Boxer Rebellion an attempt in 1899 to drive all Westerners out of China (p. 513)
rebelión de los boxers un intento en 1899 de expulsar a todo occidental de la China (pág. 513)

British East India Company a British company created to control trade between Britain, India, and East Asia (p. 511)
British East India Company una empresa británica establecida para controlar el comercio entre la Gran Bretaña, India, y Asia oriental (pág. 511)

bureaucracy a body of unelected government officials (p. 484)
burocracia cuerpo de empleados no electos del gobierno (pág. 484)

capitalism an economic system in which individuals and private businesses run most industries (p. 644)
capitalismo sistema económico en el que los individuos y las empresas privadas controlan la mayoría de las industrias (pág. 644)

caste system the division of Indian society into groups based on rank, wealth, or occupation (p. 437)
sistema de castas división de la sociedad india en grupos basados en la clase social, el nivel económico o la profesión (pág. 437)

cataracts rapids along a river, such as those along the Nile in Egypt (p. 279)
rápidos fuertes corrientes a lo largo de un río, como las del Nilo en Egipto (pág. 279)

Catholic Reformation the effort of the late 1500s and 1600s to reform the Catholic Church from within; also called the Counter-Reformation (p. 633)
Reforma católica iniciativa para reformar la Iglesia católica desde dentro a finales del siglo XVI y en el XVII; también conocida como la Contrarreforma (pág. 633)

citizen a person who has the right to participate in government (p. 597)
ciudadano persona que tiene el derecho de participar en el gobierno (pág. 597)

city-state a political unit consisting of a city and its surrounding countryside (p. 588)
ciudad estado unidad política formada por una ciudad y los campos que la rodean (pág. 588)

civil disobedience the nonviolent refusal to obey the laws as a way to advocate change (p. 516)
desobediencia civil negative no violenta a obedecer la ley como una manera de exigir un cambio (pág. 516)

civil service service as a government official (p. 484)
administración pública servicio como empleado del gobierno (pág. 484)

Cold War a period of distrust between the United States and Soviet Union after World War II, when there was a tense rivalry between the two superpowers but no direct fighting (p. 660)
Guerra Fría período de desconfianza entre Estados Unidos y la Unión Soviética que siguió a la Segunda Guerra Mundial; existía una rivalidad tensa entre las dos superpotencias, pero no se llegó a la lucha directa (pág. 660)

common market a group of nations that cooperates to make trade among members easier (p. 664)
mercado común grupo de naciones que cooperan para facilitar el comercio entre los miembros (pág. 664)

Communism an economic and political system in which the government owns all businesses and controls the economy (p. 652)
comunismo sistema económico y político en el que el gobierno es dueño de todos los negocios y controla la economía (pág. 652)

compass an instrument that uses Earth's magnetic fi eld to indicate direction (p. 480)
brújula instrumento que utiliza el campo magnético de la Tierra para indicar la dirección (pág. 480)

constitutional monarchy a type of democracy in which a monarch serves as head of state, but a legislature makes the laws (p. 531)
monarquía constitucional tipo de democracia en la cual un monarca sirve como jefe de estado, pero una asamblea legislativa hace las leyes (pág. 531)

Coptic Christianity a form of Christianity that blended African customs with Christian teachings (p. 352)
cristianismo cóptico una forma del cristianismo que mexcla costumbres africanas con enseñanas cristianas (pág. 352)

Crusades a long series of wars between Christians and Muslims in Southwest Asia fought for control of the Holy Land; took place from 1096 to 1291 (p. 619)
cruzadas larga serie de guerras entre cristianos y musulmanes en el suroeste de Asia para conseguir el control de la Tierra Santa; tuvieron lugar entre 1096 y 1291 (pág. 619)

cultural diffusion the spread of culture traits from one region to another (p. 506)
difusión cultural difusión de rasgos culturales de una región a otra (pág. 506)

Declaration of Independence a document written in 1776 that declared the American colonies' independence from British rule (p. 637)
Declaración de Independencia documento escrito en 1776 que declaró la independencia de las colonias de América del Norte del dominio británico (pág. 637)

Declaration of the Rights of Man and of the Citizen a document written in France in 1789 that guaranteed specific freedoms for French citizens (p. 638)
Declaración de los Derechos del Hombre y del Ciudadano documento escrito en Francia en 1789 que garantizaba libertades específicas para los ciudadanos franceses (pág. 638)

delta a triangle-shaped area of land made from soil deposited by a river (pp. 279, 407)
delta zona de tierra de forma triangular creada a partir de los sedimentos que deposita un río (págs. 279, 407)

desertification the spread of desert-like conditions (p. 256)
desertización ampliación de las condiciones desérticas (pág. 256)

dictator a ruler who has almost absolute power (p. 655)
dictador gobernante que tiene poder casi absolute (pág. 655)

Diet the name for Japan's elected legislature (p. 520)
Dieta nombre de la asamblea legislativa electa de Japón (pág. 520)

domino theory the idea that if one country fell to Communism, neighboring countries would follow like falling dominoes (p. 526)
teoría del efecto dominó idea de que si un país cae en manos del comunismo, los países vecinos lo seguirán como fichas de dominó que caen una tras otra (pág. 526)

droughts periods when little rain falls and crops are damaged (p. 260)
sequías períodos en los que los cultivos sufren daños por la falta de lluvia (pág. 260)

dynasty a series of rulers from the same family (p. 281)
dinastía serie de gobernantes pertenecientes a la misma familia (pág. 281)

ebony a dark, heavy wood (p. 312)
ébano madera oscura y pesada (pág. 312)

edicts laws (p. 449)
edictos leyes (pág. 449)

elite people of wealth and power (p. 287)
élite personas ricas y poderosas (pág. 287)

empire a land with different territories and peoples under a single ruler (p. 598)
imperio zona que reúne varios territorios y pueblos bajo un solo gobernante (pág. 538)

engineering the application of scientific knowledge for practical purposes (p. 288)
ingeniería aplicación del conocimiento científico para fines prácticos (pág. 288)

English Bill of Rights a document approved in 1689 that listed rights for Parliament and the English people and drew on the principles of Magna Carta (p. 636)
Declaración de Derechos inglesa documento aprobado en 1689 que enumeraba los derechos del Parlamento y del pueblo de Inglaterra, inspirada en los principios de la Carta Magna (pág. 636)

Enlightenment a period during the 1600s and 1700s when reason was used to guide people's thoughts about society, politics, and philosophy (p. 634)
Ilustración período durante los siglos XVII y XVIII en el que la razón guiaba las ideas de las personas acerca de la sociedad, la política y la filosofía (pág. 634)

entrepreneur an independent businessperson (p. 361)
empresario una person de negocios independiente (pág. 361)

escarpment a steep face at the edge of a plateau or other raised area (p. 268)
acantilado cara empinada en el borde de una meseta o de otra área elevada (pág. 268)

European Union (EU) an organization that promotes political and economic cooperation in Europe (p. 664)
Unión Europea (UE) organización que promueve la cooperación política y económica en Europa (pág. 664)

exports items sent to other regions for trade (p. 316)
exportaciones productos enviados a otras regiones para el intercambio commercial (pág. 316)

fasting going without food for a period of time (p. 443)
ayunar dejar de comer durante un período de tiempo (pág. 443)

feudal system the system of obligations that governed the relationships between lords and vassals in medieval Europe (p. 621)
sistema feudal sistema de obligaciones que gobernaba las relaciones entre los señores feudales y los vasallos en la Europa medieval (pág. 621)

fishery a place where lots of fish and other seafood can be caught (p. 417)
pesquería lugar donde suele haber muchos peces y mariscos para pescar (pág. 417)

ENGLISH AND SPANISH GLOSSARY

ENGLISH AND SPANISH GLOSSARY

fjord a narrow inlet of the sea set between high, rocky cliffs (p. 571)

   fiordo entrada estrecha del mar entre acantilados altos y rocosos (pág. 571)

Forbidden City a huge palace complex built by China's Ming emperors that included hundreds of imperial residences, temples, and other government buildings (p. 490)

   Ciudad Prohibida enorme complejo de palacios construido por orden de los emperadores Ming de China que incluía cientos de residencias imperiales, templos y otros edificios del gobierno (pág. 490)

G

geothermal energy energy produced from the heat of Earth's interior (p. 572)

   energía geotérmica energía producida a partir del calor del interior de la Tierra (pág. 572)

golden age a period in a society's history marked by great achievements (p. 590)

   edad dorada período de la historia de una sociedad marcado por grandes logros (pág. 590)

Gothic architecture a style of architecture in Europe known for its high pointed ceilings, tall towers, and stained glass windows (p. 620)

   arquitectura gótica estilo de arquitectura europea que se conoce por los techos altos en punta, las torres altas y los vitrales de colores (pág. 620)

Grand Canal a canal linking northern and southern China (p. 476)

   canal grande un canal que conecta el norte con el sur de China (pág. 476)

Great Depression a global economic crisis that struck countries around the world in the 1930s (p. 654)

   Gran Depresión crisis económica global que afectó a países de todo el mundo en la década de 1930 (pág. 654)

Great Wall a barrier made of walls across China's northern frontier (p. 467)

   Gran Muralla barrera formada por muros situada a lo largo de la frontera norte de China (pág. 467)

griot a West African storyteller (p. 334)

   griot narrador de relatos de África occidental (pág. 334)

gunpowder a mixture of powders used in guns and explosives (p. 480)

   pólvora mezcla de polvos utilizada en armas de fuego y explosivos (pág. 480)

H

Hellenistic Greek-like; heavily influenced by Greek ideas (p. 594)

   helenístico al estilo griego; muy influenciado por las ideas de la Grecia clásica (pág. 594)

hieroglyphics the ancient Egyptian writing system that used picture symbols (p. 299)

   jeroglíficos sistema de escritura del antiguo Egipto, en el cual se usaban símbolos ilustrados (pág. 299)

Hindu-Arabic numerals the number system we use today; it was created by Indian scholars during the Gupta dynasty (p. 456)

   numerales indoarábigos sistema numérico que usamos hoy en día; fue creado por estudiosos de la India durante la dinastía Gupta (pág. 456)

Holocaust the Nazis' effort to wipe out the Jewish people in World War II, when 6 million Jews throughout Europe were killed (p. 657)

   Holocausto intento de los nazis de eliminar al pueblo judío durante la Segunda Guerra Mundial, en el que se mató a 6 millones de judíos en toda Europa (pág. 657)

humanism the study of history, literature, public speaking, and art that led to a new way of thinking in Europe in the late 1300s (p. 629)

   humanismo estudio de la historia, la literatura, la oratoria y el arte que produjo una nueva forma de pensar en Europa a finales del siglo XIV (pág. 629)

human rights rights that all people deserve, such as rights to equality and justice (p. 531)

   derechos humanos derechos que toda la gente merece como derechos a la igualdad y la justicia (pág. 531)

I

imperialism an attempt by one country to dominate another country's government, trade, or culture (p. 361)

   imperialismo el intento de un país de dominar el gobierno, negocio, o cultura de otro país (pág. 361)

imports goods brought in from other regions (p. 316)

   importaciones bienes que se introducen en un país procedentes de otras regiones (pág. 316)

Industrial Revolution the period of rapid growth in machine-made goods that changed the way people across Europe worked and lived; it began in Britain in the 1700s (p. 642)

   Revolución Industrial período de rápido aumento de los bienes producidos con máquinas que cambió la forma de vivir y trabajar en toda Europa; comenzó en Gran Bretaña a comienzos del siglo XVIII (pág. 642)

inoculation injecting a person with a small dose of a virus to help build up defenses to a disease (p. 456)
    inoculación acto de inyectar una pequeña dosis de un virus a una persona para ayudarla a crear defensas contra una enfermedad (pág. 456)

island hopping the strategy used by U.S. forces in the Pacific during World War II that involved taking only strategically important islands (p. 525)
    saltar de isla en isla estrategia de las furezas de Estados Unidos en el Pacífico durante la Segunda Guerra Mundial que consistía en tomar sólo las islas importantes desde el punto de vista estratégico (pág. 525)

isolationism a policy of avoiding contact with other countries (p. 492)
    aislacionismo política de evitar el contacto con otros países (pág. 492)

ivory a white material made from elephant tusks (p. 312)
    marfil material blanco procedente de los colmillos de los elefantes (pág. 312)

karma in Buddhism and Hinduism, the effects that good or bad actions have on a person's soul (p. 440)
    karma en el budismo y el hinduismo, los efectos que las buenas o malas acciones producen en el alma de una persona (pág. 440)

kente a hand-woven, brightly colored West African fabric (p. 337)
    kente tela muy colorida, tejida a mano, característica de África occidental (pág. 337)

loess fertile, yellowish soil (p. 412)
    loess suelo amarillento y fértil (pág. 412)

M

mandate of heaven the idea that heaven chose China's ruler and gave him or her power (p. 466)
    mandato divino idea de que el cielo elegía al gobernante de China y le daba el poder (pág. 466)

manor a large estate owned by a knight or lord (p. 622)
    feudo gran finca perteneciente a un caballero o señor feudal (pág. 622)

Mau Mau a violent movement in Kenya during the 1960s, led by Kikuyu farmers, to rid the country of white settlers (p. 368)
    Mau Mau movimiento emprendido por los agricultores kikiyu con el fin de expulsar de Kenia por medios violentos a los agricultores blancos (pág. 368)

meditation deep, continued thought that focuses the mind on spiritual ideas (p. 443)
    meditación reflexión profunda y continua, durante la cual la persona se concentra en ideas espirituales (pág. 443)

Mediterranean climate the type of climate found across Southern Europe; it features warm and sunny summer days, mild evenings, and cooler, rainy winters (p. 564)
    clima mediterráneo tipo de clima de todo el sur europeo; se caracteriza por días de verano cálidos y soleados, noches templadas e inviernos lluviosos y más frescos (pág. 564)

mercenary a hired soldier (p. 448)
    mercenario soldado a sueldo (pág. 448)

merchant a trader (p. 316)
    mercader comerciante (pág. 316)

metallurgy the science of working with metals (p. 456)
    metalurgia ciencia de trabajar los metales (pág. 456)

Middle Ages a period that lasted from about 500 to 1500 in Europe (p. 618)
    Edad Media período que duró aproximadamente desde el año 500 hasta el 1500 en Europa (pág. 618)

Middle Kingdom the period of Egyptian history from about 2050 to 1750 BC and marked by order and stability (p. 292)
    Reino Medio período de la historia de Egipto que abarca aproximadamente del 2050 al 1750 a. C. y que se caracterizó por el orden y la estabilidad (pág. 292)

Middle Passage the name for the voyages that brought enslaved Africans across the Atlantic Ocean to North America and the West Indies (p. 356)
    Paso Central viaje en el que los esclavos africanos atravesaban el océano Atlántico hasta llegar a América del Norte y las Antillas (pág. 356)

missionary someone who works to spread religious beliefs (p. 446)
    misionero alguien que trabaja para difundir sus creencias religiosas (pág. 446)

monsoon a seasonal wind that brings either dry or moist air (p. 409)
    monzón viento estacional que trae aire seco o húmedo (pág. 409)

mosque a building for Muslim prayer (p. 331)
    mezquita edificio musulmán para la oración (pág. 331)

mummy a specially treated body wrapped in cloth for preservation (p. 286)

momia cadáver especialmente tratado y envuelto en tela para su conservación (pág. 286)

N

nationalism a devotion and loyalty to one's country; develops among people with a common language, religion, or history (p. 648)

nacionalismo sentimiento de lealtad al país de uno; se desarrolla entre personas con un idioma, religión o historia en común (pág. 648)

nation-state a country united under a single strong government; made up of people with a common cultural background (p. 625)

nación-estado país unido bajo un solo gobierno fuerte; formado de personas con una cultura común (pág. 625)

navigable river a river that is deep and wide enough for ships to use (p. 568)

río navegable río que tiene la profundidad y el ancho necesarios para que pasen los barcos (pág. 568)

New Kingdom the period from about 1550 to1050 BC in Egyptian history when Egypt reached the height of its power and glory (p. 292)

Reino Nuevo período de la historia egipcia que abarca aproximadamente desde el 1550 hasta el 1050 a. C., en el que Egipto alcanzó la cima de su poder y su gloria (pág. 292)

nirvana in Buddhism, a state of perfect peace (p. 444)

nirvana en el budismo, estado de paz perfecta (pág. 444)

noble a rich and powerful person (p. 284)

noble persona rica y poderosa (pág. 284)

nonviolence the avoidance of violent actions (pp. 441, 516)

no violencia rechazo de las acciones violentas (págs. 441, 516)

O

oasis a wet, fertile area in a desert where a spring or well provides water (p. 252)

oasis zona húmeda y fértil en el desierto con un manantial o pozo que proporciona agua (pág. 252)

obelisk a tall, pointed, four-sided pillar in ancient Egypt (p. 300)

obelisco pilar alto, de cuatro caras y acabado en punta, propio del antiguo Egipto (pág. 300)

Old Kingdom the period from about 2700 to 2200 BC in Egyptian history that began shortly after Egypt was unified (p. 283)

Reino Antiguo período de la historia egipcia que abarca aproximadamente del 2700 hasta el 2200 a. C. y comenzó poco después de la unifi cación de Egipto (pág. 283)

oral history a spoken record of past events (p. 334)

historia oral registro hablado de hechos ocurridos en el pasado (pág. 334)

P

pans low, flat areas (p. 270)

depresiones áreas bajas y planas (pág. 270)

papyrus a long-lasting, paper-like material made from reeds that the ancient Egyptians used to write on (p. 299)

papiro material duradero hecho de juncos, similar al papel, que los antiguos egipcios utilizaban para escribir (pág. 299)

partition division (p. 517)

partición división (pág. 517)

periodic market an open-air trading market that is set up once or twice a week (p. 269)

mercado periódico mercado al aire libre que funciona una o dos veces a la semana (pág. 269)

pharaoh the title used by the rulers of Egypt (p. 281)

faraón título usado por los gobernantes de Egipto (pág. 281)

pope the spiritual head of the Roman Catholic Church (p. 619)

papa jefe espiritual de la Iglesia Católica Romana (pág. 619)

porcelain a thin, beautiful pottery invented in China (p. 479)

porcelana cerámica bella y delicada creada en China (pág. 479)

Protestant a Christian who protested against the Catholic Church (p. 633)

protestante cristiano que protestaba en contra de la Iglesia católica (pág. 633)

proverb a short saying of wisdom or truth (p. 335)

proverbio refrán breve que expresa sabiduría o una verdad (pág. 335)

pyramid a huge triangular tomb built by the Egyptians and other peoples (p. 288)

pirámide tumba triangular y gigantesca construida por los egipcios y otros pueblos (pág. 288)

R

Raj the British rule of India from 1757 until 1947 (p. 511)

Raj gobierno británico en la India desde 1757 hasta 1947 (pág. 511)

Reformation a reform movement against the Roman Catholic Church that began in 1517; it resulted in the creation of Protestant churches (p. 632)

Reforma movimiento de reforma contra la Iglesia Católica Romana que comenzó en 1517; resultó en la creación de las iglesias protestantes (pág. 632)

Reign of Terror a bloody period of the French Revolution during which the government executed thousands of its opponents and others at the guillotine (p. 638)

Reino del Terror período sangriento de la Revolución Francesa durante el cual el gobierno ejecutó a miles de personas, oponentes y otros, en la guillotina (pág. 638)

reincarnation a Hindu and Buddhist belief that souls are born and reborn many times, each time into a new body (p. 439)

reencarnación creencia hindú y budista de que las almas nacen y renacen muchas veces, siempre en un cuerpo nuevo (pág. 439)

Renaissance the period of "rebirth" and creativity that followed Europe's Middle Ages (p. 628)

Renacimiento período de "volver a nacer" y creatividad que siguió a la Edad Media en Europa (pág. 628)

republic a political system in which people elect leaders to govern them (p. 597)

república sistema politico en el que el pueblo elige a los líderes que lo gobernarán (pág. 597)

rift valleys places on Earth's surface where the crust stretches until it breaks (p. 258)

valles de fisura puntos de la superficie de la Tierra en los que la corteza se estira hasta romperse (pág. 258)

Rosetta Stone a huge stone slab inscribed with hieroglyphics, Greek, and a later form of Egyptian that allowed historians to understand Egyptian writing (p. 299)

piedra Roseta gran losa de piedra en la que aparecen inscripciones en jeroglíficos, en griego y en una forma tardía del idioma egipcio que permitió a los historiadores descifrar la escritura egipcia (pág. 299)

S

sanctions economic or political penalties imposed by one country on another to try to force a change in policy (p. 373)

sanciones penalizaciones económicas o políticas que un país impone a otro para obligarlo a cambiar su política (pág. 373)

Sanskrit the most important language of ancient India (p. 435)

sánscrito el idioma más importante de la antigua India (pág. 435)

savanna an area of tall grasses and scattered trees and shrubs (p. 256)

sabana zona de pastos altos con arbustos y árboles dispersos (pág. 256)

scholar-official an educated member of China's government who passed a series of written examinations (p. 484)

funcionario erudito miembro culto del gobierno de China que aprobaba una serie de exámenes escritos (pág. 484)

seismograph a device that measures the strength of an earthquake (p. 472)

sismógrafo aparato que mide la fuerza de un terremoto (pág. 472)

Senate a council of rich and powerful Romans who helped run the city (p. 597)

Senado consejo de romanos ricos y poderosos que ayudaban a dirigir la ciudad (pág. 597)

Sikhism a monotheistic religion that developed in India in the 1400s (p. 509)

sijismo una religion monoteísta que se desarrolló en la India en el siglo XV (pág. 509)

silent barter a process in which people exchange goods without contacting each other directly (p. 322)

trueque silencioso proceso mediante el que las personas intercambian bienes sin entrar en contacto directo (pág. 322)

silt a mixture of fertile soil and tiny rocks that can make land ideal for farming (p. 250)

cieno mezcla de tierra fértil y piedrecitas que pueden crear un terreno ideal para el cultivo (pág. 250)

sphere of influence an area of a country over which another country has economic control (p. 513)

esfera de influencia la area de un país sobre cual otro país tiene control ecónomico (pág. 513)

sphinx an imaginary creature with a human head and the body of a lion that was often shown on Egyptian statues (p. 292)

esfinge criatura imaginaria con cabeza humana y cuerpo de león que aparecía representada a menudo en las estatuas egipcias (pág. 292)

subcontinent a large landmass that is smaller than a continent (p. 406)

subcontinente gran masa de tierra, más pequeña que un continente (pág. 406)

suffragettes women who campaigned to gain the right to vote (p. 646)

sufragistas mujeres que hicieron campaña para obtener el derecho a votar (pág. 646)

sundial a device that uses the position of shadows cast by the sun to tell the time of day (p. 472)
reloj de sol dispositivo que utiliza la posición de las sombras que proyecta el sol para indicar las horas del día (pág. 472)

superpower a strong and influential country (p. 660)
superpotencia país poderoso e influyente (pág. 660)

Swahili an African society that emerged in the late 1100s along the East African coast and combined elements of African, Asian, and Islamic cultures (p. 353)
swahili sociedad Africana que surgió a finales del siglo XII a lo largo de la costa africana oriental; combinaba elementos de las culturas africana, asiática e islámica (pág. 353)

taiga a forest of mainly evergreen trees covering much of Russia (p. 581)
taiga bosque de árboles de hoja perenne principalmente que cubre gran parte de Rusia (pág. 581)

tariff a fee that a country charges on imports or exports (p. 529)
arancel tarifa que impone un país a las importaciones y exportaciones (pág. 529)

textile a cloth product (p. 644)
textil producto de tela (pág. 644)

townships crowded clusters of small homes in South Africa outside of cities where black South Africans live (p. 373)
distritos segregados grupos de pequeñas viviendas amontonadas ubicadas en las afueras de las ciudades de Sudáfrica, donde vivían los sudafricanos negros (pág. 373)

trade network a system of people in different lands who trade goods back and forth (p. 316)
red comercial sistema de personas en diferentes lugares que comercian productos entre sí (pág. 316)

trade route a path followed by traders (p. 293)
ruta comercial itinerario seguido por los comerciantes (pág. 293)

trade surplus when a country exports more goods than it imports (p. 529)
excedente comercial cuando un país exporta más bienes de los que importa (pág. 529)

Treaty of Versailles the final peace settlement of World War I (p. 650)
Tratado de Versalles acuerdo de paz final de la Primera Guerra Mundial (pág. 650)

trench warfare a style of fighting common in World War I in which each side fights from deep ditches, or trenches, dug into the ground (p. 650)
guerra de trincheras forma de guerra comúnmente usada en la Primera Guerra Mundial, en la cual ambos bandos luchan desde profundas zanjas, o trincheras, cavadas en el suelo (pág. 650)

tsunami a destructive and fast-moving wave (p. 416)
tsunami ola rápida y destructiva (pág. 416)

veld open grassland areas in South Africa (p. 270)
veld praderas descampadas en Sudáfrica (pág. 270)

woodblock printing a form of printing in which an entire page is carved into a block of wood, covered with ink, and pressed to a piece of paper to create a printed page (p. 480)
xilografi a forma de impresión en la que una página completa se talla en una plancha de madera, se cubre de tinta y se presiona sobre un papel para crear la página impresa (pág. 480)

zonal organized by zone (p. 256)
zonal organizado por zonas (pág. 256)

Index

INDEX

INDEX

INDEX

Credits and Acknowledgments

Acknowledgments

For permission to reproduce copyrighted material, grateful acknowledgement is made to the following sources:

Bantam Books, a division of Random House, Inc., www.randomhouse.com: From *The Bhagavad-Gita,* translated by Barbara Stoler Miller. Copyright © 1986 by Barbara Stoler Miller.

CNN: From "Taiwan: War bill a big provocation," from *CNN.com* Web site, March 14, 2005. Copyright © 2005 by Cable News Network LP, LLLP. Accessed September 22,2005 at http://edition.cnn.com/2005/WORLD/asiapcf/03/14/china.npc.law/

Doubleday, a division of Random House, Inc.: From *The Diary of a Young Girl, The Definitive Edition* by Ann Frank, edited by Otto H. Frank and Mirjam Pressler, translated by Susan Massotty. Copyright © 1995 by Doubleday, a division of Random House, Inc.

Foreign Affairs: From "A Conversation With Lee Kuan Yew" by Fareed Zakaria from *Foreign Affairs,* March/April 1994, vol. 73, issue 2. Copyright © 2004 by Council on Foreign Relations. All rights reserved.

HaperCollins Publishers: From *Antarctic Journal: Four Months at the Bottom of the World* by Jennifer Owings Dewey. Copyright © 2001 by Jennifer Owings Dewey. From *The Endless Steppe* by Esther Hautzig. Copyright © 1968 by Esther Hautzig.

David Higham Associates Limited: From *Travels in Asia and Africa 1325–1354* by Ibn Battuta translated by H. A. R. Gibb. Copyright © 1929 by Broadway House, London.

Alfred A. Knopf, Inc., a division of Random House, Inc., www.randomhouse.com: From *Shabanu: Daughter of Wind* by Suzanne Fisher Staples. Copyright © 1989 by Suzanne Fisher Staples. From *Crossing Antarctica* by Will Steger. Copyright © 1991 by Will Steger.

Lonely Planet: From "Hungary" from the *Lonely Planet WorldGuide* Online Web site. Copyright © 2005 by Lonely Planet. Accessed at http://www.lonelyplanet.com/worldguide/destinations/europe/hungary/.

The Jewish Publication Society: Exodus 20: 12–14 from *Tanakh: A New Translation of the Holy Scriptures According to the Traditional Hebrew Text.* Copyright © 1985 by The Jewish Publication Society.

National Geographic Society: From *Geography for Life: National Geographic Standards 1994.* Copyright © 1994 by National Geographic Research & Exploration. All rights reserved.

Naomi Shihab Nye: "Red Brocade" from *19 Varieties of Gazelle: Poems of the Middle East* by Naomi Shihab Nye. Copyright © 1994, 1995, 2002 by Naomi Shihab Nye.

Penguin Books Ltd.: "Quiet Night Thoughts" by Li Po from *Li Po and Tu Fu: Poems,* translated by Arthur Cooper. Copyright © 1973 by Arthur Cooper. From "The Blood Clots" from *The Koran,* translated with notes by N. J. Dawood. Copyright © 1956, 1959, 1966, 1968, 1974, 1990 by N. J. Dawood.

G. P. Putnam's Sons, a division of Penguin Group (USA) Inc.: From *Time Enough for Love, the Lives of Lazarus Long* by Robert Heinlein. Copyright © 1973 by Robert Heinlein. All rights reserved.

Estate of Erich Maria Remarque: From *All Quiet of the Western Front* by Erich Maria Remarque. Copyright © 1929, 1930 by Little, Brown and Company, copyright renewed © 1957, 1958 by Erich Maria Remarque. All rights reserved. "Im Western Nichts Neues" copyright 1928 by Ullstein A. G.; copyright renewed © 1956 by Erich Maria Remarque.

Scribner, an imprint of Simon & Schuster Adult Publishing Group: "The Snows of Kilimanjaro" from *The Short Stories of Ernest Hemingway.* Copyright © 1938 by Ernest Hemingway; copyright renewed © 1966 by Mary Hemingway.

United Nations: From the *Preamble to the Charter of the United Nations.* Copyright © 1945 by United Nations.

Sources Cited:

Quote from *Seeds of Peace* Web site, accessed August 23, 2005, at http://www.seedsofpeace.org/site/PageServer?pagename=BakerEvent.

From "Adoration of Inanna of Ur" from *The Ancient Near East, Volume II* by James D. Pritchard. Published by Princeton University Press, Princeton, NJ, 1976.

From *The River* by Gary Paulsen. Published by Random House, 1991.

From *Aké: The Years of Childhood* by Wole Soyinka from www.randomhouse.com Web site. Published by Random House, 1981.